Feasting on the Gospels
John, Volume 1

Editorial Board

A Feasting on the Word™ Commentary

Feasting on the Gospels

John, Volume 1
Chapters 1–9

CYNTHIA A. JARVIS and **E. ELIZABETH JOHNSON**

General Editors

WESTMINSTER
JOHN KNOX PRESS
LOUISVILLE · KENTUCKY

© 2015 Westminster John Knox Press

2015 paperback edition
Originally published in hardback in the United States
by Westminster John Knox Press in 2015
Louisville, Kentucky

15 16 17 18 19 20 21 22 23 24—10 9 8 7 6 5 4 3 2 1

Scripture quotations from the New Revised Standard Version of the Bible are copyright © 1989 by the Division of Christian Education of the National Council of the Churches of Christ in the U.S.A. and are used by permission. Scripture quotations marked CEB are from the Common English Bible, © 2011 Common English Bible, and are used by permission. Scripture taken from *The Message.* Copyright © 1993, 1994, 1995, 1996. Used by permission of NavPress Publishing Group. Scripture quotations marked NIV are from *The Holy Bible, New International Version.* Copyright © 1973, 1978, 1984, 2011 by Biblica, Inc.® Used by permission. All rights reserved worldwide. Scripture quotations marked RSV are from the Revised Standard Version of the Bible, copyright © 1946, 1952, 1971, and 1973 by the Division of Christian Education of the National Council of the Churches of Christ in the U.S.A., and are used by permission.

Book design by Drew Stevens
Cover design by Dilu Nicholas

Library of Congress Cataloging-in-Publication Data

Feasting on the gospels—John : a feasting on the WordTM commentary / Cynthia A. Jarvis and E. Elizabeth Johnson, general editors.—First edition.
    volumes cm
  Includes index.
  Contents: Volume 1. chapters 1-9 -- Volume 2. chapters 10-21.
    ISBN 978-0-664-23553-6 (v. 1 : hbk. : alk. paper) — ISBN 978-0-664-26036-1 (v. 1 : pbk. : alk. paper) — ISBN 978-0-664-23554-3 (v. 2 : hbk. : alk. paper) — ISBN 978-0-664-26037-8 (v. 2 : pbk. : alk. paper)
 1. Bible. John—Commentaries.   I. Jarvis, Cynthia A.   II. Johnson, E. Elizabeth.
  BS2615.53.F43 2015
  226.5'077—dc23

                                                                           2014031603

Contents

Publisher's Note

Feasting on the Gospels is a seven-volume series that follows in the proud tradition of *Feasting on the Word: Preaching the Revised Common Lectionary*. Whereas *Feasting on the Word* provided commentary on only the texts in the lectionary, *Feasting on the Gospels* will cover every passage of the four Gospels. *Feasting on the Gospels* retains the popular approach of *Feasting on the Word* by providing four perspectives on each passage—theological, pastoral, exegetical, and homiletical—to stimulate and inspire preaching, teaching, and discipleship.

Westminster John Knox Press is grateful to the members of the large *Feasting* family who have given so much of themselves to bring this new series to life. General editors Cynthia A. Jarvis and E. Elizabeth Johnson stepped from their service on the editorial board of *Feasting on the Word* to the editorship of *Feasting on the Gospels* without missing a beat. Their commitment, energy, and unflagging enthusiasm made this work possible. The project manager, Joan Murchison, and project compiler, Mary Lynn Darden, continued their remarkable

work, bringing thousands of pieces and hundreds of authors together seamlessly.

The editorial board did enormous work under grueling deadlines and did it with excellence and good humor. The hundreds of writers who participated—scholars, preachers, and teachers— gave much of themselves to help create this bountiful feast. David Bartlett and Barbara Brown Taylor took the time and care to help conceive this new project, even as they were finishing their excellent work as general editors of *Feasting on the Word*.

Finally, we are again indebted to Columbia Theological Seminary for their partnership. As they did with *Feasting on the Word*, they provided many resources and personnel to help make this series possible. We are grateful in particular to seminary President Stephen Hayner and Dean of Faculty and Executive Vice President Deborah Mullen.

It is with joy that we welcome you to this feast, in hopes that it will nourish you as you proclaim the Word to all of God's people.

Westminster John Knox Press

Series Introduction

At their best, people who write about Scripture are conversation partners. They enter the dialogue between the biblical text and the preacher or teacher or interested Christian and add perspectives gained from experience and disciplined attention. They contribute literary, historical, linguistic, and theological insights gathered over the millennia to the reader's first impressions of what is going on in a text. This conversation is essential if the reading of Scripture is to be fruitful in the church. It keeps reading the Bible from being an exercise in individual projection or uncritical assumption. That said, people who comment on the Bible should never become authorities. While a writer may indeed know more about the text than the reader does, he or she nevertheless writes from a particular perspective shaped by culture, ethnicity, gender, education, and theological tradition. In this regard, the writer of a commentary is no different from the writers and readers of Scripture.

The model for this series on the Gospels is the lectionary-based resource *Feasting on the Word* (Westminster John Knox Press, 2008–2011), now widely used by ministers as they prepare to preach. As central as the task of preaching is to the health of congregations, Scripture is the Word that calls the whole community of faith into being and sends out those addressed as witnesses to the Word in the world. Whether read devotionally by those gathered to pray or critically by others gathered to study, the Bible functions in a myriad of ways to undergird, support, and nurture the Christian life of individuals and communities. Those are the reasons that Westminster John Knox Press has taken the next step in the *Feasting* project to offer *Feasting on the Gospels*, a series in the style of *Feasting on the Word* with two major differences. First, all four Gospels are considered in their entirety, a *lectio continua* of sorts that leaves out nothing. Second, while *Feasting on the Word* is addressed specifically to preachers, *Feasting on the Gospels* is addressed to all who want to deepen their understanding of the Gospels—Bible study leaders and class members, seasoned preachers and seminarians, believers and skeptics.

The advantage of *Feasting on the Gospels* is that the reader encounters multiple perspectives on each

text—not only the theological, exegetical, pastoral, and homiletical emphases that shape the essays, but also the ecumenical, social, ethnic, and cultural perspectives of the authors. Unlike a single-author commentary, which sustains a particular view of a given interpreter throughout, *Feasting on the Gospels* offers readers a broad conversation that engages the text from many angles. In a church as diverse as the twenty-first-century church is, such deliberate engagement with many voices is imperative and, we hope, provocative.

A few observations about the particular challenges posed by the Gospels are in order here. The Gospels were written in a time when fledgling Christian communities—probably in their second generation—were just beginning to negotiate their relationships with Judaism (within which they were conceived and born), a community that was itself in the process of redefinition after the destruction of the Second Temple in 70 CE. Some of that negotiation was marked by great tension and sometimes outright hostility. The temptation for Christian readers to read anti-Semitism into texts that portray intra-Jewish conflict has beset the church almost from its beginnings. Our editors have been particularly mindful of this when dealing with essays on texts where the temptation to speak contemptuously of Jews and Judaism might threaten faithful interpretation. In these two volumes on John, readers will also find a helpful essay by Jaime Clark-Soles, a member of the editorial board and a Johannine scholar, about the troublesome language of "the Jews" in the Fourth Gospel and how faithful interpreters might deal with it.

A second observation involves the New Testament manuscript tradition. In *Feasting on the Gospels* we identify and comment on significant manuscript variants such as Mark 16:9–20 and John 7:53–8:11, something we did not have to contend with in *Feasting on the Word*. We identify those variant readings the way the NRSV does, except that we talk about "other ancient manuscripts" rather than the "other ancient authorities" of the NRSV notes.

The twelve members of our editorial board come from a broad swath of American Christianity: they are members or ministers of Presbyterian, Baptist, United Church of Christ, Roman Catholic, and Disciples of Christ churches. Some of them are academics who serve on the faculties of theological schools; others are clergy serving congregations. All of them are extraordinarily hardworking, thoughtful, and perceptive readers of Scripture, of the church, and of the world. The writers whose work comprises these volumes represent an even wider cross-section of the church, most of them from North America, but a significant number from around the world, particularly the global South.

We could not have undertaken this work without the imagination, advice, and support of David Dobson, Editorial Director at Westminster John Knox Press, and his colleagues Don McKim, Marianne Blickenstaff, Michele Blum, and Julie Tonini. We are deeply grateful to David L. Bartlett and Barbara Brown Taylor, our mentors in the *Feasting on the*

Word project, who continued to offer hands-on assistance with *Feasting on the Gospels*. We thank President Stephen A. Hayner and Dean Deborah F. Mullen of Columbia Theological Seminary and the congregation of The Presbyterian Church of Chestnut Hill in Philadelphia, Pennsylvania, who made possible our participation in the project. Joan Murchison, who as Project Manager kept all of us and our thousands of essays in order and enforced deadlines with great good humor, is once again the beloved Hammer. Mary Lynn Darden, our compiler, who corralled not only the essays but also information about their authors and editors, brought all the bits and pieces together into the books you see now.

To the preachers, teachers, Bible study leaders, and church members who will read the Gospels with us, we wish you happy feasting.

Cynthia A. Jarvis
E. Elizabeth Johnson

"The Jews" in the Fourth Gospel
Jaime Clark-Soles

The Problem of Translation

John's Gospel refers seventy-one times in sixty-seven verses to *hoi Ioudaioi*.[1] The phrase appears in every single chapter of John except the Farewell Discourse (chaps. 14–17) and chapter 21. The NRSV usually translates this phrase "the Jews," although the phrase resists facile translation, because it does not mean the same thing each time it occurs. Numerous scholars have suggested various meanings for *hoi Ioudaioi* in the different instances in John, and these have been considered and categorized by Urban von Wahlde.[2]

"The Jews." First, the "national" sense refers to religious, cultural, or political aspects of people. When an event occurs in the time frame described as a festival of *hoi Ioudaioi*, it may be fine to translate it as "the Jews," because indeed the Festival of Sukkot (Booths or Tabernacles), for example, is a Jewish occasion, not a pagan one. Additionally, when Jesus declares to the Samaritan woman that "salvation is from the Jews" (4:22), he invokes the whole ethno-socio-religious history of God's covenant with Abraham and Sarah, Isaac and Rebekah, and Jacob and Rachel and Leah. This usage is ethically neutral and merely descriptive. Von Wahlde includes the following passages in this category: 2:6, 13; 3:1; 4:9a, 9b, 22; 5:1; 6:4; 7:2; 11:55; 18:20, 35; 19:21a, 40, 42.

"The Judeans." Sometimes, though, it is better to translate *hoi Ioudaioi* as "the Judeans." Von Wahlde calls this the "regional" sense. If one changes the Greek *I* to an English *J* (as we do with Jesus' name), one can practically hear the word "Judea." At times the term is used to designate those who are geographically connected to Judea. This usage also is ethically neutral and merely descriptive and can be found in the following verses: 3:22, 25; 11:8, 19, 31, 33, 36, 45, 54; 12:9, 11; 19:20.

Here is where it begins to get complicated, though, because it is clear that Jesus comes into conflict with the leaders of his own tradition, whose symbolic (and literal) seat of power was located in Jerusalem, which, of course, is in Judea. As the three-year ministry of Jesus is narrated, notice that Galilee is a safe haven of sorts for Jesus, whereas each time that he goes to Jerusalem (or even contemplates it), ominous music begins to play in the background. In 1:19 we read: "This is the testimony given by John when *hoi Ioudaioi* sent priests and Levites from Jerusalem to ask him, 'Who are you?'" One might argue that this should be translated as "the Judeans," since the party comes from Judea.

"The Religious Authorities." The example from 1:19, however, raises another translation possibility. It is not everyone in Judea who sends priests and Levites; it is patently the religious authorities. The same is true in 7:13, and in both cases it would be best to translate *hoi Ioudaioi* as "the religious authorities." They are not the only religious leaders, though, as even 1:19 makes clear with the mention of priests and Levites. There are also high priests, rulers, and Pharisees. This brings us to von Wahlde's third category, which he designates the "Johannine use" of the word; most instances of the phrase *hoi Ioudaioi* fall into this category, so it is worth explicating, if briefly.

First, in these instances, the term does not have the national meaning, since these "Jews" are distinguished from other characters in the narrative who are also Jewish in the national sense. In other words, taken in a literal ethnic or religious sense, it makes no sense to translate these instances as "the Jews," because that does not distinguish them from anyone else in the Gospel: apart from the centurion and Pilate, everyone in the narrative is Jewish (even the Greeks in chap. 12 may be Greek Jews), both those who believe in Jesus and those who do not. Second, this usage is characterized by hostility toward Jesus. Passages that depict hostile or skeptical religious authorities include 1:19; 2:18, 20; 5:10, 15, 16, 18; 7:13, 15; 9:18, 22a, 22b; 18:12, 14, 36; 19:38; 20:19. Third, in these instances, the authorities labeled "the Jews" think and act en masse: "they represent a single undifferentiated reaction."[3] This use includes 2:18, 20; 7:35.

---

1. John 1:19; 2:6, 13, 18, 20; 3:1, 22, 25; 4:9 (twice), 22; 5:1, 10, 15, 16, 18; 6:4, 41, 52; 7:1, 2, 11, 13, 15, 35; 8:22, 31, 48, 52, 57; 9:18, 22 (twice); 10:19, 24, 31, 33; 11:8, 19, 31, 33, 36, 45, 54, 55; 12:9, 11; 13:33; 18:12, 14, 20, 31, 33, 35, 36, 38, 39; 19:3, 7, 12, 14, 19, 20, 21 (three times), 31, 38, 40, 42; 20:19.

2. Urban von Wahlde, "The Johannine 'Jews': A Critical Survey," *New Testament Studies* 28 (1982): 33–60; "'The Jews' in the Gospel of John: Fifteen Years of Research (1983–1998)," *Ephemerides Theologicae Lovanienses* 76 (2000): 30–55. See also Joshua D. Garroway, "*Ioudaios*," in *The Jewish Annotated New Testament*, ed. Amy-Jill Levine and Marc Z. Brettler (New York: Oxford University Press, 2011), 524–26.

3. Von Wahlde, "The Johannine 'Jews,'" 47.

Religious Authorities or the Common People?
Another issue that always arises in the debate about *hoi Ioudaioi* in John is that, after one has moved through the national and regional meanings (which are ethically neutral) and has extracted the passages that refer rather clearly to religious authorities, one still has a batch of verses to address. With those, it is less clear whether the author has in view the religious authorities or the common people. This becomes even further complicated because sometimes the author blurs the line between *hoi Ioudaioi* and the "world" (*kosmos*). The "world" is another complex character in John's Gospel, sometimes believing and sometimes not. "He was in the world, and the world came into being through him; yet the world did not know him" (1:10). Some interpreters conflate "the [unbelieving] Jews" with "the [unbelieving] world." Such a move is not helpful.

For our purposes, one of which includes reading the New Testament ethically, trying to determine which instances might refer to the common people instead of the authorities is not productive and can, in fact, lead to a reasoning that results in a seemingly "partial" anti-Semitism: "Well, it is not Jews per se who are to be maligned, but just their leaders; or maybe just the Jews who did not accept Jesus; or maybe just the Jews who do not accept him now." Faulty logic quickly becomes deadly logic. That said, with respect to the "debatable" instances, von Wahlde argues that, with two exceptions (6:41, 52), they likely refer still to "the religious authorities" rather than "the common people." These are 7:1, 11; 8:22, 48, 52, 57; 10:24, 31, 33; 11:8; 13:33; 18:31, 38; 19:7, 12, 14, 31.

We have now accounted for all of the occurrences of *hoi Ioudaioi* and shown the variety of meanings and the problems in attempting a reasonable translation in each instance. Two further observations should be made. First, because John's passion narrative has been a particularly thorny text with respect to Christian anti-Semitism, it may be worth noting that even there varieties in meaning inhere. The "Johannine sense" of *hoi Ioudaioi* appears in the following, according to von Wahlde: 18:12, 14, 31, 36; 19:12, 14, 31. The following use one or another of the other senses discussed earlier: 18:20, 33, 35, 39; 19:3, 19, 20, 21a, 21b, 21c, 40, 42.

Untranslated. Second, regarding the meaning of the seventy-one occurrences of *hoi Ioudaioi*, there is actually a surprising level of general agreement among scholars about the "Johannine uses." The

following seven, however, remain the most contested: 3:25; 8:31; 10:19; 11:54; 18:20; 19:20, 21. So riddled with difficulties is this translation issue that many scholars simply leave the phrase untranslated in those cases. Several authors of the essays in these volumes have made precisely that choice.

The Importance of Context

The Fourth Gospel evinces numerous tensions within itself, obvious literary seams, responses that do not answer the question posed, and so on. There are apparent strata, and scholars posit a lengthy and complicated composition history. Let us take a moment to sort out at least three of these strata chronologically.

1. Jesus of Nazareth is born, conducts his ministry, and dies at the hands of the Roman governor Pontius Pilate in about 30 CE.
2. Post-Easter, Jesus' disciples preach publicly about Jesus' identity, words, and deeds.
3. These oral traditions are committed to writing and eventually are drawn together into the narrative we know as the Gospel of John. Tension with the parent tradition remains high as the community discerns its identity vis-à-vis that tradition.
4. Sometime after the composition of the Fourth Gospel, the Epistles of John are penned, reflecting a later stage of the community. The issues now center on internal church conflict among the leaders, apostasy, and docetic Christology.

At the time of Jesus, the temple in Jerusalem is still standing, and numerous varieties of Judaism exist. The power of the Sadducees is temple-based; thus, when the temple is destroyed in 70, they fade from power. The Zealots, Sicarii, and the Fourth Philosophy are nationalists who oppose Roman occupation and favor civil war. The Essenes are a reformist, ascetic sect residing primarily at Qumran near the Dead Sea. The nationalists and the Essenes are decimated by the Roman army in the war of 66–70. The Pharisees are Torah-based teachers whose power derives from their ability to interpret the law—kind of a cross between lawyers and Bible scholars. When the temple is destroyed, they are the ones best positioned to assume leadership. The destruction of the temple effectively ends the period known as Second Temple Judaism and makes way for rabbinic Judaism, the kinds of Judaism that perdure to this day.

The original Johannine community consisted of Jews who worshiped in synagogues with their fellow Jews; they were Christian Jews because they believed that Jesus was the Messiah. Claiming that "the" or "a" Messiah had come was certainly not foreign to first- and second-century varieties of Judaism. John of Gischala in the first century and Simon Bar Kochba in the second were declared Messiahs. This was not grounds for dismissal from the Jewish community. So what happened? It is impossible to say with certainty, but clearly the Johannine community began to experience conflict with its parent tradition. The author of the Fourth Gospel claims that the members who made up John's community were put out of the synagogue, *aposynagōgos* (a word unknown in early Jewish or Christian literature apart from John 9:22; 12:42; 16:2), due to their high Christology, perhaps even confessing Jesus as God. It is clear that a full confession of the identity of Jesus as defined by John led to extremely painful conflict between the parent tradition and the sect that formed as a result of their expulsion from the synagogue.

According to J. Louis Martyn,[4] John can be read as a two-level drama. First, there is the story of the historical Jesus, what happened "back then." Second, there is the reality that the Johannine community is experiencing near the end of the first century, sixty to seventy years after Jesus' death and twenty to thirty years after the temple has been destroyed; the Pharisees (not the Sadducees) are in power, and the synagogue (not the temple) is the seat of power for the religious authorities. The story of the Johannine community living in the late first century gets retrojected onto the story of Jesus and the first disciples.

For example, when one is reading in chapter 9 the story of the blind man being persecuted and put out of the synagogue, unsupported by his parents, one should imagine a Johannine Christian who is openly professing faith in Christ and being persecuted by members of the parent tradition. The story is anachronistic, because the Pharisees and the synagogue were not such centers of power in Jesus' own day; the Sanhedrin and temple were. It is also anachronistic because no one could give a confession of Jesus as Lord (as the blind man does), Son of God, God (as Thomas does), Messiah, Son of Man, and more until *after* the passion, resurrection,

sending of the Paraclete, and return of Jesus to God. In other words, the story could not have happened historically the way it is narrated. One should therefore be careful about making historical assumptions based on texts that have a different rhetorical aim. Certainly the text caricatures anyone who opposes Jesus, the hero of the narrative. The Pharisees are not excused from the Fourth Evangelist's lampooning.

While certain aspects of this reconstruction have recently been contested,[5] important conclusions and warnings can nevertheless be drawn from it. First, the Fourth Gospel reflects an intra-Jewish debate, not a debate between "Christians" and "Jews"; they are all Jews. This is the way sects develop. The Johannine community makes sense of itself as a Jewish community in categories drawn from the Hebrew Bible and Jewish markers of all kinds. Remembering this is crucial when reading this text. Those who choose to ignore the concrete social setting of the New Testament will find it easy to justify anti-Semitism by drawing on John. His violent, seething language about "the Jews" has been used and still is used to charge Jews with all sorts of wickedness.

Second, remember that the Gospel is a story and follows narrative conventions, including characters drawn for symbolic purposes, conflict that the hero must overcome, and so on. It is not a historical rendering, and it takes great poetic license in its depiction of history. Interpreters will be able to understand that only when they learn about the historical context from historical sources that, happily, scholars have provided in abundance.

The Insidious Problem of Anti-Semitism

Easter has always been a potentially dangerous time for Jews, as Christians accuse them of being guilty of deicide, of being Christ-killers, and, thanks to John 8, of being murderous children of the devil. In a post-Shoah world, it is ethically incumbent upon all Christians, especially those who preach and teach, to address and to battle anti-Semitism. There are at least three ways that the Gospel of John may fuel anti-Semitism. We have already addressed the first problem: the repeated use of the phrase *hoi Ioudaioi* in primarily pejorative ways.

The second problem is Johannine dualism. It begins already in chapter 1, where "grace and law"

---

4. J. Louis Martyn, *History and Theology in the Fourth Gospel, Revised and Expanded*, New Testament Library (Louisville, KY: Westminster John Knox Press, 2003).

5. See the work of Adele Reinhartz, for example: *Befriending the Beloved Disciple: A Jewish Reading of the Gospel of John* (New York/London: Bloomsbury Academic, 2002); and "John," in *The Jewish Annotated New Testament*, 152–96.

and "Jesus and Moses" are presented as opposites: "From his fullness we have all received, grace upon grace. The law indeed was given through Moses; grace and truth came through Jesus Christ" (1:16–17). Other dualistic categories include light and darkness, truth and falsehood, life and death, God the Father and Satan the father, above and below, not of this world and of this world. Jesus and the disciples are associated with all of the good categories; "the Jews" are primarily associated with the negative trait in each pair.

This contributes to a third problem that arises in the Fourth Gospel: the use of typology in a way that leads to Christian supersessionism.[6] Jesus is depicted as like, but superior to, numerous Old Testament figures, including Moses (chaps. 1, 5, 6), Jacob (1:51; chap. 4), Abraham (chap. 8), and Woman Wisdom herself. Jewish symbols and rituals now find their fulfilled meaning only in Jesus: his incarnation is a tabernacle (1:14); his body is now the temple (chap. 2); he is the bread from heaven celebrated in the Passover; he is the Passover lamb (which is why he dies a day earlier in John than in the Synoptics); he is the King of the Jews. He has fulfilled or replaced everything worthwhile in Judaism. In this way, John may be accused of being anti-Jewish, if not anti-Semitic. Helpful is the following from the Jewish Johannine scholar Adele Reinhartz:

It must be emphasized that the Gospel is not anti-Semitic in a racial sense, as it is not one's origins that are decisive but one's beliefs. Nevertheless, it has been used to promote anti-Semitism. Most damaging has been John 8:44, in which Jesus declares that the Jews have the devil as their father.... While John's difficult rhetoric should not be facilely dismissed, it can be understood as part of the author's process of self-definition, of distinguishing the followers of Jesus from the synagogue and so from Jews and Judaism. This distancing may have been particularly important if the ethnic composition of the Johannine community included Jews, Samaritans, and Gentiles. This approach does not excuse the Gospel's rhetoric, but it may make it possible for readers to understand the narrative's place in the process by which Christianity became a separate religion, to appreciate the beauty of its language, and to recognize the spiritual power that it continues to have in the lives of many of its Christian readers.[7]

The authors and editors of the two John volumes of *Feasting on the Gospels* have worked diligently to bear such convictions in mind as they worked through this rich and complex Gospel to offer preachers, teachers, Bible study leaders, and interested Christian readers guidance through the thicket of language and images that historically have divided Christians from Jews and frequently resulted in Christian violence against Jews.

---

6. Supersessionism is a theological claim that Christianity supersedes or replaces Judaism in God's plan of redemption. Sometimes it is called fulfillment or replacement theology.

7. Reinhartz, "John," 156.

Feasting on the Gospels
John, Volume 1

John 1:1–9

¹In the beginning was the Word, and the Word was with God, and the Word was God. ²He was in the beginning with God. ³All things came into being through him, and without him not one thing came into being. What has come into being ⁴in him was life, and the life was the light of all people. ⁵The light shines in the darkness, and the darkness did not overcome it.

⁶There was a man sent from God, whose name was John. ⁷He came as a witness to testify to the light, so that all might believe through him. ⁸He himself was not the light, but he came to testify to the light. ⁹The true light, which enlightens everyone, was coming into the world.

Theological Perspective

The prologue to John is high Bible, full of majesty and complexity. Some of the complexity is theological. Within the prologue's eighteen verses the evangelist sets in motion some of the biggest theological issues in the Bible: the divinity of Christ, the Trinity, mediation of creation, the antithesis between light and darkness, salvation by grace, incarnation, and the revelation of God the Father by "God the only Son."

Verse 1 unfolds the majesty and mystery with a classic declaration: "In the beginning was the Word." *Ho logos* (the Word) had deep resonance within Greek philosophy, representing the rational principle or power that is the glue of the universe. "In the beginning" also echoes Genesis 1, where God's first action is to speak—in fact, to speak light into darkness. So the first clause of verse 1 is AC current to Greeks and DC to Jews.

A third resonance of verse 1 has to do with "the word" itself. In John's Gospel Jesus will say at least five times (3:34; 7:16; 8:26; 12:49; 14:24) that his words are not his own, but reproduce the words of his Father who sent him. Just as he is "the way" and "the truth" (14:6), he is also "the word." He speaks for God.

For patristic writers who framed the church's doctrine of the Trinity, verse 1 was irresistible. If the Word is both God and with God (Gk. *pros*, "toward,"

Pastoral Perspective

Bob Woods tells the story of a couple who took their son and daughter to Carlsbad Caverns. The tour of this wonderful national park includes a dramatic moment at its deepest point underground. Upon reaching the lowest point, the guide turns off the lights, to show just how dark darkness can be. Enveloped in complete darkness, the little boy began to cry. Immediately was heard the quiet voice of his sister, "Don't cry. Someone here knows how to turn on the lights."[1]

Verse 5 is our affirmation that there truly is Someone who "knows how to turn on the lights." One could go so far as to say that the true power of the Christian faith is grounded in the simple statement, "The light shines in the darkness, and the darkness did not overcome it." Not only does Someone know how to turn on the lights, Someone has. In response, questions that follow for us are: Do we live in such a way that the inextinguishable light is evident? Are we able to bring assurance to those who are overcome by the darkness of this world? Are we willing to enter into the dark and unfriendly parts of our communities in order to bring hope to those who feel "overcome" by darkness?

---

1. Craig Brian Larson, ed., *Illustrations for Preaching and Teaching* (Grand Rapids: Baker Books, 1993), 133.

Exegetical Perspective

"In the beginning was the Word." With this opening phrase, the Gospel of John intentionally evokes Genesis. The first two Greek words of John, *en archē*, repeat not only the first two words of Genesis in the Septuagint (or any other Greek translation of the period), but also the book's title, since the opening words of a biblical book served as its title. The connection between the opening words—and perhaps title—of John and the first book of the Jewish Scriptures is unmistakable. John intentionally and explicitly places the beginning that he is narrating alongside the beginning that Genesis narrates. His story is a retelling of the story of creation.

To take the connection between Genesis 1 and John 1 as our interpretive starting point invites us to think about John 1 first and foremost as a story, as Genesis is a story. Nevertheless John 1:1–18 is rarely interpreted as a narrative. Instead, John's opening verses are most commonly interpreted as an introductory hymn and read loosely as poetry instead of prose. In this common way of reading, John 1:1–18 does not belong to the unfolding of the Gospel narrative, but is a "prologue" to the Gospel narrative. John 1:1–18 is read as a self-contained unit that stands apart from the rest of the Gospel. The crucial interpretive focus is then on the nature of the hymn, its origins, and its function as a prologue

Homiletical Perspective

Chaim Potok opens his novel *In the Beginning* with this simple sentence: "All beginnings are hard."[1] While Potok's wisdom is hard to debate, the author of John's Gospel has his own unique perspective on beginnings. Echoing the creation hymn of Genesis 1:1–2:4a, John opens his Gospel with the affirmation, "In the beginning was the Word." Beginnings may be hard for humans, but not for God in John's theological poetry. In fact, verses 1–9 remind us that God refashions chaos into order. This Logos hymn celebrates the beginning of life, but this time in a way that will not be despoiled, as happened after God sang the world into being at creation.

The theme of life begun anew will recur throughout John's Gospel, in such prominent stories as the encounter between Jesus and Nicodemus in chapter 3 and Lazarus stripping off his burial garments in chapter 11. Preachers who come to John's prologue in contemporary society often do so with a deep societal suspicion that life is ultimately no more than what we make it. In the prevailing wind of human self-achievement, God is not the source of new beginnings or new life; we are. John invites preachers to tell a different story, a far more life-giving story, a story that has the power to transform into new life

1. Chaim Potok, *In the Beginning* (New York: Random House, 1975), 1.

Theological Perspective

God, suggesting intimate fellowship), then this being is simultaneously the same as God and also distinct from God. In a second verse, John repeats for emphasis that the Word is not a creature: "He was in the beginning with God." (See also 17:5.)

At the outset of John's Gospel, there are two who are eternally God, really intimate and really distinct. The Word was with *ho theos* (the God), and the Word was *theos* (God). The Word is not the same object or person as God, but is, nonetheless, whatever God is. (Verse 18 will disclose further that the two belong, roughly speaking, not only to the same genus, but also to the same family.)

Theologians have always spotted here a living root of the doctrine of the Trinity. Frederick Dale Bruner remarks how the epistles and the other Gospels build up their testimony to the divinity of Christ by increments.[1] Yet for John, Wham! He needs only two verses to give us Trinitarian distinction-within-unity and the eternality of the being he will identify in verse 17 as Jesus Christ and in verse 18 as "God the only Son."

In verses 3 and 10 John states that the Word/Son is mediator of creation. This is a biblical and theological angularity attested in major strands of Hebrews (1:1–3) and Paul (1 Cor. 8:6; Col. 1:15–17) and here in John. What does it mean? One theological suggestion is that he is called "the Word of God" because he reproduces the words of the One who sent him. At least twice Paul calls him "the wisdom of God" or its kin (1 Cor. 1:24; Col. 2:2). The intertwined concepts of word and wisdom suggest that the work of Jesus Christ represents the intelligence and expressiveness of the triune God.

John's Gospel will go on to show that the Father is "in" the Son and the Son "in" the Father, and that the Paraclete represents the life and intelligence of both. The Gospel tells us that between the Father and Son and, by extension, the Paraclete, self-giving love is the dynamic currency of the Trinitarian life of God. The persons within God exalt each other, commune with each other, defer to one another. Each person, so to speak, makes room for the other two. Early Greek theologians described the glorious Trinitarian dynamism with the term *perichoresis*, stating that each person *harbors* the others. In a constant movement of overture and acceptance, each person envelops the other two. You might say that the Trinitarian persons show each other *hospitality* in this way of thinking.

Pastoral Perspective

Frequently the church is more like the little boy than the older sister: trembling at the depths of the darkness, instead of remembering that there is One who not only knows how to turn on the lights, but who truly is the Light. For people in the post-Christendom context of the West, it is much easier to feel overwhelmed by the darkness than to recall the power of the Light.

The old Christendom assumptions caused many to believe that the church would always be at the center of society. People would always flock to the church because of its cultural importance. From this confidence, it was easy to believe that anyone who did not belong to a faith community was strange and a problem to be solved. Some went so far as to assume the stranger to be the enemy. Now a different reality has come. The church no longer is central. Instead, it is surrounded by strangers who do not look or behave like those in the church. This new context may even cause some to believe that the darkness is returning.

However, the Gospel tells us that the darkness cannot prevail (v. 5) and that we never meet anyone who is completely unenlightened by the true Light (v. 9). In other words, no one can be a stranger to Christ. He has already met them and touched them in some way. If that is true, no one need be a stranger to those who are in Christ. With the dawning of this Light, all should be approached and all should be welcomed. With the dawning of the true Light, we may begin to see the strangers not as dangerous but as magnificent creatures already touched by the power of God.

C. S. Lewis expressed this insight memorably: "There are no *ordinary* people. You have never talked to a mere mortal. Nations, cultures, arts, civilizations—these are mortal and their life is to ours as the life of a gnat. But it is immortals whom we joke with, work with, marry, snub, and exploit—immortal horrors or everlasting splendors."[2]

How different would our congregations be, how different would *we* be, if we took seriously the reality of John's words that the true Light, that is Jesus Christ, has intervened, has touched everyone who comes into this world? This is not a call to naiveté, not a summons to ignore the realities of sin in ourselves and others. Far too often we have succumbed to that false gospel of progressiveness, that self-delusion that we are all basically good and doing the best that we can. That is not John's message.

---

1. Frederick Dale Bruner, *The Gospel of John: A Commentary* (Grand Rapids: Eerdmans, 2012), 13.

2. C. S. Lewis, *The Weight of Glory and Other Addresses* (New York: Macmillan, 1975), 19.

Exegetical Perspective

to the Gospel. Is the hymn a pre-Christian hymn to Wisdom/Logos that John has adopted for a Christian context? How do verses 1–18 divide into strophes (hymnic verses)? Where in the hymn does the focus shift from a hymn to Wisdom to a hymn to the incarnate Word? How do the prose "insertions" about John the Baptist fit with this hymn?

However, this interpretive bent ignores the shaping role of the cadences, form, and content of Genesis 1 on the Gospel's "beginning." Nowhere else in the Gospel is there a self-contained liturgical piece, but there are many places where John repeats the cadences, form, and content of a biblical story to tell the story of Jesus (e.g., the connections between manna and Passover texts in John 6). The same narrative pattern and technique of retelling a biblical story shapes John 1:1–18. These verses are a midrash on Genesis 1:1–5, not a hymn.[1]

A midrash is a retelling of a root biblical text for a homiletical purpose, often with a secondary text to inform the retelling. For John, the root biblical text is Genesis 1:1–5, the secondary text is Proverbs 8:22–31 (Wisdom's role at creation), and the homiletical purpose is to show how the story of the incarnate Word of God continues the story of the creative Word of God. The story of the creating power of God's Word in Genesis provides the form and the content for John's midrash; John's repetitions and rhythms echo the repetitions and rhythms of the Genesis 1 text.[2] Genesis 1:1–5 tells the story of God's creation of light and so demonstrates the creating power of God's Word; John 1:1–5 remembers and retells the story of that creating Word. Where Genesis shows God speaking (Gen. 1:3) and calling (Gen. 1:5) creation into being, John repeatedly names the creating power and presence of the Word (*logos*) with God (vv. 1–3). Genesis 1:4–5 tells the story of the separation of light from darkness, and this same creation story is repeated in John 1:4–5. John 1:1–5 is a reimagining of Genesis 1:1–5.

John begins the Gospel with a celebration of the God whose Word has ultimate creative power. By retelling Genesis 1, John simultaneously gives his story cosmic significance and roots it deeply in the story of the God whose works are already known to John's readers.

1. See the important article by Daniel Boyarin, "The Gospel of Memra: Jewish Binitarianism and the Prologue to John," *Harvard Theological Review* 94 (2001): 243–84. In Boyarin's reading, John 1:1–18 is "a homiletical retelling of the beginning of Genesis, and therefore interpretive and narrative in its genre and not hymnic and cyclical, that is, liturgical" (264). The readings offered in each of my three essays on John 1 play out Boyarin's suggestions.
2. Boyarin, "Gospel of Memra," 270.

Homiletical Perspective

even what is dead within us and around us. It is a story worth telling in any age.

Another approach to preaching John 1:1–9 would engage preachers with the new electronic publishing tool called the "Wordle." This device generates "word clouds" from texts. The cloud gives greater prominence to words that appear with greater frequency in the text. John 1:1–9 would render a fascinating "Wordle." In nine verses, recurring words and themes pepper John's poetry, not just "beginning" and "life," but "word," "into being," "light," "darkness," "testify." Like "beginning" and "life," each of these words and themes is revisited frequently throughout John's Gospel and plays a major role in this evangelist's theology.

Too often, preaching is a prosaic exercise. Perhaps, the Wordle approach to John's prologue might provide for more poetic or musical possibilities, as the preacher focuses on these Johannine themes in fresh and creative ways. This approach might also open the imaginations of the worship leader and the worshiper, leading them to engage this text artistically, from employing the visual arts and liturgical movement, to experimenting with a service that moves from near darkness into full light. In whatever ways preachers and worship leaders proclaim this text, it will be a missed opportunity if the liturgy and proclamation stay at the level of the prosaic.

Preachers would be wise to heed one word of caution as they wrestle with the prevalent themes in John's beginning. When expounding on the Johannine themes of "darkness" and "light," it is tempting to flatten these rich apocalyptic images into one dimension, missing their polyvalent meanings. Without a full appreciation of their apocalyptic import, preachers can advance, even innocently, the damaging racial connotation of everything "dark" being associated with chaos and evil, while everything "light" is associated with whiteness and purity.[2] There are already enough treacherous racial/ethnic challenges in John's Gospel without preachers making this unfortunate homiletical choice.

Advent and Christmas offer another fine homiletical portal into this text. If read during the season of Advent, this text notes the critical role that John the Baptist plays in pointing to the light, while never making the mistake of pointing to himself as the source of the light. Moreover, this text from the prologue of John expands on traditional themes of the season of Advent. Taking direction from John's

2. See Barbara Brown Taylor, *Learning to Walk in the Dark* (San Francisco: Harper One, 2014)

John 1:1–9

Theological Perspective

If hospitality thrives within God, how does it spread to creatures? The one who spreads it is a "mediator," a person who works "in the middle." We ordinarily think of Jesus Christ as the mediator of salvation, but John 1:3 reveals that the agent of redemption is also the agent of creation. Christ is the person designated to work in the middle both times.

"Word of God" and "wisdom of God" are profound metaphors for the Godly intelligence and expressiveness of the Holy Trinity spread to creatures through both creation and redemption. According to God's intelligence, the way to thrive is to cause others to thrive; the way to fulfill yourself is to spend yourself. Throughout the Gospel, John will show the self-spending Jesus going to work for others: he will make wine for them, wash their feet, hand them bread, and carry his cross to The Place of the Skull (19:17).

This self-spending principle also explains the role of John the Baptist. Like Jesus, John was "sent from God" (v. 6), but not to be the light of the world. John's role was to point to the light of the world—to exalt him, glorify him, defer to him. He is witness and then martyr. John had to display humility to display the glory of Christ. He had to hide his little light to testify to the true light that was coming into the world.

In an age of self-acclaim (we used to have the Me generation, but after three generations of self-exaltation it is now the Me Me Me generation) John shows one of the virtues we seldom prize. John the Baptist shows us the virtue of voluntary obscurity.

Nevertheless, in the end, obscurity eluded him: just Google John the Baptist.

CORNELIUS PLANTINGA JR.

Pastoral Perspective

John reminds us that there is a darkness that would overwhelm us if we were left to ourselves and our own efforts at self-improvement. The glorious good news is that we are not alone, that there is Someone who knows how to "turn on the lights." Most importantly, a light that is Light, the Light that was in the beginning, has dawned in the fullness of time over two thousand years ago. Jesus Christ is the Light who has triumphed over the darkness that causes us to fail to recognize strangers as our brothers and sisters and simultaneously renders us unable to properly grasp our own value in him.

If Lewis is correct that there are no *ordinary people*, that includes those who are in the church as well as everyone else. We are free to explore the splendor of living when we walk in the Light that dawns in Jesus. We are empowered to refuse to take the destructiveness of human sin as the final answer. That darkness has been overcome by the divine intervention of the Triune God. We are therefore invited and enabled to live life in a new way that insists upon the triumph of God's Light—the Son of God, Jesus Christ.

How do we allow the light to shine in us so that we may see strangers as people who have also been touched by the true Light? The answer to that is to begin in the beginning. Before any problem ever presented itself, the Word had been spoken and the Light had dawned. All our sin, all our problems, are significant. At the same time, they are only plot twists in the grand narrative of the gospel, which promises the triumph of the Light and grants us the grace to live as those who believe God is the One who, in Jesus Christ, has "turned on the light."

PHILIP D. JAMIESON

Exegetical Perspective

This is the God to whom John the Baptist bears witness in verses 6–9. When John 1:1–5 is read as a midrash on Genesis 1:1–5, verses 6–9 are not an awkward interruption, but are the next essential step in the story John is telling. In each of the Gospels, John the Baptist is the voice crying out in the wilderness, calling people to light over against darkness (cf. Luke 1:76–79), preaching "a baptism of repentance for the forgiveness of sins." John's depiction and role in verses 6–9 is consistent with his presentation in the Synoptic Gospels: before the advent of Jesus into the world, "he came as a witness to testify to the light, so that all might believe through him" (v. 7). John witnesses at the edge of light and darkness, his prophetic role shaped by his awareness of how easily darkness can overcome the light.

"In the beginning" is more than a phrase that John repeats to open his Gospel. The repurposing of this phrase is part of a complete retelling of Genesis 1:1–5 and provides the frame for understanding all that follows in the Gospel. In John 1:1–9, John firmly places his story in the story that early Christians shared with Judaism—God's creating Word, the light of God that is in the world, the prophets who bear witness to that light and that Word. These verses remind the reader that while John will soon celebrate the story of something new—the incarnation of the Word of God—this newness can be understood only when it is located in the story of the first newness, God's creation, the power of God's Word. As intensely christological as the Gospel of John is (and it will take the christological turn at 1:14), its "beginning" in Genesis 1:1–5 is a reminder that it is also profoundly theological.

GAIL R. O'DAY

Homiletical Perspective

prologue, Advent is not only a season of peace, hope, joy, and love, not only a season of watching, waiting, and wondering. It is also a season of testifying, "He came as a witness to testify to the light, so that all might believe through him" (v. 7).

For the many who have lost all religious connotations of the word "testify," and who connect "testify" with what happens in a courtroom drama, this classic text affords the opportunity for preachers to bring listeners into a new understanding of what it means to testify. What if preachers were to help their listeners reclaim the ancient art of bearing witness as an essential Advent discipline?

In many liturgical traditions, this Johannine text serves as an alternative, certainly a nontraditional, reading on Christmas Eve or for Christmas morning worship. John's "Christmas" story is missing a visitation and Magnificat, magi and shepherds, a "No Room" sign, even Mary and Joseph. Still, in many ways, John's story is the theological back story for Matthew's and Luke's Christmas narratives. John grabs hold of the imagination and takes us back, long before Bethlehem, indeed long before time, to when there was nothing but chaos. In his Genesis revisited, John tells the story of order (*logos*) emerging out of chaos (darkness). Is there a more powerful or more important Christmas story to tell than the one John portends in these verses: "The true light, which enlightens everyone, was coming into the world" (v. 9)?

Christmas is often associated with "belief," in particular with the childhood belief in a Santa Claus, a belief that is abandoned long before adulthood. In this text, John invites us to reclaim Christmas as a season of "belief" for those of all ages. John would have us believe in the "logos" who will speak and wine will flow from casks of water (chap. 2), who will speak and a disabled man of thirty-eight years will stand up on his own (chap. 5), who will speak and those with nothing to eat will be eating their fill (chap. 6). John's prologue is a perfect Christmas morning text, because there is no question about who is the source of our Christmas joy. The only question in chapter 1 and continuing through chapter 21 is whether we will believe in this life-giving, new-beginning "logos." John will preach that truth throughout his Gospel, and preachers would be wise to do the same.

GARY W. CHARLES

John 1:1–9

7

John 1:10–13

¹⁰He was in the world, and the world came into being through him; yet the world did not know him. ¹¹He came to what was his own, and his own people did not accept him. ¹²But to all who received him, who believed in his name, he gave power to become children of God, ¹³who were born, not of blood or of the will of the flesh or of the will of man, but of God.

Theological Perspective

These verses tell us of a great biblical tragedy and then of God's partial salvage of it. "The true light, which enlightens everyone, was coming into the world" (v. 9), and the world told him to get lost. The world hung up on him, slammed doors on him, turned their backs to him. The Gospels say that pious people plotted against him, that Judas betrayed him, that three disciples fell asleep on him, that witnesses lied about him, and that Peter denied him. They tell us that Pilate flogged him, and that soldiers mocked him. Then, when the soldiers got tired of kneeling in front of Jesus and belting him in the face, they led him out to crucify him. After all, mockery mortifies the human spirit so devastatingly that crucifixion is just a way of finishing it off.

This is what happened to the true light coming into the world. In a few verses of immeasurable heartbreak and of breathtaking understatement, John says that the world "did not know him" (v. 10b), that his own people "did not accept him" (v. 11b).

The Gospels give us one innocent reason for this unknowing and unaccepting. They tell us that Jesus Christ can be known, but he is hard to know. He is elusive, unpredictable, untamable, unguessable. He teaches in stories, an indirect medium, and at least once suggested that he did so to keep people off balance. He falls silent at crucial times. Given that he is

Pastoral Perspective

These four verses of John 1 reveal a puzzle that is central to human existence: humanity is alienated from the very creation of which it is a part. We do not recognize the Creator, and thus we cannot recognize the web of relationships that are central to the creation. For this reason, we are alienated from our neighbor and ultimately from ourselves. It is a special problem of knowledge. We have the capacity to know many things through our observation of the created order. Modern science is predicated upon that. What verse 10 states is that in spite of all the things that we can know through observation, we are unable to know that which is most important, that which is the key to all proper perception: who we really are and who we are meant to be. That inability is related directly to the human powerlessness and unwillingness to recognize God in our midst.

To say it another way, creation is silent at the very point where we require a definitive word. Our powers of observation fail us when we need them the most. The natural order truly is glorious; it really is a marvel. However, it simply does not provide us with the key to understanding that which can unlock the greatest mysteries. In other words, it cannot help us recognize the gracious nature of the Creator. Reflecting on Genesis 3:8 ("They heard the sound of the LORD God walking in the garden at the time of the

Exegetical Perspective

John 1:10–13 is a transitional unit in the opening verses of the Gospel of John, positioned between the preincarnation story of verses 1–9 and the incarnation story that will begin with the dramatic announcement of 1:14. A long-standing issue in Johannine studies is determining at what point the prologue begins to talk about the incarnate Word. When the prologue is read primarily as a hymn, interrupted twice by narrative fragments about John the Baptist (vv. 6, 15), this issue becomes particularly convoluted. Since John the Baptist belongs most properly to the Jesus story, the "interpolations" of verse 6 must introduce the incarnation, even though such an interpretation mutes the dramatic power of the confession of verse 14.

If one approaches verses 1–18 freshly, reading them not as a hymn or poem, but as a narrative, one discovers that "a strictly chronological narrative interpretation of the text rather than a lyrical, hymnic one makes for a much better reading."[1]

As noted in the entry on John 1:1–9, John 1:1–5 can be read as a midrash on Genesis 1:1–5. John 1:1–2, like Genesis 1:1–2, begins outside of time, in the cosmic realm before God called time (light and darkness) into being. John 1:3–5 retells the first day

1. Daniel Boyarin, "The Gospel of Memra: Jewish Binitarianism and the Prologue to John," *Harvard Theological Review* 94 (2001): 265.

Homiletical Perspective

Preachers would be wise to note that John 1:10–13 comes in the middle of a carefully crafted theological prologue to the Fourth Gospel. To read only verses 10–13 from John's prologue is not unlike walking unprepared into an intense family debate. Preachers who tackle this text from John might consider expanding the reading, reaching back to verse 1, even if the focus of the sermon is largely on verses 10–13. One example of such a homiletical strategy is apparent when preachers consider John's witness in verse 9, a witness that sets up expectations for what will follow in verses 10–13. After talking about the witness of John the Baptist, the evangelist promises, "The true light, which enlightens everyone, was coming into the world." With consummate finesse, in verse 9 John sets up his readers to expect great things to happen when the world finally experiences the "true light."

As our text opens, the great hope that John generates in verse 9 is quickly doused—or at least delayed. Not only is the "world"—a recurring theme in the prologue—oblivious to the "true light" when it arrives, but the world has no excuse for such blatant unawareness. In his dance with time, John tells us that the "true light" is not only coming but is already here; in fact, "the world came into being through him" (v. 10). "The world," then, is culpable

John 1:10–13

Theological Perspective

"God the Son," he needs to pray a lot more than you would expect. Somebody asks him a question, and he responds by answering a different question. In John's Gospel, uniquely, Jesus speaks in long, stylized discourses on an altogether different plane from that of his fellow travelers.

Jesus Christ can be known, but he is hard to know. He is God *with* us, so he may be known; but he is also *God* with us, which means he is way beyond us.

In this way he is exactly like his Father. God may be known, but God may not be comprehended. God may be known, but God's greatness is unsearchable. We know *something* of God, but there is much more we do not know, perhaps will never know, and in our finiteness *cannot* ever know, even in eternity. Karl Barth famously put it that God is both veiled and unveiled, and that God remains veiled even in unveiling.[1]

Yet why would the world not know at least the unveiled part of Jesus? In John's terms, that would include Jesus' word, work, love, glory. How could the world have missed these things?

Here is the mystery of iniquity that includes willed ignorance and self-deception. Self-deception is a form of corrupted consciousness, wrote popular theologian Lewis Smedes, which like a skillful computer fraud, doubles back to cover its own trail: "first we deceive ourselves, and then we convince ourselves that we are not deceiving ourselves."[2]

"The world did not know him" (v. 10b). Here is one of the oldest and most tragic of missed opportunities. Despite his teaching, his signs, his prophetic edge, his manifest love, the world did not know him.

Some of this unknowing is perennial, and some of it is in the church. Why else do new revised standard versions of God keep emerging? Why else does God emerge in the church as racist, sexist, nationalist, socialist, capitalist? If we are poor, God is a revolutionary; if we are propertied, God is night watchman over our goods. If we are intellectuals, God is a cosmic Phi Beta Kappa. If we are anti-intellectual, then "Show me an educated Christian and I will show you a backslider." The gods of the Persians always look like Persians.

"The world did not know him" (v. 10b), and too much of the world is in the church.

Pastoral Perspective

evening breeze, and the man and his wife hid themselves from the presence of the LORD God among the trees of the garden"), Ray Anderson makes two important points. First, "there never was a time when humans were solely dependent on the impersonal, created world to expound the nature and purpose of God." That is, God does not leave us alone in our ignorance, but comes to us and would reveal God's self to us. Second, Genesis 3:8 also expounds the human proclivity to flee the very God who graciously and personally comes to us.[1]

Therefore, what verse 10 states should not surprise the reader. The inability to recognize the Word is basic to the human dilemma. God comes into our midst, and we hide, fearing the very One who has created and loves us. God's overtures are misunderstood because humanity has no means of understanding the nature of God and yet insists on basing its understanding on its own inadequate resources.

It is this very problem of the fragility of human knowledge that should make us suspicious of our judgments regarding our neighbors. No doubt, verse 11 references the first people who failed to recognize the Word made flesh; a faithful pastoral reading will insist upon turning attention to ourselves and how we continue to fail to recognize Christ in our midst. We, who have been given power to become children of God, know only enough to leave ultimate judgments about eternal things to God. We simply do not have the capacity, absent God's revelation in Christ, to understand ourselves or others in a proper manner.

Verse 12 contains the verb that is central to faith: "gave." The children of God have received and accepted. They have not earned this remarkable change of status: from those who are alienated to those who belong to the Creator God. No one can work his or her way out of such self-alienation; the power to do so always comes as a gift. It is a gift that is revealed as a new relationship. This change in status implies a movement from outside the family to inside; it implies a new way of living, founded upon a new relationship to God and ultimately to all of creation.

The new status granted to those who have become God's children through the agency of Jesus Christ has tremendous implications for congregational life. The new status of child can be difficult to accept by those who are accustomed to earning and withholding love. Those who have become acclimated

---

1. See Karl Barth, *Church Dogmatics* I/1 (Edinburgh: T. & T. Clark, 1975), 176–81.
2. Lewis Smedes, *A Pretty Good Person* (San Francisco: Harper & Row, 1990), 74.

1. Ray Anderson, *The Soul of Ministry* (Louisville, KY: Westminster John Knox Press, 1997), 6.

of creation and so brings the story from the cosmic into the beginning of the created order. With the creation of light, of day and night, morning and evening, time can now begin to be calculated. John 1:6–9 brings the Gospel of John fully into the historical present. John the Baptist is the narrative link between the time before the incarnation and the time after the incarnation.

Chronology and the movement of time from the eternal into the time-bound and time-specific is a central dynamic throughout John 1:1–18. Creation and God's creating Word set the context for everything that follows in the Gospel, but John the Baptist sets the story's time. John the Baptist and his witness mark the transition from the common creation story, shared by all who claim Genesis as a sacred text, to a more particularized story of God in the world. His prophetic witness is a reminder that even in the face of the awesome creative and creating power of God, people still chose not to receive what God has offered.

Can verses 10–13 be read as part of a narrative, chronological reading? In the mid-twentieth century, C. H. Dodd advocated this type of reading, noting that verses 9–13 continue the story of the preincarnate Word.[2] Read this way, verses 10–13 do not recount a story specific to the incarnation; they do not describe the particular reception of the incarnate Word. Rather, they narrate the regular and repeated story of the fate of the Word in the world. Verse 10 restates the creating power of the Word, yet also notes the world's inability to know the Word. Verse 11 repeats the same claim in slightly different language (cf. the repetition in 1:1–3). The Word comes to creation, but creation does not recognize the Word. Yet the fate of the Word is not thoroughly negative. Verses 12–13 describe what happens when the Word is recognized: there is a renewal of creation, as those who receive the Word become children of God.

This dynamic of recognition and nonrecognition, reception and rejection, is the story of the Word in the world; it is a pattern repeated in the prophets and throughout the stories of the Jewish Scriptures. It is the story of Wisdom searching for a home.[3] It often seems to be a pattern without an end; for every story of rejection, there are complementary stories of acceptance. For every story of acceptance, there are also stories of rejection. It is the same story that the writer of Hebrews recalls: "Long ago God spoke

for its ignorance of the one who is the source of its creation. While this is tragic behavior, according to John, it is not new behavior for "the world." Raymond Brown notes, "The rejection of the Word by men [sic] in vs. 10 is quite similar to the rejection of Wisdom by men [sic] in En xlii 2: 'Wisdom came to make her dwelling place among the children of men and found no dwelling place.'"[1] Preachers can cite verse 10 to speak to the often tragic and mysterious disconnect between the good intentions of God and the egregious ignorance of God by humanity. More specifically, they can address Jesus as the "light" of the world and wonder why the world so often chooses to ignore the light and dwell in darkness.

If preached in isolation from the rest of the Gospel, verse 10 and the verses that immediately follow might be proclaimed as a gospel of tragedy, a Johannine dirge over the ignorance and opposition of "the world." However, John will soon transform this potential dirge in verses 10–13 into an occasion for celebration when Jesus will declare: "For God so loved the world that [God] gave [God's] only Son, so that everyone who believes in him may not perish but may have eternal life" (3:16). God does not send the "light" into the world to condemn the world to continue to stumble about in "darkness." God sends the life-giving and transforming light into the world to illumine a world that is easily seduced by the dark.

At several junctures in John's Gospel, including these verses, the author points to the tragic separation of the "world" from God, but at no point does the author conclude that the world's darkness has or will prevail. "The light shines in the darkness, and the darkness did not overcome it" (1:5). Thus preachers of the prologue need to be nimble as they pay close attention to the tragic components of the text at hand, while also listening to the entire witness of good news in this Gospel.

While John 1:10–13 affords preachers the opportunity both to name the darkness that still prevails in the world and to point to ways in which God's light is penetrating that darkness, this text also invites preachers to speak to a recurring frustration among the faithful who bear witness to the "light." Why is it that some people hear the promise of Jesus, that he is the long-promised light of the world, as the good news they have always hoped to hear, while others see any talk of Jesus as so much nonsense? Although it may offer little comfort to listeners, verse 10 invites

2. C. H. Dodd, *The Interpretation of the Fourth Gospel* (Cambridge: Cambridge University Press, 1953), 281.

3. E.g., *1 Enoch* 42:1–2. Boyarin, "Gospel of Memra," 277–78.

1. Raymond E. Brown, *The Gospel according to John I–XII,* Anchor Bible 29 (Garden City, NY: Doubleday & Co., 1966), 30.

John 1:10–13

Theological Perspective

The world did not try to put out the true light because Jesus puzzled them or because it simply did not *want* to know him or accept him. No, the very people he created came to *resent* him. The true light is a reproach to us in our worldliness, because his light contrasts so sharply with our darkness. In Johannine terms, we love darkness rather than light because our "deeds [are] evil" (3:19). In the presence of glory and light, our irremediable shabbiness is revealed, our selfishness, our evasion of the truth about ourselves. A police officer who shines a flashlight into a pulled-over car is likely to meet resentment. A news photographer filming police brutality is likely to meet resentment.

The darkness resents the light. Who is this man Jesus, who calls our works evil and who says that he and the Father are one? What makes him think he is anything more than a mortal like ourselves?

Envy knows how to deal not only with claimed superiority but also with real superiority. If real glory exposes my inglorious self, I will resent it, I will lie about it, and then I will kill it.

"His own people did not accept him" (v. 11b). To say the least.

Then comes the marvelous turn in the prologue toward believers, accepters, knowers of Jesus, to whom he "gave power to become children of God" (v. 12b). Theologically speaking, what kind of power can cause a second birth? What kind of power can pierce puzzlement, self-deception, envy turning to hatred turning to murder?

So thick is our corruption, so hard our hearts, so intractable our will, that only a supernatural, God-almighty, Holy Ghost power can do it. Without the miracle, our will simply and imperially wants what it wants. Therefore the power that softens our will is going to have to be no less astonishing than the power that created the world or the power that raises the dead.

The reason is that the regeneration of a hard human will *is* a resurrection of the dead into a whole new creation where all things have been made new.

CORNELIUS PLANTINGA JR.

Pastoral Perspective

to living on the "outside" of acceptance may need some time fully to acknowledge this profound gift. It may take a good deal of time to shed the old ways of judgment and rejection, of bias and fear. Too many Christians, forgetting their graciously given status as God's children, may find it hard not to retreat to the more natural ways of hiding.

Those who are mindful of their new status as children are empowered to treat others in a different manner. Those who have been given power are empowered to reach out to those who are without power. These verses raise important pastoral questions. First, do the members and constituents of the congregation recognize their new status and its gifted nature? Are they able to know and act according to the knowledge that the Creator God is also their loving Parent? All too many Christians act as if God barely tolerates them and is only looking for an excuse to break relationship with them. However, that is not the relationship that God both desires and has established through Christ in the power of the Holy Spirit. The good news of verse 13 is that the children of God have neither created nor instigated their new status. They need only receive it as the unexpected and remarkable gift that it is.

A second and equally important question is also raised here. Founded upon the gracious knowledge that the Creator is also the loving Parent, are these children of God treating others in a new way? Once again, all too many Christians are happy to claim a new status, but are hesitant to treat others in a way consistent with that status. Those who are the children of God, those who have not labored for the new relationship, must be willing to view all others as potential children of God and therefore people of infinite value. Verse 13 removes human striving from the salvation equation.

PHILIP D. JAMIESON

Exegetical Perspective

to our ancestors in many and various ways by the prophets" (Heb. 1:1). The Gospel of John starts "in the beginning" of this story, and in verses 10–13 brings the reader to the ever-repeating middle. John brings the reader face to face with the human story before God. The creative and creating power of the Word is rebuffed as regularly as it is embraced, even when the embrace means one becomes a child of God.

If we take this narrative, chronological reading one more step, it is intriguing to imagine that verses 10–13 do not belong to the Gospel's explicit commentary, but are instead words spoken by John the Baptist. John the Baptist's traditional role in the Gospels is to proclaim the fate of the preincarnate Word in the world and so "prepare the way." These verses can be read as John's depiction of that role. To give John the Baptist such prominence at the beginning of the Gospel of John conforms to the beginnings of the other canonical Gospels. He is the voice that indicts the present failure of the world to embrace the Word of God, the voice that demands more, and the voice that proclaims what comes next in God's ongoing story with God's people.

In a narrative, chronological reading of John 1:1–18, there is a definite and defined movement from point A to point B. John tells the story of the Word, from its initial appearance at creation to its repeated appearances throughout the human story. It is not a simple story of failure, because there are moments in the history of the Word where the Word is recognized and received, and those who receive the Word become children of God. However, it is also not a story of complete success, either. The Gospel of John has set the stage for a dramatic turn in the story of the Word, when the Word of God no longer only speaks, but dwells among us.

GAIL R. O'DAY

Homiletical Perspective

preachers to name a centuries-old conundrum. According to John, the world has no excuse to offer for its disregard and dismissal of Jesus; yet it still happens. For those who get discouraged as they try to follow Jesus and try to persuade others to do the same, this verse is confirmation that such evangelistic hope will not always be met with exuberance.

In 1:11 John focuses on the great mystery that Jesus, a Jew, came as a light to his own nation, but many chose to disregard the light and even sought to extinguish the light. This is a theme that John will revisit numerous times throughout the Gospel. Before preaching on this complex and sensitive subject, preachers would do well to read the excursus on Jesus and "the Jews" at the beginning of this book. This excursus will provide valuable wisdom to those proclaiming these perplexing verses, lest the church continue a sad history of harmful and ill-informed interpretations of Jesus and "the Jews."

Preachers have often turned verses 12–13 into a Johannine altar call, celebrating that the days of the Abrahamic and Davidic covenants are over and that in Jesus, God has initiated a new and better covenant, the covenant of the heart (Jer. 31:31–34). I hope that preachers will now dig deeper before preaching with such homiletical hubris as they listen to these verses within the entirety of the Johannine witness.

In verses 12–13, John points to the power of God to bring people to faith, regardless of their religious pedigree or lack thereof. Just as God is able to penetrate the deepest darkness with an indestructible light, so God is able to penetrate the darkness of unbelief and disbelief with the power of faith. Surely, this is good news for people of lots of faith and people of little faith at any time and in any place.

GARY W. CHARLES

John 1:14–18

¹⁴And the Word became flesh and lived among us, and we have seen his glory, the glory as of a father's only son, full of grace and truth. ¹⁵(John testified to him and cried out, "This was he of whom I said, 'He who comes after me ranks ahead of me because he was before me.' ") ¹⁶From his fullness we have all received, grace upon grace. ¹⁷The law indeed was given through Moses; grace and truth came through Jesus Christ. ¹⁸No one has ever seen God. It is God the only Son, who is close to the Father's heart, who has made him known.

Theological Perspective

The classic Christian doctrine of the incarnation of the Son of God describes "a love so amazing, so divine" that it seems downright paradoxical; and so it is.

The classic doctrine states that the eternal second person of the Holy Trinity, himself of "one substance" with the Father, "became flesh." John's choice of *sarx* may have been intended to rout early Docetists who regarded Jesus' humanity as a phantom, a mere appearance. In any case, John insists on Jesus' flesh. The high one became a low one. The one who had lived in triplicate hospitality and verve, in a constant outpouring of spirit upon spirit, became flesh— real flesh, messy flesh, entirely fleshy flesh.

So maybe God the Son now hammers nails in Joseph's carpenter shop, whacks his thumb, howls with the pain of it—especially because it is hay-fever season. The one who had existed from all eternity is born of a woman. The omniscient second person of the Trinity now has to "grow in knowledge and favor" with human beings and, even after much growth, still does not know when the end of the world will happen. In some towns the omnipotent Son of God cannot get anybody to believe and once had to heal a blind man in two stages because he did not quite get it right the first time. There seems to be almost a metaphysical leakage at the joint between divinity and humanity.

Pastoral Perspective

New Testament scholar Rudolf Schnackenburg has written: "The absolute term *flesh* is not merely a circumlocution for *human being* . . . but in Johannine thinking an expression for what is earthly and limited, frail and transitory."[1]

In other words, for the Logos to become flesh means that God has not drawn near to us as an invulnerable human being. He does not stride through life moving from one victory to another. The orthodox teaching of "fully divine and fully human" does not imply a person who is one of us, while at the same time *not* one of us. It does not mean a superbeing, distant and remote. No, the enfleshed Logos is human as we are: always subject to forces beyond human control. The one without whom "not one thing came into being" (1:3) is now acted upon by the very things created through him. He is now subject to economic downturns, to governmental oppression, to illness and death. As the author of Hebrews reminds us, "For we do not have a high priest who is unable to sympathize with our weaknesses, but we have one who in every respect has been tested as we are, yet without sin" (Heb. 4:15). Christ does not succumb to the temptations to

1. Rudolf Schnackenburg, *Jesus in the Gospels* (Louisville, KY: Westminster John Knox Press, 1995), 290.

Feasting on the Gospels

Exegetical Perspective

In John 1:14, "word" (*logos*) reappears in the Gospel narrative for the first time since verse 1. This reintroduction of the central theme of the unfolding story underscores the pivotal importance of the announcement/confession of this verse. The Word was in the beginning, and now "the Word became flesh." A dramatic change has taken place in the story of the Word.

This change can be seen most clearly by observing the use of the verbs *eimi* ("to be") and *ginomai* ("to become") in the opening verses of John. In 1:1, the verb *eimi* is used three times: "in the beginning was [*ēn*] the Word, and the Word was [*ēn*] with God, and the Word was [*ēn*] God." In 1:3 *ginomai* is used to describe the process of creation and the Word's role in that creative process: "Everything became [*egeneto*] through the Word, and without the Word, not one thing became [*egeneto*]" (my trans.). In 1:6, *ginomai* is used to introduce John the Baptist, "There was [*egeneto*] a man, sent from God, his name was John." The verb choice signals that John the Baptist belongs to the time-bound realm, like creation in 1:3, and not the eternal realm, like the Word in 1:1. In 1:14, the verb *ginomai* replaces *eimi* to speak about the Word: "And the Word became [*egeneto*] flesh." This shift in verbs perfectly embodies what is new and dramatic about the Word in verse 14. The Word has moved from being the creative, eternal

Homiletical Perspective

The close of John's masterful prologue offers up a homiletical feast. For preachers who wish to address major doctrines of the faith, John 1:14–18 is a compelling invitation to consider the doctrine of the incarnation. At the opening of John's prologue, we learn that the Word has been with God since the beginning of creation. As the prologue closes, John insists that the eternal Word entered the bounds of the material world, as the Word "became flesh and lived among us" (v. 14a). The Johannine God does not disdain the material world, existing only in the realm of the spirit, does not enter the world in the guise of human flesh, as do many of the gods in Greek and Roman mythology, but instead "became flesh and lived among us."

In even more vivid imagery of this incarnated God, John points his readers back to Exodus 25:8–9 when he insists that the eternal Word of God "pitched a tent" (*skēnoun*) among us. In Jesus, God "pitched a tent," choosing not simply to visit or to observe, but to dwell within the human community. The story of the incarnation is not a story of a God who supplies believers a transport system through which to escape the evil, material world. According to John, the Word of God decisively and intentionally enters the material world and, by doing so, reminds us of the refrain about the newly fashioned

Theological Perspective

Some of us exult in the paradoxes of the incarnation—Sylvia Dunston, for example, in her marvelous hymn "Christus Paradox" ("shining in eternal glory," "beggar'd by a soldier's toss").[1]

Of all the paradoxes of the incarnation, think about the paradox of Jesus Christ's glory—"the glory as of a father's only son, full of grace and truth" (v. 14). How hard it is to see real glory when we think glory is all about making a splash! We miss the real thing because we get our standards from people who have glory mixed up with publicity—people like pro athletes and entertainers, or hard-charging winners in business who then want to star in their own TV show. In ordinary life, glory is reputation, and it is built on publicity and peer review by people just as fouled up as we are.

John has a different view of glory. In his Gospel, Jesus changes water to wine at a wedding to make people joyful. He washes his disciples' feet, hoping to model and ignite a heart of service in them. He feeds the disciples bread at the table where they reclined—including Judas—and then submits himself to arrest.

In all three cases—the wine (chap. 2), the bathwater (chap. 13), the bread for a traitor (chap. 13)—the evangelist tells us that it was a sign of his glory. This is a glory he shares with his Father. Jesus makes lots of wine at Cana because he comes from a wine-making family. Every fall God turns water into wine in France and Chile and the Napa Valley. C. S. Lewis said that at Cana Jesus just did a small, speeded-up version of what God does all the time in the great vineyards of the world.[2]

Glory in the wine of Jesus, and glory in the washbasin of Jesus. Has not God always been humble to serve us, even when our sin has led us into terrible trouble? "Have mercy on me, O God, according to your steadfast love; according to your abundant mercy blot out my transgressions. Wash me thoroughly from my iniquity, and cleanse me from my sin" (Ps. 51:1–2). Jesus on his knees before his disciples is just doing what he sees his Father doing, and the gospel finds glory here, because it is so much like God humbly to clean people up.

Bread for a traitor? Does not God do this all the time—sending rain on the fields of unjust people so that their crops will grow and *they* will grow too as they feed on God's gifts? Jesus hands Judas a piece of bread because he just does what he sees his Father

Pastoral Perspective

which flesh is subject, but he does understand and experience completely human frailty and need.

So here in this little word, "flesh," we see a foreshadowing of Christ's pastoral encounters and the signs of his identity: the healing of the official's son (4:50–54), the paralytic at Beth-zatha (5:1–18), and the man born blind (9:1–17), and weeping at Lazarus's grave (11:33–37). God has identified with us in all of our pain and infirmity. This is a God who will not shun the brokenness of our human situation.

Perhaps it is the second part of verse 14 that may strike some of us as the oddest statement. It is in the very taking up of the human frailty of flesh that "we have seen his glory, the glory as of a father's only son, full of grace and truth." Reflecting upon this passage, Karl Barth twice identifies the miraculous with God's mercy:

> So we say that when the Word becomes flesh, we are concerned with a miracle, an act of God's mercy. There takes place in the created world the unforeseen, that which could not be constructed or postulated from the side either of the world or of God, the work of the love of God to a world distinct, nay divided from Him, to a creature which He does not need, which has nothing to offer Him, to which He owes nothing, which rather is permanently indebted to Him for everything, which has forfeited its existence in His eyes.

Then Barth writes, "'The Word became' if that is true, and true in such a way that a real becoming is thereby expressed without the slightest surrender of the divinity of the Word, its truth is that of a miraculous act, an act of mercy on the part of God."[2]

The pastoral implications of this relationship between miracle and mercy are immense. God's glory is not separated from God's mercy. To be even more precise, God's glory is best known in God's mercy. To anticipate the example of Lazarus's return from death, in the Word becoming flesh we see that God's strength and beauty are made known as much in Jesus' weeping as in his ability to raise Lazarus from the dead. God is seen, God is made known (v. 18) in Jesus' tears as much as in his shout for Lazarus to "come out!"

In other words, the incarnation is not merely something that happened once and then was finished. The incarnation is an ongoing summons to the church that, even as it is the body of Christ, it may be only the type of body that is revealed in

---

1. Sylvia Dunston, "Christus Paradox," in *Glory to God, The Presbyterian Hymnal* (Louisville, KY: Westminster John Knox Press, 2013), #369.
2. See "Miracles," in *God in the Dock: Essays on Theology and Ethics*, ed. Walter Hooper (Grand Rapids: Eerdmans, 1970), 29.

2. Karl Barth, *Church Dogmatics* I/2 (Edinburgh: T. & T. Clark, 1956), 136 and 159.

Word to being part of creation. The Word *becomes* flesh (v. 14).

This is a dramatic redirection of the story, a redirection made necessary by the story of the Word's reception as narrated in verses 10–13. Those verses are a reminder that the eternal Word has moved from place to place, from time to time, seeking unsuccessfully to find a home, a dwelling place, with God's people. Notice that the verb used to describe the light in 1:9–10 is *eimi*, confirming that the light moves through the world but is not part of the created order.

In the dramatic announcement of 1:14, however, the Word enters the created order, the realm of the flesh, and significantly, given the world's previous inability to know the light (1:10), has made a home ("has dwelled with us"). John 1:14 is in continuity with the story of faith that has led to this moment; God's creative and creating Word remains the central focus, and the central goal remains for that Word to make its home "among us." However, there is also a significant shift: in becoming flesh, the Word is now located in time, no longer the determiner of time (cf. Gen. 1:3–4). Moreover in becoming flesh, the story of the Word shifts from being only a theological story to being a christological story as well (cf. Heb. 1:1–2).

The christological story is the subject of verse 14b ("we have seen his glory") through verse 18. These verses introduce the metaphor of Father and Son that govern the christological story (vv. 14, 18). Father/Son language is language of incarnation, but also recalls the themes of 1:1: the Son shares in the fullness of the Father ("a father's only son," 1:14; "the one and only," 1:18 NIV), just as the Word shares fully with God ("the Word was God"). The Son is "close to the Father's heart" (v. 18), just as "the Word was with God" (1:1). The christological story is one of continuity with the story of the Word (*logos*) and God (*theos*), but the incarnation is also a radically new moment in that story.

To understand verses 14–18 as the beginning of the christological story provides a useful interpretive context for the reference to John the Baptist in verse 15. As noted in the earlier entries on John 1, many Johannine scholars view the references to John the Baptist as prose interpolations into the "hymn" of the prologue, but to do so misreads the function of these references to John. The two appearances of John the Baptist (1:6–9, 15) are consistent with the movement of the opening verses of John. In verses 6–9, John fulfills his preincarnation role of prophet, a role he also plays in the other Gospels (e.g., Luke

world in the first Genesis creation story: "And . . . it was good" (Gen. 1:10, 12, 18, 21, 25, 31).

Whatever the incarnation means for John, it means that God enters the material world fully and blesses it. This is an important correction to much of the docetic preaching done today, in which Jesus only seemed to be human and entered human form just long enough to lead believers out of this corrupted, bound-for-destruction world. For John, much is wrong with the world, but in the incarnation, God does not come to condemn the world (3:17); God comes to redeem and recreate everything and everyone that is broken and marred in the world. Preach that good news to those who are broken and to those who too easily give up on others who are broken— and marvel at the power of incarnational preaching.

What better time is there to preach on the incarnation than at Christmas? Yet John 1:14–18 is rarely heard from pulpits in the land on Christmas Eve or Christmas Day. The lectionary suggests that we do so, and Lamar Williamson articulates why: "The Fourth Gospel has no birth narrative, but its prologue is appointed to be read on Christmas Day because it announces the mystery of the incarnation. Nativity says what happened; incarnation says what it means."[1] As Christmas becomes more and more a secular holiday in our society, this text offers preachers not so much an opportunity to rail against unbridled Santa consumerism, but an occasion to bear witness to the profound gift of the incarnation. Rather than settling for a tinselly holiday that skates on the surface of sentimentality and specializes in syrupy stories, read the entire prologue as an alternative Christmas story, reminding all who will listen that "grace and truth came through Jesus Christ" (v. 17b).

Prior to the Christmas celebration, this text could also provide a powerful witness during Advent. The story of John the Baptist as rendered by the Synoptic Gospels is a recurring story during the Advent season. Preachers can provide a fresh perspective on the Baptist by focusing on John 1:14–18. In these verses, we learn little about the man, but we hear the content of his preaching. He is the voice of one pointing to "grace and truth" that is incarnated in the person of Jesus. "Grace and truth" will be theological themes that make frequent appearances throughout John's Gospel and find their locus in the person of Jesus.

The traditional Advent question is this: "For whom are you waiting?" John 1:14–18 declares that

---

1. Lamar Williamson, *Preaching the Gospel of John* (Louisville, KY: Westminster John Knox Press, 2004), 7.

Theological Perspective

doing, and the gospel finds glory here, because it is so much like God to feed enemies even while you oppose their evil.

The gospel finds glory where we are not looking—in the wine, and the water, and the bread, and even in the blood of Jesus. In John 12 death is in the air. The Son of Man will die and fall into the earth in an event so devastating that it will seem to turn creation back into chaos; but Jesus says that this is the hour in which the Son of Man will be *glorified*. We grope for his meaning. Getting glorified on a cross? Is that like getting enthroned on an electric chair? Is it like being honored by a firing squad?

Glory in the cross of Jesus Christ sounds almost grotesque. Jesus, the friend of sinners, was crucified between his kind of people in a godforsaken place where all the lights go out from noon to three. Yet the gospel wants us to find glory in this disaster, because Jesus Christ is pouring out his life for the world God loves.

The Word became flesh, full of grace and truth. Full of grace upon grace, grace added to grace, grace following hard after grace. Full of truth too—of faithfulness, reliability, unwaveringness. None of this is different from the grace and truth that are God's signature virtues among the children of Israel. None is different, because Jesus is "exegeting" or interpreting his Father. He makes his Father known in a way finally expectable from a Son who is "close to the Father's heart" (v. 18b).

CORNELIUS PLANTINGA JR.

Pastoral Perspective

vulnerability. That is, the church is a fleshly body, one that is subject to forces outside its control. A church that shuns human weakness is not, and truly cannot be, the body of Christ.

The Logos becoming flesh summons the church to seek its Savior in the places of weakness and infirmity. If Christ's church would participate in the ongoing mission of God, it must abide with the widows and the orphans, the addicts and the felons. If only the enfleshed Logos has revealed the "Father's heart" (v. 18b), then God abides and can be found only where human brokenness is understood and not shunned.

As the church is summoned to embody flesh as the Logos is flesh, the church must not understand this summons as drudgery or grim work. Instead, the church is invited to participate in the true glory revealed in vulnerable human flesh with joy, even as God in Christ has participated with joy in God's glory through becoming human. In the words of the great Christmas hymn, "Veiled in flesh the Godhead see; hail th' incarnate Deity, pleased with us in flesh to dwell, Jesus our Emmanuel."[3] God is pleased to abide with us. God is pleased to set aside the status and privileges of divinity in order to enter into human frailty. God is pleased to assume human weakness and accomplish the miraculous through it.

So the question before any Christian congregation, and before each one who has any part in Christ's body, is simply this: Where are the places where you may best behold Christ's flesh? What are the parts of your towns and cities where human frailty is on full display? Do we shun the flesh, or with joy do we abide especially with those lives that are fragmented and crushed? Are we pleased to join Christ in his joyful mission of becoming, as flesh is redeemed and lives are renewed?

PHILIP D. JAMIESON

---

3. Charles Wesley, "Hark! The herald angels sing."

Exegetical Perspective

1:16–17; 3:7–14). Chronologically, John first testifies to the light (1:7; cf. Luke 1:76–79), to the presence of God in the world; and then he testifies explicitly and directly about the incarnate Word, about the presence and ministry of Jesus (v. 15; cf. Luke 3:15–17). John the Baptist connects both parts of the Gospel story: he had a role in the theological story of the Word and God, and he has a role in the christological story of Father and Son. Read in this way, John 1:1–18 flows smoothly into John 1:19, where John's witness continues.

Yet it is important not to draw too sharp a distinction between the theological story and the christological story. Verses 14–18 are an announcement and confession spoken by a particular community ("lived among us," "we have seen," "we have received"), and the language with which this community names what it sees and receives is in complete continuity with what is revealed about God in the preincarnation story: glory, grace and truth, grace upon grace, "the law indeed was given through Moses; grace and truth came through Jesus Christ" (v. 17). These are not new gifts; they continue the gifts that shaped the earlier story of God and God's Word. The trajectory of the Hebrew Bible could be mapped with the language of glory, grace and truth, and the gift of the law; verses 14–18 carry that trajectory forward into the story of the incarnate Word. John 1:14–18 makes clear that the trajectory of the stories of Scripture is not left behind in the new christological story but is the foundation on which it is built.

Outline of John 1:1–18:

1:1–5: The creating power of the Word
1:6–9: John's witness to God's light in the world
1:10–13: The troubled story of the creative Word of God in the world
1:14–18: The incarnate Word of God dwells with us

GAIL R. O'DAY

Homiletical Perspective

he has already come and will come again, and "from his fullness we have all received, grace upon grace" (v. 16). For John, the eternal Word does not arrive as a visiting angel to gather up our Christmas wishes or to deliver us from the evil world. Instead, "Jesus Christ" (v. 17) arrives fully human to give content to all our Advent longings and a redemptive shape to all our desires.

Another homiletical approach to this text is to celebrate how God is revealed in the incarnated Word, Jesus. In Hebrew Scripture, Moses is as close to God as any figure, but even Moses does not behold the glory of God. To look upon God in Hebrew Scripture is to die. In the person of Jesus, says John, we behold God's glory but rather than die, we are given a pathway to life. A sermon series based on the prologue, and how the prologue plays itself out thematically in the rest of the Gospel, could offer preachers a rich opportunity to help people "see" God as God is revealed in the person of Jesus.

John's language is not nuanced, nor is it judiciously diplomatic; it is polemical and aimed at making his case as a skilled attorney would do in any court of law. John is convinced not only that God is most fully revealed in the person of Jesus Christ, but that it makes all the difference in the world for people of faith to share that conviction.

When preaching from John's Gospel, it is critical for preachers to remember that John was writing in a time when the church was differentiating itself from the synagogue. John was not interested in presenting Jesus as one among many ways that God reveals God's self. For John, Jesus is the incarnated, eternal Word of God, and is therefore the only way that people come to know God fully (14:6). Preaching John's Gospel in the twenty-first century will include a passionate testimony to how Jesus reveals God, but it will not stop there. Preachers can adopt John's passionate testimony without adopting John's restrictive understanding of revelation. It will require nuanced and careful preaching, but in the end, there is no other reasonable way to preach from this Gospel.

GARY W. CHARLES

John 1:19–28

[19]This is the testimony given by John when the Jews* sent priests and Levites from Jerusalem to ask him, "Who are you?" [20]He confessed and did not deny it, but confessed, "I am not the Messiah." [21]And they asked him, "What then? Are you Elijah?" He said, "I am not." "Are you the prophet?" He answered, "No." [22]Then they said to him, "Who are you? Let us have an answer for those who sent us. What do you say about yourself?" [23]He said,

"I am the voice of one crying out in the wilderness,
  'Make straight the way of the Lord,'"
as the prophet Isaiah said.

[24]Now they had been sent from the Pharisees. [25]They asked him, "Why then are you baptizing if you are neither the Messiah, nor Elijah, nor the prophet?" [26]John answered them, "I baptize with water. Among you stands one whom you do not know, [27]the one who is coming after me; I am not worthy to untie the thong of his sandal." [28]This took place in Bethany across the Jordan where John was baptizing.

Theological Perspective

How does one recognize the divine presence among us? Where does one look to "see" God in a real, tangible, and concrete way? Those are certainly questions that have come to the forefront in the postmodern era and will most certainly be on the minds of those who engage this passage. However, there is a sense in which these are universal questions, as old as theological reflection itself. In fact, the Gospel of John might be seen as a sustained theological discourse on these questions from a Christian perspective. Thus the themes of Christology and the identity of Jesus are central to this Gospel and to our passage.

In the first eighteen verses of chapter 1, the author uses an introductory prologue that artfully lays out his Christology. Jesus is the Word, the *logos*, God's wisdom that "became flesh and lived among us" (v. 14a). Jesus is the incarnation of God, the one in whom we see the divine fully. The author wants to establish the identity of Jesus at the outset, for his interest is not to address historical questions as such but to elicit faith within his community of concern (20:30–31). Now, with verses 19–25, the author begins to develop the themes of identity and Christology, beginning with the identity of John the Baptizer.

* See "'The Jews' in the Fourth Gospel" on pp. xi–xiv.

Pastoral Perspective

"Who are you?" That is the question posed by the priests and Levites to John. It begins a series of powerful questions in the first chapter of John's Gospel that speak to the human condition. The first question is perhaps the most profound question in life: "Who are you?" Many of us spend a lifetime answering this question. How do we answer it? On the surface it can be answered through family identifiers or employment. "I am an attorney." "I am a mother." "I am an only child." It can be answered by religious affiliation. "I am a Christian." "I am a Presbyterian." The most direct answer is our given name. There are many possible responses to the question "Who are you?"

How does John the Baptist answer the question? He begins by saying who he is not. He is not the Messiah. He is not Elijah. He is not the prophet. Clarity around defining who we are not is indeed part of defining who we are. Had John not possessed the clarity to know who he was not, he could never have understood who he was. It is often easier to define who we are not than who we are. Clergy often find themselves saying who they are not. "I am not your Savior." "I am not a miracle worker." Congregations and denominations can also seek to define themselves by who they are not: "We are not like that church." "We are not about that kind of Christianity."

Exegetical Perspective

Following the prologue (1:1–18), the prose narrative begins at 1:19. The unit before us connects to the prologue through the figure of John the Baptizer, introduced at 1:6–8 as "one sent from God" to give "testimony" (*martyria*) to the Light. His voice has earlier interrupted the meter of the prologue poem (v. 15) to make an important announcement about the Logos: "This was he of whom I said, 'He who comes after me ranks ahead of me because he was before me.'" Indeed, this *exact* announcement of the Baptist will be repeated in verse 30, forming a frame for the material in between, where what is at stake is the true identity of *both* the Logos and his harbinger, the Baptist.

The unit begins in courtroom-like gravity: "This is the testimony [*martyria*] of John," the one sent by God to testify (cf. vv. 6–8) concerning the Light (cf. v. 9). The term "to testify" (*martyrein*) with its cognates appears forty-five times in the Gospel, four times prior to this verse, communicating both the force and the consequences of the Gospel message. Repeatedly it is "testimony"—the witness of and about the true God (3:33)—that is borne, heard, received, or rejected as the life-and-death drama of the Gospel unfolds. Into this courtroom atmosphere comes a query directed to John by "priests and Levites from Jerusalem" (1:19) that begins a volley of

Homiletical Perspective

From the lofty perch of the prologue, the reader is given an insider's view of the character and other-worldly origin of the incarnate Word, come to reveal the Father while living among his own in the person of Jesus Christ. The perspective shifts as the sky-cam zooms in on Bethany across the Jordan, where the cosmic drama begins to unfold. The opening scenes elaborate several subjects previewed in the prologue: God's envoy, John; the identity of the Word made flesh; and varying responses to the Divine-become-human Sojourner. Flanking the Baptizer's introduction of Jesus (vv. 29–34) are two passages that depict the questioning and questing that occur throughout the narrative. Homiletical possibilities for the first of these (1:19–28) include the themes of witness, the identity of John, and the challenge of "the Jews."

Exemplary Witness. Given the pervasive witness motif, some scholars have proposed reading the entire Gospel as a trial narrative.[1] As the curtain rises, the Baptizer is being questioned by priests and Levites from Jerusalem regarding his identity and ministerial authority. In a fearless, threefold confession that contrasts with Peter's later triple disavowal of his discipleship, John describes himself in terms of

---

1. See, for example, Andrew T. Lincoln, *Truth on Trial* (Peabody, MA: Hendrickson Publishers, 2000).

John 1:19–28

Theological Perspective

Levites come from Jerusalem asking questions about this one who is baptizing. They want to know who he is and by what authority he is baptizing people—pertinent questions, since the reader is given very little information. We are told only that his name is John; he has been sent from God to be a witness to the light that is Jesus; and his witness to Jesus is connected with the practice of baptism by water. John answers in the negative when asked if he is Elijah or one of the prophets, but then in verse 26 he shifts the questions about his identity to the identity of Jesus. "Among you," the Baptizer says, "stands one whom you do not know." The Christology of this Gospel is often identified as a "Christology from above." That is, the author's understanding of Jesus is approached not from the perspective of how could this human person be divine, but rather, how is this divine being, the preexistent Word, recognized and comprehended? Hence, to know, to see, to understand, to comprehend—these words are all part and parcel of the same theological conundrum for the author of this Gospel. The divine presence has come into the world, but the world cannot see it. Why? How could one not see God if God were standing "among you"? For the author, the theological issue is where one looks; one must look at the light that is Jesus Christ.

There are a number of unique challenges from this passage that bear fruitful theological reflection. First, the words "witness" and "testimony" connected with John the Baptizer are legal language and foreshadow the trial of Jesus before Pilate (18:28–38). The irony of the later passage is who or what is actually on trial. While it may appear that Jesus is on trial, it is really Pilate who is on trial; religious legalism is on trial; the world is on trial—because none of these could recognize the divine presence. Ultimately, it is *truth* that is on trial (18:38), the truth that Jesus Christ is the Messiah, the Son of God. Of course, since the author wants to elicit faith in believers, this work is directed to "insiders," to those who, though they have not physically seen Jesus, have indeed seen the Lord and "come to believe" (20:29).

Thus we are witnesses; we give testimony to the truth that is Jesus Christ. The task before us is to "flesh out" the truth that is Jesus Christ, in our proclamation, our work, and our communal life together. However, contained in this task is a challenge. Can we give witness to the truth that is Jesus Christ in a way that affirms the uniqueness of this truth without also falling prey to a kind of theological exclusivism that undercuts the universal nature of that truth?

Pastoral Perspective

Yet self-definition is seldom found by exclusively traveling the *via negativa*.

Knowing who we are not is important, but at some point the question must be answered in the positive. How does John do this? He turns to the story of his faith, to Isaiah 40. When asked a second time, "Who are you?" John replies, "I am the voice of one crying out in the wilderness." He understands himself as the voice that calls from outside the world as it is, to announce the coming of a different world. He is the voice from the margins, from the wilderness, called to point to the one who brings a new tomorrow and to prepare the way for that one's arrival. Borrowing from Luke's Gospel, we are reminded that John has been doing this since before the day he was born! John has a clear sense of his identity. He knows who he is: the messenger called to prepare the way for God's tomorrow.

How can such clarity be found? How can we develop such self-understanding? Psychologically our identity is shaped by our families of origin. From the perspective of family-systems theory, the DNA passed on from generation to generation and the emotional process of each generation before us shape our identity. It is self-definition. This is true on both an individual and an organizational level. Ron Richardson identifies self-definition as "the personal task of defining who we are within our emotional systems . . . [which] means identifying the beliefs, values, commitments, and life principles on which we will base our life."[1] He goes on to say, "Life in the family of origin . . . is a tremendously powerful experience for everyone. And the impact of that experience is not restricted to childhood. The way we see ourselves, others, and the world is shaped in the setting of our family of origin. The views we develop there stay with us throughout life."[2] Parents, grandparents, siblings, extended family all play a role in shaping self-understanding and defining identity. In understanding these dynamics, one begins to answer the question "Who are you?" They are "the cards we are dealt," so to speak. Yet we have the freedom and responsibility to choose how to play the cards dealt to us. By so doing, we define who we are not, as well as who we are.

From a theological standpoint, faith teaches a primary identity beyond our families of origin. In 1998, the General Assembly of the Presbyterian

---

1. Ronald W. Richardson, *Becoming a Healthier Pastor: Family Systems Theory and the Pastor's Own Family* (Minneapolis: Fortress Press, 2005), 59.
2. Ronald W. Richardson, *Family Ties That Bind* (Bellingham, WA: Self-Counsel Press, 1995), 1.

identity-seeking questions that will dominate the next three units of text and even beyond them to include the entire Gospel narrative: "Who are you?" they ask. With no prompt but the question itself, the Baptist answers in a manner fitting high court proceedings: "He confessed and did not deny but confessed, 'I am not the Christ'" (v. 20, my trans.). Follow-up questions posing alternate identities receive shorter and shorter responses: "Who then? Are you Elijah?" "I am not." "Are you the prophet?" "No" (v. 21). A final, more open-ended inquiry follows, revealing the questioners' motive: "Who are you, then, so that we may give answer to those who sent us?" (v. 22).

The Baptist's answer is now more expansive but less direct. Citing Isaiah 40:3 (LXX) he responds, "*I am* the voice of one crying in the wilderness, 'Make straight the way of the Lord,' as the prophet Isaiah said" (v. 23). Despite the positive "I am," a locution of great significance for the Gospel, John's answer does not satisfy the delegates, who fixate instead on the three previous denials. Why does he baptize, they wish to know, if he is not the Christ, nor Elijah, nor the prophet?

Various problems attend the threefold denial: First, the questioners themselves do not introduce the term "Christ" (*Christos*), "messiah," and yet the Baptist presents and denies *this* title first, giving priority to messianic identity in the interrogation to follow.

Second, to deny that he is Elijah is to put this passage at odds with the Baptist/Elijah connection in the Synoptics (cf. Mark 1:2–3; Matt. 11:14; Luke 1:17), where Elijah is explicitly associated with the Baptist's role as messianic forerunner. Why, we wonder, does the Baptist embrace the desert forerunner typology from Isaiah but deny the Elijah title? Is there in the background an Elijah-type messiah whose mantle the Baptist eschews? Does his denial concern a popular view that John is *literally* Elijah returned to the world? Perhaps the geography of John's ministry raises eschatological expectations pointing to Elijah's return; the detail in verse 28 that "these things happened in Bethany beyond the Jordan" places the Baptist's ministry in proximity to the place of Elijah's assumption into heaven in 2 Kings 2:5–14, "across the Jordan."

Third, the denial concerning the Baptist's identity with the prophet (*ho prophētēs*) raises the question, which prophet? The definite article points to a *particular* one, perhaps the "prophet like Moses" mentioned in Deuteronomy 18:15: "The LORD your God will raise up for you a prophet like me [i.e., Moses]

his relationship with Jesus. Claiming to be "the voice" of Isaiah 40:3, he deflects attention from himself to the eminent Coming One he announces. In the Fourth Gospel, John's baptismal activity and function as prophetic forerunner—both of which figure prominently in the Synoptics—are overshadowed by his role as witness to the Word. *Martyreō* ("testify") and cognates refer to John seven times in verses 6–34 and bracket his declaration. As the first of a parade of witnesses that includes the Father, the Scriptures, miraculous works (5:31–39), and the believing community, John successfully carries out his divine appointment by testifying to the truth of God's self-revelation in Christ. A sermon on this passage might stress the importance of bold verbal testimony in bringing others to faith and explore additional forms of effective witness. The preacher may encourage listeners to consider the following questions: As Christ-followers, have we waived our right to remain silent? In the absence of a witness protection program, what risks does the confessing church assume? How might persecuted Christians throughout the world hear this text? Using John the Baptizer as a model, how do we rate as the Lord's witnesses?

Identity Crisis. John's baptizing calls for a decision on the part of religious officials. Who is he, and what are his credentials, the emissaries want to know. The Messiah? Elijah (Mal. 4:5)? The prophet, perhaps (Deut. 18:18)? His triple negation (*egō ouk eimi, ouk eimi, ouk*) makes it clear that John is no "I" witness. Denying that he is any of these eschatological figures, he acknowledges his own subordinate status and the honor derived from performing even the most menial service for the exalted one he heralds. John's self-effacing language looks ahead to his commentary on Jesus' growing following: "He must increase, but I must decrease" (3:30). Under no illusions as to his own importance, he remains in the limelight just long enough to redirect the beam to the actor who is about to take center stage.

This text invites reflection on John's example of humility and the challenges posed by a "me-focused" culture. "It is not about me," quips the popular motto, but experience suggests that egocentricity is alive and well, in the church as elsewhere. Cardinal Jorge Bergoglio's choice of Francis as his papal name highlights the need for church renewal in light of this basic Christian value. Alternatively, the preacher might lead congregants in considering that most fundamental of human questions: Who are you? What defines us? How does affiliation ("adoption")

John 1:19–28

Theological Perspective

Here then is the second theological challenge that grows out of reflection on this passage. Does the author want to affirm that the *logos* as made manifest in Jesus is the *only* point of contact between the Divine and the human? The short answer is yes; or, at least that the *logos* revealed through Jesus is the lens through which the divine presence is filtered. Any talk of seeing God in the smile of a newborn, in sunset walks on the beach or staring at the world from the grandeur of a lofty mountaintop, or even seeing God at work in movements toward peace and acts of justice, would all seem to be secondary at best. One thinks here of Calvin's image of the Scriptures as the "spectacles" through which God and the world are viewed correctly.

Applying Calvin's image to John's Gospel, the universe is a cold, harsh, and impartial place; it is only through an encounter with the Son that one can then sing, "This is my Father's world." Likewise, one imagines the author of John would eschew any Eastern notion that in our search for the divine presence we are all climbing a mountain on different paths, and all paths lead to the same place. The analogy that befits this Gospel is that the world is in darkness and there is one light. Yet, as R. Alan Culpepper writes, "because the Gospel presents Jesus as the Incarnation who made known the work of the Logos from the creation and through all time, it undercuts the triumphalism of claims that Christendom has a monopoly on the revelation of God."[1] Therefore the question we need to confront is this: does the light that is Jesus Christ overpower all other light, or does it ultimately illumine and help us to recognize the divine presence wherever that presence may manifest itself? Thoughtful reflection on this passage will look for ways both to challenge and be challenged by the theology herein.

BURAN PHILLIPS

Pastoral Perspective

Church (U.S.A.) adopted a study catechism for children entitled "Belonging to God." The first question of the catechism is the same question posed to John the Baptist: "Who are you?" There are many possible responses within the life of faith. Some Christian traditions teach that the appropriate response to the question is, "I am a sinner." Defining self in such a way can have tragic consequences, distorting self-understanding in very unhealthy ways. The catechism offers a different response: "I am a child of God." The church's faith teaches us that this is our primary identity, beyond any worldly category, beyond family function or dysfunction, beyond even our own self-understanding.

Of course, pastorally we live in between these realities; between who we are as a product of our family systems and who we are as beloved children of God claimed in Christ by God's grace; between our penultimate self-definition and our ultimate identity; between the world as it is and the world as it shall ultimately be. Life seldom offers the clarity of identity John demonstrates in this Gospel reading. While there are moments when self-definition is clear and concisely stated, more often than not, life is lived in the tension between who we are and who we are not, who we have been and who we hope to be.

Each and every day the circumstances of life confront us with the question of the priests and the Levites, "Who are you?" Who we are in relationship with one another, how we spend our time and with whom, where we spend our energy, how we spend our money—in answering these questions each and every day we define who we are, for better or worse. In the midst of such a wilderness world, facing the realities of today, people of faith are ultimately called to join John in pointing to the hope that is God's tomorrow.

JOSEPH J. CLIFFORD

---

1. R. Alan Culpepper, *The Gospel and Letters of John* (Nashville: Abingdon Press, 1998), 302.

Exegetical Perspective

from among your own people" (cf. Deut. 18:18). Already in the Dead Sea scrolls, pre-Christian eschatological hopes attached to this coming Moses-like prophet (4Q175 *Testimonia*) in addition to a Davidic messiah. Likewise, in Acts 3:22, the eschatological coming of Messiah Jesus is explicitly identified with the promise of the coming prophet like Moses.

Even though John's Gospel never identifies Jesus as the Moses-like prophet, Moses typology is strongly present in the first half of the Gospel. While the connection is at first positive, Moses references become increasingly polemical until they cease in a standoff between the disciples of Moses and the disciples of Jesus in 9:28–29, a fact that may signal the intra-Jewish debate taking place in the Johannine community. If, as many experts suggest, the Baptist can be associated with the Dead Sea sectarians, a connection to eschatological Moses expectations (as in *Testimonia*) would be apt. However, in the Gospel neither John nor Jesus is correctly thus identified. In general, the compilation of messianic figures and forerunners—Christ, Elijah, the prophet-like-Moses—reflects the heightened eschatological interest the Baptist excites, even as he denies the titles for himself. They point to the Lord whose way he prepares in the desert.

Why, then, the interlocutors "from the Pharisees" ask, does John baptize if he is not himself one of these eschatological figures (v. 25)? John's answer relies on the Isaiah prophecy he has just cited: his baptism in water (*en hydati*, v. 26) alone is in preparation for the Lord, the one who comes after John and whose sandals John is not worthy to unlace. This single use of the term "worthy" (*axios*, v. 27) in John's Gospel parallels the term "adequate" (*hikanos*) in Synoptic triple tradition. Acts 13:25 uses the same expression, "worthy" (*axios*), as Paul recounts the Baptist's words in strikingly similar terms: "I am not he. But after me one is coming, the sandals of whose feet I am not worthy to untie." Commentators agree that the image of stooping to untie another's sandals is one of extreme subservience, relegated in the ancient world to slaves alone. The image is exaggerated by an ironic detail unique to John's Gospel, where true *gnōsis* (knowing) connects the knower to God: the One who merits such honor is standing in their midst and is yet *un*known (v. 26).

ALEXANDRA R. BROWN

Homiletical Perspective

with God through Christ shape the believer's identity? How can we avoid identity fraud and become our "child-of-God selves" (1:12 *The Message*)?

The Challenge of "the Jews." Knowing from the prologue that not all will accept the Word, the reader approaches the opening exchange alert to the characters' responses. John's encounter with the Pharisees' envoys hints at the conflict between the divine Envoy and the Jerusalem establishment later in the narrative. Resistance seems to be the initial reaction to perceived "trouble in River City." Rapid-fire questions demanding an explanation for John's unusual baptizing suggest an interrogation. His testimony reveals that the Father's Exegete (1:18, NRSV "who has made [the Father] known"), unknown to "the Jews," is already among them. God's radical intervention is in progress, but they fail to recognize it.

This passage offers an opportunity to expose and combat uncritical anti-Semitic readings of the Fourth Gospel, by examining the narrative function of "the Jews" as representatives of the unbelieving world (see the essay on "the Jews" at the beginning of this volume). At issue is not ethnicity but blindness and rejection of God's self-revelation. The preacher might also explore what makes us slow to see God at work in fresh, surprising ways.

In a liturgical setting, this dialogical text could easily be presented as a reader's theater, with participants assuming the roles of John, the Jewish messengers, and the narrator. To reinforce the theme of witness, ancient creeds or denominational confessions of faith might be given special emphasis. The time-honored practice of testimony, crucial in the revitalization of the Salvadoran church under Archbishop Romero, forms an integral part of worship in the black church and in some evangelical circles. The late Thomas Hoyt Jr. acknowledges its value "in a society where many voices sound yet where public speech that is honest and empowering is rare." Personal anecdotes of God's transformative power told against the backdrop of Scripture "keep alive the truth—that life is stronger than death, that people can change with God's help, that God is worthy of our thanks and praise."[2] Preachers themselves are among the "great cloud of witnesses" that link congregational story with the metanarrative of our faith.

KAREN M. HATCHER

---

2. Thomas Hoyt Jr., "Testimony," in *Practicing Our Faith: A Way of Life for a Searching People*, ed. Dorothy C. Bass (San Francisco: Jossey-Bass, 1997), 91–103.

John 1:29–34

²⁹The next day he saw Jesus coming toward him and declared, "Here is the Lamb of God who takes away the sin of the world! ³⁰This is he of whom I said, 'After me comes a man who ranks ahead of me because he was before me.' ³¹I myself did not know him; but I came baptizing with water for this reason, that he might be revealed to Israel." ³²And John testified, "I saw the Spirit descending from heaven like a dove, and it remained on him. ³³I myself did not know him, but the one who sent me to baptize with water said to me, 'He on whom you see the Spirit descend and remain is the one who baptizes with the Holy Spirit.' ³⁴And I myself have seen and have testified that this is the Son of God."

Theological Perspective

The first chapter of the Gospel of John develops the themes of Christology and the incarnation that grow out of the author's unique understanding of the identity of Jesus. Those themes continue in these verses with the ongoing work of John the Baptizer. The Baptizer continues to subordinate his work and his own self so that the focus might be on Jesus and so "that he might be revealed" (v. 31), a subtle but significant point for the Gospel of John. The purpose of ministry, of witness and testimony, is to make known this One who has come to dwell among us in the flesh.

The day after John was baptizing in the Jordan, he sees Jesus approaching and immediately recognizes him as the "Lamb of God" (v. 29). There is no indication that Jesus himself is baptized, or that the two of them (cousins, according to the Gospel of Luke) even know each other. Nonetheless, when the Spirit descends and remains on Jesus, it confirms for the Baptizer (as the One who sent him has told him) that this one is the "Son of God" who will baptize others with the Holy Spirit. Baptism with the Holy Spirit does not appear to be connected with any kind of emotional state, nor the bestowal of any particular gift or ability, although later the reader is instructed that the Spirit will "guide you into all the truth" (16:13). As with most things in the Gospel of John,

Pastoral Perspective

"Do you know Jesus?" This is a question often posed by evangelical Christians seeking to offer their witness to unbelievers. At the most intense end of that spectrum, it is posed by street preachers as a way of engaging passersby. John the Baptist serves as the inspiration for many of these intense evangelists. In fact, www.officialstreetpreachers.com references John as the model for their work as voices crying out in the wilderness. Given their identification with the hairshirt-wearing, locust-munching preacher, they are no doubt informed by John's fiery sermon in Luke's Gospel. It begins, "You brood of vipers! Who warned you to flee from the wrath to come? Bear fruits worthy of repentance" (Luke 3:7–8). Such is the hellfire and brimstone "good news" that too often defines the public Christian witness.

In the Fourth Gospel, John the Baptist takes a very different stance. He does not lambaste onlookers with calls for repentance, fueled by warnings of hell. He does not give specific marching orders for what repentance looks like, as does the counsel offered in Luke 3: "Whoever has two coats must share with anyone who has none" (Luke 3:11). He does not even begin with "Do you know Jesus?" In fact, he goes as far as to say, "I myself did not know him"—not once, but twice in these five verses. In the Fourth Gospel, John's is a simple witness: "Behold

Exegetical Perspective

"The next day" (v. 29) begins the second of a three-part narrative of revelation that opened with John's baptizing activity in the wilderness beyond the Jordan. Intense interest in the true identities of both Jesus and the Baptist continues in this unit. In ironic contrast to the unknowing Jewish delegates from Jerusalem, the Baptist is prepared by his origin (sent from God, 1:6) and the sign of the dove (also from God, 1:32) to recognize Jesus as the "Lamb of God who is taking away the sin [*hamartia*] of the world" (v. 29, my trans.). The christological title "Lamb of God" (*amnos tou Theou*) occurs in John alone among the Gospels and otherwise in the NT only in the book of Revelation, where a different Greek word for lamb (*arnion*) is used.

Jewish sources called to mind by the image include Isaiah 53, where God's Suffering Servant is said to be like a sheep (LXX *probaton*) led to slaughter and a lamb (LXX *amnos*) silent before its shearers (Isa. 53:7) who "bears the sin [LXX *hamartia*] of many" (Isa. 53:12). It also brings to mind Exodus traditions of the unblemished paschal lamb (LXX *probaton*) whose blood marked the doorposts of the Israelites to spare them the fate of the Egyptians (Exod. 12:1–20). Raymond Brown suggests that the *historical* Baptist may have had in mind the apocalyptic Lamb of Jewish apocalyptic works like *Enoch*

Homiletical Perspective

In the chapel of the Unterlinden Museum in Colmar, France, visitors will find the impressive Isenheim altarpiece painted by Matthias Grünewald in 1515. The crucifixion scene, seemingly drawn from the pages of the Johannine Gospel, portrays the dying Christ surrounded by his mother, the Beloved Disciple, and Mary Magdalene. Surprisingly, the artist has also included the figure of John the Baptizer. Facing the viewer, he holds the open Scriptures in one hand, while with the other he points to Jesus on the cross. At his feet stands a lamb, cross in the crook of a foreleg, ancient symbol of the Agnus Dei. The image illustrates John's role as Christ's "point man," showing as well as telling onlookers who Jesus is. This is precisely what he does in these verses. This christocentric text serves as the central panel of a triptych whose wings depict characters that come to reject (vv. 19–28) and to accept (vv. 35–51) the one to whom John witnesses. This passage offers homiletical options on the interrelated themes of Jesus' identity and his baptism.

John Introduces Jesus. On the day after his interrogation by "the Jews," John sees Jesus approaching. Having described him in the previous pericope as a supreme dignitary en route, yet mysteriously present, incognito, among the people, John introduces

Theological Perspective

baptism with the Spirit is about "seeing." It is to be born anew/from above, which enables one to see that Jesus is the One sent from God, the One who has "words of eternal life" (6:68), which for the author is less about the quantity of life in the hereafter and more about the quality of life in the here and now.

However, note here that Jesus' baptism with the Holy Spirit is connected with Jesus' own identity. In the Synoptic Gospels, the true identity of Jesus is something that gradually unfolds, and is not fully confirmed until his death and resurrection. In John's Gospel, we are met almost immediately with several titles for Jesus in the first chapter: the Word, Son of Man, Son of God, the Messiah, the King of Israel. In these verses we encounter the intriguing phrase "The Lamb of God who takes away the sin of the world" (v. 29). No doubt this is an expression that has very early worked its way into Christian consciousness. Further, even though eucharistic imagery is rich throughout the Gospel of John (see 6:35–58), the author seems to have no specific reference in mind other than a general allusion to sacrifice. Hovering over this expression, however, is the larger question of what it means, for the author and for us, to say that the Lamb of God takes away human sin.

Twenty-four years of parish ministry has confirmed for this writer that a close second to questions of theodicy (Why, God? Why do bad things happen to good people?) is questions about the atoning work of Christ. They are not articulated as such, but they are there. Exactly "how" does the death of this man Jesus on a cross take away human sin? What does that sacrifice really mean beyond an act of heroic love? New Testament theology in general certainly connects the death of Jesus with the forgiveness of sins and salvation, but is not explicit about exactly how one affects the other. Of course, theologians throughout church history have offered several theories about the atoning work of Christ, and the more popular and well-known ones include the satisfaction theory, associated with Anselm, which sees Jesus' death as satisfying the righteous demands of a God offended by human sin; and the substitutionary view, attributed to the Reformers, which understands Jesus' death as the death of God's innocent Son, offered on our behalf or in our place. Another well-known theory is often called the moral influence theory, associated with Peter Abelard, which sees the death of Jesus as the ultimate expression of the depth of God's love, saving us insofar as the realization of that love transforms us and our world.

The Gospel of John offers a unique perspective that might be called an incarnational theory of the

Pastoral Perspective

the Lamb of God who takes away the sin of the world!" (v. 29). He testifies to what he has seen and what he has been told. He saw the Spirit descend on Jesus and remain upon him. He was told that whomever that happened to was the one who baptizes with the Holy Spirit. In the Fourth Gospel, John's is a ministry not of proclamation but rather of testimony. He is a witness, testifying to what he has seen.

Looking at the world, what do we see? What do we witness? Do we see the poverty of the world? Do we glimpse in our own cities and rural communities the devastating reality of a world where the vast majority of people live on less than $10 a day? Do we acknowledge the growing divide between rich and poor? Is the growing education achievement gap, perhaps better referred to as the "opportunities gap," on our radar? Are we aware of the scale of violence that defines this world, of the innocent victims of war, of the suffering, of those civilians struck down by drones? Do we see a world where one in four women experiences domestic violence? Do we see a nation that spends $718 billion on defense, more than Medicare, more than the next thirteen highest countries combined?[1] Do we acknowledge the millions of Americans who live without health care, or do we just see a political issue to be "owned" in the next election? Do we see the sin of the world? Are we willing to testify to it?

More importantly, do we see the Spirit of God at work in the midst of such a broken world? Do we see Christ in the hungry, the sick, the alien, the prisoner? Can we perceive the Spirit alighting upon them? Can we imagine the risen Christ, the Lamb of God taking away the sin of the world? If John's assertion is true, that Christ is present, then the church, the body of Christ, must embody this presence. The church is called to be the incarnation of self-giving love that has the power to overcome the sin and violence of this world. The church must invest its life in making a difference in the midst of the world's brokenness.

Are we capable of being a church that embodies this testimony? In his book *The Witness of Preaching* Tom Long quotes Paul Ricoeur, who identifies four biblical claims made upon witnesses. Summarizing Ricoeur, Long points out that witnesses are not volunteers; they are summoned and sent to testify. Second, their testimony is ultimately not about human experience, but about God and God's claim upon life. Third, the testimony is for the benefit of

---

1. Brad Plumer, "America's staggering defense budget, in charts," *Washington Post*, January 7, 2013.

90, where the conquering Lord of the Sheep comes to vanquish sin and evil at the end time, an image present also in the book of Revelation (e.g., Rev. 17:14).[1]

The Gospel as a whole reinforces elements of both Exodus and Isaiah in its lamb/sheep typology without forfeiting the apocalyptic overtones the Baptist may himself have intended. Since there is a doublet of the announcement "Behold the Lamb of God" in the next unit (1:36), now *without* the relative clause, "who takes away the sin . . . ," some speculate that the evangelist has added that clause to the simpler, original saying of the Baptist, that is, "Behold the Lamb of God."

Despite the temporal specificity of the setting "on the next day," the unit presents a kaleidoscopic series of events that resist precise temporal ordering. Immediately after the announcement of recognition in the present tense (John sees [*blepei*] Jesus coming [*erchomenon*], v. 29), we are directed to *past* events that explain how the Baptist, despite not knowing Jesus (v. 31), came to perceive what he now testifies, that "this is the One who ranks before me because he was before me" (v. 30, my trans.).

Here, as in the opening verses of the prologue ("In the beginning was the Logos"), the "One" is defined by time as *eternal*. That is, in mundane time he comes *after* John, but his inception eternally *predates* this mundane hour. As Logos, he was "*in the beginning*," a designation that for this Gospel points backward beyond a starting point for creation to his presence with the Creator. It is this dignity of primordial presence that accounts for the Baptist's comparison of rank in verse 30. Because the Logos was with God "in the beginning," he is also "before" the Baptist in the sense of "greater than."

The drama of identities revealed continues in verse 31 with an explanation of how the Baptist came baptizing with water "in order that he be revealed [*phanerōthē*] to Israel." In this reference to Israel, as in 1:49 and 3:10, the earliest layer of the Johannine community is likely in view; the Messiah, it was thought among some early Jewish messianists, would be identified by signs made known to Israel.[2] Now the Baptist presents the revelatory evidence by which he came to his own testimony (*martyrion*). Sandwiched between the two confessions of ignorance— "I did not know him" (vv. 31, 33)—he reports, "I saw [*tetheamai*] the Spirit come down as a dove from

him to unspecified listeners with titles that offer additional insight into his identity. Explaining Jesus' superior status with an allusion to his preexistence (v. 30), John recognizes him as both possessor and purveyor of the Holy Spirit through baptism. In testifying to Jesus as the Son of God, he highlights the intimate relationship that uniquely qualifies him to make God known (1:18). Perhaps most striking is the appellation "Lamb of God" and the designation of Jesus as the world's sin-remover.

This multifaceted metaphor stirs the imagination. Is this a twist on the ram supplied by God in the story of Abraham's near-sacrifice of his "only son" Isaac (Gen. 22:1–19)—"a ritual-mythical pattern come full circle in this New Testament material [with] the son tak[ing] the place of the sheep who took the place of the son"?[1] Could it be instead the triumphant lamb of Jewish apocalyptic that overcomes evil at the last judgment, as in the book of Revelation? Is the evangelist linking Jesus to the Suffering Servant of Isaiah 53:7, who goes like a lamb to the slaughter (cf. Jer. 11:19)? Is the reference to the slain paschal lamb, which, though it did not take away sin, symbolized deliverance?[2] Does it picture the cosmic Householder come into the world to mark the doorposts and lintel of "his own home" (1:11, alternate trans.)? Preachers might delve into the rich interpretive heritage of this Christian icon as they consider how the text's collage of images contributes to an understanding of Christ.

Another sermon angle involves juxtaposing John's initial introduction of Jesus with Pilate's presentation of him at the end of the narrative. In the procurator's pronouncement, "Behold the man" (19:5 KJV, RSV), we hear discordant echoes of the Baptizer's "Behold, the Lamb of God" (1:29 RSV). Is Jesus merely human, or is he I AM's definitive Word on the human condition? Preachers may follow the evangelist in challenging listeners to resolve the all-important issue of Jesus' identity for themselves.

Jesus' Baptism Recalled. In this Gospel's distinctive account John testifies to Jesus' baptism as a remembered event confirming the revelation of God. The enigmatic text leaves John's role in the incident open for debate, portraying his water baptizing primarily as a vehicle for recognizing the Unknown One. Having received in advance a divine communiqué—"This

1. Raymond E. Brown, *The Gospel according to John I–XII*, Anchor Bible 29 (New York: Doubleday & Co., 1966), 58–59.

2. For this theory and its sources, see J. Louis Martyn, *History and Theology in the Fourth Gospel* (Nashville: Abingdon Press, 1968), 117.

1. J. Levenson, *The Death and Resurrection of the Beloved Son* (New Haven, CT: Yale University Press, 1993), 208.

2. Raymond E. Brown, *The Gospel according to John I–XII*, AB 29 (Garden City, NY: Doubleday, 1966), 58–63.

Theological Perspective

atonement. That is to say, the incarnation is at the heart of the Christology of the Gospel of John. The death of Jesus on a cross is not unimportant, obviously, but it is the uniting of the Divine and the human in this man Jesus that makes salvation possible, possible because the divine life has entered human life and now the possibility of new life exists for all. To see the light and truth the Word-made-flesh reveals, to believe, is to participate in this new life. Further, the Christology of this Gospel reminds us of something often neglected in discussions about the atoning work of Christ. Most theories of the atonement reflect rather ghastly images of God. God and Jesus are two independent agents, with God either offering the Son as the innocent scapegoat to be brutally killed or actually doing the punishing in what seems like a kind of cosmic child abuse.

For the Gospel of John, however, the Lamb who is sacrificed, the one who suffers and dies on the cross, is not something or someone independent from God. This is the death of the "Word [that] became flesh" (1:14). That is, much like the notion articulated in Philippians 2:6–11, Jesus' death is a divine self-emptying, God's giving of God's own self, put to death by those who were too blind to see. Hence, rather than saying Jesus died "for" our sins as an innocent substitute or to appease the wrath of an angry God, it might be more in line with this Gospel's Christology to affirm that Jesus died "because" of our sins. If blindness is indeed the great spiritual sin of the world, then the Lamb takes away sin by shining light into our spiritual darkness and making new life possible . . . as if one were born again.

BURAN PHILLIPS

Pastoral Perspective

all people. Finally, the testimony is not merely one of words, but demands speech and action. Long concludes, "The whole life of the witness is bound up in testimony."[2] As witnesses, those called to offer our testimony in the midst of this broken world in which we live, this world filled with war and rumors of war, poverty beyond comprehension, famine and disease, do we see a world God loves enough to enter and redeem? How does our witness reflect this reality?

Poet and professor Christian Wiman embodies this faithful witness in the midst of a broken world. *My Bright Abyss: Meditation of a Modern Believer* is his spiritual autobiography. It is his testimony, written in the midst of his battle with an incurable blood cancer, a diagnosis he received less than a year into his marriage. He offers a powerful witness, for as is true of good poets, he tells what he sees and hears in a potent and profound way.

One of his poems, authored during his struggle with cancer, embodies his compelling witness. It is entitled "Every Riven Thing." "Riven" is an old word that speaks of brokenness, of what is rent asunder. Wiman offers this repeated phrase throughout the poem: "God goes belonging to every riven thing he's made."[3] It is offered five times with different punctuation each time, illuminating the many ways God is found in the broken spaces of life, in essence holding us together. If the church is called to be the body of Christ in the world, perhaps the most powerful witness the church offers is when the church embodies that presence in the midst of this riven world. That is where we belong.

JOSEPH J. CLIFFORD

2. Thomas G. Long, *The Witness of Preaching* (Louisville, KY: Westminster John Knox Press, 1989,) 42–43.
3. Christian Wiman, "Every Riven Thing," in *Every Riven Thing* (New York: Farrar, Straus & Giroux, 2010), 24–25.

heaven and remain on him" (v. 32, my trans.). While John still did not know him, the One who sent John interpreted the sign in this way: "the One on whom the Spirit [dove omitted here] descends and *remains* [*menon*] *is* the one baptizing in the Holy Spirit" (v. 33, my trans.).

The contrast drawn here between baptizers, together with the Baptist's repeated denials, reflects polemic against some who continue to follow John, not Jesus: John baptizes with water, but Jesus baptizes with the Holy Spirit. Moreover, John's testimony attests that the authorizing Spirit (*pneuma*) is not fleeting but *remains* on this one who baptizes in the Spirit. This first appearance of the Spirit (of twenty-two) in the Gospel confirms above all the divine origin and identity of Jesus (cf. 4:24, where "God is spirit"). That the Spirit is said to "remain" (*menein*) points ahead to the Gospel's exhortation to "remain" in Jesus as branch upon vine for divine sustenance (chap. 15) and to the sustaining role of the Advocate (*Paraclētos*), sent to the disciples by God after Jesus' death (chap. 14). The account famously omits the *actual baptism* of Jesus by John, perhaps to mitigate sectarian claims of John's disciples that John is superior to Jesus.

Finally, in the several verses from verses 31–34, notice the piling up of the verbs "to know" and "to see," all governed logically by the main action of the unit, to reveal, *phaneroun*. These culminate in the perfect indicative of the verb "to see" (*horan*), "I have seen" (*heōraka*, v. 34), which renders not merely grammatically, but also theologically, "I know." To *see* as the Baptist saw is to *know* the Son of God or, in the manuscript tradition favored by some, "God's Chosen One."[3] The testimonial that began in verse 19 with clarification of the Baptist's own identity (vv. 19–24) culminates in verse 34 in perfect tenses that carry the continuing effect (from John to the Gospel to its reader) of the divine revelation: I have seen and I have testified, "This is God's Son."

ALEXANDRA R. BROWN

will be a sign for you"—he has his senses primed to perceive the heaven-sent dove that marks Jesus as God's Spirit-possessing chosen one (v. 34, alt. trans.; Isa. 42:1). Careful, intentional sight (*tetheamai*, v. 32) leads to insight as vision corroborates voice. John witnesses with spoken word to the divine word he has heard and the Word-made-flesh he has seen. Hailing Jesus as Spirit Baptizer and, by implication, agent of Israel's renewal (Ezek. 36:25–27), John concludes his testimony, ceding the witness stand to others. The one who expresses solidarity with humanity in the Jordan's murky waters now sets out toward a baptism of another sort (Mark 10:38).

This passage invites preachers to explore with congregants the deep meaning of baptism, lest the rite be viewed as little more than a membership card into the local church. The following questions may provide a point of departure: What is the significance of Jesus' baptism(s)? If the sacraments are "visible preaching," as Augustine claimed, what message do we proclaim through baptism? How does your congregation's particular baptismal practice influence your interpretation of this passage? In what times and cultural contexts has the witness (*martyria*) of baptism resulted in martyrdom or persecution? How might this passage be personalized by drawing from your congregants' baptismal stories?

This passage has been interpreted extensively in Christian art, which offers a treasury of paintings, sculptures, and stained-glass images suitable for a liturgical context. The Agnus Dei motif can be supported with musical selections ranging from gospel hymns to Handel's "Behold the Lamb of God," according to worship style. In planning a baptismal service, preachers may wish to incorporate this passage and related time-honored materials like the following prayer, penned by eighteenth-century Baptist pastor and hymnist Benjamin Beddome:

Eternal Spirit, heavenly Dove,
On these baptismal waters move,
That we, through energy divine,
May have the substance with the sign.[3]

Baptism offers an ideal opportunity to recall a pivotal moment in the Jesus movement, as John does, and to renew our call to be "on point" in a holy endeavor.

KAREN M. HATCHER

3. Brown, *Gospel according to John I–XII*, 57.

3. Benjamin Beddome, "Eternal Spirit, Heavenly Dove," *The Hymnary*, http://www.hymnary.org/text/eternal_spirit_heavenly_dove; accessed March 31, 2013.

John 1:35–42

³⁵The next day John again was standing with two of his disciples, ³⁶and as he watched Jesus walk by, he exclaimed, "Look, here is the Lamb of God!" ³⁷The two disciples heard him say this, and they followed Jesus. ³⁸When Jesus turned and saw them following, he said to them, "What are you looking for?" They said to him, "Rabbi" (which translated means Teacher), "where are you staying?" ³⁹He said to them, "Come and see." They came and saw where he was staying, and they remained with him that day. It was about four o'clock in the afternoon. ⁴⁰One of the two who heard John speak and followed him was Andrew, Simon Peter's brother. ⁴¹He first found his brother Simon and said to him, "We have found the Messiah" (which is translated Anointed). ⁴²He brought Simon to Jesus, who looked at him and said, "You are Simon son of John. You are to be called Cephas" (which is translated Peter).

Theological Perspective

The heart catheterization process is an extraordinary thing to experience and witness firsthand on the overhead monitor. The dye injected into the body slowly but surely begins to move throughout every vessel, every vein, until all are filled. This procedure reminds one of the marvels of technology, but also serves as a powerful image of what is happening theologically in the Gospel of John.

The incarnation affirms that the divine presence "became flesh" (1:14); now that it has been, as it were, set loose in the world through the Christ, the divine presence/spirit/wind is surely and steadfastly hallowing or "holy-ing" all creation. This process of sanctification is slow, perhaps to the point of being imperceptible to the world, except to those who can truly believe and see. This process also highlights an important element for the Gospel of John in general, the doctrine of election, and the way the doctrine is "fleshed out" in this particular passage through the themes of identity and discipleship.

"You did not choose me, but I chose you," says Jesus in the fifteenth chapter (15:16). Because John's theology is imbued with theology of the Hebrew Scriptures, there is a strong sense throughout this work of the providence of God. We do not see a philosophical argument juxtaposing divine sovereignty over against human agency so much as an overriding

Pastoral Perspective

"What are you looking for?" That is the question Jesus poses to Andrew and his friend in John 1:38. They had been following John the Baptist for quite some time and had come to John to be baptized. In preparation for the coming of the Messiah, the one who would bring the kingdom of God, they needed to repent from their sins. What were they looking for? They were looking for redemption; they were looking for the Messiah.

What did they want from the Messiah? Maybe they were looking for adventure, for new experiences, to see the world beyond the sleepy little village where they had spent all their lives. Maybe they were looking to make a difference, to be a part of a movement to resist the Roman occupation and the corrupt leadership of Judea. Maybe they were looking for meaning and purpose in their otherwise aimless lives. Perhaps they were looking to "find themselves," so they joined the cult of John the Baptist with visions of utopia dancing in their heads. While Scripture does not reveal what they were looking for, is it possible they were looking for some of the same things twenty-first-century churchgoers seek?

People come to church looking for something. Some are looking to get out of church by twelve o'clock to beat the traffic to a favorite brunch spot. Some are looking for community, for a place to

Exegetical Perspective

On the following day, Jesus appears once more, again to be addressed by the Baptist, who fixes his gaze (*emblepō*) upon him and announces, "Behold, the Lamb of God" (v. 36 RSV). The repeated title is one of several "doublets" that mark the chapter. In this case the doubling may suggest distinct layers of tradition around the title (cf. 1:29), but like several other doublets in the preceding verses (1:15 and 1:30; 1:25 and 1:31; 1:31 and 33), it also has the effect of amplifying the Gospel's central questions of identity and testimony: what is seen elicits confession.

In the rich epistemological vocabulary of the Gospel, seeing clearly leads to knowing truly, and what is known gives rise to testimony. Evangelistic consequences of the Baptist's confession are immediately evident. His own two disciples, Andrew and another unnamed, heard the address being spoken, "Behold, the Lamb of God," and *heeded* it, following Jesus (v. 37). Both the verb "to hear" and the verb "to follow" are rendered here as grammatical aorists, whose action may be either constative or ingressive; so "they heard" or "they began to hear and continued hearing" (*ēkousan*), and "they followed" or "they began to follow and continued to follow" (*ēkolouthēsan*). In either case, the two terms together, "to hear" and "to follow," mark out distinguishing and ongoing activities of discipleship.

Homiletical Perspective

This passage follows John's powerful testimony to the one whose identity has been revealed to him through baptism. As a result of his faithful execution of his God-given task as witness, others "see the light" (1:6–7) and set off to discover for themselves who Jesus is. This pericope and the subsequent one introduce Christ's first followers and offer a glimpse of "those who received him" (1:12). Preachers might develop a sermon on the pattern these verses establish for the growth of the believing community: *seeing, seeking, staying, speaking.* Other homiletical options include the themes of quest, discipleship, and evangelism.

A Searching Question. The call narratives of the Synoptics have been recast as quest stories in the Fourth Gospel, which is permeated with the seeking motif. Here Jesus does not recruit but rather rewards potential followers that seemingly take the initiative. As the scene opens, John notices Jesus walking by and points him out to two of his own disciples as the "Lamb of God," a title linking this episode with his testimony of the preceding day. Seeing leads to seeking, an invitation to stay the day, and further insight into the true greatness of this "rabbi."

The disciples' inquiry about Jesus' abode foreshadows the promise of his abiding presence (1:38; 14:23).

John 1:35–42

Theological Perspective

element of the doctrine of election. God calls, God sends, and so forth, and all human response is just that, a response to the prior divine initiative, as the divine plan carefully but surely unfolds. It continues to unfold here with John's understanding of discipleship, for disciples are those who have been called to "see" and then give testimony to what they have seen.

Verses 35–42 continue to establish the identity of Jesus with an account of the first disciples who follow him. When Jesus notices that two of John the Baptizer's disciples are following him, after the Baptizer has again acknowledged Jesus as the "Lamb of God," Jesus turns and asks them, "What are you looking for?" Normally a question such as this is a simple question. However, in John's Gospel, questions such as these have different layers to them.[1] The pace of the narrative in this first chapter, and the fact that all the titles ascribed to Jesus are used by people who have never seen him before, are just a few of many stylistic details that should alert us to the reality that John is writing not with the eye of a historian but with the heart of an artist. John wants to paint a picture of a world that one would have to see to believe.

In this world, a simple question like "what are you looking for?" is a question that also invites existential reflection upon the human condition. The human condition is defined by spiritual blindness; *that* is the fundamental sin. Whether one chooses the darkness (3:19) or is born blind (chap. 9), humanity cannot see that the divine presence as revealed in Jesus is what it is looking for. Humanity is looking for purpose and meaning, but most of all a sense of permanence amid the vicissitudes of life and the fact of death and decay.

This permanence for John is expressed in metaphors throughout the Gospel. For example, we are looking for bread to eat so as never to be hungry again (6:50–51), for water to drink that will forever quench our thirst (6:35), for words of eternal life (chap. 6), and a house with many rooms (chap. 14), to name but a few of the metaphors. Humanity is looking for the presence of God in a real, tangible, "fleshly" way; for the author of John, coming to know and understand this presence in the here and now is to find eternal life.

The disciples' response to Jesus' question seems awkward, to say the least. "Where are you staying?" is not an answer to what they might be looking for.

Pastoral Perspective

belong, to connect with other people, and connect more with God in the process. Some are looking for a foundation upon which to build their lives; others for a connection with the Divine; others for a connection with the past, with what life was like when they were growing up. Some are looking for the healing of body or soul or both. Some seek redemption, new life on the other side of mistakes made or opportunities missed. People come to church looking for many things.

Jesus' question carries great power, because everyone is looking for something. At the turn of the eighteenth century, theologian Friedrich Schleiermacher wrote of humanity's quest for something beyond themselves, describing it as "a taste for the infinite."[1] In the twentieth century, Paul Tillich would speak of God as "the ground of being," the subject of life's "ultimate concern," or concern for that which is ultimate, that is, beyond one's self.[2] These great thinkers of the faith point to the truth that human beings long for something beyond themselves.

"What are you looking for?" People long for identity, for purpose, for meaning, for healing. They are looking for redemption, for love, for life. The world is ready and willing to offer solutions to the search. Media and the market offer myriad possibilities. Can it be found in a big salary and the corner office? How about in that dream house in the perfect neighborhood? The potential solutions are endless. The problem is that every human solution misses the life for which human beings were made. Until it is recognized that the human heart longs for the ground of being, the ultimate concern, for a life lived in relation to God and God's will, the heart will never find what it is looking for.

"What are you looking for?" asks Jesus. Andrew and his friend offer no answer. They respond with another question, "Where are you staying? Where have you pitched your tent? Where do you dwell?" Perhaps they do not exactly know what they are looking for, but they know they have found something of it in this Lamb of God. Perhaps they know wherever he is going, they just might find what they are looking for. "Come and see," invites Jesus. "Come and see."

They do come, and do they ever see! They see miracles—water turned into wine, five thousand fed with a few loaves and some fish. They see Samaritans

---

1. See R. Alan Culpepper, *The Gospel and Letters of John* (Nashville: Abingdon Press, 1998), 121ff.

1. Friedrich Schleiermacher, *On Religion: Speeches to Its Cultural Despisers*, 2nd ed., trans. from the first German ed. of 1799 by Richard Crouter (Cambridge: Cambridge University Press, 1996), 39.
2. Paul Tillich, *Systematic Theology* (Chicago: University of Chicago Press, 1951–63), 2:10.

Responding to the action of the disciples, Jesus turns, and seeing (*theasamenos*, v. 38; cf. 1:32; 6:5) them following him, speaks for the first time in the Gospel: "Whom do you seek [*zēteite*]?" The disciples respond without answering the question directly: "Rabbi, where are you staying?" "Rabbi" (translated here *didaskalos*, "Teacher") is used frequently and positively in this Gospel, especially in the so-called Book of Signs (1:19–12:50).[1] The inquiry, "Where are you staying?" employs the same term (*menō*) that described the dove-borne Spirit descending and remaining (*emeinen*) on Jesus in verses 32–33. The alert reader will already have begun to sense the rich double entendre of the expression "to stay" in this Gospel, for this key term—used thirty-four times in even distribution across the narrative—connotes not only a relation to physical space but a connection to spiritual presence. For example, in chapter 15, the one who "stays in Jesus" is promised the "Father's" abiding and nourishing presence in return, just as the branch is nourished by the vine (15:4–6).

Jesus' answer, "Come [*erchesthe*] and see [*opsesthe*, v. 39]," is the first instance of a formula that echoes throughout the Gospel—in the Samaritan woman's call to "Come [*deute*] and see [*idete*] a man who told me all that I ever did" (4:29, my trans.), in the invitation *to* Jesus to "come [*erchou*] and see [*ide*]" the tomb of Lazarus in 11:34, and even Jesus' postresurrection utterance, "Come and eat breakfast" (!) in 21:12. In each instance, the expression prepares for the revelation of divine identity. Through this literary pattern of seeking-invitation-revelation, the Gospel portrays evangelistic success even as opponents of Jesus, who "do *not* seek [*zēteo*] the glory that comes from the only God" (5:44, my trans.), take counsel [*zēteo*] to kill him (5:18).

The disciples' response—"they came and saw where he was staying [*menei*] and stayed [*emeinan*] there with him that day" (v. 39, my trans.)—invokes, once again, the double meaning of *menō*, "to stay." It points again to that sort of abiding with Jesus that concerns the Gospel as a whole. If the "tenth hour" is reckoned from daylight (6:00 a.m.), the time indicated is four in the afternoon, a time of no obvious symbolic significance.[2] What stands out is that the disciples both see (*eidan*) and stay (*emeinan*) *with* Jesus for an extended time.

Having remained with him, Andrew is able to recognize him as God's Anointed and to proclaim him to his brother Simon. Jesus' first utterance in the Gospel—"What are you looking for?" (v. 38)—is more than a simple query that propels the story forward. It is an existential question whose answer is determinative for the characters'—and readers'—life choices.

More to the point is the similar question Jesus poses to Mary Magdalene at the end of the narrative proper: "*Whom* are you looking for?" (20:15). What counts is the object of the quest. Citing Bultmann's assertion that "human life is—consciously or unconsciously—impelled by the question about God," John Painter observes, "From the standpoint of faith, authentic existence (the question of myself) can only be realized in relation to God because 'our heart is restless until it rests in [God].'"[1] Having been hard wired for that relationship, the seeker will find no satisfaction until she or he can echo the disciples' cries of discovery: "Eureka!" (NRSV "We have found," v. 41); "My Lord and my God!" (20:28).

Preachers may challenge congregants to consider how they would answer Jesus' question. What are they seeking, both individually and corporately? How should this text be understood in view of the tension maintained in the Gospel between choosing and being chosen (15:16)? Given the evangelist's paradox-permeated world, is it possible that the seeker turns out to be the one sought (cf. Luke 19:1–10)?

Change of Allegiance. This account differs from the Synoptic version not only in how the disciples come to Jesus but where and who they are. The incident presumably takes place near the Jordan (1:28), not the Sea of Galilee, and the first two followers are Andrew and an unnamed disciple, adherents of John, who defect with his blessing (3:25–30). In a few verses, the evangelist masterfully depicts the developmental nature of discipleship, beginning with leaving and culminating in believing. Following is defined not as a one-time decision but in terms of relationship. Understanding deepens over time as those who abide with the light are enlightened (1:9) and come to faith (2:11).

The transformational power of the process is suggested by the renaming of Simon. Upon meeting him, Jesus looks at him with the penetrating gaze (*emblepsas*, v. 42) of one who reads hearts (2:24–25)

---

1. Raymond E. Brown shows that in the Book of Glory (13:1–20:31) this title is replaced by "Kyrios" (*The Gospel according to John I–XII*, Anchor Bible 29 [Garden City, NY: Doubleday & Co., 1966], 75).

2. Ibid.

1. Rudolf Bultmann and Augustine, quoted in John Painter, "Inclined to God: The Quest for Eternal Life," in *Exploring the Gospel of John*, ed. R. Alan Culpepper and C. Clifton Black (Louisville, KY: Westminster John Knox, 1996), 353.

Theological Perspective

Again, we see the author almost playing with words. To stay, to dwell, to abide—all of these have to do with the divine presence. Where is Jesus abiding and dwelling? Where is the divine presence to be found? Here is a foreshadowing of chapter 15: the divine presence, God, abides in Jesus, who has come to dwell with humanity. Those who obey the commandments of Jesus abide/dwell in God's love, and God's love abides/dwells/stays in them.

"Come and see" is Jesus' response to the question of where he is staying. More than a general statement, it is an invitation to discipleship. "Come and see," first of all, is an invitation to experience the gospel in order to understand. For John, to "see" or to "believe" is not merely an intellectual assent to certain propositions; it involves the totality of the self. This does not mean that faith is nonrational; rather, it means that faith is not attained at the end of an argument. That is why, for example, Jesus and Nicodemus talk past each other in chapter 3. Jesus is talking about openness to the Spirit, while Nicodemus is trying to figure out how one might literally be born again.

"Come and see" also reflects John's emphasis on developing one's vision for discipleship. Again, disciples are those who have come to believe through the gift of faith and then, by their witness and good works, enable others to come to believe. All of this is part and parcel of God's providential mission unfolding throughout history. To discover this is to discover one's own identity. Notice the end of our passage, where the disciple Simon is now to be called Cephas or Peter. Reminiscent of, or perhaps informing, Calvin's notion that the knowledge of God and of self are intricately bound together, this name change returns to the theme of identity. We discover our identity when we come to see who Christ is, and as we come to see who Christ is, our spiritual vision is developed to see the divine presence both in him and wherever creation itself is being hallowed.

BURAN PHILLIPS

Pastoral Perspective

and outcasts welcomed by a Jewish holy man. They see the lame walk, the blind see, the lepers cleansed, even on the Sabbath day. They see him wash their feet and speak of betrayal. They see him hang on the cross and breathe his last on a Friday. On the first day of a new week, in a room filled with scared disciples, with the rest of the eleven, save for Thomas, they see alive him who was dead, risen from the grave.

In the late 1980s, the Irish rock group U2 released what would become one of their best-selling songs, "I Still Haven't Found What I'm Looking For."[3] The song's best version is arguably the recording that includes the Harlem Gospel Choir, found on their *Rattle and Hum* album. Its lyrics speak of that search inherent to the human condition. The song also speaks of a belief in the coming of God's kingdom. Ultimately it expresses an experience that seems to be inherent in the human condition: finding what we are really looking for proves to be an elusive quest.

The world offers many possibilities—wealth, power, material possessions, the list goes on and on—but they are ultimately found wanting, for they are dead idols. They cannot fulfill what the human heart ultimately seeks. If Schleiermacher is right, if the human quest is ultimately for the Infinite, then the search will not be resolved on this side of eternity. Nevertheless, with Andrew and his friend, those who would follow Jesus are invited on a journey. "Come and see," calls the Christ. Join the journey, for in the quest itself, there is life to be found in the one who journeys with us; and from time to time, by God's grace, one just might glimpse in him what every human being is looking for.

JOSEPH J. CLIFFORD

3. Bono, "I Still Haven't Found What I'm Looking For," *The Joshua Tree* (Dublin: Danesmoate House, 1987).

Exegetical Perspective

In verse 40, the scene changes abruptly. Andrew appears, as if for the first time, as "one of the two who heard John speak and followed *him*." (Here, the pronoun "him" could refer either to John or to Jesus, but context favors Jesus; cf. v. 38.) Reference to the prior testimony of the Baptist brings what follows into the chain of revelatory events narrated from 1:19. Andrew first finds his brother Simon and announces, "We have found [*heurēkamen*] the Messiah (which is translated, the anointed One)" (v. 41, my trans.). As J. Louis Martyn suggests, the statement "We have found the Messiah" in this Gospel probably presupposes an expectation, alive in the earliest synagogue-based Johannine community, of a Messiah-Moses typology where the Messiah is to be recognized through his miracles (signs, *sēmeia*).

Such a tradition merges OT expectations of the coming prophet like Moses, who "worked signs and wonders" (Deut. 18; cf. 1:21), with eschatological expectations such as those at Qumran, where a prophet like Moses *and* two Messiahs are expected (1 QS 9:10f). Early rabbinic sources reveal the explicit *merging* of Moses and Messiah typologies.[3] If early in this community's history, Jewish evangelists persuaded some in the synagogue that Jesus was the expected Prophet-Messiah like Moses, a collection of signs like those narrated in 1:19–12:50 would have provided evidence for this crucial identification (2:11, 18, 23; 3:2; 4:48, etc.).

Having "found" and announced the Messiah, Andrew continues the chain of evangelism that began with the Baptist's testimony by bringing his brother Simon to Jesus (v. 42). As the unit ends, Jesus looks at (*emblepsas*) Simon, identifies him, perhaps prophetically as "son of John" (cf. Jesus' recognition of Nathanael in 1:48), and renames him "Cephas," an Aramaic word meaning "rock," which the narrator translates into the Greek word for "rock," *Petros*. Peter's appearance alongside but *after* the appearance of the unnamed disciple has led to speculation that the unnamed is the disciple who bears a special authority in John's Gospel, the Beloved Disciple (e.g., 18:15; 21:20–24).

ALEXANDRA R. BROWN

Homiletical Perspective

and gives him the moniker Cephas, a gesture reminiscent of I AM's renaming of Abram and Jacob. The irony is not lost on the initiated reader, for Peter is anything but a rock in the narrative. Yet this pronouncement of the Logos creates a new reality, as in the beginning, and the postresurrection Peter lives into it. The preacher might invite congregants to experience this story by slipping into the role of the mysterious, nameless disciple. In the Synoptics, Jesus' followers leave behind nets and familial networks; here, they leave behind their involvement in John's renewal movement. What ties might commitment to Christ require your congregation to sever? The evangelist claims that the identity of those receiving and believing Christ has been radically redefined (1:12). What does it mean to be rechristened with his name in today's world?

Evangelism. This passage bears out Paul's assertion that faith comes through hearing the word about Christ (Rom. 10:17). John's testimony has a ripple effect as two of his disciples reach the same conclusion about Jesus, based on personal experience. Convinced that he has found the Messiah, Andrew cannot keep the news to himself, and he brings his brother Simon to meet him. A similar scenario will play out the next day between Philip and Nathanael. Having seen and sought and stayed, they also speak out about whom they have discovered, inviting family and friends to "come and see." Evangelism appears as a ministry of introduction, flowing naturally from the followers' relationship with Jesus.

Two millennia later, this is still the modus operandi of the church, as the faithful tell their own unique versions of the ancient quest, "We have found the Lord!" In an age when the term "evangelism" evokes images of Great Awakening tent revivals, stadium crusades, and religious television broadcasts, this passage reminds us of the power of conveying that message to our intimates. An evangelistically oriented sermon might be supported with missionaries' often dramatic anecdotes of encountering Christ in the field. Given the implicit tagline of this invitational text—RSVP—a time of response may be an appropriate component of the worship service. As congregants are sent forth, preachers may wish to highlight their commission as envoys of the divine Envoy (20:21), heralds of hope to a world desperately in need of the life-giving Word.

KAREN M. HATCHER

3. "How long do the days of the Messiah last? Rabbi Akiva said: Forty years. Just as the Israelites spent forty days in the wilderness, so will he [the Messiah] draw them forth and cause them to go in the wilderness" (*Tanchuma 'Ekeb* 7, cited in J. Louis Martyn, *History and Theology in the Fourth Gospel* [Nashville: Abingdon Press, 1968], 109).

John 1:43–51

⁴³The next day Jesus decided to go to Galilee. He found Philip and said to him, "Follow me." ⁴⁴Now Philip was from Bethsaida, the city of Andrew and Peter. ⁴⁵Philip found Nathanael and said to him. "We have found him about whom Moses in the law and also the prophets wrote, Jesus son of Joseph from Nazareth." ⁴⁶Nathanael said to him, "Can anything good come out of Nazareth?" Philip said to him, "Come and see." ⁴⁷When Jesus saw Nathanael coming toward him, he said of him, "Here is truly an Israelite in whom there is no deceit!" ⁴⁸Nathanael asked him, "Where did you get to know me?" Jesus answered, "I saw you under the fig tree before Philip called you." ⁴⁹Nathanael replied, "Rabbi, you are the Son of God! You are the King of Israel!" ⁵⁰Jesus answered, "Do you believe because I told you that I saw you under the fig tree? You will see greater things than these." ⁵¹ And he said to him, "Very truly, I tell you, you will see heaven opened and the angels of God ascending and descending upon the Son of Man."

Theological Perspective

The basic story here is not confusing: Jesus calls Philip to follow; Philip fetches Nathanael; Jesus and Nathanael have a chat. That conversation is the enigmatic part. Something weighty is going on, but what is it? It depends either on action offstage or on terms whose meanings are not self-evident.

This is a passage where Reformation approaches to biblical interpretation prove helpful. One is the interpretation of Scripture by Scripture: when one passage is a bit foggy, look for help from other passages that are clearer on the topic. Another, typology, is more a perspective than a technique: Old Testament events were understood to be related to events of the New Testament like shadows cast backward through time, and both can be shadows of things eschatological. These approaches may not bring perfect clarity here, but they are illuminating.

When Philip tells Nathanael that Jesus is the one foretold by Moses and the prophets, Nathanael responds, "Can anything good come out of Nazareth?" It sounds sarcastic, even bigoted. However, trying to compare this passage with clearer passages, we find Nazareth is never even mentioned in the Old Testament. Nathanael seems to be asking an honest question about messianic expectation. How could Jesus be the promised one if his town is not in the Bible?

Pastoral Perspective

Nathanael does not start out as part of the crowd. He is not one of the many that follow Jesus for what they can get, like fishes and loaves, a healing, or a miracle. When we first encounter Nathanael, he is better described as curious. He is willing to draw a little closer to see what the claims about Jesus are really about. He is curious enough to listen to Philip's testimony and engage in the conversation. There is no hint of debate or quarrel, just a single question: Can anything good come out of Nazareth?

The sticking point for Nathanael is not so much the assertion that Jesus is the one about whom Moses and the prophets wrote. The obstacle to acceptance is his place of origin. He doubts if anything good can come out of a place that is routinely disregarded. Nazareth is not mentioned in the Law or the Prophets. It is not on a major travel route and is therefore isolated from the mainstream. In reality, it is a small village, not even a city, with only about five hundred people.

Perhaps Nathanael feels as if someone of importance should come from someplace important. At least important people must be familiar with the person. Thinking like this makes public opinion the arbiter of truth. In the absence of public acclaim, there is suspicion. By the same token, belief based on public acclaim leads to a bandwagon mentality. If

Exegetical Perspective

This passage is the third of three distinct but related scenes in John 1:29–51. After the formulaic introduction (1:1–18), the narrative begins in 1:19–28 with John the Baptist as an uncredentialed person of suspicion under investigation by religious leaders. He defends himself by displacing his importance through an assertion of his inferiority to another. "The next day" introduces each of the subsequent three scenes (vv. 29, 35, 43). In each, a series of related people recognizes some aspect of Jesus' identity: John (vv. 29–34); Andrew, another unnamed disciple of John, and Peter (vv. 35–42); and Philip and Nathanael (vv. 43–51).

Each scene of this expanding circle of witnesses relates various aspects of Jesus' identity: "the Lamb of God" (vv. 29, 36); "the Son of God" (vv. 34, 49); "rabbi" (vv. 38, 49); "Messiah" (v. 41); and "King of Israel" (v. 49). Throughout John's Gospel, Jesus' identity continues to be a primary concern, central to which is his divine origin; he incarnates God's word (1:14) and speaks often about whence he has come and whither he will return.

John's incarnational theology departs from traditional conceptions of divine transcendence. Beginning in 1:1–18 and then throughout the Gospel, John's Jesus fully incarnates and is in no way lesser or secondary in relation to God (as one would

Homiletical Perspective

The Gospel of John has always seemed to many people like an alternate universe to the Synoptic Gospels. It seems to occupy a different dimension and has caused readers to be skeptical of John's approach to Jesus. According to some, he tends to deify Jesus and diminish his humanity, so much so that it can make a person nervous. In church cultures that make Jesus so divine that he loses touch with humanity and with the world, the incarnation loses its fundamental meaning. Since in these churches Jesus is not grounded in the world, the church culture is free to sanction racism and neo-slavery, to oppress women, to repress homosexuality, and to worship materialism and militarism. In John's Gospel, these churches find a Christ who really is interested not in this world but rather in the world to come.

Having grown up in such a church, I must say that as I entered these stories of the calling of the inner core of Jesus' disciples in this first chapter of John, I felt as though I had stepped right into that alternate universe. Even though New Testament scholars like Susan Hylen and Deborah Krause have helped me to see my cultural captivity in regard to John and have urged me to listen anew for the Spirit speaking to me in John's Gospel, I still wrestle with the otherworldliness of John's Jesus.

Theological Perspective

When Nathanael comes near, Jesus exclaims, "Here is truly an Israelite in whom there is no deceit!" If the Nazareth comment were in fact snarky, Jesus' words would seem to be an affirmation of Nathanael's candor. Now we need to look further afield.

What does it mean to say Nathanael has no deceit? In both testaments "deceit" is a strong word for sin, and often enough the Septuagint uses the same Greek word that John uses here. It can be a human disposition to deceive (Ps. 109:2 [LXX 108:2]; 2 Cor. 12:16), one of a summary list of sins (Mark 7:22; Rom. 1:29), the spiritual intention of the devil (Acts 13:10), or in poetic parallelism, an equivalent to injustice and oppression (Ps. 10:7 [LXX 9:28]; Ps. 43:1 [LXX 42:1]). To proclaim that Nathanael is without deceit is high praise. More than a comment on Nathanael's frank tongue, it amounts to a proclamation of his righteousness.

Small wonder, then, that Nathanael asks how this stranger knows his heart so well. Jesus' answer again holds a mystery: "I saw you under the fig tree before Philip called you." He refers to events that we can never really know. It is like dramatic scenes in fiction where characters prove their identity by revealing facts known only to intimates.

Is the fig tree the key? The phrase carries some consistent symbolic weight in Scripture. As stripping of the fig trees speaks of God's judgment (e.g., Amos 4:9), sitting in the shade of one's own fig tree is a trope for the blessed life in the promised land (e.g., Mic. 4:4, Zech. 3:10). Jesus saw Nathanael in a place connoting peace and prosperity.

What did Jesus see Nathanael doing there? It convinced him of Nathanael's innocence. Perhaps we should think of Psalm 32:1–5, where lack of deceit means honest confession leading to blessed forgiveness. Maybe Nathanael had been in prayer, admitting his sins. Speculate as we might, it remains a private moment.

Nathanael, though, is moved to find that Jesus saw him, guileless, under that fig tree. He bursts out with the third public confession of Jesus' messianic role recorded in John's Gospel.

Jesus seems ambivalent about these early professions of faith. Rather than welcoming Nathanael's affirmation, so boldly given on such a small basis, Jesus turns him toward the future. Someday, Jesus promises, Nathanael will see much more: "Very truly, I tell you, you will see heaven opened and the angels of God ascending and descending upon the Son of Man" (v. 51).

Pastoral Perspective

everyone else is for it, one jumps on it. Yet this devotion to public opinion will also necessitate jumping off when others feel the ride is over. One gives up her own judgment, substitutes another's testimony for his own, and may thereby miss the opportunity for a real encounter with the Lord.

It is important to note that Nathanael simply raises the question. It is an honest question. He has not answered it already or shut down the discussion. He may not know yet whether God is at work in Jesus, but he is also not prepared to say where God is not or could never be. Nazareth is a questionable locale, and Jesus' association with Nazareth makes him questionable too. It seems to be an unlikely place for the Christ to call home; yet Nathanael does not assume he can determine where God can act, the people among whom God can be, or the things God can do. Instead, he is curious enough to accept Philip's invitation to "come and see."

What a masterful witness Philip is! He does not try to convince or cajole. He does not even try to answer Nathanael's question. No, Philip invites Nathanael to join him on this faith journey and answer the question for himself. In effect, Philip tells Nathanael to come and see if what he is saying is true. Nathanael is not obligated to take his word for it; he can find out for himself; and he must, because, when all is said and done, Nathanael will need his own encounter with Jesus. Philip cannot be his mediator. Nathanael will need more than a "borrowed faith"; he will need one that is reliant upon his own experience of and testimony to the God who has come to him in Jesus Christ.

Philip's response should cause us to consider how often we refuse to share the good news because we think our job is to answer every question. It begs the question of how many people's faith journey has ended at the point of curiosity because we received their questions as a threat, a refusal to believe, or a challenge that must be answered with righteous indignation. Like Philip, we must recognize that questions are an opportunity to help the people who are curious venture into the ranks of those who are willing to come and see. Our job is not to think for people; it is only to invite them.

Philip takes Nathanael to a place where he can encounter Jesus for himself. To his amazement, in Jesus' presence Nathanael discovers he is already known. Jesus identifies him as an "Israelite in whom there is no deceit" (v. 47b). Jesus sees that Nathanael is not a mere skeptic wishing to disprove his friend. He is a curious seeker. Although the testimony Philip

think from reading the Synoptics). Jesus claims, for example, "The Father and I are one. . . . The Father is in me and I am in the Father" (10:30, 38b); "Whoever has seen me has seen the Father. . . . I am in the Father and the Father is in me" (14:9b, 10a). People come to see and believe this by hearing testimony and seeing Jesus' acts, which demonstrate his identity (4:48–54; 5:36; 10:25, 37–38; 14:8–11).

At the end of his life, Jesus promises that God's presence and power, the presence and power that the believers have witnessed and experienced through him, will not cease with his absence, but will continue in the Spirit of love and truth that binds the community together (see 7:39; 14:15–26; 17:20–26; 20:21–22). So John's narrative arc ultimately asserts the radical immanence of the Divine to the community of believers, first in the person of Jesus and then in the spirit of the Advocate or the communal bond of love.

John 1:29–51 unfolds according to the basic shape of this narrative. In the first scene John the Baptist identifies Jesus as the subject of his previous testimony, calling him both Son and Lamb of God (vv. 29, 34). His testimony results in an expanding set of witnesses that culminate with Nathanael's repetition of John's confession: Jesus is "the Son of God" (v. 49). Two of John's disciples respond to his testimony by following Jesus (v. 37). One, Andrew, then finds his brother Peter and spreads the news: "We have found the Messiah" (v. 41).

The NRSV may wrongly specify the subject of verse 43 as Jesus, since the closest antecedent is Peter. If it is Peter, then he repeats the pattern by finding Philip. In either case, Philip certainly repeats the pattern when he reacts to the command, "Follow me" (v. 43), by finding Nathanael and testifying, "We have found him about whom Moses in the law and also the prophets wrote, Jesus son of Joseph from Nazareth" (v. 45). The word "follow" in verses 37, 38, 40, and 43 should be taken both literally and metaphorically for the life of discipleship, as Jesus uses it later (8:12; 12:26).

John's story is thus about people responding, not initially to calls from Jesus as in the Synoptics, but to testimonies from others about Jesus' identity. Testimony leads people to encounter Jesus as the incarnate spirit of divine love and truth, and then to enjoy life with others in a community bound together by that same spirit. The communal boundary is neither fixed nor impermeable. As soon as people are called in, they go out. Philip is commanded, "Follow me" (v. 43), and then his next action is reported: "Philip

I should add that I do like John's approach to these "call" stories. Matthew and Mark have very brief call stories—Jesus tells folk to follow, and they do it right away. John joins Luke's Gospel and seeks to give us some insight into these calls. In chapter 5 of Luke, we see some dialogue between Jesus and Peter, offering some explanation of why Peter (and we) can say yes. Why would people drop everything and follow Jesus? In John's account there is dialogue not between Jesus and Peter, but rather between Jesus and Nathanael, a character not mentioned in the Synoptic Gospels. Perhaps the best way to preach this passage is to follow the relationships.

Jesus goes to Galilee and tells Philip to follow him, and Philip finds Nathanael and tells him about Jesus the Christ. It is one of John's powerful themes: those who are called by Jesus, in turn call others. In the first chapter of John, we saw that the core of Jesus' disciples come from the circle of John the Baptizer. This tradition continues in Jesus' encounter with the Samaritan woman in chapter 4 and in healing the blind man in chapter 9. Indeed, this is how it works; the gospel of Jesus Christ is not only for individuals. It is relational also—not just "me and Jesus," but rather "we and Jesus." As the Samaritan woman tells her friends: "Come and see a man who told me everything I have ever done" (4:29).

For all the ethereal streams that run through John's Gospel, the author of John brings us right down to earth in the encounter between Jesus and Nathanael. When Philip goes to find Nathanael to tell him the great news about Jesus, Nathanael responds as if he were a postmodern, jaded cynic: "Can anything good come out of Nazareth?" In spite of Nathanael's skepticism, he does follow Philip because of their relationship, because of the community building that has already taken place. He is friends with Philip, and while Philip may be wrong about Jesus, Nathanael honors their relationship and comes to check Jesus out.

As Nathanael approaches him, Jesus makes a judgment about Nathanael. Is it his divine nature that gives him knowledge of Nathanael, or is he an astute observer? Nathanael retains his skepticism and wants to know how Jesus did it; but like all of us, he is easily flattered and takes Jesus' word to mean that it is obvious from looking at Nathanael that he is a fine person.

Instead of promising to make Nathanael a "fisher of people," as he does those whom he calls in the Synoptics, Jesus pulls out an apocalyptic image (v. 51) built on Jacob's ladder (Gen. 28:12) and the

John 1:43–51

Theological Perspective

This final line of the passage is the final mystery as well. It takes the form of a clear allusion to an Old Testament passage: the vision of Jacob at Bethel, where, with a rock for a pillow, "he dreamed that there was a ladder set up on the earth, the top of it reaching to heaven; and the angels of God were ascending and descending on it. And the LORD stood beside him and said, 'I am the LORD'" (Gen. 28:12–13). Jesus is telling Nathanael that he will have a vision like that of the patriarch Jacob. That is interesting on two levels, both best understood in light of later passages in John's Gospel, especially in the eighth chapter.

First, Nathanael and Jacob are given the same vision, though the men are typological reverse images of each other, like a photograph and its negative. Unlike Nathanael, Jacob had nothing but deceit (see Gen. 27:35), receiving his vision while on the run after tricking his brother out of both his birthright and their father's dying blessing. The patriarch's vision includes the promise of becoming a great people and a blessing (Gen. 28:13–14). We infer that the disciple, typologically the true descendant of Abraham (8:31–59), is also being given a promise and a calling.

More interesting, though, is what Jacob saw: a ladder that linked earth and heaven, convincing him that the place was sacred: "Surely the LORD is in this place—and I did not know it!" he declares (Gen. 28:16).

Now Jesus promises Nathanael a vision showing the "Son of Man" as the link between earth and heaven. This is the first use of the title in John, so Nathanael cannot know Jesus claims it for himself (8:28), but he surely knew it as a biblical messianic title. Soon Jesus will say, "Before Abraham was, I am" (8:58), helping us as readers understand that Nathanael, like Jacob, was truly in God's presence. The meaning of the vision becomes plainer with Jesus' later claim, "I am the way. . . . No one comes to the Father except through me" (14:6). The verbal metaphor matches the vision, with Jesus himself as the highway for humanity to travel to God.

GARY NEAL HANSEN

Pastoral Perspective

gives does not add up, he is willing to be proven wrong. He is man without deceit. There are no ulterior motives. He is seeking answers about Jesus, but he is no stranger to Jesus.

Jesus knows who Nathanael is at the character level. He gets to the core of his identity. Jesus also knows where he has been. By revealing Nathanael to himself, Jesus fulfills what is perhaps one of the greatest human needs: to be known. It is clear that Jesus' words strike the heart of Nathanael, because he quickly moves from the posture of "come and see" to confession. Unlike Philip, Nathanael identifies Jesus as "Son of God" rather than the son of Joseph. The true Israelite recognizes the true King of Israel. With his own experience of Jesus, he can now testify.

Nathanael's journey does not end here. This is just the beginning. Should he continue in the presence of Jesus, make the next transition from confession to commitment, he will see even "greater things." Like Jacob's ladder, Jesus is the portal between heaven and earth, human and divine interaction. Like Jacob's ladder, "ev'ry round goes higher, higher." As our faith seeks understanding and our curiosity causes us to come and see, we encounter new aspects of who God is and what God is up to in our lives and in the world. We confess Christ as Lord of our lives and commit to keep following him. Another round (curious → come and see → confess → commit) is made, and we go higher, higher!

RAQUEL ST. CLAIR LETTSOME

Exegetical Perspective

found Nathanael and said to him . . ." (v. 45). Perhaps Philip simply disobeys the command, or perhaps John intends to portray an intrinsic relationship between following on one hand, and finding and testifying on the other.

Nathanael is a curious character. He appears nowhere else in the Bible. His name means "God has given," and some read him as a symbol for Jews who believe and have "no deceit" (v. 47). His response to Philip's testimony is clearly comical and captured in his most memorable line, "Can anything good come out of Nazareth?" (v. 46). This anticipates others who will not accept that Jesus could be the Messiah because he was from Galilee and not Bethlehem (7:41–52), as well as the Gospel's deep concern with Jesus' true, divine origin. Yet by verse 49 Nathanael converts from question to confession.

One can read him as half of a frame for John, matched at the end by Thomas, both stories of conversion from question to confession. Both receive similar responses from Jesus. To Nathanael: "Do you believe because I told you that I saw you under the fig tree? You will see greater things than these. . . . You will see heaven opened and the angels of God ascending and descending upon the Son of Man" (1:50–51). To Thomas: "Have you believed because you have seen me? Blessed are those who have not seen and yet have come to believe" (20:29). Jesus tells Nathanael that the ground for belief is less in what Jesus saw of Nathanael, and more in what Nathanael will see in Jesus. In an allusion to Jacob's dream (Gen. 28:12), Nathanael will see the incarnational image of Jesus as the ladder connecting heaven and earth, the embodied, human presence of the Divine. Jesus' response to Nathanael suggests that the life of faith is not carried out in response to some particular incident that initially sparks belief, but is instead a response to the summons "come and see" (1:39, 46), and to the promise of greater, presently unknown revelations of the Divine.

DAVIS HANKINS

Homiletical Perspective

Human One ("Son of Man" from Dan. 7:13–14). Is Jesus belittling Nathanael here, or is he reminding him (and us) that if he follows Jesus, this journey will be much deeper and more harrowing than just a bit of psychic wizardry? Here we see an early sign in this Gospel that following Jesus means taking a path into the depths of ourselves—and even more importantly, into the depths of life itself. It works! Nathanael becomes part of the inner circle (though not in the Synoptics) and gathers at the end of the Gospel on the shores of the Sea of Galilee after the crucifixion and (rumored) resurrection of Jesus.

This passage raises many questions for the preacher, but one question is fundamental: How do we know that it is Jesus who is calling us? There are voices of many powers and forces in our lives, asking us for our loyalty and passion. John's answer rests in the relational nature of our lives; most of us first encounter Jesus in community. That is why we make promises at the sacrament of baptism to help those being baptized to know who Jesus is. In this first chapter, there is a long chain of relationships: John the Baptizer to Andrew to Peter to Philip to Nathanael.

John offers us a high view of the purpose of the church: "Sir, we would see Jesus." It is also terrifying, because we are always seeking to reshape Jesus to fit our image, rather than seeking to reshape ourselves to fit Jesus' image of us. Which Jesus are we sharing? The nonviolent Jesus? The white, male Jesus? The capitalist Jesus? The Jewish Jesus? The poor Jesus? The church has great potential here, but our history has indicated that our community sharing is filled with both promise and peril. The promise is what we see here in Nathanael's coming to know Jesus. The peril is that, in all ages and all places, the church often seeks to capture Jesus in its image. Thank God, Jesus continues to come to us to rock our world, as he does in John's Gospel.

NIBS STROUPE

John 2:1–12

¹On the third day there was a wedding in Cana of Galilee, and the mother of Jesus was there. ²Jesus and his disciples had also been invited to the wedding. ³When the wine gave out, the mother of Jesus said to him, "They have no wine." ⁴And Jesus said to her, "Woman, what concern is that to you and to me? My hour has not yet come." ⁵His mother said to the servants, "Do whatever he tells you." ⁶Now standing there were six stone water jars for the Jewish* rites of purification, each holding twenty or thirty gallons. ⁷Jesus said to them, "Fill the jars with water." And they filled them up to the brim. ⁸He said to them, "Now draw some out, and take it to the chief steward." So they took it. ⁹When the steward tasted the water that had become wine, and did not know where it came from (though the servants who had drawn the water knew), the steward called the bridegroom ¹⁰and said to him, "Everyone serves the good wine first, and then the inferior wine after the guests have become drunk. But you have kept the good wine until now." ¹¹Jesus did this, the first of his signs, in Cana of Galilee, and revealed his glory; and his disciples believed in him.

¹²After this he went down to Capernaum with his mother, his brothers, and his disciples; and they remained there a few days.

Theological Perspective

After Jesus' baptism and the calling of his first disciples, the Gospel *seems* to show life getting back to normal. They all go to a wedding, and then they go back to Jesus' hometown.

This is, on the contrary, a very important story, set in the midst of ordinariness. John points to its significance at the end, when he tells us that, in this first miraculous sign, Jesus "revealed his glory" (v. 11). The statement in the same verse—that the disciples believe in him—is far less important. John the Baptist, Andrew, Philip, and Nathanael had already declared some form of faith (1:29, 36, 41, 45, 49), and in the next passage a whole crowd will do so too (2:23). The conclusion of these affirmations is a statement that Jesus distrusted them (2:24–25).

How did this particular wondrous act reveal Jesus' glory? Just what is glory, anyway? It seems to have a wide range of meanings in Scripture. Any one of the Bible's authors might well cite Humpty Dumpty, who said to Alice when talking of this very word, "When I use a word . . . it means just what I choose it to mean—neither more nor less."[1]

What Jesus revealed was not the earthly glory of a king or the heavenly glory of his ascension. Nor

* See "'The Jews' in the Fourth Gospel" on pp. xi–xiv.
1. Lewis Carroll, *Alice's Adventures in Wonderland and Through the Looking Glass* (London: J. M. Dent & Sons Ltd., 1954; repr. ed. 1961), 185.

Pastoral Perspective

Nobody looked for Jesus until the wine was gone. Old wine was still wine, even if it was not new wine. Old wine was enough to keep them from seeking Jesus. Sometimes it is the old, not the empty, that gets in the way of somebody seeking the Lord—old attitudes and actions, old habits and hurts, old insecurities or old information, old rituals and rules that coalesce to create old, dry religion. Old wine. We tell ourselves that it is still wine, even though it is not new wine, forgetting that the old wine is enough to keep us from seeking Jesus.

As long as there was food, music, and wine, nobody thought about the Lord. John records no special greeting for him. He was not the guest of honor. No one asked him to give a toast or even acknowledged his presence until the wine ran out. Then again, we should not be surprised. There are many people who do not seek Jesus until something runs out. Prayer and congregational worship often increase when finances, jobs, health, relationships, and solutions to life's problems run out.

Chances are, we have all experienced some form of running short. It is the rare person who has always had enough or had what it takes to make it in, through, or out of a particular situation. If we cannot think of a time when we have run short, the Bible testifies that we all fall short: "For all have sinned and

Exegetical Perspective

This story presents interpretive challenges, not because its sense is difficult to determine, but because it makes so much sense. The many interpretive options are wide ranging. Just after Jesus' promise to Nathanael that he "will see greater things" (1:50), this passage records "the first of [Jesus'] signs . . . [that] revealed his glory; and his disciples believed in him" (v. 11). John's Gospel clearly states the significance of such signs for the purpose of belief and life in Jesus (20:30–31). That Jesus in John performs signs, not miracles, is no mere variation in terminology. The signs often signify and illustrate some aspect of his identity. Jesus raises Lazarus and claims, "I am the resurrection and the life" (11:25); he heals the man born blind and claims, "I am the light of the world" (9:5); he feeds five thousand and claims, "I am the bread of life" (6:35, 48). However, any potential connection between this revelation of divine glory (2:11; cf. 1:14) and the miraculous production of wine for wedding guests who had drunk the supply secured by the groom seems less clear.

The miracle in Cana also seems qualitatively different from Jesus' other signs in John. Is the miraculous production of wine at a wedding a revelatory act of God's glory, similar to the granting of sight to a man born blind (9:1–41) or the healing of an official's son (4:46–54)? Some modern commentators

Homiletical Perspective

Who is this guy? The newly called disciples of Jesus are likely asking this question. The author of John has already given us many names for Jesus in chapter 1: "the Lamb of God," "rabbi," "Messiah," "Son of God," "King of Israel." Here the author uses a story from a wedding in Cana to reveal what he calls "the first of his signs," among several used to show who Jesus is in "his glory," as the author puts it (v. 11).

This first sign, this first miracle, is a rather odd one. No healing of a person who cannot see; no restoration of strong legs for someone who cannot walk. Instead, a mundane (although no less spectacular) miracle of changing water into wine. The details are so interesting! Jesus and his disciples seem to have been invited to the wedding, but their arrival is problematic: the wedding hosts have run out of wine. Did Jesus and his friends overwhelm the wine supply, or was this problem already existent? Whatever the answer, Jesus' mother seems hopeful and tells Jesus about the problem. From the written text, we cannot tell where her emphasis is: reporting a fact, making a request, or expressing dismay. Jesus takes her report as a request for relief and gives what seems to be a difficult response to his mother: "Woman, what concern . . . ?" (v. 4).

It appears to be a strange way to speak to his mother, and commentators scramble to assure us

Theological Perspective

Pastoral Perspective

again was it the paradoxical glory of the cross. John had made one earlier reference to Christ's glory, at the climax of the prologue: "And the Word became flesh and lived among us, and we have seen his glory, the glory as of a father's only son, full of grace and truth" (1:14). John uses the story of the wedding at Cana to illustrate what he means by this glory. In the end it is the same quiet glory Luke shows us with the babe in the manger. It is the glory of the incarnation itself, with all its earthy implications.

Both sides of the incarnation are firmly in evidence. The power of the divine Word is clearly shown in the miracle; if ordinary people could turn water into wine, no one would ever get anything done. Most of the passage focuses instead on the human side: the wonders that happen in human and earthly realms because the divine Word is here, becoming human flesh in the midst of fleshly concerns.

We might have imagined the result would be a great disruption of the human and earthly orders. Instead, we find their great fulfillment. The passage shows all creation lifted up and honored by the Word who comes near.

Jesus attends the wedding of an unnamed couple. Doing so, he honors human relationship and marriage. Clearly he does not come intending to do anything showy, as he tells his mother in verse 4. It is the fact of his presence we should note with awe. No more can we consider a wedding a merely earthly and civil contract. When these two people enter this most basic partnership, the Word made flesh shows up personally, lifting it up to a holy state. That is glorious.

Jesus honors his mother as well, by doing what she asks of him. He does this despite his disagreement about the relevance of the lack of wine, and despite the inconvenience to his own sense of timing. He simply does what God's own commandment says to do (Exod. 20:12; Deut. 5:16); but in doing it as the Word made flesh, he shows that the commanded action reflects God's own character. In the process, he lifts up both parenthood and childhood by his divine attention. Honoring parents is an imitation of God. Glorious again.

Jesus shows his glory as he honors ordinary people, quietly, wondrously tending to them. Jesus honors the bridegroom whom he saves from social disgrace. If the wine were allowed to fail, people would notice. He would hear about it at every holiday dinner for the rest of his life. Jesus honors the otherwise easily ignored servants whom he makes the only real witnesses to the miracle. Jesus even

fall short of the glory of God" (Rom. 3:23). The issue is not being empty. The issue is not being depleted. The issue is not even running out. The issue is whether or not we will go to Jesus to be filled. When the wine ran out, Mary went to find Jesus.

Mary is in the right place, knows the right person, and thinks it is the right time. Jesus says otherwise, says that it is not his hour. His ear is open to her request for help, but Jesus has to move according to his timetable. This leaves Mary with many unknowns. She does not know how Jesus will supply the need, what he will require in order to do it, or when he will act. However, the critical issue for Mary is not what, when, where, or how. Her calmness is the result of knowing who. This is perhaps the only question for which she does have an answer. At the very least, she knows her son. Therefore, Mary is neither upset nor unnerved by Jesus' response. She seems confident that he will act on her petition. Consequently, she does not leave before ordering the servants to do whatever Jesus tells them.

Mary's parting words are informative for us all. They remind us that if we want the Lord to move in our lives, we must be prepared to do what he says. We soon see that what he says does not make obvious sense. Perhaps this is when obedience is the hardest—when it has to be mixed with faith. For the people at the wedding, the lack of wine is the problem; yet Jesus commands the servants to fill the jars with *water*. If one does not know the end of the story, a request for so much water in the absence of much needed wine does not compute. However, their compliance will show us that obedience to uncommon commands often yields uncommon results.

Jesus takes an empty and inadequate situation and makes the best out of it. He takes the water they have and makes the wine they need. This story encourages us to quit looking at what we have lost or do not have and look to Jesus, putting what we have into his hands. At the very least, we have some life, health, strength, and maybe even some sanity. What we have may not be the wine we need. Perhaps, it is some water; but if we bring it to him, the Lord can do something miraculous with it. After all, Jesus takes the water they have and gives them way more than they need—120 to 180 gallons of wine—when there is not even a grape left. He exceeds their expectations in both quantity and quality.

The results of this sign are far-reaching. Everyone at the wedding is affected by a miracle that on the surface seems to be of benefit only to the host. The lack of wine would have surely been a social disaster.

labor extensively to contextualize this act within the honor-shame sociocultural context of first-century Palestine. This thus becomes a story about Jesus saving the groom from the dishonor he would suffer for failing to provide his guests with wine.

While informative, such contextualization comes up short if it implies that the story is primarily about Jesus acting to save a groom from potential social damage. It seems unjust if not obscene to grasp this story as a kind of sociological counterpoint to, for example, Jesus' act that heals a man of a thirty-eight-year disease (5:1–18). To consider another sign story where Jesus miraculously produces abundance, is supplying an excessive quantity of wine to festive guests at a wedding party the same kind of act as feeding five thousand hungry people in Galilee with scant resources?

While the text does not directly address such questions, there is some textual support for distinguishing them. For example, the end results differ. In one case Jesus provides an abundance that satisfies all; in the other he supplies an exorbitant abundance above any possible calculation of present need, demand, or even desire (cf. the great catch of fish in John 21). Plus, Jesus asks what concern the wine is to him (2:4), but never asks similar questions about the official's son, the blind man, or others. Jesus seems to recognize something different about this act. The uniqueness of the act, however, only raises further questions about its significance and why it receives pole position among Jesus' signs.

In addition to the sociological approach, scholars also try to understand the significance of this sign by reading it symbolically. Beginning with the mention that the wedding occurs "on the third day" (v. 1), nearly every detail has been mined for its potentially deeper significance. Does the replacement of wine for water in stone jars used for Jewish rites of purification suggest a critique of such rites, a critique of Judaism; or should one stress continuity and see here the emergence of something new (wine/Jesus) within and from the old (jars/Judaism)? Why are the jars so big, far exceeding the amount necessary for purifying attendants at even the largest wedding in Cana? Is this enough water to cleanse the world that God so loves (see 3:16)? Why does John devote such attention to the jars' description if not to signify through them some deeper meaning? The jars are six, one less than seven, so perhaps the story intends Jesus as the seventh that will fully and perfectly purify Israel before God. Should the wine be read in relation to the use of wine in early Christian Communion, or

that Jesus is not being disrespectful to his mother. Yet there definitely is tension in their conversation. Jesus' mother (she is never called Mary in John's Gospel) has an idea about her son's power, and she is hoping that he can rescue the situation. Jesus seems hesitant or irritated (or both) at this request. Perhaps he wants his first sign to be a bit more glorious or controversial (controversy comes soon enough in the next story). Maybe he is even beginning to imagine how long the list of requests for action will be, once the word gets out that he has special powers. His answer to his mother—"my hour has not yet come"—indicates that this miracle is a bit premature for Jesus.

His mother seems to take Jesus' resistance in stride. After all, she has birthed him at great risk and has led him through adolescence, so she knows his foibles and moods. She also seems to have authority over the servants in someone else's home, and some have taken this to mean that one of her relatives is in the wedding party. His mother knows that, despite his resistance, Jesus will take care of her request. She tells the servants to follow his instructions, and they do. Verses 6 and 7 seem to be too much information (TMI) and extraneous. Why do we need to know the number and the size of the water/wine containers? These jars are used for holding water for Jewish folk to wash their hands in order to be ritually clean. This prompts two responses to the accusation of TMI.

First, the sheer quantity of water that is changed into wine is so huge that we cannot dismiss it with any charge of trickery or magic. Second, this is the initial step of Jesus' movement to replace the former religious rites with new ones. Since our Christian history is so tainted with violence against Judaism, the preacher would be well advised to deemphasize Jesus' replacing Judaism. Whether the author intends that meaning here, contemporary life in the church is filled with similar issues: Noisy worship or dignified silence? iPads or flat screens or hymnals? Casual or formal dress? Finish worship in an hour or go longer? Then, of course, there is Jesus' own metaphor about the difficulty of pouring new wine into old wineskins (Mark 2:21–22).

The initial audiences of this story would hear the enormous quantity of wine as an occasion for joy and celebration. Weddings would often last a week, so we are witnessing a festive occasion. In noting the struggles behind the scene of this first sign of the glory of Jesus, we should not lose sight of the fact that in a wedding celebration that includes Jesus of Nazareth, God is moving in a new and decisive way.

Theological Perspective

honors the creation, doing his miraculous work with the most basic of elements: stone, in the shape of jars, and water. Glory shines when the presence of the Word turns the basic into the sublime.

The glory shown in the miracle itself is more than water turned to wine, sublime as that fact is. It even goes beyond the fact, as the expert witness testified, that what he made tasted like the best vintage wine—much better than the cheap stuff served early on. No, the glory of the presence of Word made flesh is in the unbridled exuberance of the miracle. With "six stone water jars . . . each holding twenty or thirty gallons" (v. 6) filled to the brim, Jesus has blessed this reception with no less than 120 gallons of wine. The sheer volume makes the whole thing sound like an enormous practical joke.

That overwhelmingly generous gift, the equivalent of 605 bottles of the very best wine, is the way the Word made flesh honors human celebration itself. Because Jesus is present, God is present. Because God is present, let the good times roll.

The glory revealed at Cana, John shows us, is Jesus' display of his own character. This scene from the Word's incarnate life reveals things about what God is like that are hard to find so clearly elsewhere. Jesus is earthy, humble, and generous. God in flesh is ready to care for others, both up close and at a distance. He gives really quirky gifts. Jesus, the incarnate Word, affirms the very human, the ordinary, and the mundane.

There's glory for you.

GARY NEAL HANSEN

Pastoral Perspective

However, Jesus not only saves the reputation of the host; he provides enjoyment for the guests. John tells us that, in this sign, Jesus' "glory was revealed," and his disciples, who have responded to his command to follow him, now also "believe in him." Yet at the heart of this story is a mother who believes Jesus will do something and a few servants who are willing to obey him. The result is that everyone at the event profits from the actions of a few.

Numbers can be deceptive. A big crowd can give a false sense of security. A couple of people can give a false sense of defeat. Signs and wonders do not inherently require a large group, an entire church, or a whole household. Sometimes a few folk who will do what the Lord says is enough. The life-changing ministry of many churches and social movements is the consequence of a few, not the majority. It is the result of a few folk who stay and pray at a prayer meeting when the many go home; a few folk who give of their time, talent, tithes, and offerings while the many leave only a token; a few folk who are willing to worship while the many sit and watch; a few folk who catch the vision of what could be, while the many criticize, based on what already is. They may not have much—perhaps only some water—but they bring it, and they see the glory of the Lord.

RAQUEL ST. CLAIR LETTSOME

otherwise in relation to Christian symbolism for Jesus' blood? Should it be read against those OT texts that associate abundant wine with the arrival of God's promised future restoration (Joel 3:18–21; Amos 9:13–14)? Should one consider Dionysus and a Greco-Roman mythological background for this scene? Could we read the episode as a parable for Jesus, bridegroom of the church, who belatedly brings the good wine? After all, John refers to Jesus as the bridegroom (3:28–30); and such imagery has important OT antecedents (e.g., Isa. 54:1–8; 62:1–5) and is present in other early Christian literature (e.g., Matt. 8:11; 22:1–4; Luke 13:29; 14:15–24; Rev. 19:9). Is the story more about Jesus' capacities as creator (see 1:3)?

Further questions arise from the odd abruptness and indirectness of Jesus' exchange with his mother. If this Gospel were all we had, we would not know her name. She appears only here and at the cross, where Jesus ensures care for her after his death (19:25–27). She speaks only twice; once to Jesus ("They have no wine," v. 3) and once to the servants ("Do whatever he tells you," v. 5). For some, she figures Judaism and expresses its desires for a kind of Messiah that Jesus rejects. For others, her interests represent a system of honor and patronage that he rejects. His response to her is ambiguous, but clearly suggests that her interests are at cross-purposes with his concerns and his hour. Yet he does not refuse but meets her implicit desire that he supply wine. Furthermore, this act is deemed first of his signs and revelatory of his glory (v. 11).

In the end, the meanings this story elicits are too many and diverse to be synthesized. At the very least, this story exposes a number of productive tensions animating Jesus' life and ministry: between Jesus and Judaism, Jesus and his family, and Jesus and his sociocultural context. These tensions never quite break into complete divisions, and through them Jesus reveals his glory. Jesus never operates above the fray; others impinge upon him, affecting his disposition and altering his concerns, and it is in the fray of such tensions that abundance is produced, unexpected goodness enjoyed, and glory revealed.

DAVIS HANKINS

The tension in this first sign should not prevent us from seeing that there is an emphasis on the joining of the flesh and spirit. Here "the Word became flesh and lived among us" (1:14). What better way to emphasize this foundational view than at a wedding, where the unity of spirit and flesh are affirmed and celebrated!

A wedding is a sign of the uniting of flesh and spirit. There are the delights of the flesh: companionship, friendship, and sexuality. There are also the difficulties of the flesh: in the course of our engagement with one another we will encounter things about our partner and ourselves that we do not like. The struggle of the spirit often begins in mutual disappointment. What do we do with these conflicts, these blocks? Do we use them as opportunities for growth, or do they become stumbling blocks? The vows of marriage stress this—for better, for worse, in good times and in bad—and these vows point to the importance of the flesh as well as the necessity of the spirit.

This first sign is a clue to the "fleshliness" of the Word. For those like me who believe that John's Gospel is too ethereal, we should note that the first miracle meets a "fleshly" need—indeed, for some a questionable fleshly need. This first sign is not feeding the starving but rather providing wine to those who may already be a bit tipsy! How audacious and surprising of Jesus and God to do this! That certainly seems to be John's point here. In the midst of the grinding and messy run of human life, God's power is coming. Behold the Lamb of God!

NIBS STROUPE

John 2:13–25

¹³The Passover of the Jews* was near, and Jesus went up to Jerusalem. ¹⁴In the temple he found people selling cattle, sheep, and doves, and the money changers seated at their tables. ¹⁵Making a whip of cords, he drove all of them out of the temple, both the sheep and the cattle. He also poured out the coins of the money changers and overturned their tables. ¹⁶He told those who were selling the doves, "Take these things out of here! Stop making my Father's house a marketplace!" ¹⁷His disciples remembered that it was written, "Zeal for your house will consume me." ¹⁸The Jews then said to him, "What sign can you show us for doing this?" ¹⁹Jesus answered them, "Destroy this temple, and in

Theological Perspective

When, at the wedding at Cana, John says Jesus gave his first "sign," it is obvious that he refers to Jesus' turning water to wine. John indicates that the story of the cleansing of the temple is a sign as well: it is, he says afterward, "because they saw the signs that he was doing" (v. 23) that the crowd began to believe in him. This is a different sort of sign, however, delivering a different sort of message. It tells us that Jesus claims ownership of the place of worship—and that he has a distinct distaste for religion driven by market forces.

We tend to gloss over the magnitude of Jesus' disapproval here. He did not act impulsively. He stopped. He found some good rope. He made his own personal whip. Then, fully prepared, he went well and truly berserk. To appreciate this, it helps to imagine the scene happening in one's own house of worship. If someone came in on a Sunday morning armed even with a whip, upended the furniture and drove everybody out, the story would end with incarceration or hospitalization. It might just make the national news.

When Jesus cleansed the temple, questions arose, and the conversation turned to signs. When they asked what sign he could give to justify his behavior,

*See "'The Jews' in the Fourth Gospel" on pp. xi–xiv.

Pastoral Perspective

Many people like to journal, to express their thoughts, prayers, questions, hopes, happenings, and gratitude on clean, crisp, white pages. Some of these journalers do not want any type of writing or ornamentation on the paper. They want to be the first to mark the page. For this reason, they write only on unlined paper.

Some people marvel at their choice. They cannot seem to write straight across the page. The trick, however, is to write the first word straight and line up the rest with it. Most people tend to line up the new word with the preceding word. They do not go back to the beginning to check if the word is straight. They assume that because the new word matches the previous word it is in line with every word on the page. Often they are deceived because they miss the subtle incline or decline of a word only a few words into the writing.

When this happens, they must decide whether they will continue writing on the angle until they get to the end of the page or make midcourse correction. Most choose the angle because at least all the words are moving in the same direction, even if they are not in line with the dimensions of the paper. Few have the courage to "mess up" the page by straightening out the next line, which will make the writing look inharmonious.

three days I will raise it up." ²⁰The Jews then said, "This temple has been under construction for forty-six years, and will you raise it up in three days?" ²¹But he was speaking of the temple of his body. ²²After he was raised from the dead, his disciples remembered that he had said this; and they believed the scripture and the word that Jesus had spoken.

²³When he was in Jerusalem during the Passover festival, many believed in his name because they saw the signs that he was doing. ²⁴But Jesus on his part would not entrust himself to them, because he knew all people ²⁵and needed no one to testify about anyone; for he himself knew what was in everyone.

Exegetical Perspective

This passage recounts one of the rare events attested by all four canonical Gospels (Matt. 21:12–27; Mark 11:15–33; Luke 19:45–20:8). In the Synoptics it occurs at the end of Jesus' life and ministry, which is no less dramatic than in John, where it is the first time Jesus clearly acts of his own accord. John begins with stories of others impinging upon Jesus' ministry. In 1:35–51 John the Baptist's disciples follow him and gather others without direct invitation or instruction. In 2:1–12 Jesus' mother transforms the lack of wine at the wedding from no concern of his (2:4) to the first occasion for his glory's revelation (2:11). Here it seems that Jesus' interests alone motivate his actions, and the end of the story reports his refusal to be impinged upon by others (v. 24).

John seems to present this story, as the report of Jesus' first freely initiated act, as particularly indicative of his initial sense of vocation. Yet the narrative context matters, for this story of aggressive action reads differently when placed after other stories where he adjusts his attention in accordance with those around him. While the earlier interactions do not lessen the importance of this text for indicating his vocation, they do color the reader's perspective on his disposition toward his vocation. The narrative context compels one to understand Jesus' disruptive opposition to the religious authorities and the temple

Homiletical Perspective

This is one of the most striking passages in the Gospels. It shows Jesus on the verge of violence as he drives the money changers out of the temple. It is a blow struck at the heart of his religious tradition. It is a powerful memory in the church, for it is found in all four of the Gospels. In the Synoptics this story is found toward the end of Jesus' ministry, after he has entered Jerusalem on Palm Sunday. Here in John it is placed at the beginning of Jesus' ministry, and it points out a main difference between John and the Synoptics. In the other three Gospels, Jesus goes to Jerusalem only once, but in John's Gospel, he goes several times and celebrates three Passover seasons there.

This second sign in John is a dramatic shift from the joy, celebration, and abundance of the wedding in Cana. Here we move to a prophetic, tension-filled sign. In some years during Lent, I set up a card table at the front of our sanctuary. I put some plastic cups and plates and metallic objects on it, and as I begin the sermon, I turn the table over forcefully. It has the desired effect! It wakes people up and gives them a sense of the tension in this story. Because Jesus' actions are a direct challenge to the temple-centered focus of the Judaism of his time, we see "the Jews" questioning him about his actions. As we have warned before, given the horrific history of persecuting Jewish people in the name of Jesus the Jew,

John 2:13–25

Theological Perspective

Jesus gave his first allusion to his resurrection: destroy the temple of his body, and he would raise it up again. The sign would be found in the acts that bring salvation.

John also points to salvation as the context by mentioning twice that the events happened at the Passover (vv. 13, 23). It seems odd when John calls it "the Passover *of the Jews*," since that was the only Passover around. However, for the early Christians to whom he writes, the great events of Maundy Thursday, Good Friday, Holy Saturday, and Easter Sunday are the *Christian* Passover.

John is telling us that Jesus' actions were a sign of this new Passover. In cleansing the temple, as in his passion and resurrection, he was bringing his people through a new exodus, a new deliverance from what binds them. Clearly, one of the ways God's people were bound into slavery was by a religion that had been co-opted by market forces.

Jesus was not objecting to religion, or to the particular religion they were trying to practice. They were buying the offering specified in God's law for the ritual acts specified in God's law. Jesus objected to the misidentification of the temple with a marketplace, a place people go to get conveniently what they want or need. That was not the purpose of the temple.

One can find various analogies to modern Christian practice here. It would seem like easy picking to note the groups selling fair-trade goods as a mission initiative, or selling unrelated things to fund mission projects. Perhaps we will be okay, by the standard of the passage, if we keep all these good causes in the fellowship hall and out of the sanctuary.

The more subtle issue is the pervasive marketing mentality in today's North American version of Christianity. When we move to a new town, or when we get fed up with our old church, we go "church shopping." We want our needs met; so we shop around to see what the different outlets have to offer. Using the phrase, we make ourselves consumers aiming to buy a bit of religion.

Those of us in mainline churches point our fingers outward to huge nondenominational churches for just this reason. We think that they have given in and are offering entertainment instead of the gospel, with interest-focused programming that looks like recreation.

Some in the big nondenominational churches make the same accusation of the so-called mainline denominations, and with equally good reason. Our small homogeneous churches seem like boutiques

Pastoral Perspective

The challenge we have on paper is also the challenge we have with our discipleship. There can be a subtle decline of our individual and corporate faith and worship without our recognizing it, because we go back only a few years, maybe a generation or so, and line up our practices from there. We do not go back to original practice or intent, to translate it into faithful action in our time and place. Then the jarring moment occurs when someone has the audacity to go back to the "first word on the page," and we see we are askew. Now we must decide whether we will continue on the slanting journey that contradicts the dimensions of our page, or make the midcourse correction at the expense of revealing our sloping tendencies. As there is "nothing new under the sun" (Eccl. 1:9), we are not the first to experience this tension. I believe this same dynamic is at work in the temple scene recorded in John 2.

Somehow along the way the purpose and priorities of temple worship were changed. What was ancillary to temple practices—the changing of money for paying the temple tax and buying the animals needed for sacrifice, with all of the buying and selling that ensued—became the main event. Jesus reminds the people that the temple is the "Father's house." It is the house of God, the same God who was in the beginning with the Word and was the Word (1:1). Therefore, God's purpose and agenda are to be the "first Word on the page." Rather than going back to its original intent and keeping that primary, the people began slanting toward economic profit at the expense of spiritual gain. In the end, worship was co-opted by commerce. The temple became a marketplace, rather than a place to meet God.

In steps Jesus. He does not "cleanse" the temple; there is no evidence that the buying and selling stopped. His actions are symbolic. They point to the slanting nature of the temple practices. The problem is that not only the temple is slanting; the culture is slanting also. All the writing on the page is moving in the direction of money making at the expense of the Father's agenda of aiding the poor, reaching out to the "least of these," practicing social and economic justice, and worshiping God in Spirit and in truth. Jesus' actions confront them with the slanting nature of their worship. Now that they know, it is decision time. They must decide whether they will continue askew because all the words on the page are moving in the same wrong direction, or whether they will make a midcourse correction.

What Jesus is trying to get them to see is that they need to get their priorities straight. The business

Exegetical Perspective

complex in light of, for example, his miraculous, festive production of an exorbitant amount of wine at a wedding.

In fact, the two scenes in chapter 2 form a pair that it is instructive to consider together. Both end with reports about Jesus' signs that lead to belief (2:11, 22–23); few grasp the full significance of the signs. They depict a portrait of numerous contrasts: Galilee versus Judea, Cana versus Jerusalem, a home versus the temple, a wedding versus Passover, the positive transformation of water into wine versus the negative transformation of "my Father's house" into "a marketplace." Through their juxtaposition John invites us to consider them together, just as the triumphal entry into Jerusalem introduces and so colors the temple incident in the Synoptics with a particularly political valence.

In the Synoptics Jesus critiques the temple for becoming a den of robbers instead of a house of prayer (Matt. 21:13; Mark 11:17; Luke 19:46). Jesus' indictment in John is not limited to dishonest or exploitative economic practices, but judges economics/commodification as such: "Stop making my Father's house a marketplace!" (2:16). John takes readers from the miracle in Cana to the marketplace in Jerusalem. The former fills up Jewish vessels in a way that clearly exceeds market logic; the latter pours out market-based instruments from a Jewish vessel (temple) in anticipation of an alternative Jewish vessel (temple/body) that will host social and religious life apart from such commodification.

This episode is the first of many times that John mentions the festival of Passover (6:1–71; 11:55–57; 12:1–8; 13:1–19:42). By the first century, Passover had merged with the festival of Unleavened Bread into a celebration, rooted in the tradition of the exodus from Egypt, of God's preservation and protection of God's people against all forms of oppression, danger, and evil. Passover had transitioned from a localized family ritual into a national pilgrimage festival centralized in Jerusalem (cf. Exod. 12–13 to Deut. 16:1–8 and 2 Chr. 35:1–19). All able adult men and their households were expected to travel to Herod's newly expanded temple in Jerusalem for the weeklong holiday. On the 14th of Nisan most families would sacrifice a lamb or kid, which they would consume for dinner along with unleavened bread. For the next week they would avoid food with leaven, make various sacrifices, and joyously celebrate the holiday with prayers, music, and assemblies. Pilgrims could buy animals to participate in worship, and so did not need to travel with them.

Homiletical Perspective

preachers must take care here. Take the story where it should lead us: as a challenge to all religious establishments captured by the powers of the world.

John's version of this story opens with a lively scene of a marketplace in the court of the Gentiles at the temple during Passover in Jerusalem, when thousands of pilgrims are there for the festival. People have come to celebrate and to pay the temple tax, a per capita fee assessed on every Jewish family in order to maintain the temple. The problem is that only shekels are accepted to pay the tax—no Roman coins, no Greek coins. The money changers at the temple will be glad to exchange and convert the coins—for a fee, of course. Many pilgrims also want to offer an animal sacrifice at the temple for Passover. They have brought their own animals or bought some in town, but the animals to be sacrificed must be without a blemish. There are animal inspectors at the temple, and it should come as no surprise that the animals brought for inspection rarely ever pass. Yet, thank God, the temple has unblemished animals for sale!

Jesus comes into this raucous process and upsets it all, driving out the animals, the money changers, and the inspectors. He makes a mess. The pilgrims cannot celebrate Passover properly, and the temple loses revenue. Again, it should also come as no surprise that the religious leaders question him about this brazen attack on the temple. Jesus' answer both is puzzling and is taken by the establishment to be an even greater affront: "See this temple? I can rebuild it in three days!" The religious leaders take this literally and are shocked. It enrages them, and they remember it. Matthew and Mark tell us that this is the only specific charge brought against Jesus at his trial later that week; and of course, it is thrown back in his face by his tormentors as he dies on the cross (Mark 15:29). The author of John tells us, the readers, that Jesus meant this metaphorically, speaking of his body, and that his disciples remembered this and figured it out later.

Even as a metaphor, Jesus' answer is a threat to the religious establishment. It indicates that Jesus is making the claim that his life, death, and resurrection will replace the temple as the location of the dwelling place of God—a bold and outrageous claim indeed. Here we can see why John places this story at the beginning of the ministry of Jesus. While the Synoptics may be historically correct in their placement of the story in Holy Week near the end, John lifts up the foundational meaning of this event by placing it toward the beginning of Jesus' ministry. Jesus' purpose is not just to clean up the

John 2:13–25

Theological Perspective

carefully designed for people who share the same tastes.

Our planning and strategizing often sound more like marketing than theological reflection. When we want to grow, we do demographic studies and try to figure out what our target groups will be interested in. We hire a youth leader or a Christian education director because we believe young families will choose a church based on programming that meets their perceived needs. We start a new service with a different style of music, a projector and screen, convinced that somehow people with current tastes and a desire for technology will find their way through our doors and feel at home.

It is not just one part of Christianity that buys and sells in the place that should be devoted to worship. It is an attitude in our culture that we absorb with every billboard and commercial. In the time of John's Gospel, as now, people were going to the place of worship to get something. They wanted to buy sacrificial offerings and needed the right kind of coinage. We want sermons that make us feel confident, or give us useful guidance about parenting, or give us insights into the biblical world.

Jesus did not say they should reverse the emphasis and come to give instead of coming to get. Here in John's version of the story, he simply emphasized that the place was his "Father's house" and a "temple." The place belonged to God—and so he claimed it for his own. The people of God were to come there to encounter God, turning their attention to God in all the movements of soul we call "worship."

God calls people to gather and attend to the presence of God. We respond with praise and confession. We find ourselves listening, trusting, obeying, and asking for help. Turning to God and responding is worship. Anything else misses the mark.

One by one in these first two chapters, and now here in great numbers, people confessed faith in Jesus. He did not take their profession very seriously. We want him to take our trust in him seriously. One good step in that direction is to leave behind our sense of what we are shopping for and direct our full attention to God's presence as we gather every Lord's Day.

GARY NEAL HANSEN

Pastoral Perspective

of the temple must be the business for which God has established it. They cannot allow the culture to dictate its agenda, its leadership, its mission, or its standards. They must be prepared to follow God, even when it means moving against the culture. They must be prepared to follow God, because things will not stay the same. Change is coming.

The forty-six years of temple construction will come to naught. Business as usual will not continue. The practices they are fighting to preserve cannot continue. The Jerusalem temple will be destroyed, but the temple of the Jewish man crucified outside Jerusalem will be raised to stand forever. This means that "the presence of God in the world is no longer to be identified with a *place* but now with a *person*."[1]

This passage reminds us all to look at the first word on the page, the Word who was in the beginning with God, was God, and became flesh to live among us (1:1, 14). He continues to enter our individual and corporate lives and interrupt business as usual. When he does, it is important that we use the 20/20 hindsight we have been given. We must see his actions as an opportunity to put things right and prepare for what God is about to do. For the glory and presence of God will not be found in the sloping practices and protocols in which we have found comfort. Rather, they will be found in the first Word on the page. Let us line up our lives with him.

RAQUEL ST. CLAIR LETTSOME

---

1. Robert Kysar, *Augsburg Commentary on the New Testament: John* (Minneapolis: Augsburg Fortress, 1986), 51.

Exegetical Perspective

Therefore many money changers were required to accommodate various currencies.

By the time John was compiled, the Romans had destroyed the temple, and Passover had begun to transition once again into a home ritual, now without the practice of sacrifice. For John's community, Jesus was the definitive paschal sacrifice. In John, Jesus dies at the precise moment the lambs are being slaughtered in the temple in preparation for the Passover meal (19:14, 30–31). Likewise, Jesus' critique at this first Passover endures (up to today), for it attacks the creep of market logic, forces, and values into spheres of social life where their presence poisons the values and goods that such spheres provide. Jesus goes to temple to celebrate Passover; so he is not rejecting Judaism or the temple. Instead, like numerous OT prophets (e.g., Jer. 7:1–15; Zech. 14:21), Jesus rejects temple practices corrupted by market valuation and practices.

The reactions of two groups are reported: his disciples and the Jews. Everyone in the story is a Jew, so "the Jews" means those Jewish authorities that Jesus indicts. The Jews ask Jesus to prove that he has the authority necessary to justify his actions as, presumably, a substantial critique rather than a brazen tantrum (v. 18). As is typical in John, Jesus gives an enigmatic response—"Destroy this temple, and in three days I will raise it up" (v. 19)—that he intends in a symbolic sense but that is misunderstood and taken in its literal, straightforward sense (cf. 3:3–5). No one apparently understands until after his death, when his disciples take it as about "the temple of his body" (vv. 21–22). The interpretation refers not only to Jesus' resurrected body but also to the community, which would provide the unique dwelling for God's presence after Jesus' death and the temple's destruction (see 17:20–26). Verse 22 also reveals the ongoing process of interpretation undertaken by the community after Jesus' death and prior to the Gospel's compilation.

Verses 23–25 raise the vexed issue in John about the relationship between seeing Jesus' signs and belief. In 2:11 signs seem sufficient for belief. Jesus suggests that signs are necessary for belief in 4:48: "Unless you see signs and wonders, you will not believe." However, then he says to Thomas, "Blessed are those who have not seen and yet have come to believe" (20:29). John 2:23–25 suggests that belief through signs alone is insufficient. This issue remains crucial in the following exchange with Nicodemus.

DAVIS HANKINS

Homiletical Perspective

temple. His resurrected body will replace the temple, a claim as fraught with difficulty now as it was then. John is emphasizing that the Christ event—his life, death, and resurrection—changes everything, especially long-established religious traditions and understandings.

John places this story near the beginning of his account in order to emphasize to readers in every age that the Christ event calls into question all facets of our existence, including the religious aspects, which seek to answer the deepest questions and mysteries of our lives. Indeed, in the very next story, Jesus tells one of the religious leaders, who is afraid to be seen with him in public, that he must be born again in order to find the meaning of his life. He must start all over!

This is heavy and dangerous stuff for all institutions and systems. In our modern world, which emphasizes the marketplace and money as the keys to life, this passage should serve as a strong warning about our captivity to the systems of this world. In this story one can almost hear the prophetic power of Amos's harsh words: "I hate, I despise your festivals. . . . Take away from me the noise of your songs. . . . But let justice roll down like waters" (Amos 5:21, 23a, 24a).

This second sign of Jesus in John's Gospel is threatening to systems in all ages and all places, but it is especially difficult for us in our culture, which is saturated with a belief in the salvific power of money. This is a troublesome passage to hear and to preach, so the preacher should be forewarned: if the congregation hears the Word from this passage and is not disturbed by it, the preacher has tamed this passage way too much.

NIBS STROUPE

John 3:1–8

¹Now there was a Pharisee named Nicodemus, a leader of the Jews.* ²He came to Jesus by night and said to him, "Rabbi, we know that you are a teacher who has come from God; for no one can do these signs that you do apart from the presence of God." ³Jesus answered him, "Very truly, I tell you, no one can see the kingdom of God without being born from above." ⁴Nicodemus said to him, "How can anyone be born after having grown old? Can one enter a second time into the mother's womb and be born?" ⁵Jesus answered, "Very truly, I tell you, no one can enter the kingdom of God without being born of water and Spirit. ⁶What is born of the flesh is flesh, and what is born of the Spirit is spirit. ⁷Do not be astonished that I said to you, 'You must be born from above.' ⁸The wind blows where it chooses, and you hear the sound of it, but you do not know where it comes from or where it goes. So it is with everyone who is born of the Spirit."

Theological Perspective

The life of faith is born of the Spirit (v. 5). It is not something we manufacture for ourselves. It is not an achievement for which we can take credit. Like birth, the new life of faith is a mysterious gift. It is a birth from above. The Greek word translated "from above" (v. 3) can also mean "again," which is how Nicodemus initially understands Jesus' call for a new birth (v. 4). What sense does it make to be born all over again? How is this possible for someone who has already "grown old"? There is nothing unreasonable about Nicodemus's questions. Throughout John's Gospel, Jesus' teachings elicit one misunderstanding after another, as his hearers try to make sense of his appeals to the things of ordinary life—birth, water, bread, light, sheep—to talk about God's extraordinary love and grace. "Flesh" does not have negative connotations in John, as it often does in Paul's writings. To be "born of the flesh" (v. 6) is simply to receive God's gift of physical life. To be "born of the Spirit" (v. 8) is to receive God's gift of eternal life, a transformed mode of life that begins already now.

The Spirit is God's power and life operating in creaturely existence to transform it; but how and where is the Spirit at work? Christian theology affirms a double-edged view of the Spirit. On one

* See "'The Jews' in the Fourth Gospel" on pp. xi–xiv.

Pastoral Perspective

Nicodemus comes to Jesus "by night." When Nicodemus later appears at Jesus' tomb, John makes it a point to remind us of this: "Nicodemus, who had at first come to Jesus by night, also came" (19:39). Is Nicodemus afraid of the ramifications of being seen with Jesus? Perhaps. Perhaps the Gospel is providing us with a portrait of what takes place when an insider, a church member, a pastor, comes face to face with Jesus, "the light of all people" (1:4). When read through this lens, the story of Nicodemus's darkened encounter with Jesus can open the reading community to an as-yet-unimagined future.

One of the gifts, and burdens, of this text is its familiarity. For many, the words "born again" have become a slogan, a badge of honor, a tool to distinguish insider from outsider and saved from lost. It means that the pastoral challenge in faithfully hosting this text is, at least, twofold. On the one hand, those who are confident in their understanding of the passage because they claim a born-again experience will benefit from an invitation to have their eyes opened all over again. On the other hand, those who have closed their ears to the text after too many "Have you been born again?" inquisitional questions may be surprised by what they discover upon being invited into a close reading of the narrative.

Exegetical Perspective

This scene opens with immediate reference to a particular Pharisee, a "leader of the Jews" called Nicodemus. John frequently portrays the Pharisees as foils who challenge Jesus' authority. Those who read the Gospel in sequence will have noted that in John 1:19, John emphasizes that "this is the testimony given by John when the Jews sent priests and Levites from Jerusalem to ask him, 'Who are you?'" A few short verses later, he adds that "they had been sent from the Pharisees" (1:24). Thus the Pharisees are introduced early in the narrative in a questionable light. That John specifically identifies Nicodemus by name signals the importance of this particular Pharisee in John's Gospel. Nicodemus will have a recurring role in this Gospel and in some ways will defy John's typical image of a Pharisee.

Although they are certainly not alone in this regard, the Pharisees are often portrayed by John in terms of their ignorance, which is thematic in a Gospel whose prologue declares that the *logos* "was in the world, and the world came into being through him; yet the world did not know him" (1:10). In John 2:18–21, Jesus is questioned by "the Jews," that is, the Judean leadership at the temple, who misunderstand the meaning of his answers. Nicodemus will demonstrate a similar level of ignorance, but John casts him in a decidedly more benevolent light.

Homiletical Perspective

Nicodemus is a patron saint for preachers who have lots of questions. Why did you not pay more attention in seminary—especially during the class on change and conflict? Should you have become an Episcopalian when you had the chance? Why did you fail to nail down the vacation policy with the personnel committee? What would you do differently if you could rewind your life? What would you change if you could be born again? If I could start all over, I would skip junior high football, the last five minutes of my first date, and the second semester of Hebrew. I would read more Jürgen Moltmann and less Dear Abby, skip the *Beverly Hillbillies* in favor of PBS, and listen to more Ray Charles and save the $6.00 I spent on a Bee Gees album.

Every once in a while the people in our congregations realize that their lives could be different and plan to turn over a new leaf. They make a list of everything that has to go, everything that will not be part of their new life, and a list of everything they are going to do more of—exercising, reading great books, spending time with the people they love. Their new resolutions work for a while, maybe for a couple of days. They also have moments when they realize that even if they could stop doing everything wrong, even if they did everything right that they wanted to do right, even if they kept all the rules that

John 3:1–8

Theological Perspective

hand, the Spirit is like the wind, which "blows where it chooses" (v. 8). (In Hebrew and Greek, one word means both "spirit" and "wind.") The Spirit is loose in the world in surprising and disruptive ways, transcending human understanding and control. No human rules or traditions can contain the Spirit. Like fire, the Spirit is powerful and unpredictable, bringing light and warmth to cold and dark places. The Spirit's reach is universal. No corner of creation is off limits to the Spirit's transforming power. Kalbryn McLean calls the Spirit the "wild child" of the Godhead.[1]

On the other hand, the Spirit has an institutional affiliation, as the One who both indwells the church and is given through the church as a means of grace. The concrete rituals and practices that structure life in the Christian community are "habitations of the Spirit,"[2] places where the Spirit transforms us personally and corporately. The Spirit's power is channeled through prayer and sacraments, through acts of mercy and outreach, even through potlucks and communal governance. John 3:5 says that new life comes through being born "of water and Spirit," likely a reference to baptism. In and through the church's practice of baptism, the Spirit is at work bringing new life. Through the things of earth— water, bread, wine, oil—comes new life from above. These two edges of Christian teaching about the Spirit, the "wild child" and the institutional, should both be affirmed, not set in opposition to each other.

Nicodemus brings an impressive set of institutional credentials to his nighttime meeting with Jesus. He is a Pharisee and a member of the Sanhedrin, the highest governing body of the Jewish people (v. 1). He is "a teacher of Israel" (v. 10), a keeper of its rituals and practices. The arrangement of John's Gospel invites us to contrast Nicodemus with the next person Jesus engages in conversation, the Samaritan woman in John 4. The contrast is not flattering to Nicodemus. Unlike Nicodemus, the Samaritan woman is female and unnamed. Even worse, she is a morally disgraced member of a theologically suspect group. She has zero religious capital. Yet she meets Jesus in broad daylight (4:6), rather than in the dead of night, and immediately has the courage to give public testimony about him to her own people (4:39). Through the mysterious work of the Spirit, she is born from above.

1. Kalbryn A. McLean, "Calvin and the Personal Politics of Providence," in Amy Plantinga Pauw and Serene Jones, eds., *Feminist and Womanist Essays in Reformed Dogmatics* (Louisville, KY: Westminster John Knox Press, 2006), 122.
2. Craig Dykstra, *Growing in the Life of Faith: Education and Christian Practices* (Louisville, KY: Westminster John Knox Press, 2005), 63–64.

Pastoral Perspective

Nicodemus, the religious leader, assumes that he is enlightened: "Rabbi, we know that you are a teacher who has come from God" (v. 2). In response, Jesus points to his blindness: "No one can see the kingdom of God without being born from above" (v. 3). Nicodemus is in the dark. The transformative voltage that flows through this text puts at risk the status quo of any reader, or reading community, who comes to it assuming sight. Seeing the kingdom of God and therefore seeing how one's citizenship is to be lived in the new world of God's rule will, says Jesus, require a rebirth, a radical break, a new identity.

This is, of course, more easily said than done. Those who are prepared to take the risk of a new birth are, most often, those who admit that they are in the dark, in trouble, lost. This is the reason that 12–step groups begin with an admission of powerlessness and a turning over of life to a higher power. Sobriety will require something other than simply trying harder. It will require a radical reorientation of life "from above." Perhaps such insight into our own blindness is the first sign of rebirth.

Nicodemus does not get it. He is a literal reader. Metaphors are beyond him. He wants to know how it is biologically possible to reenter the womb of his mother. The text assumes that Jesus is not easy to understand. His way of seeing and of speaking confronts our assumptions and expectations. It is not easy for a religious leader like Nicodemus to understand Jesus. This is oddly reassuring. As church leaders we too often struggle to understand the gospel. Sometimes we simply continue to trumpet our misunderstandings, rather than prepare ourselves for the new life Jesus intends. We assume that our rebirth to newness has already taken place when we are, even now, standing alongside Nicodemus in the dark.

Jesus moves the conversation from the question of seeing to that of entering the kingdom of God: "Very truly, I tell you, no one can enter the kingdom of God without being born of water and Spirit" (v. 5). It is one thing to see what is needed. It is another thing to do it. How often this is true for the church. We see the way of Jesus. We hear his command to forgive. We are drawn to his walk with the poor, the outcast, the marginalized. Still, we find old habits, family patterns, and cultural norms beyond our power to break and change. We see but cannot dare to enter the new world that is the kingdom of God.

Entry into the kingdom of God, Jesus says, requires birth of water and Spirit. A Gospel that has begun with Genesis—"In the beginning was the Word" (1:1)—now reminds its readers of how God begins

Exegetical Perspective

It is noteworthy that John presents Nicodemus as a religious leader who is positively disposed toward and genuinely interested in learning more about Jesus, whom he addresses, as do Jesus' disciples, as "Rabbi." Nicodemus not only acknowledges the "signs" that Jesus performs, he speaks for more than just himself when he acknowledges their significance: "'Rabbi, we know that you are a teacher who has come from God; for no one can do these signs that you do apart from the presence of God'" (v. 2). Still he has questions, which should not come as a surprise in a Gospel that contends that signs alone are inadequate for understanding Jesus (20:30–31).

Nicodemus approaches Jesus "by night." Some see in this reference the implication that Nicodemus seeks Jesus out secretly, that is, only by cover of darkness. Others read it as indication simply that Nicodemus is yet "in the dark" about Jesus. Perhaps the most direct path to John's meaning is the one laid out in John 3:19–21, where the author writes,

And this is the judgment, that the light has come into the world, and people loved darkness rather than light because their deeds were evil. For all who do evil hate the light and do not come to the light, so that their deeds may not be exposed. But those who do what is true come to the light, so that it may be clearly seen that their deeds have been done in God.

By coming to Jesus as he does, Nicodemus the Pharisee is illustrative of one who does "what is true" and whose deeds are "clearly seen." He comes in darkness to Jesus the light. Although he does not immediately grasp all that Jesus teaches, he approaches the one he calls "Rabbi" in all sincerity.

Jesus meets Nicodemus's humble greeting with an unsolicited lesson on the kingdom of God that recalls the birthing imagery introduced in John 1:12–13 and underscores the necessity of being born "from above." Although the term *anōthen* can be translated as either "from above" or "again," the former meaning makes most sense here, as the contours of John's Gospel adhere to the binary separation of the realm above from the world below. When Nicodemus, understandably confused, asks, "How can anyone be born after having grown old? Can one enter a second time into the mother's womb and be born?" (v. 4), Jesus speaks to Nicodemus not about rebirth but about new birth from above, that is, from the realm of the Spirit. To be "born of water and Spirit" (v. 5), with water serving as a probable allusion to baptism, is to be born anew, not again.

Homiletical Perspective

they made for themselves, something would still be missing.

Our churches include people who like Nicodemus keep the rules, but know something is still missing. This story offers an opportunity to encourage them, like Nicodemus, to take their questions to Christ. Jesus and the disciples are sitting in an olive grove after a busy day and a long walk. They have finished dinner—fish again—when they hear Nicodemus making his way up the hill, twigs snapping under his feet. Nicodemus is uncomfortable being there so late at night. Jesus gestures for him to go ahead. How do you begin a conversation with Jesus? Nicodemus starts, as debaters often do, with a compliment, "Jesus, we know that you are a remarkable person with rare gifts for teaching. You do extraordinary things." He is having trouble getting to what he wants to ask. Jesus thinks it is too late for a long, drawn-out analysis, so he cuts to the chase: "What the whole thing boils down to is that unless you are born from above, you might as well give up."

This is not the response Nicodemus is expecting: "I came here for a serious conversation at considerable risk to my reputation, and you start posing riddles. What do you mean? How are you supposed to be born again when you are pushing retirement age? How can you be born from above when it is a challenge just to get out of bed in the morning?"

Jesus explains, "The wind blows where it will, and you hear it, but you do not know where it comes from or where it goes. That is how it is with everyone who is born of the Spirit." Jesus is playing on the word *pneuma*, which means both spirit and wind. God's Spirit is as uncontrollable and unknowable as the wind. The new life that Jesus has in mind is elusive, mysterious, and entirely God's doing. The incomprehensible wind of the Spirit blows where we do not see. People experience God's grace in more ways than we understand. We worship a wind that blows where it will.

We preach new life that is not about knowledge or accomplishment, but about the uncontrollable wind of the Spirit. Being born from above is not the same thing as acting like a nicer person, learning more, or working harder. We cannot give ourselves a new start. No one can enter the kingdom of God, or even see it, without being born from above, of water and Spirit (vv. 3, 5). If everyone in the world read the Bible, joined a church, and said hello to their neighbors, if we were all as good as Nicodemus, something would still be missing. Life is a mystery beyond our understanding, a gift that only God can give.

John 3:1–8

Theological Perspective

It has been tempting for Christian interpreters (especially Protestant ones) to see Nicodemus's institutional affiliations as a barrier to the work of the Spirit. On this reading, the Spirit spurns the "legalism" of Pharisees like Nicodemus and blows into unlikely places, like the life of a disgraced Samaritan woman. This classic move in Christian anti-Judaism does justice neither to Nicodemus nor to Christian understandings of the Spirit. Nicodemus appears two more times in John's Gospel, once to defend Jesus' right to a hearing on the basis of Jewish law (7:50–51), and one last time to anoint and prepare Jesus' body "according to the burial custom of the Jews" (19:39–40). Nicodemus never abandons the rituals and practices that structure life in his religious community. In and through them the Spirit blows, creating space for Nicodemus to find and express his devotion to Jesus. Jewish burial customs become habitations of the Spirit. Through the things of earth Nicodemus is born from above. His journey, which begins in darkness and incomprehension, ends in faith.

"Do not be astonished" (v. 7), Jesus says to Nicodemus, about his need for new life. To the church, Jesus says, "Do not be astonished at the many ways this life 'from above' comes. Do not be astonished when ancient traditions become habitations of the Spirit. Do not be astonished when the Spirit shows up in new and disturbing places. However and whenever faith and new life appear, know that they are 'from above,' gifts of the Spirit. Give thanks for all the gifts of the Spirit." As Hildegard of Bingen declares, the Spirit is "radiant life, worthy of praise, awakening and enlivening all things."[3]

AMY PLANTINGA PAUW

Pastoral Perspective

again. New creation begins with the wind/spirit/ breath of God sweeping over the face of the waters (Gen. 1:2). The waters are storm waters of trouble. They are like the waters of the Red Sea that God holds back so that the people can pass through. They are like the storm waters of Galilee that Jesus calms in the face of the disciples' fear. They are like the baptismal waters in which, says Paul, we drown to our old way of life and rise to walk with Christ in "newness of life" (Rom. 6:4). Rebirth—whether personal or congregational, cultural or political—requires a break, an ending, a risky journey to new life.

No wonder Jesus says that this birth must come from above. This is not the kind of transformation that can be programmed or taught. Its source and activity is mysterious—as unpredictable as the wind. Nicodemus is not told what to do in order to be reborn, because rebirth is beyond his control. It is the inexplicable, incredible gift of God.

In this regard, rebirth is no different from birth itself. It is beyond our control. It comes through the waters of the darkened womb. It is reliant upon the divine gift of breath/spirit. The eyes to see and the power to enter the world we are born into are given to the newborn freely, as gifts. Could it be that the personal rebirth we long for, the rebirth of the dying church we know and of the troubled world we inhabit, is the great gift of God in Jesus Christ for those with eyes to see?

EDWIN SEARCY

---

3. Fiona Bowie and Oliver Davies, eds., *Hildegard of Bingen: An Anthology* (London: SPCK, 1990), 118.

Exegetical Perspective

Birthing imagery captures the Gospel's thematic emphasis on the role of the *logos* in creation: "In the beginning was the Word [*logos*], and the Word was with God, and the Word was God. He was in the beginning with God. All things came into being through him, and without him not one thing came into being" (1:1–3). By expanding upon the prologue's initial references to the life that comes from the *logos*, John makes clear that the creative activity of the *logos* is ongoing. Jesus' use of the second person plural, "you must be born from above" (v. 7), not only responds to Nicodemus's use of the first person plural (v. 2); it also recalls the prologue's concern for humanity writ large, "What has come into being in him was life, and the life was the light of all people" (1:3b–4).

The first sign that Jesus performed—changing water into wine at the wedding in Cana (2:1–11)—served to illustrate astonishing transformation and abundance. Here in chapter 3, Jesus' first extended teaching in the Gospel emphasizes human transformation. Jesus presents an understanding of new life as that which is both abundant and rooted in and generated by the Spirit. Being born anew cannot be compelled, controlled, or managed by human initiative. As John writes, "The wind blows where it chooses, and you hear the sound of it, but you do not know where it comes from or where it goes. So it is with everyone who is born of the Spirit" (v. 8). Using the same Greek word, *pneuma*, for both wind and Spirit, John evokes the image of the wind or Spirit of God that "swept over the face of the waters" (Gen. 1:2) at the opening of the first biblical account of creation. John's message is clear: the *logos* and Spirit who brought life into being at the very beginning of all things continue to bring new life to all humankind. The creative and life-giving work of God is powerful, unpredictable, and ongoing.

MARY F. FOSKETT

Homiletical Perspective

Any life we know comes as a gift of God. Hope and joy come from God. The same Spirit who gave life in the first place gives life over and over again.

What does it mean for us to preach about being "born from above"? Perhaps in your church there are two women who seem to have similar lives, but the first is incredibly overworked. She is a legal assistant, married with two teenagers. She is tired most of the time. She teaches a children's Sunday school class, and is tired of that too. She feels burned out in just about everything. The second woman does not feel trapped. She works as an office manager, divorced with two small children. She is busy, but she finds time to teach an adult Sunday school class. She enjoys life and the people around her.

The two women's lives are alike in most respects, but the first woman thinks hers is dull, and lives out of a sense of duty. Maybe the boredom she feels is the Spirit calling her to a better way, but she does not recognize it. The second woman thinks of her life as a gift, and lives out of gratitude. Pinning down the difference between the two women or the ways in which we play both parts is hard, but it has something—or everything—to do with the hope of being born from above. The change we want and the life we need are gifts from God.

When we feel burned out and feel no joy, we should ask God to be born from above. We should preach that the dullest day given to God has meaning. The emptiest week committed to love has purpose. The most hopeless life given in faith finds hope.

BRETT YOUNGER

John 3:9–15

Theological Perspective

John 3:9–15 presents two teachers talking to each other about matters of faith. Jesus is "a teacher who has come from God" (3:2), and Nicodemus is "a teacher of Israel" (v. 10). It would be more accurate to say that one teacher is talking over the head of the other. Nicodemus is having a hard time following Jesus' lesson. It is easy to sympathize with Nicodemus's plaintive question in verse 9: "How can these things be?" He has tried, to no avail, to follow Jesus' lesson about birth and wind in verses 3–8. Even "the earthly things" (v. 12) are too hard for him to understand. This "teacher of Israel" is out of his league, and he knows it.

Nicodemus is not alone. When it comes to understanding matters of faith, we are all out of our league. Karl Barth encouraged his fellow theologians not to take themselves too seriously. He wanted them to recognize the humor in all human attempts to understand the things of God. He imagined the angels' giggling about his prodigious theological efforts, and the relief of one day being able to dump his enormous *Church Dogmatics* "on some heavenly floor as a pile of waste paper."[1]

In verses 11–12, Jesus the teacher seems exasperated with his student. We speak of the truth that

1. Eberhard Busch, *Karl Barth: His Life from Letters and Autobiographical Texts*, trans. John Bowden (Grand Rapids: Eerdmans, 1994), 489.

Pastoral Perspective

"How can these things be?" Nicodemus speaks for a wealth of insiders and outsiders who wonder at the impossible possibility of a new future. How is real newness possible? It is a question that saps the energy of lone souls in despair, of congregations in decline, of families in dysfunction, and of peoples under oppression. Nicodemus names Jesus "a teacher who has come from God" (3:2) but this teaching is more than he has bargained for. It is one thing to be taught to live a more faithful life. It is another thing to learn that the future calls for rebirth "from above" (3:7). Those who know too well what it is to endure cycles of abuse and those who witness the continued degradation of the planet by human consumption wonder with Nicodemus how anything truly new can be.

Jesus appears surprised: "Are you a teacher of Israel, and yet you do not understand these things?" (v. 10). Jesus imagines that Nicodemus should be well schooled in the rebirth of a people. From the barren future of Abraham and Sarah to the grinding oppression of Pharaoh's system and the dry bones of utter loss in exile, the memory of Israel is well stocked with stories of impossible newness from above. After the long season of Christendom, the church we know also has fallen victim to the amnesia that affected Nicodemus. Teachers of the church often find that they too do not understand

Exegetical Perspective

This passage records the second portion of the dialogue between Jesus and Nicodemus. Nicodemus once again initiates the conversation with a question, but then falls silent. Clearly puzzled by Jesus' teaching about being born from above by water and Spirit, he asks Jesus, "How can these things be?" (v. 9). It is difficult to determine the precise tone of Jesus' retort. On the one hand, it is clearly meant to challenge Nicodemus. On the other hand, it acknowledges Nicodemus's seemingly considerable stature in the community. Translated literally, Jesus' designation for Nicodemus could be taken as titular. He asks, "You are the Teacher of Israel [*ho didaskalos*], and you do not know these things?" Even as he admonishes Nicodemus for his lack of understanding, he recognizes Nicodemus's importance as a teacher among those to whom Jesus himself has been sent (1:31). Most importantly, John uses the brief exchange to turn the reader's attention to the extended monologue by Jesus that immediately follows. Nicodemus effectively disappears from the scene when Jesus' monologue begins (he reappears twice more in the Gospel, in 7:45–51 and 19:39–42). The author's primary interest is in readying his readers to listen to Jesus as if he were no longer speaking to Nicodemus, but addressing them instead.

The passages that follow, 3:11–15 and 3:16–21, outline key aspects of John's understanding of Jesus'

Homiletical Perspective

Nicodemus has a complete set of *Feasting on the Gospels* on his shelf. He is one of us. Nicodemus is chair of the religion department and a mover and shaker in the ministerial association. He has a blog called "Religion for Grown-ups." Being a professional expert on God is good work if you can get it. Nicodemus is adept at articulating the intricacies of religion and detecting the logical shortcomings in other people's faith. Yet, like the rest of us, if he does not understand that life is God's gift, then he had better start over again. Nothing is more basic than knowing that God is a wind beyond our understanding. None of us is an expert on the Almighty.

Nicodemus's coming to see Jesus is surprising, because as far as the ministerial association is concerned, Jesus is a troublemaker. His only status with the local clergy is as a pain in the neck. Just last week he kicked over some tables during a big stewardship campaign at the temple. Nicodemus knows that there are social risks in coming to see Jesus; so he decides that with his reputation to uphold, it might be smart to pay his visit at night. As a result of his decision, many preachers have been unable to resist the temptation to title sermons on this story "Nic at Night." Nicodemus is a good person, who does not do the things you are *not* supposed to do and does the things you *are* supposed to do.

John 3:9–15

Theological Perspective

comes from God, he says to Nicodemus, and we testify to what has been revealed. You have read the Scriptures. Why is this teaching so hard for you to receive? If you cannot grasp the basics, how are you going to handle the more advanced subjects? Nicodemus has undoubtedly read the Scriptures, but he is still having a hard time connecting the dots. Again, it is easy to sympathize with Nicodemus's perplexity. Like the Christian poet George Herbert, we long to know how all the lights of Scripture combine, so that we can see "not only how each verse doth shine / But all the constellations of the storie."[2]

In verses 13–14 Jesus provides Nicodemus with two guide stars in the biblical constellations: Moses and Woman Wisdom. The role of personified divine Wisdom in Proverbs and the deuterocanonical writings is to teach humanity "heavenly things" (v. 12) and lead them to abundant life. As Wisdom declares about herself in Proverbs 8:35, "whoever finds me finds life and obtains favor from the LORD." More than any other Gospel, John aligns Jesus with the figure of Woman Wisdom (see Prov. 30:4), "who descended from heaven" (v. 13) to offer light and truth to humanity. When Jesus, the Son of Man, "has ascended into heaven" (v. 13), this will mark a return to his heavenly origins.

In verse 14 Jesus teaches Nicodemus about the significance of his upcoming death on a cross with a story about Moses from Numbers 21. Israel is crying out in the wilderness for deliverance from a plague of deadly serpents. God tells Moses to craft an image of a serpent and lift it up on a pole. Paradoxically, all who look upon this symbol of death find healing and life. Jesus too will be "lifted up" (v. 14), on a cross, a symbol of death. Through his death, he becomes the source of life and salvation for all (12:32). When Moses wrote about God's gracious acts of healing and deliverance, Jesus says later, Moses "wrote about me" (5:46).

The ascension and the crucifixion are difficult lessons. We can imagine Nicodemus responding to Jesus' mysterious teachings about these "heavenly things" yet to take place with the same question he had before: "How can these things be?" Christians living on the other side of the crucifixion and ascension of Christ often have Nicodemus's question too. Even the best teachers among us need remedial help to grasp the heavenly mysteries. We long for our teacher Jesus to open our minds to

Pastoral Perspective

these things. Being "born again" is regularly reduced to a one-time personal experience of the individual, when it holds the promise—and threat—of radical renewal for whole communities being born anew into the kingdom of God.

Now Jesus enters the witness box. The dialogue with Nicodemus gives way to Jesus' singular testimony. The encounter is no longer framed as teacher and student. Nicodemus slips quietly off the stage of the text until later in the Gospel (7:50; 19:39–40). Now we, the reading community, become the jury who must weigh the evidence before us. Jesus swears to tell the truth, the whole truth, and nothing but the truth: "Very truly, I tell you, we speak of what we know and testify to what we have seen" (v. 11). This is the foundation upon which our life together will be lived. This is how we will know it is true. We will know it is true because we witness the testimony of Jesus' life, death, and resurrection and judge it to be the truth.

Trusting in Jesus to bring new life is not easy for jurors who witness strong countertestimony from a "real world" in which rebirth is an impossibility. Such countertestimony is often convincing, even to those who long to place their trust in Jesus. It saps courage for change, drains energy for risk and sacrifice, feeds the twin cancers of apathy and despair. Jesus notices the jury's hesitancy, the heads shaking "no" in response to his vision of life born from above (v. 11). The reception of Jesus' testimony as the truth—as a faithful depiction of the real world in which we live—is a critical pastoral issue facing the church, whether gathered in worship or scattered in mission. This is the reason that congregations benefit from honest testimony in which doubt and uncertainty are safely given voice. Witnesses are to be protected in God's sanctuary. Their proclamation is not canned. In this way the community comes to trust the testimony that says yes to Jesus and confirms the truth of his way.

Jesus pushes on. His testimony about rebirth has been "about earthly things" (v. 12). Now he will tell the truth about "heavenly things." First he has testified that the kingdom of God requires human beings to be born from above into a new world. Now he says that there is One who has bridged the chasm between heaven and earth: the Son of Man. Here we receive the two most audacious claims of Christian faith: that Jesus is "descended from heaven" (v. 13) and that broken, flawed, sinful humankind can be reborn, saved, made new. We will not be surprised if the jury—whether outsiders or insiders—often arrives at a verdict of disbelief.

2. George Herbert, "The Holy Scriptures (2)," in *The Complete English Poems* (London: Penguin Books, 2005), 52.

identity and purpose. In the first of these two units, Jesus makes use of both first- and second-person plural address: "Very truly, I tell you, we speak of what we know and testify to what we have seen; yet you do not receive our testimony" (v. 11). Although the precise meaning of the "earthly" and "heavenly" things to which Jesus refers in John 3:12 is unclear, the meaning of the contrast between the two is not. The dualistic language places Nicodemus not only among those persons who do not understand Jesus, but among those who do not believe or accept him. Where Nicodemus initially appeared as earnest but lacking insight, he is now cast as resistant. The change in tone is abrupt and surprising, especially since John resumes his more benevolent portrayal of Nicodemus later in the Gospel (7:45–51; 19:39–40).

To a large degree, then, John 3:11 seems to be speaking less to the unfolding story of Jesus in his day and more to some tension in John's historical context, a tension rooted in differences in belief within John's own community or between his group and outsiders. John seems to be speaking through the figures of Nicodemus and Jesus in order to represent differing religious perspectives. Jesus' point of view aligns with the religious perspective of John and his community, while the position that Jesus characterizes through his use of the second person plural ("you," vv. 11–12) conveys the writer's generalizing take on those who refute the claims to which he and his community adhere. John uses the scene to draw a sharp distinction between those within and without his religious community. What then follows points to the Johannine understanding of "heavenly things" (v. 12), that is, to God's purpose in sending Jesus into the world.

John 3:13 indirectly but effectively identifies Jesus as the Son of Man and clarifies what distinguishes him from all others: "No one has ascended into heaven except the one who descended from heaven, the Son of Man." Jesus is the only one who has ascended into heaven, precisely because he is the only one who has come from heaven. Charles H. Talbert observes that John draws a clear contrast between his understanding of Jesus' uniqueness and those ancient Jewish and Christian traditions that held that Moses or Isaiah had themselves experienced heavenly ascents. Philo, for example, refers to Moses' ascent into Mount Sinai as "the calling above of the prophet," and "a *second birth* better than the first . . . or, as we have said, the *divine birth*" (*Questions and Answers on Exodus* 2.46). As Talbert notes, "Here Philo contrasts the first birth from the earth

Nicodemus visits Jesus because he knows that there has to be more.

Nicodemus's last words to Jesus make him sound like all of the ministers who are not sure how to begin anything we are not in charge of: "How can this be?" Jesus sounds surprised, "You are a teacher, and you do not understand this?"

Most preachers recognize Nicodemus. We have treated our opinions as God's. Sometimes we speak about God as if God is no harder to understand than anyone else. We have beliefs that we have held for so long that we think that if they are not God's, they ought to be. We begin to believe that if we do not know something, then it does not matter. We share Nicodemus's ability to judge what others think on the basis of how close it is to what we think.

Like Nicodemus, we can speak truth without feeling the Spirit, but we also have moments when we hear the one who descended from heaven. We, like others in our congregation, experience this difference as we gather as a church. Sometimes we go out of habit. At other times, the people who care for us bring us into God's goodness. We see the difference in how we serve. Sometimes we do good because we want to think of ourselves as the kind of people who do good. At other sacred times we care for others because God's love flows through us. We see the difference in how we give. Sometimes we figure out the smallest amount we can give without feeling guilty. On other blessed occasions we realize that what we give away is the best money we spend. We see the difference in how we treat the people closest to us. Sometimes we stay with them only because we have promised to. At other times we ask God to help us love them more each day. We know the difference when we come to worship. Some Sunday mornings we tell ourselves, "It's only an hour." However, there are also moments when we feel the gentle breeze of God's Spirit.

God will lead preachers away from Nicodemus's assumption that we can know and control it all and lead us toward heavenly things. The writer of the Gospel of John says this hope is like the strange story in Numbers 21 with the copper snake. Christ is lifted up so that all can see the hope of God. The cross, the Son of Man lifted up, reveals the depth of God's mercy for all of us who are snake-bitten by the power of death. Unlike the author of the Fourth Gospel, most Old Testament scholars protect their reputation by ignoring the snake story. The ones brave enough to comment work hard to make it clear that the writer of Numbers is not saying that the snake heals anybody. The people's decision to

Theological Perspective

understand the Scriptures, as he did for his first disciples (Luke 24:45).

Fortunately, eternal life in Jesus (v. 15, following the NIV translation) does not require perfect understanding, but simply belief. In her "Reflections on the Right Use of School Studies with a View to the Love of God," Simone Weil notes that we do not start with an intellectual verification of heavenly things, and then proceed to belief. Faith starts in the dark, without light, just as Nicodemus's encounter with Jesus did (3:2). Faith does not depend on certitude and understanding—these are the fruit of faith, not its precondition. Trusting our teacher Jesus, we take the leap of faith before we can see exactly where it is all going to lead. Spiritual certitudes "are arrived at by experience," Weil insists.

The Israelites dying of serpent bites in the wilderness (Num. 21:6–9) did not first understand how a serpent on a pole could save them, and then put their faith in God's surprising mode of deliverance. They first trusted that God would deliver them, and their experience of being healed led to certitude about the efficacy of Moses' strange action of lifting up the serpent. Likewise, we do not have to understand the cross and ascension of Christ before we can be saved by them. There are no honors students in the school of Christian discipleship. Our confidence is in God, not in the strength of our intellects. Yet spiritual progress is possible. Trusting God, we can grow in the life of faith. As Weil insists, "the best support for faith is the guarantee that if we ask our Father for bread, he does not give us a stone."[3]

AMY PLANTINGA PAUW

Pastoral Perspective

Disbelief comes with a cost. Disbelief leaves those who do not trust Jesus' testimony living in the status quo, the rat race, the real world in which new life "from above" is, by definition, impossible. Belief in him, on the other hand, will lead to life "from above." The One who has descended from heaven must be "lifted up," just as Moses lifted up the serpent in the wilderness (Num. 21:9). The text prefigures the lifting up of Jesus on the cross and from the grave so that a world poisoned by the powers of death may be healed, saved, reborn. Trusting the Son of Man who is lifted up will result in life with a capital *L*, new life lived in the real world of the kingdom of God, life that is eternal.

This language is thick. John's Gospel is at once accessible and inaccessible, familiar and unfamiliar, clear and opaque. For many, the word "belief" has come to mean accepting certain statements about God as true. When communities are learning to live this text, they will need to redefine belief that leads to eternal life as risky, courageous trust in Jesus to lead his people into a new way of being. Then eternal life will not be defined by chronological time and restricted to life after physical death. Then eternal life will describe the time on either side of death when lives are lived on the cruciform path of Jesus. Then believing in Jesus will not lead those who entrust their lives to him on a path out of the suffering world. Instead, trust in the testimony of Jesus will lead believers into the suffering world as witnesses who have seen the shape of life eternal. Their lives and deaths will then testify to the newness that lies on the other side of dying to the ways of the world and being born from above into the way of Jesus Christ.

EDWIN SEARCY

---

3. Simone Weil, *Waiting for God*, trans. Emma Craufurd (New York: G. P. Putnam's Sons, 1951), 107.

Exegetical Perspective

with the second birth from above."[1] John's Gospel opposes such reasoning and contends that the only one who can ascend into heaven is the one who is born of the realm above. Therefore, by extension, readers are to understand that the new birth from above that John 3 describes owes itself not to the spiritual knowledge and heavenly ascent that a human person attains, but to the activity of the incarnate Word (*logos*) and Spirit of God.

John then proceeds to focus his reader's attention on the integral relationship that he sees between divine initiative and human belief. He emphasizes not heavenly ascent, but human assent, when Jesus says, "And just as Moses lifted up the serpent in the wilderness, so must the Son of Man be lifted up, that whoever believes in him may have eternal life" (vv. 14–15). Jesus alludes to the biblical story of how the Lord told Moses to make a bronze image of a poisonous serpent and raise it up high with his staff so that the Israelites who had been bitten by venomous snakes in the wilderness could gaze upon the image wrapped around Moses' pole and be healed (Num. 21:8–9).

The analogy points to Jesus as the one who is to be lifted up, not on a pole or staff, but on the cross. The meaning for John is clear: those who gaze upon the incarnate *logos* and believe him to be Son of Man will find eternal life. John casts the cross itself as an instrument of healing. No wonder, then, that this Gospel refers to the crucifixion as the "hour" in which Jesus will be glorified (2:4; 12:23). For John, Jesus' death is analogous to that of the Passover lamb. It provides liberation from death to those who believe. In this manner, John attaches the creative activity of the Spirit and the concept of new birth to human belief, a motif that he develops further in the passage that follows.

MARY F. FOSKETT

Homiletical Perspective

look is what matters. When people look to God, they find life. The cross does not heal so much as the love behind the cross heals. Whoever believes in this love will find their way to eternal life. Jesus leads us to preach heavenly possibilities.

The Gospel of John does not tell us what Nicodemus felt as he left Jesus that night, but after Jesus died, Nicodemus came to the cross and cared for Jesus' body. Nicodemus did not understand God, but somehow the wind beyond his understanding led him to hope.

A retired minister lives in a cottage in New England on the side of a mountain. He can see forty miles to the east. There is a mountain range to the west, and there are two lakes in the distance to the south. One Sunday evening a congregation from nearby comes to have a sunset vespers service there on the mountaintop. As one woman looks at the view, she begins crying. The minister leans over and quietly says, "It is a lovely view." She replies, "No. You do not understand. I have lived within twenty miles of this view all of my life, and I never knew it was here."

We can preach things that are accurate, but if we do not preach the one who has been lifted up, the one who brings life, the one who is hope, then we are like someone twenty miles from a gorgeous view who never climbs the mountain.

BRETT YOUNGER

---

1. Charles H. Talbert, *Reading John. A Literary and Theological Commentary on the Fourth Gospel and the Johannine Epistles* (London: SPCK Publishing, 1992), 100–101.

John 3:16–21

16"For God so loved the world that he gave his only Son, so that everyone who believes in him may not perish but may have eternal life.

17"Indeed, God did not send the Son into the world to condemn the world, but in order that the world might be saved through him. 18Those who believe in him are not condemned; but those who do not believe are condemned already, because they have not believed in the name of the only Son of God. 19And this is the judgment, that the light has come into the world, and people loved darkness rather than light because their deeds were evil. 20For all who do evil hate the light and do not come to the light, so that their deeds may not be exposed. 21But those who do what is true come to the light, so that it may be clearly seen that their deeds have been done in God."

Theological Perspective

"For the world has Me; I am its God." That is how Martin Luther summarized God's "inexpressibly beautiful message"[1] in John 3:16. God's own being and nature is love (1 John 4:8), and God's declaration of unconditional love for the world sets the tone for the whole of verses 16–21. The evil and darkness of the world (v. 19) can seem overwhelming, but they cannot overcome the light of God's love. The supreme manifestation of God's love is the giving of Jesus. The declaration that God "gave [God's] only Son" (v. 16) refers both to the incarnation and to the cross. The Son is both "given" to the world as the Word who "became flesh and lived among us" (1:14), and "given up" to death on the cross (Rom. 8:32). Jesus is given up to death, so that the world may have eternal life (v. 16). Jesus is the face of God turned toward a hurting and alienated cosmos.

To a world enshrouded by death-dealing powers, the love of God is a light shining out of darkness. According to Raymond Brown, the purpose clauses in verses 20–21 do not provide the subjective reason why people come or do not come to the light. For example, those who "do what is true" (v. 21) do not come to Jesus to have it confirmed to everyone

1. Martin Luther, *Sermons on the Gospel of St. John*, ed. Jaroslav Pelikan, in *Luther's Works* (St. Louis: Concordia Publishing House, 1957), 22:376, 373.

Pastoral Perspective

What an extraordinary announcement: "God so loved the world that he gave his only Son" (v. 16). We are accustomed to stories of the gods who are, at best, indifferent and, at worst, hostile to the world. We assume that if God loves anyone, it will be those who love God; but the text does not read, "God so loved the church" or "God so loved the faithful" or "God so loved the pure." The focus is out beyond the horizon of the church. This story is about God's deep and abiding love for the world. This is the missional energy, the *missio Dei*, that is meant to be the heart and soul of the church's witness. No wonder so many use the shorthand "Jn 3:16" as a signpost pointing to the new world of the gospel.

This outpoured love of God for the world is revealed in the gift of God's only Son. As revealed in the opening chapters of John's Gospel, this one who comes to dwell with us is the Word become flesh (1:14). He is the incarnation in human form of the divine Word that speaks and, in speaking, creates. God gives of God's very essence to the world in an act unheard of among the gods, an act of self-sacrifice on behalf of the world. We expect the creation to give back in love to its Creator. Instead, it is the Creator who, in Jesus, reaches out to a lost and broken creation.

Exegetical Perspective

This unit begins as a dialogue between Jesus and Nicodemus and ends as a monologue centered on Jesus alone. Its final section opens with what is perhaps the most famous verse in the New Testament. John succinctly summarizes the divine intention embodied by Jesus and his mission: "For God so loved the world that he gave his only Son, so that everyone who believes in him may not perish but may have eternal life" (v. 16). The declaration of God's fundamental love for the world hearkens back to the creation motif that pulses throughout the Fourth Gospel. John's good news is that the world that came into being through the *logos* (1:10) remains the object of divine love. Just as John understands the creative activity of the Word to be ongoing, he perceives God's love for the world in Jesus to be continuing and profound.

The second half of John 3:16 details the specific connection between the incarnation of the Word (*logos*) and God's love for the creation. According to John, recognizing and believing in the Word made flesh opens the door to eternal life. Belief functions as the vehicle for the new birth from above of which John 3:3–8 speaks. Its absence signals the opposite, which is the threat of perishing.

It is not that the world and ordinary human existence are evil. John will not make such a claim

Homiletical Perspective

We have so many choices that we have trouble taking our decisions as seriously as the author of the Fourth Gospel does in this passage. Consider how many inconsequential questions we deal with each day: Will that be cash or credit? Do you want that for here or to go? Should we take the freeway or drive through town? Do I wear tennis shoes or dress shoes? Should I go to the gym or Marble Slab? Can I think of something new to preach about John 3:16?

We can change our minds; so we tend to forget that our choices have consequences. Even the important decisions may not turn out to be as permanent as we first think. If we do not like the college we choose, we may transfer. If we do not like our job, we can look for another. If we do not like where we live, we can try to move. The people to whom we preach are tempted to miss the permanency to their decisions. During one of his speeches, then–vice president Dan Quayle said, "I believe we are on an irreversible trend toward more freedom, but that could change."[1]

Admitting that some directions are irreversible is difficult. That is why we find it hard to bring ourselves to say, "This one thing I do." Like Robert Frost in his most famous poem, we keep standing at

1. *The Wall Street Journal*, May 26, 1989.

Theological Perspective

that their deeds are good. Rather, the idea in verses 20–21 is that the light of Jesus exposes what everyone is: "Jesus is a penetrating light that provokes judgment by making it apparent what a [person] is."[2] Those who have quietly gone about doing deeds of mercy and justice, like the bewildered sheep in Jesus' parable in Matthew 25:34–40, are revealed as those whose "deeds have been done in God" (v. 21).

On the other hand, the light of Christ also shows the world's evildoers for who they really are, and they stand condemned. In the penetrating light of Jesus, there is nowhere to hide. All the shabby and shameful things we might wish to keep secret are out in the open. Yet condemnation is not the purpose of Christ's coming, nor is it God's last word on humanity. The Son of God comes not to condemn the world but to save it (v. 17). The world's sin is not only exposed for what it is; it is also dealt with. Jesus is "the Lamb of God who takes away the sin of the world" (1:29).

Christians are those who have "believed in the name of the only Son of God" and face no condemnation (v. 18). They have "come to the light" (v. 21), and have already received the gift of eternal life from God (v. 16), a transformed mode of life that starts now. The image of coming to the light might suggest that Christians turn their backs on the darkness of the world and spend all their time reveling in the light of Jesus. In 1 John, the sending of the Son is oriented toward the Christian community: God's aim is that "we might live through him" (1 John 4:9).

While God's love is abundantly experienced in the church, it is not restricted to the church. The Gospel of John makes clear that the aim of God's sending the Son is universal in scope. God's love encompasses everyone, even those who "love darkness rather than light" (v. 19). God's ultimate aim is for all humanity to be drawn to Jesus (12:32). This means that Christians are not to keep the "inexpressibly beautiful message" of God's love to themselves. Rather, they are sent into the world to share it with others. As Letty Russell puts it, the church is "a P.S. on God's love affair with the world."[3]

Christians come to the light of Jesus, and when they go out into the world, Christ is the light by which they see. You can think of Christians as spelunkers and Jesus Christ as the headlamp that they put on to guide them. Followers of Jesus do not sit

Pastoral Perspective

The pastoral implications of God's out-reaching love are massive. It means that God is to be found where the Son of God is to be found, living incognito in the world. Notice that in the space of two chapters in John's Gospel Jesus is found first meeting in the dark of night with the Jewish leader Nicodemus, a classic insider, and then in the noonday sun with a Samaritan woman, a forgotten outsider. While he can sometimes be found in the synagogue and the temple, Jesus is usually seen in the streets, where he is feeding, healing, teaching, forgiving. He has been given to the world to embody—to incarnate—the love of God for the world. The church that claims his name is called to be a daring witness with this true testimony: that God loves *the world*.

Yet how often the world hears a different message! How often the gospel sounds not like love but like condemnation! How often the church comes across as "holier than thou"! It can seem as though God is eager to divide, to judge and separate, to save some and abandon the rest. Jesus reacts to such misunderstandings: "Indeed, God did not send the Son into the world to condemn the world, but in order that the world might be saved through him" (v. 17). The *missio Dei* is life-giving and life-saving. This is not a rejection mission. It is a rescue mission. This is the inclusive love of God. It is life from above for all who are perishing.

Yet not all who are perishing want this life or trust the One who offers it. Therefore, there is a judgment, a dividing line between those who trust the One who comes bearing the love of God and those who cannot place their trust in him. The inclusive love of God will not force itself upon those who opt out. There is a judgment, says Jesus. There is condemnation (vv. 18–19), but it is not the judgment of God. God does not damn. The judgment occurs whenever we choose to hide from the light of God's sacrificial love. Choosing to stay in the darkness is an act of self-condemnation. It means condemning oneself to more of the same old, same old.

Some of us who love the darkness live imagining that eternal life is to be found in the accumulation of possessions or of prestige or of power. For some of us the darkness is a land of addiction to short-term fixes that can never fully mask deep, long-term pain. Even the church finds itself wandering in this dark place when it tries to domesticate Jesus, telling him what he can and cannot say and telling him whom he can and cannot save. More often than not, the evil deeds that are done in the dark have become so habitual, so commonplace, so much a part of our

---

2. Raymond E. Brown, *The Gospel according to John, I–XII* (Garden City, NY: Doubleday & Co.), 148–49.
3. Letty Russell, *Human Liberation in a Feminist Perspective* (Philadelphia: Westminster Press, 1974), 158.

Exegetical Perspective

about that which God has created. Rather, it is that ordinary human existence and perception are limited and finite, unable in and of themselves to generate the knowledge and experience of the fullness of God. Thus the anthropological implications wrought by the Gospel's way of conceiving reality in terms of the binary divisions of light and dark, heavenly things and earthly things, eternal life and finitude, come more fully into view in this passage. For John, the realm below is in need of salvation and aid that only God can provide.

John outlines the purpose and impact of the incarnation. Jesus' presence in the world and what he reveals as the distinction between that which derives from the realm above and that which is rooted in the realm below are not intended to function as the equivalent of a divine game of "Gotcha!" Instead, Jesus' coming into world signals God's loving action and initiative: "Indeed, God did not send the Son into the world to condemn the world, but in order that the world might be saved through him" (v. 17). Here the NRSV translates the verb *krinō* ("to judge") as "condemn" in order to sharpen the contrast it forms to "might be saved." John's emphasis in this verse is on the salvation that God extends to the world through Jesus.

The following verse, however, introduces the negative implications of John's perspective: "Those who believe in him are not condemned; but those who do not believe are condemned already, because they have not believed in the name of the only Son of God" (v. 18). Belief, the path to transformation, comes to function as a new dividing line. John's language underscores the tension between condemnation and salvation, and between judging and not judging, which this Gospel struggles with and does not fully resolve (see 8:15–16). On the one hand, John paints reality in terms of pairs of binary opposites, with each element being representative of one realm to the exclusion of the other. On the other hand, he portrays Jesus as the one who comes from the realm above to that which lies below, precisely to save the world that is created and loved by God. With the incarnate Word bridging the two realms, believing functions as a mechanism for both exposing and overcoming their separation.

The closing verses in this scene redirect the reader to consider judgment in a different light. Here judgment is less about divine authority to render a verdict and more concerned with the human response that Jesus elicits and what that response reveals. Jesus' words focus on human initiative and

Homiletical Perspective

junctures where two roads diverge and want to go down both at once. We find it painful to decide to do *this* when we know it means we will never be able to do *that*. Convincing ourselves that all of the paths end up converging is comforting. We are tempted to believe that it does not matter what anyone decides, that everything will turn out the same in the end, but that is not true to our own life experience or our observations of others.

The decision Jesus puts before us is a choice with consequences for this life and the life to come. Death or eternal life? Believing or being condemned? Good or evil? Light or dark? The choice to live with or without God is built into the very essence of our existence, but the power of that decision is so overwhelming that we want to think that we must be mistaken.

When theologians address questions of eternity, they are understandably uncomfortable with the idea that people make decisions that are of eternal significance. Why do you think people are attracted to predestination—the idea that eternal destiny is unrelated to human choice? I believe it is from thinking that big decisions should not be left to human beings; let God make all the decisions. In much the same way, universalism, the belief that God automatically accepts everyone into eternity, is attractive because it lessens the significance of our decisions.

This passage in John sounds peculiar to modern ears, because the difference between life and death is a decision. Preaching this familiar text is difficult, because taking the choices we make this seriously is difficult. For Christians, Jesus is the defining revelation of God's love and mercy, and the one about whom we must make a decision. All of our choices ultimately turn to Jesus.

John 3:16 is the declaration that God *has decided* to love the whole world. God does not love just those who gather on Sunday, not just the religiously inclined, not just those who have heard the name of Jesus, but the whole world; so God comes in Christ to show the way of life in the midst of death.

God's love does not coerce us into relationship, but does require us to choose whether we will love God in return. A stepping stone can also be a stumbling block. A healing presence can be a disturbing presence. Every light casts a shadow. God comes to our death-bound situations, where we can see the life God offers. We have to decide how we will respond to God's love.

Sometimes we choose to live without God's love. We cherish grudges, even as we wish we could let

John 3:16–21

Theological Perspective

in a dark corner of the cave with their headlamps in their laps, mesmerized by its glow. Their focus is not on their personal experiences of Jesus but on the vision of the world that he makes possible. Jesus directs their attention toward the world God loves. Walking in Christ's light, Christians find in themselves a deepening commitment to the whole world God has made. They begin to see all people in the light of God's love.

In our own day, we have come to recognize that the world that God so loves is larger than the world of human creatures. The cosmos is not simply an elaborate stage setting for the drama of human redemption. Our human creaturehood does not set the terms for God's relation to the rest of creation. The light of Christ exposes our indifference and greed toward our fellow creatures who, like us, are God's beloved. As long as we try to hide from Christ's light and pretend that "earth care" is not part of doing what is true in God's sight (v. 21), we stand condemned. Even so, God did not send the Son into the world to condemn us (v. 17). God calls us instead to put away works of darkness and "live as children of light" (Eph. 5:8). We do so, trusting that God's love is the first and last word on all of creation, including us.

AMY PLANTINGA PAUW

Pastoral Perspective

way of life, that we barely recognize that this way of life is out of sync with Jesus. Yet believing in Jesus, trusting him, means being in sync with him, living in harmony with God's extraordinary love for the world.

This is a difficult passage. It presents real pastoral challenges. Some come to the text having received messages that they are "no good," "going to hell," "God-damned." They need to be shown the text's emphasis on God's expansive, inclusive love, open to all who trust it to be true. Others come to the text having heard that there is no judgment, no condemnation, no living hell. They need to see that the love of God revealed in Jesus demands a decision to believe, or not to believe; to live in response to the sacrificial love of God for all people, or not. To say no to the love of God in Jesus is to choose a life in the familiar darkness of the world we have been taught to call reality. It is to be condemned to the living hell of the "real world."

It is worth noting that the Easter conclusion of John's Gospel returns to these themes of God's love for the world and of our response in belief. The risen Jesus breathes new life on his disciples while commissioning them as ministers of God's reconciling love: "If you forgive the sins of any, they are forgiven" (20:23). Then Jesus responds to the doubt and the faith of Thomas with a new beatitude: "Blessed are those who have not seen and yet have come to believe" (20:29). Trusting belief in Jesus' power to make new is, it turns out, a mysterious blessing to be received. So too is the forgiving love that is Jesus' fingerprint in the world.

EDWIN SEARCY

activity. What men and women do reveals what they believe and where they stand:

> And this is the judgment, that the light has come into the world, and people loved darkness rather than light because their deeds were evil. For all who do evil hate the light and do not come to the light, so that their deeds may not be exposed. But those who do what is true come to the light, so that it may be clearly seen that their deeds have been done in God. (vv. 19–21)

It is what people do that proves to be the true measure of their relationship to the light, which John clearly identifies with Jesus, the Word incarnate. The importance of this teaching cannot be overemphasized, for what John introduces here finds expression again in the Gospel's final and summary lesson.

In chapter 21, John concludes his Gospel by telling the story of the final encounter between Peter and the risen Jesus. He writes, "When they had finished breakfast, Jesus said to Simon Peter, 'Simon son of John, do you love me more than these?' He said to him, 'Yes, Lord; you know that I love you.' Jesus said to him, 'Feed my lambs'" (21:15). Three times Jesus asks Peter if he loves him, and three times he responds to Peter's answer with instruction to care for his people. To love Jesus is to care for others, to act on their behalf and for their sake. John's closing scene reminds his readers that disciples of Jesus are to imitate the one whose name they confess. It is only after this exchange that Jesus says to Peter (and by extension, to John's readers), "Follow me" (21:19). In the end, belief-as-action trumps mere assent to believing in Jesus. God's love for the world finds expression in Jesus. The love human persons are to return is to be conveyed through their imitation of that same Jesus.

MARY F. FOSKETT

our anger go. We value our independence, even as we wish we cared more for others. We stay in a dark but comfortable corner, even as we wish we lived in the light. Our story from beginning to end is selfishness, consequences, repentance, and life. God has given us the wonderful, painful gift of choice. When we do not have the courage to choose what is best, but act as if our choices do not matter, we make no progress even on the smoothest path. When we choose courageously, we go forward even on the roughest road.

From the first choice we make in the morning until we choose to go to sleep at night, we are making the decisions that form our lives. We choose in the words we speak or do not speak, the people we love or do not even see, the thoughts we entertain or reject, the deeds we do or leave undone. God has chosen to help us choose eternal life.

God has decided to allow preachers to encourage others to turn to life in an amazing variety of ways. Feel. Dream. Breathe deeply. Work joyfully. Spend an afternoon with a dear friend. Wear tennis shoes. Go for ice cream. Read G. K. Chesterton. Read the Gospels. Listen to Adele. Sing along with Frank Sinatra. Ask God to help you feel grace again. Sing loud in worship. Try a new ministry, even though you do not think you have the time. Pray with gratitude. Pray for peace. Take risks. Give better gifts. Give away more money. Call your mother. Notice small things. Do kind things. Hug someone. Laugh. Listen to the wind of the Spirit.

We choose to build up or tear down, love or ignore, heal or hurt, bless or curse. On Sunday, preachers have the amazing privilege of sharing the invitation to life.

BRETT YOUNGER

John 3:22–30

²²After this Jesus and his disciples went into the Judean countryside, and he spent some time there with them and baptized. ²³John also was baptizing at Aenon near Salim because water was abundant there; and people kept coming and were being baptized ²⁴—John, of course, had not yet been thrown into prison.

²⁵Now a discussion about purification arose between John's disciples and a Jew.* ²⁶They came to John and said to him, "Rabbi, the one who was with you across the Jordan, to whom you testified, here he is baptizing, and all are going to him." ²⁷John answered, "No one can receive anything except what has been given from heaven. ²⁸You yourselves are my witnesses that I said, 'I am not the Messiah, but I have been sent ahead of him.' ²⁹He who has the bride is the bridegroom. The friend of the bridegroom, who stands and hears him, rejoices greatly at the bridegroom's voice. For this reason my joy has been fulfilled. ³⁰He must increase, but I must decrease."

Theological Perspective

In the Gospel of John, John the Baptist is the original and paradigmatic witness to Jesus Christ. This is clear from his introduction in the prologue, where we are told that John was sent by God "as a witness to testify to the light, so that all might believe through him" (1:7). He is the first to point to Jesus as the Lamb of God who takes away the sin of the world (1:29) and to declare him to be the Son of God, on whom the Spirit descended, who baptizes by the Spirit (1:32–33). He also directs two of his own disciples to follow Jesus, and one of these, Andrew, brings his brother Simon Peter to follow Jesus (1:35–42). Even though John came before Jesus, he places Jesus before himself in rank and honor (1:30) and declares that his sole purpose in baptizing is to bear witness to Jesus, "that he might be revealed to Israel" (1:31). Consequently, John claims nothing for himself, and explicitly denies that he is the prophet, Elijah, or the Messiah (1:19–25), so that he might direct all of Israel to Jesus Christ.

The distinctive character of John's account is illuminated by comparison with Matthew's version, where the relationship between John and Jesus is much more complex and fraught with tension. In Matthew, Jesus is baptized by John, which locates

* See "'The Jews' in the Fourth Gospel" on pp. xi–xiv.

Pastoral Perspective

With John the Baptist as a guide, the faithful can look beyond self-interest and embrace a mission greater than themselves. In this higher purpose, God is revealed.

A pastoral understanding of this text directs us to Aenon (v. 23), a fertile place for discussion and new insights. In this place, we encounter disciples of John the Baptist who are not convinced that Jesus' way is a better way than the one they have been following. The tension created by two parallel ministries is unique to the Fourth Gospel. In the other Gospels, the ministries of John and Jesus do not overlap, as Jesus' ministry begins *after* John's imprisonment. The discussion recorded in this Gospel may reflect theological concerns or tensions within the Johannine community itself, or between it and rival groups. Most scholars believe that Jesus' followers in the Johannine community coexisted with rival followers loyal to John the Baptist.

In this context, the discussion about purification between John's disciples and a Jew may describe the kind of conflict often present whenever one group's views differ from those of another. The person identified as a "Jew" could even represent another group among those who came to believe in Jesus (2:23; 4:1), as well as diverse groups within Judaism in Jesus' or John's day. The substance of the discussion

Exegetical Perspective

Continuity in the Ministries of John the Baptist and Jesus (vv. 22–24). After the wedding at Cana of Galilee, the overturning of the tables in the temple in Jerusalem, and an encounter with Nicodemus, John turns to focus on Jesus' active ministry with his disciples among the populace and in relationship to the figure of John the Baptist. Because the history between Jesus and John is fresh in memory (1:19–36), these transitional verses can focus on the activity and symbolism of baptism. The evangelist first signals the continuity between the ministries of Jesus and John the Baptist by locating them both in Judea, not in Jerusalem but in the countryside. John's Gospel is distinct in its portrayal of the ministry of Jesus as a constant movement back and forth between Galilee and Judea (cf. the focus on Jesus' ministry in Galilee in the three Synoptic Gospels). Given John's careful use of geographical markers, "the land of Judea" (RSV) is best taken here as "the Judean countryside outside Jerusalem" (expanding slightly the NRSV). John 2:23 clearly states that Jesus' prior location was Jerusalem and not Galilee or any other territory outside of Judea proper.

John 3:22 is the only testimony to Jesus having a baptizing ministry. Other than the reference to the Judean countryside, the precise location of this ministry is not given. The evangelist does tell us that

Homiletical Perspective

"He [Jesus] must become greater, I must become less" (v. 30, my trans.). Many have echoed this assertion by John the Baptist down through the centuries. Those words are the final interaction between John the Baptist and his disciples as uniquely recorded in this Gospel. There is a stark contrast between the envy of these disciples toward Jesus and John's deference to Jesus leading up to his statement.

Jesus and his disciples have been baptizing in the Judean countryside while John and his disciples were baptizing further north. The two groups were performing this action in close proximity to each other. A parenthetical note is that this was before John was put into prison (v. 24). This Gospel does not recount John the Baptist's imprisonment and subsequent martyrdom. The significance of this section is that these are the last of the Baptist's words in the Gospel of John, and once again he points in the direction of Jesus.

The interaction between John and his disciples is precipitated by an argument between his disciples and a certain Jew about ceremonial washing. As a result John's disciples come to their rabbi and express envy of Jesus and his ministry. John had previously pointed out Jesus: "Here is the Lamb of God who takes away the sin of the world!" (1:29). John's disciples refer to Jesus only as "the one who was with

John 3:22–30

Theological Perspective

him as a disciple of John. Jesus does not begin his public ministry until John is arrested, and the message he proclaims is the same as John's: "Repent, for the kingdom of heaven has come near" (Matt. 3:2; 4:17). Moreover, John begins to have serious doubts about the preaching and work of Jesus, and the last we hear of him is his apparent disappointment with what he has heard about Jesus, so that he sends his disciples to ask Jesus, "Are you the one who is to come, or are we to wait for another?" (Matt. 11:3).

In the Gospel of John, all of these tensions are absent. John does not baptize Jesus, nor does he preach the same message that Jesus later preaches, about the kingdom of heaven coming near; rather, he speaks directly about the coming of Jesus himself. Jesus does not begin his public ministry after John is arrested, but while John is still baptizing in the Jordan. All of this would seem to diminish any rivalry or tension between John and Jesus, as John clearly places himself beneath Jesus.

However, Jesus and his disciples seem to act in such a way as to provoke a rivalry between John and Jesus. They baptize with water and not explicitly, as foretold by John, with the Holy Spirit. They also apparently baptize in close proximity to where John and his disciples are baptizing. Even though we are told that "people kept coming and were being baptized" by John (v. 23), it is evident that more people are going to Jesus and his disciples to be baptized by them. This clearly bothers John's disciples, and they come to John to make clear to him that they view Jesus as a serious threat to their own work and mission. "Rabbi, the one who was with you across the Jordan, to whom you testified, here he is baptizing, and all are going to him" (v. 26).

The overlapping ministries of John and Jesus remind us of the relationship between Saul and David. Both had been anointed as kings by Samuel, and yet the one who came after Saul was clearly emerging as being above Saul in the eyes of the Israelites. When the women of Israel celebrate David's great victories over the Philistines by singing, "Saul has killed his thousands, and David his ten thousands," Saul becomes very angry, and sees the success of David as a direct threat to his own rule. "So Saul eyed David from that day on" (1 Sam. 18:6–9). Indeed, Saul spends the rest of his life trying to subdue and even kill David, out of the intense envy David's success fuels in him. It seems that the disciples of John want him to see Jesus in the same way, as a direct threat to his and their own ministry; hence they seek to fuel John's envy of Jesus' success,

Pastoral Perspective

is unclear, but the context, as Lamar Williamson notes, "suggests a debate about whose ritual washing is most effective for spiritual cleansing: that of official Judaism, that of John the Baptist, or that of Jesus."[1] In Aenon, conversation flows freely in different directions.

Entering pastorally into the text, we might hope for an empathetic ear from each of the parties involved, but our experience reminds us that this kind of listening is not a given. Even in a fertile place, debate can be unproductive. What is the tone of this discussion? Does the conversation flow respectfully toward a mutual understanding? Even lacking complete agreement, are the different groups able to build some bridges between them? More problematically, is further conversation diverted by an emotional cutoff? We who live in a time when civil public discourse, both political and theological, is often lacking can easily imagine a polarizing end to this discussion. Entrenched positions bring dialogue to a halt. In fertile Aenon, the discussion could become dry and lifeless.

From a pastoral perspective, we hope for a better result in their time and in ours. We have our own examples of failed attempts at dialogue between various groups. The differences present within and among our own faith communities come to mind as we overhear the discussion about purification. Purity, holiness, righteousness: we might hope that these are words that bring opposing parties closer to "what has been given from heaven." From experience we know that many times these are in fact *fighting words* within the church. With a longing for Christian unity, a pastoral response to the discussion in this text leads us to ask: who among us is calling the divided Church to a ministry that looks for what has been given from heaven, a mission from God that joyfully brings us together?

As we search for these spiritual guides, we can consider John the Baptist, whose humility offers a way forward in our search for unity and cooperation among different faith communities. As a spiritual guide, John *the humble* says of himself in relation to Jesus, "I must decrease." Humbly, he embodies a style of leadership that lifts up the other, specifically lifts up Jesus, and encourages a shared identification with a greater good. With a generosity of spirit, he points to the leadership role of another. In this way, a leader becomes a friend, "the friend of the bridegroom,

1. Lamar Williamson Jr., *Preaching the Gospel of John* (Louisville, KY: Westminster John Knox Press, 2004), 42.

John and his disciples were baptizing at Aenon near Salim, but the precise location of Aenon (the name means "spring") remains unknown. John indicates that it was adequate for water. It was surely on the western side of the Jordan River, in the Judean countryside and not "across the Jordan" (as in 1:28 and 3:26). The following discussion between John and his disciples (vv. 25–30) does not encourage us to think that Jesus and John were baptizing disciples in the same precise area, but only within the bounds of the Judean countryside.

Despite the apprehensions Jesus' ministry seems to raise in John's disciples, John the Baptist affirms the essential continuity between his ministry and that of Jesus. This continuity is implied by the direct statement in verses 22–23, "[Jesus] spent some time there with them and baptized. John also was baptizing." The Gospel writer does not deem it necessary until later to give fuller details: "although it was not Jesus himself but his disciples who baptized" (4:2). The baptizing ministry of Jesus symbolizes the continuation of John's call to the work of God's renewal of the people through this chosen agent: Jesus, the Lamb of God (1:29). Jesus, mighty in acts of creation (1:2; 2:7–9), sustaining the created order (1:4; 2:19), and redeeming humanity (1:12; 3:14–16), continues to reorient people and call followers through his own baptizing ministry.

Heaven's Work, Not Competition (vv. 25–27). Given the location of the ministries of John and Jesus in the Judean countryside, it is best to read "Jew" here (3:25) as "a Judean." An unspecified Judean has seen Jesus' baptizing ministry in a nearby locale and now reports and discusses it with John the Baptist's disciples. The issue involves "purification," but the absence of details leaves us with little to go on besides inferences from the human interactions that follow. The natural human inclination to choose sides, to seek channels of authority and priority, and to protect or claim "derived power" seems evident in the question of John's disciples to their leader. They speak of Jesus obliquely as "the one who was with you" and "to whom you testified." Their exaggerated statement—"and *all* are going to him!" v. 26b—suggests that they are threatened. This "comment" has an implied question: "They go directly to him and not through you (us). What should be done (to keep our place)?" John's reply calls his disciples to examine their own hearts and (strikingly!) to testify "against" themselves ("you yourselves are my

you across the Jordan" and report, with exaggeration, that "*all* are going to him" (v. 26).

Envy arises, as it often does when comparison takes place. Envy may surface within a congregation when an individual desires the ministry of others or when a person is not invited to a leadership position and instead another person is chosen. Envy threatens ministry. It can show up in the preacher's life when focusing on attendance numbers and baptismal statistics. The bane of ministry conferences is hearing about all the "successful" growing ministries measured by head count. A competitive spirit arises where one ministry tries to outdo another or there are accusations of "sheep stealing."

Preachers can use this passage to help congregational members reflect on envy within the Christian community and to explore their God-given roles within church and society. John the Baptist corrects and counters his disciples, highlighting his role in relationship with Christ. First, he declares that the source of all things is from above. Therefore, his vocation is from God. Second, John clarifies the vocation he does not possess: he is not the Christ (cf. 1:20–27). He does not possess the savior complex or overreach his calling. John aims to fulfill his calling. Third, he functions as a forerunner to the Messiah, testifying to the person and the message. As a witness, he prepares people for the coming of the Messiah by presenting a message of repentance. Fred Craddock rightly notes that, while the Gospel designates John's role as the one who baptizes, John's most important role is as a witness.[1] In fact, baptizing is subsumed under his broader role as witness. Pointing people to Jesus is at the heart of witness and evangelism.

John uses the image of the friend of the bridegroom who assists the bridegroom to describe his relationship with Jesus. He does not usurp the groom's role. He rejoices with him. We easily see the modern analogy to the best man at the wedding, assisting the groom and members of the wedding party. Rather than take center stage, he draws attention to the main characters of the wedding. It goes too far to portray the church as the bride of Christ in this analogy. John's focus here is clearly on John's role in relationship to Jesus.

John dramatically and climactically concludes, "He must become greater, I must become less" (v. 30, my trans.). The classic King James Version states, "He must increase, I must decrease." John humbly

---

1. Fred B. Craddock, *John*, Knox Preaching Guides (Atlanta: John Knox Press, 1982), 32.

John 3:22–30

Theological Perspective

to embitter him toward Jesus so that he might defend his own honor.

In light of the understandable envy both Saul and John's disciples experienced, John's reply to his disciples is astonishing. He does not show a hint of envy or defensiveness, but rather begins by pointing out that all who are going to Jesus have been given to him by God (v. 27). Moreover, those whom John is baptizing do not belong to him, but rather to Jesus. John is the friend of the bridegroom, not the bridegroom himself. Israel is the bride, and is to be wed to Christ; so when more Israelites start going to Jesus than to him, this does not embitter John with envy but, rather, leads him to rejoice: "For this reason my joy has been fulfilled. He must increase, but I must decrease" (vv. 29–30). John is the first and paradigmatic witness to Jesus, because he is joyfully willing to become nothing so that Christ might become everything.

Those of us who are called to bear witness to Christ have much to learn from this response of John. We often act as though the goal of our ministry is to make ourselves great by means of the proclamation of Christ, so that we may continually increase, while those around us decrease. We view the success of other witnesses to Christ the way Saul eyed David—with envy, anger, and bitter suspicion. Would that we might learn from John to free ourselves from the poison of envy. Would that we might rejoice when others are drawn more to Christ than to our particular practice of religion. Would that we could rejoice in willingly making ourselves nothing, so that we and our envy might get out of the way of leading others to the love of God in Jesus Christ.

RANDALL C. ZACHMAN

Pastoral Perspective

who stands and hears him, [who] rejoices greatly at the bridegroom's voice" (v. 29).

In Aenon, John sees no tension between his ministry and that of Jesus. The potentially contentious discussion becomes instead an occasion of shared joy. Imagining himself as the friend of the bridegroom, John invites his followers to celebrate this spirit of unity. More than just agreeing to disagree, John affirms a shared ministry and in so doing reveals the ways of God. Joyfully, he calls his followers beyond feelings of self-importance. He is secure enough to embrace the good work of another. The happiness of another becomes a reason for John to rejoice.

In my study, I have a picture of a groom and his best man. Taken during the wedding reception, the picture shows the bridegroom with his arm resting comfortably around the shoulder of his best man. These two are brothers and my sons. Looking at the picture, I have to think for a moment about which son is the groom and which one is the best man. Their shared joy makes it difficult to discern their roles, but there is another issue too. This particular wedding picture sits on the shelf near another wedding photo of these same two sons striking a very similar pose; only in this photo their roles are reversed. The best man is the groom in the other wedding picture, and the groom is the best man. The expressions on their faces are remarkably the same.

I understand that there are limits to this analogy with regard to the text. John the Baptist does not assume the role of the Messiah. He is very clear about this! However, his humility in relationship to Jesus' ministry reminds me of my sons, each of whom comfortably assumed the role of the friend at the other's wedding. Sibling rivalry—or any other for that matter—does not reign supreme when a higher purpose comes into view. In a place of joy and abundance, it is possible to receive what has been given from heaven. With John as a spiritual guide, it is worth considering that which is greater than our own self-interest. What God has joined together, let no one break apart.

CRAIG S. TROUTMAN

Exegetical Perspective

witnesses").[1] John remains true to what we have heard him say emphatically in 1:29–34: John knows his is not the central place; John is first in the historical sequence, but the priority is Jesus first and then John. The renewal of the people of God is now being directed by God from heaven through Jesus. The evangelist will develop the theme of the *work of God,* present among human beings as gift, in the Farewell Discourse (chaps. 14–17; esp. 14:8–17).

A Picture of Cooperation (vv. 28–30). Gospel narratives in general and John's Gospel in particular do not attempt to persuade only through declarative statements. In these verses, John the Baptist reiterates his own position of subservience to Jesus through metaphor and a compact story regarding an impending wedding. This image is well known to all. Some have pointed to the obvious nature of John's words here: "He who has the bride is the bridegroom" (v. 29a). However, John's statement is no mere banality. It sets up the universal story, invites the use of the imagination, and makes possible the recognition of deeper meaning. Who are the other players in the wedding story? Ah, look, the friend of the bridegroom, the best man.

John the Baptist contents himself (and calls his disciples to content themselves) with his supporting role—like a best man to the bridegroom. "Preparing for the Lord" (cf. 1:23 with Mark 1:3) has universal applicability—friendship, loyalty, and the inner peace and integrity that bears no guile, but truly rejoices with abandon at the happy moment. Heaven's good work is to renew the people of God—once again to prepare the bride (cf. Ezek. 16:8–14; Hos. 2:16–23)—in and through and for the bridegroom, Jesus. John the Baptist has had a central and leading role in that preparation, but now the bridegroom has come, and John is ready to take a lesser role, that of the supporting and trustworthy best man: "He must increase, but I must decrease." A successful and joy-filled wedding is a picture of well-ordered cooperation. John knows his place.

ROLLIN A. RAMSARAN

Homiletical Perspective

spoke earlier of "the one who is coming after me; I am not worthy to untie the thong of his sandal" (1:27). That is a good direction for disciples of all ages. We are not to use Christ to gain status in the church; instead, Christ gains prominence in and through one's personal life, one's relational life, and one's life in community. In our day, ministers may rise to superstar status with prominence and recognition, but it is important for the preacher also to echo and model John's relationship to Jesus.

The congregation and preacher should take time to ponder the meaning of John's words in various spheres of life. How does this relationship take shape in the worlds of commerce or politics, as well as in the congregation itself? How can congregations model this way of life and witness in a world where so many seek to draw attention to themselves, even sometimes using their faith for personal gain?

Proclamation of this passage may naturally turn toward the biographical. Biographies often connect in a powerful way to people's lives. Appropriate biographical preaching, however, should follow the tenor and direction of the passage. In a congregation where I preached on this passage, people had time to share testimonies of what God was doing in their lives. Many recounted specific provision and help they had received from Christ during the week. Testimonies that point to Jesus can complement preaching on this passage when they are focused on Jesus' work in and through the person's life.

John the Baptist clearly articulates the role that he has embodied in relation to Jesus, beginning in John 1, by baptizing and witnessing. While John draws the attention of many followers, he does not do so in order to cause others to focus on him and his example but to point to Jesus. John's response to his disciples gives us clear and compelling insight into the nature of true discipleship. John the Baptist—or better, John the witness—is a central character in this passage. In keeping with the thrust of the passage, however, the sermon should focus on increasing the visibility and prominence of Jesus Christ rather than on John. The challenge to congregations is to exclaim with John, "He must become greater, I must become less," and then see how that translates into life.

DANIEL L. WONG

---

1. Note the *past tense* verb in John's "I said" (v. 28)—which should not be construed with the sense of the present continuing tense, "I say/am saying." So John's disciples hear and bear testimony to what was previously said, most certainly pointing to the initial testimony of John regarding Jesus in 1:29–34.

John 3:31–36

³¹The one who comes from above is above all; the one who is of the earth belongs to the earth and speaks about earthly things. The one who comes from heaven is above all. ³²He testifies to what he has seen and heard, yet no one accepts his testimony. ³³Whoever has accepted his testimony has certified this, that God is true. ³⁴He whom God has sent speaks the words of God, for he gives the Spirit without measure. ³⁵The Father loves the Son and has placed all things in his hands. ³⁶Whoever believes in the Son has eternal life; whoever disobeys the Son will not see life, but must endure God's wrath.

Theological Perspective

We need to keep clearly in mind the radical nature of the claims made about Jesus in John's Gospel, especially in light of its negative portrayal of the response of the Jews to Jesus. Those of us who accept the testimony of John to the person and work of Jesus must remember how hard it is to harmonize the claims this Gospel makes about Jesus with the history of God's relationship to Israel.

Jesus in the Gospel of John is the one who comes from God and returns to God (13:3). As the one who comes from God, he is the only one who has seen God (1:18), and so it is only by his testimony about what he has seen and heard of God that anyone can know God: "The one who comes from heaven is above all. He testifies to what he has seen and heard" (vv. 31–32). Thus, even though John the Baptist is the first and prototypical witness to Jesus, John himself tells us that Jesus is the one and only true witness to God the Father. "Whoever has accepted his testimony has certified this, that God is true" (v. 33). Jesus bears witness to the Father by what he says, for "he whom God has sent speaks the words of God, for he gives the Spirit without measure" (v. 34). Jesus will also bear witness to God through what he does (5:36). Consequently, whoever believes in the Son, and in his testimony to God, has eternal life. Whoever disobeys the Son must endure the wrath of God (v. 36).

Pastoral Perspective

John the evangelist testifies to the Father's love for the Son, and the faithful share in this love both now and forever. Placed in the narrative as the Baptist's final witness, John testifies with clarity and certainty. Having bound himself to Jesus, John certifies (v. 33) what he believes to be true about God. In his testimony, we hear an echo of a more famous passage, John 3:16—a proclamation of God's saving love for the world made known to us through the Son. At the conclusion of the third chapter of the Fourth Gospel, John the evangelist proclaims this witness to the world: "the Father loves the Son and has placed all things in his hands" (v. 35).

Many Christians are uncomfortable with the concept of witnessing if it involves convincing others that their beliefs are wrong. Living in a nation with people of many religious faiths (as well as people of no religious faith), many Christians within the mainline tradition are not comfortable challenging the beliefs of another. John's words in this passage, by contrast, make an all-or-nothing claim about belief in the Son. His unwavering affirmation resounds throughout this witness. Without hesitation, John the evangelist says, "Whoever believes in Jesus has eternal life; whoever disobeys the Son will not see life, but must endure God's wrath" (v. 36). Are there any questions?

Exegetical Perspective

Once Again: Who Is Speaking? It is not clear whether this passage represents a continuation of John's words to his disciples or a comment from the narrator of the Gospel. The same issue has been raised with regard to John 3:13–21: is the narrator commenting after Jesus' discussion with Nicodemus, or is the discussion a continuation of Jesus' own words? The speeches of both Jesus and John the Baptist show some indication of our author's own hand with regard to vocabulary and style. Not surprisingly, then, this section demonstrates much commonality with both John's prologue (1:1–18) and Jesus' response to Nicodemus in 3:13–21.

While we in the twenty-first century mostly *read* Scripture, the Gospel of John was routinely *performed orally* in large narrative sections—if not in its entirety—to audiences that would readily identify and correlate repetitions of vocabulary, key phrases, and developing perspectives. The narrator's voice is strong at the beginning (1:1–18) and the end of the story (20:30–31; 21:24–25) but fairly subdued within. It seems best, then, to see 3:31–36 as a continuation of the words of John the Baptist, yet fully formed and shaped within the Gospel writer's understanding of the larger story of God's renewal of the people of God through the heavenly agent, Jesus.

Homiletical Perspective

Who is Jesus Christ, and what does he mean for us and for the redemption of the world? Among the many opinions regarding the identity of Jesus Christ, he is considered a good teacher, healer, prophet, even Messiah, or by others just a mortal human. This passage highlights the exalted position of Jesus Christ, the Son of God whom the Father loves, and the one around whom we must order our lives in order to gain eternal life. Because it develops themes already set forth in 3:16–21, this section is an apt conclusion to the Nicodemus story (3:1–21) and the testimony of John the Baptist (3:22–30). John the Baptist makes Jesus the focus of attention with the climactic statement, "He must become greater, I must become less" (v. 30, my trans.). The author of the Gospel now develops this theme still further, announcing that Jesus is the one who comes from heaven, who is both from above and above all.

While these verses may continue John the Baptist's instruction to these disciples, they are also clearly written from the perspective of John the evangelist, for they draw a contrast between Jesus and John the Baptist. Jesus is from heaven; John is from the earth. Jesus *is* the divine witness; John has a *derived* witness.

One approach to the passage might focus on the details of the description of Jesus. This passage reveals

John 3:31–36

Theological Perspective

The claims that Jesus makes about himself in relation to the Father are astonishingly bold. By stating that he is working even as his Father is working, Jesus makes himself equal to God (5:17–18). By claiming to be God's Son, he states that he is one with the Father, and thus makes himself God (10:30–33). The words he uses to describe himself are equally bold and shocking, especially when he proclaims, "Very truly, I tell you, before Abraham was, I am" (8:58). Those who do not believe that Jesus is I AM will not inherit eternal life (8:24). Lest we make any mistake about the radicality of this claim, the Gospel tells us that when Isaiah saw the Lord enthroned in the temple, he actually saw the glory of Jesus and spoke about him (12:41; cf. Isa. 6:1). Jesus also tells us that when Moses wrote about the Lord, he was actually writing about Jesus (5:46).

It is not hard to see why Israelites would be deeply offended by the claims that Jesus makes about himself. The way Jesus identifies himself with YHWH would be seen as blasphemous. After all, Isaiah told them that the pride of the king of Babylon was so great that he dared to take the divine name to himself (Isa. 47:10). The arrogance of Antiochus IV Epiphanes was great enough to trigger the end of days (Dan. 7:8–11), but as he lay dying in great agony "he began to lose much of his arrogance" and realized, "It is right to be subject to God; mortals should not think that they are equal to God" (2 Macc. 9:11–12). Herod Agrippa met a similar fate when he did not object to but, rather, accepted divine honors from the people and was immediately stuck down and died (Acts 12:22–23).

The claim of Jesus to be I AM, the one who revealed himself to Moses in the burning bush and to Isaiah in the temple, raises yet more problems for Jewish belief. If Jesus is YHWH, then who is the God who sent him? Israelites would also be offended when Jesus tells them that they have never heard the voice of the Father or seen his form (5:37). Moses reminded the Israelites that they hear the voice of God every time they hear the law delivered at Sinai (Deut. 4:12, 33), and Moses himself beheld the form of God (Num. 12:8). The claim that no one has seen God contradicts the many times Jacob, Moses, and others are said to have seen God and lived (Gen. 32:30; Exod. 24:11).

John's perspective is that "no one has ever seen God. It is God the only Son, who is close to the Father's heart, who has made him known" (1:18; cf. 3:32). The most we can learn from Moses and the prophets is about the one who is I AM, which Jesus

Pastoral Perspective

Like most mainline churches, our Moravian congregation does not ask its members to testify to another's disobedience. When we give our testimony, we usually do not think that it entails persuading another that he or she is wrong or wrongheaded. *The Moravian Covenant for Christian Living* suggests a nonjudgmental approach to evangelism. In this statement, Moravians agree that "we will at all times be ready cheerfully to witness to our faith."[1] John the Baptist, in contrast, seems to take a much more aggressive, even judgmental approach. We should, however, notice the other dimensions of John's witness within the wider context of this passage, especially the sense of joy that pervades John's message (v. 29), as well as the way John has borne witness to Jesus through his practices.

Through the centuries the church's witness to Christ has been most faithful when its joy was also evident. This understanding of witness has as much to do with our way of living as with our doctrinal beliefs. In our very living, we proclaim the message of the gospel. One thinks of the quote popularly attributed to Francis of Assisi: "Preach the gospel at all times, and if necessary use words."

As a witness, more welcoming than rejecting, we emphasize the joy that is present when we believe and follow in the way of Jesus. "Whoever believes in Jesus has eternal life" (v. 36). With John the evangelist, Christians can affirm that eternal life is a present reality. In this life, we share in the benefits of Jesus' redeeming work. By affirming the grace of God through "the one who comes from above" (v. 31), we live with an awareness of the eternal that is not limited to "the sweet by-and-by." Eternal life includes that which brings happiness to the present moment.

In this life we offer a witness to that which we know, but "the incomprehensible grace of God"[2] means that the eternal is greater than what we know. With John, we can understand eternal life as a present reality and testify that the future has been placed in the Son's hands (v. 35). By emulating Jesus' life of service to others and believing his testimony, we attest that eternal life is both present and future.

As the Fourth Gospel makes clear, Jesus' testimony is not accepted by all (v. 32). Indeed, people known to us—neighbors, friends, family members—do not accept this testimony. John declares that, in Jesus, God has given "the Spirit without measure"

---

1. To read the entire document, see http://www.moravian.org/the-moravian -church/what-moravians-believe/moravian-covenant-for-christian-living.html
2. *The Ground of the Unity*, a doctrinal statement adopted by the worldwide Moravian Church in 1957 and revised in 1995.

Exegetical Perspective

Of Greater and Lesser Things (vv. 31–33). The opening verses of this section further elucidate 3:30: "He must increase, but I must decrease." John confirms the worldview he has named moments before: God's heavenly presence is involved with worldly events (3:27: "what has been given from heaven"). John's words in verse 31 recall the discussion between Jesus and Nicodemus about being born "from above" (3:3, 7) and Jesus' more recent comments on the heavenly descent and ascent (3:13). There is craft in the structure of verse 31: the equivalencies of "from above" and "from heaven" fully enclose the lesser position of "the earth." No strong duality is intended between spatial realms or moral categories. Rather, these two men, Jesus and John, both participate in the good and active plans of God, but Jesus' origin makes him greater and gives him a unique place as agent for God. Jesus' heavenly origin, as opposed to John's earthly origin, indicates a special relationship to the Spirit, to God as Father, and to destiny.

We are used to hearing about the witness of John the Baptist, but in verses 32–33 we have John the Baptist speaking of the witness and testimony of Jesus. These verses echo the prologue at 1:10–11: Jesus' testimony to the plan and purposes of God to redeem from darkness will be flatly rejected by humanity. This grim reality is moderated here by *the exceptions* that, in truth, carry the plan of God along: "no one accepts his testimony" is followed by "whoever has accepted his testimony" (!).

In Spirit and in Truth (vv. 34–35). John the Baptist's words here speak of him "whom God has sent," echoing the prologue in 1:9 ("The true light . . . was coming into the world") and 3:13–21 ("God did not send the Son into the world to condemn it"). The word "to send" (*apostellō*) is important to the Gospel writer. The initiator is God, who sends, and the object is Jesus or the Spirit. The recipients, those benefiting from the sending, are the renewed covenant people of God, of whom Jesus is the catalyst. Here then John indicates that God sends the Son, who proclaims God's purposes, along with a full measure of God's Spirit that "remains" upon him (1:32–33).[1] We recall earlier that this is done out of God's love and concern for the world (3:16), but here in verse 35 we also see that "the Father loves the Son." Jesus, the heavenly one, brings knowledge,

---

1. There is no report of John directly baptizing Jesus, but John does testify in 1:32 that the Spirit descended as a dove and "remained on him." In 3:34, the Spirit is given "without measure," that is, not in installments. Jesus has had from beginning to the present a full measure of the Spirit.

Homiletical Perspective

much about the person of Christ. Jesus is from above and above all. Therefore, Jesus is a reliable witness to both God and the gospel. He is the sent one, God's Son ("Son" appears three times in the passage), and he is loved by the Father. He is the one who testifies to what he has seen and heard, speaking the words of God and giving the Spirit without measure (v. 34). This portrait is foundational for belief in him.

This passage closely connects with John's expressly stated purpose for this Gospel: "Now Jesus did many other signs in the presence of his disciples, which are not written in this book. But these are written so that you may come to believe that Jesus is the Messiah, the Son of God, and that through believing you may have life in his name" (20:30–31). These verses in John 3 are thus central to the purpose of the whole Gospel. John declares that "whoever believes in the Son has eternal life" (v. 36). It is believing in the person of Christ, not beliefs about the person of Christ or agreeing to a series of doctrinal statements, that coincides with the experience of eternal life now.

A second approach to the proclamation of this passage thus might focus on the contrast of believing and disbelief in Jesus' divine identity (vv. 32–33, 36). If the focus is on the specific response of believing in Jesus, then this section can be paired with John 3:16–21 as further explanation of the necessity and consequences of believing.

"Eternal life" is the specific term used in verses 31–36 to describe the outcome of believing. The preacher can expand on the meaning of "life" in John's Gospel. The specific designation in this passage is "eternal life" (cf. 3:16; 5:24; 17:3). "Passed from death to life" (5:24), abundant life (10:10), and "life in his name" (20:31) are some of the descriptions of life used by John. The focus of this passage is life lived in relation to God and life freed of death's dominion as a present possession. This has more to do with quality of life than future destination or duration. The message that "eternal life" is a current experience is necessary for proclamation. Eternal life is too often seen as a future hope rather than a present occurrence. Living out life in the Son is a matter of day-by-day living, here and now, in God's love and power, not a disembodied life in God after death.

The most challenging part of preaching this passage is explaining and applying the consequences of unbelief : "whoever disobeys the Son will not see life, but must endure God's wrath" (v. 36). "Disobeys" is understood as disbelief in the Son of God. Those without belief stand under condemnation (3:18). These are stark alternatives: believe in Christ

John 3:31–36

Theological Perspective

attests is himself (5:39). The one seen by Abraham, Moses, and Isaiah is Jesus, not God. Only Jesus can reveal the God who sent him, as no one knows this God until Jesus reveals him. This is why Jesus tells the Jews who believed in him (8:31) that they cannot hear his testimony (8:47). Only Jesus can bear witness to the God who sent him, as no one knows this God until Jesus reveals him.

These descriptions of the relationship of Jesus to the God of Israel, unique to the Gospel of John, are very hard to harmonize with the rest of the Bible, including the rest of the New Testament. The New Testament assumes that the God who appears in Jesus is the very same God who appeared to Israel. Peter tells the Israelites in the temple, "The God of Abraham, the God of Isaac, and the God of Jacob, the God of our ancestors has glorified his servant Jesus" (Acts 3:13). The Gospel of John, on the other hand, tells us that the only one revealed to Abraham, Moses, and Isaiah was Jesus, and that God was never revealed to anyone until Jesus came. We need to place John in the context of the larger witness of the New Testament to the unity of the God revealed in Christ with the God revealed to Abraham and Moses, and the identity of this God as YHWH, the one who delivered Israel from Egypt and gave them the Law through Moses. Only in this way can we address the legitimate question raised by the Jews in John's Gospel: "We know that God has spoken to Moses, but as for this man, we do not know where he comes from" (9:29).

RANDALL C. ZACHMAN

Pastoral Perspective

(v. 34). Yet we know of others who speak of inspiration as that which comes from the human spirit. This spirit, in lowercase, also motivates people to do good works. What are we to say about this? How might we offer a witness to the one who speaks the words of God (v. 34)? Witnessing to God's love for the world—the first testimony (John 3:16) many of us learned—we can let the words of the song, "He's got the whole world in his hands," inform our response.

Our congregation hosts a community outreach program known as the Flower Shuttle. Begun seven years ago, this program takes flowers that would otherwise be discarded—arrangements once on display at weddings, funerals, and banquets, as well as in local florist shops—recycles them into small bouquets, and delivers the arrangements to people in the community who are living with sickness, terminal illness, disability, and poverty. In nursing homes, hospice facilities, hospitals, and homeless shelters, volunteers share their witness, one that has become well known in our community.

After a local newspaper article about the Flower Shuttle identified our church as the location of this program's work, one of the volunteers who is not a member of our church complained about the publicity given our congregation. "The Flower Shuttle is not about religion; it's about flowers," she said. Some of our members took her comment to be a rejection of what our church believes; but others, more congenial, allowed that uniformity of belief among the volunteers is not something the Flower Shuttle requires. "And anyway, this program isn't about religion for me either," one volunteer explained. "It's about bringing some joy into places that can be quite depressing; it's about touching another person's life with a beautiful reminder of the grace of God." This volunteer, in line with Christian witnesses from John's time to the present, gives testimony not to a religion or a church, but to the grace of God, whose love for the whole world is available now and forever. "The Father loves the Son and has placed all things in his hands" (v. 35)—and as one witness to the gospel might add, "The Father's love also includes placing flowers into the hands of others."

CRAIG S. TROUTMAN

is fully imbued with power, and is wholly trusted to orchestrate the redemption of the world for God, who "has placed all things into his hands."

Echoing John 3:16–18 (v. 36). While emphasizing the superiority of Jesus, the evangelist establishes parity between the message and activity of Jesus and John the Baptist. What was started through John now continues through Jesus, and John's words testify accordingly. John's words both in 3:16–18 and in this concluding verse provide a summation of God's activity through Jesus to this point in the story, as did Jesus' words in John 3:13–21. Here, as there, the Gospel writer emphasizes the "crisis moment" that faces each person in his or her encounter with God's actions in Jesus. Now John indicates that belief in Jesus (the Son) brings life with God that extends into eternity (v. 36a; cf. 3:16). John's words, which across the canonical Gospel traditions have a moral edge, express lack of belief in terms of "not obeying."

With John 3:18 still ringing in our ears, we recognize that those who do not obey the Son judge themselves and exclude themselves from what God so strongly desires to give to humanity—life. John 3:36 is the only reference in the Gospels to "God's wrath" (although John the Baptist speaks of "the wrath to come" [Matt. 3:7; Luke 3:7]). In its context and on analogy with John 3:18, the "wrath of God" appears to be the already-occurring exclusion from God's gifts and presence caused by unbelief/disobedience—an event surely no less tragic in God's eyes than our own.

The final verse anticipates the following engagement between Jesus and the Samaritan woman. Jesus' suspicion of a disobedient ruling structure within Judea, now heightened by the presence of Pharisees, will be the catalyst for his movement to Samaria. It is here that belief and life will be offered to and accepted by anyone who worships God in spirit and in truth. The agent of God's renewal is the Son (4:25–26), the one who comes from heaven and brings eternal life (3:31; 4:14).

ROLLIN A. RAMSARAN

and have eternal life; reject Christ and receive the consequences.

This serves as a warning even for those in congregations, many of whom have yet to truly believe. Recently I preached a sermon on this text, having in mind a person in the congregation who thus far has not expressed faith in Jesus. He did not grow up within a Christian family or have much exposure to Christian teaching before coming to North America. He has been in this congregation for several years. I talked with him after the worship service and urged him to place his faith in Christ. He replied that he needed to know more about Christianity.

Believing in Jesus is not a call to join the Christian religion, but a call to faith, a call to conform our lives to the one who comes from above. Christianity is not the issue, but rather the foundational conviction that Jesus is the one who shows us God, the one in whom we place our trust, the one who is the source of all our life—eternal life. In time I anticipate this man will place his faith in Christ. This text is a powerful motivation to share the gospel, extending the offer of eternal life to others. We want to testify, individually and in our life together, to what we also have seen, heard, and experienced in Jesus.

The good news in this passage is the blessing of believing in the person of Christ and the promise of eternal life here and now. How can we help our congregations discover and experience this life and bear witness to its source, so that we may be living expressions of this life for those inside and outside of the church?

DANIEL L. WONG

John 4:1–6

¹Now when Jesus learned that the Pharisees had heard, "Jesus is making and baptizing more disciples than John" ²—although it was not Jesus himself but his disciples who baptized— ³he left Judea and started back to Galilee. ⁴But he had to go through Samaria. ⁵So he came to a Samaritan city called Sychar, near the plot of ground that Jacob had given to his son Joseph. ⁶Jacob's well was there, and Jesus, tired out by his journey, was sitting by the well. It was about noon.

Theological Perspective

The Gospel of John agrees with Matthew, Mark, Luke, and Acts that a fundamental difference between John the Baptist and Jesus lies in the fact that John baptizes with water, whereas Jesus baptizes with the Holy Spirit (1:33). John is unique among the Gospels in having John the Baptist bear witness to Jesus as the Lamb of God and Son of God, but without baptizing him with water. John's distinctive orientation is also represented in the reasons given for why John baptizes with water. In Matthew (in agreement with Josephus), John baptizes with water for repentance; Mark and Luke specify that John proclaims a baptism of repentance for the forgiveness of sins. Since John's Gospel presents John the Baptist as the original witness to Christ, his baptism finds its ultimate meaning in making Jesus known. "I came baptizing with water for this reason, that he might be revealed to Israel" (1:31).

One might therefore expect that once John the Baptist reveals Jesus to Israel and directs his own disciples to follow him, he would have no further reason to continue baptizing in the Jordan. One might also expect Jesus and his followers to abstain from baptizing with water, since the priority of Jesus over John is established by the claim that he will baptize with the Holy Spirit, whereas John baptizes with water. All of this makes the scene in the Judean

Pastoral Perspective

In his commentary on the Gospel of John, Raymond Brown labels the first three verses of this chapter "A Transitional Passage."[1] Entering pastorally into this text, we can acknowledge the transitions that occur on any given day. I think, for example, about a day in the life of a parish pastor. One moment you are proofreading the Sunday morning bulletin; the next you are answering a call from a frantic parishioner whose husband has been rushed to the ER. One moment you are engaged in a mundane task, the next in a life-and-death drama. In the life of a parish pastor, this roller-coaster ride also moves in other directions. One moment you sit at your desk entranced by a particularly inspiring phrase from the assigned Gospel reading that will be your sermon text, and then the reverie is interrupted by a four-year-old from the preschool who walks into your study holding a picture she has drawn.

Is there such a thing as a "typical day" in the life a parish pastor or in the lives of any of us? The natural rhythms and seasons of life also include transitional passages along the linear path we are presumably following. In the passage before us, Jesus moves in a straight line, traveling from Judea back to Galilee.

1. Raymond E. Brown, *The Gospel according to John I–XII*, Anchor 29 (Garden City, NY: Doubleday & Co., 1966), 164.

Exegetical Perspective

On the Move Again (vv. 1–3). In this Gospel, Jesus has been on the move: from primordial time to the present ("In the beginning," 1:1–2); from heaven to earth ("And the Word became flesh and lived among us," 1:14); from Jerusalem in Judea to Galilee (1:43). This repeated pattern of Jerusalem to Galilee and back again demands our attention. Jesus is drawn to Jerusalem by the feast days and presumably to Galilee for rest, renewal, and safety. Jerusalem is the place of challenge and confrontation with the Judean ruling structure and its retainers (1:19, 24; 2:13–23; 3:10–11), while Galilee—especially Cana of Galilee—is the site of sign and faith, God's movement of renewal through Jesus (2:1–12; 4:3).

Here in John 4:1 we pick up once more a hint of suspicion and challenge. The narrator once again introduces a setting change and movement on Jesus' part. Care should be taken to notice Jesus' importance in relation to John the Baptist, even as the story moves on and John is left behind. John's narrative highlights Jesus' priority, power, and connection with God. John's image of Jesus[1] resonates with key themes of the previous verses: he is the one from above, empowered with the Spirit to speak,

---

1. This depiction of Jesus is consistent with designations of Jesus as "Lord" that occur as the story moves forward (among others, 9:38; 20:28).

Homiletical Perspective

Many of us love to travel. Travel brings us new adventures and opportunities to learn about various cultures and even learn more about ourselves. When we realize God at work in our travels, we may view travel in a new light. On the surface, John 4:1–6 appears to be a travel narrative of Jesus' journey northward from Judea to Galilee through Samaria. On closer examination, we see Jesus led to go through Samaria, a geographic area that could be and often was avoided by faithful Jews. This passage sets the stage for an encounter with a woman and people in need of the gospel.

These verses follow the extensive narrative of Jesus' interaction with Nicodemus about the Pharisee's need to be "born from above" (3:3) and the description of John's ministry of baptism. John 4:1–6 could be preached on its own, but it belongs most clearly in this larger context that is focused on baptism, as well with the following story of living water. It is most often preached, however, as part of the larger narrative of 4:1–42. A sermon on the whole story might bring out the background of the Samaritans and describe their doctrine and practices. It would trace Jesus' conversation with the woman that answers her concerns and questions leading up to Jesus' revelation to her that he is the Messiah. She in turn becomes the evangelist who invites the

John 4:1–6

Theological Perspective

countryside more puzzling. John and his disciples are baptizing with water in the Jordan; Jesus and his disciples are also baptizing with water in the Jordan; and the Pharisees are told, "Jesus is making and baptizing more disciples than John" (v. 1b). Why would John continue to baptize and make disciples after he revealed Jesus to Israel and has directed his own disciples to follow him? Why would Jesus baptize with water when John proclaimed that the one coming after him would baptize with the Holy Spirit?

One reason for this puzzling scene may be to help the audience distinguish between baptism by water and baptism by the Holy Spirit. If Jesus or his disciples baptize with water before the Holy Spirit is given, this means that baptism by water is not the same as baptism by the Spirit. When Jesus tells his disciples that the Father will send the Spirit in his name (14:26), or that he will send them the Spirit from the Father (15:26), he does not mention baptism by water at all. Moreover, when he does give the Spirit to the disciples, he does so by breathing on them, not by baptizing them with water (20:22). John underlines this distinction in yet another way: in John the Holy Spirit is not given with the water of baptism when Jesus' disciples baptize and make more disciples than John, but is given only after Jesus is lifted up and glorified on the cross (20:22).

It is ironic that the text that is most often used to show that baptism by the Spirit coincides with baptism by water is found in the Gospel of John. Right before the scene of Jesus and his disciples baptizing, Jesus tells Nicodemus, "Very truly, I tell you, no one can enter the kingdom of God without being born of water and Spirit" (3:5). This verse has traditionally been used to claim that baptism by the Spirit occurs when the church baptizes with water. From one perspective, this claim can be heard to domesticate the gift of the Spirit, by seeming to place the Spirit under human control. Jesus, however, tells us that others will not know where the one born of the Spirit comes from, nor where she goes (3:8). If the church believes itself to be the giver of the Spirit by the waters of baptism, then the church can also claim to know precisely where those born of the Spirit come from and where they are going: they come from and go to the church.

From this reading of the text and its institutional consequences, clarifying the distinction between baptism by water and baptism by the Spirit is critical for the life and health of the Christian community. John is not the only New Testament writer to make the distinction more clearly than we realize. Even

Pastoral Perspective

For Jesus, the direct route home goes through Samaria, though the direct path is not preferred for most Jews. Division and controversy keep Jews at a distance from Samaritans; so in this transitional portion of the text the question arises: why does Jesus choose to go through Samaria?

Does the parish pastor have to answer the phone call when she is attending to a task? If she is very engaged in sermon preparation, for example, why not keep the door to her study closed and remain unavailable for a time? Does Jesus disregard the boundary between Jews and Samaritans because he is in a hurry? Does this explain why "he had to go through Samaria" (v. 4)?

While a sense of urgency on Jesus' part could explain the use of the words "had to," in other places within the Fourth Gospel the word translated as "had to" is associated with God's plan (e.g., 3:14, 30; 9:4).[2] This association provides another way to interpret the transition that leads Jesus to Samaria. Like Jesus, those of us who view life through the lens of vocation know what it means to move from one task to another with an awareness of a plan more significant than the one we were following. Routine tasks and decisions may be understood in relation to the greater purpose that is God's loving concern for the world (cf. 3:16).

In congregations, ministry is the shared task of clergy and laity, and much of the routine work within the parish is directed by committees. Church members who serve on these committees often transition to this work after having spent a demanding day in the office or at home. In the text before us, it appears that Jesus may have been eager to move away from a difficult situation in Judea (vv. 1–2). Similarly, church members may arrive at a committee meeting hoping for a better experience. In any event, like Jesus, they can be tired from their day's journey, however it has gone. What motivates them to serve?

Betty and Laura, members of the Christian education committee, were assigned the task of coordinating the annual Sunday school teacher appreciation breakfast. On the night before the Saturday morning breakfast, the two of them drove to the church to arrange tables and chairs in the fellowship hall. Having already worked an eight-hour-plus day, they were tired, but the task of creating a welcoming space for the Sunday school teachers brought renewed energy. A plan came to life as they brought out linen

2. Gail R. O'Day, "Luke and John," in *The New Interpreter's Bible* (Nashville: Abingdon Press, 1995), 9:565.

Exegetical Perspective

bear testimony, and judge the faithful and unfaithful—themes that push forward in chapter 4 to the climactic description of Jesus as "the Savior of the world" (4:42).

While we have been given the impression that Jesus does indeed baptize like John, now curiously the narrator draws a distinction: Jesus himself does not baptize; rather, he directs baptisms by his disciples. Thus the influence and success of Jesus grow, and the Pharisees, who watched carefully and questioned the actions of John, take notice. Jesus, sensing a challenge and confrontation coming, chooses to depart from Judea for the less dangerous confines of Galilee. The dance between Judea and Galilee continues in Jesus' ministry until the midpoint of the Gospel, when "his hour had come" (13:1). From that point onward, Jerusalem will be the final destination and the climactic setting of the story.

An Intermediate Stop (vv. 4–5). The evangelist simply notes that Jesus "had to go through Samaria." While this may seem like common sense (as the middle of Palestine, Samaria separates Judea from the Galilee), the comment provides another important cue for the interpretation of this narrative. Jesus moves about freely and at the will of the Father, without the need to circumvent the area of Samaria by taking a route along the Trans-Jordan to Galilee. The Greek word meaning "must, have to" (*dei*) suggests that Jesus is moving according to divine necessity and call toward Samaria. Indeed, the following story of Jesus and the Samaritan woman indicates that Jesus comes to understand himself as "the Savior of the world" amid a broad field ready for harvest (4:31–38)—a ministry not confined to Judea and Galilee.

John identifies the setting still more specifically with the Samaritan city of Sychar. We lack details regarding Sychar, but we can infer by the mention of the patriarch Jacob that we are dealing with the region around the Samaritan capital of Shechem. The mention of Joseph's field suggests that Sychar is an area nearby. This correlates well with the larger narrative when the Samaritan woman draws Jesus' attention to the Samaritan place of worship on Mount Gerizim (4:20), which would presumably have been visible. Despite common ancestry and traditions, Jews (i.e., Judeans) considered Samaritans a people of mixed and impure traditions, stemming from events surrounding their captivity by the Assyrians in the eighth century BCE. Jesus' decision to go through Samaria represents a bold move

Homiletical Perspective

townspeople to Jesus. This sermon might also contrast Jesus' approach to the Pharisee Nicodemus and the Samaritan woman at the well.

John 4:1–6 makes significant contributions to this larger story. The first contribution is the key expression in verse 4: "But he had to go through Samaria." Although this was the shortest route, Jesus does not take this route because of human necessity or geographical convenience. There is, rather, a divine necessity to go through this area. The Greek *dei* in John's Gospel often involves divine intention and direction. Jewish people usually avoided traveling this route, preferring to take a longer route to avoid contacting the Samaritans, whom they regarded as a mixed race of people following a false religion oriented around an alternative temple. Fred Craddock affirms that Jesus' decision to follow this route "is not a statement about historical or geographical necessity. Jesus' obligation to pass through Samaria is a theological statement, consistent with 'for God so loved the world.'"[1] Jesus is inaugurating the expansion of the gospel beyond the Jewish people. There was a different route that could have avoided "those" people. "But he had to go" (v. 4).

From God's directing God's Son Jesus to Samaria, we may draw an analogy to the way God directs our own lives, often along more difficult routes, particularly to the areas where we might meet people's needs by living out and presenting to them the gospel. This movement or travel beyond our comfort zone applies to us both as individuals and as communities of faith. Are we willing to venture out beyond our comfortable pews? Beyond the routes we usually follow to and from church? Often this means crossing cultural lines, taking us into areas where we do not feel at home. God challenges congregations to go through Samaria in order to discover and bear witness to the depth and breadth of God's love for the world.

The challenge is to minister to people of different socioeconomic groups, races, ethnicities, genders, or other backgrounds. A choice can be made to bypass Samaria, to avoid close encounters with the "other," to play it safe. Faithful ministry requires meeting the challenge of the new, the different, and the unexpected. Instead of becoming bastions of isolation, many congregations have embraced opportunities to engage directly with their community. They realize that they have been called to ministry in that location and at that time for a divine purpose. In this

---

1. Fred B. Craddock, *John*, Knox Preaching Guides (Atlanta: John Knox Press, 1982), 36.

John 4:1–6

Theological Perspective

the book of Acts, where baptism and the gift of the Spirit are often correlated (e.g., Acts 2:38; 9:17–18; 10:44–48), begins with the risen Jesus reminding the disciples of the difference between baptism by water and baptism by the Spirit: "for John baptized with water, but you will be baptized with the Holy Spirit not many days from now" (Acts 1:5). When Jesus baptizes the disciples with the Spirit, he fulfills the astonishing claim made by the prophet Joel, that in the last days God will pour out the Spirit of prophecy on the old and the young, on men and women, on slaves and free (Joel 2:28–32; Acts 2:16–21), and thereby fulfills the wish of Moses when he cried, "Would that all the LORD's people were prophets, and that the LORD would put his spirit on them!" (Num. 11:29).

The disciples know that God freely gives the Spirit through Christ; nevertheless, they are continually surprised by the way God gives the Spirit, especially when God pours the Spirit out on the Gentiles as well as on the Jews. "And God, who knows the human heart, testified to them by giving them the Holy Spirit, just as he did to us" (Acts 15:8–9). Had the disciples thought that the Spirit was given only through the waters of baptism, it is doubtful that the Gentiles would ever have been included in the community of believers.

By having Jesus' disciples baptize with water and make more disciples than John before the Spirit has been given, the Gospel of John invites us to rethink the connection we typically presume between baptism by water and baptism by the Spirit. The disciples can decide whom to baptize with water; but only Jesus can ask the Father to send the Spirit upon those to whom he wills to send it. Jesus gives us an anticipation of what the freedom of the Spirit might look like when he leaves Judea for Samaria, in order to call the Samaritans to faith in himself.

RANDALL C. ZACHMAN

Pastoral Perspective

tablecloths and napkins, individual place settings, and floral centerpieces. After several hours, the fellowship hall was transformed, enabling them to imagine the celebration that would take place in less than twelve hours.

Tired and happy, the two women eagerly headed out the door, the last task accomplished in what had been a long day. Approaching their cars, they were startled by the movement of a person standing in the shadow of one of the entrances to the church. As they turned in that direction, a woman stepped toward them and said, "Ah, you caught me." The young woman, in her twenties, was wearing a thin jacket and carrying a small suitcase. On a brisk evening in early March, she had planned to sleep on the church grounds. On the run from an abusive boyfriend, she had hitchhiked as far as our city but was heading 250 miles west to a town where a family member would house her while she decided what to do next.

The woman had not eaten that day, so Betty and Laura took her to a nearby restaurant and then to the bus station, where they purchased a one-way ticket that with stops would arrive at this woman's destination early the next morning. Indeed, it was about that time of day when I heard her story. "You had to have been scared when you saw someone on the church grounds," I said. "Oh, we were frightened, all right," Betty admitted. "But to be honest, once I saw who it was, my next thought was: 'I'm too tired to deal with this.'" "I felt the same way," Laura added. "I looked at Betty, and we both shook our heads. You know, here's one more thing to do." Laura sighed. "But then I realized that she was so alone and in such need. We had to help her."

In a manner of speaking, the young woman was not the only one who had been "caught" in this situation. Two women of faith, recognizing the divine imperative in this moment, *had* to help.

CRAIG S. TROUTMAN

Exegetical Perspective

to cross boundaries and extend God's activity to include even those people who, although related, are alienated from the Jews whose hopes are focused on the temple in Jerusalem.

Intrigue and Expectations (v. 6). This transitional passage culminates with a verse that establishes more specifically the setting for the story to follow in 4:7–42. Jacob's well becomes the focal point of the story and the interaction between Jesus and the unnamed Samaritan woman. Most modern translations do not translate the Greek word *houtōs* ("thus, in this way"), which is an important element in John's "storytelling style": "Now, Jesus, who was wearied from his journey, was sitting *in this way* beside the well" (v. 6a, my trans.). Moreover, it was in the heat of the day ("about noon")! A long journey. A happenstance coming upon a well in foreign territory. Thirst. Jesus, apparently without provision to draw water. Sitting down to wait to see what will happen. So John's audience (and we, if we know the biblical traditions of Isaac, Jacob, and Moses, as they did!) joins Jesus in this story of intrigue and anticipation. Sitting and waiting for a providential meeting, a match-making encounter between Jesus and a woman come to draw water.

Jacob had met Rachel at a well (Gen. 29:1–14). Before Jacob, Abraham's servant, sent to find a bride for Isaac, succeeded when he stopped at the well outside Haran and met Rebekah (Gen. 24:1–27). After Jacob, Moses, fleeing to Midian, at a well had chanced upon seven daughters, from whom he was given Zipporah as a wife (Exod. 2:15–22). So this context is rich with expectations and opportunities. What will transpire? Whom will Jesus (the future bridegroom!) meet, and what will be the outcome of the relationship that is established? What might be a happenchance moment will, as in stories before, be an occasion for God to lead toward purposes unforeseen.

For the Samaritan woman, nothing about this encounter will be business as usual; it will instead become an opportunity for "living water." For her it will not be another "husband," but rather a meeting with the Messiah. For an excluded and marginalized people, the Samaritans, it will be an introduction to "the Savior of the world."

ROLLIN A. RAMSARAN

Homiletical Perspective

way they both heed God's call and make incarnate their witness to God's Son. As preachers we too must enter our Samaria. This may involve addressing our prejudices, often in the guise of preferences. It is relatively easy to tell others what to do, but difficult to model living out and sharing the good news ourselves.

A second contribution of the passage to the overall narrative is the involvement of the disciples in baptizing others. John 4:2 notes that it was not Jesus but his disciples who were baptizing. The Pharisees credit Jesus with the baptisms (v. 1), but this ministry was carried out by the disciples. The Scriptures do not state that John's disciples baptized. Here Jesus' disciples carry out an important delegated ministry, just as we are often called to be the hands and feet of Jesus to serve others. Our preaching should aim to empower others to serve in response to the opportunities they encounter, using the gifts they are given.

A third contribution of this passage to the story John tells is the observation of Jesus' humanity described in verse 6. Here we find Jesus seated at the well, tired from his journey. John mentions that it is the sixth hour (noon). We can imagine the midday sun beating down upon him. Jesus is thirsty as well as hungry. Jesus is like us in our need of physical necessities—rest, water, and food. Even in this state he is willing to reach out to others, to initiate conversation that leads others to the living water (4:10–15). Jesus is the model for us and readies us to spread the gospel in response to his saying at the end of John, "As the Father has sent me, so I send you" (20:21). We may be called in times when we are physically weak like Jesus. It may be when we do not think that we have enough knowledge to present the gospel or the ability to answer searching questions. Sometimes we just do not feel like it.

At the well we see the traveler Jesus, in an unusual place and burdened with human weakness, yet divinely positioned to serve others. So we too see ourselves and our congregations in places by divine appointment, aware of our human weakness, yet poised to serve others.

DANIEL L. WONG

7A Samaritan woman came to draw water, and Jesus said to her, "Give me a drink." 8(His disciples had gone to the city to buy food.) 9The Samaritan woman said to him, "How is it that you, a Jew,* ask a drink of me, a woman of Samaria?" (Jews do not share things in common with Samaritans.) 10Jesus answered her, "If you knew the gift of God, and who it is that is saying to you, 'Give me a drink,' you would have asked him, and he would have given you living water." 11The woman said to him, "Sir, you have no bucket, and the well is deep. Where do you get that living water? 12Are you greater than our ancestor Jacob, who gave us the well, and with his sons and his flocks drank from it?" 13Jesus said to her, "Everyone who drinks of this water will be thirsty again, 14but those who drink of the water that I will give them will never be thirsty. The water that I will give will become in them a spring of water gushing up to eternal life." 15The woman said to him, "Sir, give me this water, so that I may never be thirsty or have to keep coming here to draw water."

Theological Perspective

The dialogue between Jesus and the Samaritan woman at the well (4:1–42) spreads a theological feast of amazing bounty. John's explanation of Jesus and of the Spirit through the figure of Wisdom; the importance of prophecy in communal experience and in the portrait of Jesus; the meaning of baptism; the startling assertiveness of women in this Gospel; the deeschatologizing of the judgment; hope for the restoration of Israel; the meaning and problems of Christian "universalism": all are woven throughout the dialogue. Its first exchanges (vv. 7–15) lay the ground for these multiple associations, but focus especially on Wisdom.

Until recently, scholarly readings of John have not been generous with either the Samaritan woman or the dialogue as a whole. Although John Chrysostom recognized her as a woman of wisdom (*Homilies on the Gospel of John* XXXI.4–XXXII.1, 2) and Eastern Christians awarded her the name Photine ("enlightened") and a lurid martyrdom, scholars and preachers of the modern Western churches generally have treated her as an example of spiritual obtuseness and sexual sin. Yet a careful reading of the text reveals her as the most persistent and astute of all Jesus' interlocutors in this Gospel.

* See "'The Jews' in the Fourth Gospel" on pp. xi–xiv.

Pastoral Perspective

Good news happens in unexpected places and often in chance encounters. Jesus is off the beaten path, not in the usual areas of his life and ministry, Judea and Galilee. Earlier in this chapter, John mentions that Jesus was journeying from the typical locations of his ministry and had to go through another territory, Samaria. In this foreign place and tired from the journey, Jesus sits at a well while the disciples are sent off to search for food. Here, in this place outside the bounds, a gospel conversation occurs.

Not only is this conversation in an unexpected place; it occurs between two individuals of very different status and social standing. The animosity and discord between Jews and Samaritans and the difference in social standing of a man and a woman would have been well known by the early Gospel readers and have been well documented for those who study Scripture today. The woman's comment to Jesus poignantly notes that this meeting is beyond convention and across boundaries: "How is it that you, a Jew, ask a drink of me, a woman of Samaria?" (v. 9). In case the reader misses the point, John parenthetically adds, "Jews do not share things in common with Samaritans."

As the church, we often live in a world of controlled conversations that we imagine happen mainly within the confines of the calendars on our

Exegetical Perspective

Readers know from the beginning that Jesus is the Word made flesh who "lived among us . . . full of grace and truth" (1:14). Characters within the narrative, however, do not initially share that knowledge. This leads to ironic statements like the one we hear from the Samaritan woman in this passage: "Are you greater than our ancestor Jacob, who gave us this well?" (v. 12; cf. 8:53; see also Gen. 48:22; Josh. 24:32).

The question of Jesus' identity is woven through John's Gospel. This essay traces some of those narrative threads, particularly as they connect to chapters immediately before and after the story of the woman at the well.

Like Nicodemus (chap. 3) some people come to Jesus on account of his signs (e.g., 2:23; 6:2), although they do not always understand what they are seeing (6:26). Others, during the festivals in Jerusalem, listen to his teaching, grapple with its meaning, and wonder who he is and where he comes from (7:40–44). The Samaritan woman, for her part, encounters Jesus in the midst of her daily routine. At first his identity is as baffling to her as it is to others.

The episode, found only in John, incorporates a number of Johannine terms (eternal life, truth, seeing, believing, the hour), as well as narrative themes and motifs (the true identity of Jesus, irony, movement from misunderstanding to believing).

Homiletical Perspective

Many persons have had the experience of being shunned, ostracized, and isolated. It may happen not just because of how people have made us feel or treated us, but because of a distorted perception of oneself or a sense of having been victimized. Teenagers with a simple pimple or blotch on the skin may feel worse than the frog or the ugly duckling. Adults who grew up in dysfunctional family units may continue to wrestle with serious issues of self-esteem and self-perception. Persons who have been the victims of sexual assault and abuse, such as rape, may experience an overwhelming sense of shame and guilt that can seriously hamper their ability to handle social relationships in positive ways.

The woman in this story seems to have known the experience of being ostracized and isolated. Jesus was passing through Samaritan territory when he decided to rest by a well. He was tired from the journey and feeling very thirsty, as it was the noon hour. The sun would no doubt have been quite hot. No sooner had Jesus settled down to rest than the Samaritan woman approached to fetch water.

As those who have lived under such conditions know, one does not usually fetch water at that time of day. This is a task for the morning hours and the late afternoon or evening, when the temperature is more hospitable. So we may ask what she was doing

John 4:7–15

Theological Perspective

In contrast to Nicodemus, who comes to Jesus by night, this woman comes to the well at the brightest point of day (4:6), and leaves utterly illumined (4:28–29). The scene is set by the note that Jesus' disciples baptize (4:2) and by the location at Jacob's well (4:6). Jesus asks the woman for a drink, and the woman tells the reader what is wrong with his request: this man is a Jew, while she is both a Samaritan and a woman, and they are alone; can his motives be good?

Jesus then reverses his demand: "If you knew the gift of God, and who it is that is saying to you, 'Give me a drink,' you would have asked him, and he would have given you living water" (v. 10). The woman replies with two questions. The first and more obvious one is where and how he will get this living water. The more important—indeed, the supremely right—question is the second: "Are you greater than our ancestor Jacob?" (v. 12). The earliest Christian readers and hearers must have understood that she was indeed coming to know the one who spoke to her, as they gladly answered, "Yes!"

Jesus answers her double question with a single offer to her and to any willing to accept it: the offer of a drink that differs from all other water, a drink that becomes a source, a continual spring within herself. This single offer enshrines a twofold promise: first, the pledge of an unending, life-giving drink; second, the proclamation that this drink will become, and will make the believer, a source of life. Later in the Gospel, at the feast of Sukkot, Jesus makes the same twofold promise. First he cries: "Let anyone who is thirsty come to me, and let the one who believes in me drink"; then, "As the scripture has said, 'Out of the believer's heart shall flow rivers of living water'" (7:37–38). The narrator identifies the living water: it is a drink of the Spirit, promised for the postresurrection future of the readers, both early and late (7:39).

Both aspects of this drink echo and trump the many offers voiced by Wisdom in biblical and early Jewish texts. Particularly striking is the long poem in Sirach 24. There Wisdom speaks in the first person, recounting her heavenly origin, her role in creation, her search for an earthly dwelling, and her tenting upon Zion (Sir. 24:4–12), and describing her luxuriant flourishing there as tree and vine (Sir. 24:13–17). Then she calls:

> Come to me, you who desire me,
>   and eat your fill of my fruits.
> For the memory of me is sweeter than honey,
>   and the possession of me sweeter than the
>   honeycomb.

Pastoral Perspective

smart phones or the walls of our sanctuaries. We who are people of faith attempting to keep up with the pressures of everyday life while managing faith commitments often schedule and routinize our lives in such a way that there remains little time for the unexpected or off-the-plan encounters. We stay within comfort zones of time management and safe locations, too rarely wandering off the beaten path into unfamiliar and even dangerous places. The encounter between Jesus and the Samaritan woman provokes and confronts the imagination to see that gospel encounters happen unexpectedly and in places beyond the expected and usual.

By locating this unexpected encounter in the region of Samaria, John's narrative spurs congregations to move out beyond the cozy confines and daily routines of the church building or membership to the places and people beyond the bounds. It invites attentiveness to the unexpected, a willingness to risk stepping outside borders, and an openness to the Spirit that blows where she wills. While this may seem a simple truism, the human tendency to flock together with birds of a similar feather and to stay comfortable with the known is in constant need of challenge and provocation. The story of Jesus and the Samaritan woman induces communities of faith to risk crossing boundaries and to be open to chance encounters where good news can be shared.

Out there, not only will we find those who are eager for the good news. We will also find Jesus. Depending on how we read and are read by this story, we as congregations can find ourselves both as bearers and receivers of the gospel. Students of John's Gospel have shown that it is full of irony, which is seen clearly here in the interplay between Jesus and the Samaritan woman. Their statements and questions seem to shoot past each other; throughout she remains very literal, while Jesus moves on a different level of understanding. Yet she is seeking what Jesus has to offer, and he does not water down his message of living water that quenches thirst forever.

As followers of Jesus, we often read the story from the perspective of Jesus; that is, as the church, we imagine that we are like Jesus in this story. Moving out into unexpected places, we encounter those who are searching, even if they are not quite sure what they are searching for. The temptation is to morph the language of the gospel, to translate it in such a way that it meets the felt needs of the hearer. Instead of the radical news of living water, we offer buckets of advice in terms that reduce the gospel to effective steps or ordered plans. Jesus, however, never

Throughout the extended dialogue, the woman is bold to ask several questions as Jesus reveals truths about his identity and the gifts of God that are available to believers through him.

The pericope overflows with vocabulary related to water: "well," "spring," "bucket," "drink," "thirsty," "living water," "water gushing up." An *inclusio* in verses 7 and 15 ("came to draw water"/"coming here to draw water") frames the section and focuses attention on the woman's desire to procure this fundamental element of life, even if she must retrieve it in the heat of the day (literally "the sixth hour," 4:6). It also provides verbal linkage to the first sign at Cana, barely two chapters earlier, where Jesus revealed his glory at the wedding feast when he commanded the stewards to "draw out" (*antleō*) the water-turned-wine and show it to the bridegroom (v. 7a; 2:8).

Identities are at the forefront as the woman hints that Jesus is crossing too many social boundaries: "How is it that you, a Jew, ask a drink of me, a woman of Samaria?" (v. 9). Lest readers miss the significance of her remark, the evangelist inserts the equivalent of a stage whisper: "Jews do not share things in common with Samaritans" (v. 9; similar asides appear at 1:38, 42; 2:21; 11:2; 18:9; etc.). Jesus does not respond directly to her spirited challenge, but raises a challenge of his own. If only she knew who he really was, *she* would have asked *him* for a drink, with a satisfaction greater than the contents of any bucket could offer.

At the heart of the dialogue is Jesus' offer of "living water" (v. 10) that becomes "a spring of water gushing up to eternal life" (v. 14). What he means by this is not clarified during the conversation, but John 7:37–43 explicitly connects living water with the giving of the Spirit after Jesus is glorified, that is, after his death and resurrection. The image echoes Isaiah's promises of deliverance and restoration: "with joy you will draw water from the wells of salvation" (Isa. 12:3) and "everyone who thirsts, come to the waters" (Isa. 55:1). It also suggests the practice of baptism for those who receive "power to become children of God" (1:12).

The woman misunderstands, focusing on water's material substance rather than its spiritual significance. Her confusion is reflected in the double meaning of the Greek, "living water" or "flowing water" (*hydōr zōn*, v. 10), which she interprets in the latter sense. She sees only a well like a "cistern" (*phrear*, vv. 11–12)—in contrast to a "spring" (*pēgē*, v. 6), as it is called by the narrator and Jesus (v. 14)—suggesting that true knowledge about the identity of Jesus is more than meets the eye.

there and why she was alone. Tradition suggests that noon was the hour when persons who were socially ostracized or ashamed would go to the well, so they would not have to face the harsh and cold treatment of the other women of the community. As the story unfolds, we discover why this woman may have been subject to such ostracism.

Jesus did something most unusual in his culture, but not uncharacteristic of him. He ventured beyond the boundaries of the religious and cultural taboos of his day and began a conversation with the woman. In the first place, a Jewish rabbi did not have conversation with a woman in the public arena; second, a Jew was not expected to interact with a Samaritan in any familiar fashion. Jesus here broke the convention and engaged her in an exchange that would allow her to redefine herself and her mission that day, thereby changing the course of her life.

Jesus asked her for a drink of water, and the woman, perhaps taken aback and surprised, tried to draw up a dividing wall, a partition: "How is it that you, a Jew, ask a drink of me, a woman of Samaria?" (v. 9a). Jesus did not follow along the line she pursued. Yet he also did not want to push her away. He wanted to establish a relationship with her; perhaps he saw within her potential, possibility, and goodness. Jesus countered with an offer, an olive branch: "If you knew the gift of God, and who it is that is saying to you, 'Give me a drink,' you would have asked him, and he would have given you living water" (v. 10).

Jesus' words carry a depth of meaning to which the woman responded at a superficial and materialistic level. Jesus used the very ordinary symbol of water, the drink, to open to her deeper truths. John presents Jesus as the life-giving water that replaces the "stagnant" or "standing water" of her worldview and religious orientation. Jesus is "the water of life," a new movement of God for the well-being of God's people.

Missing the level to which Jesus had taken the conversation, the woman returned the conversation to the ordinary element of water: "How are you going to offer me water? You have no bucket, and the well is deep. Are you suggesting that you have a better alternative to offer than Jacob who gave us this well?" Was she giving Jesus what she considered a reorientation to reality, suggesting that his claim was more that he could deliver?

Jesus continued to clarify and deepen the conversation by speaking of "living water" that can spring up to eternal life. What he was offering is not just material or for the immediate moment, but

John 4:7–15

Theological Perspective

> Those who eat of me will hunger for more,
> and those who drink of me will thirst for more.
> (Sir. 24:19–21)

Wisdom offers herself as a gift of life like food, like drink; divine life and being we can take into ourselves, and she becomes us. She offers a new realm of desire; those who taste her will continually long for her. Jesus' offer echoes hers, but radically exceeds it, proclaiming that the one who drinks the Holy Spirit and eats the living bread will never hunger or thirst: "whoever comes to me will never be hungry, and whoever believes in me will never be thirsty" (6:35).

To this offer, the woman gives the perfect answer: "Give me this water, so that I may never be thirsty" (v. 15). Both the earliest and modern readers and hearers have recognized this response as their own. Her plea helped to make the woman the model for the baptismal candidates in the early churches, and won the dialogue a place in the ancient baptismal lectionary that is revived in the Lenten lectionaries of Year A. Many commentators misread the second part of her answer as a sign that she has not (or not yet) understood, assuming that her desire not to return and draw water shows that she continues to think in material terms. However, the progress of the dialogue and indeed the meaning of the water suggest that the Samaritan woman has received her drink of the Spirit, and it gushes up in her, a source of life for herself and others.

The central role of Wisdom in the dialogue and in John's Christology began to be recognized only in the mid-twentieth century, and Sirach was relegated to apocryphal status during the Reformation. Even so, the Wisdom Christology enshrined in John lived on in Christian piety. From the combination of Sirach 24:19–23 and John 4:14 come the first verse of the medieval hymn "Jesu Dulcis Memoria" and its English version, "Jesu, Joy of Man's Desiring, Holy Wisdom, Love Most Bright." In a nineteenth-century hymn still much in use, Jesus as Wisdom repeats his offer to new generations of believers:

> I heard the voice of Jesus say,
> "Behold, I freely give
> the living water; thirsty one,
> stoop down and drink, and live."[1]

MARY R. D'ANGELO

Pastoral Perspective

moderates the mystery and power of the gospel. Consistently he confronts the woman with the good news of life offered through him. As Augustine said, "our hearts are restless until they rest in thee"; in the terms of our passage, we are thirsty until we drink of the Living Water. Offering anything less means not quenching the underlying thirst.

In his book *Waiting for Gospel*, Douglas John Hall suggests that the church has lost the conviction of the gospel as being truly good news and thus is offering something watered down and ineffective.

This is not an easy calling. It will be easier for men and women who (perhaps to our own surprise) find ourselves called to be witnesses to this gospel—it will be much easier for us to preach homilies full of musts and shoulds and ought-tos, to lace our sermonettes with television-inspired one-liners, to deliver from our pulpits gently challenging admonitions to self-improvement. After all, that's what everybody has come to expect from preachers! It will be easier for us to become "professional Christians" and do all the things that people in our congregations could be doing, often better than we could do. It will be easier to play the role of the activist or the psychoanalyst or the spiritual court jester than to aspire to "make known with boldness the mystery of the gospel" (Eph. 6:19).[1]

Communicating the gospel forthrightly and compassionately, as Jesus does, is the promise and hope of his encounter with the woman at the well.

When we cross boundaries and participate in unexpected conversations that break societal conventions, there is an irony that awaits us in John's story: our own understandings are transformed and changed as we, like the Samaritan woman, encounter the Christ who offers us living water. Our watered-down buckets are filled with living water that flows, no less gushes forth, and we realize how thirsty we have become in our safe and controlled worlds.

THOMAS W. WALKER

---

1. Horatius Bonar, "I Heard the Voice of Jesus Say," stanza 2.

1. Douglas John Hall, *Waiting for Gospel: An Appeal to the Dispirited Remnants of Protestant "Establishment"* (Eugene, OR: Cascade Books, 2012), 10.

Exegetical Perspective

Her confusion mirrors that of Nicodemus, one chapter earlier, who tripped over the dual meaning of being born again or from above (*anōthen*, 3:3–4). Beyond their shared confusion, however, Nicodemus and the Samaritan woman are a study in contrasts. He is named, she is not. He is a man of high status, a Pharisee, who comes to Jesus in the dark of night to query him about his identity. She, on the other hand, is an outsider, a Samaritan, who has a chance encounter with Jesus in the middle of the day. At the end of their respective conversations with Jesus, Nicodemus sneaks off into the night and says very little. In contrast, the woman's testimony about Jesus leads people from her village to believe in him (4:39).

Looking ahead in the Gospel, the dialogue between Jesus and the woman anticipates a conversation between Jesus and the crowd following the feeding of the five thousand. In both cases, the heart of Jesus' gift is eternal life. Like the woman, the crowd wants to know more: "What sign are you going to give us then, so that we may see it and believe you?" They wonder how his gift compares to that of their ancestor, Moses (6:30–32; cf. 4:12). The water will be a spring gushing up to eternal life, and the bread is that which comes down from heaven and gives life to the world (v. 14b; 6:33). Those who drink this water will never be thirsty again (v. 14a), just as those who receive the bread shall not hunger (6:35). The woman and the crowds respond to Jesus' promises in virtually the same way: "Sir [*Kyrie*], give me this water, so that I may never be thirsty or have to keep coming here to draw water" (v. 15); "Sir [*Kyrie*], give us this bread always" (6:34).

At this point in the conversation, the woman does not yet recognize the fullness of Jesus' gift, nor his true identity. However, she is beginning to discern the answer to her opening question, "Are you greater than our ancestor Jacob?" There is more to this boundary-crossing traveler than meets the eye.

AUDREY WEST

Homiletical Perspective

something that has eternal implications. The woman again misunderstood the qualitatively different substance Jesus was speaking of and stayed with the ordinary and superficial: "Give me this water so that I never have to make this trip again." She understood this living water to be flowing water that fulfills domestic needs, an alternative to the standing water of the well. Perhaps we could think of it almost like getting indoor plumbing. Jesus was offering something quite different.

The preacher may take note of the fact that Jesus has not yet brought about any profound changes in the life of this woman, nor has he judged her. Rather, he has demonstrated the inclusiveness of his life, his love, and his mission, which crosses ethnic, cultural, religious, and gender barriers—whatever constitutes the social divide. The story clearly calls the church to reach out in inclusive ways, challenging the many boundaries and barriers that we encounter or even create in the context of our communities, our culture, our nation—even the barriers we create in what has become the global village. Jesus focuses here, in particular, on how we might engage those who are of other faiths, without arrogance and bigotry.

Sharing the faith with persons who do not share our convictions or who have no particular faith commitment may not lead to any perceptible change. However, the very act of engagement may affirm the value of the human person within the love of God, challenging the isolation, shame, and ostracism they may live with every day. In this interaction of Jesus with the Samaritan woman, we observe the sowing of a seed that can grow into the harvest of a life transformed.

HOWARD K. A. GREGORY

John 4:16–21

¹⁶Jesus said to her, "Go, call your husband, and come back." ¹⁷The woman answered him, "I have no husband." Jesus said to her, "You are right in saying, 'I have no husband'; ¹⁸for you have had five husbands, and the one you have now is not your husband. What you have said is true!" ¹⁹The woman said to him, "Sir, I see that you are a prophet. ²⁰Our ancestors worshiped on this mountain, but you say that the place where people must worship is in Jerusalem." ²¹Jesus said to her, "Woman, believe me, the hour is coming when you will worship the Father neither on this mountain nor in Jerusalem."

Theological Perspective

The first exchanges in the dialogue between Jesus and the woman at the well (4:7–15) reveal Wisdom as the source of the Gospel's understanding of Christ, of the Spirit, and of the disciple. In the second set of exchanges, 4:16–21, two issues in particular emerge: the first is Jesus' knowledge of what is in the human being (cf. 2:25); the second is the restoration of Israel enacted by the encounter between Jew and Samaritan. These two features of the dialogue have largely been obscured by a focus on the woman's supposed sexual degradation—something that plays no role in the dialogue itself.

Past readers have identified the woman as a sinner on the basis of the exchange in which Jesus sends the woman for her husband (or "man," *anēr*), and she denies that she has one. Affirming her answer, Jesus replies that she has had five men, and that the one she has now is not hers. Commentators frequently dwell on both answers, asserting that the woman must be a sexual outcast; some even claim that she was at the well at noon (and not at the more usual times of morning and evening) only because she was ostracized by other women. Some go so far as to suggest that her acknowledgment of Jesus' prophecy (v. 19) is a ploy to change the subject. Even Chrysostom takes Jesus' words to be reproof, though he makes her response an occasion to praise her

Pastoral Perspective

The first congregation I served was located in a large capital city. It was full of leaders in all realms of the community, from politicians to business women and men to philanthropists. The folklore of the church was that more business of state happened in the fellowship hall coffee hour between morning worship services than down at the state capitol. The church also had a cadre of retired pastors who took the new, young associate under their wings. One day, one of those retired pastors asked, "What would you do if you found the text leading you to some place for a sermon that you knew would offend some of the leaders of the church? What would you do if they were sitting on the front row? What would you say? Would you risk telling the truth?"

As the conversation between Jesus and the woman at the well continues, the focus moves to their speaking plain truth to one another. In the earlier part of their conversation, Jesus and the Samaritan woman seem to be talking past one another; she talks about buckets and wells, while he speaks about living water that quenches thirst eternally. Everything Jesus says is loaded with potential for misunderstanding, yet carries deeper meanings. This new phase of their engagement begins with Jesus' simple request of the woman to get her husband. Jesus notes that her declaration is truthful: she has no husband.

Exegetical Perspective

In John's account of the dialogue between Jesus and the Samaritan woman at the well, the matter of Jesus' identity continues to weave its way through the conversation. Up to this point the woman has not recognized Jesus' significance, despite her ironic question of whether he is greater than Jacob, their shared ancestor (4:12). She continues to speak boldly with him, despite the interruption to her daily work.

This portion of the passage may be divided into two parts: (1) the marital status of the woman and her many prior relationships (vv. 16–18); and (2) the proper location of worship, whether "on this mountain" (Mount Gerizim) or in Jerusalem (vv. 20–21). The hinge between the two is the woman's declaration of Jesus' significance: "Sir, I see that you are a prophet" (v. 19).

The first part of this passage has more to do with the identity of the woman than with Jesus, but it has received a good deal of exegetical attention. Traditional interpretations highlight the supposed immorality of her marital history.[1] Her appearance at the well during the midday heat—rather than the more traditional morning or evening hours, when other

---

1. For an overview of the history of interpretation, see Luise Schottroff, "The Samaritan Woman and the Notion of Sexuality in the Fourth Gospel," in *What Is John?* ed. Fernando F. Segovia, vol. 2 of *Literary and Social Readings of the Fourth Gospel*, SBL Literature Symposium Series (Atlanta: Scholars Press, 1998), 157–69.

Homiletical Perspective

This passage constitutes a second act or scene in an ongoing drama. Jesus has already gained the attention and growing confidence of the Samaritan woman. Their conversation, however, has been between two persons who speak from differing points of reference, which results in a conversation that sounds like a very disjointed exchange. The woman has asked Jesus to let her have the water that he professes to be able to provide for her and that will satisfy her in such a way that she will never be thirsty again or need to return daily to draw water from the well. Jesus now moves the woman toward a point of self-confrontation as a way of bringing home to her the reality and life-changing impact of his offer (v. 16): "Go, call your husband, and come back." The woman is quick with her response: "I have no husband."

Jesus receives her comment and responds out of the depth of his knowledge of her situation. How? We do not know, but perhaps we may consider the fact that John wants us to see in it the operation of Jesus' divine intuition, the ability to see into the nature of her situation, in the same way that he could see Nathanael under the fig tree (1:43–51), or his understanding that he should not entrust himself to those who believed in him because they saw the signs he was doing, for "he himself knew what was

John 4:16–21

Theological Perspective

exemplary wisdom and meekness (*Homilies on the Gospel of John*, 32.2). Speculating or focusing on the woman's sexual sin distorts the dialogue. While the Bible offers examples of innocent wives of multiple husbands (Sarah in Tobit, the levirate wife of seven husbands in Mark 12:18–27), it is still more significant that the Gospel shows no interest in the woman's supposed sin; she never expresses repentance, and Jesus says nothing about forgiveness.[1]

More weighty evidence for the Samaritan woman's probity is the Gospel's summary of the judgment, which in John is a present reality. The plot in John turns on a double trial: Jesus is on trial before the world, and the world is on trial before God. These trials function as one, described in the conclusion to Jesus' dialogue with Nicodemus:

> This is the trial [judgment, *krisis*]: that the light has come into the world, and human beings loved the darkness rather than the light because their works were evil. For all who do evil hate the light and do not come to the light, lest their works be accused. But the ones who do the truth come to the light, that their works may be made manifest, that they are done in God. (3:19–21, my trans.)

Both the woman's arrival at noon and her approach to Jesus show that she chooses to come to the light and that her deeds will bear its scrutiny.

The focus of these exchanges is Jesus' extraordinary knowledge of who she is; she will later say, as the old spiritual intones, he "told me everything I've ever done" (4:30). Because he knows her, she knows him: "I see that you are a prophet" (v. 19). A similar exchange of recognition appears in John 1:46–51; Jesus knows Nathanael as a guileless and true Israelite, having seen him "under the fig tree." This basis for judgment is totally opaque to the reader, but completely illuminating to Nathanael, who at once knows Jesus as "Son of God, King of Israel" (1:49). The woman's recognition of Jesus as prophet is not of less significance than Nathanael's messianic salutations; in John, Jesus is the prophet like Moses, expected as deliverer by both Samaritans and Jews (1:21; 6:15–16; Deut. 18:15–22; 4Q *Testimonia*).

Even more importantly, both Jesus' knowledge and the woman's reflect the experience of the first audiences; one function of early Christian prophecy was knowledge of the human heart. As Jesus knew what was in the human being (2:25) and the woman

---

1. See D'Angelo, "(Re) presentations of Jesus and the Gospels: John and Mark," in *Women and Christian Origins*, ed. R. S. Kraemer and M. R. D'Angelo (New York: Oxford University Press, 1999), 134–35.

Pastoral Perspective

He then goes on to declare more of the truth about her life. Jesus' truth-telling leads the Samaritan woman to proclaim that he is a prophet.

This text asserts a direct link between truth-telling and prophecy. Here, prophecy is not fortune telling or predicting the future, but forth-telling or naming reality. Biblical prophets invite honest speech and action about the world and our lives. They challenge our everyday narratives of reality, inviting new visions that give rise to hope. Given that much is invested in the shared conventional understandings of reality, prophecy carries inherent risk as it speaks truth to power both small and large.

Prophecy as naming truth directly impacts our understanding of pastoral ministry, both as leaders and participants in communities of faith. At any level, forth-telling can be difficult and risky. In this passage, risk is already present in a conversation that is outside the bounds and between two individuals of different social standing. Many times, taking the risk to tell the truth about a relationship, instead of all the stories we tell ourselves to make everything OK, can be a pivotal moment on the road to healing, forgiveness, and restoration. An honest word can remove blinders and open eyes. In the verses immediately following this conversation, the Samaritan woman invites others to come and see Jesus, precisely because he has spoken the truth about her life. This truth-telling leaves her wondering if Jesus is the promised one, the Messiah, who brings God's rule to earth.

The transformative power of truth-telling works not only individually, but corporately. One of the ironies of many communities of faith is that most people put on their "Sunday best" to attend worship services. This Sunday best extends not only to our clothes, but to the presentation of the state of our lives. Rambunctious kids are made to sit up straight and be overly polite. Conversations focus on how wonderful life is. Just below this projected surface calm, there is struggle, hurt, brokenness, and more. Even in a community based in no small part on forgiveness, the pressure to maintain the pretense of propriety makes it difficult to tell the truth. This is true despite the honesty about our human condition found throughout the Scriptures, from the early stories of Genesis to personal lament psalms to this encounter between Jesus and the Samaritan woman. As a pastor once said in echoes of Augustine's words, the church is called to be a hospital for sinners, not a rest home for saints.

At face value it may seem that only reasons like job security, salary, college funds, and politeness

women would be there too—is offered as further evidence of her ill repute.

Some interpreters observe, however, that Jesus never speaks condemnation against the woman; indeed, the practice of levirate marriage could explain her situation (Deut. 25:5–10; cf. Mark 12:18–27). Unmarried women, especially older widows, were particularly vulnerable, and she may have been forced into these relationships in order to survive. By acknowledging her tragic situation—indeed, by crossing the social, ethnic, and religious boundaries that divide people (see 4:9b)—Jesus demonstrates his solidarity with all who are vulnerable or outcast. The woman is freed from cultural strictures and is empowered to become one of the first witnesses to Jesus' true identity (4:39).

The Samaritan woman may also be viewed as a symbolic figure, although interpreters differ on what she symbolizes. To some interpreters, five husbands represent five books of the Pentateuch comprising the Samaritan canon; to others, her outsider status represents the Gentiles who ultimately become part of the church. According to 2 Kings 17:24, after the Assyrian exile in 722/21 BC, colonizers from five cities settled in Samaria and intermarried with those who had remained behind, bringing with them their worship of pagan gods ("five husbands"). This OT connection, as well as the mention of "true worshipers" (4:23), leads many interpreters to suggest that the woman's current situation is a metaphor for the continuing apostasy of those Samaritans (in Jesus' day or at the time of John's Gospel) who have not yet returned to the true God of Israel.

The story also echoes Jacob and Rachel's first encounter (Gen. 29:1–20), which itself echoes an earlier meeting to arrange the marriage between Isaac and Rebekah (Gen. 24:10–61; cf. Exod. 2:15b–21). These OT betrothal scenes differ in detail from one another and from the Johannine account, but share broad strokes. A stranger stops beside a well, where he meets a woman. Somebody draws water. The woman returns home to report the encounter to her kinfolk. The stranger is invited for a meal, after which the stranger and the woman are betrothed to one another.[2] Details in John's Gospel underscore the betrothal/wedding theme: Jesus' first sign at the wedding in Cana (2:1 ff.), John the Baptist as "the friend of the bridegroom" (3:29), and a second reference to the Cana wedding later in chapter 4 (4:46; for Christ as bridegroom, see Mark 2:19–20 and par.;

2. Robert Alter, *The Art of Biblical Narrative*, new and rev. ed. (New York: Basic Books, 2011), 62.

in everyone" (2:25). Jesus confirms her direct, honest reply: "You are right in saying, 'I have no husband.' You have had five, and the one you now have is not your husband" (vv. 17–18). As the expression goes, "You could have knocked her over with a feather."

The truth of the woman's situation is now out in the open, undeniably so. The preacher may choose to explore what such a moment of disclosure can mean and has meant in the life of the church. Consider for a moment also what many Christians might have to say to this woman. What might this kind of revelation mean to us, if one of the ex-husbands were related to us, or if we were friends of the man with whom she was now living? Here then is probably the reason why she had to come to the well to fetch water at high noon. Notice, however, what comes from the mouth of Jesus. He raises up the truth about her situation so that she can face it, but without a word of condemnation and judgment.

Jesus' lack of condemnation does *not* thereby indicate his approval of her way of life (in contrast to what some Christians argue: that without explicit disapproval, the church tacitly endorses unchristian behavior). Jesus' perspective seems to be that until the individual is able to bring her way of life into the light and acknowledge it, no significant inner change is going to take place.

The woman is taken aback by the depth of Jesus' knowledge of her situation and is probably a bit flustered. Nevertheless, she recognizes and names him as a prophet. Her discomfort with the revelation of the truth about herself and her situation seems to make her want to change the subject again, to divert the attention away from herself to another issue. We should not be too surprised that she uses a discussion of religious dissension and conflict to shift the conversation to less personal terrain. Oh, how hard it is to deal with the truth about ourselves and our situation! Her question focuses on a perennial topic of conflict between Jews and Samaritans, namely, whether Jerusalem or Mount Gerizim is the more appropriate place to worship God.

It often seems inevitable that Christians too will turn our historical and doctrinal differences, both large and small, into profound matters of faith. The history of the church, past and present, is full of instances in which conflicted issues within a local congregation or denomination are given theological or biblical spins, and baptized as eternal truths, leading inevitably to another expression of schism. Religion may often be introduced into a conversation by a nonbeliever or one who does not share

John 4:16–21

Theological Perspective

knows him by his knowledge of her, the gift of prophecy allowed insight into thoughts and desires of human beings (1 Cor. 14:24–25), as well as into the divine plan, the deep things of God (1 Cor. 2:10).

With her recognition of Jesus' prophetic role, the woman emerges as a theologian, laying before this newly discovered prophet *the* theological issue between his people and hers, between the Samaritans and the Jews, the two disunited branches of Israel. John does not regard the Samaritan woman as a foreigner, and certainly not as Gentile. Nor does she see Jesus as an alien. Rather, she has stressed their common heritage: "Are you greater than our (common) ancestor Jacob?" (4:12, parentheses mine). Her question now is where God was to be worshiped, the one place the one God of Israel had chosen to dwell: the ancient sanctuary at Mount Gerizim, the successor to the altar prescribed by Deuteronomy (11:26–30; 12:13–14; 27:1–8), or Solomon's temple at Jerusalem (1 Kgs. 9:3), painfully rebuilt after the first destruction and so recently made new by Herod's spectacular reconstruction.

Jesus' answer begins with prophecy: "the hour is coming," he promises, "when you will worship . . . neither on this mountain nor in Jerusalem" (v. 21). This is a prediction that must have struck awe into the hearts of the first readers and hearers of the Gospel. They would have known that the first part had been fulfilled when the temple at Gerizim had been destroyed (by John Hyrcanus sometime in the early decades of the second century BCE), long before the dialogue between Jesus and the woman is supposed to have taken place. Even more poignantly, the second part had been fulfilled in their own time. The Romans had destroyed the Jerusalem temple and excluded the Jews from the temple mount within the memory (70 CE) of at least some of those who first read or heard the Gospel. For them, Jesus' prophetic status was dreadfully confirmed by these words. For later readers, the prophecy is a reminder of the traumatic loss that marked the Gospel's context.

MARY R. D'ANGELO

Pastoral Perspective

might force pastors to hedge their bets about forth-telling. Like the woman at the well, pastors may be revealing only part of the truth, hoping that those who hear will not force an engagement with a deeper truth. Yet, truth be told, a little dose of reality is needed here as well. Like the woman at the well, those of us in the pastoral ministry stand in need of a little truth-telling, a little telling of the fuller story of our lives, by Jesus.

When we encounter the fuller story, we find that we are deeply and heavily invested in the narratives of the world. We preach the weakness, vulnerability, and servanthood of Christ, yet rarely allow others to see our own brokenness. We often are tempted by prestige and position in our local communities. We proclaim Sabbath, but rarely practice the rest and renewal that Sabbath offers. We speak of calling and vocation, yet burn ourselves out in amazing numbers. We teach a gospel of grace and forgiveness, but perhaps too seldom allow that same truth to penetrate and impact our work and relationships.

In Doug Marlette's cartoon *Kudzu*, one of the main characters is the Reverend Will B. Dunn. Rev. Dunn is the shepherd of the flock in Bypass, NC, and fancies himself as a spiritual guide for the community. In one strip, Rev. Dunn is pondering the possibility of confronting one of his members, Big Bubba Tadsworth, the largest business owner in town, about his corporation's unfair practices and harming of the environment. As Rev. Dunn muses, the dilemma is clearly evident on his face. Finally, the last frame reveals that Rev. Dunn has been deliberating this conundrum in a hot tub, and he says something like, "It's hard to be objective . . . especially in the Tadsworths' hot tub."[1] It is hard to tell the truth, but Jesus tells the truth and invites all who will follow him to do the same, for it is in telling redemptive truth that we encounter the Messiah.

THOMAS W. WALKER

---

1. Doug Marlette, *Preacher: The Wit and Wisdom of Reverend Will B. Dunn* (Nashville: Thomas Nelson Publishers, 1984), n.p.

Matt. 25:1–13; Rev. 19:7; 21:2, 9). Even the titles used by Jesus and the Samaritan woman to address one another (*kyrios, gynē*) may be translated respectively as "husband" and "wife." In addition, the Samaritans invite Jesus to stay for two days (4:40).

The discussion about her life situation leads the woman to exclaim, "Sir ["Lord" (*kyrios*), an address she uses throughout], I see you are a prophet." This assertion puts her in good company among Johannine characters (6:14; 7:40; 7:52; 9:17; cf. 4:44). Coupled with Jesus' response ("Woman, believe me . . . ," v. 21), it sets up a conventional Johannine pairing of *seeing* and *believing*, repeated most notably at 6:40: "This is indeed the will of my Father, that all who see the Son and believe in him may have eternal life; and I will raise them up on the last day" (cf. 2:23; 12:45; also 4:48; 6:36; 11:40; 11:45; 20:25–26).

The dialogue then shifts suddenly from singular to plural subjects: "*Our* ancestors worshiped . . . but *you* [plural] say . . ." No longer does the conversation concern one man and one woman; it encompasses their respective (and opposing) communities as well. For generations Jews and Samaritans have been at enmity over the location of the temple and their respective claims to be the true people of God: Jews at Jerusalem and Samaritans at Mount Gerizim. Now, in Jesus, their longstanding hostility is about to be undone: "The hour is coming when you [plural] will worship the Father neither on this mountain nor in Jerusalem" (v. 21). Instead of two opposing alternatives and the necessity of choosing between them, together with the intractable conflict that such choices engender, Jesus suggests that a future with him is a future of new possibilities.

The woman has progressed in her understanding of Jesus' true identity. In the beginning she knew only that he was a Jew, an outsider to her people and a man with whom she probably should not be talking (4:9). Now she recognizes him as one who speaks the things of God, who opens up a future she has never before imagined. There is still more for her to learn and know, but before the day is over, her own future and that of her townspeople will be forever changed.

AUDREY WEST

our religious commitment to see how we handle the issue. The sensitivity and sense of grace and love that are brought to the discourse can make all the difference in the outcome of such a relationship. Christians who feel that they need to lay down the law and set the issues straight, without any understanding of where the other person is coming from, may cause far more damage than good and even alienate the other from possible further engagement with the faith we intended to share by our words and actions.

Jesus takes the issue of religion raised by the woman in a different direction. He points toward a day when the things about which we generate controversy and division no longer have their power. Disputes about the right mountain will no longer be an issue, because the hour is coming, indeed is here, when God will be revealed beyond the restrictions and confines of any mountain. The true worshipers will not be the ones who have the national or religious pedigree, but the ones whose worship flows from sincerity of heart, from "spirit and truth." This will happen when God's saving work is revealed in the life, death, and resurrection of Jesus and in the sending of the Holy Spirit.

In our contemporary world, which is religiously pluralistic and full of tensions, prejudices, and persecution, the preacher may challenge the faithful to explore what Jesus' approach to the woman and her different religious perspective may have to say to us as we engage in multifaith relations and dialogue. There are no seeds here for the divisive conflict and radicalism that is evident among so many Christians and some persons of other faiths, a conflict that only causes harm and fails to bear witness to the God who calls us to worship together in spirit and truth.

HOWARD K. A. GREGORY

²²"You worship what you do not know; we worship what we know, for salvation is from the Jews.* ²³But the hour is coming, and is now here, when the true worshipers will worship the Father in spirit and truth, for the Father seeks such as these to worship him. ²⁴God is spirit, and those who worship him must worship in spirit and truth." ²⁵The woman said to him, "I know that Messiah is coming" (who is called Christ). "When he comes, he will proclaim all things to us." ²⁶Jesus said to her, "I am he, the one who is speaking to you."

²⁷Just then his disciples came. They were astonished that he was speaking with a woman, but no one said, "What do you want?" or, "Why are you speaking with her?" ²⁸Then the woman left her water jar and went back to the city. She said to the people, ²⁹"Come and see a man who told me everything I have ever done! He cannot be the Messiah, can he?" ³⁰They left the city and were on their way to him.

Theological Perspective

This final set of exchanges between the Samaritan woman and Jesus confirms the woman's share in the Spirit and displays the source of Wisdom and life she fosters within herself. Yet these verses also raise acute questions about Christian claims of universalism.

When the woman asks Jesus the one place for the worship of Israel's God, his reply first recalls the destruction of the temple of Gerizim and "predicts" the destruction of the Jerusalem temple (4:21). He then offers a remedy for these disastrous losses, one available now, even before the Jewish war: "The hour is coming and is now here" (v. 23). Worshiping in spirit the God who is Spirit not only repairs the loss of the holy places, but also heals the split between Samaritan and Jew, between Jerusalem and Gerizim: God seeks worshipers in spirit and truth (vv. 23–24). The holy places that once divided true worshipers are no more, but also are no longer needed.

So complete an answer to her query leads the woman to a new conclusion. The redeemer expected by the Samaritans was a revealer, a prophet like Moses. Knowing that this anointed one "will proclaim all things to us" (v. 25), she suggests what she has deduced from his responses, but does not ask, "Are you the Christ?" Even so, Jesus answers, "I am"

* See "'The Jews' in the Fourth Gospel" on pp. xi–xiv.

Pastoral Perspective

As much as things change, they seem to remain the same. In a casual observation of this text from John's Gospel it would not be hard to imagine that Jesus and the Samaritan woman are engaged in a worship-war conversation. Although they are not talking about types of music or the role of liturgy, the verses right before this passage signal a disagreement (common between Jews and Samaritans) about where appropriate worship happens. Is it this mountain or that mountain, drums or organs, praise bands or choirs? In John 4:21 Jesus shifts the conversation from these details of worship—the whats, whens, and hows—to the object of worship, "the Father." By naming who is to be worshiped, the conversation moves into a different direction.

Our passage picks up on this change in direction. As has happened throughout this encounter at the well, Jesus speaks in terms and language that carry meaning beyond the obvious. At some level his words connect the nature of worship to the character of God. In other words, worship is shaped by who God is and is to reflect God's nature. Jesus' final response to the woman, which features the language of God's name from Exodus 3, "I am he," sparks our recognition that worship is to reflect the character of Jesus. While this is not surprising, given the rest of John's Gospel, it invites a change in the nature of the

Exegetical Perspective

The conversation between Jesus and the Samaritan woman at the well reaches its climax in this third section of the dialogue. In response to the woman's tentative assertion (is she hoping against hope?) that a Messiah is coming, Jesus proclaims, "I am he" (v. 26). Despite her remaining questions, the woman returns to the city and invites her fellow Samaritans to "come and see" (v. 29).

This passage opens with a statement that appears to inflame first-century worship wars by pitting Samaritans against Jews: "You [plural] worship what you do not know; we worship what we know" (v. 22). For a moment, at least, readers are wrenched back to the woman's initial words, where she wondered aloud that a Jew would ask a Samaritan for a drink (4:9). Jesus' statement draws attention to the long-standing enmity between their two peoples.

The purpose of this statement, however, is not ultimately to divide, but rather to reunify these conflicted cousins-in-the-faith and to make them children of God through the person of Jesus. Parallel construction in the Greek (vv. 21 and 23) makes this clear. No longer will true worshipers be determined by geography—"in [*en*] Jerusalem" for the Jews, or "on [*en*] this mountain" for the Samaritans—but rather by their abiding in God, "in [*en*] spirit and truth." Already the Johannine Jesus has identified his

Homiletical Perspective

The temple and the sacred mountain, which the Samaritan woman had presented as religious barriers, no longer stand as issues. Now the woman pursues another tangent, the coming of the Messiah. Here, however, she raises an issue that establishes some common ground between herself as a Samaritan and Jesus as a Jew. She acknowledges that when the Messiah comes, all truth will be revealed. Remember, she has already been gracious enough to call Jesus a prophet, but at this point she is still unable to go any farther to identify Jesus the prophet with the Messiah. Her response to Jesus is, therefore, that, despite Jesus' demonstrations of prophetic insight and power, there is still one coming who will supersede him, the Messiah, who will reveal the ultimate truth. Hearing this, Jesus declares, "I am he!"

The moment of revelation and transformation has occurred. John portrays this moment of light dawning as a disclosure that leads the person to whom the revelation comes to do what seems incredible, if not irrational. Her reaction may be likened to the response of Peter in chapter 21. Although he is naked, when he realizes that Christ has been raised and is present in their midst, he puts on his clothes and jumps into the water to greet the risen Jesus. When the light dawns on this woman, she immediately abandons the purpose of her visit to the well. She finds a new

John 4:22–30

Theological Perspective

(v. 26), confessing to her what Peter confesses to Jesus in Mark 8:29.

At this dramatic juncture, the disciples return from their search for nourishment and wonder, without asking, what Jesus wants from the woman. The woman, on the other hand, has found all that she came for. She leaves behind her water jar, since she no longer is thirsty; nor does she need to come for water (4:15). Beginning the missionary harvest not yet understood by the disciples (4:31–39), she summons the people of her city and proclaims the messianic sign she has been given. "Come and see a man who told me everything I have ever done!" she says, and invites them to the conclusion she has drawn: this is the Christ (vv. 28–29). They respond, and go out to see what she has seen (v. 30).

The woman at the well has become a source of life for the Samaritans, a font of the Wisdom they also will possess (4:42). Living waters flow from her breast (7:37–39); she seems to enact the words of the sage:

> As for me, I was like a canal from a river,
>   like a water channel into a garden.
> I said, "I will water my garden
>   and drench my flower-beds."
> And lo, my canal became a river
>   and my river a sea. (Sir. 24:30–31)

So too in John's Gospel, the believer possesses and becomes a channel of the Spirit, bringing life to others and flowing to the great sea of wisdom.

So far this account has omitted verse 22, where Jesus castigates the Samaritans' ignorance of the One they worship, declaring, "Salvation is from the Jews." Its effect is highly ambiguous. On the one hand, this proclamation asserts Jesus' Jewish identity and offers a mild check to this Gospel's frequent and violent presentation of "the Jews" as the opponents—even the murderers—of Jesus.[1] On the other hand, dismissing Samaritan wisdom displays an early version of cultural chauvinism. As Christianity joined the empire, the idea of replacing the two contested and lost ancestral shrines with spiritual worship became a form of identity theft. "Universal" Christian missions too readily partnered with the "civilizing" imperial powers. In the long history of Christian missions in Africa, the universalizing proclamation that Jesus is the "savior of the world" (4:42) takes on an imperialist cast, and the charge that "you worship what you do not know" evokes older Christian

1. See Adele Reinhartz, "John," in *Searching the Scriptures 2: A Feminist Commentary*, ed. Elisabeth Schüssler Fiorenza with Shelley Matthews (New York: Crossroad, 1983), 595–97.

Pastoral Perspective

conversations that we continue to have about worship. Instead of asking questions about what is most enjoyable or attractive, or what makes us distinctive and unique when compared to the church down the way, this narrative welcomes questions about what is communicated in worship: does worship reflect the nature of God, the grace, forgiveness, and love experienced in Jesus Christ? Using language from earlier in this conversation, does worship pour forth the living Water that quenches thirst eternally? Is the focus so much on form that sight is lost of the God whom we worship and who shapes our very lives?

I once heard a pastor talk about a group of American cattle ranchers visiting their counterparts in Australia. The Australian ranchers toured their colleagues from across the sea around their ranches, showing them their operations. Finally, near the end of the day, one of the visitors said, "In America, we brand our cows and build fences, so that we can keep them separate and know whose is whose. Where are your fences?" One of their hosts proclaimed, "We don't build fences here. We dig wells." Jesus' conversation with the woman at the well about worship invites us to wonder if we have spent too much time on the fences in worship, instead of the well of living Water.

In continuing to look at this text through the lens of worship, we find that the direction of the conversation between the woman and Jesus may speak to another way of understanding the role of worship in our daily lives. Jesus continues to speak in language that is not completely understood by the woman until possibly his final words to her, "I am he, the one who is speaking to you." Instead of recording her direct response to Jesus, John turns our attention to the return of the disciples. Simultaneously, after Jesus' revelation of his identity, the woman leaves her water jar behind (perhaps an indication that she recognizes who Jesus is in part) and runs to tell those in the city to "come and see a man who told me everything I have ever done." Intriguingly, the narrative connects our worship of God with the revelation that Christ knows all about us.

Perhaps worship is, therefore, not only the place where we tell the truth about God and reflect God's nature, but also where we are told the truth about ourselves, where our lives are revealed. Each week different narratives, from the culture and Scripture, seek to write the script for the lives of the congregation. For example, consider the ways we talk about our lives that suggest that an individual's value and worth are directly related to that person's usefulness and productivity. These narratives suggest that we

own body with the temple of God (2:21). There is a contrast, then, between two types of temples: those that are located geographically, and the true temple that is the person of Jesus.

"The hour is coming, and is now here, when the true worshipers will worship the Father in spirit and truth. . . . God is spirit, and those who worship him must worship in spirit and truth" (vv. 23–24). The language here is allusive. As the Word made flesh, Jesus is "full of grace and truth" (1:14; cf. 1:17), and he is "the way, and the truth, and the life" (14:6). God, who is spirit (v. 24), will send another Counselor, the "Spirit of truth" (14:17; 15:26), who will "guide you into all the truth" (16:13; also 15:26–27). Further, this Spirit is associated with the gift of living water (7:38–39), which Jesus has just offered to the Samaritan woman (4:13–14; cf. 3:5). It is "a spring of water gushing up to eternal life" (4:14).

From the beginning of their conversation, the woman has progressed in her knowledge of the truth about Jesus. At first she knows only that Jesus is a stranger who boldly crosses sociocultural boundaries (4:9). (Readers should note that the woman acts boldly as well.) Jesus suggests that her knowledge is incomplete, as his mission goes beyond boundary crossing. "If you knew [oida] the gift of God, and who it is that is saying to you, 'Give me a drink,' you would have asked him, and he would have given you living water" (4:10). Although the woman does not fully comprehend his meaning, she dares to ask for this water (4:15). Moments later she sees (theōreō, "perceive") that he is a prophet (4:19). Certainly this is a step in the right direction, but Jesus points out that her knowledge is still deficient, for she and her people "worship what you do not know [oida]" (v. 22).

At this point the woman asserts something that she *does* know: an anointed one [Messias] is coming, who will proclaim all things (v. 25). Jesus validates her assertion and steps things up a notch by identifying himself as this anticipated Messiah (v. 26; cf. 20:31). His response, "I am he [egō eimi], the one who is speaking to you," is the first of several Johannine occurrences of "I am" (egō eimi), sometimes with a predicate nominative (e.g., "bread of life," 6:35; "light of the world," 8:12; "the gate for the sheep," 10:7; "the resurrection and the life," 11:25; "the way, and the truth, and the life," 14:6; "the true vine," 15:1) and other times, such as here, without (8:58; 13:19; 18:5). The phrase echoes the divine name found in the OT, for example, "God said to Moses, 'I am who I am' . . ." (Exod. 3:14, egō eimi, LXX; cf. Isa. 51:12).

orientation for her life and a new mission. She leaves her water jar and all the domestic demands that await the water and rushes back to the city.

In the joy of our encounters with God in Christ, the priorities of our life are likely to undergo drastic changes. The response may seem irrational to the onlooker and be dismissed without attributing any authenticity to the experience. The things to which we have given primacy of place may undergo dramatic change. The moment of transformation, while deeply personal, impacts our relationships as well. The revelation of Jesus Christ transforms and makes new a whole network of relationships between this woman and her community. She probably came to the well at midday so that she could avoid contact with the people of her community, but now she goes to fetch the same community so that they can meet Jesus.

Notice what she says to the people of her community: "He told me everything I have ever done" (v. 29). Jesus did no such thing! Yet when Jesus shines the light on our life, every corner and crack is illumined and everything that was in shadow seems to come to the fore. When we encounter Jesus, we cannot hide from the reality of our lives.

The woman never reports any word of judgment and condemnation to her community. The approach of Jesus affirms that making space for people to face their issues is far more liberating than calling down judgment upon them. There is also an important dimension of mission present in this story: the Christian experience of Jesus Christ cannot be a privatized experience. Our encounter with Christ may cause us, like the woman at the well, to experience a new sense of freedom and therefore to leave behind the water jar or other burdens of this life. She hurries to invite the whole community to come and share her experience and to ask her question, "Can he be the one [the Messiah]?" Apparently she has become infected with a spirit that makes it impossible for her not to leave her daily tasks behind and rush back to her village with a new purpose. As she steps back to her community, she is not thinking about the water jar she has left behind.

The woman's response to Jesus underscores what it means for the church to be a part of the *missio Dei*. In a world of individualism, it is so easy to see faith as a personal faculty that one nurtures in a private world. While the church can become preoccupied with itself, its membership, and its institutional well-being, in this story we see an example of what it means to be the bearer of the good news of God's salvation for the world.

John 4:22–30

Theological Perspective

assumptions that mission fields hold "darkness" and ignorance that can be remedied only by eradicating indigenous spiritual wisdom.

Musa Dube, a feminist and postcolonial interpreter from Botswana, has interrogated traditional readings of John 4:1–42.[2] She offers a decolonized rewriting by Mositi Totontle, a novelist of Botswana. In Totontle's reading, Jesus is replaced by a prophetess, Mother Mary Magdalene; the woman who comes to the well receives the name Mmapula. Mother Mary Magdalene affirms rather than denigrates Mmapula's ethnic identity and explains why Mmapula has no husband: her husband belongs to the South African mines. Unlike John's Jesus, the woman prophet both takes the drink she has asked of Mmapula and hands it back to her. The healing that Mother Mary Magdalene announces to the people of Mmapula's village finds its source in themselves.[3]

Totontle's rewriting embodies ways that privileged twenty-first-century Christians might reread this narrative in the interests of less lethal approaches to a universal mission for Christian faith. First, such a rereading would affirm Jesus' Jewish identity, while refusing to oppose it to that of the Samaritans, and so would restore dignity and identity to both the Samaritans and the Jews who are defamed or vilified in the Gospel. Similarly, it would conceive mission in reverse, as a call to go out and hear the word of God's wisdom in the intense, particular, and prophetic wisdom of all peoples, but especially of the impoverished. Such a reading would reject gender and sexual status as criteria for spiritual authority and would recognize the complex and painful relations of sexual arrangements to exploited labor. Like Totontle's women, who each take the drink the other offers, this reading would not allow spiritual thirst to obscure the desperate and growing need of so much of the world for clean and potable water.

Jesus' dialogue with the Samaritan woman at the well offers a true feast, affirming the promise of a drink of the Spirit that becomes a source in believers, leading the churches into truths they have not yet been able to bear (16:12–13). Any future Christian universalism must know that the Spirit comes from and goes where it will (3:8), as believers become channels into the great sea of Wisdom.

MARY R. D'ANGELO

Pastoral Perspective

are loved directly in proportion to how much we deserve to be loved. In contrast, each week in worship we encounter and are renarrated by the God who knows everything about us, whose nature is defined by love, and who loves us even knowing all that we have done. The gathered community in worship proclaims and is claimed by this deep truth of God's love, revealed in Jesus.

In the late seventies, I was a youth on a leadership team for a large youth retreat in our denomination. As people gathered for the retreat, they were given a sign to wear around their neck where the letters IALAC were written boldly. The letters were an acronym for "I am lovable and capable." During the day, if anything happened that made you feel less than loved or capable, you were supposed to tear off a piece of the sign. By the end of the evening, as we gathered in worship, most of us had battered and torn signs. As we worshiped and once again engaged God's truth about our lives, we were given another sign to face the next day, again with the letters IALAC written boldly. Worship not only reflected the nature of God, but also renarrated the story of our lives by the love of the One who knew everything about us and made us whole again.

For the Samaritan woman, the encounter with Jesus does not simply end at the well. She goes to the city and, using the language of witness that occurs throughout John's Gospel, invites the people of the city, "Come and see." Worship is not only an encounter with God that renarrates our lives, but one that also sends us out to invite others to come to the well and drink the living Water.

THOMAS W. WALKER

---

2. Musa W. Dube, "Reading for Decolonization (John 4:1–42)," *Semeia* 75 (1996): 37–59.
3. Mositi Totontle, *The Victims* (Gaborone: Botsalo, 1993), 72; based on Dube's citation and analysis.

Exegetical Perspective

When the disciples reappear on the scene (they had left earlier to go into town to buy food, 4:8), they are astonished that Jesus is speaking with a woman. They do not mention that she is a Samaritan, and they do not ask questions. Their initial silence contrasts with the woman's testimony to the people of her city: "Come and see" (v. 29; for the same phrase rendered using different vocabulary, see Jesus' invitation, 1:39).

Although some of Jesus' opponents (and perhaps John's earliest readers, as well) view Samaritans in a negative light (8:48), Jesus' encounter with the Samaritan woman challenges that view. Like the Samaritan leper who returned to give thanks for healing (Luke 17:11–19) or the traveler in Jesus' parable who offered aid to the man left for dead beside the road (Luke 10:29–37), the Samaritan woman in John becomes an exemplary character, a model of responsiveness to the revelation of Jesus. Although she still has doubts ("He cannot be the Messiah, can he?" [v. 29]—the Greek suggests that she anticipates a negative answer), her lingering question does not keep her from sharing what she has experienced.

Leaving behind her water jar (in her haste? or perhaps because *living water* needs no jar?), she returns to the city and testifies to the people about Jesus. The passage ends as they go out to meet him (v. 30). A few verses later the episode continues as the Samaritans of that city invite Jesus to abide with them (*menō*, 4:40; NRSV "stay"). Their experience serves as a narrative preview of Jesus' later words: "This is the Spirit of truth. . . . You know him, because he abides with you, and he will be in you" (14:17).

Due to the woman's boldness in continuing to speak with and listen to Jesus, and her testimony about him to her neighbors, readers of John's Gospel may recognize that the Samaritans of her city are to be numbered among "those who received him, who believed in his name," to whom he gives "power to become children of God" (1:12). Perhaps exegetes should call her the Johannine Good Samaritan.

AUDREY WEST

Homiletical Perspective

So many Christians offer excuses about why we cannot share the faith with others: "I do not know enough. I am new." Talk about new! This woman is as new as they come, but she has experienced something that is too good to contain within a little part of her private self called the heart. What a challenge to us who claim to have experienced Christ!

The return of the disciples and their discovery of Jesus in conversation with this woman at the well introduce a different focus. Their sense of surprise that Jesus is speaking with a woman, a Samaritan woman, is informative. Perhaps they are here expressing their cultural prejudices, even while trying to keep their concern to themselves. It may be that this is a moment of revelation for them too. They come to acknowledge once more the inclusiveness of the love and mission of Jesus, which will shape their own ministries later as they lead the church to cross all kinds of borders and boundaries.

At the same time, the response of the disciples may be one of concern for a tired and weary Jesus. Their concern about him and his food seems to suggest that there is no ill intent on the part of the disciples, but mostly caretaking and protection of Jesus. Christians also face the temptation to think we need to defend God from the assaults of people around us. Perhaps instead we need to step back and allow God to do God's work through Christ in the lives of people, albeit in ways that may break with our conventions and defy the ways we would choose.

HOWARD K. A. GREGORY

John 4:31–38

³¹Meanwhile the disciples were urging him, "Rabbi, eat something." ³²But he said to them, "I have food to eat that you do not know about." ³³So the disciples said to one another, "Surely no one has brought him something to eat?" ³⁴Jesus said to them, "My food is to do the will of him who sent me and to complete his work. ³⁵Do you not say, 'Four months more, then comes the harvest'? But I tell you, look around you, and see how the fields are ripe for harvesting. ³⁶The reaper is already receiving wages and is gathering fruit for eternal life, so that sower and reaper may rejoice together. ³⁷For here the saying holds true, 'One sows and another reaps.' ³⁸I sent you to reap that for which you did not labor. Others have labored, and you have entered into their labor."

Theological Perspective

In that great school playground that is the New Testament, the Gospel of John is the bespectacled and awkward kid who hardly ever got invited to play with the others and, instead, hovered around the teacher. Picture it: Matthew, Mark, and Luke are playing king of the narrative mountain on the theological jungle gym. The Pauline Epistles are arguing with the book of James about faith and works on the orthodoxy/orthopraxis seesaw. Hebrews and Revelation are trying to see how dizzy they can get on the eschatological merry-go-round. The Pastoral Epistles are arguing with the three John brothers about who has the bigger dad. Jude is by himself over by the fence doing, well, whatever it is that Jude does, while the Gospel of John is wandering around, watching the others (especially Matthew, Mark, and Luke) and humming a tune he sometimes seems to be making up as he goes.

Think about it: when the Gospels lined up, John was last. When the Revised Common Lectionary picked teams, all the Gospels got a year of their own except John. When they told their stories to each other, John could not seem to keep his narrative together: he interrupted his story of the Samaritan woman at the well from John 4:1–30, only to return to it in verses 39–42. Then when they picked their passages from the Scriptures to reinterpret, everyone

Pastoral Perspective

It is so easy to recognize ourselves in the disciples as they engage with Jesus in the dailiness of life and in routines as simple as eating lunch. We can almost taste the box lunch of falafel, pita, and hummus, but John is multitasking in this fourth chapter. We are mindful of the amazing drama unfolding just offstage as the Samaritan woman, now a witness for Jesus, is bringing the people of her village, old enemies of the Judean disciples, to meet this man who in her growing faith she imagines might be the Messiah. John invites us into this amazing enactment of Jesus' announcement that the time is no longer coming—it now is!—when God dwells everywhere among us, inviting all people, even our enemies, to life in its fullness.

The question is, will we notice and step into the possibilities? These eight verses are a kind of dramatic aid to help us "look around and see," as Jesus would say. How easily we might routinize our vocation over box lunches at the mission committee meeting and miss the larger drama of the life God's dwelling among us makes possible.

Jesus redirects an invitation to share lunch into a conversation about the linkage between identity and vocation—a linkage we baptized Christians have heard before. When we are welcomed into communities of faith with the sacrament of baptism, it

Exegetical Perspective

Literary Considerations. In this pericope Jesus teaches about divine nourishment and the ministry it sustains. The discussion takes place just after Jesus' conversation about living water with the Samaritan woman at Jacob's well (4:1–30) and just before the encounter with believers from Sychar (4:39–42). Narratively, this pericope marks time, giving those whom the woman has convinced of Jesus' greatness time to move from the city to the well. Earlier in the narrative, the disciples left Jesus at the well to go into the city and find food (4:8). They return (4:27) and immediately question Jesus' judgment in conversing with the woman, who leaves to recruit people from the city to come out to greet Jesus (4:28–30).

The disciples must have secured provisions, because they urge Jesus to eat something (v. 31). Jesus answers their urgings with a cryptic statement that he has food, literally meat (*brōsis*), of which they are not aware (v. 32). Like the woman's response to Jesus' assertion that he has water to give (4:10–11), the disciples assume that Jesus means someone else has brought him food. Jesus' explanation that his sustenance is to do the will of the one who sent him (v. 34) briefly draws on the same logic as his discussion of living water: Jesus is not concerned with material water and food.

Homiletical Perspective

The disciples are mystified. What is this food Jesus possesses unbeknownst to them? Jesus lives, he says, not to eat, not to satisfy his own needs, but to do God's will and to complete it. Can they see the grand picture of what Jesus is about? Do they understand that they are a part of something much greater than themselves? He invites them to enter into this grand work with urgency.

There is a story told about a basketball coach. One day early in practice, he made the whole team lie down on the gym floor and close their eyes. "Just imagine exactly what it is like to win the championship," he told them. "See it. Feel it. Hear the sounds." One of the players said, "This is a waste of time." The coach responded, "If you cannot imagine winning a championship, you cannot win it."

When Jesus says, "My food is to do the will of him who sent me and to complete his work," he is urging the disciples to envision God's will fulfilled and to understand that it is so in him. He is helping them to understand their ministry with him as helping to bring that fulfillment now. They may believe they are just beginning to plant seeds. Jesus wants them to see that it is harvest time. What they add to the effort is important.

In a basketball game every point counts, but that basket that wins the game in the last second takes

Theological Perspective

else picked *texts* to reinterpret—stuff like "a voice cries in the wilderness," "make a way for the Lord," or "You shall love the Lord your God with all your heart, and with all your soul, and with all your mind." John? John picked *images*, like the serpents in the wilderness from Numbers 21 (3:14) or this passage's harvest imagery from Isaiah 27 and Joel 3, in order to give Jesus the chance to answer a question that nobody is actually asking him. John is, euphemistically, "an unusual boy."

Like many a bespectacled and awkward kid, though, John is also a deep and deliberate thinker. When he interrupts one story to tell another, he has reasons. When he chooses his images, he has reasons. When John's Jesus answers questions that nobody has asked, he has reasons. John 4:31–38 is reason filled, even if not all those reasons are readily apparent.

Take the interruption. Certainly one of the rhetorical purposes for situating Jesus' conversation with the disciples about food between the people leaving the Samaritan city in verse 30 and arriving in verse 40 is to build suspense: what will the people say and do when they meet Jesus? (The answer is given in v. 41.) Verses 31–38 provide—both literally and literarily—traveling time.

Yet situating verses 31–38 where he does serves other purposes. It lets John draw parallels between the woman at the well who misunderstands Jesus' claims about water (vv. 7–15) and the disciples' misunderstanding Jesus' claims about food. Indeed, the disciples reveal themselves to be more foolish than the woman, as the text never suggests they understand Jesus' statement, let alone connect his claims to their own lives. It lets John bring the disciples back onto the scene after they have apparently completed the food-finding task they began in verse 8; in doing this, John underlines the connection between work and reward that Jesus develops in verse 34 and following: "My food is to do . . . [God's] work." The disciples work to find food for living; Jesus' work is food for life. Centrally, it loads those two most basic of human activities—eating and drinking—with salvific import. If, in Jesus' presence, even these activities are full of saving power, then surely nothing in ordinary human existence is beyond the transformative power of God.

All this suggests a possible reason as to why John's Jesus reinterprets the Old Testament images as he does. Though sowing and harvesting images are plentiful in both testaments, John pushes them into each other and disrupts the anticipated ordering

Pastoral Perspective

is as disciples who will bear witness to the love that calls us into being and names us as God's own. We then spend the rest of our lives living into this vocation—deepening our understanding of the grace that marks this gift and the possibilities into which the Spirit invites us.

This story about a brief stop for lunch by Jacob's well is an invitation to reconsider our own vocations and the practice of looking around and seeing as Jesus sees. The disciples and Jesus are taking the most direct route to Galilee through Samaria, a land occupied by a people who share a mutual enmity with Judeans, already generations old by the time this event takes place. Perhaps we can identify with the disciples who simply want to move on through to their destination point, avoid contamination, and resume their ministry in Galilee among their own kind. Surely these Samaritans are not people to whom their God would call them to minister. Moments before the disciples arrive with lunch, we, of course, overhear Jesus describe a God not confined to either Jerusalem or Samaria, but now present everywhere in spirit and truth.

John invites us to consider how our imaginations about God's love may be too narrow to embrace opportunities to bear witness or to receive the witness of those whom God also loves but we do not. Samaria is not simply a shortcut for Jesus; it provides an opportunity to bear witness to the breadth of God's love to disciples and Samaritans alike. The enmity between the Judeans and the Samaritans was deep and harsh and sometimes violent, though their ancestry shared the witness of the patriarchs. This drama plays out, after all, at Jacob's well.

In his award-winning book *The Dignity of Difference*, Jonathan Sacks, chief rabbi of London, wrote that the most important challenge facing our time is learning to see the face of God in those who do not look like us.[1] We hear echoes of Isaiah reminding us that God's ways are not our ways (Isa. 55:8), and we can imagine Peter horrified at the thought of eating food that was unclean, only to find himself taking a deep breath and going in to baptize Cornelius and his family (Acts 10). We were not baptized to bear witness only to those whom we think God loves and whom we love or pity.

What Rabbi Sacks names and what Jesus invites the disciples and us "to look around you and see" (v. 35) is the breadth of God's love already at work well beyond boundaries comfortable for us. Both

1. Jonathan Sacks, *The Dignity of Difference: How to Avoid the Clash of Civilizations* (London, New York: Continuum, 2002).

This exchange also continues the trope that the disciples, while well-meaning, do not understand Jesus' ministry with the same sophistication as the implied reader. In other words, the characterization of both the disciples and the woman highlight for the reader a sense of his or her own spiritual maturity. By recognizing that Jesus provides living water and nourishes himself with the Father's work, the reader identifies herself or himself as a more enlightened follower than even the disciples. John's readers know that Jesus is food and drink for spiritual life!

This discussion of food prepares readers for the challenge that Jesus issues in the next few verses, as the writer connects the meat that is the work of the Father's will to an imminent grain harvest (vv. 35–38), extending the metaphor further. Jesus paints a vivid picture of agrarian life: those connected with agriculture sow seeds, tend their early growth, and then watch with a discerning eye for the optimal harvest time. The Greek word that the NRSV translates "ripe" is literally "white" (*leukos*); green fields of grain turn a golden yellow or near white color when they are ready for harvest.

Jesus' explanation of this harvest imagery takes a commodified turn when he suggests that the harvester is already drawing wages from the fields, even fields that one did not plant. Jesus' explanation in verse 38 that he sends the disciples to reap that for which they did not labor raises questions about how to parse the theological, historical, and political referents in the metaphor of sowers and reapers. Verse 37 vaguely references a division of labor between sowers and harvesters—a division that verse 36 suggests is cause for mutual rejoicing—yet the narrative does not parse out who did the sowing and who harvests, let alone in which fields the sowers are sowing and the harvesters are reaping.

Sociopolitical Interpretive Frameworks. In the sociopolitical context of first-century-CE Roman Palestine (where factions are drawn along lines created by both Roman imperial power and imperial regimes from centuries previous) the Samaritans were not the most likely group for a visit from Jesus. John, the Gospel writer, also makes it clear that in his factional politics—which are geographically removed and five to six decades later than the time period in the narrative itself—the Samaritans are not the most likely group to recognize Jesus as Messiah. Some commentators suggest that in this sociopolitical context Jesus sends the disciples to harvest among even the most despised of peoples. Thus the harvest imagery

on particular meaning. Jesus is inviting the disciples, and therefore us, to see our discipleship as part of the final act of the emerging reign of God. Every act of kindness matters especially now. The reign of God is at hand, and we are part of it.

For Jesus, the goal right before them is to complete the work that God has begun in him. If the disciples can see the fulfillment as he does, they can participate fully with energy and focus appropriate to the outcome at hand.

Jesus is excited about the possibilities—too excited to eat. His motivation comes from envisioning the completion of God's work. He seems to be saying, "I cannot think about food at a time like this! There is work to be done!"

Do you ever forget to eat? What would it be like to be that excited about being part of God's work in the world?

Sometimes the immediate needs of congregants, or the demands of an aging building, or the mere survival of a congregation, become dominant in a congregation's (or pastor's) mind—like the disciples wondering where the next meal will come from. Instead, Jesus represents a bolder view of mission that involves completing God's work in the world. Jesus does not expect bold vision to belong to the faraway future. He urges his followers to join in creating that future already in our midst.

What would your community look like if God's will were more fully realized right now in you? How might God's reign be visible already in you and your congregation? What mission has God given to the particular group of people that gathers with you for weekly worship? Where do the needs of the community and the passions and skills of the congregation dovetail for good? How big are you thinking? How far down the road are you imagining?

Perhaps your congregation has already begun looking beyond your own immediate need. You see that the fields are indeed "ripe with harvest." Your challenge might be that you are overwhelmed by the extent of the need. It is hard to know how to get started. John helps by focusing our attention on Jesus himself, on recognizing him as the one sent from God, who represents God, who is the word of God. Just as God's work is food and drink to Jesus, so Jesus is food and drink to us. In John's Gospel, Jesus sums up God's will with the simplest of all commands: love one another. Completing God's work will involve demonstrating self-giving love for one another in the church and outside the church in the wider community, just as Jesus did. Though the

John 4:31–38

Theological Perspective

of the work. Sower and reaper rejoice together and seemingly do their work at the same time, rather than separated by months of growing/tending/pruning time.

Other Gospels offer a vision of time in which a sequential series of events leads, eventually, to salvation (i.e., first birth, then life, then death on a cross, then burial, then resurrection). In so doing, they imagine time as what comes before eternity and the eschaton as something still to come that will replace history and ought to be eagerly anticipated—especially by those who find themselves on the underside of history.

John, though, mashes the eternal into the temporal: wherever Jesus is and whatever he is doing, eternity is already present. Contra British historian Arthur Toynbee, history is not just one damned thing after another; it is the house in which eternity resides. The eschaton is not something still to come, so much as something already around us. The very fields that are being sown are already ripe for harvesting.

This vision of the relationship between time and eternity transforms the way Christians engage the world. Rather than squinting into the future, hoping for glimpses of a kingdom to come, we learn to observe the kingdom already in place: apocalyptic vision, more than prophetic clairvoyance, becomes the most basic way Christians see the world. Rather than dreaming of what is not, we celebrate what really is: gratitude, more than hope, motivates Christian action. Rather than anticipating an end to come, we attend to the end that is already here: purposeful work, more than patient waiting, shapes the fundamental virtues of Christian life. These are the answers of the Johannine Jesus to questions not being asked.

This way of thinking about the relationship between time and eternity has both strengths and weaknesses. As a strength, it encourages us to imagine a world in which God is already sovereign. As a weakness, it can encourage either a kind of placidness that does not take injustice seriously or a kind of arrogance that assumes that we know more—and can therefore do more—than other people. It is good to have an unusual boy like John around—and also good that he is not the only kid on the school playground.

MARK DOUGLAS

Pastoral Perspective

the Samaritan woman and the disciples who return with lunch to find Jesus talking to her are astonished when Jesus engages her in conversation because he is transgressing ethnic, religious, and gender codes meant to divide and demean.

Such codes remain entrenched in religious institutions, governments, and cultures. Religious extremists in each of the world's major religions have perpetrated violence in the name of religions that espouse peace, compassion, and justice. Epidemic levels of violence against women and children continue in families and countries shaped by each of the world's religions, including the United States. Religious institutions, governments, and businesses are deeply insinuated by patterns of racial and ethnic bias with clear material and emotional consequences.

"Look around you, and see," Jesus says (v. 35). Everywhere the fields are ripe for harvesting—not later but now. The human community is ripe with longing for love that honors the human dignity of each person and offers generosity and grace and freedom from the hierarchies that divide and demean human communities. This harvest is possible, not due to the work of these disciples, but because of the longing for love the Spirit has sown in human hearts—including theirs and the hearts of the Samaritan villagers who are about to reenter the scene at Jacob's well. Even more challenging, this immediate "harvest" is sown not by them but by a Samaritan woman who experiences in Jesus someone who takes her seriously and offers her hope that is real.

When we look around and see through Jesus' eyes, who is rounding the bend that does not look like us? How might we open our hearts to receive the gift of relationship with them as persons whom God also loves and in whom we will be invited to see the face of God?

NANCY J. RAMSAY

Exegetical Perspective

becomes a missional directive to the disciples that the "harvest" in Samaria is ripe for recognizing Jesus.

With this directive Jesus' ministry transgresses the geopolitical and religious boundaries of Judea and Galilee.[1] In other words Jesus' ministry extends to the ends of the earth, and even the most despised heretics are included and welcomed as followers of Jesus the Messiah. Jesus' work, labor, and toil come to fruition in the "harvest" of faithful followers, regardless of geopolitical, social, and religious boundaries. The disciples reap the reward of Jesus' labor.

Other commentators caution that this kind of missional impulse trades on colonial structures of power that require the Samaritans to dissociate with their cultural, political, and social customs in favor of a foreign, yet more powerful set. Thus, as outsiders to Samaria who claim that salvation comes from their Judean/Jewish lineage (4:22), the disciples devalue Samaritan subjectivity. Jesus and the disciples talk about the Samaritans without including them in the discussion of their future, even if that future is following Jesus. It is as if the Samaritans were commodities for harvest, rather than partners in ministry. Thus our interpretive focus should shift to the Samaritan woman's work as a prophet and teacher among her own people, as one who brings good news in her own idiom and using her own resources.[2]

Seen in this postcolonial framework, Jesus' commentary on the labor of sowing and tending fields highlights the faith of the Samaritan woman, whose labor among her friends brings them out to greet Jesus. She preaches and teaches about Jesus while the disciples wait for the harvest to come to them (as it will in 4:39–42). Of course, such an interpretation also raises questions for contemporary Christians about the value and recognition of women's evangelistic work. What kinds of work do church leaders claim for themselves? How might we see those who labor but who are often unseen in our institutional structures?

Summary. As Jesus discusses the food of God's will and the harvest that creates such food, interpreters must attend to our geopolitical frameworks within the text. Placing the Samaritan woman at the heart of the harvesting metaphor honors her work as disciple, preacher, and teacher.

KATHERINE A. SHANER

1. Craig R. Koester, "The savior of the world (John 4:42)," *Journal of Biblical Literature* 109 (1990): 665–80.
2. Musa W. Dube, "Reading for Decolonization (John 4:1–42)," *Semeia* 75 (1996): 37–59.

Homiletical Perspective

mission of completion may seem overwhelming, it is Jesus who completes. Our focus is on the part of it we can do, knowing that there are other workers as well.

Sometimes we struggle to act on God's will, because we carry in our heads an abstract concept of Jesus that has no power to move us. We love the idea of Jesus, but we have yet to enter into a real relationship with a present Christ. Yet just as the disciples served a living leader, so we meet the living Christ face to face at the Lord's Table. There we are fed. There we hear Christ's call to extend God's love to the community at large. At the Table with Jesus we look at the world and see it through God's eyes with all God's children gathered and whole. We are renewed and ready to take our part.

The disciples in this story are distracted by the physical needs of the moment. Jesus, by contrast, is focused on a compelling view of the fulfillment of God's work. He is committed to completing what has been started. He sees many who could help now if they can only grasp the nature of the challenge.

This passage invites us to turn our eyes toward the harvest at the ready, just outside our churches. It calls us to notice the hunger for God's love as Jesus presents it to us. In presenting the challenge he also encourages us with good news. The results of God's love are already visible. The fields are ripe for harvesting. Many are ready to know the word of God in Jesus as his followers speak it and act it out.

It is a team effort: some sow, others reap. Now is reaping time: time to set aside personal needs and focus on the readiness of the community to receive the word that God is love; to understand God's love through the story of Jesus, made real through the witness of his followers.

SHARON WATKINS

John 4:39–42

[39]Many Samaritans from that city believed in him because of the woman's testimony, "He told me everything I have ever done." [40]So when the Samaritans came to him, they asked him to stay with them; and he stayed there two days. [41]And many more believed because of his word. [42]They said to the woman, "It is no longer because of what you said that we believe, for we have heard for ourselves, and we know that this is truly the Savior of the world."

Theological Perspective

What does an evangelist look like? In the book of John—itself a peculiarly evangelical text—it looks like a shunned, serially married, uppity Samaritan woman whose midday project of drawing water from a well outside of town is disrupted because of an odd conversation with an even odder stranger. Rather than a smooth-talking, socially accepted, well-connected man, John presents as evangelist a vaguely combative, socially rejected woman with too many marital connections from her past and all the wrong tribal connections in the present.

Sharing her own brief testimony about a recent conversation, she succeeds beyond all previous Johannine measures. Offering a narrative about Jesus, she persuades good parts of her town to come and meet Jesus. In earlier evangelical moments in the Gospel, the invitation to come and see either induces curiosity (1:45–46) or lacks a mediating presence (2:23). In John 4, a woman about whom Jesus seems to know everything, but for whom we do not even have a name, shares a story so compelling that "many Samaritans from that city believed in him because of the woman's testimony" (v. 39).

What could make her testimony so compelling? Could they actually see a shift in her tenor or presence that compelled them to believe what she said about a man they still had not met? Perhaps. After

Pastoral Perspective

In this passage John continues to build the dramatic power shaping the fourth chapter as he invites us to imagine breathtaking transgressions against long-standing codes of behavior and the Roman Empire that shape the drama. This passage bespeaks a truly transformative experience for the Samaritan villagers. In response to the witness of a woman who is one of them, they come to see and listen to Jesus for themselves. They hear enough to ask Jesus to stay with them. After two days, the villagers turn their world upside down as they make this astonishing assertion about Jesus: "This is truly the Savior of the world" (v. 42). The Samaritan people had experienced a succession of five colonial powers and now were enduring life under Roman occupation. With the power of an adverb, "truly," they make it clear that they find in Jesus one whose power is trustworthy and beyond the scope of Roman authorities such as Caesar, who claimed the same title, "savior of the world," for himself.[1]

Perhaps this story unfolds further what John means in the first chapter of his Gospel when he lifts up the amazing fact of God's incarnation: "the Word became flesh and lived among us. . . . From his fullness we have all received, grace upon grace

1. Warren Carter, *John and Empire: Initial Explorations* (London and New York: T. & T. Clark, 2008), 188–91.

Exegetical Perspective

These verses form the conclusion of the story of Jesus' encounter with the Samaritan woman at Jacob's well near Sychar (4:5–30). At the end of their conversation, the woman leaves Jesus to go into the town and tell others about the remarkable person at the well (4:28). She suggests to those who will listen that he might be the Messiah (4:29). Meanwhile, the disciples and Jesus discuss the work of gathering followers with harvest imagery (4:31–38). As the pericope opens, we hear that the woman has been quite successful in her efforts to gain followers (v. 39). In fact, she is so successful that a group forms to come out to the well, greet Jesus, and ask him to stay for some days (v. 40).

This invitation can be understood both in the context of everyday hospitality expectations in first-century regional practices and in the context of civic rituals for greeting Roman imperial visitors.[1] In ancient literature, strangers traveling through unknown lands would often seek hospitable accommodations at the local water source when first coming to town (see Gen. 18:1–16; 1 Kgs. 17:8–24). These travelers in the first century often found themselves tired, hot, dusty, hungry, and thirsty, especially when traveling in the midday sun—thus Jesus' need

1. Andrew E. Arterbury, "Breaking the Betrothal Bonds: Hospitality in John 4," *Catholic Biblical Quarterly* 72 (2010): 63–83.

Homiletical Perspective

There are several jumping-off points for the preacher in this short text. It concludes the "woman at the well" story from earlier in the chapter. The woman's testimony can be where the sermon begins: "He told me everything I have ever done" (v. 39b). That Jesus talks to her at all is of note. She is drawing water at an unusual time of day. We assume this is because of her inappropriate living situation with a man to whom she is not married. Most people would not socialize with her. Jesus—a man and a person of a different nationality—was even less likely to engage her. Yet he does. It is astonishing that he would engage in conversation with her. More surprising still, even though Jesus has never met her, he can see straight through her. He seems to be a prophet or seer.

Her testimony, therefore, says something about who she is and who Jesus is: "He told me everything I have ever done." She has struggled in life. It is possible that she has made some bad decisions, possible that life has presented her with few good options. In any case, Jesus knows her situation—and spends time with her. Jesus knows her—and still cares about her. He not only has the knowledge of a prophet; we can imagine that he brings a life-changing affirmation to one who has been left out and shunned.

In congregations where this passage is preached, people may identify with the woman in ways known

John 4:39–42

all, radical transformations are more obvious than subtle ones, and everyone loves stories of a reformed sinner. Did her very marginalization give her the courage—or even the permission—to speak about Jesus in such persuasive ways? Perhaps. After all, she had less to lose than the socially upright and politically connected members of the community. Were her storytelling abilities that good? Perhaps. After all, she had demonstrated herself as an able and subtle interlocutor with Jesus at the well. Yet the text does not name her personal transformation, her social location, or her rhetorical gifts as reasons for her evangelical effectiveness.

It may be that this is part of John's point: to give reasons for the effectiveness of the Samaritan woman's testimony is to risk turning a story into a how-to manual for evangelism. The only thing we know she told the town is, "He told me everything I have ever done" (v. 39). Her words are hardly generalizable for others to use: "Come meet a man who knew everything about that woman over there."

As if to reinforce this point, John eventually gives the townspeople their own voice: "It is no longer because of what you said that we believe, for we have heard for ourselves" (v. 42). Here, then, may be part of John's understanding of evangelism:

- Because it is about a person, it cannot be thought of in terms of a particular body of information that, once shared, will result in faith. Evangelical testimony can serve only as a ready example for others who are developing their own way of speaking about their relationship with Christ. Evangelism in John is *personal*.
- Because evangelism is an expression of relationship, it treats time as a gift in which those relationships can blossom ("they asked him to stay with them; and he stayed there two days," v. 40), rather than an obstacle to overcome or a threat to counter before it is too late. Evangelism allows others to live with God as their lives unfold at their own pace. Evangelism in John is *patient*.
- Because evangelism is so oriented around the words of "the Savior of the world," it need not be constrained to a particular set of ritually spoken human words about that Savior. Evangelical language reveals its fruits in the first-person stories of others even more than the third-person creedal statements of the believing community. Evangelism in John is *testimony*.

Unsurprisingly, John's approach to evangelism meshes well with his encompassing theological

. . . grace and truth" (1:14a, 16, 17b). Clearly relationship with this Jesus creates unprecedented and unimagined possibilities. It would be easy for us to miss the way the entire scene of the Samaritan woman bearing witness to her village would leave first-century readers (and the Judean disciples) beyond amazement.

Her witness parallels that of John the Baptist in its effectiveness, for, as with him, the people respond to her invitation and in turn come to believe.[2] The Gospel writer sweeps aside formerly unquestioned religious and gender codes in the simple description of her witness. How might we make sense of this in our own contexts? Are there individuals or social groups whose witness would be unimaginable to us? If rules as certain as purity codes and gender norms lose their power to divide and subordinate one to another in the human community God intends, what does this mean for our own abilities to witness? It appears that the Samaritan woman's experience with Jesus is so profound she overcomes her initial incredulity at the encounter Jesus initiates. Are there religious and cultural barriers that limit our relationship to this embodied presence of God?

Beyond such codes for behavior and relationships, what does it mean that this scene takes place in Samaria, the context of long-standing religious and ethnic enmity between Judeans and Samaritans? We know from the parable of the Good Samaritan in Luke's Gospel (Luke 10:29–37) that Jesus has also used this deep enmity as a foil to disclose the power of God's love. This parable of unprompted and generous compassion challenged the smug presumption of religious superiority among the Judean elites. This time we see Jesus choose to go through Samaria not simply because it is the shortest route but because bearing witness to God's love is what he is called to do. Precisely in such a place as Samaria he discloses the unimaginably universal scope of God's love that judges every pretense of privilege we humans create.

Both the Judean disciples looking on and the Samaritans who are equally sure of their biases are caught up short by this dramatic enactment of Jesus' claim to the woman at the well (4:21–24) that "the time has come and now is" when old assumptions about revelation are pushed aside. God's love is wider than the imaginations of either group. Instead, God's Spirit works wherever it is able to create possibilities for God's love to be received.

---

2. Gail O'Day, "Gospel of John," in *Women's Bible Commentary*, 3rd ed. rev. and updated, ed. Carol Newsom, Sharon Ringe, and Jacqueline Lapsley (Louisville, KY: Westminster John Knox Press, 2012), 522.

of food and water (4:10, 31). Such travelers often found refuge with kind strangers, who offered them drink, a meal, and shelter. Frequently travelers were urged to stay a few days and rest. The Samaritans, in keeping with these customs, offer this same hospitality to Jesus (v. 40). In the Synoptic Gospels and Acts, the disciples' ministry depends on this system of hosting traveling strangers (see Matt. 10:5–42; Mark 6:10–11; Luke 9:1–6; 10:1–18; Acts 16:14–15).

This pericope also draws on another hospitality practice from the first century CE, namely, receiving and welcoming a visiting ruler. Josephus relates that during the Jewish revolt in the late 60s CE, when Vespasian arrived in Tiberias, the population of the town went out to meet him before he reached the city gates.[2] They then escorted this imperial visitor into the city. John surely knows of this practice as well and plays on it in crafting his narrative as a way of pointing out Jesus' royal, messianic stature.

Another way that John draws on imperial imagery comes at the end of the pericope. John reports that at the end of Jesus' stay in Sychar, many more had heard his words and believed, calling him the "Savior of the world" (ho sōtēr tou kosmou, v. 42). While modern readers hear the phrase as a christological title for Jesus, the phrase was relatively common in the ancient world. For example, Philo uses the exact phrase as a characteristic of God (*Spec. Laws* 2, 198). The title "savior" describes deities in antiquity (e.g., Zeus, Isis, Asklepios).

Additionally, the phrase is often associated with Roman emperors in the first two centuries CE. Inscriptions from the region around ancient Samaria name Roman emperors from Augustus to Hadrian as "savior and benefactor of the whole world" (*ho pantos kosmou sōtēr kai euergetēs*).[3] The Samaritans' designation of Jesus as "Savior of the world" underscores the honor, respect, and power ascribed to Jesus. He is divine. He is imperial in stature. John's use of this imperial title certainly emphasizes Jesus' importance and gives his readers a way to understand Jesus' power. Of course, the title also gives John's readers a sense of subversion, in that Jesus, the one whose power is not recognized on the political landscape of the first century, is the true imperial power of the cosmos (*tou kosmou*).

and unknown to the preacher. It is certain that people carry pain and embarrassment from poor decisions. Others may feel bound by limiting situations. We, like the woman, can be assured that Christ knows us and loves us nonetheless.

Furthermore, the woman at the well is transformed by her encounter with Jesus. From the solitary figure drawing water, she becomes the one who runs into town telling everyone she meets about the life-changing encounter with one who knows her, yet values her. Such transformation is possible for us, as well.

The interplay between the woman's testimony about Jesus and Jesus' own words about himself also provides homiletical substance. Having been introduced to Jesus by the woman, the people respond. They believe, the passage says. However, they do not let the relationship stop there. They invite Jesus to stay, so they can get to know him on their own. Now they believe "because of his word" (v. 41). While the people of Galilee and Judea—Jesus' own people—will require "signs and wonders," the Samaritans take Jesus at his word.

The experience described here is different from what we can experience in the twenty-first century. After hearing the testimony of the woman, the Samaritans had the opportunity to learn directly from the words of Jesus himself. Their face-to-face experience with Jesus validated what the woman had said. For us there is not the physical face-to-face validation. For us the "word" of Jesus has to take on life and validity in a different way. The sermon may become the opportunity to explore how Jesus comes alive for us today.

How do we go from the belief passed on by others to incorporating belief truly into our lives? Jesus may come alive for people today through the reality of the gospel the church shows forth as the body of Christ. What are the tangible ways in your community that people, through interaction with the church, can come to know the living Christ?

The theme of meeting the living Christ face to face also provides an opportunity to explore with members of the congregation how their spiritual life may bring them into closer relationship with Christ. This is a chance to explore the powerful experience of listening for the word of God through prayer or by dwelling in Scripture or by meeting the living Christ face to face at the baptismal font or the Table. Jesus' words can speak to us just as powerfully as they did to the Samaritans during Jesus' earthly life.

Finally, we find in the Samaritans' witness material for preaching. In the biblical context, the

---

2. Josephus, *J.W.* 3.9.8§459. For more on the trope of imperial visitors, see Helmut Koester, "Imperial Ideology and Paul's Eschatology in 1 Thessalonians," in *Paul and Empire: Religion and Power in Roman Imperial Society*, ed. Richard A. Horsley (Harrisburg, PA: Trinity International, 1997), 158–66.

3. For a more extensive list of "savior" titles used for Roman emperors in inscriptions, see Craig R. Koester, "The savior of the world (John 4:42)," *Journal of Biblical Literature* 109 (1990): 665–80, at 667.

John 4:39–42

Theological Perspective

vision. It is a character-centered set of narratives in which *kairos* and *chronos* time are blurred and in which Jesus spends more time talking about himself and the relationships he is in—with God, with the disciples, and with the world—than he does about the kingdom of God, the demands of love and justice, or the shape of the community of faith.

However, this hardly settles things. After all, just two chapters earlier, John was quite clear: "But Jesus on his part would not entrust himself to them, because he knew all people and needed no one to testify about anyone; for he himself knew what was in everyone" (2:24–25). How could it be that John would seemingly forget something he had written so recently such that, by chapter 4, Jesus was relying on the woman at the well, entrusting himself to a Samaritan village for days, and letting the townspeople develop their own testimonies about him?

This question gets to the crux of a theological tension within John and for the early church: how to name the incarnate and crucified one as both sovereign (and thus in no need of support from any others) and human (and thus relational and vulnerable to others). John addresses this tension uniquely, by so emphasizing both sides that they are joined into each other. John's Jesus is so sovereign that even the crucifixion is an expression of divine glory: he does not even need support in his otherwise horrific death. At the same time, John's Jesus is so human that he will ask for water from a Samaritan woman with a bad reputation because he is thirsty (an act, incidentally, that foreshadows his last request from the cross in 19:28). This sovereign, John suggests, is fundamentally relational.

All of which helps make sense of John's evangelical sensibility. Testimony about Jesus (of the very sort that John shares throughout his Gospel) is about neither Jesus' need for a witness (though we may need to share our witness) nor our need to gain some good from him (though we do gain great goods). Instead, it is an organic outgrowth of our relationship with this intrinsically relational sovereign. Like the Samaritan woman, we have stories to tell. Like the Samaritan villagers, we believe because Jesus, himself, has entered our own stories.

MARK DOUGLAS

Pastoral Perspective

Try to imagine the experience of the disciples, who wanted to get through Samaria as quickly as possible, having as little contact as possible with these "unclean" people. Now they find themselves living among the Samaritan villagers as guests and witnessing how God is at work in them. In this experience, of course, God's Spirit was not only opening the hearts of the Samaritans. God's Spirit was transforming the enmity and suspicion deep in the hearts of the disciples, who had grown up knowing they wanted to avoid contaminating themselves with these heretics. Surely John invites us to "stay with Jesus" and open our lives to this transformative power of God's love. For example, what if a suburban congregation enters into covenant with an urban congregation to resist the burden of racial and class marginalization. Together the congregations seek an opportunity to experience God's power in shared witness that resists the barriers that ordinarily divide us.

John concludes this scene in the dramatic fourth chapter with a startling acclamation by the Samaritans about Jesus, "This is truly the Savior of the world." (v. 42) It is a celebration of Jesus' witness to a universal worshiping community that bears witness to God's love because it is no longer confined to the codes and privileges of the Judean community. At the same time, this acclamation is a rejection of Rome's claims to its imperial authority over them. Caesar and others may claim this title, but the world they intend pales in comparison to the power of the creator of the world to which the Samaritans refer.[3] Surely John invites us to imagine making this acclamation our own. Our privileged location in the United States among the world's Christian communions situates us more closely with the disciples in this scene, who begin to realize that the privileged position they have presumed is now shared with all people. Similarly, the power of empire in the background of this story invites us to consider how living within the authority of the U.S. government shapes our expectations about God's saving power.

NANCY J. RAMSAY

3. Carter, *John and Empire*, 190–91.

Exegetical Perspective

Some modern readers, however, ask whether imperial power, even the subversive version of it, describes our own conceptions of power rather than Jesus'. This question arises when we foreground the most vulnerable person in the story, the Samaritan woman. John says that the crowd comes out to the well to greet Jesus because of the woman's testimony (v. 39). From what John reports of her teaching, she has characterized Jesus as clairvoyant, a kind of fortune-telling Messiah. After Jesus stays with the Samaritans for a couple of days, they declare to her that they believe Jesus because of their own encounter instead of her chatter (*lalia*, v. 42). The Greek word for "chatter," *lalia*, signifies that the woman's words are silly words, a kind of idle loquacity verging on tale-telling. In addition, John's story notes that Jesus' new followers only *believed* (*pisteuō*) the woman's silly words. After hearing Jesus in person, they *know* (*oida*) he is the Savior. This vocabulary shift signals a profound change in certainty. The fact that the woman engenders only belief dismisses the work she did before Jesus' arrival. She fades into the background, not as an evangelist or a preacher or teacher, but as a chatty woman with a questionable past.

In the conclusion of this story John chooses to highlight Jesus' subversive messianic power that crosses geopolitical boundaries, yet part of the story discredits the Samaritan woman. Why is the Samaritan woman not recognized, praised, and celebrated as a witness to this power? Interpreters should take care, however, not to contrast Jesus' acceptance of the woman with the Samaritans' response. Such an interpretive move plays into power structures that pit foreigners who are less enlightened about women's authority against readers who identify with Jesus. While some may suggest that John's sociocultural context keeps him from characterizing the Samaritan woman as a witness, we need also to ask who our sociocultural context makes vulnerable, characterizes as silly, or dismisses as ignorant. We may be missing an insightful witness to Jesus' power in our own day.

KATHERINE A. SHANER

Homiletical Perspective

Samaritans at first glance are the least likely people to believe. They are not Jesus' own people. In fact, they are people who are despised by Jesus' own—not quite the right faith, not quite the accepted ethnicity. Yet they are the ones who understand him to be Savior "of the world." This is important. The longing for a savior was the hope of a particular community. Yet the Samaritans recognized Jesus as Savior not just of a few but of all the world. This is another way that John lets us know, early in the Gospel, that "God so loved the world"—the whole world. Jesus comes not just to his own, but to all.

The belief of the Samaritans based on the woman's testimony—and then their own experience with Jesus that leads to their confession of faith—gives us the opportunity to think of the ways in which we keep others from that confession. It spurs us to think of our own reticence to share with others what we know about the love of God. It helps us to reflect on what we may miss in the way of inspiration and wisdom when we listen only to one voice.

In a world that becomes smaller and smaller through technology and ease of travel, we have more opportunity than ever to learn from the testimony of many people. The extensive racial/ethnic and generational diversity new to the early twenty-first century will only increase, giving us the chance to experience diversity as a gift. This passage challenges us to go beyond the comfort of our own community and our "own people," however defined, to extend the boundaries of our thinking and experience. The preacher has the opportunity to invite the congregation to learn how God is acting in the lives of many, and thereby to experience the living Christ through his surprising encounters with unexpected people. The confession of the Samaritans may help us expand our understanding and experience of the transformative power of Jesus.

SHARON WATKINS

John 4:43–54

⁴³When the two days were over, he went from that place to Galilee ⁴⁴(for Jesus himself had testified that a prophet has no honor in the prophet's own country). ⁴⁵When he came to Galilee, the Galileans welcomed him, since they had seen all that he had done in Jerusalem at the festival; for they too had gone to the festival.

⁴⁶Then he came again to Cana in Galilee where he had changed the water into wine. Now there was a royal official whose son lay ill in Capernaum. ⁴⁷When he heard that Jesus had come from Judea to Galilee, he went and begged him to come down and heal his son, for he was at the point of death. ⁴⁸Then Jesus said to him, "Unless you see signs and wonders you will not believe." ⁴⁹The official said to him, "Sir, come down before my little boy dies." ⁵⁰Jesus said to him, "Go; your son will live." The man believed the word that Jesus spoke to him and started on his way. ⁵¹As he was going down, his slaves met him and told him that his child was alive. ⁵²So he asked them the hour when he began to recover, and they said to him, "Yesterday at one in the afternoon the fever left him." ⁵³The father realized that this was the hour when Jesus had said to him, "Your son will live." So he himself believed, along with his whole household. ⁵⁴Now this was the second sign that Jesus did after coming from Judea to Galilee.

Theological Perspective

For a *narrative* about Jesus, the Gospel of John plays awfully fast and loose with time and space. Jesus jumps from place to place along time lines that do not make sense. For example, after a "first day" in 1:24–28 in which John the Baptist talks about Jesus, 1:29, 1:35, and 1:43 all begin with "the next day," but 2:1 begins with "on the third day" (third day after what? the second "next day"?). To make the various sites of those days possible, Jesus and the disciples must have been ultramarathoners, well deserving of their rest in Capernaum in 2:12. Then, from the end of chapter 2 to the end of chapter 3, we discover that Jesus has traveled to Jerusalem, decided to return to Galilee in 4:3, and only shortly thereafter veered off into Samaria for a few days. The text is as peripatetic as its protagonist—which may be part of John's point. As we wander through the text, we join the wandering Messiah to whom the text points. The text, by its very structure, encourages us to identify with Jesus and the disciples.

By 4:43, though, Jesus and the disciples seem to be following a coherent route. They leave Samaria to resume their journey to Galilee and stop in Cana (where, the text reminds us, Jesus had turned water into wine, as if to drive home the point that this particular lap of Galilee and Judea has come to an end), only to be asked by a royal official to return to

Pastoral Perspective

John concludes the drama of chapter 4 with yet another opportunity to help us understand the distinctiveness of Jesus and the nature of the power that he exercises. We come to Cana with the acclamation of the Samaritans ringing in our ears: Jesus is "truly the Savior of the world" (4:42b). What sort of salvation does this Savior offer in contrast to the Roman, self-described saviors such as Caesar?

We are introduced to a royal official whose religious identity is left provocatively ambiguous. He is in the employ of Rome. Is he a Gentile? Does it matter? That his employment comes from Rome seems to be John's focus, and it helps us understand more of the distinctiveness of Jesus' identity and power. This official, related to the empire, comes to Jesus as a father utterly desperate to secure physical healing for his son. Rome cannot offer this power. The empire has power to extract whatever wealth it can and to impose taxes that further impoverish the poor. John demonstrates to us that while the father simply seeks physical healing, Jesus has the power, in contrast to the empire, to bring health and wholeness.[1] His power is generous and life giving.

Yet again in this chapter John invites us to imagine with the people of Cana and this desperate

1. Warren Carter, *John and Empire: Initial Explorations* (London, New York: T. & T. Clark, 2008), 29.

Exegetical Perspective

The initial verses of this pericope are travel-ing verses. Jesus has just spent two days with the Samaritans on his way to Galilee from his encounter with John the Baptist in the Judean countryside (3:22–24), and now in 4:45 Jesus comes into Galilee. Verse 44 inserts a curious aside about why Jesus left Samaria, reminding the audience of Jesus' words that a prophet has no honor at home. The aside is curi-ous, because Samaria is not Jesus' home territory, yet John's narrative clearly depicts a warm greeting in Galilee. Both the Synoptic and extracanonical Gospels relate this saying of Jesus in fuller detail, but in those versions Jesus is met with suspicion not enthusiasm (Mark 6:1–6; Matt. 13:53–58; Luke 4:22–24; *Gos. Thom.* 31). John includes this saying and implies its importance, but the sentiment does not fit with the larger narrative arc, particularly as Jesus returns to Galilee.

Some scholars suggest a different source of suspi-cion for John, namely, the authorities in the temple rather than the faithful in Galilee. John contrasts this warm welcome in Galilee with the cold question-ing of the Judeans (*Ioudaioi*) after Jesus' outburst in the Jerusalem temple during Passover (2:13–22). Those who welcome him witnessed these and pre-sumably other actions (4:45). John does not name the outburst in the temple or any other particular

Homiletical Perspective

This is the return to the scene of Jesus' first sign in the Gospel of John, at Cana. Now a second sign wid-ens the circle of belief. Jesus is back in his hometown area. His own people will require physical proof, beyond his word alone, which had proven adequate for the Samaritans, if they are to believe.

A royal official approaches Jesus. His son is sick. The father believes that Jesus can heal the son. Jesus expresses exasperation, saying unless you see signs and wonders you will not believe. The official begs for the life of this child. Jesus is his last hope. Jesus tells the man to go and that his son will live. The man believes and heads back toward home. His slaves meet him on the road and tell him the child is alive. When did the boy start to recover? The hour that Jesus pronounced it so. Now the man believes for sure, and his whole household too. A second sign. The circle of belief deepens and widens.

Although the passage includes a sign—a heal-ing—it lets us know that miracles are not always necessary, or even desirable, for belief. The father believes, sight unseen, that his son will be healed. He goes to Jesus in the first place believing Jesus will help. He talks to him and receives his word that the deed is done. At this point, the father trusts that Jesus will follow through. He does not need to drag

Theological Perspective

Capernaum. Rather than further retrace his steps, though, Jesus stays put, which is a little odd, since this trip would not be too great and the purpose of the trip—to heal the official's son—certainly seems a worthy endeavor.

Having heard that Jesus has returned from Judea to Galilee (the text once again emphasizes the most recent journey), the royal official comes begging. This agent of the empire, undoubtedly used to receiving petitions and giving commands, is reduced to offering his own petition in the hopes that Jesus will come to Capernaum and give the command that leads to the boy's health. Yet Jesus remains. Indeed, Jesus commands neither the boy to get well nor whatever forces are inducing illness to depart. Instead of a command, Jesus offers a report: "Go; your son will live" (v. 50). The official departs but this particular wandering Jew stays put. Whatever else is going on, this Jesus is clearly in control of his own travel plans—recognition of which will be useful later in John, as Jesus' travels take him up onto the cross.

John's Jesus is also clearly in control of other forces. Almost regardless of the royal official's faith, Jesus' initial words to him are sufficient for the boy. No laying on of hands. No "Little boy, arise." No sweat or tears. No sign or wonder that leads others to believe.[1] Just a statement of fact that, the text strongly suggests, Jesus is adequate to the task, as the father would later realize that the boy's healing had occurred at "the hour when Jesus had said to him, 'Your son will live'" (v. 53a).

This is, then, an unusual healing story. We do not see Jesus do anything; he refuses the very request—to come to Capernaum—that is made of him. We do not meet the healed one; like the royal official, we simply hear a report. It does not lead to the official's belief; the official first believes in the very way Jesus says does not happen and then seemingly rebelieves after talking with his slaves. Apparently this is the second sign Jesus performs after coming to Galilee (v. 54), though the text is silent about the first sign. John plays as fast and loose with this healing narrative as he does with time and space

---

1. The referent of the plural pronouns "you" in 4:48 is ambiguous. Do the pronouns refer to the royal official? If so, why plural? Do they refer to all those around him when the royal official begs Jesus to come heal his son? If so, why does Jesus talk to "him"—in the singular—in 4:48? Do they refer to all the agents of the empire? If so, why is the official so quick to believe? Do they refer to John's audience (including us), a group of people who have not seen signs and wonders but are asked to believe on the basis of a word? Perhaps. However, this would also imply that we are supposed to identify with the royal official. If we are supposed to identify with this official, in what ways are we to identify him? As royal, à la the royal priesthood of 1 Peter 2:9? As having to surrender our own authority and control and come, begging, to the one who heals? As those whose faith cannot be based on signs and wonders? The text baffles.

Pastoral Perspective

father what it means to enter into relation to God's presence living among us, the Word made flesh who answered the Samaritan woman's hope for the Messiah with the breathtakingly simple, "I am" (4:26 NRSV note). Many of us do not live in arid land or under crushing poverty, and few of us have experienced the oppression of a harsh colonial power. In fact, we know more about the privileges of a powerful government. How might we imagine the Galileans' longing for healing and wholeness? Surely their imaginations were fed by the poetry of Isaiah's images of springs of water in the desert, the blind seeing, the deaf hearing, the lame leaping, the absence of fear, prisoners released, oppression ended, and the establishment of peace and justice (Isa. 35, 42). Are the hopes imagined by these images really so foreign to our hearts? Like the desperate father, in a time of crisis we might settle simply for healing, but wholeness is so much more—perhaps so much more that we dare not acknowledge its absence.

John opens yet another dramatic scene and draws us in. Jesus' exploits with the elite Judeans profiting in the temple in Jerusalem had been satisfying to the Galileans who had witnessed them. They welcome Jesus home. We can imagine a people whose difficult economic and political circumstances are apparent in their bodies and clothing, even as they greet Jesus, and we can then imagine the arrival of a "royal official" likely traveling with an escort of some type and likely well fed and clothed. The inversion of circumstance catches our attention; cloaked in the guise of power, the official comes to plea for healing. Perhaps he kneels before Jesus, who would surely be showing the signs of travel as well as his simple economic means. He stands in the midst of those who suffer under the weight of the colonial power the official represents.

Can you imagine the feelings of the Galileans as they make way for the official and his escort? Here comes yet another presuming privilege. How does the word spread as the official approaches and makes his case? Does it make a difference when he speaks as a parent desperate for his son—a desperation many of them know, with only the simplest medical resources at hand? Can you imagine the desperation of this father? Can you imagine the longing that drives him to make the journey of twenty challenging miles from Capernaum to Cana? What has he heard of Jesus? What might it cost him if his Roman employers know he has made a public plea to Jesus? His job and future employment can well be on the line. Is he fearful as he makes his way through the Galileans, implicated as he is in their oppression?

action, perhaps because of a kind of ambivalence in John's Gospel (and thus in John's Jesus) about faith that relies on Jesus' actions, whether philanthropic or political. If we remember that historical political divisions between Galilee and Judea were not erased in the first century CE, Jesus' disruption at the very heart of the Judean religiopolitical world might just delight Galileans.

As he arrives again in Cana, John reminds readers of the water-into-wine miracle (2:1–12), perhaps as a way of setting the scene for the second of Jesus' signs (4:54). John's narrative throughout chapter 4 emphasizes Jesus' influence among multiple constituencies: festival-goers in Jerusalem (2:23; 4:45), Samaritans (4:1–42), Galileans (4:45), and a royal official (4:46). This emphasis shows that all kinds of people recognize Jesus' importance. This plurality of people sets up John's polemic against the Judeans (*Ioudaioi*), whether we understand that term as a political, religious, or ethnic designation. Exegetes should weight the ethical value of this polemic quite carefully.

This story has many parallels to the Synoptic story of the centurion's slave (Matt. 8:5–13; Luke 7:1–10). All three stories depict someone of some rank in the political structure. The centurion (*hekatontarkos*) in the Synoptic stories is an officer in the Roman imperial army. While the Greek word is different in John's story (*basilikos*) and connotes connection with royalty rather than military, Herod Antipas ruled Galilee from 4 BCE to 39 CE as a kind of vassal king under the Romans. *Basilikos* was often used in the Greek-speaking world to designate the emperor or regional ruler. Most scholars think John's use of the term points to someone in Herod's administration.

As the story moves forward, the royal official asks Jesus to heal his son (*huios*) who lies dying in Capernaum (v. 47). In his second entreaty, the official uses the term "boy" (*pais*, v. 49). Matthew uses this same word, "boy" (*pais*, Matt. 8:6). Both instances of the term "boy" are often translated as either "child" or "young child," yet the term can often imply enslavement. Luke explicitly uses the word "slave" (*doulos*, Luke 7:2). Although modern ears hear a deeper affection in the term "son" or "child" than in the term "slave," the distinction between slaves and sons, especially in their youth, was not always clear to ancient readers. The royal official/centurion, as head of his household, held similar power over both his sons and his slaves. Both sons and slaves added economic value to the household. John's choice of the term "son" in verse 47 may convey inheritance lines, yet the term "boy" in verse 49 slips an ambiguity

Jesus physically off to Capernaum to have him actually lay hands on the boy.

Over the course of this story, the man's belief in Jesus deepens to a point we might call trust. Belief may be a matter of the head. It may have to do with weighing evidence, such as the signs and wonders that Jesus scorned, to come to a conclusion. It may have to do with following a logical argument that leads to a particular way of seeing the world.

Belief may also be a matter of the heart. When one spouse says to the other spouse, "I believe in you," it does not mean "I believe you exist." It means "I trust you." This is the kind of believing we see in the royal official. Understanding the official's belief as "trust" in Jesus opens some riches in this passage. Trust is what a child has in his or her parents. You see it when the small hand reaches up without the child's head even turning up to look, knowing that the mom's hand will reach back—an unquestioning confidence that she will be there. Trust is being in a relationship in which a person can be completely vulnerable and open, knowing with utter certainty that he or she will not be unfairly used.

The royal official has only a little evidence, but he comes to Jesus believing Jesus can heal his son. When Jesus refuses to go with him, the man takes Jesus at his word, trusting Jesus with the life of his son. The passage invites us to explore our own level of belief and/or trust in God through Jesus Christ. Many of us in North America may not be at this point of deepest trust. Our level of material security is often strong enough that, even while we love God and believe in the Jesus story, we participate in the "circus" of life with a net. We may go forward with such a security backup that we never completely get to the point of trusting our whole lives to Jesus.

Henri Nouwen once talked about trapeze artists who swing up high in the air, holding on to the trapeze until just that moment when they have to let go and fly through the air, unsupported, in order to be caught by the hands of the other artist. Trust is in that moment of letting go.[1] Complete trust is letting go without a net.

In many parts of the world, Christians place their trust in God without the net of material security. Interestingly, these are the very places where Christianity is growing fastest. For a long time the world center of Christianity was in the Northern Hemisphere. In the early twenty-first century, it is

1. http://www.yale.edu/divinity/news/070319_news_nouwen.shtml, accessed May 3, 2014.

John 4:43–54

Theological Perspective

during Jesus' earlier travels. Why get Jesus back on track geographically if only to complicate his path vocationally?

Perhaps, though, this is part of John's point, albeit one made in a peculiarly abstruse rhetorical way. John gives us ample opportunity to identify with various characters throughout his Gospel, but then, having identified with them, structures his stories so that we feel the very upheaval that they must have felt in encountering Jesus. Our own paths of comfortable faith and satisfied life will be disrupted when a Samaritan-woman-engaging, royal-official-answering, young-boy-healing Messiah travels past. These unruly narratives recounted in the first several chapters of John not only push us into puzzlement about the story; they invite us to attend to the puzzles of our own lives.[2]

Best, though, not to tarry while puzzling. By 5:1, Jesus is on the road again, returning to Jerusalem and trailing puzzled disciples behind him.

MARK DOUGLAS

Pastoral Perspective

This is likely one of those "betting the farm" propositions, when nothing else is as important as the possibility that his beloved son may recover. Notice that he addresses Jesus with deference, "sir," and that he, employed by Caesar, "begs" for healing from the one John discloses to be truly the Savior of the world (4:42).

How do we who live in a country identified with the benefits of a modern-day empire experience this drama? How does this story help us imagine Jesus as truly the Savior of the world?

Jesus seems to lift up the common humanity of the official and the crowd, for he responds to the official's request in the plural, as if he knows the gathered Galileans, and perhaps we share this same need of assurance: "Unless you see signs and wonders you will not believe" (v. 48). Then he enacts the sign: "Go, your son will live" (v. 50a). Jesus offers more than healing. His use of the word "live" makes plain that the true Savior of the world offers healing and life in it fullness, as those inviting metaphors in Isaiah suggest. The entire household of the royal official recognizes that the sign of healing points beyond itself to Jesus, and they believe in him. Jesus has now enacted two signs in Cana of Galilee: when abundance is signaled at a wedding as water becomes excellent wine, and when healing and wholeness are extended to the dying son of a royal official—and to all of us who long for such healing and wholeness ourselves. These signs convey to first-century readers and to us the meaning of John's Gospel when it says that in relationship with this man, Jesus, we experience God's "grace and truth . . . grace upon grace" (1:14b, 16b).

NANCY J. RAMSAY

2. This may hint at why John inserts 4:44 where he does. Whereas Luke connects the prophet Jesus being rejected by his own to a story in which his own actually reject him in Luke 4:16–39, John connects it to a story in which he is welcomed by his own. Perhaps accepting and rejecting are twinned attitudes that run within individuals, rather than opposing attitudes that distinguish one group from another.

Exegetical Perspective

about the status of the sick child into the story. Whereas in the Lukan version of the story the centurion is trying to preserve an obedient slave under his authority (Luke 7:8), John gives few details and little sense of motivation for the official's request.

John, Matthew, and Luke all use the basic structure of this story to show that politically powerful people recognize Jesus as still more powerful. Each Gospel writer changes details to fit with his own persuasive goals. In John's case the story marks a brief commentary on the "signs and wonders" (*sēmeia kai terata*) that recur throughout the Gospel.[1] John does not emphasize the official seeking out Jesus as a healer. Rather, John's version of the story implies that the official seeks Jesus' help because the official needs to see "signs and wonders" in order to believe in Jesus (v. 48). This subtle dig implies that the official asks for a sign (*sēmeion*) as proof that Jesus is the Messiah, yet 4:50 states that the official believed Jesus' word despite the chiding in verse 48.

The narrative continues with the official ascertaining precisely when his son was healed. As a response to the revelation that it was the same hour that Jesus spoke, the official and his whole household believe (vv. 52–53). This sequence of events illustrates the ambivalence in John's Gospel about belief, especially belief that is connected to signs. Does the official believe the word that Jesus spoke (v. 50), and thus the son is healed? Is it after the official puts together the timetable for Jesus' healing the boy that he believes? We often read John's ambivalence around signs as a blessing on those readers (modern ones included) who believe without seeing signs and wonders. Nevertheless, as readers we should also ask ourselves, what do we believe or doubt in John's story of Jesus? What signs do we expect to witness?

KATHERINE A. SHANER

Homiletical Perspective

in Africa.[2] While Christianity stagnates or declines in North America and Europe, it grows exuberantly in the Southern Hemisphere. In many communities where Christianity is growing, people have no illusion about material security. They place their trust in God for a life that is meaningful and complete. They are ready to share the security and life they know in Christ Jesus. The circle of belief widens.

A related theme is introduced with the healing of the boy. Jesus is the giver of life. The father has been right to trust Jesus with the life of his son. In previous stories, in his conversations about water and food, Jesus has talked indirectly about being the life of the world. Jesus now literally brings a boy back from the brink of death. He restores him to fullness of life now. Life in Christ is not something for which we have to wait. Jesus brings eternal life, beginning immediately, to those who believe, to those who trust their lives to him. The experience of the royal official invites us to trust Jesus completely with our own lives. It invites us to reflect on how trusting in Jesus brings us to life in the first place.

This story helps us ask how a trusting relationship with Jesus brings life to us as individuals or as church or as we reach out to our communities. How does reflection on trust in Jesus help us come to terms with our dependence on material security for our happiness? Does our dependence on a "net" of material security keep us from life-giving involvement in our community? In order to maintain our own security, do we stay quiet or stay home when we might otherwise be advocates, in the name of Christ, for life-giving changes for our neighbors and community?

In many important ways, this passage invites us, as believers, to deepen our own belief, to let go and fly, trusting that God will surely catch us.

SHARON WATKINS

---

1. The other signs include the miracle at Cana (2:1–12), healing at the pool of Bethsaida (5:1–9), feeding of the five thousand (6:1–14), giving sight to the man born blind (9:1–17), Lazarus's resurrection (11:1–46), Jesus' entry into Jerusalem (12:12–36). John assures readers that Jesus did many more signs than these (2:23; 20:30).

2. http://www.pewforum.org/2011/12/19/global-christianity-exec, accessed Dec. 1, 2014.

John 5:1–9a

Theological Perspective

The narrative about the pool of Beth-zatha provides a stark contrast between a view of miracles common to many cultures and perspectives and the place of miracle in the new life that Jesus Christ brings. In the testimony of the Gospel of John, the Word brings people to wholeness, freeing them from bondage to the cruel status foisted upon them by an unjust society and human misperception. Like living water and many other signs in the Gospel of John, healing from Jesus brings life and freedom.

The pool of Beth-zatha had a tradition of healing. Others experienced healing in the pool prior to the paralyzed man's tenure of disappointment. Apparently enough people found healing in the pool to keep the paralyzed man waiting at poolside and crawling somehow toward the water's edge time after time. The waters would stir, and upon immersion one or more needy people would receive their desired cure. Each stirring had some quota on healings; however, the paralyzed man never managed to drag himself soon enough to the pool before one or more got ahead of him. The paralyzed man had never been first, or soon enough, into the water, and therefore he remained unhealed.

Pastoral Perspective

It is a Jewish feast day and we join Jesus in Jerusalem—a point that ought not be overlooked. "Why?" one might ask. Jesus' location does become a point of conflict with the religious elite in the next passage (5:9b–15) because he performs a healing miracle on the Sabbath. From a pastoral perspective, there are many rich images in this episode, but I will focus on three: (1) the sense of hopelessness portrayed by the man enduring a thirty-eight-year illness; (2) the lack of imagination in this man, who responds to Jesus by stating that there is no one to take him to the pool when the waters are stirred up (v. 7); and (3) the human desire to be healed, which is often accompanied by a sense of hopelessness or inertia, because the familiar illness is in some ways easier to cope with than a cure that represents an unknown or uncertain future. Though it is tempting to draw baptismal images out of the reading of this text, one needs to attend to the reality that for this disabled man, water did not provide the cure; rather, Jesus commanded him to "stand, pick up his mat, and walk around" (v. 8, my trans.).

Raymond Brown[1] suggests that the disability of the man at poolside is a case of atrophied limbs. We do not know why they became atrophied or if there

---

* See "'The Jews' in the Fourth Gospel" on pp. xi–xiv.

1. Raymond E. Brown, *The Gospel according to John I–XII* (Garden City, NY: Doubleday & Co., 1983), 207–8.

Exegetical Perspective

Identifying Jesus: A Community in Crisis. John's Gospel is marked by a conflict between Jesus and "the Jews." Its context reflects a time when tension began to sever relations between emerging Christian sects and post–70 CE rabbinic Judaism (9:1–23). The primary point of conflict centered on a situation where those who believed and confessed Jesus was the Christ were in serious disagreement with those who passionately rejected this christological claim. The text refers to those who refuted the claim that Jesus was the Messiah as "the Jews." The term "the Jews" does not reflect the Jewish people. Rather, it represents those characters in John's Gospel who advocated against the theological and christological claims made by Jesus' followers. "The Jews" emphasizes the ideas represented by the other side of the argument and thus is more of a reflection of the christological debate at the end of the first century. It is widely held that it may not accurately report the experiences of the historical Jesus and his fellow Israelites during Jesus' lifetime.[1]

This text is a healing story that continues to illustrate the Johannine community's understanding of Jesus' identity as the Messiah/Son of God. The passage sets the stage for the theological and

1. See Francis, J. Moloney, *The Gospel of John*, ed. Daniel J. Harrington, SJ, Sacra pagina 4 (Collegeville, MN: The Liturgical Press, 1998), 9–11.

Homiletical Perspective

The account of Jesus healing the invalid at the pool of Beth-zatha—so memorable yet on closer inspection so full of puzzles—is rife with temptations as well as promise for the preacher. On the one hand, archaeological discovery of a pool quite precisely matching the one in the narrative suggests a concrete location in space and time: the significance of this story does not appear to lie simply in symbolism, but in a real individual to whom Jesus reached out. Jesus really does show mercy in practical ways.

On the other hand, obscurity regarding various details—what feast was in view? what among the many options was the name of pool?—suggests that these historical particularities are not critical to the meaning of the passage and should not occupy much of the preacher's time. They might, nonetheless, be mentioned in passing, not least because people using varying translations may be puzzled; and some who have been assailed by excessive skepticism may be helped by knowing that the setting was not imaginary.

More serious at the pastoral level is the temptation to psychologize Jesus' question in verse 6: "Do you want to be made well?" A preacher fascinated by the reality and power of psychosomatic symptoms and seeking to demonstrate up-to-date understanding of the influence of the mind over the body may

John 5:1–9a

Theological Perspective

The tradition of healing at the pool of Beth-zatha reveals a common belief in and about miracles that borders on superstition. Miracles are jackpots handed out capriciously. Some are healed but many continue to suffer, perhaps with the added sense of rejection. Common belief about miracles sounds good on the surface: someone gets relief. However, the implications for the unhealed are cruel. Added to the mystery of why one suffers in the first place, is the question of why one's suffering does not end, even though someone else's does. Theologically, the questions implicate God in suffering: Why do people suffer at all? Why do some suffer more while others suffer less?

Then there is the inaction that implicates human beings in suffering. If someone had helped the paralyzed man into the water, he might have gained his cure. There is a social-ethical dimension in the situation. No one has helped this man, and the common "theology" of miracles remains silent on the basic injustice to any and all left behind. Worse yet, the capriciousness of miracles would seem to excuse the injustice of the man's abandonment, marginalization, and existence in a less-than-whole state. Since miracles capriciously separate the rewarded from the rejected, many others assume they are mere bystanders.

In contrast, Jesus' healing of the man reveals God's will for human wholeness and reveals what human love and responsibility look like. Without the revelation of God's will for human wholeness in Jesus, people can move logically from the question of suffering directly to questions of God's will and God's justice (e.g., Is it fair for God to allow suffering? Why does God not fix it?). They also can subtly excuse their own culpability and that of fellow humans for not helping neighbors in need.

In the beautifully stark and simple contrast between Jesus' healing and the miracles at the pool of Beth-zatha we behold the gift of healing and human wholeness in Jesus Christ available to all. From light and bread and gates and shepherds, to a host of other images, John's Gospel presents signs that God's love is not limited in the ways enshrined in all other mythic systems of the ancient world. Jesus is completely different; his gift of healing is a miracle of a very different sort: the miracle of eternal life revealed within the confines of mortal life, thereby showing and enacting the love of God who dwells with us.

Against the injustice of being left behind in the competitive scramble into the pool, Jesus addresses

Pastoral Perspective

is any correlation between the disability and the man's own actions. When one wants to address the human experience of hopelessness in twenty-first-century life, there are many circumstances that end in despair; the discussion of this passage does not need to be limited by the fact that the disabled man has a physical ailment. From what other conditions (e.g., spiritual, mental, emotional) of atrophy does hopelessness arise? What disabilities does a contemporary believer live with that may not even be recognized as disabilities? Technology, for example, provides opportunities for us to think of ourselves as members of "global communities," but it also makes it possible for us to avoid person-to-person "real-time" conversation. Thus it may be that our relationships experience atrophy over time, as do our congregational communities, in direct proportion to the amount of time spent in "virtual reality."

To experience atrophy is to experience a kind of wasting away that is a result of inadequate nourishment. In what ways do our relationships waste away as a result of choices we make? Like the man who responded to Jesus with excuses, in what ways do the demands of earning a living provide for us an excuse for not seeking help for our atrophied spirits? What nourishment is offered by our church communities as an antidote or part of the cure for what ails us? What does healing look like in our communities of worship?

Hopelessness, synonymous with despair, brings to mind mental disorders such as depression. The very nature of a mood disorder suggests that a person will lack the energy or desire or imagination necessary to pursue a cure, even when the person yearns for health. The inability of the man at poolside to seize the opportunity for healing is analogous to a struggle with mental illness. Yet the experience of enduring illness in our culture may suggest not a lack of energy, desire, or imagination, but the lack of financial resources or the presence of fear concerning the transformation necessary if healing is to take place.

In many ways, little has changed concerning human empathy for those who are chronically ill; there is a tendency not to blame the social order but to blame the one who suffers. Thus, like the ancient people of faith, we tend to draw a one-to-one correspondence between sin and disease or faith and health. This text invites us to discuss what it is about disability or disease that makes us uncomfortable. It also affords us an opportunity to think about healing as something other or more than a physical cure. How does our own lack of imagination prevent us

christological debates between Jesus and his followers and "the Jews." John's Gospel makes much of
signs (*sēmeia*) and their role in legitimating Jesus'
divine authenticity (1:43–51; 2:1–11; 2:13–22; 2:23;
3:1–2; 4:46–54). Signs refer to "miracles confirming
the claim of a savior or prophet sent by God; they
are meant to awaken faith and are demanded or
prompted rather than requested."[2]

Although a healing narrative, this story is not
named as a "sign," and it leads not to belief but to
indifference and disbelief. After performing this
miracle, Jesus is not heralded as the Messiah or the
Son of God. Rather, "the Jews" seek to persecute and
kill him for healing on the Sabbath and making himself "equal" to God. Nevertheless, with a strategic use
of language, the author uses messianic indifference
toward Jesus to offer insight into his identity as the
Christ and the subsequent challenges that he and his
followers must endure and, at times, embrace.

Do You Want to Become Well? (vv. 1–9a). After
Jesus heals the royal official's son in Cana, he travels
to Jerusalem to attend a "festival of the Jews." The
text does not specify which festival. Rather, we learn
that Jesus' first stop in Jerusalem is at a healing pool
known as Beth-zatha. The pool has five sections, and
in each section are people who are blind, lame, and
paralyzed. At Beth-zatha Jesus encounters a man
who for thirty-eight years has suffered a debilitating
illness. At first glance, it appears that John is using
a healing story as a sign to elicit belief in Jesus and
thereby verify him as the Messiah. We observed
this thematic purposing in the previous narrative
(4:46–54), in which John recounts an instance where
Jesus healed the son of a royal official, resulting in
the official, along with his entire household, accepting Jesus as the Christ. Instead, today's lesson takes
an unexpected turn.

Unlike the previous healing account, where
the royal official recognizes Jesus and asks him to
heal his son, in this narrative Jesus approaches the
afflicted man and asks, "Do you want to be made
well?" (v. 6b). The man does not answer Jesus in the
way we might expect. Jesus' question assumes the
man's healing is a matter of his will, which is one
aspect of faith. However, the man's response suggests
that it is not at all a matter of his will. This is not a
question of faith. The issue is with his ability or the
lack thereof. When the waters are stirred, the man
has no one to help him into the pool, and even when

convey the impression that those who are suffering
from various maladies are not healed because, down
deep, they do not really want to be. The sufferer is
then left with guilt and hopelessness added to physical misery. The problem is not that such a diagnosis
is always wrong, but that a sermon is too blunt and
nonspecific an instrument to use for judgments
requiring the most careful and skillful discernment.
Furthermore, putting the emphasis on the psychosomatic side undermines the text's emphasis on Jesus'
actual power to heal. Angles on the narrative more
likely to be constructive for the sermon involve the
power and initiative of Jesus and the opening of
the invalid to new possibilities in a way that fully
engages him rather than leaving him in his long state
of helplessness.

With respect to Jesus' power, we note that he
specifically selects a man who has been disabled
for what must have been most of his life. While we
cannot be certain that his knowledge of the man's
malady is supernatural, it likely is, given John's frequent suggestion that Jesus has supernatural insight.
Choice of such a "hard case" shows both the greatness of Jesus' ability to heal and his mercy toward
one who is especially in need. One might note that
persons who frequent the pool are disabled in the
ways that keep them from partaking (v. 3) in the
temple ritual, thereby increasing their isolation. This
particular man appears to be friendless, having no
one to assist him (v. 7). Thus he fits the pattern of the
especially needy, for whom Jesus takes special care.

With respect to initiative, we see that it is all on
Jesus' side. The man makes no request, shows no
hope, exercises no faith—quite unlike the royal official in the immediately preceding account (4:46–54).
Indeed, he could not have faith in Jesus, for we soon
discover that he does not even know who Jesus is
(v. 13). Here is powerful counterevidence to the
"only-believism" that correlates healing neatly with
faith. Healing is more mysterious than that, resting
far more on the Lord's own purposes than on the
human capacity for belief. Sometimes Jesus does
indeed work through faith as an instrument, but
sometimes he does not. Sometimes strong faith is
disappointed (e.g., 2 Cor. 12:8). Here a single disabled person is selected out of very many who are
also in need of help and who are no more ignorant
of Jesus than the one who is healed.

With respect to opening the man to new possibilities, we might see Jesus' question in verse 6 as
directed to that end. Here lies a man whose hopes
have been so thwarted that he can scarcely find

---

2. "Semeia," in H. Balz and G. Schneider, eds., *Exegetical Dictionary of the
New Testament* (Grand Rapids: Eerdmans, 1990), 2:239.

John 5:1–9a

Theological Perspective

the paralyzed man, not as less than human because of his infirmity, nor as someone who is about to become magically more than anyone thought possible. Jesus addresses the paralyzed man as a whole person, with integrity and value even though he is not a winner in the usual "theology" of miracle. Jesus regards him within his God-given opportunity to live in a new way. Taking up his mat to walk is indeed a miracle over against paralysis, but it is also liberation from waiting by the pool of capriciousness. To walk as Jesus said is to live with a purpose and determination that the pool cannot give.

Common views would consider the paralyzed man's thirty-eight years of paralysis to be God's judgment against him as a sinner. Even if healed one day in the pool, the thirty-eight years of disability could carry social stigma. The man would forever be the healed paralytic. The character of the gift from Christ is much more than a new label upon an old condition. It is a whole new life, begun on the day when he first stood and walked, and embodied human wholeness.

To be "made well" through Jesus Christ is, according to the Gospel of John, to be given the life abundantly given all creation by God. In eternal life revealed in the Word made flesh, one sees one's value as God sees it: as one for whom God gave the Son. Paralysis is not sin, but to live in paralysis of spirit is. The gift of Jesus to the man by the pool of Bethzatha, the second miraculous healing story in the Gospel of John, stands with many other such gifts throughout the Gospel of John. They are all species of God's love, sealed and accomplished by the sign of the cross. No stirred pool is needed, now or ever. Instead, the cross of Christ restirs the waters of creation, so that all may live in the power of God's love, no longer defined as broken, unwell, and left behind.

GILSON A. C. WALDKOENIG

Pastoral Perspective

from hearing or seeing what may be helpful to the ones who suffer? In what ways do we assist those who feel paralyzed by their disabilities or "diseases" (understood as anything that unsettles us or becomes an annoyance physically, emotionally, or spiritually) at a time that is rife with anxiety?

This passage also invites us to think about the anxiety that affects the national psyche: natural disasters of epic proportion, acts of terrorism within our borders, and medical diseases that are treatment resistant, to name just a few of the headlines that clamor for our attention. The headlines fade from view, but the conditions and struggles often persist, and those who struggle are soon forgotten by many who do not suffer or who have the resources to provide assistance for themselves.

We may want to understand this episode as an example of faith healing; but the reality is that the man did not know who Jesus was, did not think to ask for Jesus' name, and did not at any point articulate his own faith. Moreover, he never truly answered the question Jesus posed, "Do you want to be cured?" (v. 6). He replied instead with an excuse about why he had not been cured after thirty-eight long years. One may even want to infer that in Jesus' question the man heard a reprise of the belief that his sickness was his own fault. His faith did not cure him; the power of Jesus did. This text underscores the immediacy of Jesus' power, but his identity and relationship to the Law of Moses remain hidden until verse 14 in the next passage.

One final point worth observing is the fact that the evangelist tells us that Jesus knew this man had been sick for a very long time (v. 6), underscoring a Johannine theme: Jesus' extraordinary knowledge of people. We are also known by Jesus; like the disabled man we may lack the energy necessary to pursue a cure, but nourishment is offered by caring communities of faith.

CAROL L. SCHNABL SCHWEITZER

Exegetical Perspective

he attempts to crawl or drag himself into the pool, someone steps down ahead of him.

Of course the man wants to be healed, but here the desire to be healthy is not an admission of faith. Instead, the man does not possess the ability to secure his health. Hence, John's emphasis shifts from the man's will to Jesus' ability. Jesus commands the man to stand up (*egeire*, v. 8), take up his mat, and walk (*peripatei*). On Jesus' word, the man is made healthy, and he obeys Jesus' command. However, his obedience is not an indication of his belief, and it is significant only because Jesus has performed a miracle.

Beyond Belief. Regardless of the man's lack of faith, Jesus performs the work of the Messiah. For instance, on the one hand, *egeire* can be translated as "rise" or "stand," but it also can mean "awaken." As a metaphor, *egeire*/"awaken" can be understood as the cessation of a way of thinking that belongs to the realm of death and an entering into the sphere of life (5:24). John plays on each of these possible translations. Jesus does in fact command the man to stand up and thus restores his capacity for independent physical activity. Jesus also restores the man's ability to live and engage in relationships as one who carries a sense of personal agency (vv. 10–15).

Moreover, this same duality of meaning is present in Jesus' command for the man to walk (*peripatei*, v. 8). On one level, *peripateō* simply means to "walk" or "walk around." The text tells us that on Jesus' command the man takes up his mat and begins to "walk/walk around" (v. 9a). However, figuratively the word means "to conduct one's life" in a certain way. The significance of *peripateō*'s figurative meaning for this healing narrative and its role in identifying Jesus as the Messiah becomes evident in verse 14. At this juncture the narrative simply illustrates Jesus' healing power; it is not intended to display people's belief in him as the Messiah. Instead, 5:1–9a prepares us for the looming conflict between Jesus and "the Jews."

MONYA A. STUBBS

Homiletical Perspective

energy even to desire a different future; it costs too much actively to expect something that appears to have been permanently denied. Even the idea that healing really can come must be introduced anew. The man responds in terms of set ideas about how things happen and how he has been perennially frustrated (v. 7); he can see no other way. That he actually responds to Jesus' healing command (vv. 8–9) is an impressive demonstration of renewed life, given, received, and acted upon. Jesus gives what he demands, but he does not do so without engaging the recipient as a whole person.

The sermon's primary focus might be on the divine initiative in all its efficacy, mercy, and mystery. It might emphasize that grace comes without our deserving it—sometimes when we are not even seeking it, and even when we have given up on it ever coming to us. It might suggest that healing for the one serves as a sign for the many: those who are not healed may see what the Lord can do and may, if they trust in his character, trust that his purposes for them also are good and will in the end be accomplished. Such a sermon will hold up Jesus as one in whom we may have confidence, seeking thus to reassure those who have grown weary from their own long-unanswered prayers or self-punitive in their doubts and struggles.

Alternatively, the sermon might take up the secondary theme of the man's grasping of a new possibility. It might imaginatively enter into the man's situation—his sense of futility, his inability to imagine a way forward, his response to the seeming absurdity of this stranger's question, and yet his need for outside input to rekindle hope, and his final seizing of proffered help. The man without hope now picks up his mat and walks into a brand-new future.

MARGUERITE SHUSTER

John 5:9b–15

^{9b}Now that day was a sabbath. ¹⁰So the Jews* said to the man who had been cured, "It is the sabbath; it is not lawful for you to carry your mat." ¹¹But he answered them, "The man who made me well said to me, 'Take up your mat and walk.'" ¹²They asked him, "Who is the man who said to you, 'Take it up and walk'?" ¹³Now the man who had been healed did not know who it was, for Jesus had disappeared in the crowd that was there. ¹⁴Later Jesus found him in the temple and said to him, "See, you have been made well! Do not sin any more, so that nothing worse happens to you." ¹⁵The man went away and told the Jews that it was Jesus who had made him well.

Theological Perspective

Restored to wholeness and walking on his own, the "man who had been cured" now finds himself caught between religious authorities and the man who made him whole, whose name he does not even know yet. The narrative in John 5:9b–15 exposes the social-ethical dimensions of what Jesus did in John 5:1–9a, further highlighting the contrast between life in its fullness and the oppressive schemes of religious authorities.

The cured man goes through a short version of what plays out at length in John 9. He finds that telling the truth about the wholeness of life he has been given brings him back around to meet Jesus again. In the presence of the one who healed him, he hears that his ongoing freedom coincides with his resistance to sin. Meanwhile, just as in John 9, Jesus counters reigning religious authorities.

It is best to read the passage using the word "Judeans" instead of "Jews" in verse 10. The reference is to religious authorities representing the common and dominant religious perspectives of the day. John was not speaking of the opposition of the Jewish people in general to "Christians." Therefore it cannot be said too often that the contrast of Jew and Christian in the third millennium of Christianity

---

* See "'The Jews' in the Fourth Gospel" on pp. xi–xiv.

Pastoral Perspective

At this point in the story of the healing of the man at poolside, the focus shifts from the *miracle* of healing to a *violation* of the Sabbath. The joy of the healing is overshadowed by the violation of a religious rule. The man who is healed is himself Jewish; so "the Jews" who want to know who has performed this healing here refers to the religious authorities. The act of carrying his mat on the Sabbath is a violation of the prohibition against working on the Sabbath. None of the religious authorities rejoices with this man who is healed; rather, he is told that he should not be carrying his mat around. In response to those who question him he protests, "But the man who healed me told me to carry it!" He is simply and somewhat mindlessly following instructions without ever stopping to think about or question what has happened. His life has been changed. His response is akin to a person in shock. He has no idea who his healer was; surprisingly it never occurred to him to ask.

In the first part of this story Jesus' extraordinary knowledge of people is emphasized; in the latter part of the story the emphasis is placed upon being "found" by Jesus—a soteriological theme in John's Gospel. Thus it is Jesus who returns to the man, presumably identifies himself, and then commands the man, "Sin no more!" Why? The evangelist tells us only that the man returns to the authorities after

Exegetical Perspective

Renegotiating Sabbath Practices. In this text John sharpens his argument about Jesus' identity by situating the discussion in opposing views about acceptable Sabbath practices. The narrator displays no concern for the faith status of the man. The relevant issue here is the day on which Jesus performs the miracle. "But that day was the Sabbath" (5:9b; also see 9:1–14; 7:22–23). "The Jews," who are likely the religious authorities, come on the scene with an accusation against the healed man. He is unlawfully carrying his mat on the Sabbath. However, the man does not take responsibility for his actions. It is not necessarily his will to carry his mat on the Sabbath. Rather, it is the will of Jesus; he only did what Jesus commanded him to do.

His obedience, though, does not constitute belief. Again, we notice that the healed man does not appear to regard Jesus with any special affinity. The healthy man has not moved beyond his initial impression of Jesus. He offers no indication that he views Jesus as anything more than a helpful stranger. "The Jews" want to know the one who not only infringes on Sabbath practices, but also empowers others to do the same. The narrator announces that the man did not know the one who had healed him. We are left pondering, who is Jesus, and by what authority does he renegotiate Sabbath practices?

Homiletical Perspective

The continuation of the account of the man healed at the pool of Beth-zatha presents different, though not fewer, challenges than the narrative of the healing itself. All of the persons involved behave in ways that we might not have expected, ways that might, if carefully handled, provide a direction for a sermon.

First, we encounter certain religious leaders who, as commentators tend to be fond of noticing, seem less interested in a major miracle than in a seemingly minor violation of Sabbath law. However, we miss opportunities to proclaim the gospel if we presume these characters challenge only the failings of others. If—rightly rejecting the disproportionate response of the religious leaders—we end up dismissing the genuine importance of religious practices that shape life and character, we have made a significant mistake. Maybe we need to be a good deal more careful than we generally are with respect to our observing of the Lord's Day.

A sermon relating to proper Sabbath observance might well note that while Jesus appears to have chosen the Sabbath for this seemingly nonemergency healing to make a point, the point for Christians is not that one might just as well spend Sunday mornings at the beach or at soccer practice. Rather, he shows that even nonurgent acts of mercy are proper ways to honor God, on the Lord's Day as always. He

John 5:9b–15

Theological Perspective

continues to be mired in misappropriated categories that come from centuries long after the Gospel of John. In John 5:9b–15 the term "the Jews" clearly refers to religious authorities who pursue and engage the cured man as the rest of the passage verifies. In this passage it is best to think of "the Jews" as being the religious authorities, rather than an ethnic category. (Please refer to the excursus on "the Jews" at the beginning of this volume.)

Whereas people were neglectful of their needy neighbor at the pool of Beth-zatha, evidenced by charging past the paralyzed man in selfish pursuit of their own healing, the religious authorities who close in on the man immediately following his cure are no better. They take aggressive action to try to undo the wholeness Jesus has established. Their weapon is their interpretation of God's law. While there are some prohibitions in the law concerning what one may do on the Sabbath, the Sabbath prohibition against carrying things appears for the first time in Jeremiah 17:19–27. It is worth noting that the objection of the authorities did not have to do with the healing but with the healed man's act of carrying something on the Sabbath. Reading this story in the context of a society in which judgmental attitudes about disabilities persist, we are instead struck by the authorities' inability to rejoice that a suffering person has been restored to wholeness.

The nature of healing is a theological issue for contemporary readers of the passage. Many today, as in ancient times, avoid the social-ethical implications of suffering and healing. Instead of facing the fact that neighbors and society fail to help those who suffer, people lay blame for suffering on individuals or on God. In restoring the man to wholeness, the "cure" Jesus offers is the gift of a robust life lived in response to God's love, which immediately extends to brothers and sisters: that is the ethical implication of the theology of love in the Gospel of John. God loved the world, and therefore we may love. The ethic of love is supreme in the Gospel of John.

Sabbath rules are the presenting excuse for confronting the man's newfound freedom. It is unlawful to carry a mat, they say. Mat-carrying is the command of Jesus that restores the whole life of the paralyzed man in verse 8. Pious dedication to religious strictures notwithstanding, the religious authorities display little regard for the cured man. They offer nothing like the regard Jesus gives to him.

John 5:9b–15 stands with other Sabbath-challenging stories, like Jesus' healing of the blind man on the Sabbath in John 9. As Paul will later

Pastoral Perspective

his encounter with Jesus in the temple, informing them that it was Jesus who cured him—an ancient example of "no good deed goes unpunished!"

In what follows I will examine two ways in which one may want to think about the pastoral implications of this text. First, in what ways do we still attempt to draw a one-to-one correspondence between sin and disease, or health and salvation? More importantly, what are the dangers of doing so? Second, in what ways are we so focused on the letter of the law in our communities of faith that we overlook opportunities for joyful celebration when someone is healed? Another way to reframe this question is to ask, in what ways do we use the letter of the law as an exclusionary device to draw boundaries between insiders and outsiders?

How does one respond to questions about the correlation of individual sin and disease or corporate sin and natural disasters? Disease and disaster were understood by ancient people of faith to occur as a form of God's punishment for sin; these attitudes may not prevail in contemporary communities of faith, but the questions still linger there. Some facts in the text are clear. The man was ill for a long time—thirty-eight years! As Jesus heals the man, the occasion is marked by an imperative: "Sin no more!" The imperative is followed by a caution that if the man does not clean up his act, something worse may happen the next time. We may be inclined to conclude that in this case there was a correlation between the man's condition and his behavior. We may wonder about what could be worse than thirty-eight years of physical disability and consider the harshness of Jesus' cautionary words. Finally, we may want to question the man's complacency and whether or not his social location contributes to his condition. Either he was really oblivious, lacking in imagination, or he had become hopeless after all those years.

What are the implications for us? Are there certain behaviors that may lead to diminished health? Yes. This is not new information. Is it the case, for example, that all individuals with lung cancer were smokers? Emphatically, no. A pastoral perspective requires that we suspend our judgments concerning *how* an individual becomes sick or has diminished capacities and instead focus on the reality of the illness and restoration to health. We may also want to provide some education about how to prevent situations of diminishment in the future. If the situation is more corporate in nature, the same realities apply. We respond to the realities of suffering with judgment suspended

Righteous Intentionality: A Discussion in the Temple. Although it appears that neither the narrator nor the Johannine Jesus has any interest in the coming to faith of the man, the most arresting comments in these verses at least hint at a concern for the man's spiritual well-being, in relation to Christ. For instance, later Jesus finds the man in the temple and again initiates contact with him. The scene lacks continuity and separates the actions from the surrounding narrative. There is no mention of the Sabbath, but this scene actually points back to 5:8–9a. It is here that the author explains the figurative meaning of Jesus' command that the man *peripatei* (NRSV "began to walk")—that he conduct his life in a certain manner.

Jesus reminds the man that he has been made healthy, and then adds that he should sin no more, or he might find himself in a more desperate condition than that from which he has just recovered. Jesus' response to the man's healing moves beyond the physical event and the issues it raises about Sabbath. In Jewish tradition, sickness and death are often interpreted as God's punishment for sinful behavior. Jesus breaks the traditional link between physical dysfunction and God's punishment; the man's physical problems have been eliminated. However, sinful behavior creates situations and circumstances much more degrading than physical illness.

While Jesus does not speak in terms of belief or faith, we are reminded of what he says later in 11:9–10, where *peripatein* ("live in a certain way, walk") is also used in a figurative sense. Jesus encourages the man to move forward with his life in a way that suggests he walk or live as if he sees the light of this world (11:9), and not stumble through the night, lacking the protection and wisdom of God because the light of the world is not in him (11:10). Jesus, in effect, reminds the man to live his life in accordance with the will of God so that he is able to navigate the vicissitudes of life in a steady and deliberate manner.

Having established the man's ability to be responsible for his actions, in 5:14 Jesus holds him morally accountable for his behavior. Jesus is not suggesting that the man's actions caused his illness, but Jesus demands from the man, who has encountered the healing power of God, a certain righteous intentionality in his movements through the world. The righteous intentionality that Jesus emphasizes is important because it carries eschatological and soteriological significance. For instance, in 5:25–29, as Jesus explains his relationship to "the Father" and describes the end times, the soteriological promise

is, we might say, recalibrating the measuring rod, but we should not thereby assume that he is throwing out altogether the observance of the Lord's Day. Indeed, if we see the Lord's Day as no more than divine sanction for a much-needed break, we likely have the proportions seriously wrong ourselves.

Second, we see the man who was healed, but whose behavior is hard to interpret. Is he mainly afraid and preoccupied with saving his own skin, since Sabbath violations could be capital offenses? Is he a bit of a numbskull, not perceiving that identifying Jesus to those unsympathetic to him puts Jesus as risk? Is he actively betraying Jesus, perhaps to curry favor with those he sees as being in power? In any case, he is hardly an admirable character; and we may observe that fear and self-interest may be as effective instruments of evil as outright malice. We ought not too quickly to excuse his, or our own, moral weakness.

Also significant is the insufficiency of a miracle to produce faith. In fact, it is quite astonishing how regularly people who have experienced a dramatic deliverance of any sort pick up their lives as if nothing had happened. Here again, we may contrast this man with the royal official of John 4:46–54. His daughter's healing does bring the official to belief in Jesus (4:53). The restored invalid in John 5, however, gives no evidence whatever of faith or even gratitude after his healing.

Many people insist that if only they had sufficiently dramatic evidence, they would believe, implying that God is guilty of failing to give them what they need. Others who are denied something they earnestly believe they had sought in faith feel betrayed and turn away in anger and disappointment. Still others live lives of such terrible difficulty that the real miracle is their continued trust in God. We cannot predict from God's interventions, or failures to intervene, in people's lives, whether they will follow Jesus. Anyone coming to this narrative thinking, "If only such a thing happened to me, I would believe," should be confronted with the negative outcome of the account in that respect.

Third, we find Jesus again taking the initiative, confronting the healed man in the temple with strong words. He seems to link sin and sickness, as well as sin and something worse than sickness. The preacher will want to be absolutely clear that not all sickness results from sin, as John 9:3 says plainly. Ill people do not need preachers adding guilt to their maladies. However, the preacher should not backpedal too fast and too far, for sometimes sin quite

John 5:9b–15

Theological Perspective

write to the Galatians, the basic message is, do not submit again to the yoke of slavery. The Sabbath laws do not express the heart of the Sabbath. The Sabbath is about living in fullness of life, which may sometimes involve walking and mat-carrying and telling the truth to religious authorities.

Jesus makes a pastoral call to follow up with his client. This pattern will happen again in John 9, in a more elaborate version of the same sequence: healing; religious controversy; Jesus' follow-up. Jesus recommends not sinning, so that nothing worse happens. Jesus is not reinterpreting what took place. The man gains wholeness by a free gift in God's love, not by virtue of his acceptance of Jesus. However, the man's faith is a part of the health and wholeness that is given him by God's grace. The command not to sin again is another side of being "made well" by Jesus, whose healing and forgiveness are inextricably bound together.

Beyond the pool, there is a new horizon, which Jesus indicates is the ongoing work of God. Jesus is working as his Father is working, and new life is given to all who believe. The follow-up of Jesus to the man, plus the identification of Jesus' work with the ongoing work of the "Father," not only provides a sharp contrast to the human neglect and competition that has previously left the man behind; his claim also gives the authorities a further reason to seek his death. The continuing revelation of Jesus' relationship with his Father deepens the divide between those who believe and live in response to the eternal life that has come to them in Jesus and those who persist in unbelief.

Preachers and teachers may ask hearers of the text to assess the degree to which the passive acceptance of their own brokenness affects their sense of worth; or how their disregard for neighbors in need of healing and wholeness diminishes the health and well-being of the community of faith; or what it means today to carry one's mat and walk in wholeness of life, whatever one's physical condition. How is God still working today to make people whole?

GILSON A. C. WALDKOENIG

Pastoral Perspective

and, if needed, offer education for improved lifestyles in the future. The importance of a pastoral perspective is that we do not draw conclusions that are not supported by facts, so that we do not exacerbate suffering by blaming the one who suffers.

The correlation between sin and sickness is difficult, but not as difficult as considering the nature of our own uses of legalism to exclude others and/or overshadow joy that accompanies healing. In a culture where traditional mainline Protestant churches continue to experience decline, it may be a more difficult task to explore just how our own practices as communities of faith serve to exacerbate the decline. Anxiety about the future drives individuals to cling to positive memories of the past and to fear change in the present or future. Then, like the authorities in this text, we overlook the moments of joy and ask at least metaphorically, "Who told you to do this?" The question itself is accusatory and sets our defense mechanisms on high alert.

The discussion of this passage does not need to stir up more anxiety; rather, the teacher or preacher needs to point out what is obvious and overlooked. Even the man who took no initiative on his own behalf was found and healed by Jesus. This is a point to be celebrated! Jesus seeks us out and we are called to invite others into our communities where they may be known and healed. In studying this story, the church would do well to ask how not to become mirror reflections of the authorities of Jesus' day, who were unable or unwilling to focus on the priority of human need over the practice of religious rule and ritual. Like the man who was afflicted, Jesus knows our afflictions, Jesus finds us, and Jesus makes us whole. In response and shaped by gratitude, we are called to look beyond ourselves and find new ways to share this grace with others.

CAROL L. SCHNABL SCHWEITZER

Exegetical Perspective

for humanity centers on "works" that are defined either by a righteous/morally excellent intentionality or by an evil/morally base intentionality:

> "Very truly, I tell you, the hour is coming, and is now here, when the dead will hear the voice of the Son of God, and those who hear will live. For just as the Father has life in himself, so he has granted the Son also to have life in himself; and he has given him authority to execute judgment, because he is the Son of Man. Do not be astonished at this; for the hour is coming when all who are in their graves will hear his voice and will come out—those who have done good [*agatha poiēsantes*], to the resurrection of life, and those who have done evil [*phaula praxantes*], to the resurrection of condemnation." (5:25–29)

So, while this encounter does not appear to alter the man's understanding of Jesus as simply a "helpful stranger," Jesus' authoritative comments do reveal the interest he has in the man's faith life, and they also highlight the exceptional claims he makes for himself as the appointed life-giver and judge (vv. 29–30).

The Mark of the Messiah. The man leaves Jesus and returns to "the Jews," the religious authorities. He informs them that it was Jesus who made him healthy. Still though, there is not a sense of belief or faith on the man's part. He does not offer Jesus a word of thanksgiving or gratefulness. His report on Jesus to the religious authorities is not filled with reverence and awe. Although Jesus reveals himself as one who transcends the Sabbath, the man does not describe Jesus as one who acts with divine authority. However, the man's indifference is not without exegetical significance. The mark of the Messiah is not simply to elicit belief through healing miracles or other miraculous signs. John reminds his readers that the Messiah must heal, deliver, and encourage, without regard for accolades or acceptance. In fact, sometimes the work of the Messiah leads to contention, conflict, and disbelief.

MONYA A. STUBBS

Homiletical Perspective

obviously leads to sickness, as when disease is transmitted by dirty needles used by those addicted to illegal drugs. Sometimes, someone else's sin leads to sickness, as when farmworkers' children are harmed by pesticides. Sometimes harbored resentments and the like really do produce physical maladies. Maybe, when an ill person asks if God is punishing them, it is better first to ask if there is any reason why God should, before hastening to give reassurance.

In the case of the healed invalid, we cannot be sure whether the sin Jesus speaks of preceded or continued throughout his long disability, or whether Jesus is commenting on what may have been his ungrateful and self-interested response to his healing. The "something worse" than his disability that Jesus spoke of (v. 14) could be taken to refer to final judgment; physical healing in this life is not all that counts! This is another reality preachers may be tempted to avoid. However, doing so is to fail in one's responsibility to preach the whole counsel of God, for Jesus has a great deal to say about judgment. Sin will not go unpunished forever. Justice will come. The merciful Lord who seeks out and helps the needy is the same Lord who sees the heart and will not be deceived.

Because these various themes have aspects that rightly make preachers and their hearers anxious, one strategy would be to take up only one of them, carefully playing out what we learn here of a godly Lord's Day observance; or the question of character, miracle, and faith; or the interrelationship of sin, sickness, and judgment. Alternatively, the preacher could use a faceted design, taking up different perspectives held by the various characters in turn, with the final facet carrying the major emphasis of the sermon.

MARGUERITE SHUSTER

John 5:16–18

¹⁶Therefore the Jews* started persecuting Jesus, because he was doing such things on the sabbath. ¹⁷But Jesus answered them, "My Father is still working, and I also am working." ¹⁸For this reason the Jews were seeking all the more to kill him, because he was not only breaking the sabbath, but was also calling God his own Father, thereby making himself equal to God.

Theological Perspective

The story about the man freed from paralysis, the pool of Beth-zatha, and the reaction of the religious authorities concludes with three verses that suggest three different theological themes. The first theme concerns the ongoing nature of revelation. The second theme returns to the conflict between those who believe in Jesus and those who remain in unbelief: how can we understand the theological conflict in John's community in contrast to centuries of murderous misunderstanding? Finally, there is John's central belief that the Word was in the beginning and was with God and was God (1:1). Taking the theological themes verse by verse, we will first consider John 5:17 by itself, which can be read as a conclusion to the Sabbath challenge lodged against the cured man and Jesus in the narrative just prior. Second, verses 16 and 18 draw the conflict with the religious authorities to a close, at least temporarily, though the line John draws between belief and unbelief is a line we still draw in the theological sand. Again it must be said that it is best to think of "the Jews" in the text as religious authorities, not an ethnic group. (See the excursus on "the Jews" at the front of this volume.) Finally, verse 18 broaches the unity of Jesus and God, a theological motif in the Gospel of John.

*See "'The Jews' in the Fourth Gospel" on pp. xi–xiv.

Pastoral Perspective

The entire fifth chapter of John's Gospel is devoted to a discussion of Jesus' Sabbath work. Thus a question for those of us who live in the twenty-first century is, what does it mean to honor the Sabbath? The words "he did this sort of thing" ("he was doing such things," v. 16 NRSV) need to command our attention. These words remind us of the healing of the disabled man at poolside on the Sabbath. An inquiring mind will want to know what other types of healings (or work) Jesus performed that are not recorded for us but nevertheless drew the ire of those religious authorities who did know of their occurrence. The healing events disrupted the status quo to the extent that the religious authorities in Jerusalem were willing to persecute Jesus. It was not simply Jesus' apparent disregard for the Sabbath that garnered hostility against him; it was their interpretation of his claim that insofar as God, his Father, was at work, so too would he be at work, bestowing the power of life upon those who needed healing.

The transition to twenty-first-century life from such a brief text may present a significant challenge. From a pastoral perspective one may want to address the importance of finding a way to maintain Sabbath practices (e.g., worship and rest) in a cultural context that makes it difficult. One may also want to examine the manner in which established churches

Exegetical Perspective

Oneness with God: An Interpretive Misunderstanding. The story returns to the interaction between Jesus and his opponents. The narrator states that because of Jesus' work on the Sabbath, "the Jews"[1] begin to strategize his demise. Jesus' opponents move on two fronts. As indicated by the term *ediōkon*, "the Jews" started harassing and annoying Jesus, and they also initiated legal action against him. The imperfect use of *ediōkon* ("started persecuting," v. 16 NRSV) suggests that the "persecution" was a consistent agitation. Jesus defends himself against his accusers by revealing an inflammatory truth: "My Father is still working, and I also am working" (v. 17). After Jesus' response, the narrator states that hostility by "the Jews" intensifies against him. No longer are they only persecuting him; they now want to kill (*apokteinai*, v. 18) him (7:1; 8:37, 40; 11:53). Read in light of Jewish Sabbath theology, the religious authorities' charge that Jesus' words are blasphemous seems more reasonable. For instance:

> It was clear to Jewish thinkers that God could not rest on the Sabbath. Creation continued, people died and were thus judged; children were born, and thus life was given. Despite Genesis 2:2–3

1. Francis J. Moloney, *The Gospel of John*, ed. Daniel J. Harrington, SJ, Sacra pagina 4 (Collegeville, MN: The Liturgical Press, 1998), 9–11.

Homiletical Perspective

In these few verses we come to the crux of the account of the disabled man healed at the pool of Beth-zatha: the question of Jesus' identity. Make no mistake; if Jesus was a mere man, his opponents had reason to oppose him: he was a dangerous man, a lawbreaker, and a blasphemer—and all the more dangerous if people, rightly or wrongly, thought him to have impressive powers. Consider cult leaders of past and recent memory whose orchestrated "miracles" have drawn droves of followers, sometimes with disastrous results. One cannot unhesitatingly trust works of power. Jesus as well as his opponents would know the Old Testament teaching (Deut. 13:1–3) that even prophets whose prophecies came true must not be believed if what they advocated led away from the one God. Impressive results were not enough. The true prophet of God, Jeremiah, forbade carrying burdens on the Sabbath (Jer. 17:21–27). One could not let this kind of thing go.

Nor, it would appear, did Jesus intend that his choice of the Sabbath for performing this healing be let go. He had in a sense provoked conflict by doing on the Sabbath what did not have to be done on the Sabbath. A man who had lain by a pool for thirty-eight years could lie there one more day without overwhelming harm. Furthermore, if all Jesus had in mind was promoting a more generous,

John 5:16–18

Theological Perspective

The middle verse of the three, verse 17, contains Jesus' affirmation that he and his Father are "still working." The aphorism is a fitting retort to the challenge raised in the previous verses that the man Jesus cured was breaking Sabbath law by carrying his mat and walking about. The story links to other Sabbath-breaking challenges, and the rejoinder in verse 17 asserts the ultimate settlement to all such challenges. With the author of the Sabbath, Jesus is still working. The work that Jesus does is on par with the original creative work of God, with which the Gospel of John begins; and the creative work of God never stops.

The ongoing work of Christ and of God has many times been a central theological claim, whenever renewal or reform movements push practice or belief beyond present understanding and into new horizons. Theological traditions differ on the duration and content of the ongoing work. Pentecostal movements claim the continuance or restart of the normative work of God through the work and power of the Spirit. Others identify the normative work of God primarily with the work of God revealed during the time narrated in the New Testament. Therefore ongoing expressions of God's work are mediated through church, ministry, sacraments, and witnesses as they display conformity with the original work. A fruitful discussion might invite hearers to consider whether God is at work in the world today and by what authority they have reached their conclusions.

The contrast of Jesus and the religious authorities in John 5 gives preachers and teachers an opportunity to invite hearers into a deeper understanding of the issues and conflicts shaping John's community. An important model for contextual understanding is offered by Pauline scholar Brigitte Kahl in her *Galatians Re-Imagined*.[1] Kahl asks who the Galatians really were; likewise readers might ask who the followers of Jesus really were in the Gospel of John. Kahl shows that the Galatians were oppressed people in the Roman Empire. Paul's advice that they not submit to Jewish law was not a recommendation to be a Christian rather than a Jew; rather, it was a challenge to be a Galatian in full view rather than "hiding" as something else.

While John's Gospel clearly is a different context, a parallel effort to read John without coded categories could help the focus of preaching and teaching to be on the liberation message to the disciples, rather than on the rejection of those who did not believe in Jesus. Such a reading would be in keeping

1. Brigitte Kahl, *Galatians Re-Imagined: Reading with the Eyes of the Vanquished*, Paul in Critical Contexts (Minneapolis: Fortress Press, 2010).

Pastoral Perspective

continue the practices of those ancient gatekeepers of the faith, thereby creating a tension between the rules for practicing faith and the relationships in faith communities. If contemporary Christians are to understand the seriousness of the charges against Jesus, they need to have a deeper appreciation of the significance of Jesus' violation of the Sabbath.

What does it mean to "keep Sabbath" in a world that makes it difficult? Sports tournaments for young people take families away from their congregations on weekends. Others are reluctant or unable to turn down opportunities for employment that require them to work on the Sabbath. Still others become disillusioned with the rhetoric and behaviors of so-called believers, including faith-community leaders. Thus they leave organized religion altogether. Misconduct scandals, identification with perceived liberal or conservative values, and at times intolerance for difference are among some of the excuses and criticisms (valid or not) that lead the disillusioned away from church. These "violations" do detract from the life of the community, even if they occur outside the normal worship time.

Jesus' perceived violations of Jewish Sabbath laws infused life and health into his community. What are the sorts of actions or behaviors that we would perceive as violations of "Sabbath" that are simultaneously life-giving? An obvious response is medical personnel or other human services personnel who work during worship times and need alternative times for Sabbath taking. Other possibilities include mission trips and programs that require commitment from the faithful beyond the worship hour. We need to be cautious, however, that we do not use attendance at worship as a litmus test for faith.

This leads us to consideration of a second and somewhat riskier pastoral concern that arises from the text: In what ways do we, like the ancient religious leaders, prioritize rules over relationships? What are the rules about our worship or faith practices that we cling to and defend adamantly? The responses to this question will vary from congregation to congregation, but the constant is that many will be able to describe a rule that is deemed inviolable.

Another way to engage this question is to consider what challenge to current worship practices or preferences would likely lead to division and hostility in the congregation. Attention need not be focused solely on worship practices. Consider, for instance, what the "rules" of church membership are, both written and spoken, as well as unwritten, unspoken

God could not cease to be active, even on the Sabbath, or else history would come to an end. This prerogative of God, though, could not be usurped by any creature. Sabbath was a "memory" of a creating and redeeming God rendered present to a people. It celebrated God's sovereignty as creator and redeemer and called on the people to recognize this sovereignty publically. Sabbath existed for the celebration of the unique sovereignty of Israel's Deity.[2]

Following this perspective, Jesus' opponents rightly understand his statement as both admitting to breaking the Sabbath and equating himself with God. Jesus breaks the Sabbath, however, not to do away with it. He breaks (*elyen*, v. 18) it in the sense that he "loosens" or "releases" it from the accepted interpretation. The loosening or releasing for John has to do with Jesus' identity. John's great christological claim is not that Jesus and God are equal, that is, equality in the sense of Jesus perceiving himself as another god. While Jesus does boast oneness with God, it is not because he understands himself independent from God. He cannot act independent of God. Jesus' relationship with God is one of radical dependence (5:19). Jesus is God's Word, God's big idea and ideals, made flesh and interjected into human history. Jesus gives life to the dead, restores health to invalids, and refashions estranged relationships. Jesus is empowered by the "Father," with the glory and honor of an only Son, to enact and/or imitate the Father's work (*ergazetai*, v. 17).

To Work and to Love. The focus on "work" is important. It is associated with christological and eschatological concerns. On numerous occasions, the Gospel of John ties performing the work of God to Jesus' identity as the Messiah; John also ties work to people's belief in Jesus as the Son of God and therefore to their eternal salvation. Consider John 4:31–34 and 6:27–35, two passages that bookend Jesus' healing of the lame man. In 4:31–34, Jesus' disciples encourage him to eat. He responds, "I have food to eat that you do not know about. . . . My food is to do the will of him who sent me and to complete his work [*ergon*]." Jesus explains that the work of the one who sent him is to invite *all* (he is in the midst of the Samaritans, 4:39–42) people into the favor of God's love. Those who follow Jesus must also hold this work as their life's mission; it is the bread that enables their life and sustains their future.

2. Moloney, *Gospel of John*, 170.

mercy-centered view of what was proper for faithful persons to do on the day of rest, he could easily have argued for expansion of the interpretation of those passages that already did allow essential, life-saving activity even on the Sabbath. No, something more than mercy was as stake here. Jesus' identity, the sovereign authority by which he acted, was the larger issue. *What* he did could not rightly be understood apart from *who* did it.

This identity question comes to the fore when Jesus, giving answer to his opponents' implied challenge to his behavior, speaks of God as "*my* Father." Jews, like Christians today, understood God as *their* Father; that was not a problem. However, using the singular in an emphatic construction, implying a unique relationship to God not shared by others, was indeed a problem. The Jewish leaders heard Jesus as making a blasphemous claim of equality with God, a sin much worse than the already serious offense of Sabbath breaking and one that cut at the heart of their monotheistic convictions. Jesus did not correct them. They were alarmed, not because they heard Jesus wrongly, but because they heard him rightly.

Exegetes and theologians will properly wrestle at length with what a text like this means with respect to Jesus' equality with the Father. However, exploring the nuances of Trinitarian theology will probably not be the preacher's most productive approach to this passage. It would be better to focus more simply on the clear implication that Jesus does what God does, and that we see the work of God uniquely in Jesus. In him, we have not a mere imitation of God, like the imitation of Christ to which Christians are often enjoined, but a true manifestation of God.

The specific thing this passage says God does is continue to work, including on the Sabbath—obviously a problem if one reads Genesis 2:2–3 as involving cessation of all activity on God's part when the initial creation was complete. Jewish interpreters had long wrestled with this problem themselves; for they, like Christian interpreters, tended to suppose that the whole of creation would simply collapse, were God to cease sustaining it in existence. The rabbis came to some creative solutions, like the suggestion that the God who filled and encompassed all spaces could not be accused of "working" by moving anything from one domain to another. Taken alone, then, the idea that God continues to work need not be problematic. The problem was that Jesus gave to himself God's own prerogatives.

In fact, that God never ceases to be engaged with creation is an especially important affirmation in

John 5:16–18

Theological Perspective

with freedom regarding the Sabbath laws in the previous verses and would reinforce the basic intent of a gospel of new life throughout this passage and the whole Gospel of John. The message of fresh and ongoing life, from Christ and for people, resonates in dimensions yet unheard when *freed from* the confines of the self-interest that beset religious authorities of any age and *freed for* the abundant life that follows from a theological commitment to love neighbors, just as Christ in the Gospel of John loved the world.

The end of verse 18 broaches the unity of Jesus and God, a central theological affirmation throughout the Gospel of John. Beginning with the first verse of the prologue and continuing through the many "I am" statements of Jesus, which are identified with the I AM spoken from out of the burning bush to Moses on Horeb (Exod. 3:6), John rings the changes on the unity of the Son and the Father, and on the Word that was in the beginning and the Word that came to dwell among us in the fullness of time. In the preceding story, Jesus simply said his Father and he were still working. Later in the Gospel of John, Jesus will say that he and the Father are one, and the one who has seen Jesus has seen the Father. In Jesus' prayer on the eve of his crucifixion, he begins with the petition that the Father glorify the Son so that the Son may glorify the Father (17:1). Subsequently, parties in the church seeking scriptural warrant for a higher Christology and a closer tie of Jesus Christ with God have turned to the Gospel of John for that warrant. The text in this case is not enforcing a high Christology such as would later become an issue, but is citing the reason that Jesus' oneness with the Father was an offense in the religion of his day.

Each verse by itself invites the preacher, teacher, and reader of Scripture to ask what is at stake today in believing that God is still working as Christ is alive and working in the world God so loved.

GILSON A. C. WALDKOENIG

Pastoral Perspective

but understood. How do we engage with one another around these rules as members of a faith community? Our responses to questions about who belongs and other questions like them often highlight the qualities of those individuals who are deemed to be ideal members in our faith communities. We draw invisible boundaries that define who is an insider and who is an outsider or exile in the community of faith. As we examine this reality in our own congregations, we mirror what is happening between Jesus and religious authorities in these verses. As members identify unexpectedly with the religious authorities in relationship to insider rules, they also may be able to experience the offensiveness of the gospel.

Thus, if one chooses to focus on this second concern, one needs to be prepared for the reactions that may ensue. Speaking a prophetic word with a posture of humility that acknowledges the teacher's own struggles with the issues and questions at hand is an act of invitation that may lead others to do the same.

Jesus responds quite plainly to those who interrogate him, claiming that his life's work is the work of salvation. There are many ways one may choose to interpret Jesus' saving work, including a restoration of health, practices of love and forgiveness, a call to justice for the oppressed, and the creation of communities where God's word is not only heard but practiced in ways that glorify God. Thus a final pastoral consideration for twenty-first-century Christians is to examine how their lives and work contribute to, or detract from, God's work in the world to bring about wholeness and reconciliation. Sabbath keeping and holy living are not limited to one hour on the day when the faithful gather for worship. Acts of hospitality, practicing forgiveness, attending to the aging, ecological awareness, and appropriate stewardship of personal resources are some of the many opportunities we have to reflect on our own vocations as being life-giving.

We will give way to sinful behaviors, but on those occasions we need to remember that Jesus extended grace to all, so that we would have plenteous opportunities to live life abundantly. How do our own lives give testimony or provide evidence to the casual observer that we have received a gift from Christ that is truly transformative?

CAROL L. SCHNABL SCHWEITZER

Exegetical Perspective

John 6:27–35 describes a teaching moment between Jesus and his followers. After a feeding miracle, Jesus warns his followers against seeking him for mere physical gain. He instructs them that they must work (*ergazesthe*, 6:27) not for food that perishes or food that simply fills their stomachs. Jesus reminds them that there is a form of nourishment that transcends physical bread, and it is for this bread that they must work. The people ask Jesus what they must do to perform the "works of God." Jesus responds: "This is the work [*ergon*] of God, that you believe in him whom he has sent" (6:29; also see 3:17–21).

Scholars argue that John is offering an alternative to Israel's belief that the Law provided life for those who lived by it and they labored on the Law so that they might have life.[3] Fresh manna in the wilderness authenticated Moses. The people want to know what sign Jesus will perform so that they might engage the work of believing in him (6:30). Jesus corrects their logic. He does not need to perform a sign; he is the sign. Moreover, it was not Moses who provided the bread from heaven, but God provides the true bread that gives life to the world (6:32–33). Jesus is the bread of life, and the only way to do the work of God is to believe in the one whom God has sent (6:35).

In Sum: Participating in Love. John 5:16–18 captures the heart of the argument between those who understood Jesus to be a new and definitive revelation of God in the world and those who did not. The passage inaugurates an ideological conflict that will be unto death. However, couched in the deep schism between the opposing perspectives about Israel's messianic hopes is a passionate plea for a renewed understanding of God's activity in the world. John's unyielding call for people to accept Jesus as the Messiah/Son of God is ultimately a call for people to participate in the life-giving work/energy (*ergon*) of God in the world. Jesus is the embodiment of God's big idea (*logos*) of love. John asks that people subject themselves to God's love and in doing so free themselves to experience eternal life.

MONYA A. STUBBS

Homiletical Perspective

a day when many people seek to deal with alleged conflicts between science and religion by making the (deistic) assumption that the Creator, having set things in motion and established their physical laws, then left them to run on their own. Taking this tack not only gives the scientific explanation of all things exhaustive scope, right back to the moment of anything at all coming into being; it also rules out miracle from the start.

By contrast, a God understood to be continually at work in creation does not act, even in miracles, as One who intrudes suddenly from the outside, but as the ever-present God who sometimes chooses to make that presence known in perceptible and surprising ways. Thus Christians may see an analogy between Jesus' healing miracles, which were not granted to all, and God's dealings with the world in general. That we do not understand the "why" of particular manifestations is not an argument that they do not occur, but an expression of the mystery of God's freedom—and perhaps of that freedom God grants to us.

The unsettling character of this mystery, in a world so full of pain and evil, makes it especially important that we have confidence in God's character. Elsewhere (14:9) Jesus says that the one who has seen him has seen the Father; here the implication is that the Father's work and Jesus' work are intimately related. We gain confidence in God's character, then, by looking at Jesus. If Jesus abrogated a strictly interpreted law of Sabbath observance, he did so in a way that drove home the truth of a God more concerned for mercy and restoration of the creation than Jesus' contemporaries had discerned in their determination to preserve proper worship of this God. Moreover, he did so not as a mere man offering one more opinion for discussion, but as one who was speaking of his own Father and was himself acting in the full power and authority of that relationship. Who Jesus is and what God is like were both critically at stake in this confrontation.

MARGUERITE SHUSTER

---

3. Moloney, *Gospel of John*, 209.

¹⁹Jesus said to them, "Very truly, I tell you, the Son can do nothing on his own, but only what he sees the Father doing; for whatever the Father does, the Son does likewise. ²⁰The Father loves the Son and shows him all that he himself is doing; and he will show him greater works than these, so that you will be astonished. ²¹Indeed, just as the Father raises the dead and gives them life, so also the Son gives life to whomever he wishes. ²²The Father judges no one but has given all judgment to the Son, ²³so that all may honor the Son just as they honor the Father. Anyone who does not honor the Son does not honor the Father who sent him. ²⁴Very truly, I tell you, anyone who hears my word and believes him who sent me has eternal life, and does not come under judgment, but has passed from death to life."

Theological Perspective

Questioning the identity of another person is a basic human instinct, because we want to know with whom we are dealing. When we hear a knock on our door, we ask, "Who is there?" When we interview a person for a job, we ask, "What are your credentials?" It is human nature to want to know with whom we are dealing; so we ask, "Who are you?" This is also a question that humans have asked of God for generations. Jacob pleaded for the name of the one with whom he wrestled, and Moses asked God to speak his name.

Jesus faced similar questions, questions that remain with us today. Who is this Jesus? Why does his life matter? Is he God, or is he human? The religious authorities referenced in the text as "the Jews" not only questioned Jesus; they also persecuted him and looked for reasons to get rid of him. They found a reason when they discovered a man whom Jesus had healed on the Sabbath. They interrogated this man, asking, "Who did this? Who is the man who said to you, 'Take up your mat and walk'?" (5:12). When they learned it was Jesus, they became infuriated and anger raged in their hearts, for they believed Jesus had made "himself equal to God" (5:18).

One suspects this argumentative group was already wrestling with questions about Jesus' identity. The man's answer provoked an intense reaction.

Pastoral Perspective

One morning in worship, the lay liturgist read aloud the assigned Scripture passage. It was the liturgist's custom to say, at the conclusion of the reading, "This is the word of the Lord." On one occasion the liturgist instead turned to the preacher and remarked, "I sure hope you are going to tell us what in the world this means"—to which the congregation on autopilot replied, "Thanks be to God."

It could have been this passage from the Gospel of John that perplexed that cheeky liturgist. There is no story line in these verses. There is no parable. There is no miracle. There is only Jesus talking about himself and his relationship to God the Father. Frankly, trying to follow the metaphysical claims Jesus makes here could give some readers an actual physical headache.

It helps to note the context for Jesus' discourse. Barely into chapter 5 of the Gospel, the tension is mounting. Jesus arrives in Jerusalem and immediately raises the hackles of the powers that be. The Sheep Gate is swarmed with the sick and lame. One imagines them complete with cardboard signs and coin-filled cups befitting their strategic position on the busy thoroughfare. In conversation with Jesus, one sick man is made well, only to be stopped by the religious authorities for walking with a mat on the Sabbath. The man explains that Jesus told him to do it. If someone is to be blamed, it should be Jesus.

Exegetical Perspective

Following his healing of a paralyzed man, Jesus is challenged by the authorities for working on the Sabbath (5:16–18). God had rested on the Sabbath and commanded the Israelites to do the same (Gen. 2:2–3; Exod. 20:8–11). On what basis could Jesus command someone to work on the Sabbath (by carrying a mat) or do so himself? Contemporary Jewish interpreters asserted that God continued to work on the Sabbath by giving life and sustaining the universe. Jesus here claims that he may work on the Sabbath, because the Son does what the Father does. That claim merits the accusation that Jesus "makes himself equal to God" (5:18), that he falsely exalts himself to a status not rightly his. Jesus then explains not only why he acts as the Father does, but even expands his claims to include the divine prerogatives to give life and to judge (vv. 21–24).

The Son's Life-Giving Work (vv. 19–21). Jesus opens his discourse with an emphatic doubled "Amen," asserting that "the Son can do nothing on his own" (cf. 5:30). Jesus does not work independently of God; indeed, he cannot work without God's authority. In asserting his dependence on the Father's authorization, Jesus also asserts his unity with God. The Son never works apart from the Father; Jesus' work is therefore the work of God. Jesus further describes

Homiletical Perspective

This passage is positively riddled with typically Johannine pitfalls. It is no wonder it appears neither in the Revised Common Lectionary nor in the newer Narrative Lectionary. Though these words mark the opening of Jesus' first fully developed discourse in John's Gospel—and thus deserve our attention—still they do not tend to capture our imaginations at first blush. This is perhaps because we know full well how much thick and cumbersome, even *tiresome*, discourse is yet to come in John's telling of the Gospel, and we have little patience for such tedious talk.

Sunday worshipers are likely to feel the same. If all the recent demographic research is true, it is just this sort of overtly theological, doctrinal, and *dogmatic* discourse that has contributed to the widespread sense among many modern Americans that the church has nothing relevant to say about life anymore. Combine such well-worn concepts as *eternal life* and *judgment* with the added ingredient of a seemingly rigid androcentrism (*Father, Father, Father, Son . . .*), and you have a recipe for a sanctuary full of either the sleepy or the offended.

However, it need not be so. The first step in reengaging with this discourse is to understand (and for the preacher to make explicit to the congregation) its *setting*. Jesus does not speak here in a vacuum. Rather, he responds specifically to the persecution,

John 5:19–24

Theological Perspective

They wanted to kill Jesus. How one answers questions about Jesus' identity can lead to all kinds of reactions. At one end of the spectrum is the apostle Paul; with great zeal he advanced the good news of Christ, who did not count equality with God a thing to be grasped (Phil. 2:6). At the other end are the religious authorities (authorities that once included Saul before his conversion), as seen from John's perspective, who believed Jesus was equating himself with God.

So Jesus responds directly to their questions by describing his relationship to God. He describes it as a relationship like that of a parent and a child, where instructions are regularly provided. Parents often teach their children lessons through their words and actions, and they are certainly no strangers to having their children imitate them. Children often repeat words they hear, copy mannerisms, and even dress up in their parents' clothes. Children also get into a fair amount of trouble, especially when they break the rules and fail to follow through as they were instructed. Jesus emphasizes that the Son perfectly follows through with the Father's instructions. There are no exceptions, because the Son's actions are like that of the Father. In fact, the Son's actions offer a clear reflection of God the Father. Jesus understands his own identity as that of one who lives with "unqualified obedience to the Father's will."[1]

This unqualified obedience is visible to us through the actions of the Son. That means we have an idea of what God the Father is like by looking at Jesus the Son. For example, the way Jesus responds to sin or the way he ministers to people in need provides us with not only a glimpse of how God acts, but also an example for us to emulate.

The text names two specific activities of the Son: he is to give life and to stand as judge, and these activities are often thought of as the "greater works" (v. 20) cited by John. Giving life and judging are understood in Jewish tradition as the activities of God that continue even on the Sabbath.[2] God does not rest from this work, because it is a part of God's character. God is working to bring life to all; to do so, judgment is required. Judgment challenges us. It says to us, "What you have done is wrong," and then demands we change our ways. Judgment can also be an act of affirmation. It says to us, "What you have created is good," and so we should continue doing it.

1. C. H. Dodd, *The Interpretation of the Fourth Gospel* (Cambridge: Cambridge University Press, 1953), 327.
2. Gail R. O'Day, "John," in *The New Interpreter's Bible: John* (Nashville: Abingdon Press, 1995), 9:584.

Pastoral Perspective

"For this reason," the Gospel writer tells us, "the Jews were seeking all the more to kill [Jesus], because he was not only breaking the sabbath, but was also calling God his own Father, thereby making himself equal to God" (5:18). In verse 19 and following, Jesus answers these accusations. He does not back down, but defends his healing work and confirms his equality with God.

Before going further, it is important to be reminded that the Gospel writer sets up "the Jews" as the straw-man villains in this text and throughout the Gospel narrative. Preachers and teachers need to parse with care the conflict John's Gospel sets up between Jesus and the Jews. Surely the good news of Jesus Christ does not hinge on the knocking down of Jewish straw men, that is, religious authorities.

The substance of this passage articulates Jesus' claims about his sonship and relationship to the Father. The church has long wrestled with questions of the Trinity and Christology. The faithful have argued over the claims Jesus makes about his works and the works of the Father. Do they both raise the dead to life? Is the Father alone responsible for judgment? How is it that showing disrespect to the Son necessarily disrespects the Father? These questions are the subject of controversy and heresy, and out of these debates come the creeds of the church that help us speak of the God we trust.

That is Christianity 201. We live in an era, however, when the number of people who in polls check "none" as their religious affiliation is on the rise. Many of those in the pews on Sunday morning are not "churched"; that is, they have not grown up steeped in the faith. Most do not come to church because they are eager to relive the debates that occurred at Nicaea and Chalcedon. Most are not kept up at night wrestling down the philosophical question of how Jesus can be separate from God while simultaneously being the same as God.

In reality, if people in our pews have lost sleep, it is because of the still unpaid medical bills or the pregnancy test that came back negative again. The tossing and turning is the parent at his or her wit's end or the unbearable stress at the office. It is the heart broken open by grief or the aches of an aging body that chased any hint of sleep into hiding. These dear souls come to church to hear the good news of Jesus Christ. They come in search of hope. They come to be reminded yet again of the difference Jesus might make in their lives.

Fortunately, entangled in Jesus' confusing words about himself are several strands of good news. The

his relationship to the Father with a picture of a son imitating his father, perhaps as an apprentice who learns his father's trade or craft. The son learns well because the father, in his love, shows or teaches the son everything. Here Jesus is the Son who learns from the Father. The Son does the Father's work because the Father has shown him his work. The Father and Son work in unity and in love.

The far-ranging scope of the work that Jesus does is emphasized as well: the Son does *all* that the Father does; the Son's subsequent works will be "greater" than those he has just done, causing those who see them to be astonished. It is typical of the Gospel to underscore that Jesus has been given *all things* by God (*panta*, vv. 20, 22; cf. 1:3; 3:35; 6:39; 12:32; 13:3; 16:15). That claim in turn lays the groundwork for Jesus' universal mission to all people (1:12; 6:40; 12:32).

The "greater works" (v. 20) are raising the dead and giving life (v. 21). Lazarus and Jesus are both said to be "raised from the dead," brought back from death to life in the present (12:1, 9, 17). They come out of the grave. While the verb translated here "to give life" (*zōopoieō*) typically refers in the New Testament to future resurrection (e.g., Rom. 4:17, 8:11; 1 Cor. 15:22, 36, 45), the emphasis here falls on participating in God's own life by means of faith (17:3). While eternal life properly belongs to the time following resurrection, that life is experienced in the present in fellowship with the life-giving God (17:3).

In the Scriptures the power to give life uniquely characterizes God. The epithet "living God" contrasts the Lord who creates the world with "dead idols" made by human hands (e.g., Jer. 10:8–10; 23:36; Isa. 40:18–20; 41:21–24; 44:9–20, 24; 45:16–22; 46:5–7). In an echo of Genesis 1:1, John asserts that "all things" (*panta*) are created by God through the Word (1:1–3). This life-giving and living God is the God of resurrection; the God who creates life is also the God who raises the dead to life. Jesus now exercises that unique divine power to give life in unity with the Father.

The Scope of the Son's Work (vv. 22–24). Jesus introduces a second divine prerogative that he has been given by the Father, namely, the power to judge. The word translated "to judge" (*krinō*) can also be rendered "to condemn." Jesus has been given the power to pass a sentence of judgment that acquits or accuses. Jesus' mission is to save, not to condemn (3:16–17). While elsewhere the Bible speaks of God's power to take life (2 Kgs. 5:7; cf. Deut. 32:39; 1

even death threats, that his opponents direct at him following the Sabbath healing of 5:1–9. His opponents focus their deadly ire on Jesus for two reasons, according to John: "Because [Jesus] was not only breaking the sabbath, but was also calling God his own Father, thereby making himself equal to God" (5:18). Thus the entire discourse, which runs through the remainder of the chapter, is Jesus' attempt to answer for his actions and to explain his unique relationship to God.

Already our interest is piqued, if for no other reason than that controversy stories are far more interesting than abstract speeches. Even so, more work needs to be done. In inviting the congregation into the tension of this moment, we must be clear on where we stand as modern participants. Given the long and ugly history of anti-Semitism in the church (not to mention the more general habit we have had of reading nearly *all* Scripture as congratulatory, rather than challenging), let us place ourselves in the role of Jesus' opponents. We are, our listeners are, the current religious establishment. We are the ones who hold tightly to tradition and custom under pretense of honoring God. Though we may not often resort to death threats, we do expend a great deal of time and energy foreclosing new possibilities for the church, the community, and the world.

When we see ourselves as Jesus' opponents, we begin to hear not only the strongly judgmental tone of this passage, but also its deep undercurrent of hope. This hope for the world (even for us, his opponents) arises out of the unique relationship Jesus has with God. Understanding this relationship gets us to the theological and homiletical heart of this passage—even to the heart of the Gospel itself, as our long centuries of theological reflection can attest. Yet we need not descend into the depths of historical theology to speak about the relationship of Jesus to God. Rather, we may give witness to Jesus' vital connection to God *in terms he himself used*, which is to say, *relational* terms.

Worshipers will wake up for this very radical claim: that the Maker of heaven and earth not only *has* relationships, but in a very real sense *is* a relationship. Jesus of Nazareth—first-century Palestinian Jew, carpenter's son, would-be revolutionary, agitator—is the very power and presence of God in the world. Therefore, when he defies tradition to heal, it is *God* defying tradition to heal; when he speaks of life and death, it is *God* speaking of life and death; when he reaches out in love to the world, it is *God* doing that too. This last thing, love, is crucial. The

John 5:19–24

Theological Perspective

Both understandings lead to life, and both are integral to the identity of Jesus.

When Jesus healed the sick soul who was unable to walk, he was criticized for breaking the Sabbath, even though he was simply doing what God is always doing. God is working to bring life to all, in both a physical and a spiritual sense. Jesus shares in this work and continues it, even on the Sabbath, because it is a fundamental part of God's character. God does not take a day off from this work, because God is always working to bring life to all people, including those in need like the lame, blind, sick, and poor. Jesus does the same, offering God's gracious gift of eternal life to all who believe his word and believe in the One who sent him. This gift is not earned; it is not a consequence of human action. It is grace granted by God through Jesus Christ.

The identity of Jesus matters because it shapes our identity as his disciples. His life and ministry shape our life and ministry, and when we imitate his actions, we participate in the great work of God, which brings life to others. The identity of Jesus takes us to those who are hurting and suffering, like the lame, blind, sick, and poor, and demands that we share life. Participating in this work is ironically where we find our fullest life. We find that we are living within the life of Christ, which is where our identity lies.

Reflecting on the identity of Christ helps us better understand our identity as children of God who play a vital role in sharing life with the world. As we share in this work of Christ, we are empowered to share life and bring good news to others. This may lead to questions or even criticisms, but we need not fear, because we are not alone. We are surrounded by a rich tradition and a great cloud of witnesses who stand with us and who share our identity with Christ.

MARK D. WHITE

Pastoral Perspective

Son, like the Father, gives life. Life, we remember from the prologue to John's Gospel, is the light of all people. That light shines in the darkness, and the darkness has not overcome it (1:5)—very good news for our terror-stalked, grief-filled, fear-studded lives.

Verse 21 tells us that all judgment has been given to the Son. We do well not to perpetuate the heresy of a wrathful God who demands retribution and the sacrificial lamb of a Son who indulges that demand. Rather, we rejoice in the knowledge that through the power of Christ's death and resurrection, all sin and death have been defeated. We have been found guilty and yet are redeemed. The judgment we well deserve will not be exacted upon us. Thanks be to God.

Finally, Jesus tells us, "*anyone* who hears my word and believes [in] him who sent me . . . has passed from death to life" (v. 24). This statement is full of good news. First, life is available to anyone and everyone who hears and trusts in God. Second, that life is available now. The English translation "has passed" does not connote the full effect of the tense. The perfect active indicative denotes a past action whose effect continues into the present. The passage from death to life has already happened, and that movement continues to exert its effect on us here and now. The movement of salvation is not contained on a cross two thousand years ago, nor is it a future promise for which we wait. The move from death to life is felt now, experienced now, lived now.

That promise holds us more surely than the lonely darkness of our sleepless nights. In Christ Jesus we have life and light in our present. Light shines in the darkness, and the darkness does not overcome it.

JESSICA TATE

Exegetical Perspective

Sam. 2:6), John emphasizes the life-giving power of God in the face of death. The work that the Father accomplishes through the Son is giving life. In the Scriptures (among many passages, Gen. 49:16; Exod. 18:13, 22, 26) God does delegate to others the power to rule and to judge. However, in John, the one who judges also has the power to determine who lives; the power of judgment is the power of life. Somewhat astonishingly, the Father has given his entire authority to judge to the Son; the Father "judges no one" (v. 22).

Because Jesus carries out God's work of giving life and judging, it is appropriate to honor (*timaō*) him even as one honors God. In John's view, to fail to honor Jesus is to fail to honor God. The Old Testament commands to honor God (*timaō*) and to give God glory (*doxa*, LXX Pss. 28:1; 95:7; *doxan kai timēn*, Pss. 29:1; 96:7) now also include Jesus. Therefore, hearing the word of Jesus is linked to believing the Father who sent him (v. 24). For even as the Son does what he has learned to do from the Father—to give life to the dead—so he also speaks what he has heard from the Father—words that give life. Those who hear the word of Jesus "pass from death to life," because he is the embodiment of the life-giving Word of God (1:1–3) and speaks the words of eternal life (6:68).

While the Father and Son have different roles—the Father teaches and shows the Son what he is to do—they merit the same honor, further testimony to their unity. Cities or provinces of the Roman Empire often sought permission to offer "divine honors" to a living emperor, and from Augustus onward it was customary for the emperor to refuse such honors. Here Jesus himself calls for such honors, not as an arrogant assertion of his "equality with God," but because of his unity with the Father who has entrusted his work to the Son. The Son gives life in unity with the Father who loves him. For this, the Son is honored even as the Father is.

MARIANNE MEYE THOMPSON

Homiletical Perspective

relationship between God and Jesus is founded and sustained by love. Love—not as sentiment or idea but as *act* of self-giving and receiving—is what courses through their common veins. Love is God's lifeblood.

People may be led to this understanding without much fuss. Invite them to think of their own relationships of love, which, while never able fully to capture the divine relationship, are nevertheless able sometimes to point to it, to approximate it. We may begin to understand by analogy that just as we find nearly everything about our lives formed and reformed by our relationships of love—be they parent and child, spouse and spouse, or friend and friend—in just this way is the life and ministry of Jesus underwritten and undergirded by the powerful love of God.

All of which suggests that when Christ's living presence offends us by meddling in our churches, we ought to consider that the offense itself may originate with God. This is no longer abstract discourse, but a rich and challenging word. We might ask: What is it about Christ that shakes the church to its core? Is it the social barriers brazenly broken down? What about the dogged pursuit of justice? Is it perhaps his maddening refusal to meet violence with violence or to bless our business as usual?

Whatever it is about the work of Christ that irks us, he promises more of the same: *you will be astonished!* If ever we find ourselves completely at ease with the ministry of Jesus among us, it is a likely sign that we have traded the real thing for a sham. Just as God is beyond us, so too is Christ beyond our ability to grasp, to hold, to control him. Thanks be to God, though, Jesus asks not that we grasp, hold, or control him, but rather that we believe in him. In so doing, we find our own lives swept up into the current of love, into the relationship of God and Christ, which the gospel calls *life*.

DANIEL F. LEWIS

John 5:25–29

^{25}"Very truly, I tell you, the hour is coming, and is now here, when the dead will hear the voice of the Son of God, and those who hear will live. ^{26}For just as the Father has life in himself, so he has granted the Son also to have life in himself; ^{27}and he has given him authority to execute judgment, because he is the Son of Man. ^{28}Do not be astonished at this; for the hour is coming when all who are in their graves will hear his voice ^{29}and will come out—those who have done good, to the resurrection of life, and those who have done evil, to the resurrection of condemnation."

Theological Perspective

Apocalyptic visions often anticipate a day in the future when both the living and the dead will be judged. The purpose behind some of these visions is to incite fear in people so that they may change their ways before they face the judgment seat of God. Yet we learn in the text from John that divine judgment is not just a future reality. It happens in the present as God speaks through Jesus Christ. John understands that the Father has sent the Son into the world to "execute judgment" by speaking on behalf of God, so that all people may taste salvation. Even more, John would have his readers understand that a life lived through Christ is not a life lived in fear but a life lived abundantly.

The promise of the abundant life is good news because, even though death is ever present, we need not fear it. Death is not the final word. As Paul eloquently put it, "I am convinced that neither death, nor life . . . will be able to separate us from the love of God in Christ Jesus our Lord" (Rom. 8:38–39). Life is at the heart of the Christian faith. Our faith willingly confronts death, while modern culture so often does the opposite. It ignores death, pretends it will not happen; or at least it does everything in its power to prevent the inevitable. The world seeks escape from this reality, even though it would be better off facing up to death in all its forms, both

Pastoral Perspective

What happens when we die? In 2010, journalist Lisa Miller reported that 81 percent of Americans tell pollsters they believe in heaven. We cannot know exactly what they mean, Miller writes, "beyond an automatic and understandable hope for something after death besides the terrifying end of everything."[1]

What happens to us in death? The question haunts us. It meets us at bedsides, in services that bear witness to the resurrection, at the death of a beloved pet. We face it when floods devastate neighborhoods and livelihoods or when bombs go off in the midst of innocent crowds. It follows us down the aisle when we take marriage vows and at the birth of our children. The question flits through our consciousness any time we are confronted with the mysteries of life and death. It sometimes lodges in our hearts and minds, demanding we acknowledge our finitude and cosmic insignificance.

What happens to us after death? Jesus does not say much on the subject (or at least he talks about other subjects at much greater length), and when he does address life beyond death, it is far from straightforward.

Conventional wisdom takes us directly to verse 29. What happens after death is one of two things:

1. Lisa Miller, *Heaven* (New York: Harper Perennial, 2010), xiii.

Feasting on the Gospels

Exegetical Perspective

In the long discourse that comprises the bulk of John 5, Jesus explains the character of his mission as life-giving, its origins in the Father's own work, and the Father's entrusting of judgment and giving life to the Son. In this portion of the discourse, Jesus explicates the shape of his life-giving work in two ways that, at first glance, may seem to be synonymous: in the present, Jesus' voice calls the dead to life (v. 25); in the future, Jesus' voice will bring the dead out of graves (vv. 28–29). Although these ideas are related, two different facets of Jesus' life-giving work are in view: his authority to bring people into fellowship with God, who is the source of all life; and his authority to call the dead to life at the final resurrection and at that time pass the judgment that leads to life or to death. These tasks of giving life and judging are already expressions of Jesus' unity with the Father and testify to Jesus' identity as Son of God and Son of Man.

Jesus, the Life-Giving Son of God (vv. 25–26, 28–29). Jesus first speaks of an hour that "is coming, and is now here." In Judaism at the time of Jesus, "eternal life" was widely conceived of as the life of the age to come, the life that belonged to the coming reign of God. The distinctive note introduced by Jesus is that the coming hour in which life would be given is

Homiletical Perspective

The hour is coming, and now is—a familiar trope for John. Jesus has already spoken in these terms several times. First, he protested to his mother at Cana that his hour had not yet come; later on, he spoke to a Samaritan woman of an hour in which the very character of worship in Israel would be changed forever. Now he speaks of an hour in which "the dead will hear the voice of the Son of God" and, in hearing, live.

Like so many of John's phrases, this one is shaded with subtleties of meaning and thick with interpretive challenges, not the least of which is its stubborn resistance to standard orderings of time. Is "the hour" past, present, or future? John's Jesus is never quite clear. It seems the hour is both *right now* and *not quite yet*—just at this moment and still a breath away. To his mother's request, he demurred . . . then performed his first sign anyway. To the Samaritan woman, who said, "Messiah is coming," he answered, "I am." Jesus seems perpetually unwilling both to reserve the day of salvation for the hazy, distant future, as well as to limit it to what is known today.

Far from being a merely literary issue, this question of time—of the longed-for "hour" of salvation—will immediately concern the typical Sunday worshiper. Living their lives as they do, in a world where God seems never to intervene—where past,

John 5:25–29

Theological Perspective

physical and spiritual, because the grave cannot be avoided. Death is on the attack, harassing our bodies and spirits.

This disturbs God, which is why God commissioned the Son to defeat death on the cross. It is through Christ that God speaks words that bring life to both our bodies and our spirits. However, as human beings we hear those words first as judgment rather than as words of life.

Jesus judges between those who have done good and those who have not, those who have done the will of God and those who have done evil. It is our responsibility to listen for this judgment and make our own choices. It is our duty carefully to examine a given situation or opportunity, and to decide if our actions give life or death. God has provided us with the great freedom to choose between the two, though our choosing is so much more than a personal matter between an individual and God.

Where we see places of death in the world, we are expected to respond by sharing life. Where is death visible today? How do we see death instead of avoid death? Certainly death is seen in places of war and conflict, but also in places of neglect, poverty, and extreme affluence. Death happens when one becomes blind to sin, injustice, and wrongdoing. Death is present when people stop thinking and fail to engage their minds, which often results in a refusal to receive new truth from God. Death plagues the world on many levels. It is present in countless places and situations; and while it seeks to separate us from God, the Lord is working to overcome death by speaking words of life.

Perhaps this is seen best in the example of Lazarus. When Lazarus died, Jesus was greatly alarmed by his friend's death. Death is always disturbing to God, because it is contrary to God's will for life. By no means, though, does this limit God. Jesus was not limited by his friend's death, for he came to the tomb and "cried with a loud voice, 'Lazarus, come out!'" (11:43). The power of his voice overpowered death and raised his dear friend to new life, and this same voice continues to call out to us. While it is a voice with amazing power, it is not necessarily heard as a booming sound from the heavens. Instead, the Scriptures often speak of the "still, quiet voice" of God, and in the context of this Scripture, God's voice is heard through the teachings of Jesus.

In a world consumed by voices calling for attention, why should one pay attention to Jesus' voice? John frames his answer to such a question with an affirmation of the power of Jesus' word to give life.

Pastoral Perspective

for those who have done good, there is resurrection of life (heaven), but for those who have practiced evil, there is resurrection of condemnation (hell).

Christians have long taken it upon themselves to make this distinction between people, separating the good from the evil, and using eternal condemnation as a (fairly successful) stick and eternal life as a carrot. Usually, those who are not like us or those with whom we disagree end up in the evil category. Jesus, however, makes it clear these distinctions are not ours to make. Judgment rests on his authority, and his authority comes from God the Father.

Jesus says not to be astonished by this. Many are not. For those accustomed to thinking of Jesus as the Son of God, his claim "to judge the quick and the dead" is not surprising. For those used to believing in the "resurrection of the dead and the life everlasting," the concept of life after death is not astonishing. We recite these words often, if not weekly. We teach them to our children. We believe they are important, but they do not astonish us. We know the script; we hardly need to listen to it. We hardly hear it.

However, by measures religious or scientific, what Jesus says is *astonishing*. He says, "The hour is coming, and is now here, when the dead will hear the voice of the Son of God, and those who hear will live" (v. 25). It is astonishing because Jesus rearranges the time line. Resurrection is not out there, postdeath, sometime in the future; rather, it is coming toward us even now. The hour of cosmic significance—good or evil, life or condemnation—invades our present. It is not just out there in the afterlife. It is already here in this life.

Hearing these words with post-Easter ears, we begin to understand that resurrection is not a theory of life after death. Rather, it is a way of life, in life here and now. It is life in and with the Word-made-flesh.

What happens at the end, when we die, is not the ultimate question. Life after death begins now, in our encounter with the eternal Word-made-flesh in Jesus. Pastor and best-selling author Rob Bell writes, "Eternal life doesn't start when we die; it starts now. It's not about a life that begins at death; it's about experiencing the kind of life now [by God's grace] that can endure and survive even death."[2]

"The hour is coming, and is now here" (v. 25), Jesus says. It starts now.

Shirley Guthrie cautions us against trying to understand too precisely how resurrection works. He

2. Rob Bell, *Love Wins* (New York: Harper One, 2011), 59.

Exegetical Perspective

"now here." The present hour is the hour in which "the dead" (*nekroi*) "hear the voice of the Son of God" and "live" (*zēsousin*, v. 25). The Son of God who has life speaks the words that are spirit and life (6:63), so that those who have faith in the Son have passed from death to life. That is to say, they have entered into fellowship with the very source of life, God himself. When the Son utters his life-giving words, those who hear them "pass from death to life" (v. 24); they "live" (v. 25).

However, the hour has not yet come for the *resurrection* (*anastasis*) of *all* (*pantes*) who are in the graves (vv. 28–29). The reference to those in the graves "coming out" (v. 29) is to the raising of all people in the future. Those who "have done good" rise to life; those who have done evil, rise to judgment (or condemnation). That is to say, the resurrection will seal the verdict that has already been passed. Those who have heard the life-giving word (v. 24) and voice (v. 25) of the Son of God ("have done good") will live; they will experience the "resurrection of life" (v. 29). Those who have refused to hear that life-giving voice ("have done evil") emerge from the grave to judgment. That judgment is not further described. There is no description in John of punishment for the dead; the typical New Testament words for hell or Hades do not appear. God's wrath, or condemnation (3:36) appears in the form of death.

The juxtaposition between "life" and "resurrection" can be found also in John 6:54: the one who (already) has eternal life will be raised at the last day. Similarly, at the raising of Lazarus, Jesus tells Martha that he is both "resurrection and life." Jesus can both mediate life with God in the present and ensure the future resurrection (11:25–26). In short, the promise of life is the promise that now, through hearing the word of the Son, one can participate in communion with the life-giving God. However, in the hour that is coming, all who are "in the graves" (*hoi en tois mnēmeiois*, v. 28) will come out to the resurrection of either life or judgment (*eis anastasin zōēs . . . eis anastasin kriseōs*, v. 29).

Jesus' authority to give life and to judge is further explained as God's "giving" these powers to him. In the statement "just as the Father has life in himself, so he has granted the Son also to have life in himself" (v. 26), we find the epitome of John's Christology. God is the living Father, the source of life; now the Son is similarly said to "have life in himself." The Son has life as God does, but he has it because God has given it to him. The first formulation ("life in

Homiletical Perspective

present, and future seem collapsed into a meaningless *now*—they want to know: *When? Is this the day when things will be different? When the world will be set right and God at last revealed?* The people yearn to hear the preacher speak with conviction, as Jesus does, of an all-important moment, an "hour," when *something really happens*. They yearn because ours is an anxious, and yet strangely disinterested, world. We inch to the edge of our seats and wait for a word, a summons. In its preaching, the church may echo the voice of Jesus, making the audacious claim that *today* is that day, that the promised future has arrived and is even now beating down our doors.

Our doors, however, are bolted tight. Our resistance to the coming age is not insignificant, which is why Jesus points always to the future when speaking of the present, acknowledging the fact that many ears remain stopped up, at least for now. Thus Jesus adds to the ambiguity of time an ambiguity of response, or *hearing*. At one moment it sounds as if "to hear" is to believe, to accept, or to recognize (as some but not all people do) the lordship of the Son of God (v. 25). Yet at the next moment "hearing" is something *all* the dead will do, the only difference being their various *responses* to what they have heard, that is, will they have done good or evil? As if all this uncertainty were not enough, Jesus seems unconcerned with making a distinction between the spiritually dead (v. 25) and the physically dead (v. 28)! Past, present, and future are muddled; hearing and responding are conflated; and even life and death are redefined. Ambiguity abounds.

Nevertheless, to admit that the text is ambiguous is not at all to say that it is impenetrable. One thinks of the literary density of James Joyce as a parallel. John seems to delight in his thick metaphors and intends them the way Joyce is said to have intended the obscurity of his novels. Yet, as with Joyce's writings, the keynote of John's work is actually quite clear: the voice (vv. 25, 28) is that of Jesus, the Son of God, the Son of Man. The text says that when the voice speaks, *things happen*—yesterday, today, and forever. At the word of Jesus, a brand-new thing begins to be in the world, and that new thing is . . . life.

This is precisely why Jesus has come into the world, according to John: that the people may have life in abundance (10:10). This is also the mission of the church, in preaching as in all its ministries: to witness to the new life that Jesus brings into the world. Perhaps the ambiguity of time and hearing, of life and death—of all the Johannine metaphors, in fact—is for Jesus a means to this end: that we should

John 5:25–29

Theological Perspective

His words are vitally important because they are a source of life. We should listen because they offer us abundant life now and enable us to judge between that which brings life and that which brings death.

There are great consequences, should one choose not to listen to Jesus. When his word is ignored and the voice of God is tuned out, death is lurking nearby. Ignoring the word of God in Jesus leaves one ill equipped to distinguish good from evil. This inability to discern one from the other has an adverse effect on one's behavior and ability to experience the abundant life Christ offers to us in the present. Ultimately, we will be judged by our actions, and this may strike fear in our hearts, for we are sinners and fail to live righteously. However, there is good news for us, because Jesus Christ not only judges us, but also bestows righteousness on us.

Our salvation is in God's hands; yet our ability or inability to listen to the voice of Christ directly affects how we experience the abundant life today. The text speaks of a resurrection of condemnation to those who fail to listen and a resurrection of life to those who do. Hearing and following the voice of Jesus, therefore, is life-giving and transformative, for the old is giving way to the new. We are being made into "new creations." We are being raised from our graves and given new life. Whenever we face death, either physical or spiritual, we have hope of something much better, because God desires life for all the world. God speaks words of life through Jesus that assure us that death is not the end. A rich and abundant life awaits all those who would listen to Jesus, believe in him, and center their lives in his life.

MARK D. WHITE

Pastoral Perspective

notes that even Calvin wrote, "It is foolish and rash to inquire concerning unknown matters more deeply than God wants us to know." Guthrie continues, "Where scripture places its emphasis is where we ought to place ours too—on living in the present in light of our future hope, knowing that what is going to happen to us, our loved ones, and the world will be better than the very best we can imagine in our wildest dreams."[3]

As those who live in the present reality of resurrection even while we await its coming, the paradox we face is that it becomes more painful for us to look around at a suffering world. It becomes less tolerable to see lives hunted by evil. Looking at the broken world—where gun violence reigns unchecked, where immigrants are vilified, where pressure and stress kill children, where wars and the threat of wars are barely news—the balance is always tipping between despair and hope, between the grave and resurrection, between life and condemnation.

Therefore, we need the judgment that Jesus promises to tip the scales. The judgment ensures that in the reign of God, under the authority of the Son, the practice of evil will be condemned. What will endure is life.

A young woman sat in worship for the first time, brand-new to Christianity. She was trying it out because she wanted community for her two young girls. After worship she said, "During the service, I must have misunderstood. You said that in Jesus Christ we are forgiven. That the old life has gone and new life has begun." Her eyes were shining with tears now. "I'm sure I didn't understand, because I looked around and no one looked surprised. If that's true, it is the best thing I have ever heard in my whole life."

Jesus says those who hear will live. The promised resurrection has happened already, happens now, in our encounter with the Word-made-flesh. The hour is coming and is now here.

JESSICA TATE

3. Shirley Guthrie, *Christian Doctrine*, rev. ed. (Louisville, KY: Westminster John Knox Press, 1994), 382.

Exegetical Perspective

himself") points to independence; the second formulation ("for the Father has granted" it) points to dependence: the Father gives his own life to the Son; the Son in turn gives that life to the world.

Jesus, the Son of Man Who Judges (v. 27). Jesus also speaks of his "authority to execute judgment" (v. 27), the other divine prerogative that the Father has given to the Son (v. 22). Jesus asserts that God has given him this power "because he is the Son of Man." "Son of Man" alludes to the one who is like the "son of man" (a human being, a mortal) in the book of Daniel, and to whom God *gives* dominion, glory, and kingship (Dan. 7:13–14, 27). In Daniel, this humanlike figure supplants all the beastly kingdoms that fail to offer proper homage to God and persecute God's people. After the demise of the beastly kingdoms, the humanlike kingdom receives everlasting dominion, glory, and kinship.

In John, Jesus is the "Son of Man" who comes down from heaven (3:13) and will in turn be "lifted up" or crucified on the cross (3:14; 12:23, 34; 13:31), so that he may give life (6:27, 53). This "Son of Man" is the King of Israel (1:49), the one who may properly exercise God's rule. He exercises that rule because it has been given to him by God (vv. 22, 27), who indeed distributes all power to govern or rule (19:11). Even though Jesus has the power to judge, to acquit or condemn, he always exercises that power as the Son who does the work of the living God, the life-giving Father. The one who has life in himself acts to bring life to the world. This is his commission, his mission, and his identity.

MARIANNE MEYE THOMPSON

Homiletical Perspective

listen intently for *his* voice in our lives, not assuming we know already what he will say, but rather waiting on a fresh, living word to draw us out of our confusion.

Is it too much to hope that God may usher in an occurrence of the "hour" of which Jesus speaks, the moment of new life, *precisely in our worship*, in the word proclaimed? Is this not something of what John seeks to accomplish in these lengthy discourses, with their double meanings and their strange, evocative images? Jesus himself—both in his earthly life and in his resurrection appearances—speaks a moment of decision into being. He utters a newness that demands a response. Preachers may—or rather, *must*—echo this speech.

Yet how? Certainly we would do well not to confuse the words of the preacher with the Word of God, or to presume by our own power to speak new life into the world. Still, we may in our echoing of Jesus' word of life become partakers in its work. We do this by hewing to the line of his evocative, life-giving speech: always emphatic (today!), invitational (come!), and serious (repent!).

Preachers might explore the various ways in which the question of *when* is asked in our lives: as an adolescent aches to grow up, for example, or a couple aches to conceive. More broadly, we may ask, when will the world truly live in peace, or the homeless find a home? For John at least, all our questions of *when* distill into one: is God really present in the world? The answer is an emphatic yes! Life itself, along with the still, small voice that summons us, are unmistakable signs of that presence. We are called to listen for that voice and, hearing it, to respond by following into tomorrow.

DANIEL F. LEWIS

John 5:30–38

³⁰"I can do nothing on my own. As I hear, I judge; and my judgment is just, because I seek to do not my own will but the will of him who sent me.

³¹"If I testify about myself, my testimony is not true. ³²There is another who testifies on my behalf, and I know that his testimony to me is true. ³³You sent messengers to John, and he testified to the truth. ³⁴Not that I accept such human testimony, but I say these things so that you may be saved. ³⁵He was a burning and shining lamp, and you were willing to rejoice for a while in his light. ³⁶But I have a testimony greater than John's. The works that the Father has given me to complete, the very works that I am doing, testify on my behalf that the Father has sent me. ³⁷And the Father who sent me has himself testified on my behalf. You have never heard his voice or seen his form, ³⁸and you do not have his word abiding in you, because you do not believe him whom he has sent."

Theological Perspective

Enthusiastic preachers have been known to shout from their pulpits, "Can I get a witness?" and the same phrase could very well have been spoken by Jesus. According to the text, John the Baptist is one who responds to such a question by offering his testimony. John 5 includes other testimonies, implying that people value and depend on what others say. People listen, for example, when they are in need of a good recommendation. They want someone whom they trust to vouch for a product or service. They want to hear a firsthand account.

The Scripture text, therefore, invites us to ask, What is the role of testimony in our faith? Does God use each person's life and witness for some divine purpose? Working directly through people seems to be the modus operandi of God. After all, personal stories and encounters with the Divine are at the heart of the biblical story. There is Moses, who bears witness to God by bringing forth two stone tablets. There are the prophets, who courageously speak of God's judgment and justice. There are the Gospel writers, who tell the story of people's encounters with Jesus of Nazareth. There are members of the early church like Paul, who testify to the ways in which the Holy Spirit moves in the world.

Jesus joins in with his own testimony, though he is not concerned with giving a report about himself.

Pastoral Perspective

"You have never heard God's voice. You have never seen God's form. You do not have God's word abiding in you, because you do not believe him whom God has sent." These are dramatic words from Jesus, even harsh.

John's Gospel has positioned Jesus in a high-stakes battle with the religious authorities in Jerusalem. Earlier in this same chapter the religious authorities are provoked to outrage when Jesus heals a man on the Sabbath and claims God as his Father. They cannot tolerate such disrespect to the Sabbath commandment or the suggestion that Jesus is equal to God. It is, the text says, fuel on the fire of their antagonism toward Jesus, and they are all the more ready to kill him.

This may come as a surprising narrative leap for the modern reader. The culture of the United States has long abandoned the practice of Sabbath—the practice of rest from labor and worship of God. If we persecuted all those who worked on the Sabbath, we would be hard pressed to find an innocent party. Similarly, research shows that religious belief—at least in the traditional, institutional ways religion has been practiced in this country—is trending downward. People today are not particularly interested in doctrinal claims about God and God's relationship to the Son. In their view, arguments about such matters

Exegetical Perspective

Jesus began the discourse following the healing of the paralyzed man with the claim that everything that he did was in keeping with the Father's actions and purposes. Jesus now points again to his reliance upon the Father for all that he says and does. In order to establish the truth of what he says, he also calls several witnesses to his side, including John the Baptist, his own works, and the Father himself. John the Baptist pointed to Jesus; Jesus' works point to his mission from God; and the Father, known to Jesus alone, testifies to Jesus. Here are both human and divine witnesses to Jesus' claims to judge truly and to speak the truth.

Jesus Judges Justly (vv. 30–32). Once again, Jesus makes a claim that he makes elsewhere in John: he does nothing on his own (7:17, 28; 8:28, 42; 10:18; 12:49). Jesus always acts in accordance with the will and purposes of the Father. Earlier, Jesus had claimed that the Father had given him all judgment (5:22, 27). Now he declares that, even though he has that right to judge, he exercises that judgment as an expression of the Father's judgment: he judges as he hears. That is to say, Jesus passes on the just judgment that he has heard from the Father; Jesus' judgment mirrors and enacts God's judgment.

Homiletical Perspective

Commentators have long noted the recurring trial motif in John's Gospel, which will culminate in the detailed account of Jesus' own trial in chapters 18–19.[1] At this point in the story, the indictment reads: "he was not only breaking the sabbath, but was also calling God his own Father, thereby making himself equal to God" (5:18). The entire discourse of 5:19–47 seeks to respond to this charge. These particular verses (vv. 30–38) contain the most explicitly judicial language.

As with so much of the larger discourse, and John's Gospel itself, these verses present an immediate challenge to the preacher: how can a modern-day assembly of the faithful be led to comprehend the seriousness of the charges against Jesus? Certainly few Christians today concern themselves much with Sabbath observance. Moreover, few Christians seem to struggle much with the radical biblical claim of Jesus' identity as the Son of God. It is as if both preacher and church have been summoned to jury duty for what the litigants believe to be The Trial of the Century, only to discover that we cannot really see what all the fuss is about. The reason for this is simple: the crux of the issue is a question that

1. Gail R. O'Day, "John," in *The New Interpreter's Bible* (Nashville: Abingdon Press, 1995), 9:586.

John 5:30–38

Theological Perspective

He says, "If I testify about myself, my testimony is not true" (v. 31). Instead, Jesus depends on John to testify on his behalf, in much the same way as witnesses are used in a court of law. This creates the appearance that Jesus is on trial, facing charges brought against him by a contentious group of religious authorities identified as "the Jews." Yet, if such a trial were happening, Jesus would not have been permitted to give his own testimony, because, according to Jewish law, a person cannot bear witness on his own behalf (see Deut. 19:15). Other witnesses are needed.

This raises a second set of theological questions: Does God need our testimony? Does God depend on human witnesses to further God's own work? One is hard pressed to say God needs anyone's help. The Christian faith affirms that with a word God spoke into existence all of creation. God is all-powerful and can accomplish God's work without any outside assistance; yet each person is invited to participate in the Lord's redeeming work. Christ even empowers his followers to do so, equipping them to bear witness to God by speaking words of truth, love, grace, and mercy. The witness of John pointed people to the Lord, and over the last two millennia, Christians have followed this example by embodying the good news affirmed in their baptisms. There is no one "right" way to be a witness for God or share a testimony. Instead, followers of Christ are challenged to bear witness to God in faithful and authentic ways that speak to the people of their particular contexts and cultures.

The beauty of a testimony is that it respects freedom by giving those who listen the space either to accept or to deny what they hear and see. When people share their personal encounter with God, it is an opportunity to hear and see how the Lord is working in a specific way. It is an opportunity to see that God is doing a new thing, which can be embraced or rejected. The prophet Isaiah reported that God said, "I am about to do a new thing; . . . do you not perceive it?" (Isa. 43:19). That zealous yet argumentative group found here in John apparently did not perceive it. They refused to listen to the testimonies of Jesus and John, and ultimately that meant they rejected the opportunity to see God in Jesus.

When we listen, we become open to hearing new possibilities for our lives. Jesus himself is God's testimony, for he enables us to see God in new and powerful ways. We see the will of God visibly present in his life and witness. His words and actions reflect that of God. They are good news, because God does

Pastoral Perspective

are (best case) irrelevant and (worst case) arrogant, incendiary, and hateful. It does not make sense to modern listeners that these "offenses" would be the motivator for a murder.

Even in the first-century context, the narrative leap might have been exaggerated. Throughout the Gospel of John, "the Jews" are portrayed as the narrative foe for Jesus. We do well in our explication of these texts to avoid generalizations that fuel anti-Semitism, and to focus instead on what we can learn about Jesus in his response.

Beginning in verse 19 Jesus answers the authorities, in courtroom fashion, by testifying to the relationship between Father and Son, that is, between himself and God. Any power Jesus has, he says, does not come from him, but is afforded him because he seeks "the will of him who sent me" (v. 30). Just as we are taught to pray, "Thy will be done," so does Jesus seek after the will of God. Jesus' judgment carries power because it is based in God's will.

Jesus goes on to say, "Do not take my word for any of this. Believe what John has said. His testimony is true." He reminds them that for a time, even they rejoiced in the light of John's testimony. Still, Jesus dismisses John's testimony, along with all human testimony, as missing the point. All too often we believe human testimony is the proof we need or want about Jesus. However, Jesus says the purpose of testimony is not to prove who he is. Its purpose is salvation. We are invited to share the good news of the love of God in Christ as we have heard and experienced it, but God does not need our defense. Jesus the Lord of all creation is not insecure on this matter. The purpose of any speech about God is always the salvation of God's people.

Jesus goes on. The greater testimony is found in the works that Jesus is doing (v. 36). Presumably he means teaching and healing, performing signs and wonders, and the saving work of his death and resurrection. These are the demonstration that he is sent from God.

Those who receive the testimony in Jesus' defense hear God's voice, see God's form, and have God's word abiding in them. The verb "abide" (*menō*) will come up again in chapter 15 when Jesus says, "I am the true vine, and my Father is the vinegrower." It will be extended to the followers of Jesus when Jesus says, "I am the vine, you are the branches. Those who abide [*ho menōn*] in me and I in them bear much fruit, because apart from me you can do nothing" (15:5).

To follow the metaphor, abiding in Jesus' love means seeking shelter in it, finding lifeblood in it,

Exegetical Perspective

Although Jesus judges justly because he listens to and seeks the will of the One who sent him (v. 30), he concedes that his own witness about himself cannot establish its validity. According to the Scriptures, a single witness cannot provide sufficient testimony for conviction of a crime (Num. 35:30; Deut. 17:6, 19:15), especially in capital cases. Later Jewish sources broaden this proviso, so that the witness of a single person cannot constitute valid testimony, particularly if the witness concerns oneself. On that principle, no single witness can ensure a favorable verdict. Therefore, Jesus calls on other witnesses, including John the Baptist (vv. 33–35), his works (v. 36), and the Scriptures (v. 39). Through their testimony to Jesus, one may hear and accept God's own testimony (v. 37).

Human Witness: The Witness of John (vv. 33–35). Jesus turns first to invoke the witness of the Baptist. John "has borne witness" (*memartyrēken*, v. 33) and "bears witness" (*martyrei*, v. 32; cf. 1:15). Through the pages of the Gospel, his witness continues. Ironically, while people were willing (*ēthelēsate*, v. 35) to rejoice in John's light, they are not willing (*ou thelete*, v. 40) to come to Jesus. Yet John was a lamp that was lit and went on shining, precisely so that people would see the "true Light" (cf. 1:7–8). John's human testimony (v. 34) may, however, seem to be inadequate to bear witness that Jesus speaks on behalf of God. Thus Jesus turns to a witness "greater than John's" (v. 36a).

Divine Witness: Jesus' Works and the Witness of God (vv. 36–38). Jesus next calls on his own works and on God to bear witness to him. Jesus' works, including healing, giving life, and judging, are a "greater" witness than John's because these are the works "that the Father has given me." As works that embody the divine prerogatives of giving life and of judging, they are part of the Father's witness to Jesus, testimony that the Father has given this Son these distinctive divine prerogatives (v. 36). While Jesus next refers to the witness of the "Father who sent me" (v. 37), the text does not specify exactly how the Father bears such witness. Even so, Jesus emphatically denies that his accusers have ever heard the Father's testimony.

Three statements—you have never heard his voice, you have never seen his form, you do not have his word dwelling in you (vv. 37–38)—evoke, apparently by denying, the traditions of God's giving the law to Israel at Sinai. According to Deuteronomy,

Homiletical Perspective

Christians believe was laid to rest long ago. Christians tend to think that they *already know* who Jesus is.

In verse 30, Jesus repeats a claim he has already made (5:19): that everything he does represents the will of the God who sent him, including even the judging of those who "do evil" by rejecting him. Interestingly, Jesus seems also to further underscore what may be called the "relational matrix" that unites him to the Father on the one hand and to believers on the other. The relationship works this way: Jesus learns from God what to do (how to love, how to live, etc.) and then passes on that knowledge, discloses it, to those who trust in him. As the crucial link in this relational chain, Jesus here in verse 30 goes beyond disclosing to actually *modeling* the very thing he has asked his people to do: hear, listen, and then decide (or judge).

Yet again, none of this sounds particularly controversial to our modern ears, at least not at first. We have accumulated over the centuries many well-developed creeds and confessions that explain in great detail how Christ the Son relates to the God the Father and expresses the divine will in himself. Many Christians repeat the words every week—*I believe in God the Father Almighty . . . and in Jesus Christ his only Son our Lord*, or, *true God from true God, begotten not made, of one Being with the Father*—and still we do not grasp the import of those words! In these creeds, Christians are claiming that the whole of reality coheres in the person of Jesus, that all our religious habits and claims are relativized by his living presence among us. Is that not world-changing news?

As the trial continues, one may imagine Jesus "calls witnesses" in verses 31–36. Recognizing that his own testimony in self-defense is legally insufficient, he proceeds to name others who will testify to the truth of his claims. These other witnesses include God himself, who sends Jesus and tells him what to do; John the Baptist, who, though he is vastly inferior to Jesus, still sheds some light on his claims; and finally Jesus' "works," which reveal and enact God's will for the world. While in John's story world these witnesses serve to buttress Jesus' claims in the face of opposition, we may imagine that for us they may serve a somewhat different purpose. For modern Christians, these witnesses may serve actually to rouse us from our complacency, as they testify not simply to abstract theological truths but, rather, to the utter seriousness of the life-or-death question that arises in every age: how can we be made well, made whole, saved?

John 5:30–38

Theological Perspective

not stand before us in a tangible form or speak in an audible voice. We are not afforded these luxuries, because God is always mediated. Supremely we know of God by looking at Jesus; his witness points us to his heavenly Father. A similar thing happens today. God continues to be mediated through the works of Christ that are carried out by his faithful followers.

So while we may question whether or not God needs our testimonies, the text really invites us to move in a different theological direction. It invites us to ask: to what do we testify? All of our lives point to something. One person's life may point to a successful career, while the life of another may reflect a compassionate heart. Our lives reflect what is important to us, and the aim of our witness is to reflect God. If our lives bear witness to the Lord, then we are helping others see the new ways in which God is working in our world. We are helping others experience the truth, love, grace, and mercy of God.

Therefore, it is not so much a matter of God needing our testimonies. God is not bound by our actions. Frankly, we could not stop God's work, even if we tried. God does not need our witness, but we need each other's testimony, because we are constantly in need of help. There are lessons we need to learn that can be grasped only when the truth is spoken, love is shared, grace is offered, and mercy is extended. These are all divine gifts shared in tangible ways through the witness of the church. Every testimony counts, because God can speak through each person. The text illustrates this in that the testimony of John pointed to Jesus and the testimony of Jesus pointed to his heavenly Father. Our testimonies also count, for they show others that God is indeed doing something new every time the truth is spoken, love is shared, grace is offered, and mercy is extended. So can I get a witness?

MARK D. WHITE

Pastoral Perspective

getting so entwined that we are engrafted into God. To live and remain in this love is to experience the presence of God, to experience salvation. Living and abiding in this tangle of branches, one soon finds he or she is bearing fruit.

Some among us want to speak the right words about God and say the right things about Jesus. Others want to believe the right things about God and believe the right doctrine about Jesus. To remain in words is to miss the point of the testimony, which requires the whole of our lives.

There is a singular purpose to the testimony to which Jesus refers. Its purpose is for us to know salvation in and through Jesus. Its purpose is for us to know the salvation that comes through abiding with the Word of God. Its purpose is for us to live in the salvation that enables us to bear fruit.

Later still in the Gospel (21:15–19), the risen Jesus has a conversation with Peter. Three times Jesus asks Peter, "Do you love me?" He is asking Peter about deep, self-sacrificing, abide-with-me love. Three times Peter responds, "You know I do." Three times Jesus replies, "Feed my sheep." Jesus seems uninterested in Peter's tepid response, his words about love. Instead, Jesus looks for the action that accompanies love, the fruits of salvation. "If you love me," Jesus says, "care for my people."

There is a Zen proverb that instructs followers not to mistake the finger pointing to the moon for the moon itself. Testimony about Jesus is the finger. Salvation through Jesus is even more than the moon; it is the relationship with God in which one abides.

Traversing pastureland and stiles in southwest Scotland, one comes upon sculptor Auguste Rodin's rendering of John the Baptist. John's outstretched arm and curved fingers pull you in and beckon you closer. At the same time, you are compelled to follow John's gaze, which turns you in a different direction—out, across the hillside. There your eye focuses outward on the sheep that need tending. Both are part of abiding with God. In both together we find salvation.

JESSICA TATE

Exegetical Perspective

God spoke to Israel so that they "heard the sound of words but saw no form; there was only a voice" (Deut. 4:12, 15, 33, 36). However, in John, Jesus denies that "the Jews" have heard God, seen God, or have his word within them, because they do not believe in the one whom God has sent (v. 38). John does not thereby discount the entirety of the historic revelation to Israel, but he links the manifestation of God with Jesus, so that to see the Son is to see the Father; to hear the Son is to hear the Father (14:6–8). In seeing Jesus' signs and hearing his word, one sees and hears the Father, because Jesus both embodies and speaks God's Word.

Exactly what it means to "see God" (v. 37) is not spelled out, but seeing and knowing are linked to each other. In John it is Jesus alone who has seen the Father, who therefore knows him truly and can make him known (1:18; 6:46). Indeed, in Jesus, the embodied Word of God, one may see the Father, mediated and indirectly (14:9). There are no other visions of God available. Similarly, those who have not attended to the words of Jesus cannot claim now to be hearing a word from God, either in "the Scriptures" or from Moses that does not, finally, point to Jesus (5:39, 47). These are sweeping claims for Jesus' mediation of the Father and for the singularity of the knowledge of God made available through and him in. They are grounded in the identity of Jesus as the incarnation of God's own Word (1:1–3, 14).

Because Jesus has both heard and seen the Father—that is, because Jesus has full knowledge of the Father—he can therefore speak the truth. Jesus' accusers have not believed the witness of Jesus' works (v. 36), nor have they received the witness of God (v. 37), because they have failed to heed the revelation and word that Jesus has brought (vv. 38–40). They have neither the knowledge of God gained by direct apprehension (as Jesus does) nor that gained by indirect apprehension (through listening to Jesus, the Scriptures, or other witnesses to him). Again, Jesus emphasizes his unity with and dependence on God as the validation of his mission and witness.

MARIANNE MEYE THOMPSON

Homiletical Perspective

Regarding the testimony of these witnesses, however, Jesus can be said to be somewhat ambivalent. He recognizes the need for their testimony and will certainly accept a favorable verdict (that is, *trust*) in the heart of a person, regardless of which witness sways him or her. On the other hand, he seems to assert in various ways throughout the Gospel that he wishes ultimately to call people to faith *in him*, rather than in his witnesses. It is as if Jesus implies that in closing statements the witnesses will be gone from the courtroom and there will be only this question: Do you believe this? (11:26). Do you believe in *me*?

The first step for modern preachers of this text may be to be to suggest that while we in the church today may know a great deal *about him*, we do not actually *know* Jesus, trust him, believe in him, as much as we think we do. Is not the living presence of Christ just as disruptive, even *lawless*, today as it was in the historical life of Jesus? Does not Jesus challenge our customs and habits, our comfortable arrangements of power and privilege, just as much today as then? We must reckon with the fact that we may meet him in the world today and be offended *still* by what he says and does. The charges leveled against him today could be just as serious as the original ones; he is not only breaking the status quo of church and government, of consumerism and exploitation of various kinds, but he is also claiming God's own authority to do these things!

As we sit in the jury box, the question remains: are we convinced that in this disruption, this challenge, is life? Preachers should not shy away from asking this question, nor even from adopting, at least partially, the tone of judgment with which John writes: *you do not believe*. The problem is that we see and experience all these many witnesses, these manifestations of the risen Christ among us, and yet we remain agnostic much of the time. We are like a hung jury, stuck and stalled—not for lack of evidence, of course, but for fear . . . fear of telling the truth.

DANIEL F. LEWIS

John 5:39–47

Theological Perspective

The process of realizing and constructing identities, of naming self and community, is fraught with tension. It involves acknowledging constitutive elements that inevitably result in inclusion/exclusion. Identity-based questions faced the Johannine community more than a generation after the resurrection. They had to contend with their understanding of Jesus within the context of first-century Judaism and the sacred texts they shared. How they professed allegiance to Jesus and how they interpreted these texts led to tensions that complicated relational bonds. The resulting alienation has left its traces in the pages of the Gospel according to John. While New Testament scholars offer varying suppositions regarding the form and intensity of this intra-Jewish distancing, the consequences are nonetheless painful and carry theological implications.

The differences focus on the identity of Jesus and the significance of that identity for relationships within the Jewish community. Jewish New Testament scholar Adele Reinhartz suggests that the real issue was not about faith or lack of faith in Jesus, but the centrality of faith in a Messiah in conflict with a prevailing perspective in which "messianism is only a tangential aspect of religious identity."[1] For Reinhartz

1. Adele Reinhartz, *Befriending the Beloved Disciple: A Jewish Reading of the Gospel of John* (New York: Continuum, 2001), 154.

Pastoral Perspective

Whoever follows news headlines likely harbors an unspoken question: Who is next to fall from glory? Ours is an era of skepticism. Stories of fraud and corruption are frequent, power brokers are dethroned, and clay feet abound. Human selfishness, greed, and lust for power strut their potency, motivating the actions of individuals and institutions. All too often we have been disillusioned by someone who purports to share our values, yet falls far short.

At the same time, we long to place our trust in someone who has power and influence and seems able to move things in a positive direction. How do we know who is worthy of our trust? In whom can we believe? So many voices vie for our allegiance, and vetting reveals only so much. Perpetually we are faced with the task of discernment, making good choices regarding relationships, work, church life, our beliefs, and contributions to the world.

As people of faith desiring to live with integrity, we ask ourselves, "What sources of authority shall I honor in making decisions about my life?" In particular, who is Jesus, and is he authoritative for me? No doubt early Christians faced similar questions, especially when confronted with persecution for their beliefs. Perhaps they pondered: "Is Jesus credible enough for me to risk my life because of my faith in him?"

Exegetical Perspective

This passage continues John's portrayal of the discussions between Jesus and those Jewish authorities who appear at odds with him over the interpretation of Scripture. Jesus chides them for the mistaken way in which they "search the scriptures" (*ereunate tas graphas*, v. 39). This is a technical term referring to the methods of Scripture interpretation developed in the first century of the Common Era. Careful study is motivated by the belief that the study of Scripture enables the student to find "eternal life" (*zōēn aiōnion*, v. 39), the standard Johannine term for salvation. The Gospel of John and the Jewish source *Pirke Aboth* vii, 6 agree: "Torah . . . gives to them that practice it life in this age and in the age to come." What they do not agree on is how the Scriptures are to be interpreted.

This passage concludes a monologue (5:19–47) in which Jesus explains what he meant when he said to the Jewish authorities, "My Father is still working, and I also am working" (5:18). Part of the work Jesus does is to demonstrate how to interpret Scripture properly.

The writer of the Fourth Gospel describes Jesus as if he were on trial before Jewish scholars. John offers the testimony of three witnesses in defense of Jesus. The three witnesses for Jesus are John the Baptist (5:32–35), Jesus' own miraculous deeds (5:36),

Homiletical Perspective

This passage picks up a theme introduced earlier in the Gospel. From 5:30, Jesus has been speaking about the witnesses to himself. They are John the Baptist; the works (or "signs") that Jesus has performed so far; and the Father, "who has himself testified on my behalf" (v. 37). There is a fourth now, the Scriptures themselves; for John, who is arguing for the legitimacy of Jesus, this is a crucial witness.

The Scriptures are at the heart of both Christianity and Judaism. Indeed we (Christians) are a scriptural community, because our forebears (the Jews) are also a scriptural community; so here is a point of commonality in our fundamental outlook as faithful people. For both, the Bible holds a central place, even if we interpret many texts differently. Yet witnesses, as true as they may be, are not the truth itself. For John, the Scriptures point beyond themselves to Jesus and to the Father. "Christianity is not a religion of a book, but the religion of a Word. Of a Word that is indeed written and proclaimed, but above all a Word spoken by God from all eternity and a Word who became one of us."[1]

The Scriptures, especially the Gospels, function as a two-way "icon," a window onto a greater reality, focused on God, and a window that allows that

---

1. Archimandrite Ephrem Lash, in a sermon at Great Saint Mary's, Cambridge, on February 4, 1996, reprinted in *Sourozh* no. 106 (2010): 37ff.

John 5:39–47

Theological Perspective

this privileging of Christology and messianism sets the Beloved Disciple on a collision course with Judaism that could result only in his sense of exclusion, a repudiation born of a significantly variant way of constructing Jewish covenantal identities.

Important matters of biblical interpretation are at stake in this passage from the Fourth Gospel. This Gospel places in the mouth of Jesus words that allege a misinterpretation of Scripture: "If you believed Moses, you would believe me, for he wrote about me" (v. 46). Reinhartz finds in such accusations an indication that, from the perspective of the Johannine community, "the Jews' resistance comes fundamentally from a misapprehension of God's relationship to the world and of the role of Jesus in God's plan of salvation."[2]

All sides were struggling to move forward, a task complicated by the destruction of the temple in Jerusalem by Roman imperial forces. In this circumstance, one community saw Jesus as central and sought to establish their understanding as a legitimate reading of the sacred texts of Judaism, in continuity with Jewish tradition. At the same time their language indicates attempts to persuade others of the validity of their particular interpretation. "You search the scriptures" affirms the shared nature of these texts; "and it is they that testify on my behalf" establishes the contest of interpretations (v. 39). The appeal to the authority of Moses was a familiar practice and conveys a dynamic understanding of tradition and traditioning.

Rabbi Hayim Goren Perelmuter recalls a story about Akiba, the famous late-first-century-CE rabbi. In this midrash, God situates Moses in the company of Akiba's disciples as the rabbi discourses about the law. Moses is uncomfortable and unable to comprehend the arguments. His confusion is assuaged when a student asks his rabbi for the source of his teaching. Akiba replies, "It is the law given to Moses at Sinai." Perelmuter underscores the theological point that change and continuity are interwoven; Moses may not have understood a word, but it was still being taught in his name.[3]

Considerations of identity are neither insignificant nor apolitical. Assertions of identity carry expectations with respect to word, deeds, and allegiances; and therein lay the potential for discord and conflict. How, then, are these tensions to be

Pastoral Perspective

John 5:39–47 was no doubt comforting to early Christians. It is equally useful for today's readers who are wrestling with discernment. In this dynamic text, part of a larger discourse on authority, Jesus answers his accusers, religious contemporaries who have criticized him for breaking the Sabbath by healing on that day and calling God "Father" (5:18).

In a direct, bold, confrontational style, Jesus explores sources of authority available to his accusers, in order to defend his mission and confirm that he has come in the name of God (v. 43). His argumentation is stellar; he would be a fine addition to any debate team. He goes straight to the heart of the issues, with passion and exasperation inviting listeners to consider what is credible and what the credentials are for someone purporting to speak authoritatively on religion. "Look what you are doing," he effectively insists, and points out inconsistency and hypocrisy on the part of his accusers.

As learners, educators, and preachers, what can we find in Jesus' words that speaks to our dilemmas? Sifting through his arguments, we discover potential touchstones to guide us both in weighing the merit of countless and diverse contemporary voices and in shaping our path as we strive to follow Jesus and his example, strengthen our connection to God, honor our calling, speak with integrity about the issues of our day, and bear witness to the love of God in our daily lives. The evidence Jesus proffers not only challenges his opponents' methodology and message but also reveals his own standards for his ministry, making this text foundational and of utmost significance for our ministry.

In this text, Jesus begins and ends referring to Scripture, an important focus. Jesus clearly sees himself as firmly grounded in his religious tradition and its writings, doing ministry from that platform, teaching, healing, and engaging the issues of his day. He reveals an understanding of his faith tradition as dynamic because God's revelation is ever fresh and unfolding. In fact, Jesus asserts that the Scriptures, including the words of Moses, speak of him. Against this impeccable credential, he exposes the irony that his opponents seek eternal life through the Scriptures and yet fail to understand and honor Moses' words.

How might Jesus' argument here be useful to us? As he aligns himself with the *Heilsgeschichte* or salvation history found in Scripture, does this strengthen our faith in his credibility? In our moments of discernment, how does this dynamic, evolving faith tradition speak to our situation? Looking to the past,

2. Reinhartz, *Befriending*, 86.

3. Hayim Goren Perelmuter, *Siblings: Rabbinic Judaism and Early Christianity at Their Beginnings* (New York: Paulist Press, 1989), 8. See p. 176 for the "Rabbinic Texts: Akiba ben Joseph," *Menahot* 29b.

and the witness of the Father through the Scriptures (5:37–47).

John's well-known high Christology emphasizes the divinity of Jesus by underlining the close relationship between Jesus and God. As Presbyterian scholar Lamar Williamson clearly states, "That Jesus of Nazareth was the unique revelation of God in human flesh is the basic affirmation of the Fourth Gospel and a distinguishing mark of the Christian faith."[1]

In the eyes of the Jewish leaders, Jesus' claim was offensive. "For this reason the Jews were seeking all the more to kill him, because he was not only breaking the sabbath, but was also calling God his own Father, thereby making himself equal to God" (5:18). This is the earliest of several references in this Gospel to attempts to kill Jesus. It is important to remember that the term "the Jews" in John's Gospel does not refer to all Jews in general. Instead, it refers to specific religious leaders with whom other Jews, including followers of Jesus, disagreed. This discussion reflects a sibling rivalry between two emerging forms of faith within the Jewish religious community. Only later did Christianity develop into a distinct religion. Christians who try to justify their anti-Jewish beliefs by citing passages like this from the Gospel of John are misinterpreting it.

This deep division *within the Jewish community* over the identity of Jesus underlies the whole of the Gospel of John. Certain Jewish religious leaders are the opponents against whom the Gospel writer, speaking on behalf of Christian Jews, rather stridently emphasizes the close relationship between God and Jesus. Reflecting the faith of the Johannine community, the Gospel writer says, "Anyone who does not honor the Son does not honor the Father who sent him" (5:23).

Indeed (that is probably the force of the Greek particle *kai* in v. 39), those very Scriptures studied by the Jewish scholars actually do testify to Jesus, John claims. This refers to the Scriptures as a whole (the Hebrew Scriptures that Christians call the Old Testament), rather than any specific passage.

Two very different approaches to Scripture lay at the heart of the conflict between the synagogue and the early church. The early Christians believed that Jesus was the fulfillment of the promises of God to Israel throughout those Scriptures. The problem for the Christian community was that Jewish Scripture scholars did not see Jesus as the fulfillment of the

greater reality to shine back in our direction, illuminating our lives.

What about other testimony to Jesus? The preacher can challenge the congregation to ask how else we know the truth of God that Jesus refracts and reflects. There are the living testimony of saints and heroic figures, the formative writings of the early church, and the ongoing life of the church itself. There is the testimony of those from whom we ourselves have received the Christian faith. What makes a particular testimony reliable? Since there are always those who "come in their own name," how can we tell the trustworthy from the fraudulent?

What is our own personal testimony? For most of us, there may well be some reticence about our own experience. Yet a little prompting will reveal that we have likely glimpsed the truth from at least one person who initially was rather reticent. Conviction comes in many forms that can inspire real confidence. How do we articulate in the way we speak and live "what we have heard, what we have seen with our eyes, what we have looked at and touched with our hands, concerning the word of life" (1 John 1:1)? We can be reliable witnesses in acts of peace, justice, service, self-giving, and building genuine human community.

There is no single witness. For faithful people, just as for a legal process, it is the accumulation of reliable, agreeing witnesses that convinces and convicts. The community and the testimony require congruity, and we bear witness in relationship with the church, the Scriptures, and tradition, in history and in our local communities. Our witness to the truth of God in Jesus depends on the witness of our companions on the way.

When we encounter the judgment of Jesus, we can place ourselves in the shoes of those to whom or about whom he is speaking. Such a personal reading of the Scriptures, which has a venerable tradition, often saves us from the temptation to self-reliance against which Jesus is speaking. To live fully *in faith*, to live as people who act as those who belong to God, is as notoriously hard to do in our day as it was in Jesus' time. We are just as susceptible to the opinions, both good and bad, of others, as were these rulers whom Jesus accuses.[2]

Here the preacher might explore how, just as we have faith in God, so God has faith in us. Nothing about life with God is a one-way street, even when it

---

1. Lamar Williamson, *Preaching the Gospel of John* (Louisville and London: Westminster John Knox Press, 2004), 61.

2. One ancient witness to the text of John's Gospel, the Egerton Papyrus, has the phrase "the rulers of the people" for "the Jews" in this chapter.

John 5:39–47

Theological Perspective

navigated, tensions born of differentiating identities within ancient communities who shared a fundamental bond? How can communities today avoid replicating interpretations that reinscribe the violence that was so often born of polemical stances maintained in the past? One way might entail the retrieval of an appreciation for the Jewish practice of reading the Bible in partnerships of study known as *havrutah*. Studying with a partner, even a partner with whom one often disagrees vigorously over the interpretation of the text, is just as enriching as it is challenging.

These interactive and ongoing relationships bind partners together in their commitment to sacred study. In the context of such shared study, openness to God's Word does not preclude lively discussions, debates, and even respectful disagreements. A reading of the Fourth Gospel especially invites a "search"—in Hebrew, *darash*—a seeking with care, not a hurried rush to judgment. Precisely because of the tragic legacy of noninnocent interpretations, such a "reading together" might best be accomplished in interreligious company, in study of the sacred text by Jews and Christians together.

Affirming the christological and messianic assertions of the Gospel of John establishes a set of bonds and markers constitutive of a Christian identity. Such an identity should not force our preaching, teaching, and theologizing into nourishing polemical animosities and their dangerous legacies of anti-Judaism and anti-Semitism. It does, however, call for a conscious commitment to avoid temptations to succumb to supersessionist theologies that subjugate Judaism to the status of a "replaced" faith tradition, and to recognize as kin our Jewish brothers and sisters, with whom we share a foundational bond, a complex web of relationships and a history of interpretation.

Reinhartz offers one possible direction from a Jewish perspective for moving forward theologically. She begins by recognizing the otherness of the Beloved Disciple, a move that opens her to identify with the very senses of pain and exclusion possibly experienced by the Johannine community as they sought to construct their communal identity. At the same time acknowledgment of this pain does not eliminate the Fourth Gospel as source of her own hurt or alienation; rather, it creates a space whereby centuries later it is possible for Jews and Christians to choose to study Scripture together.

CARMEN NANKO-FERNÁNDEZ

Pastoral Perspective

what is the wisdom brought forward by the faithful throughout history? Looking to the future, what is God continuing to reveal, and how does the living presence of Jesus inspire us? When we speak to contemporary issues, are we in good conscience representing this living tradition?

Jesus quickly lifts up another potential touchstone, that of having "life," foreshadowing his words in John 10:10, "I came that they may have life, and have it abundantly." What could be more elemental? According to Jesus, eternal life is found not in the Scriptures but in relationship to him, in accepting the invitation that is so central to Jesus' ministry: "Come to me" (Matt. 11:28a). How is this path, this choice, life-giving? Am I more fully human when I project myself down this road? Does our work in the world, our outward witness, bring us to a sense of richness and abundance in God's presence, and feed us? Might burnout be a sign that we are off the mark somehow?

With conviction, Jesus then goes right to the core: "I know that you do not have the love of God in you" (v. 42). An audacious, penetrating assertion, it is perhaps the ultimate touchstone, the heart of the text, the moment of truth. For Jesus, love is the absolute authority, the bottom line, the essence of God. As 1 John 4:8b says, "God is love," pure and simple. We ask, "Does the love of God dwell in this leader, this idea, this plan?" Is it love that drives our work, our public witness? Are we inner directed, heart and soul based, or, underneath it all, is personal glory in the eyes of others our motivation, feeding our insecurities? Is love the source of our power?

To bring home what Jesus is saying, might we try putting it in our own words? Perhaps it would sound something like this: "Come to me and I will give you life, for I come in God's name. I will make Scripture come alive, and connect you to God, whose love will live in you. You do not need to seek your own glory; beware of those who do. Live with integrity; shun hypocrisy; and remember, there is no truth without love, and no love without truth." If so, then how will we live, and what will be our message to others?

JEAN E. GREENWOOD

Exegetical Perspective

Scriptures. The reason for this, John argues in 5:38 with his distinctive terminology, is that "you [the Jewish authorities] do not have his word [*logos*] abiding [*menonta*] in you, because you do not believe him whom God has sent." The Johannine use of *logos* ("Word") refers to much more than a written word. As in John 1:1–5, here *logos* refers to God's self-disclosure both in the person of Jesus and in the testimony of the Holy Spirit in the hearts of believers. As unbelievers, the Jewish leaders in this scene lack *logos* and therefore do not believe Jesus' message, nor do they acknowledge the divine origin of Jesus. Believing in Jesus is the determining factor—not erudite Scripture interpretation.

John 5:41–44 discusses the vanity of erudite Scripture interpretation. The term *doxa* ("glory," v. 41 NRSV) is better understood in this verse as "fame" or "prestige." Jesus is contrasting himself with Jewish exegetes who seek to enhance their own reputations. Jesus levels a very serious charge against them by saying that they do not have love for God. Consequently they do not acknowledge Jesus as the messenger of the only true God. Jesus does not seek his own fame (5:30), but comes in the name of God, meaning that Jesus has the nature and identity of God. The Jewish authorities in this scene fail to recognize the divine glory (*doxa* in v. 44 a different sense of this term) of Jesus. Instead, they have created a mutual admiration society to promote their own fame (cf. 12:41–43).

In John 5:45–47, Jesus turns Moses, a key authority for Jewish scriptural interpretation, against his opponents. According to John, Moses stands for the Hebrew Scriptures as a whole, and they point to Jesus. By not believing Jesus, the scholars are rejecting the words of Moses. Again, the primary matter here is the interpretation of Scripture. The Johannine Jews read the writings of Moses and the prophets as witnesses to Jesus. Other Jewish interpreters do not. As British scholar C. H. Dodd points out, this passage reflects "the practice of missionary apologetics in the early Church."[2] It also reflects the vehemence with which Jewish Christians and Jewish rabbinic scholars debated about the meaning of the Scriptures.

JAMES A. BRASHLER

Homiletical Perspective

comes to faith: God has faith in us that we can meet God with the same depth of love and commitment with which God meets us in Jesus. If faith in God's promises demands a risk on our part, so faith in our response is the risk of the incarnation. Such is the love that God has for us.

This leads to another fruitful reflection on Jesus' phrase "the love of God" (v. 42). The words are ambiguous. They could mean "the love that comes from God," or they could mean "the love that human beings have for God"—or both. John's proclamation is this new, intimate relationship between the Father and us, this love that is so powerful that it can raise Jesus, and us, from the dead.

Preachers are best advised against using foreign words in most pulpits. Yet here the preacher will be helped with a little Greek. A recurring word here is the verb *lambanō*, which the NRSV translates as "accept" in verses 41, 43, and 44. While often rendered as "take," *lambanō* has about it the resonance of "receiving something as a gift" and so has much more the force of "receive" than "take" in the sense of "grasp."[3]

This invites the preacher to consider an important question. How do we "accept" or "receive" Jesus? How do our eucharistic life and our community practices reflect the way we receive Jesus? In some traditions, to celebrate the Eucharist is to be open to Jesus, even so far as to take Jesus into ourselves. Our open palms, our open mouths, our open hearts, are themselves a sacramental sign. Our willingness to be open to Jesus, in this way and in others, is another eloquent witness and worth a sermon.

PETER EATON

---

2. C. H. Dodd, *The Interpretation of the Fourth Gospel* (Cambridge: Cambridge University Press, 1968), 330.

3. In one recent, perhaps unique, revision of a liturgical text, the bishop of the Greek Metropolis of Denver provides this translation of *labete* in the Eucharistic Prayers to be used in his diocese: "*Receive*, eat: this is My Body which is broken for you, for the remission of sins" (emphasis mine). See http://www.denver.goarch.org/liturgical/fixed/ieratikon.pdf, 95 and 125.

John 6:1–15

¹After this Jesus went to the other side of the Sea of Galilee, also called the Sea of Tiberias. ²A large crowd kept following him, because they saw the signs that he was doing for the sick. ³Jesus went up the mountain and sat down there with his disciples. ⁴Now the Passover, the festival of the Jews,* was near. ⁵When he looked up and saw a large crowd coming toward him, Jesus said to Philip, "Where are we to buy bread for these people to eat?" ⁶He said this to test him, for he himself knew what he was going to do. ⁷Philip answered him, "Six months' wages would not buy enough bread for each of them to get a little." ⁸One of his disciples, Andrew, Simon Peter's brother, said to him, ⁹"There is a boy here who has five barley loaves and two fish. But what are they among so

Theological Perspective

The Gospels betray an affinity for texts that recall the feeding of multitudes. With variations, this story is found in all four Gospels, and Matthew and Mark record two versions each (Matt. 14:13–21; 15:29–39; Mark 6:30–44; 8:1–10; Luke 9:10–17; John 6:1–15). While much has been written about christological, eucharistic, and eschatological dimensions of these texts, the implications of these miracles in terms of theologies of accompaniment remain underexplored. These theological perspectives are particularly rooted and developed in the work of Latin American liberation theologians like Gustavo Gutiérrez and in the scholarship of Latino/a theologians like Ada María Isasi-Díaz and Roberto Goizueta—for example, in his book *Caminemos con Jesús: Toward a Hispanic/ Latino Theology of Accompaniment.*

New Testament scholar Sharon Ringe suggests that in the English language the expression "accompaniment" fails to communicate fully its dynamic potency. Ringe observes, however, that in Spanish this expression is quite powerful: "It evokes words like compañero/a, which designates someone with whom one shares pan—bread—and even life itself."[1] It is this life-giving relationality at the heart of theologies of

* See "'The Jews' in the Fourth Gospel" on pp. xi–xiv.
1. Sharon H. Ringe, *Wisdom's Friends: Community and Christology in the Fourth Gospel* (Louisville, KY: Westminster John Knox Press, 1999), 95.

Pastoral Perspective

How often does the real drama take place behind the scenes? In John 6:1–15, the little story about logistics, food arrangements in the face of a multitude on a hillside, becomes *the* story. The characters include Jesus, portrayed as miracle worker testing the faith of his followers; the disciple Philip, practical and realistic, doing the math and coming up short; the disciple Andrew, resourceful and observant, reporting the presence of a lad with five loaves and two fish; and the generous lad himself. The plot unfolds as the crowd comes to see more signs of healing from Jesus, perhaps to be healed themselves. This time the sign, the wonder, is Jesus multiplying the available food to feed the multitude, despite Philip's short-sighted sense of possibilities: "Two hundred denarii would not buy enough bread for each of them to get a little" (v. 7).

Where might this familiar story take us? We may choose to embrace the power and authority of Jesus. This text follows a lengthy discourse in which Jesus defends his healing on the Sabbath and his mission as coming from God, embodying God's love. So this miracle on the hillside offers evidence of who Jesus is and of his capacity to do amazing things that transcend the norm. This text, an apologetic, provides a rationale for belief in Jesus.

Moving beyond the apologetic, we might discern other, more subtle, dimensions of "miracle" that

Feasting on the Gospels

many people?" [10]Jesus said, "Make the people sit down." Now there was a great deal of grass in the place; so they sat down, about five thousand in all. [11]Then Jesus took the loaves, and when he had given thanks, he distributed them to those who were seated; so also the fish, as much as they wanted. [12]When they were satisfied, he told his disciples, "Gather up the fragments left over, so that nothing may be lost." [13]So they gathered them up, and from the fragments of the five barley loaves, left by those who had eaten, they filled twelve baskets. [14]When the people saw the sign that he had done, they began to say, "This is indeed the prophet who is to come into the world."

[15]When Jesus realized that they were about to come and take him by force to make him king, he withdrew again to the mountain by himself.

Exegetical Perspective

The miraculous feeding of four thousand or five thousand people is recorded in all three of the Synoptic Gospels (Matt. 14:13–21; 15:32–39; Mark 6:30–44; 8:1–10; Luke 9:10–17), but John is not dependent on the Synoptic tradition. Instead he relies on his own source, a collection of miracle stories, that he rewrites in his distinctive way to shine a revealing spotlight on Jesus.

The Johannine account takes the usual form of a miracle story (setting, vv. 1–4; problem, vv. 5–9; resolution of the problem, vv. 10–11; demonstration of the miracle, vv. 12–13; and the response of the crowd, vv. 14–15). However, John has supplemented the novelistic details of his source with his own features, which emphasize the nature of the miracle as a sign. In the Gospel of John, a typical Hellenistic miracle story becomes a theological statement, a sign, about Jesus as the bread of life.

John 6:1–4. Two names are given for the setting of this miracle: the Sea of Galilee and the Sea of Tiberias. Gentile readers may have been more familiar with the latter, since Herod Antipas had built the city of Tiberias on the western shore of the sea around 25 CE. We are not told how or when Jesus arrived in Galilee. He was in Jerusalem in chapter 5 and in Samaria and then Galilee in chapter 4. This

Homiletical Perspective

This story is the only miracle that is recounted by all four evangelists, two of them (Matthew and Mark) telling it twice. It was deeply embedded in the earliest, most widespread traditions about Jesus, and this observation can itself be the subject of a sermon. The fundamental theme of the feeding in all its versions is of Jesus' meeting our basic human needs, physical and spiritual.

It is always fruitful to ask where one version of a story differs from others, because we often find the way to a preaching moment in this singularity. In this case it is worth spending time with a schematic comparison. Try to avoid ill-considered reflections on the well-worn themes of "abundance-scarcity" or "no-gift-is-too-small." Although true enough, such superficiality renders this story trite.

Thomas Brodie comments on the possible significance of the geography and calendar, which are unique to John. There is the Sea "of Tiberias," which is a derivation of the name of the Roman emperor Tiberius. Then there is the timing, near the feast of the Passover. For Brodie, these two details indicate "a worldwide drama involving Gentiles and Jews, a drama of universal human need and of God's care for that need."[1]

1. Thomas L. Brodie, *The Gospel according to John: A Literary and Theological Commentary* (New York: Oxford University Press 1993), 259ff.

John 6:1–15

Theological Perspective

accompaniment that propels concrete expressions of solidarity and that inspires a consideration of the theological and ethical implications of companionship.

This story of abundance that arises from scant material resources is reminiscent of Jesus' first miraculous sign in Cana (2:1–11). In that narrative it is the mother of Jesus who reads her context and identifies a practical need that calls for attention. In this case it is Jesus, sounding like a pastoral-care professor in a ministry practicum, who identifies a communal need and asks the ministers-in-training to propose appropriate responses. Accompanying a community comes with attendant responsibilities, and limited assets may inspire creative praxis. In this situation it is Jesus—through his actions of drawing from a local resource (the boy with his bread and fish), giving thanks, distributing the food, and collecting the leftovers—who models a response that points both to the power of an accompanying God and to the concomitant mutual obligations of those being accompanied.

The relationship of food and drink to abundance, care, and communal identity is particularly evident in John's Gospel. Theologian Angel Méndez-Montoya explores this theme, among others, in his book *The Theology of Food: Eating and the Eucharist*, where he posits what he calls an "alimentary theology." Such a perspective recognizes food, nourishment, and its production as *locus theologicus*, as well as performative theology with ethical obligations to address physical and spiritual hungers in the world. Turning his attention to the multiplication of sustenance sign in John, Méndez-Montoya draws parallels with the provision of manna in the desert (Exod. 16). In both acts of feeding he sees indications of divine presence in superabundance and in deliverance. Furthermore, he asserts that liberative action experienced within the context of food sharing participates in a construction of communal identities.

In this Gospel story the acts of gathering, nourishing, and potentially redistributing signify characteristics necessary for cultivation in the embodied communal identity of those who follow and will follow Jesus. In poetic fashion, through his alimentary theology, Méndez-Montoya encourages a critical reconsideration of food in Scripture, so much so that in the nourishing Word, "Creation is a cosmic banquet and interdependent network of edible signs that participates in God's nurturing sharing."[2]

Pastoral Perspective

appear in this story and may also appear in our lives. Is it not extraordinary that this sizable crowd feels compelled to see Jesus, so drawn by the power of his presence and work that they are heedless of their physical needs? Equally extraordinary, Jesus resists the temptation to glory in the people's enthusiasm. Instead, he retreats. Furthermore, Jesus has compassion on the crowd, when perhaps he had intended simply to spend precious, much-needed restful time with the disciples. He uses the medium of ordinary food to bring forth God's grace. Jesus draws upon his wisdom and profound intuition in using the circumstances as a teachable moment.

What constitutes "miracle," the movement of the Spirit, in this story and in our everyday lives? Where might there be miracles in our interactions, moments of challenge and insight, or the sharing of our lives and our food? Do we see in our public witness gifts of grace that transcend our expectations? As poet Elizabeth Barrett Browning writes, "Earth's crammed with heaven, and every common bush afire with God: but only he who sees, takes off his shoes, the rest sit round it, and pluck blackberries."[1]

Regardless of how we understand "miracle," on an ordinary plane we are also invited by this story to consider our notion of limits and possibilities. The central contrast in this episode is between Philip's pragmatic, sensible approach that recognizes the lack of resources, and Jesus' resourcefulness that bursts the seams of the usual and expected. Jesus sheds light on the narrow-minded, limited perspectives of his disciples. For them, perhaps, the math is obvious: five loaves plus two fish divided by five thousand equals disaster—hordes of hungry, crabby people. For Jesus, though, it appears that the problem is not hunger but rather a lack of faith and, perhaps, imagination. One envisions this phrase coursing through Jesus' mind, a refrain found in other Gospels: "You of little faith" (Matt. 14:31b).

Might this text of feasting and abundance stir our curiosity about possibilities in our lives, our work, our calling, and our relationships—possibilities that we may have missed in our shortsightedness, our insufficient faith and imagination? Is this not a story about resourcefulness and generativity, about using what we have, and about the small gift having a large impact? Often we fail to see the entire ripple effect of even a minor kindness we offer. So it is faith, once again, that is imperative, faith that God's power is

---

2. Angel F. Méndez-Montoya, *The Theology of Food: Eating and the Eucharist*, Illuminations: Theory and Religion (Chichester, UK: Wiley Blackwell, 2009), ix. See chapter 4 for a detailed consideration of this Gospel text.

1. Elizabeth Barrett Browning, "Aurora Leigh," Book I, in *The Poetical Works of Elizabeth Barrett Browning* (Boston: Houghton Mifflin, 1974), 372.

Exegetical Perspective

has led some scholars to speculate that the order of chapters 5 and 6 should be reversed, but the manuscript tradition supports the order as we now have it.

John reports that the crowds follow Jesus because they have witnessed the healing miracles he has done, supposedly in Jerusalem (4:45). John 6:26 indicates that Jesus has reservations about the reason the crowd follow him. Their lack of understanding will become clearer after Jesus frustrates their attempt to make him their king in 6:15.

The reference to the Passover is a Johannine addition to his source. John shows a special interest in the Passover festival celebrated by the Jewish people in the spring of the year, commemorating their liberation from Egypt. John mentions three Passover celebrations at important points in Jesus' ministry. As Lutheran biblical scholar Robert Kysar helpfully observes, "John's use of the Passover as a setting for the ministry of Jesus stresses that in the Christ-revelation the formative event of Israel's history is completed and fulfilled."[1]

John 6:5–9. As the crowd approaches, Jesus (not the disciples, as in the Synoptic tradition) initiates a conversation by asking how the crowd will be fed. John characteristically adds the note that Jesus, fully aware of what is about to happen, is testing Philip's faith. In this way John injects the theological issue of faith into a novelistic miracle story about bread. Philip misunderstands—a typical Johannine narrative device—and fails the test. He is aware only that it will cost 200 dinarii (approximately six to eight months' wages for a day laborer). His brother Andrew emphasizes the enormity of the problem by noting that a little child (it could be a boy or a girl) has five barley loaves and two little fish, but that will be only a drop in the bucket. Both of these details are indications of the novelistic character of the miracle story in John's source.

John 6:10–11. Jesus asks the disciples to seat the people on the grass—all five thousand of them. This is another novelistic detail. John reports that Jesus takes the child's bread and fish and, after giving thanks, distributes them to the crowd. The Greek for "giving thanks" (*eucharisteō*) is the word from which the English word "eucharist" is derived. It is a translation of the Hebrew word *barak*, which was used in the blessing of the bread and the cup in the Passover meal. Again John has alluded to well-known

Homiletical Perspective

How, the sermon might ask, are we caught up in this great drama?

Then there is "the mountain." Along with the reference to the Passover, this recalls Moses and the people of Israel at Sinai. John is interested in making the connection between Moses and Jesus: he takes great pains throughout the Gospel to present Jesus as the fulfillment of God's promise in Deuteronomy 18:18 to "raise up a prophet like Moses," in whose mouth are placed God's words and who speaks in God's name. Thus the preacher could explore the continuity between Moses and Jesus. Hidden in the reference to the time of the Passover is another, harder subject to broach, but one that is crucial. Again perceptively, Brodie reminds us that "within the context of the gospel as a whole, a gospel which is built around three Passovers and which links Passover with death, the addition of such a detail cannot but be significant. . . . It is a faint reminder, even in a moment of companionship, that ultimately one must reckon with death."[2] How do we, who are fed by Jesus, who have said that we belong to him, think about and come to terms with the reality of our own death, and what that might mean?

Philip and Andrew are here, and it is easy to be dismissive of them. Much of the tension around the teachings and actions of Jesus in the Gospels arises, not because those around Jesus are doing or saying unreasonable things, but precisely because they are doing and saying *reasonable* things. Philip is right to point out the reasonable problem. The sermon could reflect on the difference between living faithfully and living recklessly: it is a vital difference, and few articulate it well. Every Christian community has to think through this difference, or the congregation will soon become unreliable and ineffective. Andrew is also attempting a solution, and he highlights the very clear intertextual connection that John makes between Jesus and Elisha, and between the man with twenty loaves of barley and ears of corn in 2 Kings 4 and the small boy with five barley loaves and two dried fish.

Jesus does the feeding himself, rather than handing the task over to the disciples. We are used to the Synoptic versions, which remind readers that Jesus is always the giver, even if the gift is mediated through us. Yet Jesus is the host as well as the fare at this eucharistic banquet, and John emphasizes this uniquely in the use of the verb *eucharisteō* (the Synoptic evangelists use *eulogeō*).

---

1. Robert Kysar, *John* (Minneapolis: Augsburg Publishing House, 1986), 90.

2. Brodie, *John,* 260.

John 6:1–15

Theological Perspective

Such participation in divine nurturing elicits a call to mutuality among those who are accompanied that ought to be lived in solidarity with the whole of God's creation. This interrelationship received particular attention from Pope Francis at a weekly papal audience that coincided with the United Nations World Environment Day in 2013. Reflecting on the feeding of the multitude, Francis focused his remarks on the dimension of regathering the fragments so there would be no loss (v. 12). His words indict what he calls a "culture of waste," where resources and people, especially the poor and vulnerable, are treated as disposable. Francis exhorts the pilgrims and visitors gathered in St. Peter's Square to accountability in global and local contexts:

> We should all remember, however, that throwing food away is like stealing from the tables of the poor, the hungry! I encourage everyone to reflect on the problem of thrown away and wasted food to identify ways and means that, by seriously addressing this issue, are a vehicle of solidarity and sharing with the needy. . . . when food is shared in a fair way, with solidarity, when no one is deprived, every community can meet the needs of the poorest. Human ecology and environmental ecology walk together.[3]

For Francis the antidote to wasteful consumerism is a "culture of solidarity" lived in the ordinary details of human existence.

¡Compañeros! ¡Compañeras! Companions! These quotidian terms tie us to each other and to our daily bread/nuestro pan cotidiano. They denote a depth of relationship that demands mutual accountability. The act of sharing nourishment is transformative at a number of levels, as the Gospel of John intimates. From a performative dimension, there is a sense that "we are what we eat." However, it is not enough to be fed. There are expectations of a community nurtured by life-giving Bread from an accompanying God. While the Gospel records that all who were fed had their fill and were satisfied, the collection of the leftovers points to those outside the circle of those who are gathered. It is a reminder that the goods of the earth are not disposable and that those who are strengthened by the Bread of Life have an obligation to alleviate the hungers of those still waiting to be fed. The question of Jesus to Philip resounds still: "Where are we to buy bread for these people to eat?" (v. 5).

CARMEN NANKO-FERNÁNDEZ

Pastoral Perspective

operative, that whatever we do matters, that goodness is never in vain. This text celebrates the power of belief—as Jesus proclaimed in another Gospel, "Your faith has made you well" (Mark 5:34).

Let us also reflect on Andrew's role in this text. He is the one who notices the lad with loaves and fish, tells Jesus about it, and then minimizes it: "But what are they among so many?" (v. 9). Have you ever questioned the significance of what you have to offer? Have you ever waited until you might have something greater to give, or until you could gather more courage, or get your act together, before doing what you feel called to do? Few among us have not. So this story is for us, along with other Gospel texts that express a similar message (e.g., Matt. 19:26b, "with God all things are possible").

This text also underscores Jesus' concern for people's practical, physical, daily needs. He is life affirming rather than life denying. Jesus cares for the whole person, not just the spirit but also the body, the fleshly dimension of life. How do we care for our bodies, as individuals and as congregations, for our physical needs as well as spiritual? Is a concern for the practical, physical, daily needs ever voiced from the pulpit? In our concern and aid for others, do we include the whole person?

Furthermore, note that Jesus does not simply meet the minimum requirements in feeding the crowd. He lavishes food—a feast—on them, filling and pleasing the people, and then some; there were even leftovers! This story is not just about abundance but about the cup being full and running over, about extravagance and pleasure. How might our lives and ministries embody this spirit of abundance?

In this text, Jesus transcends expectations on many levels, not only feeding the multitude and providing hospitality (typically the domain of women) but also embracing a child's gifts, thus defying the commonplace rationality of the adult disciples. Jesus also challenges all of us who have ever said, "It is not enough; it will never work." How fitting that the Passover was nigh, the feast celebrating God's liberation of God's people, for Jesus was at work setting the people free from hunger, from perceived limitations, and from disbelief.

JEAN E. GREENWOOD

---

3. Pope Francis, General Audience (June 5, 2013), available in English translation in "Pope at Audience: Counter a Culture of Waste with Solidarity," *Vatican Radio*, http://en.radiovaticana.va/news/2013/06/05/pope_at_audience :_counter_a_culture_of_waste_with_solidarity/en1-698604.

Exegetical Perspective

Passover imagery. It is easy to understand how the early church readily heard overtones of their own celebration of the Lord's Supper in this miracle story. In John's Gospel a miracle story has become a theological statement, a sign of God's saving power.

John 6:12–13. A powerful attestation of the miracle is that the hunger of the crowd is fully satisfied. Moreover, Jesus tells the disciples to "gather up the fragments left over, so that nothing may be lost," and twelve additional baskets are gathered. While the twelve extra baskets emphasize the magnitude of the miracle, they also suggest that the tribes of Israel have been satisfied. Furthermore, this Johannine emphasis on not losing anything is also found in 6:39; 11:52; 17:12; and 18:9. John emphasizes that Jesus does not want anyone to be left out.

John 6:14–15. The typical ending of a novelistic miracle story often has the audience celebrating the power of the miracle worker. But John turns the response of the crowd into a theological statement that says more than the crowd probably intended: "This is indeed the prophet who is to come into the world." For John, Jesus is a prophet like Moses and the Messiah, as 4:19–26 suggests. The crowd, however, sees only a potential king in the miracle worker. Jesus frustrates their misguided enthusiasm by going back to the nearby mountain alone.

The feeding of the five thousand is a compelling account within the Fourth Gospel. It introduces the sixth chapter of John with a dynamic illustration of Jesus' power to provide not simply physical bread for a hungry crowd, but the spiritual bread of eternal life for believers. A beautiful eucharistic prayer found in a first-century document called the *Didache or Teaching of the Apostles* lends witness to the significance of this story for the early church: "As this broken bread . . . was gathered up and so became one, so may your church be gathered up from the ends of the earth into your Kingdom" (*Didache* ix.4). It has remained a beloved account throughout the ages.

JAMES A. BRASHLER

Homiletical Perspective

Although the other evangelists do remark that there is grass, John says that "there was a great deal of grass." Is this expansiveness (capable of accommodating five thousand), accompanied by an instruction to have the people "recline," a hint of paradise, of the promise of restoration that occurs when Jesus gathers and feeds?

Then there is the characteristic Johannine concern for leftovers. Later in this chapter we shall hear the words, "this is the will of him who sent me, that I should lose nothing of all that he has given me, but raise it up on the last day" (v. 39). Can it be that even in so innocuous a ritual action as the reverent gathering up of the remains of a eucharistic liturgy we are acting out an eschatological reality?

Do not forget that verses 15–16 form a separate, if linked, episode to the feeding. In these two verses is a message about the kingship of Jesus. Just because those who shared this meal got it wrong does not mean that Jesus is *not* a king. Because the subject of kingship is complex, it is a biblical concept with real possibility. Here the words of Melchior in Menotti's one-act opera *Amahl and the Night Visitors* provide a good example of how we might speak of Jesus' kingship in more amenable, even Johannine, terms:

> The Child we seek doesn't need our gold.
> On love, on love alone,
> He will build His kingdom.
> His pierced hand will hold no scepter.
> His haloed head will wear no crown.
> His might will not be built on your toil.
> Swifter than lightning,
> He will soon walk among us.
> He will bring us new life
> and receive our death,
> and the keys to his city belong to the poor.[3]

The sermon could examine the nature of Jesus' kingship and the kind of kingdom that he enables us to imagine and inspires us to realize in his feeding of the multitudes. There are many homiletical possibilities in this pericope: the occasion and the nature of the congregation will guide the preacher's choice.

PETER EATON

---

3. Gian Carlo Menotti, *Amahl and the Night Visitors* (RCA Records 1952), quoted from the libretto that accompanied the CD recording. This is the recording of the first television performance on NBC, Christmas 1951.

John 6:16–21

Theological Perspective

Theological considerations of this passage in the Gospel of John typically pursue two threads that are not necessarily mutually exclusive. The first considers the apparent walk across the sea as one of the miracles of Jesus. The second regards this story as a theophany, an experience of divine self-disclosure. However, the passage leaves a striking question that is overlooked by most commentators: why did the disciples abandon Jesus and leave him alone, without a ride?

Variations of this story appear in the Gospels of Matthew and Mark. In these Synoptic Gospels, this scene occurs after the feeding of the multitudes and is reminiscent of a host cleaning up after a dinner party, sending guests home, and then seeking some quiet time. In each of these cases, Jesus explicitly tells the disciples to go on ahead of him while he disperses the crowds and then goes alone to the mountain to pray (Matt. 14:22–23; Mark 6:45–46). The text leaves no doubt that Jesus himself is responsible for his being left behind: "he made his disciples get into the boat" (Matt. 14:22; Mark 6:45).

In John, there is a hint of trouble that causes Jesus to retreat to the mountain by himself. His feeding of the multitude incites the people to consider taking "him by force to make him king" (6:15). That evening the disciples get into a boat and head for

Pastoral Perspective

Moving from Jesus' public ministry, in feeding the multitude (6:1–15), to his private life, we see him encountering his disciples on a stormy night at sea, their small vessel tossed by heavy winds. The sea can be daunting and dangerous, as we know from Jonah and other tales, and it serves as the stage for a succinct episode of high drama.

Apparently startled by a sudden change in weather, the disciples are awash in vulnerability, fearful that their boat will be swamped and they will perish. So shaken are they that when they see Jesus approaching, walking on water, they are utterly terrified, perhaps thinking it is an apparition or that they are losing their minds. When Jesus assures them it is he and there is no need to be frightened, they welcome him into their boat and find themselves instantly safe on shore.

What meaning has this text borne over time? Fear is the focus of the story. Though our era has been called the Age of Anxiety, making this episode highly relevant, one suspects early Christians found it equally compelling, as they confronted a tumultuous Roman Empire, massive social change and uncertainty, and, for some, persecution for their beliefs.

Perhaps every era feels like an age of anxiety, for human existence has always been fraught with some

Exegetical Perspective

The account of Jesus walking on the sea has parallels in Matthew 14:22–33 and Mark 6:45–52, where it is linked with the accounts of the feeding of the five thousand, as it is in John 6. This passage also bears some striking similarities to accounts of Jesus quieting the storm in Matthew 8:23–27; Mark 4:35–41; and Luke 8:22–25. Although John's description of Jesus walking on the water has several literal and structural similarities to the Synoptic accounts, the differences have led most interpreters to conclude that John used a source that is distinct from the Synoptic tradition. In comparison to the Synoptic accounts, John's version is much more condensed and focused. Because his account lacks most of the narrative details in the parallel miracle stories that appear in Matthew, Mark, and Luke, John's story is a bare and powerful account of a theophany, an appearance or visible manifestation of God.

John 6:16–17. The setting of this miracle is the Sea of Galilee, an inland lake that is approximately seven miles across at its widest point. John reports that after the feeding of the five thousand the disciples get into a boat and head for Capernaum. Mark says they are on their way to Bethsaida, and Matthew simply says they are going to the other side. The time and the weather conditions are much more

Homiletical Perspective

As do Matthew and Mark, John follows the feeding of the multitude with Jesus walking on the water. The pairing of the two incidents, recalling Psalm 107, is an early Jesus tradition. What might this pairing open up for the preacher?

Avoid the stale reductionism that so often surrounds preaching this pericope—and others. It is easy and boring—perhaps the most damning criticism a preacher can receive. As Michael Ramsey once remarked, the Bible, like Christ, "is of two natures," human and divine, and all of us who read are "Chalcedonian."[1] We cannot let John's depth escape either us or our listeners, even as he tells this story much more compactly than Matthew and Mark.

If the feeding of the multitudes is an example of Jesus' accessibility, then his walking on the water reminds us that Jesus can be neither contained nor managed. Even those closest to him experience him as mystery. What is the relationship between God's *reliability*, represented in the feeding story, and God's complete and utter *unpredictability*, represented in the story of Jesus' walking on the water? The whole concept of the mystery of Jesus is a deep well from which the preacher can draw.

1. A. M. Ramsey, "The Bible," in *Report of the Sixth Anglo-Catholic Congress* (Westminster: The Dacre Press, 1948), 3ff.

John 6:16–21

Theological Perspective

Capernaum. Why the disciples would leave their companion in the dark without a ride remains a mystery. Yet in such circumstances both their leaving and their terrified response to his reappearance might well make sense if interpreters consider the greater context of chapter 6 and the passion narrative that follows later in the story.

One key to understanding this chapter and its theological implications can be found in the question Jesus addresses to the Twelve: "Do you also wish to go away?" (6:67). Throughout the chapter there are references to Jesus being abandoned by his disciples: the disciples' departure for Capernaum, knowing "it was now dark, and Jesus had not yet come to them" (v. 17); the number of disciples who turned away because of his teachings and "no longer went about with him" (6:66); and hints of the betrayal to come from one of the Twelve (6:64, 71).

Political circumstances and the implications of being made king would certainly put Jesus and his followers on a collision course with the imperial powers and their local surrogates. The price of being considered a king resurges in the exchange with Pilate (18:33–39) and is evident in the mockery that follows (19:3), in the inscription over the crucified Jesus and the controversy surrounding the inscribed text (19:19–22). In chapter 19, the author goes to great lengths to alleviate the culpability of the Roman governor: "Pilate tried to release him, but the Jews cried out, 'If you release this man, you are no friend of the emperor. Everyone who claims to be a king sets himself against the emperor'" (19:12). It is ironic that the subjugated would dare remind the imperial representative of the threat this alleged insurrectionist posed to the empire.

With these repercussions, is it any surprise that the disciples leave behind the one whom the crowds want to force into becoming king? At first glance, terror seems an incongruous response on the part of the disciples to the reappearance of their teacher. Would not joy be a more appropriate response at seeing that a friend left behind on the shore has managed to catch up? Would bafflement perhaps more accurately reflect a reaction to the unexpected manner of his sudden appearance? Is the fear noted in this passage an acknowledgment that trouble has followed them? Not only was their attempt to ditch Jesus unsuccessful; how, the disciples may wonder, will he respond now to their abandonment? Are there echoes here of the reluctant prophet Jonah and the storm at sea that frustrated his efforts to escape his divine commission (Jonah 1:3–15)?

Pastoral Perspective

level of uncertainty in the form of threats to financial or emotional stability, health, and survival. This is certainly true in these times, characterized by a rapid pace of change, fluctuating economies, major threats to our health and physical environment, hunger and violence, terrorism on a grand scale, and escalating rates of depression and anxiety.

Understandably, we feel stressed and anxious at times, even desperate in moments, as if caught in a small boat at sea on a dark, stormy night. Absolute control over our life circumstances is beyond our reach; things do not always go as planned. Life is, and always has been, a risky venture.

Writers of Scripture have taken note of existential anxiety: "Do not be afraid," "fear not," or "do not fear" occurs in the Bible 107 times, and the word "fear" appears 314 times. Our text, one such reference, offers assurance for times of fear. One can imagine the disciples' immense relief and comfort at having Jesus present with them in that moment of vulnerability, terror, and need. Jesus has not abandoned them. His words are simple yet powerful: "It is I; do not be afraid" (v. 20). Jesus shows up as the faithful, caring teacher and friend he has always been for them, always at the most opportune moment.

Much is written about fear today, as well, a clear testimony to its prevalence. Yet the advice is varied. Shall we feel the fear and move forward anyway? Face it, embrace it, give courage our best effort? Shall we wait for an opportune moment to confront the fear, or avoid it altogether, focusing on positive thoughts or simply distracting ourselves?

On the one hand, fear plays a useful role, telling us, "Pay attention; you could get hurt." There is a time to be careful; banishing fear entirely could have dire consequences. On the other hand, we know that unbridled, constant fear can be debilitating, leading to a state of perpetual anxiety in which we may isolate ourselves, avoid those different from us, and trust others reluctantly. Such fear immobilizes us and causes us to choose inaction, lest we make mistakes or fail. If we allow our fears to control us, we may lose what control we can exercise in our lives, and compromise the life God has given us.

How then might this text help us deal with our fear? Perhaps we can identify with the terrified disciples and the feelings of abandonment that arise in the face of daunting, threatening situations. We may then find solace in Jesus' simple but comforting words. At the same time we may be stirred to consider our feelings and beliefs about Jesus. Though we lack his physical presence, do we find comfort

important than the destination of the boat. John emphasizes the darkness by beginning the account, "When evening came," and then adding, "It was now dark." Darkness is a powerful symbol in the Fourth Gospel. It is linked with unbelief and opposition to Jesus in John 1:5; 12:35; and also in 1 John 1:5–6; 2:11.

It is difficult to understand the significance of John's statement that Jesus has not yet come to them. It seems to imply that the reader would already have known that Jesus does indeed come to them later in the story. Thus the statement may be an editorial comment that John inserted into a well-known account of Jesus' appearance on the stormy water. It certainly anticipates what is about to occur moments later. It also emphasizes Jesus' absence in the midst of the darkness that engulfs the disciples.

John 6:18–19a. It is not surprising that a strong wind arises and creates a stormy sea for the disciples. Sudden storms occur frequently on the Sea of Galilee. The disciples have rowed approximately four miles (twenty-five to thirty *stadia* in Greek), which would place them in the middle of the sea, far from shore. John's laconic account focuses on the imminent danger in which the disciples find themselves.

John 6:19b–20. Dramatically, John reports that amid the height of the storm the disciples see Jesus walking on the sea and approaching their endangered boat. According to his account, it is not the powerful wind and the strong waves buffeting the boat that frighten the disciples. As experienced fishermen they probably are confident that they can navigate their boat to safety. It is the sudden and unexpected sighting of Jesus on the water that terrifies them. The disciples' terror, in keeping with biblical tradition, is a typical response to the theophany, which underscores the divine nature of Jesus.

The climactic moment comes when John attributes to Jesus a common self-identification in Greek, *egō eimi* (literally, an emphatic "I am," translated here "It is I"), to announce his presence. In Exodus 3:13–15 the Hebrew equivalent of this phrase functions as a divine name. In several key passages later in the Fourth Gospel, John will use that same phrase with very important predicate nominatives to identify Jesus, for example, "I am the bread of life" (6:35). These phrases identify Jesus as God's divine messenger who bears a message of salvation and eternal life. In John 18:5–6 the same phrase, *egō eimi*, occurs without a predicate when Jesus identifies himself to

This paradox at the heart of God needs articulation that makes sense. We say we know, or want to know, God's reliability, yet we also have some stake in attesting to the "God of surprises." How does this work in the life of the faithful community and the individual believer? Who is to say? What is the force of Jesus' announcement in verse 20, "I am"? How does this relate to God's divine name in the Hebrew Scriptures, most notably in God's encounter with Moses at Exodus 3:14?

We can take this familiar story as a paradigm for thinking about our individual and communal spiritual lives. It has all the elements that are true to our experience. First, the scene happens in the evening and in the dark, the literal and metaphorical arena of so much spiritual struggle.[2] Then there is the significance of the boat, a rich image in Christian thought, a sign of the church and a place of safety.

The disciples are without Jesus, an element of all spiritual struggle, when God seems absent from us or when we have decided to act without the companionship of Jesus. The rough sea is an obvious image for the spiritual life, and the blowing wind adds to the danger. The rowing of the disciples is a nod to the huge struggle that can be involved. As many have noted throughout the ages, prayer is hard work, and the analogy of pulling on oars is a good one that we can understand immediately.

However, even if we embark without Jesus, God will find us, just as Jesus finds the disciples. Our encounters with God are not always sweet and peaceful, and can be frightening and disorienting, especially if, in true biblical fashion, these encounters demand change from us. We come to know over and over again who Jesus is—the "I am," the perfect revelation to us of who God is—and we desire that safety and intimacy with him that is represented in the disciples' desire to take Jesus into the boat with them. The goal of the spiritual struggle is also here: we reach firmer ground at last, another step along the journey in the direction toward union with God. Sometimes that final leap, from danger to safety, from turmoil to peace, can happen almost without our realizing it.[3] Here Jesus does not calm the wind; he calms the disciples' terror.

2. Indeed John of the Cross says that the food that God gives "can only be received in dryness and darkness," as quoted in Robert Atwell, ed., *Celebrating the Seasons: Daily Spiritual Readings for the Christian Year* (Norwich: The Canterbury Press, 1999), 360. The resurrection also happens in the dark.
3. See, for a different, but similarly imaginative reading of this text, Jean Vanier, *Drawn into the Mystery of Jesus through the Gospel of John* (New York: Paulist Press, 2004), 122ff.

John 6:16–21

Theological Perspective

The response of Jesus to their action is revelatory: "It is I; do not be afraid" (v. 20). There is no rebuke, just a familiar formula that indicates the presence of God and how one should react to that manifestation. The Gospel reports that they then "wanted to take him into the boat," though it does not indicate that such a desire results in Jesus' actually getting into the boat, only that immediately they reach land (v. 21).

These references to abandonment in chapter 6 leave readers to wonder whether these are premonitions of rejections to come or intimations of the daily lived reality of the Johannine community. Some scholars suggest that vacillation, in-house discord, and desertion may have characterized the experience of this community of followers. However, the revelation is of a divine presence that continuously seeks to accompany, to chase down, to be present even to those who may flee, leaving open the possibility of return. The posture of openness expressed in the desire of just wanting to let Jesus back in makes return possible and relationship reassured.

The aversion on the part of Jesus to participate in grassroots-generated political power and the attempt of the Gospel writer to exonerate Pilate may also communicate a message. Faced with the reality of Roman power following the destruction of the temple in Jerusalem, perhaps the Johannine community was also seeking to signal to Rome that they were indeed no real threat, as if to say, "Our movement is no threat to you, mighty Rome, just an in-house Jewish squabble. Please leave us alone." In other words, the community may have wanted to convey that it had no intention of threatening the status quo or disturbing the imperial peace.

The responses of the disciples in this passage to the potential risks of discipleship reflect reasonable options: flight, fear, maybe even hope for forgiveness should one stray, because, as the Gospel suggests, "this teaching is difficult" (6:60). The question posed to the Twelve resounds across time in every context where followers of Jesus face the real-life challenges of living out faithful discipleship: "Do you also wish to go away?" (6:67).

CARMEN NANKO-FERNÁNDEZ

Pastoral Perspective

believing or sensing that his spirit abides with us? Have we ever experienced the presence of God? Do we believe in our times of terror that we are not alone and need not fear? Can we recall moments of caring from fellow Christians, standing in for Jesus and affirming that loneliness and despair need not be the final word?

These are personal questions that may or may not speak to you. If you find yourself squirming in discomfort, take heart. Perhaps there were times when you prayed, seeking answers, and no answers seemed to come. You felt alone, possibly afraid. Take solace in this fact: countless biblical writers speak of the silence or absence of God. Even Jesus himself, from the cross, cites Psalm 22, lamenting his own God-forsaken moment. For many people of faith, a sense of God's presence is evanescent. There may be moments of cherishing God's love and closeness, and other times when emptiness and loneliness prevail.

What is central to this text is the disciples' experience of connection and comfort with Jesus. One surmises they likely grew to trust that even in the silence, God's presence in Jesus would always accompany them. The essence of this story rests in the power and significance of relationships. The disciples' relationship with Jesus was the cornerstone of their faith, and his presence was absolutely compelling; they had given their lives to be with him. They experienced him fully present, physically, emotionally, spiritually.

It is incumbent on us, then, to consider the power and significance of our relationships. How comforting is our presence? Are we fully present, given the distraction of the world? As we seek to bear witness to our faith, do we embrace the importance of relationships? Do we build caring connections with people, listening to them and respecting and honoring them, regardless of who they are and what they believe? Do we understand the limited value of words in the absence of relationship?

The writer of John's Gospel has given us, in this text, a simple yet powerful story intended to bring us comfort and to strengthen our faith, our relationship to God, and our witness in the world.

JEAN E. GREENWOOD

Exegetical Perspective

the soldiers about to arrest him. Immediately they step back and fall to the ground. This raises the question of whether, for John, even a simple *egō eimi* without a predicate may have the force of the divine name. Alternatively, it may simply be a form of self-identification, as it is in the parallel accounts of both Matthew and Mark. Characteristically, John's use of this phrase has an ambiguous double meaning.

Immediately after identifying himself, Jesus adds, "Do not be afraid." The fear the disciples experience when they see Jesus coming toward them is an understandable human response to the sudden presence of deity. Nowhere else in this Gospel are the disciples afraid of Jesus. Here the greeting of Jesus and his presence dispel the disciples' fear.

John 6:21. The theophany ends just as suddenly as it has first appeared. John records only that the disciples want to receive Jesus into the boat. Without stating that they actually do so, he reports that the boat immediately reaches its destination. Roman Catholic biblical scholar Raymond Brown notes several possible allusions in John 6 to Psalm 107.[1] There, after describing waves of the sea that mounted up to heaven, the psalmist writes, "[God] made the storm be still. . . . [God] brought them to their desired haven" (Ps. 107:29a, 30b). In Brown's words, the parallels are numerous enough "to make it plausible that he [the evangelist] meant the miracle to reflect the general symbolism of the crossing of the sea at the time of the Exodus."[2]

Such parallels would only serve to emphasize further God's power as evidenced in the dramatic epiphany of Jesus walking on the stormy water. The Gospel writer focuses on the divine epiphany of Jesus rather than on particular scriptural or liturgical parallels. The miraculous landing of the disciples at Capernaum accentuates the central point of this miracle story: Jesus the incarnate Logos is one with God, and when God's presence is acknowledged, human fears and anxieties are silenced.

JAMES A. BRASHLER

Homiletical Perspective

The preacher might reflect on what it means for us to be without Jesus, especially after the experience of being fed by him. Do the disciples in this story set out on a risky trip intentionally without Jesus? Why would they not wait for Jesus to return from his withdrawal from the mountain? John does not tell us, but the fear that the disciples display in the story may convey their awareness that they were attempting something they should not have. Do we go from being fed by Jesus in word, sacrament, and community to renewed isolation and self-reliance, even when we know better? Of course we do.

At its heart, this is a showing of God, a *theophany*. Just as God tamed the primordial "deep" in creation, so the God that Jesus reveals is the God who orders chaos. Jesus walks on a sea named for a Roman emperor, not simply to calm the chaos of foreign domination and the terror it inflicts on Galilean peasants, but to show our ultimate origin in the One who makes human existence possible and who is capable of sustaining it against the forces of destruction and dissolution.

We tend to speak about experiences of God in prayer and meditation in very tame, reassuring ways. A great deal of Christian spirituality now falls under the "self-help" category of the marketplace. However, Christian spirituality was born in the harshness and danger of the desert, not in the comfort of a cushion on the carpet and a cup of cocoa. It is not surprising, therefore, that when Jesus shows the disciples who he is, as opposed to the role the crowd wanted to give him, they are scared to death. How ought we to speak of God's absolute otherness, which, to our human perception, is so foreign as to leave us with no frames of reference?

PETER EATON

---

1. Raymond E. Brown, *The Gospel according to John I–XII* (Garden City, NY: Doubleday, 1966), 255.
2. Brown, *Gospel according to John*, 256.

John 6:22–29

²²The next day the crowd that had stayed on the other side of the sea saw that there had been only one boat there. They also saw that Jesus had not got into the boat with his disciples, but that his disciples had gone away alone. ²³Then some boats from Tiberias came near the place where they had eaten the bread after the Lord had given thanks. ²⁴So when the crowd saw that neither Jesus nor his disciples were there, they themselves got into the boats and went to Capernaum looking for Jesus.

²⁵When they found him on the other side of the sea, they said to him, "Rabbi, when did you come here?" ²⁶Jesus answered them, "Very truly, I tell you, you are looking for me, not because you saw signs, but because you ate your fill of the loaves. ²⁷Do not work for the food that perishes, but for the food that endures for eternal life, which the Son of Man will give you. For it is on him that God the Father has set his seal." ²⁸Then they said to him, "What must we do to perform the works of God?" ²⁹Jesus answered them, "This is the work of God, that you believe in him whom he has sent."

Theological Perspective

This passage follows two powerful episodes in John's account of Jesus' ministry: the feeding of the five thousand (6:1–14) and Jesus' walking on water (6:16–21). John 6:22–29 leads off a series of pericopes in which Jesus identifies himself in terms of his unique relationship to God the Father and his place in the arc of salvation history. In this series the evangelist emphasizes as of central importance both human belief in Jesus as the Son and agent of God, and the agency and choice to believe that is offered to those who witness Jesus' ministry among the crowds.

The passage begins with a familiar theme: the ongoing search for Jesus' whereabouts by the crowds who have been drawn to him by signs and miracles. These crowds, which have grown in size over the course of John's narrative, include those seeking particular signs that can disclose Jesus' identity, as well as those seeking remedies for personal ills, including the sick and the hungry. In verse 22 the trail seems to have gone cold: all the clues point to Jesus' disciples' having traveled by boat to get away from the crowds, but without any evidence of Jesus' having done the same. (The reader, in contrast, knows of Jesus' alternative method of crossing the water.) Finally, the crowd spots some boats from Tiberias coming near to them, and a portion of the crowd

Pastoral Perspective

In the wake of the feeding miracle, the crowds were still hungry. They had just experienced a profound moment of nourishment, community, and transformation, and they were hoping for more. However, when they awoke the next day, they had a mystery on their hands: there was only one boat. The disciples had taken it and Jesus was not with them. They put the clues together and concluded that Jesus had disappeared, and they did what we would expect them to do: they pursued him.

Their effort was a noble one, similar to the effort many of us make when we are seeking the next profound spiritual experience. This passage is perfect for anyone in the congregation whose spiritual life has plateaued or wandered into the wilderness. It is for anyone who assesses the condition of his or her life and comes to the conclusion that Jesus has left.

So like the crowds, we engage in pursuit. We develop rhythms of religious practices, anchoring our lives in spiritual disciplines, in the hopes that these efforts will produce an encounter with Christ that will sustain us during the lean times. We pray harder, study more, and push even further to find Jesus, falling back on behavioral patterns from the past that we hope will effect a profound encounter in the present. The writer of the Gospel of John might call these efforts a search for *signs*.

Exegetical Perspective

This passage opens a long conversation (6:22–59) between Jesus and the crowds whom he fed the previous day (see 6:23). The common title, Bread of Life Discourse, is appropriate because the dialogue functions as an interpretation of the feeding scene (6:1–15). Unlike the parallel Synoptic accounts (Matt. 14:13–21; Mark 6:32–44; Luke 9:10–17), the feeding miracle in the Fourth Gospel is given an explicitly symbolic interpretation through this dialogue. Jesus' miracle is not merely a demonstration of his power but a symbol of God's eschatological feeding through the revelation of the divine word.

This passage unfolds in two sections: a narrative account of the movements of the crowd "seeking Jesus" (vv. 22–25) and a dialogue about the motivation behind such seeking (vv. 26–29). The center of the passage is the crowd's simple question about Jesus' travels: "Rabbi, when did you come here?" (v. 25). The subsequent conversation reveals that this question is far more probing, setting the context for much of the dialogue to follow. The crowd's question is a central one explored by the narrator from the opening verses of the Gospel. In this passage, Jesus argues that God works not at a point in the past, but in the eschatological present.

The initial narrative backdrop (vv. 22–25) has an important effect on the reader's experience. The

Homiletical Perspective

The church member said to her pastor, "You do a great job of preaching about what we should do for God. I wish that you would preach more about what God does for us." The words hit home. Preachers are often effective at preaching about what people can do in the areas of social justice, missions, service, ministry, stewardship, love, and so on. All of these things are about what we can do for God; but what does God do for us? That question strikes at the age-old tension between works and grace. This tension is the theme of our text from John 6:22–29.

After two amazing stories that portray the power of Jesus (feeding of the five thousand and the walking on the water), Jesus now teaches us the meaning of the events that have just occurred. A crowd has been fed and goes looking for Jesus. Realizing that the disciples crossed the sea in a boat without Jesus the night before, they look for Jesus where he fed them. Not finding him there, they do not give up easily but cross the sea in search of Jesus. They are busy scurrying around looking for the man who fed them the day before.

When they finally find Jesus, their question is about when Jesus arrived in this new location (v. 25). As is often the case, Jesus does not directly answer the question but moves the conversation to a much deeper level. He says, "Very truly, I tell you,

John 6:22–29

crosses over to Capernaum. When they finally catch up with Jesus, he responds to their query about when he arrived in Capernaum by addressing their motivation for searching him out: "You are looking for me, not because you saw signs, but because you ate your fill of the loaves" (v. 26).

Three theological issues emerge here. The first relates to the development of religious knowledge. It would be too easy to dismiss the crowds as either clueless or merely selfish or materialistic, missing the real point of Jesus' teachings. It is important to note that while the disciples may have a clearer sense of Jesus' identity and mission at this point in the Gospel, those same disciples, earlier in chapter 6, could see no way that a few loaves of bread and fish could possibly feed a hungry crowd or how Jesus could cross a lake without a boat to meet them in their time of need. For the crowds, as with the disciples, something more is going on. Here we see how the crowds have been drawn in by what they have seen and heard of Jesus, to the point of going to the waterfront and trying to piece together where he might have gone. The picture that emerges is one that reminds us that humans depend on each other in seeking after God, and that religious understanding develops progressively and incrementally. The Gospel may inspire in us patience with one another and with ourselves.

The second theological issue that arises here concerns the relationship between concrete human need and spiritual human need. Both prove to be the ground upon which Jesus meets us. At the midpoint of this story (v. 26), Jesus reminds his hearers that they have moved from witnessing Jesus' actions and power to personally experiencing them. For many in the crowd, the experience of eating as much as one wanted—until one no longer felt hungry—was probably rare. Yet they have not fully grasped the significance of their experience. Thus Jesus asks the gathered crowd to move from observing and experiencing Jesus' power and presence to recognizing its meaning and believing in Jesus as the one whom God has sent.

While Jesus exhorts them to recognize the contrast between the "food that perishes" and the "food that endures" (v. 27), he neither despises nor rejects them for seeking the former. Neither does he suggest that their tangible needs or their experience of Jesus meeting them is irrelevant or unimportant. Instead, concrete motivation and need provide opportunity for Jesus to teach his hearers and for the crowd to move to another level of religious understanding.

The response of Jesus is as puzzling as it is liberating. When the crowds finally locate him, he does not congratulate them for finding him, nor does he applaud their tenacity and their choice to continue following him. Instead, he identifies the idolatrous nature of their pursuit, names their motivation as selfish, and introduces them to the possibility of a holier life.

Pious actions are commendable, at least on the surface. However, when we perform them in order to extract spiritual benefit for ourselves—like rubbing a lamp in search of the genie or carrying a rabbit's foot with hopes for a charm—even the most disciplined spiritual practices can become idolatrous.

The response of Jesus serves as a kind of Wisdom literature for people who have become entrenched in a stale, conventional spirituality. He upended what would otherwise be considered noble behavior to say that, in the end, it is not entirely about behavior at all. Making it all about one's practice can, at the very least, lead to fatigue. At their worst, when those efforts do not produce the desired result, they can lead to emptiness, despair, and even questions about God's very existence.

The crowds, still not having fully grasped what Jesus was saying, answered the way we probably would respond. "What must we *do* to perform the works of God?" They were so entrenched in a behavior-based paradigm that they could not see any other alternatives, despite the words of Jesus. So Jesus answered once again: it is not entirely about what you do. It is all about what God is already doing. You simply have to believe.

This is a liberating message, and one that may be difficult at first for a congregation to hear. Still, it is an important word to share, for even the best-laid patterns of spiritual practice need to be uprooted from time to time.

In a congregation I once served we offered a popular Bible study series. With the completion of each year of the curriculum, students were given a pin to serve as a visible reminder of their accomplishment. Some of the students opted to display their pins on their church name tags, in an earnest way to promote the Bible study series for those who might be interested.

However, one Sunday, when a visitor to the church asked one of the Bible study "graduates" about the pin, the conversation revealed a very different perception of what the pins represented to an outside observer. The visitor thought the pins were like Boy Scout badges or stripes on a uniform:

details of the crowd's confusion about Jesus' where-abouts, and their recognition that he could not have taken the one mode of transport available, highlight a differentiation in knowledge between two audiences: the crowd searching for Jesus within the world of the narrative (the "narrative audience") and those reading (or hearing) the Gospel ("the readers"), who are "watching" the crowd. The narrative audience, unlike John's readers, is not privy to the knowledge that Jesus has walked across the Sea of Galilee (6:16–21). The reader, having witnessed this miracle, can easily answer the practical question posed in verse 25: Jesus arrived the previous night (6:21). The conversation that follows reveals the insufficiency of this answer.

A hint that the question recounted in verse 25 is more than a simple query about Jesus' travel occurs in the narrator's reference to the crowd "seeking Jesus" (zētountes ton Iēsoun). Jesus' opening words in the Gospel, "What [or whom] are you seeking?" (ti zēteite, 1:38), highlight a theme that continues throughout the narrative (see 18:4, 7; 20:15). To seek Jesus is not merely to search for his physical location; rather, it is to ask the meaning of God's revelation in Christ. The crowd, having experienced Jesus the day before, seeks an explanation.

Jesus avoids a direct answer to the question about his arrival and identifies the higher motivation behind the crowd's "seeking." He denies that their motivation is simply curiosity raised by the "signs" (sēmeia), the term used in the Gospel of John to refer to external events persons have witnessed that call for a faith decision (see 2:11, 23; 3:2). The crowd seeks Jesus because of the spiritual satiety they experienced in being fed by him. By attributing the crowd's "seeking" to their personal experience with the food he provided, Jesus strips the reader of the advantage of witnessing the crossing of the sea; advantage lies instead with those who "ate of the bread and were filled" (v. 26, my trans.).

Jesus' imperative in verse 27 upsets this advantage by clarifying that "eating" and "being filled" refer not to the past event of physical satiety, but to feeding on the teaching that Jesus, the eschatological "word of God" (1:1), offers and embodies. Jesus' miracle is a symbol of God's eschatological feeding through the sending of his Son. In dualistic terms characteristic of eschatological discourse, Jesus calls on the crowd to disregard "the food which is being destroyed" (NRSV "the food that perishes") and instead seek food that "remains [NRSV "endures"] for eternal life," offered by the "Son of Man" (a self-designation

you are looking for me, not because you saw signs, but because you ate your fill of the loaves. Do not work for the food that perishes, but for the food that endures for eternal life, which the Son of Man will give you. For it is on him that God the Father has set his seal" (vv. 26–27). With this response, Jesus brings up the subject of work. He challenges his listeners to invest their lives in working for the food that endures rather than for the food that perishes.

The preacher can linger right here for a moment and develop these words. What does the statement of Jesus really mean about our jobs and the work that we do to make a living? What do the words of Jesus tell us about our striving for power, popularity, pleasure, and possessions? Is it wrong to work hard for things that do perish, but that put food on the table and provide security for our families? Good preaching wrestles with the text, and this is a point for such an encounter. Nevertheless, we must not linger too long here, for the good news comes later and that is what the best preaching always proclaims.

The crowd often misunderstands Jesus. However, in this instance they seem to "get it"—in part, at least. Quickly the conversation moves away from working for the things that perish, as they ask, "What must we do to perform the works of God?" (v. 28). As they shift their focus away from concern about finding their next lunch, they begin to ask about the "works of God." They continue wondering about what "we must do to perform." This seems to be the age-old question, does it not? What must we do to please God?

To this day our churches are filled with people who work hard to please God with acts of justice and mercy, demonstrations of personal holiness, commitments to evangelism and missions, and time spent in prayer and worship. We say that salvation does not come by works, but every preacher can name folks who seem to live, act, and work as if eternity hangs in the balance, depending on what good work is done next. Such a mind-set is hardwired into the Protestant work ethic and the Roman Catholic traditions that pervade our land. While such an attitude keeps the church afloat, it can also become a very heavy load for folks to carry. There must be a better way.

Grace is the better way. Jesus reminds his listeners that the food that endures is what "the Son of Man will give you" (v. 27). This bread of life is not something we must earn by the work that we do; it is a gift. Grace always is. Grace is a gift given, but it also must be a gift received. Jesus makes sure that his listeners get both sides of the coin. When they press

John 6:22–29

Theological Perspective

Theologically, this passage reminds us that the hard and fast line between meeting people's tangible needs and inviting them to enter into relationship with God is a line strictly of our own making. Jesus' recognition of, and response to, human need is compassionate and comprehensive.

A final theological theme to note here is found in verses 27–29, where Jesus advises the crowd and invites them to believe. Here both Jesus and the crowd use the language of "work." In verse 27, Jesus advises the crowd, "Do not work for the food that perishes"; in verse 28, the crowd asks, "What must we do to perform the works of God?"; in verse 29, Jesus responds by defining as work belief in the one whom God the Father has sent. While John will use the remainder of chapter 6 to develop Jesus' self-identification as the one who has been sent, the emphasis here, on belief as a form of work, serves as a helpful counterpoint to theological approaches that treat faith and human action ("works") as standing in opposition to one another.

In this passage in John's Gospel, we are reminded that belief itself can be rightly understood as "work," in the sense of choice, and that the decision to believe may, for some, require considerable effort. This passage does not negate the need for grace or divine agency; as Jesus says in 6:44, "No one can come to me unless drawn by the Father who sent me." Rather, John seems to be emphasizing how the human work of belief meets its object in the one whom God freely and already acted to send. God initiates the sending of his Son and the drawing near of humankind. In response, men and women may believe.

DEIRDRE KING HAINSWORTH

Pastoral Perspective

emblems of merit and achievement—*signs*, to use John's terminology.

"These must mean you are a super-Christian," the visitor said, pointing at the pins, with all respect and earnest curiosity. That comment took the Bible study graduate aback, as a jarring dose of reality regarding how even the most sincere attempts at religious devotion can slip into religious idolatry if they go unchecked. She explained to the visitor that while the intent of her display of the pins was different, she needed the visitor's perspective to reconsider why she had been attending these Bible studies at all.

Of course, this is not to say that spiritual practice is unnecessary. Far from it! There is nothing wrong with a fervent study of the Scriptures, an integrated life of prayer, a fixed pattern of fasting, or any other kind of discipline. However, when those actions become the object of belief, rather than the means to belief, then we are making those practices more about us, and less about the one who makes those practices possible in the first place.

That is why Jesus' word to the disciples, and to us, is so liberating. "This is all God's work," Jesus said. For all Christians, there are times when engaging in spiritual practices does not produce the desired effects, when the doldrums continue and the spiritual dryness persists. If such practices are of themselves transformative, then the lack of results must mean we are performing them incorrectly.

Instead, God does all the work. While this message does not encourage us to lay aside our actions when they are ineffective or when other priorities overtake them, it does remind us that God's grace is at work, even when we feel God absent. When we sense that God has suddenly disappeared, when all evidence suggests that the boat has left without us, and when our emotions, intellect, and behaviors betray us, it is believing that covers the gap.

MAGREY R. DEVEGA

common in the Synoptics but relatively rare in the Fourth Gospel, almost always used to refer to Jesus' glorification in crucifixion; see 3:13–14; 5:27; 8:28; 12:23; 13:31) and "sealed" by the Father (an image common in eschatological texts [see Dan. 8:26; Matt. 27:66; Rev. 5:1–2; 20:3; cf. 2 Cor. 1:22]). In verse 27, Jesus shows that the food worth feeding on is not a physical element from the past, but an eschatological reality in the present.

This eschatological shift (v. 27) offers new meaning to Jesus' comment that "you were filled" (*echortasthēte*, v. 26). This language is not found elsewhere in this Gospel, but it appears in each of the parallel Synoptic feeding stories (Matt. 15:37; Mark 8:8; Luke 9:17), where satiety demonstrates Jesus' power to create so much from so little. In verses 26–27, Jesus speaks of being "filled," not by the volume of physical food consumed, but by the "food that remains [NRSV "endures"] for eternal life," which Jesus identifies as himself (6:35). In the Fourth Gospel, one becomes "filled" not by eating food but by feasting on God's word. How one can do this is explored in the rest of the dialogue.

The narrative audience first attempts to respond to Jesus' call by asking how they can do "the works of God" (*ta erga tou theou*), drawing upon Jesus' verb "work for" (*ergazomai*, v. 28). This question assumes "works of God" means "the works that God wants us to accomplish." Jesus responds by defining the singular "work of God" (*to ergon tou theou*; cf. 4:34), understood as "that which God accomplishes." God's work is the sending of Jesus, the revelation that is the grounds for the audience's (and reader's) response of belief (or faith), a central challenge of the Johannine literature (see 1:7, 12; 3:15–16; 1 John 3:23; 5:13) and the focus of the next section of the exchange (6:30–35).

The Fourth Gospel is more than a retelling of past events; it is a direct engagement of the reader at whose feet it lays the challenge of seeking Jesus not in the past but in the eschatological present. Though the reader may believe he or she knows the answer to the crowd's question in verse 25, Jesus shows that this question is answered only by an encounter with God's revelation. This Gospel asks the reader to consider not how long Jesus has been in Capernaum but, rather, how long God has been active through Jesus.

RICHARD MANLY ADAMS JR.

to know what they must do to perform in a way that is acceptable to God (works), Jesus reminds them that their "work" is to receive grace. He says, "This is the work of God, that you believe in him whom he has sent" (v. 29). The wondrous gift of the bread of heaven has been given from God's grace; now we eat of this bread and receive it by faith. With glad hearts we accept the gift of this bread, and then we are set free to serve Christ and to participate in the powerful reign of God through the offering of our lives. (See Eph. 2:8–10 for a statement that beautifully brings together grace, faith, and our works.)

If you are a preacher who has heard a parishioner ask, "What must we do to perform the works of God?" John 6:22–29 provides rich homiletical material for a sermon about what God does for us. We do not make the bread; it comes from heaven. This bread is given as a gift that brings life. The bread does not perish, but will nourish us forever. Such is the beautiful picture of what God does for us; though there is yet something that we must do for God. We eat the bread. We do this by believing and trusting in the one who is the bread of life. Faith is the "work of God" (v. 29) that we are to do. Balanced preaching that declares what God does for us and what we can do for God is proclamation that enriches the church.

DAVID W. HULL

John 6:30–40

³⁰So they said to him, "What sign are you going to give us then, so that we may see it and believe you? What work are you performing? ³¹Our ancestors ate the manna in the wilderness; as it is written, 'He gave them bread from heaven to eat.'" ³²Then Jesus said to them, "Very truly, I tell you, it was not Moses who gave you the bread from heaven, but it is my Father who gives you the true bread from heaven. ³³For the bread of God is that which comes down from heaven and gives life to the world." ³⁴They said to him, "Sir, give us this bread always."

³⁵Jesus said to them, "I am the bread of life. Whoever comes to me will never be hungry, and whoever believes in me will never be thirsty. ³⁶But I said to you that you have seen me and yet do not believe. ³⁷Everything that the Father gives me will come to me, and anyone who comes to me I will never drive away; ³⁸for I have come down from heaven, not to do my own will, but the will of him who sent me. ³⁹And this is the will of him who sent me, that I should lose nothing of all that he has given me, but raise it up on the last day. ⁴⁰This is indeed the will of my Father, that all who see the Son and believe in him may have eternal life; and I will raise them up on the last day."

Theological Perspective

Earlier in chapter 6, John illustrated how Jesus' hearers, having been miraculously fed, moved beyond merely observing to experiencing directly Jesus' power. Moreover, Jesus has urged his hearers to take the next step: to undertake the "work" of believing in the one whom God the Father has sent to the world on his behalf. Here in 6:30–40, John describes the crowd's persistent questioning, presents Jesus' self-identification as the "bread of life," and underscores Jesus' relationship with God the Father and its implications for human history.

Verse 30 continues the discussion between Jesus and members of the crowd who have followed him from place to place. In verses 28 and 29, Jesus has been asked, "What must we do to perform the works of God?" He has responded by offering just one essential task: believe. In verse 30, the crowd's question confirms their failure to comprehend what they experienced in 6:1–14, as they again ask for a sign "so that we may see it and believe" Jesus. They go on to remind Jesus of the Israelites' experience of receiving manna during their exodus from slavery in Egypt, an experience of being fed that came to be understood by the community as Moses' provision of "bread from heaven." It is unclear why the crowd, who certainly knew of or had directly experienced the miraculous feeding described in 6:1–14, would

Pastoral Perspective

In moments of duress, we seek reliability. We yearn for that which is fixed, stable, and secure, something that will endure through the highs and inevitable lows of life. In this passage from the Gospel of John, we might characterize that longing as the desire for *always*. "Sir," the crowds said to Jesus, "give us this bread *always*."

In our most desperate times, we lean toward the past; for what can be more reliable than that which has already happened? No degree of present trauma can alter what has already occurred. The people and events that have preceded us have an advantage: hardship can no longer affect them.

This may be one explanation for the popularity of genealogical studies. When we trace our lineage, unearth our roots, and rediscover our ancestral stories, we seek to learn their lessons. If they made it through tough times, we say to ourselves, then perhaps we can as well. In the process, we seek to discover who we are, and cultivate the same character that sustained our predecessors. The past can be quite comforting.

It should come as no surprise, then, that the crowds approached Jesus with their ancestry in mind. In their search for the *always*, they presented the past as evidence, a guarantee of future results. "Our ancestors ate the manna in the wilderness" (v. 31a), they

Exegetical Perspective

This passage continues the bread of life dialogue that began in 6:22. While the opening passage (6:22–29) interpreted the feeding (6:1–15) as a symbol of God's eschatological feeding, this passage explores Jesus' role. Here Jesus identifies himself as the bread sent from heaven and identifies the crowd's belief in Jesus as the "work of God" (6:29). His long discourse (vv. 32–40) serves as a response to the crowd's request for a sign (v. 30), a request that is consistent with John's portrayal of the kind of belief that forms as a response to "signs" (*ta sēmeia*; see 2:11, 23; 3:2). Jesus has acknowledged that "unless you see signs [*sēmeia*] and wonders, you will not ever believe" (4:48, my trans.; cf. 2:18–19).

The crowd offers Jewish precedent for their demand for a sign as the basis of belief. Moses miraculously provided manna as sustenance in the desert. Manna was given "so that you will know that I am the LORD your God" (Exod. 16:12, my trans.). God has provided grounds for belief in the past, even in the form of bread from heaven. If Jesus is going to demand that they believe in the one who has sent him, then he should perform a miracle at least as impressive as Moses' manna. This argument reflects the crowd's misunderstanding of Jesus as another prophet or wonder worker, their initial response to the feeding (6:14).

Homiletical Perspective

A short pericope can contain more than one theological theme, thereby calling for more than one sermon. John 6:30–40 could easily yield two sermons, one focusing on verses 30–34 and the other on verses 35–40.

Sometimes we approach God with wishful thinking, asking "What will God do for me?" Despite all the blessings that God has already shared with us, we look to what is next—wanting more. It is like the popular saying, "What have you done for me lately?" This human tendency lies at the heart of verses 30–34. This is precisely how the crowd is thinking when they ask Jesus, "What sign are you going to give us then, so that we may see it and believe you? What work are you performing?" (v. 30).

What sign? This was the group of people who had been present for the feeding of the five thousand! In fact, these were the ones who crossed the Sea of Galilee the next day to search for Jesus. They were so amazed that he had fed them that they came looking for more. Theirs was an insatiable hunger, the kind that always wants a new sign, a new amazing experience, or a new adventure. The sermon could take time to reflect on this human phenomenon.

While we sometimes approach God out of wishful thinking, we also tend to relate to God as a memory from the past. Memory is a good thing. It

John 6:30–40

Theological Perspective

require another sign at this point. What is clear is their lack of understanding.

Rather than responding with another miraculous act—the wished-for sign—Jesus instead uses the example of the manna provided in the wilderness as an opportunity to further his hearers' (and John's readers') understanding of who he is. He does so by continuing with the theme of bread, introduced not only in the earlier feeding miracle but also in the contrast he draws between food that perishes and food that endures (6:27). Jesus boldly claims in verse 32 that "it is my Father who gives you the true bread from heaven." This "true bread" not only comes from heaven, Jesus asserts, but "gives life to the world." His hearers respond by asking—politely, almost humbly—that they be given this bread "always." This sets the stage for Jesus' assertion that he, himself, is the "bread of life."

Three related theological themes, which John will develop through verse 40, have emerged by this point in the passage. The first is the expansion of the time within which God's purposes will be fulfilled. The assertion that "the bread of God is that which comes down from heaven and gives life to the world" (v. 33) speaks not only to the sustaining of life, but to life that precedes and extends beyond the bounds of history. As the repeated references in verses 39–40 to "the last day" illustrate, John anticipates both the consummation of history and life eternal (v. 40). John's Gospel is simultaneously concerned with both the concrete reality of human history and that which transcends it.

This relates to a second theological theme, namely, the complex role of Jesus within salvation history. Jesus is identified here as the bread of heaven himself, "sent" by God the Father. He exists in a relationship of reciprocal action with the Father. Thus in verse 37 Jesus states, "Everything that the Father gives me will come to me, and anyone who comes to me I will never drive away." Jesus is presented here both as an active agent in his own right and as an obedient steward, stating, "I have come down from heaven, not to do my own will, but the will of him who sent me" (v. 38). Finally, this will of God the Father is presented as attesting to and strengthening the rationale for one's acceptance of Jesus: it "is indeed the will of the Father, that all who see the Son and believe in him may have eternal life" (v. 40), and that eternal life is contingent on such belief. Implicitly, this seems to comprise belief in both Jesus' claims and his identity. The passage also raises questions about the scope of salvation that John

Pastoral Perspective

reminded Jesus. Surely if they were well cared for, then it ought to be the same for us. Right, Jesus?

The crowds had turned their ancestry into a kind of transactional theology. Their ancestors were people of the faith. That faith had produced for them security in times of distress. They were descendants of their ancestors, having inherited the faith from them. Therefore, they reasoned, they were entitled to the same security. The past is reliable; therefore it is a predictor of future promise.

The problem, of course, is that Jesus disputed that kind of reasoning. It was not their lineage that guaranteed the crowds their safety. The past, while immune from present trauma, was still not sufficient evidence for how life would turn out for them. The only lasting security to be found was in the faithfulness and compassion of God.

As if to underscore this point with basic grammar, John would invite us simply to look at the verb tenses in this passage. The people's statements are all essentially in the past tense. For the entire second half of this pericope, however, Jesus speaks about the future. Whoever comes to him *will* never be hungry. Whoever believes in him *will* never be thirsty. He *will* raise them up on the last day. This dichotomy is most evident in the present-tense response from Jesus to the crowds: "It was not Moses who *gave* you the bread from heaven," Jesus said, "but it is my Father who *gives* you the true bread from heaven."

Nevertheless, the people in our congregations are still nervous about their futures. Present-day economic realities produce troubling financial anxieties. Personal relationships that are plagued by bitterness, resentment, and betrayal often show no promise of future reconciliation. Cycles of addiction, anger, and depression can paint a future that is as dark as it is bleak. When a preacher guides people toward the future to find their hope, they often receive that message with skepticism and disbelief.

That is why Jesus' response is so liberating. When people learn to believe in possibilities, despite evidence in the past, then it matters very little what happens to them in the present. When we learn to let go of the expectations we place on God, then everything that God gives to us is a blessed surprise. When we learn to trust and believe with a faith that surpasses our capacity to understand and comprehend, then we find the true reliability, the true security, for which we are longing.

This is not to say that the past has no value, of course. Nor is it to suggest that there is no role for remembrance in the life of faith. Much of the Bible

Jesus uses the crowd's appeal to Moses as the basis for his argument, offering his own exegesis of the tradition. Jesus highlights that it was not Moses, but rather God, who was the source of manna, an argument consistent with Jewish understandings of the manna as symbolic of God's provision of life (see Neh. 9:15; Wis. 16:20). By showing that the manna was a gift from God, Jesus argues that the proper comparison is not between Moses and himself as wonder workers, but rather between the manna and himself as provisions from God.

In verse 33 Jesus begins to distinguish between manna and himself as the "true bread." Both come down from heaven (see v. 31; Exod. 16:4). However, the true bread gives "true life" to the world. The language of "life" ($h\bar{e}$ $z\bar{o}\bar{e}$) in this Gospel is almost exclusively connected to Jesus (1:4; 3:15, 36; 5:24; 8:12; 10:10); his singular mission is to provide life to the world (1:3–5). The distinction between Jesus and the manna, therefore, is the type of sustenance offered. Drawing upon his previous distinction between "the food that is being destroyed" and "food that remains for eternal life" (6:27, my trans.), Jesus shifts to the present tense ("my Father gives"), arguing that the "true bread" is not something available at discrete historical moments, but is perpetually available through God's eschatological gift. Moses' manna was temporary sustenance (a point made explicitly at 6:49); Jesus offers eternal life. Just as Jesus interprets the feeding scene (6:1–15) as a symbol for God's gift of "the food that remains for eternal life," so he interprets the manna as foreshadowing of God's provision of "true bread," now available to all in Jesus.

The crowd's request in verse 34 for physical bread betrays continued misunderstanding, recalling the misplaced requests of Nicodemus about a second birth (3:4) and of the Samaritan woman about living water (4:11–12, 15). In those instances, as in this one, Jesus' interlocutor perceives only the literal dimension of his imagery. Jesus ends the confusion by directly stating the point that has been implicit: "I am the bread of life" (v. 35; also 6:41, 48; cf. other "I am" statements: 8:12; 9:5; 10:7, 11; 11:25; 14:6; 15:1). With this statement the argument of 6:22–34 reaches a decisive point: Jesus' provision of the fishes and the loaves for the crowd (6:1–15) was a symbol of God's provision of Jesus for humanity.

Jesus closes this explanation in verse 35b by again drawing a distinction between physical and eschatological bread, using the language of Jewish wisdom traditions that connect hunger and thirst with yearning for the word of God (e.g., Isa.

is very helpful to remember all that God has done for us in the past, as our memories help to shape our faith for today. However, if our entire experience of God is rendered only in the past tense, we are missing something. If we think of God only as a force who did something yesterday, then we lose sight of the power and presence of God in our lives today. The crowd were not only hungering after a new sign, they were also focused on reliving the past. "Our ancestors ate the manna in the wilderness; as it is written: 'He gave them bread from heaven to eat'" (v. 31). Bread from heaven was the manna that came to the Hebrews who wandered in the wilderness. This bread was supplied for many years. By contrast, Jesus had provided only one meal. The crowd was comparing their recent experience to a memory, so that the past was preventing them from seeing more clearly what was happening in their very midst. The sermon could reflect further on this all too common tendency of ours.

Jesus' response to the crowd teaches us that we are to experience God in the present tense. "Then Jesus said to them, 'Very truly, I tell you, it was not Moses who gave you the bread from heaven, but it is my Father who gives you the true bread from heaven. For the bread of God is that which comes down from heaven and gives life to the world'" (vv. 32–33).

First, Jesus wanted to make sure that they knew that the manna was not from Moses but from God. More importantly, Jesus was changing tenses on them. They had talked in the future and past tense, but Jesus put the conversation in the present tense. Whereas faith is informed by our past, and ought to live expectantly about the future, the gift of the bread of heaven is for right now. It is not a meal to be remembered from yesterday or anticipated for tomorrow; it is to be experienced here in the present.

The preacher can examine these three textual illustrations, painting a homiletical picture of the first two and then pointing the listener toward a better way of believing. The bread is here for us in the present—God wants us to partake of it right now. Jesus has a conversation with us through this passage of Scripture. We preach for a response that leads people to echo the words, "Sir, give us this bread always" (v. 34).

John 6:35 introduces a new theme that the preacher can explore or pursue in a separate sermon. The subject is still the "bread of life," but Jesus now brings up the "will of God." He continues, "I have come down from heaven, not to do my own will, but the will of him who sent me" (v. 38). This turn in

Theological Perspective

leaves unresolved. Here the Gospel emphasizes both human agency in the work of seeing and believing and the understanding that it is God the Father that gives to the Son those who will be raised into eternal life (v. 37).

A final issue in this passage requires special care in theological interpretation and application. In verse 35, Jesus tells his hearers not only that he is the bread of life but that "whoever comes to me will never be hungry, and whoever believes in me will never be thirsty." For his hearers in Capernaum, fresh from the experience of having their stomach filled, this must have seemed an enormous promise. For the reader seeking to make theological sense of this claim today, the unavoidable context is that even among those who have moved from "seeing" to "believing" in Jesus, many experience the objective physical realities of hunger, thirst, frailty, and loss on a daily basis.

It is crucial to avoid two theological temptations here. First, this claim cannot be resolved by focusing on a purely spiritual promise of satisfaction and fulfillment, relativizing or dismissing the lived experience of hunger, thirst, and need. A second temptation to be avoided is to assume that the presence of physical and tangible needs connotes a lack of faith. This is a place where the text must be read within the larger framework of history and the ongoing working out of God's purposes, a framework that requires us to acknowledge both the relevance of the physical and the tangible in light of the incarnation, and the bleeding edges of need that remind us of what has yet to be fully restored and healed within history.

Together the three theological concerns identified here point to the complexity of John's incarnational theology. The Gospel that posits Jesus as the Word made flesh is deeply concerned with the comprehensive relationship that exists between the human and divine and between the corporeal and spiritual.

DEIRDRE KING HAINSWORTH

Pastoral Perspective

offers constant repetition of God's saving activity in the past, and most of the rituals and sacraments that frame the ongoing life of Christian community are anchored in what God has done. Jesus' response does not negate remembrance, but expands it in the larger context of eternal life. He called the crowds that heard him, and he calls us today, to remember not just what God has done, but what God has promised to do. It is in accepting that broader definition of remembrance that we discover the *always* that we crave: God is always near us, God is always for us, and God is giving us our daily bread, *always*.

In addition, Jesus addresses their corrupt transactional formula with one of his own. Because Jesus has everything that the Father has, Jesus will, in turn, share those things with anyone who comes to him. For Jesus, there is only one lineage that really matters. It is the one in which he assumes the critical link between creature and Creator, between redeemed and Redeemer.

Furthermore, Jesus introduces the language of divine will. It was his Father's will not to lose anything that the Father had given him. It was the Father's will that all who believe in Jesus have eternal life. In essence, Jesus was sharing with the crowds that there is really only one source of reliability and security in this chaotic world. It is not to be found in the expectation that the past will always repeat itself. It is not located in a reliance on genealogy and lineage. It is not even dependent on one's own efforts to procure it.

Rather, all security and provision is contingent on the character of a faithful, trustworthy God. It is the divine will of this God to save (to continue *always* in relationship with) all who come to Jesus Christ. That alone is sufficient evidence, and all the comfort that the people require.

MAGREY R. DEVEGA

49:10; Sir. 24). Those who eat "true bread" have no need for other nourishment. The sustenance Jesus offers need not be renewed; Jesus is "the bread that remains forever" (6:27).

Though Jesus continues to speak uninterrupted in verses 36–40, he shifts focus away from the image of bread and explores how one is to respond as a witness to this sign. Jesus' focus on the witnesses' responsibility emphasizes a second part of the manna tradition: the manna was given as a test of the people, to see "whether they will follow my instruction" (Exod. 16:4). In verses 37–40, Jesus emphasizes that "everything" that has been given to him "will be present before me" (NRSV "will come to me"), suggesting that he, like the manna, is the means of God's testing (cf. 14:6). This is not an assertion of Jesus' importance; rather, it emphasizes the sovereignty of God. It is God's will, not his own, that Jesus has come to accomplish, a common distinction in the Gospel tradition (see Matt. 7:21; 26:42) and a consistent refrain in the Fourth Gospel (4:34; 5:30; 7:17).

Not only will those who come to Jesus not be cast out; he will also "raise up" (*anastēsō*, v. 39) those who come to him. Here John employs the language used in the early church to refer to Jesus' resurrection (John 20:9; Luke 24:46; Acts 2:32) and the future resurrection of believers (1 Thess. 4:14–17). The glorification and victory won by Jesus at the cross are promised to those who come to him. The final line of the passage (v. 40) aptly summarizes the main point. Jesus was sent to offer all the chance to "see the Son" and believe in him. Jesus is a crucible of faith; he gives each person the opportunity to believe, a belief that leads to eternal life and resurrection.

This speech from Jesus was prompted by the crowd's demand for a sign as the basis of belief. Jesus does not deny the logic of their demand; a sign has been given that should prompt belief. In this passage Jesus shows that the sign is not an event of the past but an eschatological reality. Jesus is not a miracle worker who convinces witnesses that God is worthy of belief. Rather, Jesus is the sign, inviting all to belief (see 20:30–31).

RICHARD MANLY ADAMS JR.

the text gives the preacher an opportunity to turn a familiar topic in a new direction.

Many people wrestle to understand the will of God for their lives. Countless pastoral conversations have helped people sort through this subject, as people have tried to think about God's will for their personal lives, vocation, relationships, service, and discipleship. When we think about the will of God, we usually think about how God's intention will impact our own lives. Jesus turns the topic in a different way. He talks about the will of God as something that directs his life for the sake of others. He came not to do his own will, but the will of the one who sent him. What was that will? The next two verses answer the question: "And this is the will of him who sent me, that I should lose nothing of all that he has given me, but raise it up on the last day. This is indeed the will of my Father, that all who see the Son and believe in him may have eternal life; and I will raise them up on the last day" (vv. 39–40).

We live in a narcissistic culture that encourages us to focus on ourselves. It is little wonder that most of our discussion of God's will focuses on us and how we are impacted. A sermon on God's will for Jesus takes the focus away from us and reminds us of why "the Word became flesh and lived among us" (1:14) in the first place.

DAVID W. HULL

John 6:41–51

⁴¹Then the Jews* began to complain about him because he said, "I am the bread that came down from heaven." ⁴²They were saying, "Is not this Jesus, the son of Joseph, whose father and mother we know? How can he now say, 'I have come down from heaven'?" ⁴³Jesus answered them, "Do not complain among yourselves. ⁴⁴No one can come to me unless drawn by the Father who sent me; and I will raise that person up on the last day. ⁴⁵It is written in the prophets, 'And they shall all be taught by God.' Everyone who has heard and learned from the Father comes to me. ⁴⁶Not that anyone has seen the Father except the one who is from God; he has seen the Father. ⁴⁷Very truly, I tell you, whoever believes has eternal life. ⁴⁸I am the bread of life. ⁴⁹Your ancestors ate the manna in the wilderness, and they died. ⁵⁰This is the bread that comes down from heaven, so that one may eat of it and not die. ⁵¹I am the living bread that came down from heaven. Whoever eats of this bread will live forever; and the bread that I will give for the life of the world is my flesh."

Theological Perspective

In the verses following the miracle stories in John 6 (the feeding of the five thousand, Jesus' walking across water and preserving the disciples in a storm), the narrative traces various ways that the crowds following Jesus have misunderstood his claims and asked for additional signs to enable their belief. In John 6:41–51, the attitude of Jesus' hearers shifts considerably, moving from questioning and confusion to complaint and near derision. Jesus' response is an occasion for the emphatic, succinct restatement of theological claims introduced earlier in the chapter, as well as an initial allusion to the self-sacrificial dimensions of Jesus' role within salvation history. Many of the theological themes stated in this passage, particularly in verses 47–50, are restatements of claims made at greater length in verses 21–40: those who believe will have eternal life; Jesus is the bread of life; this bread of life, from heaven, will endure in a way that manna did not. Each of these claims is simply restated in verses 41–51, rather than reargued.

The initial point of contention—here attributed simply to complaints raised by the characters whom John problematically addresses only as "the Jews"—mainly has to do with the conflict between

* See "'The Jews' in the Fourth Gospel" on pp. xi–xiv.

Pastoral Perspective

Most of the time, grumbling is the result of a reality that fails to match our expectations. When events unfold that fall short of our hopes, and when we can locate a person or situation to blame, we complain. It is natural to draw parallels between the people in this passage and the Israelites who complained in the wilderness, whom Jesus references in his response. In both cases, people had targeted the person who they felt was to blame for their hunger; so they unleashed their complaints.

However, in this case, the people are questioning Jesus not only out of hunger, but out of confusion. They are struggling to reconcile the messenger with his message. They cannot come to terms with the fact that this Jesus, who is uttering profound words of wisdom, is the very same Jesus they have known since his childhood. In a sense, they are getting caught up in the same great christological controversies that will later captivate the early church: how can this Jesus be both human and divine?

I am reminded of a conversation I once had with a lifelong member of the congregation I serve. He rarely misses a Sunday, serves on numerous committees, and raised his children to be active participants in the church. Yet he rarely read the Bible and had never attended a small group Bible study. His reason? The stories are too antiquated, the language too

Feasting on the Gospels

Exegetical Perspective

This passage continues Jesus' bread of life dialogue with those whom he fed. The tone of the dialogue is more confrontational, driven no longer by the crowd's questions but by Jesus' accusations as to why they continue to misunderstand. The shift in tone is reflected in the narrator's new focus, not now on "the crowd" (6:22) but on "the Jews" (6:41), the ambiguous and problematic term John uses to describe Jesus' opponents (2:20; 5:10, 16, 18), even though Jesus and his disciples are also clearly "Jews." Though the crowd's Jewish identity is evident in the reference to "our ancestors" (6:31), the use of "the Jews" singles out those Jews who do not follow Jesus. The term is not meant, nor can it be used, to identify all Jews as opponents of Jesus, and John never equates being a Gentile with being a follower of Jesus.

The narrator characterizes "the Jews" as "beginning to grumble" (*egongyzon*, v. 41, NRSV "complain"), a new verb in the Gospel (also 6:61; 7:32), but one frequently used in the Septuagint to describe complaints in the wilderness, during the time when God was providing manna (Exod. 17:3; Num. 11:1; 14:27–29; 16:41; 17:5; cf. Isa. 29:24; 30:12). Through this description the narrator emphasizes that just as God's provision is constant, so is humanity's misunderstanding and rejection.

Homiletical Perspective

The prologue of the Gospel of John sets the table for the great feast that is to follow. Early on in this Fourth Gospel the reader is introduced to the concept of incarnation. We read that from the very beginning of time the "Word was with God, and the Word was God" (1:1). A few verses later we come to understand that "the Word became flesh and lived among us" (1:14). The rest of the Gospel of John helps us to understand how this Word lives among us.

Yet the mystery of incarnation proves difficult to comprehend. The author makes this clear in the telling of the story. Someone as smart and religious as Nicodemus struggles to understand. He has a hard time comprehending how he could possibly be born "from above" (3:3). He knows about physical birth, but the blending of physical and spiritual realities, which are at the heart of incarnation, is too much for the educated man to grasp. The woman by the well in Samaria has the same problem. She knows all about the physical reality of water and wells, but Jesus begins to amaze her by talking about the incarnational truth of "living water" (4:10). Understanding how "the Word became flesh and lived among us" (1:14) is not easy.

The crowd in John 6 is wrestling with the same incarnational mysteries. "Then the Jews began to complain about him because he said, 'I am the bread

John 6:41–51

Theological Perspective

Jesus' claims of identity in relationship with God and the hearers' observations and experiences of Jesus' human family. The issue of Jesus as "bread from heaven," a key point of confusion and clarification in the preceding verses, is largely set aside. For those raising such complaints, the potential implications of that larger claim are not even considered in the face of Jesus' challenge to existing categories of identity.

It is important to note that the earlier questions posed to Jesus also came to him, at least in part, from those within the Jewish community, as is evident from the references to the provision of manna in the journey out of Egypt. This is not at all a surprise, as John's Gospel portrays mostly Jewish characters, including Jesus, his disciples, and those who do not follow after him. Rather than representing the entire Jewish community or inviting a more general indictment of the Jewish people, the voices raised in complaint here seem to be those of a particular subgroup concerned with Jesus' origins. In verse 42, the key question is posed: "Is not this Jesus, the son of Joseph, whose father and mother we know?" Jesus' location within a particular ancestral lineage and web of family relationships in the community casts suspicion on his claim that "I have come down from heaven" (v. 38). Although Jesus asks his hearers to accept him as both related to his family and of heavenly origin, to his critics these sources of identity appear inherently contradictory.

While the later verses of this passage restate theological claims developed at greater length earlier in the chapter, three additional theological emphases in this pericope are worth noting. The first is a claim about the ways in which people come to belief. In verse 43, rather than directly refuting the complaints and questions raised about his origins, Jesus seems to be advising his hearers not to allow such concerns to become a matter of dissent among them, because the ability to believe in Jesus, in itself, is made possible by the action of God the Father. "No one can come to me unless drawn by the Father who sent me," Jesus states in verse 44.

As in preceding passages, the relative roles of human and divine agency in enabling belief are at issue, but in this scene God's role takes center stage. Those who are consumed with questions about how Jesus' earthly identity can be reconciled with his self-identification as the Father's Son are, by implication, those who have not been "drawn" to accept Jesus' claims. It is important to note that this should not lead the reader to equate the reality of faith with passive acceptance of any and all claims; throughout

Pastoral Perspective

cryptic, and the meaning much too confusing for his analytical mind.

Ironically, he shared this with me and others while sitting in the first session of his very first Bible study. He shared his feelings with earnest concern and without complaint. I thought at that moment of the number of people struggling with the confusing elements of the faith who have responded in a way that is much more negative than the way this church member responded. Consider the people in your community who would rather be anywhere but in church on Sundays, because they think Christianity is too far-fetched to believe. Think even of those in the congregation who are reluctant to live a fully committed life of discipleship, because they cannot seem to take Christian theology and practice seriously.

Jesus' response is, appropriately, quite cryptic. As is often the case in the Gospels, he decides not to address their question directly, but answers a different question altogether. He chooses not to explain how he could be both fully human and fully divine. He does not choose to engage in formal debate regarding what would later be called the christological controversy. Instead, he speaks to the deeper issue that is affecting his inquisitors, whether they realize it or not: the relationship between the grace of God and human free will.

"No one can come to me unless drawn by the Father who sent me," Jesus says. He offers them the compelling notion that they would not even be there in their state of confusion, pressing Jesus for answers, working out their struggles with the faith, were it not for the grace of God that has been operating in and through them. Their state of confusion, which they have perceived as a stumbling block that evoked their complaints, is in fact a blessed reminder of how God is actively drawing them closer to Jesus.

Anne Lamott wrote that "the opposite of faith is not doubt, but certainty."[1] Sometimes our confusion can be like a fog that seems foreboding, gloomy, and dangerous. However, it can also force us to slow down, exercise caution, and rethink our priorities in the face of the unknown.

It is true that no one can see the Father, Jesus acknowledges. There will always be things that we will not be able fully to comprehend. Nonetheless, Jesus reminds the people that "all are taught by God." We do not have to see God, fathom God, or understand God in order to be recipients of the grace of

1. Anne Lamott, *Plan B: Further Thoughts on Faith* (New York: Riverhead Trade, 2006), 256–57.

Exegetical Perspective

The narrator specifies that Jesus' opponents are upset about his claim to have come from above and conflates the statements he made in 6:35 and 6:38. How can Jesus be from heaven when he is known to be the son of Joseph? This confusion is part of a well-attested early tradition concerning the questions that were raised about Jesus' origins (Matt. 13:55; Mark 6:3; Luke 4:22). The Johannine narrative reflects this same concern (1:46), but the context allows a new interpretation that focuses on the importance of knowing Jesus' Father. The crowd focuses on the identity of his father (the phrase "and the mother" in verse 42 is missing in the earliest manuscripts and is likely a later scribal attempt to harmonize with the Matthean version). The addition of the seemingly repetitive phrase "whose father we know" highlights the misunderstanding in their grumbling. They claim to know Jesus' father, whom they assume to be Joseph (cf. 1:45), though Jesus throughout this discourse has identified God as his Father (5:17–23, 43; 6:37). The answer to their rhetorical question about Jesus' heritage, asked with the expectation of an affirmative answer, is no, not because they do not know Joseph, but because they have misidentified Jesus' Father. Jesus will argue that if they do not recognize Jesus as coming from heaven, then in fact they do not know Jesus' true Father, God (8:19; 14:7).

Jesus' response focuses on why the crowd misunderstands him. He begins by placing the initial act in the hands of the one who sent him; only those whom God "draws" (*helkysē*, v. 44) can come to Jesus. This verb can mean "to draw" as it is often translated (NRSV), but the primary sense of this language is forceful or even violent (18:10; 21:6; Acts 16:19; 21:30). Jesus argues that God must first "drag" a person to Jesus, and only then will Jesus raise him up.

Many theological debates have focused on Jesus' comment about God's "dragging" people toward him as a prerequisite for belief. It is important, though, to account for the argument in the context in which Jesus is making it. His point here is that God has already done this dragging and that the opportunity to come to Jesus is now available to all. His argument is clarified by his citation in verse 45 of Isaiah 54:13, a prophecy of hope wherein God promises to those in exile that their children will be taught the ways of God and will prosper (see also Jer. 31:33). Here in John 6, Jesus argues that God's ancient promises are being fulfilled, noting that the ability for all to come to him depends only upon hearing and learning.

Jesus' logic echoes Paul's teaching in Romans 10:14–17: it is the one who believes who comes to

Homiletical Perspective

that came down from heaven.' They were saying, 'Is not this Jesus, the son of Joseph, whose father and mother we know? How can he now say, 'I have come down from heaven'?" (vv. 41–42). From the beginning of the Gospel, we have all wrestled with the mystery of the incarnation.

Jesus gives us the answer in his language about the "bread of life." Today we use utensils to move the food from a plate into our mouths. Bread is often served at meals, but it is seen as a "starter" or a "side." Many who are watching their diets choose to forgo the bread. Therefore, when we hear that Jesus is the "bread of life," we can too easily think in terms of a metaphor for something that is as optional as a dinner roll.

The way that Jesus and his contemporaries ate was radically different from the way most Westerners eat. No utensils were used. A person ate with his or her hands. Bread was usually used to dip into the food and bring the food from the dish to the mouth. Jesus even describes this for us when he identifies his betrayer as "one who is dipping bread into the bowl with me" (Mark 14:20; the NRSV notes that the word "bread" is not in the Greek, but translators added the word because of the common eating customs of the day).

The Western mind-set allows us to think of bread as an extra that we can take or leave; but Jesus was operating with an image that was essential to the process of eating. In fact, the bread used for dipping was actually the means by which someone partook of a meal. Bread, then, was not an extra to be chosen or omitted; it was how persons accessed the food that was placed before them. According to John's Gospel, then, the incarnation is the means by which we can access and partake of the life that God offers us.

Just as John's prologue sets the table for the feast that is to follow, the concluding words that come just before the epilogue in John 21 summarize the Gospel's purpose: "But these are written so that you may come to believe that Jesus is the Messiah, the Son of God, and that through believing you may have life in his name" (20:31). The Fourth Gospel was written so that we would understand and believe in the main course, which is life. Flowing through the Gospel like a mighty river is this theme of life, abundant (10:10) and eternal (3:16). The author writes these words so that all may believe in the Messiah and through him experience life as we have never known it. Life is the main course. The "bread" is how we are able to receive the main course.

John 6:41–51

Theological Perspective

this chapter and the Gospels as a whole, Jesus is presented as willing to hear and respond to questions posed in an effort to understand the fullness of his identity and his relation to God's past engagement in human history.

This assertion that God the Father is the one who "draws" people to Jesus is located within a second, broader theological claim concerning the relative roles of the Father and the Son in relationship to human beings. The prophetic assertion that it is God who teaches humans takes on new implications with Jesus' ministry, as seen in verse 45, where the test of truly having learned from the Father is movement toward Jesus and acceptance of his claims. At the same time, Jesus identifies himself as the only one who has actually seen the Father; here, one aspect of a larger Johannine emphasis on Jesus as intermediary between God the Father and humanity becomes apparent. John presents Jesus as embodying the divine willingness and effort to be in active relationship with human beings within the realm of human history. For John, Jesus is the visible incarnation of a radically new stage in the divine-human relationship. Therefore in this section of John's Gospel, acceptance of Jesus' claims and promises comes to stand as the measure of whether or not one authentically hears the word of God the Father more generally.

A final theological theme in this passage will receive more development in subsequent verses. In verse 51, Jesus returns again to the assertion that he is the "bread that came down from heaven," but here any illusions that this is merely poetic imagery begin to be wiped away with the verse's closing words that "whoever eats of this bread will live forever; and the bread that I will give for the life of the world is my flesh." John's language constitutes Jesus' role as essential for the very life to which the Gospel repeatedly points. Later theological debates over sacraments and the presence of Christ in the Communion elements rightly find a portion of their roots here; but within the unfolding theological portrait of Jesus' identity in relation to both God the Father and to human beings, this final verse is more appropriately understood as signaling the self-giving and self-endangering implications for Jesus in his role as mediator.

DEIRDRE KING HAINSWORTH

Pastoral Perspective

God. It could very well be that the perplexing questions we bring to the table are the very evidence of God at work in us.

Jesus concludes his response with words that we consider formative for a sacramental understanding of Communion. His body is bread that is broken so that we may be whole. His life is offered so that we who receive it may live. He responds to the mystery of his dual human and divine nature with yet another mystery: how ordinary bread can become an extraordinary means of grace. What is implied in sacramental theology, of course, is that this experience of Christ's presence in the bread and the cup is a communal one, vivified in the gathering of the faithful around the table.

For those in the congregation who are struggling to make sense of the more puzzling aspects of Christian theology, the conclusion to this passage is a suitable invitation to embrace the mysteries of the faith in the context of Christian community. When we choose to share the journey with others and acknowledge our deepest questions, rather than complain about them, we discover that we are being "taught by God" and are recipients of a grace that has been at work since before we realized it.

More than a year later, my friend is still in that same Bible study group, with the same people to whom he first confessed his confusion. He reads the Bible more regularly, takes his faith more seriously, and has developed real bonds of friendship with others in the group. Recently, he shared with me how delighted he is to be part of this Bible study, and how much it has utterly transformed his life. "I have never been a part of something like this before, but I am so glad that I am." Clearly, this is the grace of God at work.

MAGREY R. DEVEGA

Exegetical Perspective

Jesus, and yet no one can believe if he or she does not hear and learn from God. He then provides the missing premise in verse 46: Jesus is the means by which God reveals God's self in and to the world. Jesus is the only one who "has seen the Father," the very point with which the Gospel began (1:1). To be taught by God, one must have access to one who knows God. The rivalry with Moses in the previous exchange (6:31–35) is implicit here. Jesus insists that now is the time God is teaching, and God is doing so in a manner more direct than when God taught through Moses and the law (1:17). The problem, therefore, lies with the crowd that is grumbling rather than listening to God's teaching.

In verses 48–51, Jesus offers a summary of this first major section of the bread of life dialogue (6:22–51). His summary here is the long-awaited final answer to the argument about Moses, raised by the crowd in 6:31. Jesus acknowledges that indeed the fathers did eat manna, but this manna provided only temporary sustenance, as the fathers died. Jesus is the bread of life whereby those who partake of him gain eternal life. The section closes with Jesus' announcement: "I will give my flesh on behalf of the life of the world," a likely reference to the crucifixion. This final line serves as the transition to the next section of the dialogue, where Jesus explores the connection between his actual flesh and the bread of life.

Thus Jesus does not argue that his opponents have no access to God. Rather, like everyone else, they live in the eschatological present wherein God is dragging people toward Jesus. Jesus began noting that the crowd comes to him because they "have been filled" by his teaching (6:26). All that remains for them to do is to listen to God's teaching and allow themselves to be "taught by God."

RICHARD MANLY ADAMS JR.

Homiletical Perspective

The preacher is called to proclaim again and again the essence of this message. It is easy for all of us to be confused about the main course. Power, success, pleasure, comfort, and wealth can easily seduce us into thinking that the main course of life is defined in very material terms. The preacher is like the author of the Fourth Gospel. We point the way to the main course, which is a life filled with abundance for all eternity. Preachers then remind people that we receive this life not based on our own actions or our own merits. The bread, Jesus, is how we get to the main course. The distinction is very clear. "Your ancestors ate the manna in the wilderness, and they died" (v. 49). Something better is now offered: "Very truly, I tell you, whoever believes has eternal life. I am the bread of life" (vv. 47–48). This offer is not a temporary solution, as was the manna. "Whoever eats of this bread will live forever" (v. 51).

This eternal life, or life of the ages, is now offered to each one of us. The main course of this life is accessible through the mystery of the incarnation. The "bread" of Jesus brings us to the "life" that we all need. Enjoy the feast!

DAVID W. HULL

John 6:52–59

⁵² The Jews* then disputed among themselves, saying, "How can this man give us his flesh to eat?" ⁵³So Jesus said to them, "Very truly, I tell you, unless you eat the flesh of the Son of Man and drink his blood, you have no life in you. ⁵⁴Those who eat my flesh and drink my blood have eternal life, and I will raise them up on the last day; ⁵⁵for my flesh is true food and my blood is true drink. ⁵⁶Those who eat my flesh and drink my blood abide in me, and I in them. ⁵⁷Just as the living Father sent me, and I live because of the Father, so whoever eats me will live because of me. ⁵⁸This is the bread that came down from heaven, not like that which your ancestors ate, and they died. But the one who eats this bread will live forever." ⁵⁹He said these things while he was teaching in the synagogue at Capernaum.

Theological Perspective

Jesus delivers an intentionally hard saying. He puts it out there, drives it home. His graphic words demand theological engagement and we had better not simply gloss over them. Resist the temptation of resorting to easy explanation—as in "relax, this is just a metaphor"—to avoid what we find distasteful in his message. The crowd had wanted to reduce the gospel to food distribution and political power (6:15, 26), but Jesus was more radical than that. The religious leaders, the characters in John's story whom he calls "the Jews," certainly understood the seriousness of the challenge. Jesus had stated, "I am the living bread that came down from heaven" and "the bread that I will give for the life of the world is my flesh" (6:51).

His claim sparks theological debate. They did not immediately recoil in disgust and plot his death. Rather, they engaged in theological argument: "The Jews then disputed among themselves, saying, 'How can this man give us his flesh to eat?'" (v. 52). It is the same question we must ask. John's added detail, that the disputation took place "while he was teaching in the synagogue at Capernaum" (v. 59), prompts the question of how earnestly we discuss biblical theology in our local churches today.

* See "'The Jews' in the Fourth Gospel" on pp. xi–xiv.

Pastoral Perspective

Jesus' listeners found themselves puzzling over his odd claims about eating his flesh and drinking his blood. How much more his words confound modern hearers! What can they mean? John's narrative lays bare multiple questions for clergy and lay ministers to ponder.

Asking, "How?" The desire to know the how of God's ways is a holy longing. Even luminaries like Abraham and the Virgin Mary, when presented with the outlandish promises of God, ask, "How?" Their honest questions become a path to deeper trust in God. In contrast to their earnest and humble desire to understand, Jesus' disputants in this passage seem to have what John Calvin calls a "passion and eagerness for quarreling." Even so, Calvin cautions us not to "attack the one word how, as if it were unlawful . . . to ask about the mode of eating." We should not "leave in their tangle those knotty difficulties which are untied for us by the Word of the Lord." Understanding the "how" is a worthwhile pursuit, as long as we keep "a moderation about the secret works of God, as not to desire to know more than [the Scriptures reveal]."[1] In our day of the new genetics, neuroscience, and digital

1. John Calvin, *The Gospel according to St. John: Part One*, trans. T. H. L. Parker (Grand Rapids: Eerdmans, 1961), 168–69.

Exegetical Perspective

Jesus has been talking of bread since John 6:26, amid crowds and questioning voices, and now the discussion is running to a close. The mention of Capernaum (v. 59) reminds the reader of where we came in (6:24), rounds off the conversation, and releases the narrative to move on. Along the way, Jesus' language shifts the discussion into a new register. After all the talk of bread, he suddenly introduces new substance for his listeners to digest: "the bread that I will give . . . is my flesh" (6:51). "The Jews"—John's problematic nomenclature for religious traditionalists in Israel—do not grasp it. "Flesh? How can this be?" they ask (v. 52). Then, as is so often the case in John, misunderstanding leads to insight. When characters in the Fourth Gospel stumble over Jesus' words, deeper layers of meaning come into view.

Jesus does not really answer the question; nor does he justify the claim he has made. John's story will do that, as it unfolds. For the moment Jesus simply presses on to explore and expand the meaning of his words, to emphasize rather than merely to explain. There are two main themes in what he says. First, he speaks of death, of "blood" as well as "flesh" (vv. 53–56). The thought is surely of sacrifice, of the separation of flesh and blood in slaughter, and of life drained away and ended, in order that life may be given and sustained. In the context of John's Gospel,

Homiletical Perspective

In these verses Jesus deepens his teaching on what it means to be the bread of life. Because the subject of the discourse is eating the flesh of the Son of Man and drinking his blood, the sacrament of Communion is bound to be the elephant in the room, even though Jesus' last night on earth is still a long ways off (and when it comes, he will be more interested in washing his disciples' feet than in feeding them supper). For this reason, it is important for the preacher to do two things before beginning to conceive the sermon: (1) clarify his or her understanding of Communion and (2) resist reading that into John. He has his own understanding.

Since "the Jews" are Jesus' adversaries in this passage, it is also important to say something about John's idiomatic use of that phrase. As Gerard Sloyan observes, the Fourth Evangelist knew whom he meant by the phrase, what he thought their problem was, and why he faulted them for it; but we do not know any of those things for sure. Consequently, Sloyan says, "referring to 'the opponents of Jesus as John sees them' and never to 'the enemies of Jesus' should handle the delicate problem best."[1] One might also note that while "the Jews" question Jesus in this passage, "the disciples" will question him in

---

1. Gerard S. Sloyan, *John* (Atlanta: John Knox Press, 1988), 75.

Theological Perspective

What can Jesus possibly mean when he invites us to eat his flesh? Those who witnessed the feeding of the crowd, when he multiplied the five loaves and two fish, connected this "sign" with the gift of manna during the exodus (6:31). As John notes that it was Passover season (6:4), the exodus tradition looms larger here in this chapter. Later in the Gospel, Passover and the story of the exodus will again play a crucial role in John's story of Jesus. Although the Gospel of John does not identify Jesus' Last Supper with his disciples as a Passover meal, it dates Jesus' death to the Day of Preparation for Passover (19:14, 31). Christians seeking to understand Jesus' grotesque language about eating his flesh should begin by considering the significance of the Passover tradition. Just as Paul insists that the Eucharist must be understood in relation to traditional Passover practices (1 Cor. 5:7–8), here Jesus presents himself as the sacrificial offering that fundamentally affirms God's covenant with his people and leads to their liberation.

Jesus does not make it easy for those first disputants or for us. To the flesh he adds his blood: "Very truly, I tell you, unless you eat the flesh of the Son of Man and drink his blood, you have no life in you" (v. 53). Jesus hammers it in, repeating the offensive phrase "eat my flesh and drink my blood" four times. The fifth time, he adds the promise, "Just as the living Father sent me, and I live because of the Father, so whoever eats me will live because of me" (v. 57). Of course, even apart from the horrific thought of cannibalism and drinking human blood, Jewish law forbids consuming the blood of animals. As the Torah teaches, "You shall not eat the blood of any creature, for the life of every creature is its blood" (Lev. 17:14; cf. Deut. 12:23).

This much is obvious: When Jesus speaks of his "flesh and blood," he is referring to himself as a living creature, a truly human "son of man" as well as the Messianic God-sent "Son of Man." Significantly, John uses the Greek word for "flesh" (*sarx*) here and elsewhere, rather than the term for "body" (*sōma*), which the Synoptic Gospels use in their narration of the Last Supper. If John had included Jesus' institution of the sacrament, it seems likely that he would have put it like this: "Take, eat; this is my flesh . . . my blood."

John's reason for reporting Jesus' words in their most raw form is soteriological, which later is essential for the church's core doctrines of incarnation and atonement. The work of Christ for salvation is accomplished in flesh and blood, from birth to

Pastoral Perspective

precision, questions of "how" are answered with striking exactness. However, in our quest to know the how of God's ways, these verses remind us that we must finally make peace with a measure of ambiguity and mystery.

Eating Well. Throughout the gospel story Jesus calls attention to the act of eating, as well as to the location and the company created by those gathering to partake of a meal together. We can learn much about a culture by observing what people eat and how they eat it. Do they eat primarily staples like rice and beans, with a few fruits and vegetables thrown in? Do they feast on the fatty meats of animals that were raised for years on the grain that might otherwise have fed hundreds of people? Do they eat food grown within a few miles of where they live and work, or do they eat out-of-season fruits, flown in from warmer climates thousands of miles away, or fish transported frozen from oceans on the other side of the planet? Do they race through the fast-food line or spend time selecting fresh foods at a local farmer's market? With whom do they eat, or do they eat alone, and why? Do they eat around a carefully set table, in an atmosphere that focuses on the meal as an event, or perhaps while standing or driving or sitting at a desk? Do they pause before eating for a ritual of gratitude, acknowledging the source of the nourishment, the food as a gift, the act of eating as sacred, or the act of eating together as formative?

If eating well is a central metaphor for abiding in Christ, then this passage surely calls us to pay greater attention to our practices of consumption and the communities that benefit from or experience the negative consequences of them. Jesus calls us to consider what we reveal and how we are formed by what and how we eat.

Eating without Consuming. Jesus says that those who eat his flesh and drink his blood abide in him, and he abides in them, which suggests the church's communion with him is both like and unlike eating. In physiological terms, when one eats,

> food is absorbed into the person and becomes that person. . . . The eating self retains its form or distinctness by destroying the identity of what is eaten. Eating, in other words, absorbs the other into me. . . . The absorption of another's form into my being introduces us to one of the great paradoxes of eating: to preserve the form of my life, the form of another's life must end. . . . We do not

where Jesus is portrayed as the "Lamb of God" (1:29), and in this chapter set at Passovertide (6:4), Jesus' words point us forward to the crucifixion. The Passover sacrifice of God's own Lamb will crown and complete all the sacrifices of the years.

Yet the intensely sensory language of eating and drinking, repeated many times in these few verses, reaches beyond the traditional images of sacrifice. For while Scripture forbids drinking blood (Lev. 17:10–16), here Jesus invites and commands it. Although his language may serve as metaphor, referring potently and graphically to faith in the Christ of the cross, the images of eating and drinking have also prompted many Christians to think of Holy Communion. In John's Gospel, the Last Supper scene (13:1–30) says nothing of the formal sharing of bread and wine, and in a way this passage in John 6 helps to fill that gap. For many readers, it roots the Eucharist in the gospel story. It takes us near to the Communion table and the cross.

The second theme in Jesus' words is the vital power of his "flesh and blood." Those who "eat and drink" will find the experience uniquely life-giving, both in the present and in the future. Without this sustenance, humanity is lifeless (v. 53). Yet in it and with it, eternal life is given—life that lasts forever and that rises in glory (v. 54). For Jesus' flesh and blood can nourish truly and profoundly, like nothing else on earth (v. 55). Earlier in the chapter we heard of bread that perishes (v. 27). Our daily food is like that; it is perishable and so are we (v. 49); but the "food and drink" that Jesus supplies sustain without end. This nourishment transcends the limits of our living and draws us into his life. We "abide" (v. 56)—we in Jesus and he in us.

Yet eventually, in our text, the swift and dense repetitions of the words "flesh and blood" end as abruptly as they began, and the conversation closes with Jesus speaking again of bread. Indeed, the last few lines that he speaks (vv. 57–58) return to points that he made a few verses earlier (6:49–51). He is heavenly bread, which has come from the Father and provides the Father's life (v. 57). Even the manna of old, the original "bread from heaven," could not prevent people from dying (vv. 49, 58). However, the strength and sustenance Jesus gives have a different quality. Those who eat do not die (v. 50), but live forever (vv. 51, 58).

It has taken a long time to get to this point from the start of the discourse in 6:26. Yet that is the way John's Gospel does theology. Ideas recur and repeat; they are held up to the light from different angles,

the next. John's Jesus is not easy to understand, even when he is talking to friends.

This opens one interesting door into the passage. For the preacher who is willing to stick with a Jesus who is hard to swallow, instead of trying to make him more palatable, these verses offer an opportunity to recover the strangeness of Communion. Early Christians were sometimes accused of cannibalism, for reasons any twenty-first-century child can understand. Offer a cup of deep red liquid to a child who is receiving Communion for the first time, say, "The blood of Christ, the cup of salvation," and do not be surprised if she says, "Yuck! No way." She may not have reached the age of abstract reasoning, but that is not her only problem. Her deeper problem is that she is a true believer. When someone tells her that Jesus' flesh is true food and his blood is true drink, she believes that proclamation enough to decide that she does not want any. When did the rest of us stop taking the language so seriously?

John seems intent on maximizing the yuck factor in these verses. By substituting "flesh" for "body," and a verb better translated as "gnaw" instead of "eat," he creates meat-eating images that are hard to domesticate. If Jesus had just stuck with the feeding of the five thousand, then he could have been the new Moses, the new *bringer* of the bread. Instead, he breaks the template by claiming to *be* the bread, with chilling implications: "Very truly, I tell you, unless you eat the flesh of the Son of Man and drink his blood, you have no life in you" (v. 53). If his listeners want the life he is offering them, they can forget being vegan. They will eat what the living Father puts in front of them.

Since Jesus in this passage is talking to unbelievers and not to disciples, his motives are worth considering. Is he confounding them on purpose, the same way he confounded Nicodemus a few chapters earlier? Is he going out of his way to use language that will offend them, so that they cannot easily appropriate what he is saying? If so, then why is he doing that? Is it because he does not *want* them to understand, or is it because he wants them to understand that what he is saying will not, by any stretch of the imagination, fit into their previous categories? Whatever they thought they knew about God, it is time to think again. It may even be time for them to give up knowing anything for a while, so that God has room to do a new thing in them.

As verses 60–71 will soon make clear, this is not a message addressed only to "the Jews." The disciples are next in line to shake their heads at Jesus'

John 6:52–59

Theological Perspective

death. When the Synoptic writers use *sarx*, after all, it is with reference to such altogether human experiences as sexual union (the two "become one flesh," Gen. 2:24) and moral failure ("the spirit indeed is willing, but the flesh is weak," Mark 14:38 and par.). Into our flesh-and-blood existence God sent his Son in order to redeem all those who will receive him. To ingest Christ is to welcome God's atoning sacrifice into our whole being.

As John writes, "In the beginning was the Word . . . and the Word was God . . . and the Word became flesh and lived among us, and we have seen his glory" (1:1, 14). Sent by God in flesh and blood, Jesus is the very Word of God. While Jesus as *logos* resonates with Greek thought, Hebrew tradition opens another window on his cryptic word, "whoever eats me will live because of me." To "eat" Jesus is to devour, digest, and be nourished by God's Word. Here Jesus evokes not Moses, manna, and Passover but Israel's prophets. Jeremiah prayed, "O LORD, . . . on your account I suffer insult. Your words were found, and I ate them, and your words became to me a joy and the delight of my heart; for I am called by your name" (Jer. 15:15–16). God said to Ezekiel, "Do not be rebellious like that rebellious house; open your mouth and eat what I give you. . . . eat this scroll, and go, speak to the house of Israel. . . . Then I ate it; and in my mouth it was as sweet as honey" (Ezek. 2:8; 3:1–3). Because Jesus is God's Word incarnate, to "eat his flesh and drink his blood" is not only to discover life's meaning, but to receive life itself, what the Synoptic Gospels call the kingdom of heaven. Feasting on the Word is the way to "have eternal life," Jesus promises, "and I will raise them up on the last day" (v. 54).

CHARLES HAMBRICK-STOWE

Pastoral Perspective

really abide with our food because in the eating of it we also destroy it.[2]

Thus "eating Jesus" must mean something other than consuming him. Though we take him into ourselves by faith, the living reality of his person remains intact. At the same time, he takes us into himself without dissolving our distinct personality. When believers partake of the flesh-and-blood Jesus, by faith, an "I-Thou relationship" is affirmed. Neither the "I" nor the "Thou" is absorbed into the other, but the two abide together in life-giving symbiosis. The gracious presence of God is not scarce, diminishing, depletable, or least of all consumable; rather, it is abundant, abiding, eternal, and inexhaustible. Jesus is not consumed as a religious commodity belonging to believers. Rather, "to consume the Eucharist is an act of anti-consumption, for here to consume is to be consumed, to be taken up into participation in something larger than the self, yet in a way in which the identity of the self is paradoxically secured."[3] The church's celebration of the Lord's Supper is the sign and seal of our participation in this greater reality; however, our nourishing relationship with Christ exists prior to and apart from the sacrament because of the faithful abiding of the One who came down from heaven.

Relocating the Supper. The editorial history of John 6 is seemingly complex. One hypothesis is that verses 51–58 constitute a redaction of John's account of the Last Supper that relocated these verses to their present location in the Gospel. Following the feeding miracle and the bread of life discourse, perhaps this text reminds us to examine what we can learn by bringing the celebration of the Lord's Supper into closer juxtaposition with the various settings in which we live, eat, consume, and relate with one another and the world. It may stand to reason that celebrating the sacrament more frequently, along with preaching that references the Table, could lead to greater facility at "relocating the Supper" into more and more contexts and places in our own lives where Jesus would abide with transforming power.

MICHAEL J. HOYT

---

2. Norman Wirzba, *Food and Faith: A Theology of Eating* (New York: Cambridge University Press, 2011), 156.
3. William T. Cavanaugh, *Being Consumed: Economics and Christian Desire* (Grand Rapids: Eerdmans, 2008), 84.

like a jewel. Bread is a sign (as in the feeding of the five thousand); it is story (as in the passage from Exodus 16, around which much of this chapter is written); and it is a symbol and sacrament of life. Almost every key idea in 6:52–59 appears earlier in the chapter (eternal life, vv. 40, 54; resurrection on the last day, vv. 44, 54: Jesus' sending by the Father, vv. 29, 57; and his coming down from heaven, vv. 33, 58). The introduction of the word "flesh" turns this short passage, where earlier themes collect and crystallize, into the climax of the entire discourse. It is in these closing verses of the discourse that we begin to see the Jesus who came from heaven as the crucified man of the cross. He will complete his human journey in dying and, through that dying, continue to communicate his heavenly love.

If we have read these verses rightly, they portray the death of Jesus as the center of John's story and as the heart and hub of the worship of Israel and the church. The crucifixion was a sacrificial dying, drawing into itself the shape and significance of Israel's ancient offerings to God. That same cross is the source of Christian sacramental worship, as the friends of Jesus share in signs that represent and recall his body and blood. All the praise of Israel and all the liturgy of the church find their focus and home in that single act, of the one who was given by heaven and who gave himself, as bread and in flesh, in death and as life.

JOHN PROCTOR

teaching, which is so repulsive that some of them decide not to go about with him anymore (6:66). The preacher who lives with constant pressure to grow the church may welcome the chance to point out that Jesus' own ministry sometimes caused numbers to shrink instead of grow.

Another door opens for the preacher who wants an opportunity to talk about the difference between reading the Bible literally and reading it poetically. In John's Gospel, almost nothing is ever simply what it seems. Water is not simply water; it is living water that springs up unto eternal life. Bread is not simply bread; it is the bread of God that gives life to the world. While the earlier verses of chapter 6 offer more support for this poetic reading than the present verses do, it is still possible to follow their trajectory by exploring the metaphorical dimensions of eating and drinking.

In his book *Mystical Christianity: A Psychological Commentary on the Gospel of John*, John Sanford points out how often the motif of eating appears in our dreams, usually after we have worked on self-understanding for some time. The reason for this, he says, is that "eating in a dream means that elements within us are now ready to be assimilated, and this requires intensive psychic preparation."[2] What is the difference between routine participation in the sacrament of Communion and deep assimilation of its elements?

One last door into the passage opens in verses 54–56, where Jesus makes twin promises to those who chew his flesh and drink his blood: eternal life and mutual abiding. How are these the same, and how are they different? Are they present realities or future ones? Christians who proudly display the prize of eternal life may benefit from thinking more deeply about the cost of abiding in someone who gives his own flesh and blood as food.

BARBARA BROWN TAYLOR

2. John Sanford, *Mystical Christianity: A Psychological Commentary on the Gospel of John* (New York: Crossroad, 1993), 162.

John 6:60–65

⁶⁰When many of his disciples heard it, they said, "This teaching is difficult; who can accept it?" ⁶¹But Jesus, being aware that his disciples were complaining about it, said to them, "Does this offend you? ⁶²Then what if you were to see the Son of Man ascending to where he was before? ⁶³It is the spirit that gives life; the flesh is useless. The words that I have spoken to you are spirit and life. ⁶⁴But among you there are some who do not believe." For Jesus knew from the first who were the ones that did not believe, and who was the one that would betray him. ⁶⁵And he said, "For this reason I have told you that no one can come to me unless it is granted by the Father."

Theological Perspective

Jesus' words are hard to swallow. The Galilean masses flocked to him, not because of his wise teaching, but "because they saw the signs that he was doing for the sick" and were miraculously fed (6:2, 26). Many identified themselves as "his disciples" (call them "small *d*" disciples, to distinguish them from the Twelve). Now it was impossible to avoid the implications of what their wonder-working rabbi was saying. They complained among themselves that his message was not only difficult but unacceptable. His utterances in the synagogue at Capernaum were just too much: "I have come down from heaven" (6:38), "I am the living bread that came down from heaven" (6:51), "eat my flesh and drink my blood" (6:54), "my flesh is true food and my blood is true drink" (6:55). The episode sparked a disputation among the religious leaders and, more strikingly, plunged his large and growing community of disciples into a crisis of faith. Aware of their murmuring, Jesus gives an acerbic reply, "Does this offend you?" (v. 61b)—and adds, in essence, "You ain't seen nothing yet!" The issues that caused many to grumble and then defect are theological in nature.

What shocks and offends is Jesus' in-your-face declaration that he was sent directly from heaven by God; that in his own flesh and blood he embodies God's infinite power, the power that created the

Pastoral Perspective

Disciples often do not want to hear the simple truth the teacher must tell us. However, Jesus' words about eating his flesh and drinking his blood may fall into the category of things we simply do not—and perhaps cannot—understand. Mark Twain is popularly said to have confessed, "It ain't those parts of the Bible that I can't understand that bother me; it is the parts that I do understand." Such is the plainspoken meaning of *skandalizei*, which appears in Jesus' query in verse 61 that the NRSV renders, "Does this offend you?"

The Offending Word. Whether the disciples fail to understand Jesus or understand him all too well, the feeling of offense is a signal that his words have approached the heart of their spiritual struggle. Indeed, Calvin suggests that their hearts, not their minds, were the problem. Feeling offended is an opportunity to humble ourselves and be open to the "guidance of the Spirit, that [God] may inscribe on our hearts what otherwise would never have entered our ears."[1]

Jesus is not trying to be obtuse, trick the disciples, or weed out the weak-minded. He later assures his friends, "I have said these things to you to keep you

1. John Calvin, *The Gospel according to St. John: Part One*, trans. T. H. L. Parker (Grand Rapids: Eerdmans, 1961), 173.

Feasting on the Gospels

Exegetical Perspective

Parts of Jesus' extended discourse about bread and the "bread of life" (6:35) proved quite contentious and difficult (6:41, 52). As chapter 6 nears its conclusion, the narrator focuses on the impact of Jesus' words and how his followers respond to his teaching. Earlier in John, we saw Jesus traveling with a group of "disciples" (2:2; 4:8; 6:16), rather like the little cluster of companions that accompanies him in the other Gospels (e.g., Mark 3:13–19). Certainly John seems to take for granted an inner group of Twelve (6:67). Jesus, however, attracted a much wider circle. Large numbers were baptized (4:1), and the "many disciples" of our text (vv. 60, 66) seem to come from the crowd that had "followed" (6:2) Jesus and whom he had fed.

Still, some of these people struggled to accept his teaching. They "complained" (v. 61), as the Hebrew people had done in the exodus from Egypt (Exod. 16:2), when God answered the people's murmuring with manna from heaven. This new complaint is aimed directly against God's "heavenly bread." Jesus has identified himself as "the bread which came down from heaven" and claimed that whoever "eats this bread will live forever" (6:58). His aspiring followers cannot accept such a claim and declare, "This is a hard saying; who can listen to it?" (v. 60; cf. 6:41–42, 52). So Jesus meets challenge with

Homiletical Perspective

John emphasizes the difficulty of Jesus' teaching in 6:35–58 by setting up concentric circles of response to that teaching: first the response of Jesus' opponents, then the response of "his disciples," and finally the response of the Twelve. Verses 60–65 focus on the middle circle, those who are counted among his followers but who do not belong to the inner circle. This means that the first decision a preacher has to make is what point of view to take. Will she stand with her congregation in the inner circle, urging them to distinguish themselves from the complainers and unbelievers, or will she stand with them in the middle circle, confessing the perennial difficulty of belief?

Either way, there are several verses that contain the seeds of whole sermons in them. The first is verse 60, in which the disciples complain, "This teaching is difficult." What teaching do they mean, exactly? Is it Jesus' revelation that he has come down from heaven, when they know who his parents are (6:42)? Is it his teaching about his singular intimacy with God (6:45)? Is it the teaching about eating his flesh (6:52)?

Even if these teachings pose no difficulties for present-day listeners, it should be easy for the preacher to come up with other difficult teachings that do. Is the virgin birth a stumbling block for anyone? How about the recitation of the Nicene Creed? Does anyone

John 6:60–65

207

John 6:60–65

Theological Perspective

universe and life on earth, the power of existence itself; that, more than the manna that nourished Israel day by day, he is the "bread of life" that gives power to transcend death and live forever. However, the crowd, like the authorities, could see that Jesus was human like them, recognizable as "the son of Joseph, whose father and mother we know" (6:42). Given the spiritual power he possessed, it was natural to understand him in terms of lofty, but still human, categories like prophet and king (6:14–15). In more recent centuries, people of a rationalist bent have focused on the Sermon on the Mount and certain parables in the Synoptic Gospels to present Jesus of Nazareth as a great ethical teacher—but still, obviously, as *just* a teacher. In light of his humanity, the claims Jesus makes for himself here seem preposterous. Disciples complain and authorities plot because of his pronouncement that (more than his healing and teaching, and underlying all he did and said) the gospel is about *who he is*.

In composing his narrative, John was also concerned to counter the opposite tendency within the Christian faith, that is, to hyperspiritualize the gospel. The Fourth Gospel stands as a refutation of gnostic movements in the early church that would minimize or deny Jesus' humanity in favor of a docetic understanding of God's sending God's Son into the world. What had become far easier for many to stomach was a "spiritual but not religious" notion of Jesus as a heavenly emissary inviting humanity into a realm of blessedness, purity, peace, and eternal life, above the sinful and painful mess of this world.

By contrast, the radically historical, flesh-and-blood personal particularity of God in Christ remains as scandalous today as it was in the first century. Incarnation and atonement are of central importance for John, and these essential doctrines depend on knowing Jesus in both his full humanity and his full divinity as he identified himself in the synagogue at Capernaum.

"Flesh and blood" and "bread," words spoken as the Passover was near, were allusions to sacrifice, with Jesus as "the Lamb of God" (1:36). Jesus referred to the mode of his sacrifice as being "lifted up," conveying the dual meaning of being hoisted on a cross and ascending to the Father (3:14; 8:28; 12:32–34). If the crowd took umbrage at his claim that he "came down from heaven," how much more confounding, after the sacrifice, that they would see him "ascending to where he was before" (v. 62). In addition, Jesus made a promise concerning all those who believe when he said, "I will raise them up on

Pastoral Perspective

from stumbling" (16:1, *skandalisthēte*). So how can a saying that so offends both ancient and modern sensibilities keep us from stumbling? Then as now, we truly stumble only if we allow questions of meaning to drive us away from Jesus. However, if our doubts and confusion incline us toward Jesus as a listening and consoling friend (15:15), if we fall into his saving embrace, then our stumbling becomes an occasion of grace.

Jesus is urging his disciples to cling to his person and to let meaning take care of itself. Like a child learning how to walk, looking with delight into the encouraging face of her parent as she unsteadily crosses the short distance before her, arms outstretched, lunging with the last stumbling steps into those familiar waiting hands, so can our stumbling become a moment of delight when we find ourselves caught up into the strong, nurturing embrace of Christ. By remembering this, we can ease our own spiritual journeys and those of our fellow pilgrims.

The Living Word. If we cling to the person of Christ through our difficulty in understanding, then we will be open to hearing and receiving the words that "are spirit and life" (v. 63b). These are not easy words or words that can be grasped in any purely rational sense. These words become an intensely personal Word that must be tasted, chewed, and slowly digested over time. The living Word is more than a proposition; it is Christ himself, whose living presence fleshes out flat statements of meaning.

The *real presence of Christ*, whether in the liturgy of sacrament or in the sacramentality of everyday life, is the only real power available to us in pastoral ministry. We do not wield this power as an instrument, but we allow ourselves to be wielded by it. The spiritual presence of the living Christ, in and through the body of—and the bodies of—believers, is life-giving to the world. The descending of the Son of Man into the flesh (*sarx*) demonstrates that the flesh is not useless when animated by the Spirit (*pneuma*). If we were to see the Son of Man ascending to where he was before (v. 62), we would know him to be the Word that was in the beginning, through whom all things came into being, and by whom all flesh is infused with eternal life (1:1–4, 14).

What may often feel to us like useless, powerless flesh contains more than meets the eye, more than is felt in the bones. We demonstrate the reality of this living Word through the pastoral ministry of the church and through the earthly, fleshly presence of the body of believers in the world, when we enter

counterchallenge. "What if," he asks, "you were to see the Son of Man ascending to where he was before?" (v. 62). That might perplex them even more. If they cannot handle what he says about earthly elements like bread and flesh, how would they respond to the sight of heaven, and to Jesus as one who is at home there? There are echoes here of his earlier encounter with Nicodemus and of his strange words there about the Son of Man (3:12–14).

"Son of Man" is an important title in the Gospels. It is found often in the Synoptics, where Jesus regularly speaks of himself in this way. In John too the phrase is quite common, and it has particular Johannine nuances. In some texts it points to Jesus' heavenly origin and to the way he opens the life of earth to the realities of heaven (1:51; 3:13). There is a parallel here to the scene in Daniel (7:13) where a "son of man" receives heavenly authority over the nations of earth. In John the words may also emphasize Jesus' full humanity, his commitment to experiencing both human life and death (6:53), and his being "lifted up" (3:14; 8:28; 12:34) in the humiliation and glory of the cross. So the "Son of Man" in John is both heavenly and human, mortal and majestic. This cryptic title sums up all Jesus' words about his being sent (6:51, 57) and his dying (6:53), and these are the claims that people cannot grasp. So "what if" they saw the process unfolding back to heaven, revealing the true dignity and destiny of the crucified one? Still they might turn away.

For only God's Spirit can turn words into life (v. 63). Human inquiry on its own cannot grasp the things of God. We have met this thought before (3:6), but it is striking to find it here, in these words. We have heard that "flesh" is life-giving (6:53); but now, just a few verses later, "flesh" is inert and useless (v. 63). The contrast, it seems, is between Jesus' "flesh" and ours. His incarnate body is flesh animated by Spirit (1:32), so that he could be a life-giver, in both his speaking and his sacrifice. Mere human nature, without the Spirit's breath, will never grasp God's truth and life. This sort of insight can only be a gift, coming to the characters in the Gospel and to the reader too in the words of Jesus (v. 63).

The theme of gift recurs a few verses further on (v. 65). When people turn to Jesus and trust in him, this is a gift from God—from Father to Son (6:37, 44; 17:24; 18:9) and from heaven to the believer (6:65). Faith is not mere human choice. We would, however, miss the depth and balance of John's theology if we were to think that God's initiative would reduce us to mere spiritual robots. Salvation in this Gospel is

have trouble with the teaching that Jesus is the only way to God? Whatever the difficult teachings are, they offer the preacher an opportunity to speak with other disciples about the role of belief in the life of faith.

Some listeners may need to be reminded that faith involves embracing mysteries that are literally beyond belief—such as the invisible presence of the Holy Spirit or the unverifiable promise of life after death. Others may need to be reassured that belief is more than intellectual assent to a set of theological propositions. The verses leading up to verse 60 offer support for both of these truths and more, but the preacher may also benefit from reviewing Howard Gardner's work on multiple intelligences or the Myers-Briggs Type Indicator, since disciples come in all personality types.

If the preacher is in the midst of a series of sermons on John 6, then verse 63 will be of interest, as it seems to contradict Jesus' teaching in verse 54. Just nine verses ago he said to his opponents, "Those who eat my flesh and drink my blood have eternal life." Here, speaking to his disciples, he says, "The spirit gives life; the flesh counts for nothing." Is Jesus offering two different teachings on the role of the flesh—one for outsiders and another for insiders—or is something else going on here?

Congregations that value close textual work may benefit from Lamar Williamson's observation that John uses certain terms (such as "world" and "flesh") in more than one way. In verse 53 the word "flesh" refers to symbolic bread on a table, representing the humanity of Jesus ("positive" flesh). In verse 63 it refers to temporal reality as opposed to divine reality ("negative" flesh). "When the intended meaning is read from the context," Williamson concludes, "the seeming contradiction disappears and the mystery of the incarnation comes into view."[1] Even without doing the word work, a preacher can make the vitally important point that verse 63 does not dismiss the value of flesh or denounce it as the natural enemy of spirit. In Jesus Christ spirit and flesh are truly one.

In his book *The Mystical Way in the Fourth Gospel*, William Countryman offers another compelling angle on the contrast between verses 54 and 63. Making no distinction between John's literary use of "the flesh" in these two verses, Countryman prefers to leave the disparity in place. Why? Because the slippage between the verses is a clear indication of John's ambivalence toward the sacraments, he says.

1. Lamar Williamson, *Preaching the Gospel of John* (Louisville, KY: Westminster John Knox Press, 2004), 87.

John 6:60–65

Theological Perspective

the last day" (6:39, 40, 54). The work of redemption required that Jesus appear in flesh and blood, but flesh and blood alone are incapable of achieving such union with God. Rather, "it is the spirit that gives life; the flesh is useless" (v. 63).

This verse has played a role in debates on sacramental theology over the centuries of church history, classically during the Reformation era, when lines were drawn not only between Catholic and Lutheran positions but also between Luther and Zwingli, followed by Calvin and others in subsequent generations. The verse refers primarily, however, to the Christology of John's Gospel, the essential importance of the two natures of Christ, human and divine, in our understanding of God's self-revelation in the person of Jesus Christ. Jesus' words about his own "flesh and blood" are "spirit and life" (v. 63).

Jesus' awareness of human nature, including individual motives and levels of commitment, is evident throughout the Gospels. John suggests that Jesus' remarkable psychological insight stems, in part, from his complete sharing in the flesh-and-blood experience of common humanity. The inescapable question arises, if Jesus "knew from the first who were the ones that did not believe, and who was the one that would betray him" (v. 64), why did he welcome them into his community at all? The answer must have to do with the message that "God so loved the world" that God "did not send the Son into the world to condemn the world, but in order that the world might be saved through him" (3:16–17).

Jesus gathers a community that is always going to be a mixed multitude, including "some who do not believe" but attach themselves for reasons of their own. "No one can come to me unless it is granted by the Father," Jesus explains. God wills that they should come. Why some have faith and others cannot quite believe, or turn hostile, remains a painful mystery, an inscrutable interface of human and divine will, with every faithful move of ours utterly dependent on God's grace. In the meantime, Jesus gathers all who will come.

CHARLES HAMBRICK-STOWE

Pastoral Perspective

into places of suffering where life is ebbing away, or is stagnant, or has been permanently scarred or brutally ended. The church does not enter these contexts so much with clear statements of meaning as with a profound personal presence, with a spiritual life that flows in a region deeper than rational comprehension. The living Word begets belief that is more relationship than comprehension, more trust than intellectual assent.

The Rejected Word. For reasons that remain a mystery, some of Jesus' disciples are able to accept his words and believe, while others are not. Jesus apparently knows not only that the disciples are complaining about his teaching; he also knows who among the disciples do not believe. Again, there is more going on here than the mere rejection of propositions, for the rejection is personal: "He came to what was his own, and his own people did not accept him" (1:11).

Had there been only confusion or disagreement about meaning and interpretation, a conversation may have ensued; but the disagreement becomes personal, and healthy communication is broken off. Jesus must intuit, even divinely perceive, that the disciples have not accepted his words. Calvin encourages us that "when we do not follow the Lord's meaning at once, the best thing to do is for us to go straight to Him, for Him to settle all these problems for us."[2] As so often happens, the disciples turn away from direct communication and grumble among themselves. This dynamic is known in family-systems theory as triangulation and in church life as a parking-lot meeting.

Even more detrimentally, when we cannot make sense of God's ways with us, our prayer life suffers or may even disappear. We may speak of God in the third person, as an idea or a proposition. Again, the restoration of belief in this text does not have to do with intellectual comprehension, but with a personal "coming to Christ," a restoration not achievable by the human heart, but only receivable as a gift from beyond, a gift generously given by the God who loves the whole world (3:16).

MICHAEL J. HOYT

---

2. Calvin, *Gospel according to St. John*, 174.

Exegetical Perspective

a relationship, and like any other relationship it asks to shape character and conduct: abide, bear fruit, keep my commands, love one another (15:9–17). The assurances of John 6 offer security and hope (6:37, 44), but they should not make us careless or complacent. Verse 64 meshes with this pattern of thought. Some of the erstwhile followers "did not believe."

It was ever thus with Jesus in the Gospels. Not everyone stayed the course. John now tells us that Jesus "knew" (v. 64) who these short-term disciples would be. He could tell when hearers had not engaged deeply with his words (2:23–25; 5:38; 6:36). "From the first" (v. 64b) he could sense when responses were superficial or hostile. Neither attitude would "abide" and "bear fruit."

More particularly and painfully, Jesus realized that one of his closest associates would eventually turn against him. We shall have to look again and more carefully at Judas Iscariot (vv. 70–71). However, for the moment it seems that Judas embodies and brings into focus the central question for all disciples: is my relationship with Jesus provisional or persistent? I can trust him. What will he find in me?

We may wonder what the Gospel's first readers made of this. Surely these verses reminded them that belief in Jesus regularly challenges and divides. The Fourth Gospel is often seen as disclosing through its narrative the situation in which John wrote and some of the conflicts through which he and his friends lived. So the text causes us to wonder whether John knew people who had slipped out of Christian belief, ones for whom the church's weighty claims about incarnation and crucifixion had proved too much to carry. Although we cannot be certain, these verses would surely remind ancient readers, as they remind us today, that Jesus always calls for persistent faith—faith that trusts in, and ultimately rests on, God's mighty and mysterious grace.

JOHN PROCTOR

Homiletical Perspective

By the time John wrote his Gospel, baptism and Eucharist were clearly established Christian rites, yet John declined to provide foundational stories for either one of them. His Gospel does not contain the story of Jesus' baptism, nor does it include the institution of the Eucharist at the Last Supper. In their place, John provides narratives that identify Jesus as living water (4:14) and living bread (6:51). "The ambiguous picture that thus emerges," Countryman concludes, "suggests that our author saw the sacramental rites as both essential and inadequate."[2] Whatever Christian tradition the preacher represents, and however that tradition views sacraments, this is an interesting theme for a sermon.

In verse 65, Jesus rephrases a teaching he offered earlier in verse 44: "no one can come to me unless it is granted by the Father." Preachers who are so inclined may use this as an opportunity to defend the doctrine of predestination, but only if they are convinced that this will be transformative for their listeners. A more interesting approach might focus on what an odd postscript this is to Jesus' indictment of the disciples for their failure to believe. Are they free to come to him, or not? If God has not granted it to them, then how can Jesus chide them?

"The real function of a spiritual friend is to insult you," wrote the Tibetan teacher Chögyam Trungpa Rinpoche.[3] Given the other slippages in this passage, this last one may offer the preacher a chance to talk about Jesus' teaching style. If he really expects his followers to understand what he is saying, then why does he make it so difficult? Preachers whose reading lists include stories about Zen or Sufi masters may recognize the technique: whenever your students get comfortable where they are, pull the rug out from under them. Eventually they will learn that comfort has nothing to do with waking up.

BARBARA BROWN TAYLOR

---

2. William Countryman, *The Mystical Way in the Fourth Gospel* (Valley Forge, PA: Trinity Press Int., 1994), 7.
3. Pema Chödrön, *The Places That Scare You* (Boston: Shambala, 2005), 155.

John 6:66–71

⁶⁶Because of this many of his disciples turned back and no longer went about with him. ⁶⁷So Jesus asked the twelve, "Do you also wish to go away?" ⁶⁸Simon Peter answered him, "Lord, to whom can we go? You have the words of eternal life. ⁶⁹We have come to believe and know that you are the Holy One of God." ⁷⁰Jesus answered them, "Did I not choose you, the twelve? Yet one of you is a devil." ⁷¹He was speaking of Judas son of Simon Iscariot, for he, though one of the twelve, was going to betray him.

Theological Perspective

One of the most frightening and neglected verses in the Gospels is the agonizing remembrance that, because of Jesus' hard sayings, "many of his disciples turned back and no longer went about with him" (v. 66). Popular support for his ministry collapsed. It would rebuild, but not without contention and opposition (7:40–44), culminating in his momentarily triumphal entry into Jerusalem (12:12–13), only to collapse again. God's activity in the world is not dependent on, or necessarily evidenced by, a high approval rating with big crowds. While Jesus is stalwart in the face of failure, his flesh-and-blood human psyche must have been wounded by such large-scale desertion.

If, "despised and rejected," he was the embodiment of Isaiah's Suffering Servant, "a man of sorrows and acquainted with grief" (Isa. 53:3 KJV), such emotions surely swept over him as he watched them pack their things and walk away. John's description of their departure is doubly apt. Not only did they stop following; they willfully "turned back." Jesus had stated that any motivation on a person's part to "come to me" is initiated by divine grace, "granted by the Father" (6:65), but it is also clear that we are responsible for our own choices and actions. Those who leave come to that decision on their own. Those who stay must determine that for themselves.

Pastoral Perspective

Turning back or being turned? Jesus' disciples are slipping out the back door faster than they come in the front. Whether John is referring only to the first followers of Jesus who "turned back" or also has in mind the apostates of his own community in the late first century (1 John 2:19), we can relate! Pastors and church leaders have experienced the disheartening pattern of church members who say all the right religious things at first but gradually stop showing up when "life gets busy," or they "travel a lot on the weekends," or they discover that "this church is full of cliques!"

Then again, every believer, if we are honest, knows firsthand the experience of turning back from following Jesus. We frequently recoil from the demands of discipleship, even multiple times a day. Still, there is a difference between the one who repeatedly fails to follow Jesus but returns to try again, and the one who makes a conscious choice to turn away and abandon Jesus completely. In the latter case, many troubling questions arise: What does the deliberate act of turning away indicate about those who turn? Were they never really chosen by Jesus in the first place? Was it not "granted by the Father" (v. 65) that these should come to Jesus? Did they turn back of their own choosing, or were they predestined to reject Jesus? Did they ever truly

Exegetical Perspective

The rather abrasive exchange of the last paragraph ends with a parting of the ways. Whereas some of Jesus' followers had questioned him earlier on (v. 60), now they quit (v. 66). He goes about in Galilee (7:1), and they take their own course without him. What, then, of the cohort of companions who have been closest to him? What will they do? That is the theme of these verses, as Jesus explores with these friends their intentions, motives, and relationship to him.

Rarely does John mention that there were twelve in the inner group around Jesus—only here and in 20:24. If John wrote in a setting where one of the Synoptic Gospels was known, and aimed to supplement its witness with his own,[1] he could assume that readers would know of the Twelve. Here they appear as a faithful remnant, adhering to Jesus as others peel away.

As happens so often, Simon Peter is the voice of the Twelve (vv. 68–69). Just as he does in the other Gospels (Mark 8:29 and par.), he declares his faith in answer to a direct question from Jesus. So there is some similarity between that Markan declaration at Caesarea Philippi and this confession in John, but in John's Gospel, Peter's words have a distinctive cast.

1. This view is set out at length in Richard Bauckham, *Jesus and the Eyewitnesses* (Grand Rapids: Eerdmans, 2006).

Homiletical Perspective

At the beginning of chapter 6, a large crowd followed Jesus around. Here at the end, the number has shrunk to twelve. God may have drawn a great many people to Jesus (6:44, 65), but only a fraction of them have decided to remain with him. To paraphrase Matthew 22:14, "Many are called, but few choose to stay."

Lamar Williamson says this makes John 6:66–71 a good passage to preach in a church that is losing members. Citing "the sifting effect of the gospel," he points out that Jesus lost a lot of members too—not only those who were offended by his teaching or found it too difficult to understand, but also those who stayed with him simply because they had no better place to go. When Jesus turned to the Twelve and asked, "Do you also wish to go away?" Simon Peter said, in effect, "What alternatives do we have?"[1]

People have lots of alternatives these days. The spiritual seekers in the congregation have ready access to wisdom from all of the world's great religions. The couples with teenagers are thinking about following their kids to the big church across town with the well-funded youth program. Even the stalwarts who have served on every committee and volunteered for every job are starting to show up a little

1. Lamar Williamson, *Preaching the Gospel of John* (Louisville, KY: Westminster John Knox Press, 2004), 88.

John 6:66–71

Theological Perspective

Jesus put it to the Twelve directly: "Do you also wish to go away?" (v. 67). With what tone of voice might he have uttered this pointed question? Accusatory? Challenging? Wistful? Heartbroken? Each of them, like a reader today engaged in the practice of *lectio divina*, would hear it with his or her own ears. The question seems to be the dark obverse of the invitation they had received from his lips in the springtime of the gospel: "Follow me" (1:43). However, Jesus is not one to revoke his call to discipleship; there is no revocation of the vocation he bestows upon his followers. His painful question was actually a renewal of the original call to follow, delivered now as they struggled in the throes of doubt, confusion, and inner and outer conflict.

Peter's response, speaking for the Twelve, indicated that he and the others understood this crucible of a situation as a moment of truth, a time for chastened recommitment and vocational renewal. Thus he blurted out, "Lord, to whom can we go?" For Peter, the experience of living closely with Jesus on a daily basis had overwhelmed all other, lesser options.

The meaning of our lives is revealed in the values or ideals with which we align ourselves, in what Paul Tillich called our ultimate concern. The notion of individual autonomy is a delusion. As Bob Dylan testified in his Christian blues-rock anthem, "Gotta Serve Somebody" (1979), "Well, it may be the devil [stating it in extreme terms] or it may be the Lord—but you're gonna have to serve somebody."[1] Peter confessed that, having come to know Jesus, there was nowhere else to go: "You have the words of eternal life" (v. 68).

In this exchange, Peter does not expressly call Jesus the Messiah. Commentators connect his confession with the one at Caesarea Philippi recorded in the Synoptic Gospels (Mark 8:29; Luke 9:20; Matt. 16:16). There, in response to the question, "Who do you say that I am?" Peter proclaimed, "You are the Messiah" ("the Messiah of God" or "the Messiah, the Son of the living God"). In the Fourth Gospel Peter begins simply, "You have the words of eternal life." These, specifically, are the very words by which Jesus has just identified himself as "the living bread that came down from heaven," the "flesh and blood" sacrifice that brings "eternal life" (6:51, 54). While many may reject Jesus' statements about himself as outrageous, those for whom Peter speaks accept them as true. Furthermore he adds, "We have come to believe and know that you are the Holy One of God" (v. 69).

Pastoral Perspective

believe, or were they fooling themselves? If their belief was genuine, if they truly had come to the Son at the bidding of the Father, was the will of the Father then thwarted when they departed? Is there hope that apostates may yet change their mind and return to following Jesus?

In this story, as with so many stories in John's Gospel, there is a mysterious interplay between human agency and divine sovereignty. The tension is not clearly resolved, in this Gospel or in the whole of Scripture. Surely, however, to eliminate all human agency would render pastoral ministry rather superfluous and make the religious life an exercise in futility. The plain sense of this text is that Jesus takes seriously the disciples' wishes and their ensuing choice.

To whom can we go? When presented with the question of their allegiance to Jesus, Simon Peter speaks on behalf of the Twelve, who are here numbered for the first time in John's Gospel. There are obvious answers to Peter's question, "To whom can we go?" Many other viable religious options are available to the disciples: the Pharisees, the Sadducees, the Essenes, and the Zealots, to name some of the Jewish possibilities. Yet Peter speaks as one whose other options have been eliminated by a powerful encounter with Jesus.

The Twelve have experienced Jesus' words as being both spirit and life for them. They cannot deny this spiritual encounter as it has resulted in their "believing" and "knowing" (v. 69) that Jesus is the one through whom God will give them eternal life. This verb combination is found elsewhere in John (16:30; 17:8; 1 John 4:16), and the two seem virtually synonymous. (However, as Raymond Brown points out, while Jesus himself is said to know God, he is never said to believe in God.[1]) The disciples' belief in Jesus as the Holy One of God is the result of an unparalleled spiritual experience. People who have breathed the fresh air of such an experience are not easily dissuaded from the knowledge they acquire, by the hot air of ridicule or the airtight logic of propositional argument. It is the privilege of pastoral ministry to give disciples the opportunity, in personal conversation or public proclamation, to profess like Peter what they have come to "believe" and "know!"

This world is with devils filled. Their public proclamation notwithstanding, disciples also experience the time of trial and the dismal failure of heart that results in betrayal. Here, and later in chapter 13,

---

1. Bob Dylan, "Gotta Serve Somebody," text at www.bobdylan.com, accessed May 21, 2014.

1. Raymond E. Brown, *The Gospel according to John I–XII* (New Haven, CT: Yale University Press, 1966), 298.

Exegetical Perspective

The term "eternal life" (v. 68) is particularly frequent in this Gospel and crops up throughout John's narrative. "Eternal" is more than mere duration; it speaks of quality—the life of eternity, of God, of the realm of heaven. This is life that knows God now (17:3) and that will rise "on the last day" (6:40, 54) to know God more deeply and directly. It comes through sharing Jesus' "flesh and blood" (6:54) and through his word and through belief in him (6:40, 68–69). To speak, then, of word and sacrament as partners in the work of the gospel is a thoroughly Johannine balance. The message preached and the elements broken and poured combine to shape the church and its life. Together they communicate God's spoken and incarnate word.

"The Holy One of God" (v. 69) is a rare title for Jesus. In the Gospels it appears in only one other episode (Mark 1:24; Luke 4:34), which occurs, curiously, in the same setting as here in John, namely, the synagogue in Capernaum (6:59). In the other Gospels the words are shouted out in fear, whereas here Peter speaks in faith, and his words fit well as part of John's good news. For Jesus is sanctified—made holy—when he is sent into the world (10:36). He carries the holiness of his Father, and passes this on to his friends, as he consecrates himself deeply and deliberately to the cross (17:17–19). Now Simon Peter wants this holiness. He recognizes it and reaches for it—demanding and even disturbing as it will surely be.

It seems that Peter has just chosen to stay with Jesus, but the truth of the matter is more complex. When Jesus asks his disciples, "Did I not choose you?" (v. 70), we find that behind Peter's decision for Jesus is Jesus' choice of Peter. "I chose you . . . to be my friends and to bear fruit," says Jesus later in John (15:15–16). In Mark, Jesus also chooses the Twelve for company and mission (3:14–15), but John speaks more fully about the dynamics of this relationship. John shows that discipleship is rooted in the life of what Christians will later identify as the Trinity— the Father's gift (6:37), the Son's call (6:70), and the Spirit's vitality (6:63). This is the framework of grace that holds us, the heartbeat of divine purpose that sustains human faith.

However, there is one desperate casualty. Judas Iscariot's story is, by any account, tragic and terrible. Whatever allowances are made for his mixed motives, misunderstandings, and later miseries of regret, his is a story of an awful mistake, of a life gone desperately awry. The Gospels consistently view him with hindsight and regularly sum him up (Mark

Homiletical Perspective

less often, citing their need to spend more quiet time with God alone.

While there are good sermons to be preached on the sifting effect of the gospel, there are other good reasons why mainline churches are losing members. Chief among them, according to this passage, is that fewer and fewer people are experiencing an upsurge of *life* in the words of eternal life. The words no longer offend or upset; most of them are as tame as house cats—even words as dangerous as "spirit," "flesh," "bread," and "blood."

In a famous exchange between Bill Moyers and Joseph Campbell, Moyers said, "We all need to tell our story and to understand our story. . . . We need life to signify, to touch the eternal, to understand the mysterious, to find out who we are." Campbell replied, "People say that what we're all seeking is a meaning for life. I don't think that's what we're really seeking. I think that what we're seeking is an experience of being alive . . . so that we actually feel the rapture of being alive."[2] A sermon that helps listeners link their experience of being alive with the living words of Jesus Christ might be a step in the right direction.

So might a sermon that calls a congregation to the hard work of exhibiting the kind of life it wants to commend to others. When Episcopal bishop Mariann Budde spoke with Yale seminarians about the challenges ahead of them, she talked about the importance of transcendent worship, of engaging the surrounding culture, and—most strikingly—of a church *liking itself* before it tries to give something of value to others. In anxious times, when visitors can smell the sweat of a congregation that is divided about how to avoid its own death, hearing the call to *like* one another right now may be more important than hearing the call to love one another to the end.

Three other themes stand out here. Two have surfaced earlier in the chapter: the role of belief in the life of faith, and the importance of choosing the God who has already chosen us. Preachers drawn to the first theme will find plenty in Peter's confession to support a full exposition of belief. Preachers drawn to the second theme will note that Jesus did the choosing this time instead of "the Father" (cf. 6:44, 65). He chose the Twelve—and yet one of them is a devil. Here, then, is a third theme: the betrayer who is an insider, not an outsider. Jesus' worst enemy is not one of "the Jews" but one of his own disciples.

2. Joseph Campbell with Bill Moyers, *The Power of Myth*, ed. Betty Sue Flowers (New York: Doubleday, 1988), 5.

John 6:66–71

Theological Perspective

Many find Jesus' words unbelievable and unreasonable, but Peter and others embraced him with both heart and mind, learning that only with faith in him does life make sense. So ontology and epistemology are profoundly christological in the Fourth Gospel. "Holy One of God" as a title is not found much in Scripture. The only other place it appears in the Gospels is from the mouth of a demoniac—an incident associated, like this one, with the synagogue at Capernaum (Mark 1:21–28; Luke 4:31–37). It may not be the most perfect title for Jesus Christ, but it served to reconfirm their vocation to follow him. The crisis of faith forced them to take their commitment, and their understanding of who Jesus was, to the next level.

Peter's declaration of the Twelve's loyalty was occasion for neither unqualified relief nor celebration. Jesus did not congratulate them. As the Reformers reminded the church in the sixteenth century, faith is a gift and not an achievement. Salvation is not a reward for good works. While the decision was theirs to cleave to him and not to leave with the others, the underlying and essential choice was Jesus' choice of them. Rather than praising them, he rooted us again in the theological ground of discipleship, the doctrine of vocation, his calling of us to live in his community. "Did I not choose you?" he said sternly to the Twelve.

Even then, all was not resolved, for Jesus was keenly aware that evil always crouches nearby. He knew that God's warning to Cain in Genesis 4 applies to all human beings: "sin is lurking at the door; its desire is for you" (Gen. 4:7). Despite having personally chosen each one of the Twelve, Jesus told them, "one of you is a devil" (v. 70b) who will betray him. Spoiler alert: John goes ahead and identifies Judas by name. The gospel is not a pretty story, and that is precisely the point. Into the real world God sends his Son in flesh and blood. Where else can we go, if we have heard the voice of the One who offers eternal life?

CHARLES HAMBRICK-STOWE

Pastoral Perspective

the Gospel writer attributes Judas's betrayal to the work of the devil. John relates that during Jesus' Last Supper with his disciples "the devil had already put it into the heart of Judas son of Simon Iscariot to betray him" and that "Satan entered into him" (13:2, 27). Nevertheless. should we single out Judas as the only devil among the disciples? In the Synoptic parallel to this scene (Mark 8:27–38), it is Peter, not Judas, whom Jesus rebukes with the words, "Get behind me, Satan!" Then, soon after this, it is Peter who thrice denies Jesus in his crucial hour. Even these closest friends, who acknowledge Jesus as the Holy One of God, are not exempt from becoming vessels of evil. It is worth remembering that in the Synoptic tradition it is an unclean spirit who acknowledges Jesus to be "the Holy One of God" (Mark 1:24).

So it is for good reason that the church's baptismal liturgy includes the renunciation of evil: "Trusting in the gracious mercy of God, do you turn from the ways of sin and renounce evil and its power in the world?"[2] The path of discipleship is littered with potholes and pitfalls, lined with enticements that call us away from wholehearted devotion to following Christ, that call us even to betrayal. Like Peter, we make bold assertions of allegiance, only to fall away. Like Judas, we are prone to aligning ourselves with the enemies of Christ. However, like prodigals of every age, we can take comfort in Jesus' affirmation that though Judas "is a devil," he still belongs to the fold: "Did I not choose you?" Despite the heartbreaking truth of Jesus' accusation and the inevitability of Judas's betrayal, even more true and certain is the unfolding of God's unrelenting love for the world in God's inexorable plan of salvation. Though Jesus may accuse, he does not condemn. "Indeed, God did not send the Son into the world to condemn the world, but in order that the world might be saved through him" (3:17).

MICHAEL J. HOYT

2. Theology and Worship Ministry Unit, for the Presbyterian Church (U.S.A.), *Book of Common Worship* (Louisville, KY: Westminster/John Knox Press, 1993), 407.

Exegetical Perspective

3:19) in terms of the way he ended up: though "one of the twelve," he was "the one that would betray him" (vv. 64, 71); in this text he is "a devil" (v. 70), a focused embodiment of evil. Apart from this, we know little about Judas. Only John mentions that Iscariot was his father's name too (v. 71; 13:2, 26). The name may come from *Ish-Kerioth*, "man of Kerioth"; there were a few places with that name. It may mean "man of the city," a Jerusalemite. These derivations are far from certain, and not very helpful, because deeper questions remain.

Judas's "betrayal"—although the word could be translated "handing over"—is surely rooted in history. That someone in the inner circle turned against Jesus is not a story the early church would have made up. Yet seeking to understand Judas is like gazing into the dark; however hard you try to see, you never get complete clarity. That Jesus chose Judas as one of the Twelve and lived with that choice, even as he realized where it would lead, is part of the strange providence of the cross. That divine goodness came about through the human sin of Judas, and of many others too, is a mystery and a paradox.

There are many paradoxes in the closing verses of John 6. For example, that a person's choice to follow Jesus can be a deliberate decision of mind and heart, and yet still reflect God's prompting and initiative, is beyond our understanding—but perhaps not beyond our intuition and experience. That God's Spirit can give insight to transcend our normal and natural wisdom (6:63), and that flesh and blood could carry the promise and power of eternity (6:54): these are truths that we cannot fully grasp, and yet they grip us and bring to us the very life of the living God.

JOHN PROCTOR

Homiletical Perspective

Did Jesus know that Judas would be a devil when he chose him? Since Jesus knows everything in John's Gospel, the most likely answer is yes, in which case Judas is indispensable to the passion narrative that is still to come. When the time arrives, Jesus will hand Judas a piece of wine-soaked bread and say, "Do quickly what you are going to do" (13:27b). Has tradition been too hard on Judas? Where would the story be without him? If God is truly sovereign, then does God not cast the villains along with the saviors?

If the answer is no, that Jesus did not know Judas would be a devil when he chose him, then Judas probably did not know either. Something happened along the way to turn this disciple against his teacher, and disillusionment is the most likely guess. Most devils are deeply disappointed people—disappointed with the way things are going and disappointed with themselves. Finding someone else to blame and bringing that person down provides a way to feel powerful again without wasting a moment on introspection. Why take responsibility for your ill will when you can make someone else responsible for it instead? An intuitive and carefully constructed sermon on Judas might help a congregational devil-in-the-making reconsider his or her strategies for taking charge of the situation.

Clergy and church members who have survived the sifting effect of the gospel may still be surprised by what a contentious place the parish can be. Plenty of us were prepared to be bruised by the world; far fewer of us were prepared to be hurt by the church. However, almost everyone has a story to tell about injuries sustained in Christian ministry. If Judas has anything to teach us, it is that he is one of us. His story reminds us that there is a potential Judas inside every disciple, waiting to be disappointed enough to want to hurt someone—but also ready to be recognized and reclaimed by those who will, with God's help, nip a devil in the bud and bring him back into the fold.

BARBARA BROWN TAYLOR

John 7:1–13

¹After this Jesus went about in Galilee. He did not wish to go about in Judea because the Jews* were looking for an opportunity to kill him. ²Now the Jewish festival of Booths was near. ³So his brothers said to him, "Leave here and go to Judea so that your disciples also may see the works you are doing; ⁴for no one who wants to be widely known acts in secret. If you do these things, show yourself to the world." ⁵(For not even his brothers believed in him.) ⁶Jesus said to them, "My time has not yet come, but your time is always here. ⁷The world cannot hate you, but it hates me because I testify against it that its works are evil. ⁸Go to the festival yourselves. I am not going to this festival, for my time has not yet fully come." ⁹After saying this, he remained in Galilee.

¹⁰But after his brothers had gone to the festival, then he also went, not publicly but as it were in secret. ¹¹The Jews were looking for him at the festival and saying, "Where is he?" ¹²And there was considerable complaining about him among the crowds. While some were saying, "He is a good man," others were saying, "No, he is deceiving the crowd." ¹³Yet no one would speak openly about him for fear of the Jews.

Theological Perspective

Throughout the opening chapters of John's Gospel, the evangelist correlates Jesus' location with the responses of his hearers. Jerusalem (2:13–25) is associated with religious leaders who contentiously interacted with Jesus, while Galilee (1:43–51) is identified as the region where Jesus was enthusiastically embraced by his followers. In Galilee, at the seashore, he fed five thousand people (6:1–14). Nearby in Cana, his mother and wedding guests marveled at his changing water into wine (2:1–11). There his disciples were confounded by his walking on water to meet them as they crossed the Sea of Galilee (6:16–21). Still, as the transitional verses leading to this passage indicate, many of his followers had begun to defect, turning back from the way proclaimed by Jesus and reembracing the ways of the world (6:66).

This desertion by Jesus' supporters anticipates the separation of Jesus from his brothers and the increasing alienation of the crowd from him. Despite their appreciation of the wonder-working power and acts of Jesus, his brothers misunderstood his mission. They affirmed the popular expectation that the Messiah would charismatically and publicly lead the people with wisdom and action in a new direction,

* See "'The Jews' in the Fourth Gospel" on pp. xi–xiv.

Pastoral Perspective

The text begins with a plot to kill Jesus (v. 1) and ends with people afraid to speak openly about him (v. 13). This situation in the first century evokes the characteristics of a police state where those in power use force and secrecy to maintain power. In such circumstances there are always citizens afraid to speak openly. Peter, for instance, was afraid to answer truthfully when, after Jesus' arrest, he was questioned about whether he knew the man (18:15–27). Compare this to another "police state": the one in which African Americans in the South lived during much of the twentieth century. Though state governments were democratically elected, blacks did not have the vote. If they claimed their rights or tried to register to vote, their lives were at risk. Many were lynched, beaten, or threatened, while the guardians of the law looked on or looked away. They were afraid to speak openly.

Jesus determined to stay out of sight because "his time had not yet come" (v. 6). Some in authority were threatened by him and his signs, and they were plotting to kill him. As with any controversial figure, there were multiple opinions about Jesus. A few appear to have believed, which in John's language means they put their complete trust in him. Others, including his own brothers, had seen his signs. They knew that the feast to which everyone was going was an opportunity for their brother to gain public

Feasting on the Gospels

Exegetical Perspective

There is no close connection between the end of John 6 and the beginning of John 7. In fact, there are more numerous connections between John 7 and John 5, such as the statement in 7:1 that "the Jews were looking for an opportunity to kill [Jesus]" (see 5:18). Therefore some scholars have suggested that the chapters have been disarranged, and that chapter 7 originally followed directly after chapter 5. However, because the narrative of the Word made flesh implies a disruption of ordinary expectations, its narrative logic may not run according to traditional expectations either.

Whatever its relation to the preceding chapters, John 7 begins a section that continues throughout rest of the narrative. Previously in John, Jesus has gone back and forth between Galilee and Jerusalem. Now, beginning with 7:14, almost the entire rest of the Gospel takes place in Jerusalem. Measured by references to the festivals (Booths or Sukkot, September–October, 7:2; Dedication or Hanukkah, November–December, 10:22; and Passover, March–April, 11:55), these events will take seven or eight months. Thus the ominous note in 7:1 inaugurates Jesus' confrontation with opponents that will climax in his "glorification" in crucifixion and resurrection.

Chapters 7 and 8 form a unity (apart from 7:53–8:11). Though these chapters begin and end with

Homiletical Perspective

This periscope is a study in confusion. There is the confusion of Jesus' brothers over who Jesus is and what his mission is. There is confusion about where Jesus should be and what he should be doing. There is confusion about whether he is a good man or a deceiver. There are only two in this narrative who know what is going on: Jesus himself and our author. He writes "so that [we] also may believe" (19:35).

We might expect better of Jesus' brothers, those raised with him and, necessarily, witnesses to his conduct and purpose. Clearly, they know he is religious, so they would expect him to do the obvious thing: go up to Jerusalem for the Feast of Tabernacles. This is one of three pilgrimages a pious Jew would have made: the Passover, the Feast of Tabernacles, and Pentecost. Where else would a religiously scrupulous person be at such a time? Surely not in Galilee, but in Judea. That is where the religious action is; it is apparently also where Jesus' disciples are located: "Leave here [Galilee] and go to Judea so that your disciples also may see the works you are doing" (v. 3). We might expect Jesus' brothers to understand him better, but "not even his brothers believed in him," regarding his purpose and mission (v. 5).

A further sign of the brothers' confusion is that they seem to think Jesus is seeking renown: "for no

away from political oppression and toward spiritual fulfillment.

While the geographical setting helps to establish Jesus' remarkable reputation, the primary context for the narrative is provided by the Festival of Booths. Celebrated as a thanksgiving for harvest and as a commemoration of the tents used by ancestors during their sojourn in the wilderness, the Feast of Booths was a seven-day autumnal festival that drew pilgrims to the temple for covenant renewal. It was recognized as the second most important Jewish festival, surpassed in significance only by Passover. Featured among the ceremonies of the Feast of Booths were rituals using water and light, which also serve as two recurrent Johannine metaphors for Jesus' self-proclamation of messianic identity.

Whether the evangelist situates events and exchanges in Galilee or Jerusalem, his theological concerns about time and messianic identity ground the circumstances in this passage and throughout chapter 7. Eschatological issues arise out of the contrast between the time of this world (*chronos*) and God's time (*kairos*), and christological questions about Jesus' identity and mission emerge from the challenges initially posed by Jesus' brothers. Although the Synoptic Gospels identify Jewish messianic expectations, Rudolf Schnackenburg observes that "it is not till the Fourth Gospel that the messianic question receives full and explicit treatment, since the evangelist is combining it with later debates between Jews and Christians."[1]

In these verses theological issues about time were initially raised by Jesus' brothers and continued to emerge in the accounts about the feast in Jerusalem, for which the covenant renewal ceremonies evoked eschatological expectations. The brothers' request for Jesus to announce himself in the context of the Jerusalem festival reflected their temporal disposition, rather than a recognition of and commitment to Jesus' eschatological mission. Although they had heard him proclaim the "words of eternal life" (6:68) and the coming time when God would be worshiped as spirit, they did not fully understand his messianic identity and mission. They did not yet comprehend that the covenant's renewal no longer was tied to the festal rituals in Jerusalem but, rather, to the incarnation of God in Jesus.

When they urged him to display his mighty works to disciples in Judea, Jesus responded, "My time has not yet come, but your time is always here" (v. 6). The judgment that follows is incisive, for Jesus insisted

1. Rudolf Schnackenburg, *The Gospel according to St. John*, vol. 2, *Commentary on Chapters 5–12* (New York: Crossroad, 1982), 146.

acclaim and possible acceptance. After feeding five thousand people bread and fish from one boy's lunch box, some people wanted to make him king. Unsurprisingly, his brothers attempt to seize the day. Jesus would have none of it, for the time was not right. Jerusalem, at least for him, was a dangerous place, not a city of festival, as it was for the multitudes.

Jesus then decided to go to the feast in Jerusalem, not publicly but privately. We learn that people were talking about him (RSV "muttering," NRSV "complaining," v. 12). No one was speaking openly; it was a whispering campaign. Some people were saying he was a good man; others said he was deceiving the people. Whatever the opinion, it was not said loudly. Jerusalem was wreathed in fear during one of the happiest, holiest feasts of the year.

So first we see that God's revelation of the Word made flesh causes crisis. When the costs of discipleship were made clear, some turned away, finding it too difficult to believe. Seeing this turning away (6:66), Jesus asked the twelve disciples, "Do you also wish to go away?" Peter replied: "Lord, to whom can we go? You have the words of eternal life" (v. 68).

Might this not characterize our generation, when our modus operandi in the church often mimics the larger society? In our perfectionist, idealistic age, we have lived too long with the notion that if the gospel is "preached correctly" then people will believe. We spend days and months tinkering with our worship or cutting the cloth of the gospel to appeal to those who have passed the church by or who threaten us with departure if we do not adhere to their agendas and inclinations.

The gospel of the Word made flesh offended and enticed; it awakened faith and enraged and sowed discord, all because Jesus came among them: "He came unto his own, and his own received him not" (1:11 KJV). Many did not believe, and the authorities tried to crush him. Now, as then, his presence creates a crisis of faith: some are drawn to him and remain faithful; others are enraged. The gospel then is the gospel now.

Second, the text invites us to acknowledge our fears and to overcome them. People are afraid to speak the truth even in love. In most (but not all) congregations, there is a prevailing mind-set (perhaps conservative, perhaps liberal, perhaps apathetic), and woe be unto those who challenge that common understanding. According to Jesus, supremely in John's Gospel, Christians are supposed to love one another as Christ has loved them (13:34), but they are often eager to set up standards,

references to secrecy and hiding (7:4, 10; 8:59), their theme is the self-revelation of the Messiah to Israel and of the Logos to the world, as seen in the words of Jesus' brothers, "Show yourself to the world" (v. 4). This revelation does not inspire universal belief, however. Instead, throughout John 7–8 there are interruptions and objections, and frequent references to decisions for or against Jesus, to divisions, and to plans to kill him. These divisions arise, in part, as people react to the contradiction between Jesus' self-revelation and his hiddenness.

Chapter 7 opens with "the Jews" seeking to kill Jesus, which raises one of the most important and difficult issues in the Gospel of John. This issue is highlighted again in verse 13: "no one would speak openly about him for fear of the Jews." Since everyone in the scene is Jewish—Jesus, his brothers, the crowds at the festival—we are presented with the peculiar image of Jews gripped by "fear of the Jews."

Such situations occur elsewhere in John (9:22; 19:38; 20:19), but nowhere else in the NT. They demonstrate that in John this term, "the Jews" (*hoi Ioudaioi*), generally does not refer to the entire Jewish people. Sometimes it may refer to Judeans as opposed to Galileans (e.g., 11:19, 31–36). Most frequently, however, it refers to Jewish religious authorities, those who make decisions that have binding consequences (e.g., 1:19; 5:9–16). It is these "Jews" whom other Jews fear and who pose a threat to Jesus' life. Often they argue with him; sometimes they seem to be identical with the Pharisees (1:19, 24; 9:13, 18).

One possible explanation for this state of affairs is that such statements reflect the context of the writer and early readers of the Gospel in the late first century—who were mainly of Jewish origin themselves but faced difficulties with local synagogue authorities—rather than the context of Jesus. This would explain references to believers in Jesus being "put out of the synagogue" (9:22; 12:42; 16:2), that is, prevented from worshiping with their fellow Jews. The reason for such an expulsion (which is not mentioned in any other ancient source) is not given, but it could reflect a desire to unify Jewish communities after the failure of the first revolt against the Romans in 70 CE.

Whatever the exact details, the Fourth Gospel's description of "Jews" who oppose Jesus and seek his life can give readers today a false and misleading picture. It may seem (as it has to Christians through the centuries) that the Jewish people *in general* were hostile to Jesus and his message, or even that he

one who wants to be widely known acts in secret" (v. 4a). They appear unaware that Jesus is in hiding because he has made strong enemies among the Jewish leaders in Jerusalem. In chapter 5, we read of Jesus healing on the Sabbath and declaring that he and the Father are equal (5:16–18). These issues, plus his subsequent railing against the Jewish leaders (5:19–47), have made for him lethal adversaries. To his brothers Jesus explains, "The world . . . hates me because I testify against it that its works are evil" (v. 7). Further, he explains, his time for a final trip to Jerusalem has not come. He bids them to go without him and remains in Galilee for a time.

Here is a confusing footnote for readers of John's Gospel. Jesus declares that his time has not come. Then, no sooner do his brothers head out of town than Jesus follows them secretly into Jerusalem. It seems his time *has* come, immediately after he gives notice that it has *not*. What is clear from this point on in the Gospel is that Jesus' return to Jerusalem is to be his last—and that this kairotic moment, which begins with his sneaking into Jerusalem, is to mark the beginning of the last episode of his life.

Further bewilderment follows. In Jerusalem, while Jesus is actually present, "the Jews" cannot find him, though they are "watching for him" and asking of his whereabouts (v. 11). Among the crowd, there is disagreement. Some speak of him as a "good man," and others are convinced he is "deceiving the crowd" (vv. 12–13); but all seem to understand that speaking about him openly will raise the ire of "the Jews." Thus they merely whisper and speculate.

What is the preacher to make of this befuddling narrative? Several homiletical directions present themselves. First, the preacher might explore the notion that the text contains much confusion about the nature of Jesus' ministry and mission. The confusion begins with those who know Jesus the best (his brothers) and continues through those who are eager to see him, but do not know what to make of him (the crowd). Jesus' enemies are a bit clearer— at least insofar as they know that Jesus means trouble for them—but they also misunderstand his purpose.

Following this vein, the preacher might examine the ways that people misunderstand Jesus' mission and purpose today. For some, he is a good teacher; for others, a world-class deceiver whose followers continue to deceive the world, even after his death. What about those of us who, like his family, know him the best? What are the ways that we also continue to misconstrue Jesus' message and demands?

John 7:1–13

Theological Perspective

that this world hates him because he declares and demonstrates that the temporal ways of the world are evil. Then, having sent them off to fulfill their religious responsibilities as pilgrims to the festival, Jesus remained in Galilee to act in accord with God's time.

The evangelist's christological concerns develop in relation to the brothers' misdirected sense of Jesus' mission. Their errant expectations also anticipated the crowd's responses to Jesus in Jerusalem, where some people were inhibited from speaking openly about him, while others wondered if he were conniving. The contrast of the responses to him signifies the polarizing potential of Jesus' message and mission. This divisiveness is vividly portrayed in the Synoptic Gospels when Jesus commissioned his disciples to stand boldly before councils and kings and to proclaim to them the good news of the coming kingdom, which, he warned, invites derision by many while exercising the power to separate brother from brother and children from their parents (Mark 13:9–13 and par.).

Throughout the Gospel the evangelist repeatedly uses festivals in Jerusalem as a framing device for presenting Jesus' theological discourses about his identity, mission, and authority. Here, though, the evangelist's account of Jesus' journey to Jerusalem for the festival introduces a theological conundrum. After Jesus had told his brothers that the time for his going to the festival had not fully come, Jesus nonetheless made the trip. This conflict between his expressed intent and actions raises questions about whether Jesus intentionally misled his brothers in order to separate from them and their misdirected expectations, or whether he newly perceived God's direction for him to make his way to the temple sooner than he had expected.

Rudolf Bultmann admits that even though it is impossible to reconcile the dissonance between Jesus' stated intent and his action, it is possible to mitigate the contrast by recognizing that the evangelist understands that Jesus did not go to Jerusalem in accord with his brothers' wishes to announce himself to the world, but that he made the journey "in secret," completing it privately rather than publicly, thereby maintaining focus on his divine mission. Whatever the narrative difficulty posed by the reversal of Jesus' intention, the theological emphasis of his action remains on the *kairos*, the transformative dimension of God's time, as opposed to the human *chronos* of his brothers' world and ways.[2]

JOSEPH L. PRICE

Pastoral Perspective

determine norms for conversation, for inclusivity, and for correct thinking that are enforced through intimidation, sarcasm, or patronizing attitudes. Many mainline denominations and congregations are rife with such behavior; perhaps this still prevents us from speaking "openly about him for fear of the authorities" (v. 13).

I suspect that every reader of these words can locate someone or some group in her congregation that is afraid to speak what truly burdens, for fear of being isolated, rejected, or disavowed. Shunning or controlling opinion is a problem when it not only diminishes the human spirit but also denies the Spirit of Christ in the body of believers. Happy are those churches where all are welcomed as sinners and as seekers after the truth, and can express their convictions without fear.

Third, knowing that the revelation of God among us can be divisive may lead us to seek to foster (with the Spirit's guidance) new communities within our churches. In such communities, people can love those with whom they disagree, people who do not fit in, and people who hold theological views against prevailing expectations. As individuals and congregations, we might begin to develop the fruits of the Spirit, rather than conform to a spirit of unanimity. Such developments may depend upon believing that the "court of highest authority" to which we are accountable is none other than Christ himself. We are not responsible for following opinion polls or for changing the rules of governance when the majority finally moves in what we believe is "the right direction." This text demonstrates that even in the context of danger and fear, which are our companions throughout the journey of our discipleship, such a way of life is invited—and expected—by the One who is the Way, the Truth, and the Life (14:6).

O. BENJAMIN SPARKS

---

2. Rudolf Bultmann, *The Gospel of John: A Commentary*, trans. G. R. Beasley-Murray (Philadelphia: Westminster Press, 1971), 294.

and his disciples were not Jews themselves (13:33; 20:19). Because this depiction represents not Jesus' circumstances but conflict decades later (and uses the exaggerated invective typical of ancient disputes), responsible interpreters must offer correctives to the hostility and prejudice that John's words have generated. A local controversy between two groups of Jews in antiquity must not continue to blight relations between Christians and Jews today.

Another puzzle here, less explosive but still difficult, is the motivation for Jesus' actions. He declines to go to the festival but then goes anyway, in secret. Is Jesus acting deceptively, or does he just change his mind? Either would seem problematic for the incarnate Logos, and in verses 1, 8, and 10 various ancient manuscripts attempt to mitigate Jesus' apparent vacillation or underhandedness. Is Jesus afraid of dying? Then why does he go to the festival at all? We may simply need to acknowledge that in John, Jesus acts on his own timing and for his own reasons, which may puzzle the other characters—and the readers (cf. 2:3–5; 11:1–15). This is related to the notion of Jesus' "time" (v. 6) or "hour" (7:30).

The lack of belief by Jesus' brothers aligns them with others in chapter 7 who are skeptical of him. (Note that in 19:25–27 he entrusts his mother to the Beloved Disciple, not to one of them.) As in 3:19–21 and 15:18–25, Jesus' message arouses unbelief, even hatred, from a world that prefers its own evil. The language is typical of John's dualism, without shades of gray. Jesus' testimony against the world's evil works consists of his own acts of obedience and love (7:17–18; see also 5:19, 30; 8:28; 12:44–50; 13:1, 34; 14:31).

"Complaining" in the NRSV of verse 12 seems overly specific. The basic sense is "murmuring" (Gk. *gongysmos*), which can have negative overtones (as in 6:41; cf. the Israelites under Moses, Exod. 17:3; Num. 11:1, etc.), but here includes both positive and negative remarks (cf. 7:32). The reader may well sympathize with these murmurers, given Jesus' mysterious behavior!

DAVID RENSBERGER

Another homiletical avenue is to follow Jesus' brothers in their well-intentioned desire to tell Jesus where to go and what to do. They seem eager to give Jesus their unsolicited and uninformed advice. How often might we be caught doing the same? The gospel is confusing; it is counterintuitive; it seems counterproductive to ordinary human progress. Surely, we think, Jesus could benefit by hearing from us regarding the best way to conduct his church's mission. After all, the incarnation was long ago, and he is out of touch. We are here now, living in a world that Jesus cannot understand. We can help him know how to build a church that meets people's needs, that answers their deepest questions, that makes the faith relevant, that gives people purpose, that makes the gospel palatable in a pluralistic age.

We might even offer Jesus advice on when his "time should come," as do those loud voices that appear every decade or so proclaiming some insider knowledge regarding the imminent return of Christ. We are very good at telling Jesus what to do. How good are we at listening to what he tells us as he testifies that the works of the world are evil?

A third approach might be to explore the ways that Jesus is hidden from us, even when he has made himself present. We can think, here, of those who claim to be spiritual but not religious—those who fruitlessly pursue spiritual pathways while assiduously steering clear of the obvious beauty of the gospel.

Whatever the preacher's approach, the lingering and pressing question is this: what is the good news to be proclaimed from this pericope? It can be this: this mystifying story is but one part of a larger narrative, the purpose of which is utterly clear. The writer pens this Gospel in order that all who read it or hear it proclaimed will know that Jesus is the Christ, the Word made flesh, the Light of the world.

CLAYTON J. SCHMIT

John 7:14–24

¹⁴About the middle of the festival Jesus went up into the temple and began to teach. ¹⁵The Jews* were astonished at it, saying, "How does this man have such learning, when he has never been taught?" ¹⁶Then Jesus answered them, "My teaching is not mine but his who sent me. ¹⁷Anyone who resolves to do the will of God will know whether the teaching is from God or whether I am speaking on my own. ¹⁸Those who speak on their own seek their own glory; but the one who seeks the glory of him who sent him is true, and there is nothing false in him.

¹⁹"Did not Moses give you the law? Yet none of you keeps the law. Why are you looking for an opportunity to kill me?" ²⁰The crowd answered, "You have a demon! Who is trying to kill you?" ²¹Jesus answered them, "I performed one work, and all of you are astonished. ²²Moses gave you circumcision (it is, of course, not from Moses, but from the patriarchs), and you circumcise a man on the sabbath. ²³If a man receives circumcision on the sabbath in order that the law of Moses may not be broken, are you angry with me because I healed a man's whole body on the sabbath? ²⁴Do not judge by appearances, but judge with right judgment."

Theological Perspective

At the beginning of this passage the evangelist situates Jesus in the center of Jewish life by locating him in Jerusalem during the middle of the popular Feast of Booths, the annual festival that celebrated covenant renewal. In so doing, the evangelist emphasizes that Jesus' teaching fully engages Jewish life and worship.

Yet the placement of this passage about the teaching and authority of Jesus in the context of the festival proves problematic, because the event that had provoked the dispute with religious authorities had occurred during an earlier visit to Jerusalem when he had healed a crippled man on the Sabbath (5:1–18). Thus, either the timing of Jesus' exchange with the religious leaders is months removed from the event, or the evangelist has blended this discourse, which is related to the cripple's cure at Beth-zatha, with an account about a subsequent visit to Jerusalem by Jesus. Because of the close thematic continuity and the festival context between this passage and the story of the healing of the cripple at Beth-zatha, Rudolf Bultmann takes the latter possibility to be more likely, and he considers the passage in conjunction with the earlier account of the Sabbath healing and Jesus' identification with

*See "'The Jews' in the Fourth Gospel" on pp. xi–xiv.

Pastoral Perspective

Jesus, who went privately to the Harvest Festival (Sukkot, the Festival of Booths), has now gone to the temple and has begun to teach. His teaching is astonishing and controversial. The crowd wonders where he has received such learning, because he has never been trained. Since all teachers of the law have been trained, they question Jesus' authority.

He answers them like this: my teaching is not mine, but the teaching of God, who sent me. When you resolve to do the will of God, then you will recognize that my teaching is from God, and not simply my own. Those who speak for themselves seek their own glory, but the one who seeks the glory of "the One who sent him" is true, and there is nothing false about him.

Then he tells them that they neither understand nor keep the law of Moses, even as he is being accused of violating the law by healing a paralytic on the Sabbath. He says that since circumcision can occur on the Sabbath, surely, in the spirit of the law, he can heal a man's whole body on the Sabbath. He knows there are some who want to kill him; when he acknowledges this, the crowd accuses him of having a demon.

The text opens a controversy for us from which the whole church can profit. Here we come face to face with a difficulty: how do we know that what

Exegetical Perspective

Continuing from the immediately preceding section, we find Jesus at the Festival of Booths (Sukkot), which lasts seven days, so that its "middle" would be day four. Jesus has allowed speculation and controversy about him to build up (7:11–13) before appearing in the temple and beginning to teach. He continues to teach and debate there through the end of chapter 8 (7:28; 8:20, 59). In the Synoptic Gospels, Jesus comes to Jerusalem for his final week, which forms the only occasion for him to teach in the temple. In John, he also acts and speaks there in 2:13–22 (at Passover). In all these instances, there are connections between his teaching in the temple and his death.

The controversies in this passage originate in 5:18–47, where the same combination of issues (the divine origin of Jesus' teaching, his doing of God's will, his glory, Moses and the law, efforts to kill Jesus, and his activities on the Sabbath) is introduced. These issues, concerning themes that were often debated by Jews of that time, inform the dispute over whether Jesus can be the one sent from God. Jesus' long speech in chapter 5 is addressed simply to "the Jews"—not the Jewish people as a whole, but authorities who enforce Sabbath law and monitor religious claims (see 5:10–18). Here he has two separate dialogue partners.

Homiletical Perspective

In the Gospel of John, all narratives, miracles, and signs point in one direction. They identify Jesus as the Son of God, come to redeem the world. Within the narratives, the author provides explanations so as to make sure that his readers understand this purpose. Whenever the author recounts Jesus' teaching, he is addressing the church with messages from God's own Word, made flesh in Jesus. This pericope is a thread within the tapestry of John's Gospel that carries the same bold message. Those who are faithful (those who "resolve to do the will of God," v. 17) will be those who understand the broad message that all of Jesus' teaching, miracles, and actions are signs that point to God.

The presenting issues in the text are, first, Jesus' teaching and authority ("How does this man have such learning, when he has never been taught?" v. 15) and, second, his healing. "I performed one work" (v. 21a) refers to the healing of the lame man on the Sabbath in 5:1–15. In John's account, this action so enraged Jewish leaders that they sought to capture and kill the man they considered a false prophet and an enemy of Mosaic Law (5:18; 7:19). Here Jesus tries to explain himself. Either his teaching and actions are in line with God's purpose and laws, or they are not. Either he is subverting the faith of Israel with new teaching, or he is presenting a clearer view of God's intentions for his chosen people.

John 7:14–24

Theological Perspective

"God his own Father, thereby making himself equal to God" (5:18).[1]

Although the chronological accuracy of the events in this passage is in question, the theological core of the passage remains essentially unaffected by its literary position in the Gospel. The theological issues that generate Jesus' interchange with the religious leaders relate to his respect for the law and his authority for instruction, and the theological question that directs his interaction with the crowd is associated with their concern about understanding his identity. Still, by placing these exchanges within the context of the Feast of Booths, the evangelist implicitly underscores Jesus' recognition of the significance of Jewish pious practices, if not faithful adherence to Mosaic Law.

Underlying the puzzlement of the religious leaders is their question about whether instructional authority can be derived apart from the law and tradition. After engaging the religious leaders on the issue of authority, Jesus denounces them for wanting to kill him because, according to them, he violated Sabbath restrictions when he healed the crippled man. In response to Jesus' accusation that they want to kill him, the crowd raises questions about his identity, not simply his authority. In today's parlance they cry, "Are you crazy? You must be paranoid if you think that anyone is trying to kill you." The crowd's response distinctly reflects the Johannine emphasis on the authority of Jesus expressed in word. In contrast to the Synoptic Gospels, which align the people's suspicion that Jesus might be possessed by a demon with the power by which he performs miracles, in this Gospel it is his words that prompt the crowd to wonder whether he is demon possessed.

Although the evangelist does not identify the content of Jesus' teaching that had prompted the religious leaders to marvel at his insight, he does provide a sample of Jesus' wisdom in response to his challengers' questions about his authority and his respect for the religious law. In Jesus' day, authority for instruction was earned from decades of devotion to careful midrashic studies with a rabbi. Unlike seminary studies today, which can be completed in a few years, rabbinical education in the first century required that a preadolescent boy apprentice himself to a rabbi, shadowing him in his studies and listening to his sermons and instruction for a decade or more. As alumni of such an educational process, the

Pastoral Perspective

Jesus says is true? His answer is one that we are particularly loath to hear. It takes away our power of decision. Jesus says that only those who do God's will know whether his teaching is from God. This does not mean that doing good works will lead us to spiritual insight, nor is it a call to salvation by good works. Instead, we are called to believe in the One whom God has sent. Then we will know the truth.[1]

We do not choose ourselves into faith. We respond and witness to the faith that is given to us. When we believe Jesus, putting our entire trust in him, then we will know that what he says is true and that he is who he says he is.

Considered another way, we are not in control of the revelation of God in Jesus Christ. It is not ours; it does not even belong to the church. The church proclaims it, lives it—always imperfectly—and rejoices in Jesus Christ, who is that revelation in word and sacrament. Still, the church does not own it.

We may not mix and match, taking some parts of the faith and leaving off other parts. We may not tailor it to suit our own purposes, our own commitments, or our own dreams. We may not decide which parts are palatable to us, which make sense to our precious postmodern sensibilities, and which do not. Instead, the revelation of God in Jesus Christ confronts us, as his teaching confronted his hearers long ago. When we respond in faith (in trust and belief), we will know that the revelation is true. The one who meets us is the great "I AM," the one who was and is and is to come, the Alpha and the Omega (Rev. 1:8). That same one meets us in the person of Jesus.

The notion that we discover truth, even divine and everlasting truth, through the study of religions, through the investigation of the universe in its macro- and microdimensions, and through explorations by communities of scholars, is pervasive in church and culture. Such an understanding concludes that if we learn to read the universe, the human mind through all the ages, and the spiritual riches of humankind, then we will arrive at truth, at reality.

This text and the Gospel of John (indeed, the entire gospel of Jesus Christ) make a different claim: we believe in order to understand. Those of us who trust that claim witness to a different reality that is prior to all the aids of scholarship and reason.

We do not reject human learning, imagination, or beauty. Rather, we know what is ultimately true, because we have made a commitment to the one whom we cannot prove, but who proves us; the one

---

1. Rudolf Bultmann, *The Gospel of John: A Commentary*, trans. G. R. Beasley-Murray (Philadelphia: Westminster Press, 1971), 273–78.

1. Lesslie Newbigin, *The Light Has Come, An Exposition of the Fourth Gospel* (Grand Rapids: Eerdmans, 1982), 95.

Exegetical Perspective

Besides the authorities who are concerned with Jesus' teaching credentials, there is "the crowd," which is unaware of the authorities' decision, reported in 5:18, and is afraid of them (7:11–13). "The crowd" seems open to faith in Jesus but has divided opinions (7:31, 40–44). Ultimately, the Pharisees, who seem equivalent to the religious authorities, contemptuously condemn them as ignorant (7:49). Thus the narrator distinguishes between authorities and common people in dialogue with Jesus; the authorities' criticism of Jesus' lack of formal training may identify him with "the crowd" (7:15, 49).

Jesus, however, does not seem to distinguish between the two groups. His tone with both is challenging and argumentative. It continues to be so and grows harsher and more hostile throughout chapters 7 and 8. Jesus' audiences respond with objections and accusations. While there are a few such passages in the Synoptics, the polemics in John are more sustained and unrelenting, reflecting the circumstances of the later Christian community for which this Gospel was written, not the circumstances of Jesus' contemporaries. Thus the background for these polemics lies not in a debate between Jesus and "the Jews," but in debates between Jewish Christians and other Jews. The contentious language used in these disputes, though it may seem inappropriate today, was not uncommon in controversies among ancient Jewish groups or Greek philosophical schools.

When asked where his teaching comes from, since he has not been formally trained, Jesus responds that it comes directly from God. Most ancient schools of thought, both Jewish and Greek, valued the ability to trace one's ideas back through a chain of teachers and regarded skeptically claims to direct divine inspiration. In John, the question of the source of and authority behind Jesus' teaching arises several times, especially in chapters 7 and 8, but also in 3:31–36; 5:19–47; 12:44–50. In all these places, Jesus is presented as claiming that his words and his deeds are "from God," that is, that he has observed and learned them from God in a way unlike anyone else.

Such claims are not found in the Synoptic Gospels, and likely represent the Johannine theology about Jesus rather than Jesus' own teaching about himself. Yet even in the Synoptics, Jesus does not cite any prior authority (note Mark 1:22, 27). Though John takes this point to its ultimate conclusion ("the Father and I are one," 10:30), for the NT church generally, the message of Jesus could not simply be incorporated into traditional patterns of inherited learning. It was a revelation from God, which led

Homiletical Perspective

The text contains a notable irony. The crowd assumes he is a man without learning and is confused by his ability to teach so authoritatively. Jesus does not deny that he is without learning, but indicates that his teaching comes directly from God. Then, in building his case, Jesus uses a sophisticated device that would be known by learned people who had studied rhetoric. He argues his case for healing on the Sabbath on the basis of analogy where a lesser thing is used to prove a greater thing. If a child can be circumcised on the Sabbath in order to incorporate him into the faith, how much more appropriate should it be for a member of the house of Israel to be bodily restored for life in faith?

The judgment of the Jewish crowd regarding Jesus' teaching and miracles is skewed because his words and actions are so extraordinary. How could they help but see them from a human perspective? Jesus tells them that so long as they view such things through their limited perspective (judging by "appearances"), they will miss what God is doing. However, those who see things with "right judgment" (v. 24) will see how Jesus' teaching and actions are in perfect consonance with God's will. It is as if they are looking at a leaf on the surface of a gentle river. The wind may be blowing the leaf in a certain direction, giving the appearance that the river flows in that direction. Looking deeper, with right judgment, it may be discovered that the course of the river is in the opposite direction.

How do we see the teachings and actions of Jesus today? Surely, we proclaim them to be signs of his unity with God. Yet do we too not need correction for seeing things as they appear, rather than with right judgment? Like the Jewish crowd, we have our own habits of misperception, born of limited judgment and the powers of habit and misinterpretation.

Countless examples present themselves to the preacher. Consider the moralistic sermon, wherein Jesus' death on the cross is reduced to an act of generous behavior. We hear it in sermons that exhort us to be more like Jesus: "If Jesus could give his life for you, can you not then give of yourselves for others?" It is reminiscent of parental martyrdom: "Do not worry about me; all I did for you was give birth to you," "I work two jobs so that you can have an education," and so forth. Such words appear to be about the good news of Christ. Judging more carefully, we see that we are not hearing good news at all. This kind of preaching is designed to produce guilt and begrudging action. The sermon may sound appropriately religious, but it is not the good news

Theological Perspective

religious leaders can hardly fathom how Jesus can be so insightful without having pursued years of study like theirs. In contrast to traditional rabbinic studies, Jesus identifies the source of his teaching with the one who has sent him, reinforcing his identity with God as his Father, a theme that runs throughout the Gospel (3:16; 5:19–24).

By ascribing authority to the one who has sent him, Jesus also deflects and rejects the accusations by religious leaders that he is seeking self-recognition through his teaching, and he further challenges them to draw their own conclusion about the one who has sent him. Continuing the incisive instruction that has wowed the religious leaders, Jesus offers this penetrating proposition: Because his words and deeds reveal God's will and ways, those who know God will recognize the source of his authority and the truth of his instruction.

Thus Jesus challenges the religious leaders to consider whether they truly are devoted to God's will or whether, in search of their own self-recognition and acclaim, they are jealous of his divine wisdom. In this way Jesus warns the religious leaders about their possible vanity in seeking glory for themselves through their own dissection of the law. While the religious leaders errantly derive assurance from their legalistic approach, they miss the reality of the law, which "is intended to make them aware of God's command and at the same time of their dependence on the glory which God gives."[2]

Turning attention then to the issue of Sabbath observance, Jesus evinces his full understanding of the law by pointing to the exception that a boy can be circumcised on the Sabbath if it is the eighth day following his birth. How much more, then, Jesus poses, would the covenant be fulfilled and the law upheld by curing a cripple on the Sabbath than by cutting an infant's flesh on that day? Reflecting on this question, Jesus enjoins the religious leaders to refrain from making superficial judgments, but "to judge with right judgment" by employing an ethic of compassion. In so doing he calls for all—religious leaders and the crowd alike—to embrace the intent of the law, rather than trying to apply the letter of its instruction.

JOSEPH L. PRICE

Pastoral Perspective

who reads us, who shows us ourselves, brings us to our senses, and calls us by name. As Matthew said of Jesus, "He taught them as one having authority, and not as their scribes" (Matt. 7:29).

As I reflected on this text, two old hymns rattled around in my head. The first, "Trust and Obey," from my childhood, was sung at revivals in country churches by folk who bore the ills of their time and place and who followed as best they could with kindness and faith. Together they sang: "Trust and obey, for there's no other way to be happy in Jesus, but to trust and obey."[2] I would not make a case for happiness as now popularly understood, but trusting and obeying Jesus leads to a confident, knowledgeable faith in the authority of his words and life.

The second hymn, anonymous, remained in mainline hymnals through the 1970s: "I sought the Lord, and afterward I knew, he moved my soul to seek him, seeking me. It was not I that found; O Savior true, no, I was found of thee."[3] Is that not the substance of the gospel? After all, the story of the human race, as recounted in ancient times and in human history, is that every human attempt to take heaven by storm, to grasp the knowledge of God, to control what is not ours, leads to disaster. So God reaches out to us and becomes, for us, the Way, the Truth, and the Life in Jesus Christ. Believing that leads us to know his teaching is true.

O. BENJAMIN SPARKS

---

2. Bultmann, *Gospel of John*, 273.

2. John H. Sammis, "Trust and Obey," *Seventh-Day Adventist Hymnal* (Hagerstown, MD: Review and Herald Pub., 1985), #590.
3. "I Sought the Lord, and Afterward I Knew," *The Psalter Hymnal (Gray)* (Grand Rapids: CRC Publications, 1987), #618.

to the idea that Jesus himself was a revelation from God. This fundamental distinction may have been part of what carved so deep a division between the Christian community and the synagogal Judaism from which it departed.

The test for validating the divine origin of Jesus' mission—namely, resolving to do God's will (v. 17)—seems so simple that we may wonder if it really means anything. Reference to John 6:35–46 may help. Early Christians reflected on why some people believed and some did not. John's solution is a dialectic between divine and human choice. In chapter 6, Jesus speaks of people being given, drawn, and taught by God; from the human side, however, one must come and must *learn*. That means being prepared to drop presuppositions about what and how God will speak, and to learn from God, not dictate to God.

There must be a willingness to accept God's will, even if it takes an unexpected form, such as the divine Logos in human flesh and a crucified Messiah. Those who open up to God's acts, instead of maintaining their own positions and seeing God only in things as they have always been, can perceive Jesus' teaching as being from God. For John, this openness is "believing." It is not a purely internal, private faith, but includes public adherence to Jesus and to the community of those who believe in him, even when that is a difficult minority position.

For all the exaltation of John's thinking about Jesus, Jesus as God's revelation continues to point toward God, rather than seeking his own glory (v. 18). Jesus' glory comes from God, not from himself (8:49–55), and this contrasts with his opponents (5:41–44; 12:42–43).

Verses 21–23 refer back to 5:1–9, a healing that took place on a Sabbath. The law is seldom a major issue in John; this is the only instance of debate over Jewish practice. It is comparable to disputes about the Sabbath in the Synoptics, such as Matthew 12:9–12. In the controversy over the divine origin of Jesus' teaching, the point may be that, even on the authorities' terms, Jesus' actions were justified; by rabbinic standards, however, it is not a strong argument.

DAVID RENSBERGER

that in Christ we have new life filled with abundance and joy.

There are other things we see darkly, without right judgment. On the way to proclaiming the true good news, it can be fitting to bring some of these things to mind. Among them might be things that feel bad to us when they actually are good for our spiritual or physical well-being; self-sacrifice that feels like a burden but often turns out to be a holy joy; being generous with our wealth that appears to be a burdensome obligation but is experienced by those who give liberally as a leap into the arms of God.

Finally, the question remains: How do Christian people learn to judge rightly? We learn by dwelling with our Teacher, listening to his word, which is the Word made flesh. His teaching may be challenged, but finally it must be embraced. When it is taken to heart, it has the power to change our heart and our capacity to perceive. To judge rightly is to look for God in all things, rather than to seek the devil behind every bush. (Note that in the Gospel of John, Jesus casts out no demons; his work is focused on pointing to God, not toward evil.) As we seek the will of God, God will appear in everything that presents itself: as an unexpected blessing in a time of misfortune, as beauty in humility, as contentment in sacrifice, as abundance in times of want, as joy in the face of adversity, as Christ in the face of an enemy. Right judgment is a habit of the heart that overrules human perspective.

CLAYTON J. SCHMIT

John 7:25–31

²⁵Now some of the people of Jerusalem were saying, "Is not this the man whom they are trying to kill? ²⁶And here he is, speaking openly, but they say nothing to him! Can it be that the authorities really know that this is the Messiah? ²⁷Yet we know where this man is from; but when the Messiah comes, no one will know where he is from." ²⁸Then Jesus cried out as he was teaching in the temple, "You know me, and you know where I am from. I have not come on my own. But the one who sent me is true, and you do not know him. ²⁹I know him, because I am from him, and he sent me." ³⁰Then they tried to arrest him, but no one laid hands on him, because his hour had not yet come. ³¹Yet many in the crowd believed in him and were saying, "When the Messiah comes, will he do more signs than this man has done?"

Theological Perspective

Despite its brevity, this passage touches upon several prominent theological themes that characterize John's Gospel. In addition to its focus on the christological issue of Jesus' messianic identity, which is the dominant theme of chapter 7, the passage also addresses issues of authority and eschatology.

At the outset of the pericope, the evangelist identifies Jesus as interacting with a distinct audience that plays a crucial role in addressing christological concerns. Elsewhere in the Gospel, Jesus is portrayed instructing his disciples, speaking to crowds, and debating with religious leaders. Here the group specified as "people of Jerusalem" makes its single appearance in the Johannine narrative. The distinction of the Jerusalemites is particularly instructive because of its contrast to the previous audience of "a crowd," who likely were pilgrims to Jerusalem during the Festival of Booths. Unlike the crowd, who had expressed disbelief about Jesus' assertion of a death threat by the religious leaders (7:19–20), the "people of Jerusalem" probably would have been familiar with and often dependent upon the penchant of the religious leaders to expose false messiahs. It is also more likely that these residents of Jerusalem would have known about the increasing hostility of the religious leaders toward Jesus, including specific threats against him.

Pastoral Perspective

In the preceding verses from chapter 7, the crowd was in conflict over whether Jesus' teaching was true. Could they trust what he said and proclaimed? He told them that they will trust the truth of his teaching when they do the will of the One who sent him.

In these verses, the controversy among the people shifts to his origin. Since he is speaking openly and the crowd knows that the authorities want to kill him, they wonder if he is the Messiah after all. The authorities have made no move against him, so maybe he is the Messiah. Yet how can that be so, since many in the crowd know where he is from? They know his address, and they also know that when the Messiah comes, no one will know where he is from.

Jesus speaks authoritatively into this confusion. He tells them that even though they know him and know his address, they do not really know where he is from because they do not know the One who sent him. Jesus has been sent to them. He has not come to them on his own accord, just as he does not speak to them on his own accord. He says that they know neither the One who sent him nor the One who gives him the words to speak.

Finally, the authorities try to arrest Jesus, but cannot because his time (his hour) has not yet come. Then those in the crowd who have been impressed

Exegetical Perspective

As in the preceding section, there seem to be two distinct groups in dialogue with Jesus here. We might think that "some of the people of Jerusalem" are identical with "the crowd" (7:12, 20, 31–32, 40–44). However, these Jerusalemites, unlike "the crowd," are aware of threats against Jesus (v. 25) and skeptical of his messianic identity (vv. 26–27), while "the crowd" remains open to believing in him. Thus the Jerusalemites seem more aligned with the "authorities" (*archontes*, v. 26, rather than "Jews" or "Pharisees") than with "the crowd." They may be citizens or natives of the city, as opposed to visitors in town for the holiday. "They" in verse 25 presumably refers to the authorities who seek to kill Jesus (7:1; 5:18). It is not clear who is meant by "they" in verse 30, whether the authorities or the Jerusalemites themselves, though obviously an arrest can only be made by people in power.

The author has constructed a dramatic scene with a variety of characters and complex levels of belief, half-belief, suspicion, and antagonism. "The people of Jerusalem" are surprised that Jesus is allowed to speak openly, and they question his messianic credentials. At least some of "the crowd" believe in him and affirm those credentials. Note that the questions in verses 26 and 31 are phrased in such a way as to expect negative answers: the Jerusalemites express

Homiletical Perspective

Jesus does something in chapter 5 that sets the stage for all that takes place in chapter 7. This has led some experts to speculate that the material in the sixth chapter of John has been inserted into the original structure of the Gospel. Regardless of the veracity of such a claim, it is clear that the healing of the invalid on the Sabbath in 5:1–18 sets a foundation for all that follows in chapter 7. It also sets the stage for a number of homiletical considerations.

In chapter 5 we are told of Jesus' second trip to Jerusalem. His first trip is recounted in chapter 2, where Jesus cleanses the temple and meets Nicodemus under the cloak of darkness. The third trip occurs here in chapter 7, beginning in verse 10 when Jesus follows his brothers to Jerusalem during the Feast of Tabernacles. The events in this pericope continue to unfold during that feast.

It was during Jesus' second trip to Jerusalem that he performed the signal event that made him enemies among the Jewish leadership. Not only did he heal on the Sabbath; he then proceeded to imply that he is one with the Father (5:17), to make that claim explicitly (5:19–27), and to accuse the Jewish leadership of unbelief (5:36–46). All of this caused the leaders to hate Jesus and seek to put him to death. As noted twice in chapter 7 (vv. 8, 30), providence protects him because his time has not

John 7:25–31

Theological Perspective

In this passage, the people of Jerusalem are perplexed about the possible messianic identity of Jesus. First, they wonder why the religious authorities, whom they already think want to kill Jesus, have not seized him, since he had made such a profound public impression. The Jerusalemites even suspect that the religious authorities might really recognize the messianic identity of Jesus, thereby prompting them temporarily to forgo an attempt at his arrest.

In general, the people of Jerusalem relied upon the religious authorities to identify the true Messiah. In one way, their dependence upon these authorities for messianic verification suggests an uncertainty about the people's own ability to discern revealed truth. In another way, as Ernst Haenchen observes, their acquiescence ultimately shifts the blame to the religious leaders for the lack of messianic recognition and for the subsequent arrest and execution of Jesus.[1]

While the people of Jerusalem looked to the religious leaders for certification of the Messiah, they also looked around for signs associated with his appearance. Because they anticipated that his arrival might be sudden (Mal. 3:1) and mysterious—that "no one will know where he is from" (v. 27)—they question whether Jesus fully fits their expectations. Their consternation specifically arises out of the conflict between their recognition of his recent whereabouts in Galilee and their anticipation that the Messiah would be born in the lineage of David and would come from Bethlehem (7:41–42).

Responding to their bewildered expressions, Jesus distinguishes his lineage and authority from their worldly perceptions. He points out that while they know him as a Galilean, they do not truly know him, because they do not know the One who has sent him, nor do they know his kinship with the One who has sent him. Although the people can identify Jesus with a geographic region, they do not recognize his transcendent origin, which can be credited, as Rudolf Bultmann points out, only when one "recognizes his authority, hears his word, and disregards his person as it appears to the world."[2] In a theological sense that the evangelist repeatedly underscores, Jesus fulfills the expectation of the mysterious origin of the Messiah because his true identity—as Logos throughout time and as the Son who is now sent from the Father—is unknown to them (e.g., 1:1–5; 1:14; 8:14; 8:23; 10:24–30).

Pastoral Perspective

by his signs wonder whether, when the Messiah comes, he will do even more signs than this man.

Confusion reigns. This is speculation run amuck.

The passage is one of several windows John throws open to let the readers see the variety of reactions to Jesus. Just as now, those who know Jesus try to understand him by putting him in categories of their own experience. They insist on their own terms—knowing him not as he presents himself, but as they want him to be. In their looking and speculating, they want to avoid being confronted by the living God. They want a human-sized God, rather than a God become flesh. There is ample evidence in the Hebrew Scriptures of just such behavior toward God's revelation to Moses and the prophets.

Similarly, we seek out the human-sized God, rather than the God become flesh. We try to pin down exactly when Jesus was born, when he lived, when and how he died. We are forever inquiring into the historical veracity of the Gospel accounts of his life, often wondering why we have only some of the existing accounts in our Scripture. We begin to question whether the testimony of Scripture is true. Perhaps the canon represents the prejudices of one sect in the church that gained dominance over other equally valid accounts of Jesus' life. Even if we have answered those questions, we are still confronted with the mystery of the Word made flesh, come to dwell among us. Divine mysteries are bigger than our human inquiries and God's presence overwhelms our avoidance tactics.

We can learn about, and write volumes on, the origin and life of Jesus. With the apostles, we may bear witness to his life, death, and resurrection. Still, we will not grasp who he is by human criteria alone. To encounter him truly, we must be grasped by him.

These verses (indeed, all of chapter 7) force us to see that speculation and argument, questioning, debating, wondering, and deciding for or against the truth of these claims amount to nothing, over against the poor woman or poor man who kneels at the feet of Jesus and begs for mercy and healing, or asks forgiveness, or reaches out in desperation.

We Christians are all too easily divided into opposing camps: liberal versus conservative, evangelical versus progressive, welcoming versus exclusionary, first world versus developing world, classical worshipers versus those who like praise music. Everywhere fault lines crisscross the fabric of the church.

Underlying all these divides is a much more fundamental question: Do we believe that we have a

1. Ernst Haenchen, *John 2: A Commentary on the Gospel of John Chapters 7–21*, trans. and ed. Robert W. Funk, Hermeneia—A Critical and Historical Commentary on the Bible (Philadelphia: Fortress Press, 1984), 15.
2. Rudolf Bultmann, *The Gospel of John: A Commentary*, trans. G. R. Beasley-Murray (Philadelphia: Westminster Press, 1971), 296.

their skepticism by doubting that the authorities acknowledge Jesus as Messiah, and "the crowd" express their openness by doubting that the Messiah will do more signs than Jesus.

This raises an issue about what credentials were expected for someone who was claimed to be the Messiah. There was no single, uniform messianic doctrine among Jews in antiquity, so there was no checklist of messianic credentials. "The Messiah" usually refers to an anointed (Heb. *mashiakh*) king expected to restore the kingdom of David and thus Israel's political independence as part of God's final intervention in history. There were diverse beliefs (including various eschatologies) about this intervention; besides the Davidic Messiah, various groups anticipated an eschatological prophet or priest or other figure (1:19–21; 7:40–41).

Within this diversity, there is evidence (albeit rather slender) for the concept of a "hidden" Messiah, whose location would be unknown (that is, his location immediately prior to his being revealed, not his birthplace). The Jerusalemites may refer to such a belief in verse 27. By contrast, in verses 41–42 some of "the crowd" refers to an expectation that Bethlehem would be the Messiah's birthplace. In either case, the fact that Jesus had come from Nazareth in Galilee was problematic, especially as there is no reference to his birth in Bethlehem in John.

The question of Jesus' origin, of where he is from, is important in John, especially in chapter 8 (8:14, 19–26, 39–42). The Jerusalemites suppose that they know where Jesus is from, which for them undermines his messianic status. Jesus repeats their claim rather sarcastically (v. 28) and proceeds to reject it. If they really knew the place from *where* he came (heaven; see 3:31; 6:32–59), they would also know the One from *whom* he came, that is, God (13:3). Their failure to recognize Jesus' heavenly origin implies a failure to know God. In John, Jesus alone knows his origin, and so genuinely knows God, from whom he comes. He shares this knowledge with those who believe in him, and thus they gain from him life-giving knowledge of God (16:26–30; 17:1–8).

As to the "signs" expected by "the crowd," there is little or no evidence that the Davidic Messiah was expected to work miracles. Miraculous signs would more likely have been associated with an eschatological prophet (Deut. 18:15), who, like Moses or Joshua, might also be associated with liberation or victory over foreign nations (6:14–15). The question, "When the Messiah comes, will he do more

fully come. However, this trip to Jerusalem marks the beginning of his kairotic time. From this point onward, Jesus remains in the area of Jerusalem up to the very end, and the pressure to capture and silence him mounts until he is arrested (18:1–12) and his passion unfolds.

There is a great irony that stands as the centerpiece of this pericope. On the one hand, the people of Jerusalem are fascinated with Jesus. They speculate on whether he is a good man or a deceiver (v. 12), whether or not he has the authority to teach (vv. 15–17), and finally, whether or not he is the Messiah (v. 26). They are impressed with his ability to heal and have a mythic expectation that the Messiah will be a miracle worker in the tradition of Moses and Elijah. They even ask, "When the Messiah comes, will he do more signs than this man has done?" (7:31).

On the other hand, the people expect that the Messiah will come from an unknown place, emerging on the scene in the last days ("no one will know where he is from," v. 27). The people's dilemma is that they *do* know where Jesus hails from. He is from Nazareth. Thus he cannot be the Messiah, even if his authoritative teaching and miracles suggest that he is.

Here is the enigmatic surprise: they think they know where Jesus is from, but they do not—or they do not fully know. They think he has merely come from Galilee. In reality, he has also come from the Father. Just as anticipated, the Messiah (who actually is this charismatic Nazarene) does come from an unknown place.

Jesus pounces on their ignorance: "Then Jesus cried out" (v. 28), declaring that he is from God. In other words (though Jesus does not use the title in his teaching), he is saying that he is the Messiah.

This is a rich irony for the preacher in the text. Christian readers have grown so accustomed to Jesus' dispute with the religious authorities in Jerusalem that we overlook how human their response to Jesus is. Why would they not be curious about him, his teachings, his miracles? Why would they not speculate about whether he is the Messiah? Why would they not live according to their traditions and myths? We might find them obtuse, but they are basing their speculations on sketchy data. While the Gospel author makes his point clearly and strongly for his readers (Jesus is God incarnate), participants in the story have no such clear testimony. They are piecing it together as they go along. What an amazing thing it is that "many in the crowd believed in him" (v. 31)! They had little to build their faith upon.

John 7:25–31

Theological Perspective

As Jesus reasons with the people about how they think they know him, he directs attention again to the One who has sent him, stating, "I have not come on my own" (v. 28). Thus he again aligns his wisdom, power, and authority with the One whom, he claims, they do not know. Whether it was this accusation or some other portion of his proclamation that angered the audience is not clear. The evangelist reports that the people tried to arrest him, but because "his hour had not yet come" (v. 30)—an apocalyptic affirmation that his life was in sync with God's time—no one was able to lay hands on him.

This first attempt to apprehend Jesus anticipates the final conflict that would arise during Passover. Although charges of blasphemy have not been connected to their desire to arrest him, Jesus' preceding discourse makes that connection, as he claims that, unlike his challengers, he knows the One who has sent him. At this point, a charge of blasphemy has not been leveled against Jesus. However, the climax of the preceding exchange between Jesus and the people of Jerusalem anticipates the religious leaders' reason for his eventual arrest on that charge, because he asserts that he knows—and is from—the One who sent has him (vv. 28–29).

Apart from the mob's action in trying to arrest Jesus, some of the Jerusalemites accepted Jesus as the Messiah (7:43), because they recognized the magnitude of his deeds: "When the Messiah comes," they wondered, "will he do more signs than this man has done?" (v. 31). Although the evangelist attributes their belief in Jesus to his having performed such marvelous acts, this point reflects early Christian arguments about the messianic identity of Jesus, because miraculous acts were not a part of Jewish messianic expectations. By contrast, Rudolf Schnackenburg avers that Jewish expectations for the messianic age held that the elimination of disease and death would be accomplished, not by a messenger or the Messiah, but by God. Consequently, the Johannine emphasis on Jesus' marvelous acts or signs reflects early Christian messianic beliefs, rather than distinct Jewish expectations about the Messiah's actions.[3]

JOSEPH L. PRICE

Pastoral Perspective

gospel that belongs to us and that we can give to others? Does our gospel provide them with salvation, or enlightenment? Is it given to make people more welcoming, or more loving, or more just? Do we possess the faith? Does, rather, that faith possess us? Does the gospel possess us, so that all we can do is bear witness, and serve each other in gladness of heart?

My first reaction to these verses was this: I feel as if I am in the midst of an argument that no one can win. Of course, from a human point of view, that is true. No one did win. Jesus was finally arrested, nailed onto a cross, died, and was buried. The disciples were scattered. Jerusalem was destroyed (which is especially ironic in John's account, since one of the rationalizations for crucifying Jesus was to save it from Roman overreach). The end of endless speculation about who the Messiah is, with chapter 7 foreshadowing his arrest and trial, is finally loss. From a human point of view, everybody lost.

However, John asks us to see from a divine point of view. God raised Jesus up upon the cross and then rescued him from its finality, therein manifesting divine glory and divine purpose. Jesus came unto his own, and they speculated about him, had arguments about him, saw him only through his signs, and, in the end, did not receive him; but "to all who received him, who believed in his name, he gave power to become children of God" (1:12).

In a world in which knowledge can hide wisdom, and grand conclusions can conceal foul purposes, what we think and say about Jesus is never above review. Perhaps theologians' and biblical scholars' words are true and useful to the church only to the extent that they themselves are willing to kneel before the cross and the empty tomb. If so, it is certainly equally true for preachers and teachers of the Word.

O. BENJAMIN SPARKS

---

3. Rudolf Schnackenburg, *The Gospel according to St. John: Volume Two, Commentary on Chapters 5–12*, trans. Cecily Hastings, Francis McDonagh, David Smith, and Richard Foley (New York: Crossroad, 1982), 149.

Exegetical Perspective

signs than this man has done?" (v. 31), seems to mix Davidic and prophetic eschatological categories or to reframe them in Christian terms; however, we need to be cautious about imposing modern analytical categories too rigidly onto ancient eschatological expectations.

The term "sign" (*sēmeion*) occurs occasionally in the Synoptics, mainly in passages where Jesus refuses to give one, such as Mark 8:11–12. John uses it more extensively and with greater complexity. Some scholars hold that this author used a source that focused on signs, editing and adapting it rather drastically; others doubt this, thinking more in terms of the author's creative use of oral tradition. In any case, it is clear that in John Jesus' miracles are considered "signs" (e.g., 2:11; 6:2; 20:30). People are attracted to Jesus because of them (9:16; 12:18) and sometimes seek or demand them from him (2:18; 6:30). As in this passage, some people believe in Jesus because of his signs (2:11; 4:53–54). However, signs can be a problematic path toward faith. They lead some only to partial belief (6:14–15), and many fail to believe despite the signs (12:37). Jesus himself sometimes seems skeptical of belief based on signs (2:23–3:12; 4:48), yet he also accepts it (4:46–50; 6:26–29).

Though signs may have been associated more with an eschatological prophet than with the Davidic Messiah, they form a significant element in John's presentation of the case for Jesus' messiahship, even if their significance is somewhat mysterious. Ultimately, it seems important in John to move beyond miracle-based belief to belief like that of Martha, who confesses Jesus as Messiah and Son of God *before* he performs the sign of raising her brother from the dead (11:20–27).

The necessity that Jesus' "hour" or "time" must come before something can take place (v. 30) is mentioned also in 7:6–8, as well as 2:4 and 8:20. The "hour" is the divinely ordained moment for Jesus to be glorified and to glorify God through his crucifixion and resurrection (12:23–28); when this hour arrives, Jesus moves into it without hesitation (13:1; 17:1). Until then, however, nothing can be done to him.

DAVID RENSBERGER

Homiletical Perspective

We might excuse the people in the story for their bewilderment and their speculation about Jesus, because we will also want to excuse ourselves for the many ways in which we confuse Jesus' identity. While John makes it clear who Jesus is, we are "prone to wander" from our certitude about Jesus. How often do we reduce his teachings to life lessons, to seven easy steps for a happy marriage, to clues for a successful leadership model, to strategies for doing what Jesus would do?

We are not eyewitnesses to the Jesus event, but we have this writer's account, whose "testimony is true" and who has given this witness so that we might believe (19:35). The irony for us is that we *do* know where Jesus comes from. We confess it and proclaim it. Yet we also deny it and turn his message into convenient platitudes and moralistic jeremiads. We can do better. Let us preach Christ, the Son of the living God.

The key to understanding this text and the very person and purpose of Jesus is to rest in the testimony that assures us where Jesus comes from. He is God incarnate; his voice is that of God; every declaration he utters is the Word of God. Let us turn our preaching on this text into bold proclamation rather than bland teaching. When Jesus said to his listeners, "You know me, and you know where I am from" (v. 28), it is not hard to imagine that he voiced this as a sarcastic question: "Really, you *think* you know me? You *think* you know where I come from? I assure you—you do not!" In our preaching on this text, we can return his statement to a firm declaration: Followers of Jesus, you *do* know him and where he comes from. Live in the love and the teaching of the Messiah. Embrace the grace that comes from the Father, through Jesus and the Spirit.

CLAYTON J. SCHMIT

³²The Pharisees heard the crowd muttering such things about him, and the chief priests and Pharisees sent temple police to arrest him. ³³Jesus then said, "I will be with you a little while longer, and then I am going to him who sent me. ³⁴You will search for me, but you will not find me; and where I am, you cannot come." ³⁵The Jews* said to one another, "Where does this man intend to go that we will not find him? Does he intend to go to the Dispersion among the Greeks and teach the Greeks? ³⁶What does he mean by saying, 'You will search for me and you will not find me' and 'Where I am, you cannot come'?"

Theological Perspective

The brief exchange in John 7:32–36 centers on two main questions: Where is Jesus going? Who can (or cannot) follow him? As with most other aspects of the Fourth Gospel, these questions are not necessarily as simple as they seem, nor are their answers easily forthcoming.

John 7:32–36 takes place in the midst of the third named festival in the Gospel of John (2:23; 6:4; cf. 5:1). This time, Jesus travels secretly to Jerusalem for the Festival of Tabernacles—the festival during which the Jewish people remember God's provision during their exodus wanderings, as well as throughout their daily lives (Exod. 23:16; Deut. 16:13–15; Lev. 23:39–43). Even before Jesus arrives, however, he is causing conflict and "grumbling" (7:12, 32; cf. 6:41, 43) among the crowd as they debate whether he is a "good man," a liar, or even the Messiah (7:12–13). It is this conflict over Jesus' identity that is still boiling in verses 32–36. That things have heated up is clear in the contrast between 7:13, where the crowd is conferring quietly out of "fear of the Jews," and 7:28–29, where the crowd's comments have grown enough to result in Jesus' crying out in response. Hearing the growing debates among the crowds of Jews gathered in Jerusalem for the festival,

*See "'The Jews' in the Fourth Gospel" on pp. xi–xiv.

Pastoral Perspective

From the vantage point of three-dimensional space and chronological time, this story is as confounding and unsatisfactory as any in the New Testament. Simple words like "with," "go," and "come" trip people up. It is as if Jesus exists in an entirely different sphere from everyone else. His "with" and their "with" do not mean the same thing at all. His "go" and their "go" operate in alternate universes. Utterly failing to grasp these differences, everyone in the story naturally locates Jesus in, and judges him by, the principles of chronological time and three-dimensional space. In a line from the movie *Cool Hand Luke*, "What we've got here is a failure to communicate."[1]

This communication problem can be addressed by accepting that John's Gospel presents a Jesus who does, indeed, inhabit a different sphere. The Jesus of this Gospel is essentially mystical; indeed, mysticism is this Gospel's very milieu.[2]

Most of the members of our congregations are no more mystically inclined than are the characters in

1. The sentence is spoken at different points in the movie, first by Strother Martin (as the Captain, a prison warden) and later Paul Newman (as Luke, a young prisoner). *Cool Hand Luke*, directed by Stuart Rosenberg (Hollywood, CA: Warner Brothers, 1967).
2. See William L. Countryman, *The Mystical Way in the Fourth Gospel: Crossing Over into God* (Harrisburg, PA: Trinity Press, Int., 1995), and other commentators.

Exegetical Perspective

John 7:32–36 presents an episode in the ongoing conflict between Jesus and the religious authorities in the Fourth Gospel. This conflict escalates in 7:1–8:59, as Jesus teaches in the temple during the Feast of Booths (7:2, 14). Also known as the Feast of Tabernacles, this festival commemorates the time the Israelites dwelled in tents while wandering in the wilderness (Lev. 23:39–43; Deut. 16:13–15). The passage begins with the religious authorities acting on their intention to capture Jesus (7:1), but it becomes clear that any attempt to silence him and obstruct the spread of his teaching is futile.

The Pharisees and the chief priests send temple officers to arrest Jesus (v. 32). In Jesus' own historical context, the Pharisees and chief priests were not close allies, and only the chief priests would have had charge over temple officers. John amplifies the Pharisees' role in opposing Jesus (7:45; 11:47, 57; 18:3) to reflect his own community's conflicts with religious leadership over the acceptance of Jesus as Messiah and Son of God. After the temple's destruction in 70 CE, rabbis, who were the Pharisees' successors, rose to greater prominence and would have represented Jewish religious authorities to the Johannine community.

The religious authorities sent the temple police because they heard the crowd "muttering" as a result

Homiletical Perspective

John 7:32–36 is a brief moment in the narrative of the Fourth Gospel. Fixing its place in that narrative is crucial for preparing a sermon on it, which makes attention to the exegetical commentary essential in early planning. For example, to avoid easy (and thus false) caricatures, the preacher must be clear regarding the ways the author of this Gospel uses the phrase "the Jews." In order to get a full sense of the weight of the questions they raise in response to Jesus' announcement that he is "going away," it is essential to recognize how often Jesus speaks of where he comes from and where he is going—and how frequently what he says is misunderstood by both friends and foes. This kind of exegetical work will help the preacher both to find relevance in these questions for proclaiming the gospel today and to appreciate that they are not far removed from what many people in the pews are asking now.

Even in our passage, it is clear that the religious leaders misunderstand Jesus, taking his talk of "going away" too literally. Looking beyond the passage, the author of the Gospel has prepared us for such a response, having demonstrated repeatedly that in the Gospel of John everyone misunderstands Jesus—at first anyway. We first encounter this literary device in the response to Jesus' words about the destruction of the temple in 2:13–22. The Jewish authorities hear

John 7:32–36

Theological Perspective

in verse 32 the chief priests and Pharisees send in guards in order to arrest Jesus and hopefully reestablish order at the holy site.

At stake in this passage are Jesus' identity and the appropriate response to Jesus. Christology is squarely at the center of the Gospel of John (20:30–31). Only when one can answer the question of Jesus' identity correctly (that is, according to the Gospel's understanding) can one answer the two main questions of our passage. In other words, in order to understand where Jesus is going, one must be able to discern whence he came (see 1:1–18). In order to follow Jesus to his destination, one must be willing to go where he leads, no matter what road he takes to get there.

Who can know Jesus' identity? To what extent can even followers of Jesus truly know him? In the Gospel of John itself, the answers seem incredibly limited. Certainly those surrounding Jesus in John 7–8 are not able to discern who he is, at least not completely. There is division among the crowd, some believing and others rejecting. Even "the Jews who had believed in him" in 8:31 eventually try to kill Jesus as a result of the conflict in 8:32–59. Moreover, John 7 follows on the heels of Jesus' being abandoned by many of his disciples in 6:60–66. Even though Peter ends that chapter with his monumental confession, the savvy Gospel reader remembers that this disciple too will desert his master when suffering draws near.

It seems, then, that those reading and listening to the Gospel, rather than the characters within, have the best chance to meet the challenge of knowing Jesus. Indeed, the Gospel repeatedly privileges its audience and underscores the importance of the Holy Spirit in this understanding with whispering asides and explicit reminders (2:22; 12:16). Given this insider knowledge, the audience seems better able to understand Jesus' cryptic words in verses 34–35, as those surrounding him flounder.

Perhaps a better question to ask, then, is *when* can one know Jesus' identity and, as a result, *when* can one follow him to where he is? This is the track taken by Augustine when he approaches John 7:36. In his *Tractates on the Gospel of John*, Augustine notes that Jesus does not say that "you will not be able" but only that "you are not able to come." He continues,

> For at that time they [the Jews] were such as were not able. And that you may know that this was not said to cause despair, he said something of the same kind also to his disciples: "Where I go you

Pastoral Perspective

the story. It is possible, therefore, to sympathize with those who do not understand Jesus and who reasonably suppose that if Jesus is going somewhere, they should be able to follow. Put differently, John's elusive Jesus and the passage's mysticism together present a genuine pastoral opportunity. They invite our sympathy, first with the Pharisees of old and, second, with twenty-first-century Christians, a great many of whom are as mystically challenged as the people of Jesus' day, including his own disciples. Those in our congregations for whom Jesus is elusive may see themselves in, and resonate with, the characters in the story.

There are confounding qualities to the Jesus of the Fourth Gospel. This mystical Jesus is slippery—not in the sense of tricky, but in the sense of tending to slip from one's grasp. He slips from the grasp of the police. His words slip from the grasp of our minds. At the same time, he commands our attention. Jesus is elusive, to be sure, but he is also profoundly compelling. Indeed, he is so intriguing that everyone reaches for him, straining to follow where he goes and struggling to understand what he says. In addition, the Jesus of this Gospel engages, surprises, and dislocates us. He challenges assumptions, makes people think, wonder, ask questions, and deeply ponder both the ways of God and the ways of the world. Jesus "blows our minds," because he is of God and is in God and is God. Fully understanding Jesus is almost certainly impossible. Following Jesus, therefore, requires a massive dose of trust.

There is some small comfort to be taken in the fact that Jesus' disciples are as dunderheaded about Jesus as is everyone else. No one understands Jesus, not even his closest followers. This softens the story's caricatures of the Pharisees. At the same time, it places those of us who are not mystics in good company. Nevertheless, it leaves everyone—Pharisee and follower, Jew and Gentile, those living then and those living now—a very long way from understanding Jesus and his words.

If the path to Jesus is a mystical path, how might we honor and engage this in our liturgies, our pastoral care, and our administrative responsibilities? How might we get from our here and now to Jesus' mystical sphere? Ultimately, if John's Jesus is in mystical unity with God, can we entice our hearers toward this state and, if so, how? Put differently, how do we dislodge our congregants and ourselves from a steady state of functional disbelief? This is a tall order for shaping disciples and caring for persons.

The passage consists of six sentences, three of which are questions. A study of this passage could

of Jesus' teaching. The vocabulary recalls the biblical background that gave rise to the Feast of Booths, "mutter" (*gongyzō*) being the same verb used in the Septuagint for the grumbling of the Israelites in the desert (Exod. 17:3; Num. 11:1; cf. John 6:41, 43, 61; 7:12). The crowd had been debating whether Jesus could be the Messiah (7:25–31), with many coming to believe (7:31). For the religious leaders, this movement by the crowd toward faith in Jesus as Messiah represents a threat that must be addressed.

Jesus' discussion with the crowd in 7:25–31 centered on his origins. In 7:32–36, the topic shifts to his destination when he departs from the world. Beginning in verse 33, the Johannine Jesus describes his death in terms of his "going away" (*hypagō*) to God (8:14, 21; 13:33, 36; 14:4, 28; 16:5, 10; cf. 13:3). At the Farewell Discourse, he will repeat to his disciples his disclosure that he will remain in the world only for "a little while" (13:33; 14:19; 16:16–19). Jesus' imminent departure lends urgency to deciding whether he is God's Messiah, as he is soon "going [*hypagō*, "I go"] to him who sent me" (v. 33).

Once he returns to God, the religious leaders who are looking for him will be unable to find him, because "where I am, you cannot come" (v. 34). The emphasis is on the place to which Jesus goes when he returns to God. Because Jesus will return to God's heavenly presence, he is going to a place the religious authorities will be unable to enter, because, unlike many members of the crowd (7:31), they are unwilling to accept Jesus as God's sent Messiah. Now is the time, while Jesus is in the world, for them to believe in Jesus. If they do not come to believe, there will soon come a time, in "a little while" (v. 33), when it will be too late (8:21–24; cf. Prov. 1:28; Hos. 5:6; Amos 8:12; Isa. 55:6; Luke 17:22).

That Jesus makes this strong claim in the temple, God's earthly dwelling, which both Jesus and the religious authorities can enter, provides a stark contrast to the future, eternal separation Jesus speaks of here. In the temple, the locus of God's presence on earth, Jesus openly reveals himself as God's Messiah (7:26; 18:20; cf. 7:4). For John, religious authorities who do not accept Jesus as God's Messiah risk forfeiting their access to God's presence in the heavenly realm.

Jesus directs his words about being separated from God's presence not toward Jews generally but to the religious leaders who oppose him. Even more concretely, verse 32 shows "the Jews" of verse 35 to be religious authorities, identified as Pharisees and chief priests, who hold positions of power from

Jesus literally, not recognizing what the disciples will *later* come to see, that Jesus is really talking about his rising from the dead. The same kind of misunderstanding appears in Jesus' conversations with Nicodemus (chap. 3), the Samaritan woman (chap. 4), and the Jewish authorities (chap. 6). Therefore, when we get to the response to Jesus in our passage, we immediately recognize that it is yet another case of misunderstanding and that they are thinking too literally—just as the others have done. It should also indicate that the author wants the readers of the Gospel of John to look carefully at what Jesus is saying—to ensure that they do not make the same kind of mistake. The disciples' misunderstanding points in this direction.

In 13:33, when speaking to his disciples during the Fourth Gospel's unique (and powerful) account of the night of his arrest, Jesus addresses them, "Little children, I am with you only a little longer. You will look for me; *and as I said to the Jews so now I say to you*, 'Where I am going, you cannot come.'" In spite of the fact that Jesus then gives the disciples the "new commandment" (13:34), with all its implications, Peter can only think to ask, "Lord, where are you going?" In 14:1–5, after hearing Jesus speak of going to prepare a place for the disciples in his Father's house, Thomas declares, "Lord, we do not know where you are going. How can we know the way?" Then in 16:17–18, in response to Jesus' saying yet again that he is going away (and returning!), some of the disciples are reduced to asking, "What does he mean . . . ? We do not know what he is talking about."

Writing a sermon on John 7:32–36 might well begin, therefore, with the questions it raises—and with the assumption that many in the congregation may find Jesus' words as perplexing as do the people in the Gospel of John. Some may have theological questions about the Fourth Gospel's language of Jesus' coming from and returning to the Father, wondering how to make sense of it beyond the language of the Bible and the creeds. Others may express such questions more personally, feeling that they are searching and not finding. Still others may even hear the words "Where I am, you cannot come" addressed to them, and feel excluded. Since such questions raise theological and pastoral issues, the commentaries on these perspectives in this volume will help the preacher reflect on their implications for preaching.

One could also explore the various ways the Fourth Gospel addresses the questions, working out from the passage itself. After speaking of "going

John 7:32–36

Theological Perspective

cannot come" [John 13:33]. Yet, while praying on their behalf, he said, "Father, I will that where I am they also may be with me" [John 17:24]. And, finally, this he expounded to Peter, and says to him, "Where I go you cannot follow me now, but you will follow me hereafter" [John 13:36].[1]

For Augustine, then, 7:32–36 is a passage of promise rather than defeat. It is a passage pointing toward a time when followers may know Jesus more completely and follow him in faithfulness. According to the Gospel of John, surely this time points toward the work of the Holy Spirit described in 7:37–52 as well as in Jesus' Farewell Discourse. Such an interpretation is important when reading the Gospel of John—a Gospel often used to foster anti-Jewish sentiments, either intentionally or otherwise. Instead of condemning "the Jews" here, Augustine discusses them in the same way he does the disciples (who are also Jewish) and everyone else who encounters the Gospel: as unable to understand Jesus completely at the present moment but with the potential to know him more fully and follow him on the way.

Nevertheless, Jesus does argue that there are those who will never know him and, quite graphically, will "die in their sins" (8:21, 24). In the closely related passage of 8:21–30, Jesus recapitulates his teachings from John 7, especially verses 32–36. He reminds his audience that they cannot come to the place he is going, because they do not know him, or, more specifically, they do not know the "one who sent" him (7:28–29). As others have noted, "sin" in the Fourth Gospel is closely tied to unbelief in Jesus as the Christ and Son of God. Nevertheless, such belief and understanding may not come when we expect them, and certainly not as a result of our own industriousness alone! Instead, John indicates the reality of confusion when one encounters Jesus and promises guidance in the form of his narrative and, more importantly, with the gift of the Holy Spirit.

ALICIA D. MYERS

Pastoral Perspective

follow in kind, consisting of at least 50 percent questions and wonderings. For instance: What does John's Gospel tell us of why the religious authorities wanted to arrest Jesus? What is at the bottom of their order to the temple police? What might it look like and feel like to live perpetually in reference to God, rather than in reference to ourselves, our jobs, and our world? How might we ponder and posit for ourselves the meaning of citizenship in heaven? Whether in the classroom or pulpit or study, the text invites us into an encounter more than it lets us explicate its meaning; it dislocates us more than it orients us.

The passage presents an additional concern. The author writes about *the* Pharisees and *the* Jews the way some people today write about *the* Republicans and *the* Democrats, or *the* Christians and *the* Muslims. He writes about them in stereotype. He writes as if the Pharisees, "the Jews," and the chief priests not only are one-dimensional, but also have achieved a meeting and melding of their minds. Obviously, that is not the case. It is likely that this stereotyping betrays real and present tensions for those to whom John is writing. This invites our reflection upon tensions in our time and our own temptations to stereotype. What groups do we think of in one-dimensional terms? Why? What might we do to investigate our own tendency to stereotype others? If others stereotype us, what unflattering traits and qualities do those caricatures presume to be ours? Why?

It is given to the followers of Jesus to handle together the mysteries of life and death, good and evil, time and eternity, self and other, meaning and memory. John's mystical Jesus invites us to take wing and explore this high and holy calling. He invites us into a state of being where these mysteries are neither resolved nor denied, but held. He invites us to follow Jesus and to trust God, while accepting the limitations of our own knowledge. Courage, Christian!

NANCY S. TAYLOR

---

1. Augustine, *Lectures or Tractates on the Gospel according to St. John*, trans. John Gibb and James Innes, ed. Philip Schaff, *Nicene and Post-Nicene Fathers 7*, Series 1 (Grand Rapids: Eerdmans, 1956), 192.

which they can authorize temple officers to pursue Jesus. It is their opposition to Jesus (and, later, to the Johannine community), not their Jewish identity, with which the Fourth Evangelist finds fault. John's narration is careful to distinguish the Jewish authorities opposed to Jesus from the Jewish crowd at the temple, whose mixed response to Jesus shows them not to be a monolithic group (7:30–31).

The misunderstanding that takes place in verses 35–36 underscores the inability of the religious leaders to be in the same place as Jesus. Throughout John's Gospel, Jesus uses ambiguous language to speak on two levels. Listeners who interpret Jesus' words at the literal, "earthly" level in fact misunderstand what he means (e.g., 3:3–10). Though Jesus speaks here of his return to God, the religious leaders assume he is speaking of traveling elsewhere in the world. Their mistaken understanding that Jesus is going to join the Jewish Diaspora and teach the Greeks (that is, Gentiles) ironically prophesies the future success of the Jesus movement among Gentiles outside of Palestine, as they unwittingly articulate what is a current reality for John's readers (cf. 11:47–52). Though Jesus had indeed "gone away" and returned to God, his word had taken hold in the Gentile world (cf. 12:20–23).

John 7:32–36 calls into question the efficacy of the power structures of the world to hinder the revelation that takes place in the person and teaching of Jesus. Jesus can assert in verse 33 that he will be in the world "a little while longer," knowing the religious leaders cannot bring about the hour of his departure ahead of schedule. When the hour arrives for Jesus' return, he goes to a place his worldly enemies cannot follow. Later, we learn that the temple police sent to arrest Jesus had not done so, because they were amazed at his word (7:45–46), further underscoring John's theme that the message revealed by and in Jesus continues to spread throughout the world, despite the best efforts of the opposition movement. Opposition from powerful sources cannot stop the Johannine Jesus from his work as sent Messiah to reveal God to the world.

GILBERTO A. RUIZ

away" in 16:29–33, for example, Jesus encourages the disciples: "I have said this to you, so that in me you may have peace. In the world you face persecution. But take courage; I have conquered the world!" (16:33). This is one of the Fourth Gospel's most dramatic declarations of the good news. In 13:31–35 Jesus links his announcement about "going away" to the new commandment (15:12), thus showing that loving one another (as just illustrated in the washing of the disciples' feet, 13:1–20) is a way to find support while living the questions. In chapter 14, the Fourth Gospel links the new commandment and Jesus' returning to the Father to the coming of the Holy Spirit, through whom Jesus is also present with the community that keeps his commandment. Since John 7:32–36 only raises the questions, tracing them throughout the Gospel may help the preacher find ways to address them in the sermon and thus help those who are wrestling with them.

An edgier way into John 7:32–36 is to start with the reference to the Pharisees, the chief priests, and the temple police—not simply to use them as straw figures, but to consider the way the Fourth Gospel sees them as religious authorities who seek to maintain power by manipulating people (Judas, for example), controlling markets (2:13–22), and colluding with secular authorities to suppress anyone who challenges their claims to power (11:45–53 and throughout the passion narrative). Coming at the text this way opens a prophetic line of interpretation, one based on the recognition that speaking to the powerful on behalf of the powerless can be an act of love. This approach may help the preacher find ways to write a sermon that allows the congregation to hear the text not simply as a word about conflicts from the past, but also as a word about contemporary conflicts—and the Spirit's work to address them through those who love Jesus and keep his commandments (14:12–17).

OLIVER LARRY YARBROUGH

³⁷On the last day of the festival, the great day, while Jesus was standing there, he cried out, "Let anyone who is thirsty come to me, ³⁸and let the one who believes in me drink. As the scripture has said, 'Out of the believer's heart shall flow rivers of living water.'" ³⁹Now he said this about the Spirit, which believers in him were to receive; for as yet there was no Spirit, because Jesus was not yet glorified.

⁴⁰When they heard these words, some in the crowd said, "This is really the prophet." ⁴¹Others said, "This is the Messiah." But some asked, "Surely the Messiah does not come from Galilee, does he? ⁴²Has not the scripture said that the Messiah is descended from David and comes from Bethlehem, the village

Theological Perspective

After baffling the Jews gathered in Jerusalem for the Festival of Tabernacles in John 7:32–36, Jesus resumes his teaching in verses 37–38. Jesus' rather oblique teaching is explained by the narrator in verse 39 before the reactions of the crowd, temple police, and the religious elite are reported in verses 40–52. On the "last" and "great" day of the festival, Jesus makes a promise of living water for those who come to him, thus summarizing various aspects of his discourses from John 4–6. The connection to earlier chapters is fitting, given the foundational role that Jesus' healing from John 5 plays in John 7–8 (7:19–24). As in preceding chapters, Jesus' teaching continues to spark confusion and conflict as those gathered around him debate his identity: is he the prophet? the Messiah? a pretender deserving punishment?

In John 7:37–38 Jesus offers a brief, albeit complex, scriptural interpretation: "If someone is thirsty, let them come to me and let them drink. The one who believes [*ho pisteuōn*] in me, just as the scripture says: 'Out of his belly will flow rivers of living water'" (my trans.). Themes from previous discourses include an allusion to Isaiah 55:1 that resonates with John 6:27, the concept of "living water" from John 4, and a demonstration of the Scriptures' testifying to Jesus' work (5:39–47).

Pastoral Perspective

The religious authorities dismiss as impossible the claim that the Messiah could hail from Galilee. They cite as evidence the sturdy triad of Scripture, law, and tradition. If the authorities are right, if Scripture says that the Messiah cannot come from Galilee, and if Jesus does come from Galilee, then can Jesus be the Messiah? The people to whom the author is writing are daily harassed by such questions, skepticism, and doubt about Jesus. Are the skeptics correct? Has John's community got it wrong? It is natural that these attacks have the effect of weakening their faith.

The author of John's Gospel writes to people not unlike many in our congregations: people for whom the claim that Jesus of Nazareth is the Messiah, the Son of God, raises nagging doubts and troubling questions. The consequences of being wrong or right are high and urgent. For his part, John does everything he can to counter the skeptics and to build and bolster his community's faith.

The author begins by taking the arguments against Jesus and addressing them each in turn. He suggests, in effect, that it is beside the point whether Jesus hails from Galilee or Gilead, from Greece or Gomorrah. Jesus' true source is from God, and his true identity is of God. Indeed, way back in the very first chapter of his story, John locates Jesus beyond

where David lived?" ⁴³So there was a division in the crowd because of him. ⁴⁴Some of them wanted to arrest him, but no one laid hands on him.

⁴⁵Then the temple police went back to the chief priests and Pharisees, who asked them, "Why did you not arrest him?" ⁴⁶The police answered, "Never has anyone spoken like this!" ⁴⁷Then the Pharisees replied, "Surely you have not been deceived too, have you? ⁴⁸Has any one of the authorities or of the Pharisees believed in him? ⁴⁹But this crowd, which does not know the law— they are accursed." ⁵⁰Nicodemus, who had gone to Jesus before, and who was one of them, asked, ⁵¹"Our law does not judge people without first giving them a hearing to find out what they are doing, does it?" ⁵²They replied, "Surely you are not also from Galilee, are you? Search and you will see that no prophet is to arise from Galilee."

Exegetical Perspective

The Feast of Booths or Tabernacles featured a water libation ritual that provides the context for Jesus' teaching in 7:37–38. During this ritual, priests processed from the temple to the nearby pool of Siloam, drew water into a golden pitcher, and returned to the temple to pour it on the altar. The ritual reenacted the miraculous moment in the wilderness when Moses struck the rock and water gushed forth (Exod. 17:1–6; Ps. 78:16). By setting Jesus' teaching within this Tabernacles context, John suggests that the unexpected has taken place again: life-giving water has come from an unforeseen source, Jesus.

The NRSV conceals the exegetical problem raised by verses 37–38. It renders the phrase *ek tēs koilias autou* as "out of the believer's heart," supplying "the believer's" where the Greek text simply has the pronoun "his" (*autou*). Two referents for this pronoun are possible: the believer and Jesus. Either could be the source of living water. Early manuscripts and patristic witnesses show that verses 37–38 can be punctuated in two different ways, each lending support to a different interpretation. One cannot turn to the quoted passage for clarity, because it occurs nowhere in the OT and could allude to any number of passages (Prov. 18:4; Isa. 12:3; 43:19–20; 44:3; 55:1; 58:11; Jer. 2:13; 17:13; Ezek. 47:1–12; Zech. 14:8). Even if the believer is understood as a source of living

Homiletical Perspective

John 7:37–52 continues the Fourth Gospel's treatment of Jesus' trip to Jerusalem for Sukkot (the Feast of Tabernacles) that began in 7:1. It opens with one of Jesus' most inviting sayings (vv. 37–38), moves to an account of the "division" within the crowd who heard it (vv. 40–44), and ends with the authorities heatedly debating what to do with Jesus (vv. 45–52). The passage picks up on the Fourth Gospel's exploration of Jesus' identity, focusing on his role as "the prophet" and "the Messiah," two related but distinct titles. It is also concerned with the interpretation of Scripture, which is explicitly mentioned in each of the three scenes in the passage. So preparing a sermon based on this passage will benefit from careful consideration of its challenges and opportunities.

Because it is so compelling, the saying in 7:37–38 will likely shape any sermon on this passage. It is reminiscent of the comforting saying in Matthew 11:28 and of such passages as Isaiah 44:2–3 and Zechariah 14:8 (a reading for Sukkot). In the Gospel of John, it echoes Jesus' conversation with the Samaritan woman, especially 4:10–15. Both passages use water metaphorically, with John 4 linking "living water" to "eternal life" and John 7 to the gift of the Spirit, a point the author makes clear in verse 39. The coming of the Spirit guarantees that those who are thirsty will continue to receive living water when

John 7:37–52

Theological Perspective

There are also a number of confusing elements in Jesus' words. Even though Jesus introduces his appeal to Scripture in a way that would lead many readers to assume he is quoting Scripture directly, there is no passage that matches exactly his words. While perhaps troublesome for contemporary readers, ancients would recognize Jesus' words as a paraphrase, a common technique in rhetorical performances. With this paraphrase, Jesus acts as an authoritative interpreter of Scripture; he knows Scripture so well that he can blend its themes and language to communicate truth. Jesus takes on scriptural voice—a most fitting feature in a Gospel where Jesus is the "Word" made flesh. Most debate, therefore, has centered on the meaning of Jesus' paraphrase.

The narrator provides some clarification by tying the living water to the Holy Spirit given after Jesus' "glorification." Nevertheless, the source of the water described remains ambiguous: is this a description of the believer's belly or of Jesus'? That one must first come to Jesus to drink resonates with the Gospel's emphasis that the source of living water is Jesus (4:10–15): the one on whom the Holy Spirit remains (1:29–32), the one from whose side water literally flows in 19:34, and the one who ultimately bestows the Spirit in 20:20–22.

Various church fathers have offered their own additional insights. For Origen, the rivers bestow immortality, for Ambrose, wisdom; for Cyril of Jerusalem, the rivers describe spiritual gifts; and for Chrysostom, they indicate the limitlessness and perseverance of grace. Augustine understands them to be "benevolence," or the desire of Christians to help others based on their own satisfaction from drinking in the love of Christ. Cyprian of Carthage suggests that this verse contains a description of the rite of baptism.[1]

Without the benefit of the narrator's aside, the characters in the text are left divided in the wake of Jesus' teaching. In verses 40–44 the crowd offers diverse opinions concerning Jesus. Some profess Jesus as "the prophet," which corresponds to earlier confessions and an expectation of a prophet like Moses in Deuteronomy 18 (v. 40; cf. 1:19–28; 4:19, 28–30; 6:14–15). Others identify Jesus as the Messiah (v. 41). Still others are preoccupied with Jesus' origins, as they were in 7:26–27. They dispute the messianic claim by noting that Jesus' Galilean origins contrast

Pastoral Perspective

the bounds of time and space. He locates Jesus in God, not in Galilee. God trumps Galilee.

The author also argues that far from dismissing the tradition, Jesus stands firmly in the tradition. After all, Jesus participates in the great harvest festival of Sukkot. By recalling the rabbinic tradition that water from the pool of Siloam was carried each year to the temple during Sukkot, Jesus himself inhabits, invokes, and fulfills the Scripture.

In addition, Jesus knows Scripture as well as, if not better than, these religious scholars. His words allude to the water from the rock in the desert (Num. 20:2–13) and to the prophetic hope of messianic deliverance (Isa. 12:3). Jesus understands and appreciates the festival more and better than anyone else. Why? Because Jesus is that living water. He is the well of salvation.[1] Indeed, he is God's Word incarnate.

What is more, Jesus wows the temple police. Having never heard anyone speak like Jesus, the police disobey direct orders to arrest him. Apparently, they are more afraid of the prospect of arresting the genuine Messiah than of being reprimanded by their bosses. Surely the behavior of hard-boiled police—their respect for Jesus, awe at his words, and hesitancy to arrest him—is a convincing witness to the power of Jesus and his words! Moreover, Jesus has wooed at least half of the ordinary people who, though unschooled in the law, seem to know God when they see God.

Finally (and here is where we come in), John's Jesus illustrates the symbiotic relationship between Messiah and believer. If, as Scripture says and Jesus quotes, "out of the believer's heart shall flow rivers of living water" (v. 38), John's Gospel cites as evidence the living waters of love and courage, of mercy and sacrifice, of prayer and praise flowing from the hearts and through the deeds of both Jesus and those who follow Jesus. Meanwhile, John hints that there is precious little evidence of such living waters trickling, let alone flowing, from those choking on the law's jots and tittles.

The arguments against Jesus in John's first-century community are not so very far from the arguments that many Christians hear and face today. In a world shaped in part by secularism, those who cannot entertain the simultaneous existence of the worlds of science and of faith sometimes describe Christians as naive and even as deceived. Furthermore, people of other faiths or no faith can be understandably

---

1. Joel C. Elowsky, ed., *John 1–10*, Ancient Christian Commentary on Scripture, New Testament IVa, ed. Thomas C. Oden (Downers Grove, IL: InterVarsity Press, 2006), 264–66.

1. Amy-Jill Levine and Marc Zvi Brettler, eds., *The Jewish Annotated New Testament* (New York: Oxford Press, 2011), 173.

water for others, this living water ultimately comes from Jesus (7:37–38a; see also 4:10–14; cf. 6:35).

Tabernacles also had an eschatological dimension that anticipated the future reality described by Zechariah: "On that day living waters shall flow out from Jerusalem" (Zech. 14:8a; cf. Isa. 12:3; Ezek. 47:1–12). For John, the day anticipated by Zechariah is inaugurated by Jesus' coming to the world and becomes realized in Jesus' death, when water flows from Jesus' body (19:34; cf. 1 John 5:7–8; Rev. 7:17; 22:1).

In verse 39, the narrator identifies the Spirit as the living water that springs forth from Jesus. Imagery connecting water and the spirit of God is found in the Hebrew Bible (Isa. 44:3; Ezek. 36:25–27). That Jesus gives the Spirit is a distinctive characteristic of the Fourth Gospel (15:26; 16:7; 20:22), but it does not become available to believers until Jesus' death, resurrection, and ascension, which John collectively refers to in terms of his glorification (12:16, 23–24, 27–36; 17:1, 4–5). John does not mean the Spirit did not exist before the cross, because the Spirit had descended on Jesus at his baptism (1:32–33). Rather, for John the Spirit does not become a reality for the community of believers until it is mediated to them by the glorified Jesus (20:22).

In verses 40–44 division arises over Jesus' teaching, centering on whether Jesus is the expected prophet in the tradition of Moses (Deut. 18:15–18) or the Messiah (John 7:25–31). One argument against Jesus' messiahship raised by the crowd is his Galilean origin, which contradicted expectations that the Messiah was to be of Davidic lineage and come from Bethlehem in Judea (2 Sam. 7:12–16; Pss. 18:50; 89:3–4, 35–37; 132:11–12; Isa. 11:1, 10; Jer. 23:5; Mic. 5:2). Knowledge of his origins also contradicted the belief that the Messiah's origins would be hidden, an issue addressed in 7:27–29.

John and his community probably knew the traditions of Jesus' birth in Bethlehem (Matt. 2:1–12; Luke 2:1–7), and ultimately John deems Jesus' heavenly origins and direct lineage to God more important than his geographical origins and Davidic lineage (1:1–18; 6:38, 41–46; 7:28–29). For John, the crowd does not know either truth, Jesus' birth in Bethlehem or his ultimate origin "with God" (1:1; cf. 8:14; 9:29), whereas John and his readers are "in the know." The question of Jesus' origins causes division, and the threat of his arrest reemerges (cf. 7:30, 32).

No arrest takes place because the temple officers sent by the religious authorities in 7:32 were amazed by Jesus' teaching (vv. 45–46). The religious authorities disapprove of the officers' response to Jesus

Jesus has returned to the Father. The Fourth Gospel develops the point in 14:15–31, where Jesus tells the disciples he will not leave them "orphaned" but will ask the Father to send them an "Advocate" [the Spirit] who "will teach you everything and remind you of all that I have said to you" (14:26). John returns to the theme yet again in 16:4b–15, where Jesus tells the disciples the "Advocate" will come and "guide you into all the truth" (16:13). Living water, therefore, is a rich metaphor in the Fourth Gospel.

If the sermon focuses on living water, the preacher might want to explore what it means to thirst and how to recognize signs of being thirsty. Spiritual thirst is frequently a longing for something more in life, a search for meaning. Signs of such thirsting are many and varied, though some may not be obvious. Anyone can show such signs, both in and out of the church. Anger, depression, anxiety, and compulsive behavior of all sorts, for example, are signs of emotional thirsting. Giving expression to these kinds of thirst allows members of the congregation to reflect on their own experiences and thus to hear more personally the invitation to "come and drink."

In order to keep the invitation from sounding (and being) empty, the sermon should explore what the "living water" that Jesus offers might be with respect to such emotional/spiritual thirsting. While the sermon might begin by opening up the meanings of "eternal life" reflected in John 4, it will be anchored in 7:37–39, showing where and how the Spirit provides "living water" for those who thirst. One might also focus on verse 38 and explore how the congregation is bringing out of its heart the "rivers of living water" by sharing the Spirit it has received through fellowship, Bible study, worship, contemplation, and counseling. If they are not already part of the congregation's mission and service, the sermon might invite the congregation to reach out to those who hunger and thirst by sponsoring food banks and other acts of charity and by working to address the causes of poverty, hunger, and thirst.

Another way to explore John 7:37–39 might be to take the water imagery more literally. In developed countries, the metaphorical meaning of thirsting for living water is likely to be the only one many will recognize. However, for significant numbers of people around the world, living water is a matter of life and death. In much of Asia and Africa, shortages of clean water endanger human life and threaten attempts to establish sustainable agriculture. Even in parts of the United States, drought conditions

John 7:37–52

Theological Perspective

what "scripture said," namely, that the Messiah "comes from the seed of David and from Bethlehem, the village from whence David was" (v. 42, my trans.).

The next reaction is that of the religious leaders, who are confounded by the temple police's decision not to arrest Jesus (vv. 45–52). The police praise Jesus' speech in verse 46, sounding much like previous responses to his words in verses 15 and 26, but the religious leaders are not amused. They respond sharply, noting their own lack of belief (*episteusen,* v. 48), and judge the crowd as "accursed" (*eparotoi,* v. 49) on account of their ignorance of the law. In the verses that follow, however, the leaders demonstrate the same division as the crowd—thus falling under their very own rebuke.

First, while they know the law, they choose not to follow its instructions when they censure Nicodemus for requesting a hearing for Jesus (v. 51). Second, their own assessment of Jesus' identity is based on nearly the same interpretation of the law made by the crowd: Jesus is from Galilee, and no "prophet" can arise from there (v. 52). They command Nicodemus: "Search [the Scriptures] and . . . see!" (v. 52). This admonition is surely ironic. Jesus has already noted the leaders' quest to "search the scriptures" in order to find life in John 5:39–41. While this search should demonstrate Jesus' own centrality to the scriptural narrative, it is in fact inhibiting the leaders' coming to him to receive eternal life; in John 7:45–52 we find the actualization of Jesus' words.

Much of the conflict in our passage, then, centers on the authority and ability to interpret Scripture rightly. Jesus acts as the authoritative teacher who offers a way of life to those who will come to him. Portions of the crowd respond positively to his words. Others, however, join the religious leaders by prioritizing their own scriptural expectations. The confusion and careless condemnation that follow should caution all interpreters of Scripture and the Christ event. John's Jesus reminds us that God often acts outside our expectations, rattling us and forcing us out of comfortable interpretations, in order to bring us truth we otherwise miss or, worse, decry as false. Instead of limiting our understanding of Scripture to a few readings spoken by those who traditionally hold positions of power, this jarring scene reminds us to be listening for the ways in which God continues to speak through others, "paraphrasing" our well-known traditions to reveal truth in and to our present world.

ALICIA D. MYERS

Pastoral Perspective

perplexed by the Christian's claim that God is three persons. Can you blame them? They scratch their heads when they hear us speak of the three persons of the triune God while we adamantly defend our monotheism.

Like John's community, we too face an abundance of challenges. Following this elusive Messiah is not easy. Understanding him is fraught and complicated. Explaining him to skeptics, nonbelievers, disbelievers, and people of other faiths is harder still. In this increasingly multifaith, interreligious, and secular world, it is natural to ask ourselves what John's community was asking themselves: Have we got it wrong? Is this Galilean peasant the real deal?

It is reasonable to assume that in every worshiping congregation there are people who lost their faith in the course of the past week, those who never had faith, and a great many for whom belief and doubt are strangely mixed together. What have we to say to such people? What does this story have to say? The stakes are high indeed. Into these challenging circumstances, John offers helpful hints, evidence, and words of assurance. He hopes, thereby, to pluck up our courage and equip our minds, hearts, and spirits for the arduous (and not so easy to defend or explain) journey of Christian discipleship.

John provides encouragement by reminding us that the rules, laws, and norms of God's world and this world are not identical. God's ways simply cannot be judged by the standards of this world. Instead, John urges us to follow Jesus, even when we do not understand him. He aches for us to listen to Jesus, even though Jesus' words and stories are perplexing. The author suggests that we trust the gentleness and openness of Nicodemus. He asks us to wonder and marvel at the defiant behavior of the temple police. He points to the uneducated crowds who find Jesus exceedingly compelling. Finally, he cites as evidence the Jesus community from whom flow living waters.

In other words, if we cannot see Jesus directly, we can at least see and experience him indirectly, through the eyes and lives of those who have risked everything, even their reputations, to follow him. Their witness is trustworthy.

NANCY S. TAYLOR

because not "any one" of them has authenticated Jesus (vv. 47–48). They also dismiss as irrelevant the crowd's response to Jesus, deeming them ignorant of the law (v. 49).

The Pharisees' presumed unanimity (not "any one," v. 48) proves to be a misstatement. One Pharisee, Nicodemus—perhaps because his prior encounter with Jesus (3:1–21) convinced him that Jesus resists any simple categorization imposed on him from commonly held messianic expectations—suggests they give Jesus a fair hearing, as their own law calls them to do (vv. 50–51). This is to no avail; his fellow Pharisees dismiss Nicodemus as they did the crowd (v. 52). The depiction of the Pharisees is scathing. While they deride the crowd for not knowing the law, they refuse to follow their own law and give the accused a fair hearing (see Deut. 1:16–17; 17:4). Their expectations provide the only valid possibility; the prophet like Moses who provides water and salvation is not to come from Galilee.

John 7:37–52 continues to portray Jesus' self-revelation and the divided response to it, showing how preconceived expectations may determine the response to such revelation; but what happens when the revelation that occurs defies such expectations? What happens if the God revered for springing surprises in history, as when God provided water in the wilderness to the wandering Israelites, does it again? What happens when the source of new life comes from an unexpected place, as when water came out of a solid rock? For John, this has happened again in Jesus, who simultaneously embodies the Scriptures and expectations of Israel, and yet cannot be wholly contained and determined by them.

The Messiah sent by God emerged from Galilee, and the new life God worked through this Messiah came in the unexpected fashion of his death, which as a result can be described as a glorification. For John, one must be open to the possibility that revelation comes from unexpected sources and in unexpected ways, for as God's prior actions celebrated in the Feast of Booths show, the God of Israel has always provided for the people's needs in surprising and unexpected ways.

GILBERTO A. RUIZ

now pose major threats to agriculture and sustainable development. In the Middle East, disputes over access to water have already become a source of political tensions that threaten people's lives and undermine initiatives for peace. Giving voice to these issues brings together the literal and metaphorical language of John 7:38 and calls on believers to join efforts to bring forth "rivers of living water" to sustain the earth and its inhabitants both at home and abroad.

With its attention to the divisions among the crowds, John 7:40–44 provides another entry into our passage. One could focus on verse 44, for example, which speaks of those who want to arrest Jesus and reminds us that confessing the faith can still be dangerous in some parts of the world. For many congregations, however, attending to the divisions among people who have differing confessional claims might be more helpful, since this remains an issue among Western churches today and creates both confusion and cynicism. Verses 40–41 refer to divisions between those who call Jesus "the prophet" and those who call him "the Messiah." The exegetical and theological entries on the passage in this volume and recent commentaries on the Fourth Gospel will inform the preacher of the significance of the titles for the communities in and for which this Gospel was written. To bring the passage to life, the sermon could show how the Gospel of John links the two titles for Jesus and thus affirms commitment to the gospel *and* social justice.

John 7:45–52 invites a sermon treating the challenges of speaking truth to power. Many in the congregation might identify with Nicodemus, recognizing how difficult it may be to profess their faith to those who belittle it. Reading verses 45–52 (along with 3:1–21; 12:42–43; and 19:39) may provide fruitful insight for exploring Nicodemus's movement toward a stronger faith. Modern examples of Christians seeking to witness in difficult circumstances could bring Nicodemus's story to life and inspire courage.

OLIVER LARRY YARBROUGH

John 7:53–8:11

[53]Then each of them went home, [8:1]while Jesus went to the Mount of Olives. [2]Early in the morning he came again to the temple. All the people came to him and he sat down and began to teach them. [3]The scribes and the Pharisees brought a woman who had been caught in adultery; and making her stand before all of them, [4]they said to him, "Teacher, this woman was caught in the very act of committing adultery. [5]Now in the law Moses commanded us to stone such women. Now what do you say?" [6]They said this to test him, so that they might have some charge to bring against him. Jesus bent down and wrote with his finger on the ground. [7]When they kept on questioning him, he straightened up and said to them, "Let anyone among you who is without sin be the first to throw a stone at her." [8]And once again he bent down and wrote on the ground. [9]When they heard it, they went away, one by one, beginning with the elders; and Jesus was left alone with the woman standing before him. [10]Jesus straightened up and said to her, "Woman, where are they? Has no one condemned you?" [11]She said, "No one, sir." And Jesus said, "Neither do I condemn you. Go your way, and from now on do not sin again."

Theological Perspective

John 7:53–8:11 is a dislocated and dislocating text. It interrupts the narrative flow of John 7–8, cutting into Jesus' teaching on the final day of the Feast of Tabernacles with never-before-seen characters[1] and an unprecedented challenge to Jesus' authority, and even adds an extra day to John's sequence of events (7:53–8:2). Scholars agree that this story is a later addition to the Gospel of John, perhaps finding a home here because of John's penchant for stories in which Jesus addresses female characters by the word "woman" (gynē), the debate surrounding the law that precedes in 7:37–52, or the repetition of Jesus' admonition to "sin no more" (mēketi hamartane) from 5:14. Yet that this beloved story is part of very early traditions concerning Jesus—hence its preservation—is also not in doubt. For this reason, 7:53–8:11 still deserves serious theological attention and reflection.

When approaching the story of "the woman caught in adultery" (NRSV heading), it is not uncommon to encounter interpretations that stress this narrative as one of unwarranted grace and as a

---

1. These characters include: the woman, the "people," and the "scribes." While other "women" are described in the Gospel (2:4; 4:7-42; 19:26; 20:13–15), this is the only appearance of this particular woman. This is also the first mention of "people" (laos) in John—the only other two occurrences will come in Caiaphas's ironic prophecy and its recapitulation in 11:50 and 18:14. This is the only mention of "scribes" (grammateis) in the Fourth Gospel.

Pastoral Perspective

Yesterday, the religious leaders had been humiliated by the refusal of the temple police to carry out their orders to arrest Jesus (7:45). Yesterday, the venerable and well-regarded Nicodemus, one of their own, had scolded them in public (7:50–51). To add insult to injury, the unlearned public is also shifting its allegiance to Jesus (7:40–41a). Worst of all, Jesus is playing a startling and starring role in the harvest festival (7:37–38). Is it any wonder that the religious authorities go home that night fuming and scheming?

By this morning, they have hatched a plan and are implementing it. They are laying a trap. They intend to prove that Jesus either does not understand the Law of Moses or, worse, flouts it. Either is a serious charge and grounds for arrest.

However, so blinded are the religious leaders by their rage and shame that they cannot see how their scheme will backfire. They cannot see how they will become hopelessly entangled in and exposed by the trap they set for Jesus. They cannot see that in their haste to judge Jesus, they are revealing their own moral hypocrisy. In their zeal publicly to expose and condemn a sinner, they display their own exceedingly ungenerous interpretation of the law by which human community under God is to be judged.

Setting a trap for Jesus and acting upon their rage and shame is precisely what these religious leaders

---

Feasting on the Gospels

Exegetical Perspective

The pericope in John 7:53–8:11 is not original to the Fourth Gospel. Stylistically it has more in common with the Synoptics (especially Luke); it is missing in the most ancient manuscripts, and different authoritative textual witnesses place it after John 7:36; 7:52; 21:25; and Luke 21:38. Because the story develops the conflict between Jesus and the religious authorities within the temple setting and resonates with various themes in John 7–8 (e.g., proper interpretation of the law, 7:19–24, 48–49; right judgment, 7:24; 8:15–16; see also Jesus' statement in 8:46), its current location became a suitable place to insert this early Jesus tradition.

The introduction (7:53–8:2) presumes Jesus teaches regularly in the temple ("he came again") and spends his nights just east of the Jerusalem city limits in the Mount of Olives, which he goes to regularly in the Synoptics (Luke 21:37; 22:39), but which is mentioned only here in John. That Jesus' audience constitutes "all the people" (v. 2) is an overstatement that signifies the presence of a large crowd, while setting up a contrast with the end of the pericope, when Jesus is left alone with the woman (v. 9).

The scribes and Pharisees, who frequently appear together in the Synoptics but not in John (which otherwise never mentions the scribes), enter the scene in verses 3–5. They address Jesus as "teacher" (again,

Homiletical Perspective

This is a wonderful story, even if it is not in the earliest Greek manuscripts of the Gospel of John or in early commentaries on it. The story is widely known today because it was in the late manuscript tradition on which the King James translation was based and in the Old Latin version of the Gospel of John that Jerome used for his translation of the Bible, known commonly as the Vulgate. Even if they are not aware of the source, most people will know the King James phrasing in verse 7 of Jesus' famous response to the scribes and Pharisees: "Let him who is without sin cast the first stone."

Indeed, this saying is likely to draw the attention of most of us preparing to preach on the text. The NRSV renders it, "Let anyone among you who is without sin be the first to throw a stone at her." Before settling on it as the text of the day's sermon, however, the preacher would do well to reread the whole story and look at it from different perspectives, opening up to other parts of the passage or gaining new insights into the familiar.

Begin by reflecting on the various characters in the story: the scribes and Pharisees, the woman, Jesus, and all the people who had gathered to hear him teach in the temple precincts. Consider also the characters who are not mentioned in the telling of the story: the woman's husband, the witnesses, and the disciples.

John 7:53–8:11

demonstration of Christ's being free of sin. While such an interpretation has its merits, it overlooks the way in which Jesus literally moves around the Pharisees' would-be "object lesson" for Jesus by means of their placement of the woman before him and the crowd. Instead of bending to their plans, Jesus demonstrates his unwillingness to allow others to be used as tools in the conflict with the religious leaders. Jesus does not engage directly with the leaders' accusation against the woman, who is acting as a stand-in defendant in their real trial against Jesus (v. 3). Rather, Jesus continually pushes attention away from her and onto himself.

If one follows the physical positioning reported in the story, one can easily become a little seasick. Jesus begins the passage "sitting" in order to teach those gathered around him in the temple (v. 2). Soon the leaders bring in a woman and make her "stand in the middle" of Jesus and his pupils, the people (*stēsantes autēn en mesō*, v. 3, NRSV "stand before all of them"). The leaders then mimic the role of students by addressing Jesus as "teacher" (*didaskale*), asking for his opinion in the case against the woman, all the while hoping to obtain a legitimate charge against him (vv. 4–6). Rather than standing to engage them, Jesus "stoops down" (*kyptō*, NRSV "bent down") and begins to write on the ground, thus drawing attention away from the standing woman and toward his finger tracing the dirt. Only after continued questioning does Jesus "look up" (*anakyptō*, NRSV "straightened up") and offer his own command to stand alongside Moses' commandment: "Let the one of you without sin throw the first stone against her" (v. 7, my trans.). Immediately, he "bends down" (*katakyptō*) again and resumes writing in the dirt (v. 8).

It is only after the leaders and the people shuffle away that Jesus rises to address the woman herself (v. 10). Now Jesus is "caught alone" (v. 9, NRSV "left alone") with her—still "in the middle"—just as she was "caught" before in adultery (*katalambanō*, vv. 3, 9). He does not accuse her or shame her; rather, he encourages her to leave and to live a life free from sin.

With its dizzying stage directions, this brief little story packs a powerful punch. While the religious leaders hope to undo Jesus' teaching moment and steal the spotlight with an accusation against him, Jesus easily outwits them. Moreover, he intercedes for the woman in a way that draws the spotlight of shame away from her and refocuses it on all those gathered around. Jesus sits, rises, stoops in the dirt, and dirties his hands as the crowd looks on—drawing their eyes from the spectacle of the woman to his

do. They find a woman in the very act of adultery, which leaves us with many questions. Have they set the woman up? If not, where is her partner in this crime? It takes two to commit adultery. If the woman has been caught in the act, surely the man was caught in the act at the same time. Why have the authorities failed to bring him to Jesus for judgment? After all, he too is guilty under the Law of Moses (Deut. 22:23–24). Finally though not least, to what brutish level have they fallen in shaming this woman and subjecting her to the possibility of death by stoning for the purpose of entrapping Jesus?

Jesus deftly reflects the attention from the accused back to her accusers. With a few words he conjures a mirror. Under the bright Palestinian sun, they see their reflection as clear as day. They see themselves snorting and fuming with righteous indignation, even as they are covered in sin. It is not a pretty sight. Then, beginning with the elders—perhaps beginning with the older and wiser among them, those somewhat mellowed by age and experience, softened by the wear of time and change—one by one they turn and walk away.

This is a story about trials. It begins with a ruse: the religious authorities putting the woman on trial. In fact, it is Jesus whom they are trying. By the penultimate scene the authorities have put themselves on trial—each is his own judge and jury, and each finds himself guilty.

John, in turn, deftly brings the story home. He brings the story to the present (from the first century to our century, and from the Pharisees to us). This is our story whenever we act out of rage and shame. It is our story whenever we are more interested in proving someone else wrong than in living as well—as righteously, morally, ethically, and generously—as we are humanly capable of living. It is our story whenever we take it upon ourselves to judge another prematurely or harshly or both.

It is also and profoundly a story about the one whom John's community and my community call Savior. It is the story of Jesus who teaches us mercy and who demands of his followers that we live lives of forbearance, of restraint and self-control.

The world eggs us on to judge others. It expects it of us. The way of the Christian is different. The way of the Christian is the way of forbearance; and because the way of forbearance is countercultural and counterintuitive, it must be learned.

Like Jesus, forbearance comes from God. Forbearance emanates from this one who is so in tune with God that he neither flinches nor judges.

common in the Synoptics but not in John; see 1:38; 20:16), though what they do is interrupt Jesus' teaching in the temple for reasons that become explicit in verse 6: they seek to test Jesus (Matt 19:3; 22:18; Mark 10:2; 12:15). They bring a woman "caught in adultery" and position her "before all of them" (v. 3).

It is telling that, though she was caught in flagrante delicto, they do not also bring the requisite two witnesses needed for a proper trial (Deut. 17:6; 19:15) or her male partner, who according to Mosaic law was also liable to face the death penalty (Lev. 20:10; Deut. 22:22–24). This shows the religious authorities' interests lie not in providing a fair trial for the woman but in getting Jesus to rule against Moses' law or against his own teachings on mercy in a public forum. Also, were he to approve of stoning the woman, such a verdict could land him in trouble with Roman authorities, if indeed it was illegal for Jews to apply the death penalty where their law requires it (18:31), which is uncertain. Either way, the woman functions as a pawn in their scheme to trap Jesus "so that they might have some charge to bring against him" (v. 6a).

Jesus' initial response is to bend down and write on the ground with his finger (v. 6b). The history of interpretation is replete with speculation about what Jesus writes (even in the manuscript tradition; see the NRSV footnote to v. 8). That the text offers no specifics indicates it is Jesus' act of writing, not its content, that matters (the scribes and Pharisees express no offense at what he writes). He might be performing Jeremiah 17:13 ("Those who turn away from you shall be recorded in the earth") as a parable in action, but primarily this act functions as a refusal to engage the scribes and Pharisees. He will not play into their thinly veiled attempt to entrap him.

The scribes and Pharisees correctly interpret Jesus' writing on the ground as an act of willful disengagement and keep questioning him for a response. In verse 7 he calls their bluff: they may stone the woman if they are sinless before the law of Moses. They are not, most immediately because they had skirted the law by seeking capital punishment without accounting for the required witnesses (who according to Deut. 17:7 had the right to throw the first stones) and her male partner. Jesus resumes writing, and his audience leaves "one by one, beginning with the elders" (v. 9a). The specification that they leave one at a time in order of seniority adds drama to their departure. Jesus is left alone with the woman, so that a scene that began with "all the people" is dramatically reduced to two individuals.

Going further still, think of those who decided to include the story of a woman caught in adultery when making their copy of the Gospel of John (or of Luke's Gospel, since the story sometimes appears in it). In considering all these actors, we might ask whose actions and attitudes would most likely mirror our own? With whom do we identify the most? Who surprises us the most? When our ministries put us in situations analogous to this one, whose actions come closest to reflecting the roles we commonly play? Asking these questions in preparation for preaching on the text may bring us to new insights and sensitivities as we open the text to others.

Reflecting on the woman's role presents us with many challenges and opportunities. She has the least to say of any of the characters, and yet has the most to lose if the situation goes against her. Quite remarkably, no one says she is innocent or that the charges against her were trumped up. Indeed, Jesus' last words to the woman, "from now on do not sin again" (v. 11), suggest he acknowledges the validity of the charge. Yet at the end of the story, when the curious observers and the agitated accusers are gone and Jesus and the woman are alone, he tells her, "Neither do I condemn you."

These are perhaps the most powerful words in the passage. How did they affect the woman? Did they change her life? Where did she go? What did she do? Reflecting on these questions may be the best way of opening up the story and finding a new way to bring it to life for people who know it well. A sermon that invites us to acknowledge the past, hear words of forgiveness, and step into the future would be a powerful word of grace for people burdened with guilt for what they have done or left undone. It will also speak to those who are haunted by the memory of belittling words of condemnation.

Focusing on Jesus' words about "throwing the first stone" presents other challenges and opportunities. Many who know the Gospels or hear them week by week in church will immediately identify the scribes and Pharisees as the villains of the story. After all, is their real concern not trapping Jesus into saying something indiscreet, so they can bring *him* up on charges (v. 6)? Are they really concerned about the woman? Do they, rather, use her as a pawn in a larger power game? (The phrase "such women" in the NRSV of verse 5 emphasizes the dismissive attitude of the scribes and Pharisees.) One way to move beyond an all-too-easy dismissal of the scribes and Pharisees is to try changing their accusations against the woman. How would we read the story if, for

John 7:53–8:11

Theological Perspective

own performance in a way that still leaves scholars guessing about what he wrote in the dust. As quickly as the Pharisees appear with the woman, Jesus has turned the tables on them. He steals the spotlight, truly takes on the role of "teacher," and instructs the Pharisees along with the crowd of their sinfulness, instead of joining in the shaming of the woman. The dubious trial—lacking prosecuting husband and co-sinning partner—disperses, and Jesus passes the verdict alone while he stands with the woman.

This solitary moment reveals even more about Jesus, however. In contrast to the culture of the day, Jesus acknowledges the woman and allows her to speak for herself. Her testimony of the scene is allowed to stand as well, and she is given the same words as the healed man in John 5, indicating belief in her equal ability to respond with faith. Moreover, Jesus' actions demonstrate his unwillingness for this woman—regardless of her sins—to be used in the machinations against him. In this way, Jesus ensures that the leaders cannot forfeit her life for a chance to dismantle his own popularity.

Jesus likewise refuses to use this situation as a chance to enhance his popularity. The only characters in the story aware of Jesus' final words are the woman and Jesus. Indeed, rather than increasing his honor, Jesus leaves himself open to scandal by being caught alone with "that sort" of woman (*toiautas*, v. 5, NRSV "such women").

Unfortunately, this story comes to us without a context. It would be fascinating to hear what happened next. Did the woman leave? Did she, perhaps, become a follower of Jesus? How did the people react to seeing this woman and Jesus alone or even later that day on the temple grounds? While all these questions are legitimate (and ultimately unanswerable aside from speculation), there is something powerful about this story as it is. It stands alone, just like Jesus and the woman, confronting its readers and forcing us to look inward as well.

ALICIA D. MYERS

Pastoral Perspective

Forbearance originates in and radiates from the deep patience of the one who quietly but firmly refuses to engage on the terms set by the accusers. It emanates from the one who in the face of pulsing temples, flaring nostrils, and veins as big as ropes, bends down, makes himself vulnerable, diverts the accusers' attention from the accused, and causes a pause in the action. He fingers the ground. Is he doodling, dawdling, or writing? Who knows?

Jesus gently invites and encourages us in living a life of humility and clear-eyed assessment of ourselves and our community. While we are constantly invited into and tempted by the world's propensity for dividing humans into us and them—good guys and bad guys, the guilty and the guilt-free, saints and sinners—in truth we are each a little of both. In truth, our life's work as followers of Jesus is learning and practicing gentleness, discipline, humility, and forbearance. Our life's work is shaping our own lives as disciples, not judging others' lives.

None of this is to say that adultery is permissible under God's law. It is not. Jesus orders the woman to sin no more (v. 11). We are led to believe that while the religious leaders' orders to the police go unfulfilled because they are given for the wrong reason (vv. 45–46), Jesus' order is fulfilled because it is given for the right reason.

Ultimately, this is a story about what it is like to live in the presence of God, where our sins, as clear as day and as visible to ourselves as to everyone else, are met with divine forbearance. This is good news for the woman caught in adultery, for her haughty accusers, for me, for you, and for any in whom there is even a smidgeon of sin.

NANCY S. TAYLOR

Exegetical Perspective

Asking if anyone is left to condemn her (v. 10), Jesus is the first person to address the woman directly. The pattern with which he addresses her is identical to how he addressed the scribes and Pharisees. In both instances he goes from bending down to write on the ground to straightening up and giving a verbal response (vv. 6b–7, 8–11). By presenting his responses to both parties in like fashion, the narration highlights Jesus' equal treatment of the woman and the religious leaders—in marked contrast to how the scribes and Pharisees had objectified her to suit their purposes.[1] So while readings of 7:53–8:11 often emphasize Jesus' merciful treatment of the woman (certainly a key element of the story), the pericope is just as much about Jesus' challenge to the religious authorities. No one, not even those of high social standing and presumed theological authority, is sinless. Everyone, be they religious leaders or accused sinners, has the chance to reexamine his or her past actions and start afresh.[2]

The woman finally speaks in verse 11, calling Jesus "Lord" (*kyrie*), an expression of her reverence for him. Jesus proceeds to acquit the woman and tells her to "not sin again" (*mēketi hamartane*, also in 5:14), offering her the possibility of a new life that is not bound by the events of her past.

GILBERTO A. RUIZ

Homiletical Perspective

example, the scribes and Pharisees had charged the woman with being an immigrant without papers? an anti-war activist? an opponent of abortion? In each situation, would *we* act like the scribes and Pharisees, or like Jesus?

Indeed, what is Jesus' role in the story? As with most stories in the Gospels, it clearly makes Jesus the hero—here not unlike the strong, silent outsider who is brought in to tame an unruly town in a classic American western. He says so little that the words he does say stand out. The action also highlights Jesus' words: he bends down to write in the dirt, straightens up to speak to the scribes and Pharisees, and then bends down again to write in the dirt. Jesus does not straighten up again until he speaks to the woman after her accusers have left. In this way, the story makes Jesus a model of matching words and actions.

Many commentaries refer to the legal complexities of the case the scribes and Pharisees bring to Jesus, noting, for example, their inappropriate application of Leviticus 20:10 and Deuteronomy 22:22. Though these passages do indicate that both partners are to be stoned, Jesus shows no concern for such matters. In spite of their persistent questioning (v. 7), he does not engage them in a debate about the law. Instead, he focuses on their attempt to manipulate it. He speaks truth to power and identifies with the weak.

The scribes and Pharisees abuse the woman taken in adultery by "making her stand before all of them" (v. 3). By the end of the story, she is alone with Jesus, "standing before him" (v. 9). What a difference! A sermon that helps a congregation recognize the difference between exposing sinners and welcoming them would be another powerful word of grace.

OLIVER LARRY YARBROUGH

---

1. See Gail R. O'Day, "John 7:53–8:11: A Study in Misreading," *Journal of Biblical Literature* 111, no. 4 (1992): 631–40.

2. "Both the scribes and the woman are invited to give up old ways and enter a new way of life. . . . The woman is invited to participate in a new future for herself that will allow her to live not as a condemned woman but as a freed woman. The scribes and Pharisees are invited to give up the categories by which they had defined and attempted to control life. . . . The scribes and Pharisees and the woman are invited to leave behind a world of judgment, condemnation, and death and enter a world of acquittal and life" (O'Day, "John 7:53–8:11," 637–38).

John 8:12–20

¹²Again Jesus spoke to them, saying, "I am the light of the world. Whoever follows me will never walk in darkness but will have the light of life." ¹³Then the Pharisees said to him, "You are testifying on your own behalf; your testimony is not valid." ¹⁴Jesus answered, "Even if I testify on my own behalf, my testimony is valid because I know where I have come from and where I am going, but you do not know where I come from or where I am going. ¹⁵You judge by human standards; I judge no one. ¹⁶Yet even if I do judge, my judgment is valid; for it is not I alone who judge, but I and the Father who sent me. ¹⁷In your law it is written that the testimony of two witnesses is valid. ¹⁸I testify on my own behalf, and the Father who sent me testifies on my behalf." ¹⁹Then they said to him, "Where is your Father?" Jesus answered, "You know neither me nor my Father. If you knew me, you would know my Father also." ²⁰He spoke these words while he was teaching in the treasury of the temple, but no one arrested him, because his hour had not yet come.

Theological Perspective

Dualism, we are told, is a pernicious mode of thought, always to be avoided. Dualisms divide a complex whole into two distinct, competing parts. The result is simple, reductionist alternatives that fabricate narrow ways of thinking and acting in the world. Mind/body dualism is one of the most notorious and harmful dichotomies, but it is not alone. Individual/group, spirit/matter, science/faith, are oppositions that present false alternatives, demanding unrefined choice. Reality is not black and white, we are told, but rather many shades of grey.

Radical dualism is no stranger to the church. In the early centuries of the church's life, various forms of Gnosticism thrived on dichotomy, none more than the Manichaean sect. Manichaean philosophy taught that good and evil were equal powers in the world, struggling against one another in a battle for dominance. The original, radical separation of good and evil, spirit and matter, light and darkness had become an intermingled reality. Human spirits were imprisoned within evil matter, and could only be liberated by spiritual knowledge and practices. Full, universal liberation would mean reestablishment of the initial division between spirit and matter, light and dark, good and evil, with the soul fully enveloped within the spiritual realm of light and truth.

Pastoral Perspective

In the age of 24-hour news cycles, it is not difficult to find someone offering sound-bite commentary on the latest headlines. Cable news shows often have two or three panelists engaged in a roundtable discussion about a current event. However, one of the things I have observed from these shows is the absence of *listening* to other perspectives. I see and hear people talking over each other, not answering direct questions, and sticking to prescribed talking points—regardless of the specific issue at hand. Very few news programs—and almost none on cable news—cultivate listening to varied perspectives.

When Jesus said to the religious leaders, "I am the light of the world. Whoever follows me will never walk in darkness but will have the light of life" (v. 12), his statement was challenged for a technicality rather than for its content. What were they listening *for*? They did not inquire about the meaning of his statement. They did not ask, "What do you mean?" or "How do you know this?" or "Why would you say that?" Instead, they shifted the focus of the conversation from Jesus' claims about his identity to the context in which he made this claim—without a witness. One may reasonably question the motives of the religious leaders. What did they intend to learn about Jesus as he taught in the "treasury of the

Exegetical Perspective

The Gospel of John employs the phrase "I am" (*egō eimi*) more than forty times. Often the statement is used without a noun to follow it (8:24; 18:5). In these instances, Jesus is connecting himself and his works to God. His words are also reminiscent of the Lord's revelation to Moses: "I AM WHO I AM" (Exod. 3:14). When "I am" immediately precedes a noun, as it does in John 8:12, Jesus speaks as one who is able to meet human needs. The Gospel writer's use of the language in these instances joins the physical presence of Jesus with what he is able to do physically for humankind. Jesus is the bread of life (6:35), the gate for the sheep (10:7, 9), the good shepherd (10:11), the resurrection and the life (11:25–26), and the true vine (15:1). In each passage, John uses this literary device to demonstrate how Jesus has come, not only that all may have eternal life, but to show Jesus as one who is able to take care of his own here and now. Jesus' statement, "I am the light of the world" (8:12), is another indication of this use of "I am."

The Feast of the Tabernacles (or Sukkot) sets the historical context for this scene, in which the Gospel writer equates Jesus with light. This autumnal feast celebrated the summer's grain harvest. The festival recalled Israel's sojourn in the wilderness after the exodus (Deut. 16:13). Lampstands symbolizing the light of God were a staple in the temple and a

Homiletical Perspective

The author of John has a deep desire for readers to know Jesus as intimate friend. Knowing Jesus deeply and trusting Jesus greatly, two aspects of genuine friendship, will enable readers to "see" Jesus reveal God as friend. Jesus is "the way" we enter a relationship with God that changes our view of ourselves, of God, and of life. John defines this relationship as redemption or salvation.

John's introduction of Jesus begins in the prologue, where we find the primary image for our text: Jesus, the light of all people. Light is the source of growth. Light overcomes darkness. Light quiets fear. The true light enlightens every human life.

"Light" captures John's description of Jesus' mission: the light that Jesus brings transforms the faith practiced by the religious leaders in Jerusalem. Jesus comes to reform faith, not initiate a new faith. As the text says, to know Jesus is to know God. The word "know" implies deep relationship, not just recognition.

The immediate context for the passage begins with chapter 7: leaders of the synagogue are looking for an opportunity to kill Jesus, and the Festival of Booths is drawing near. John introduces Jesus as a troubler of Israel, a prophetic voice of the Old Testament tradition. Jesus' teachings are disturbing to the temple authorities; even his disciples are finding his teachings difficult.

John 8:12–20

Theological Perspective

Manichaeism was an elaborate, sophisticated system that seemed to present an answer to the problem of evil in the world by providing an explanation of its power and the possibility of release from its grip. Augustine flirted with Manichaeism for nearly a decade before his baptism. While he later wrote against the Manichaeans, and while the church identified Manichaeism as a heresy, its characteristic dualistic thinking has persisted through the centuries, in the church as well as outside of it.

At first glance, John's Gospel seems to be replete with stark dualisms: flesh/spirit, above/below, heaven/earth, truth/lies, life/death, faith/unbelief, of the world/not of the world, blindness/sight, love/hate, life/death, and, prominently in this text, light/darkness. The opposition of light and darkness is introduced at the outset of the Gospel: "What has come into being in him [the Word] was life, and the life was the light of all people. The light shines in the darkness, and the darkness did not overcome it. . . . The true light, which enlightens everyone, was coming into the world" (1:3–5, 9). Throughout John's Gospel, Jesus Christ—the Word of God—is the light of the world. Is the Gospel according to John an instance of Christian dualism?

Perhaps not. After all, not all dyads are dualisms. Rejection of dualism does not necessitate the elimination of all contrasts. Dualism reduces reality to two opposing principles, one good and the other evil. Contrasting dualities, on the other hand, may clarify reality. John's use of light and darkness is not a philosophical division of reality into two opposing realms but, rather, a means to provoke theological and ethical thought about one reality: the Word made flesh in the one person Jesus Christ.

In John's Gospel, light as well as truth, life, and love, is a person, not a universal principle. "I am the light of the world" (v. 12), says Jesus; "I am life" (11:25); "I am the way, and the truth, and the life" (14:6); "I am the bread of life" (6:35). This language does not merely illustrate a truth we already know through other means. Rather, the language is richly metaphorical, opening us to know something that we cannot know otherwise. Two disparate elements—Jesus on the one hand, light (or truth or life) on the other—are placed together. The incongruous pairings change the meaning of both elements. How we understand Jesus is transformed, and how we understand light (and life and truth) is altered. Metaphors do more than put two things together; they create new insight into a new thing.

Pastoral Perspective

temple" (v. 20)? Was learning about Jesus the motive, or was there another goal in mind?

Similar questions can be asked of our public discourse today. In referring to the 24-hour news cycle, one may also reasonably question the intent of the discourse and the motives of interviewer and respondent(s). Is the intent to learn about the topic at hand by critical examination of facts, opinions, and viewpoints? Is it a fishing expedition for a "gotcha" moment? Is the intent to move beyond surface skimming into deep sea explorations of the complex societal challenges of our time? Is it just another opportunity to assert one's position with little thought given to various perspectives that inform the issue? Having a sense of the intent of the discourse can greatly influence how the hearer perceives what is being said. The Pharisees instituted a "gotcha" moment with Jesus when they invalidated his testimony (v. 13), instead of responding to the content of his message.

Jesus offers insight into the intent and validity of his testimony: "Even if I testify on my own behalf, my testimony is valid because I know where I have come from and where I am going, but you do not know where I come from or where I am going" (v. 14). Here he addresses the critique of an invalid testimony and expands the rules of engagement on the subject matter. Jesus makes it possible to bear witness to one's own experience. This has serious implications for our rules of engagement for public discourse today. It is difficult to understand someone's perspective when you do not have a sense of that person's life experiences. It is hard to understand persons when you have not attempted to understand the contexts that shaped them. If you do not understand such contexts, it will be even harder to understand their wishes and desires.

If we are to take seriously the task of understanding others' points of view, we are required to listen to them, not merely to hear the words they say, but to seek to understand the contexts and conditions that have informed them; the physical, emotional, and spiritual needs behind them; and the dreams and aspirations that fuel them. This is what feminist theologian Nelle Morton calls "hearing into speech."[1] When we make time and space to listen more fully to each other, to try and learn more about the contexts that have shaped them, we increase our chances of hearing the other more fully—and on their own terms. When we listen to each other in this way, we

---

1. Nelle Morton, *The Journey Is Home* (Boston: Beacon Press, 1986), 41, 55–66.

common feature of this and other Jewish holy days. Although the temple no longer existed by the time John records this Gospel, the writer provides cultural cues of a community dedicated to the temple as a religious and social center. Thus the reference to "Jesus as light" is no accident. Instead, John wants to give the reader a window into the religious significance of this declaration. Jesus connects himself to the temple and is also a "symbol" of the presence of God. He is the light of God for all to see.

Not only is the comparison of Jesus to light rooted in religious discourse; it also has political connotations. John's community in the late first and early second centuries existed under Roman rule. This group lived under the darkness of imperial domination. The idea of Jesus as light that has come to overthrow darkness is parallel to prophetic pronouncements of liberation and freedom, especially during exilic periods (Isa. 9:2; 49:6). Although much of the conflict in the Gospel of John centers around intra-Jewish turmoil over Christology, there are overtures of Jesus as a deliverer from imperial rule who has come to bring justice (12:12–13).

"Jesus as light" in chapter 8 is not a new theme. John first makes reference to this metaphor in the prologue (1:1–18). Here the author purports that John the Baptist was not the light, but "he came to testify to the light. The true light, which enlightens everyone, was coming into the world" (1:8–9). Again for the sake of literary and thematic consistency, what the author starts earlier now gets developed and elaborated in order to provide clarity. Whereas John anticipates in the prologue that the "true light, which enlightens everyone, was coming into the world" (1:9), seven chapters later there is no doubt that Jesus is the one who has come to enlighten everyone.

For the Pharisees, it is problematic that Jesus testifies to his unique connection to God without having anyone to witness to his testimony. According to the law (Deut. 19:15) two persons were needed to charge, convict, or validate a particular claim. The Pharisees, as religious leaders responsible for the interpretation of the Law or Torah, question Jesus about testifying on his own behalf. Their concern is that no one is present to substantiate what Jesus purports. Jesus maintains that he and God are the two witnesses who can attest to what he says and what he can do. These divine testimonies should take care of the law's requirement. What more is needed? Again, this is John underlining Jesus' identity with God, but his statement also has the effect of challenging the reigning interpretation of the law.

Pause there. Let context shape the sermon. Jesus offends, Jesus challenges, Jesus confuses—before Jesus redeems. Examine memory and the history of the congregation. Ask, "When have new ways of hearing the gospel been confusing and challenging?" Affirm that Jesus Christ is the same yesterday, today, and forever, yet also affirm that the coming of Jesus makes all things new—including our understanding of the mission of church and the will of God.

For John, Jesus is a friend, in the sense that a tough but caring coach becomes a friend, or a demanding but compassionate teacher becomes a friend. Jesus can rebuke, but he does so as his light reveals flaws and as his love brings wholeness to broken lives. Jesus as Lord and friend transforms the way disciples respond to God.

Recall the power of the light of Christ to shine into the darkness of previous generations of Christians—the darkness of racism and greed, the darkness of prejudice and discrimination, the darkness of war. Previous generations resisted hearing Jesus' teachings. Such realities are haunting reminders that disciples in every age fail to hear Jesus' proclamation of the gospel.

Listen for gospel in this passage. Notice that Jesus contradicts himself in his use of the word "judge." Gospel creates a new understanding of the relationship between God and people, a relationship that differs from the one the temple authorities practice. Gospel judges by leading those who hear gospel to repentance and confession. Repentance and confession open the hearer to the assurance of forgiveness and the gift of peace. Such is the nature of God's love, the power of God's grace.

Jesus' life, the life of God incarnate, judges everyone, and it has the power to redeem everyone. Jesus' judgment impacts people as taking a wrong road judges a traveler. A wrong turn may bring brief inconvenience for us, or a traveler may become so lost that a party is missed or a crucial business opportunity is forfeited. Taking a wrong road can even cause death. Ultimately, Jesus' judgment brings life.

John calls us to hear the gospel by asking us to see how religious leaders refused to examine the dead-end roads of their lives—personally and collectively. John then invites us to know Jesus as the light of the world, who leads us to examine the dead-end roads of our lives, our world, our time in history—and our religion. Such an examination has a power to open us to new ways of receiving Christ as redeeming light.

To proclaim gospel, invite people to name the darkness in human life and in the life of the church.

John 8:12–20

Theological Perspective

Moreover, metaphors overflow with surplus meaning that prompts us to think again, leading us to reflect more deeply. We think we know who Jesus is, and we think we know what light is, but what does it mean to say that Jesus is light? We think we know what life is, but what does it mean to say that Jesus is the light of life? John's Gospel is packed with metaphors, ranging from the conceivable ("I am the truth") to the strange ("I am the gate for the sheep"). Presented with incongruity, we strain to comprehend the something new. In the words of Paul Ricoeur, "Metaphor . . . introduces the spark of imagination into a 'thinking more' at the conceptual level."[1]

The intention of biblical metaphors goes beyond "thinking more," however; they provoke decision. The Gospel relates Jesus' actions and words "so that you may come to believe [trust] that Jesus is the Messiah, the Son of God, and that through believing [trusting] you may have life in his name" (20:31). We know what it is to stumble about in a dark room, unsure of where we are going, bumping into obstacles, and groping for guidance. We know what it is to turn on the lights and see everything clearly. Yet if Christ is the light of life, what is the darkness, what is the light, and what is life? What is the life that light reveals? What would it mean to follow Christ who is the light?

Familiarity with the Bible may dull us to the extraordinary metaphorical language that characterizes Jesus' speech, especially as it is related in the Gospel according to John. We may simply take for granted the odd pairings of Jesus with bread, vine, sheep gate, and a host of other startling metaphors. Yet metaphors are not merely illustrative images. Skimming over the surface of metaphorical incongruity diminishes our capacity to think deeply and trust fully the wonder of the Word made flesh. Providing prosaic explanations of the terms within metaphors reduces Scripture's thought-provoking language to a controlled object. Dismissing metaphors as merely illustrations that can be easily exchanged for other images fails to understand the creative function of language. Understanding the radical nature of metaphor instead enables the Gospel's language to expand thought, suggest new possibilities, and deepen commitment to "the true light, which enlightens everyone" (1:9).

JOSEPH D. SMALL

Pastoral Perspective

will often move from simplistic sound-bite explanations to learning more about the complexities of our world and its inhabitants.

What might it mean for our public discourse to take seriously the diverse experiences that shape our thoughts and perspectives? How might it change the way we see and hear each other? When we hear each other "into speech," it is easier to see each other beyond a label—black, white, straight, gay, Republican, Democrat. I have yet to meet a person that fits neatly into the stereotype of a label, yet we often make judgments about people based on very limited knowledge of who they are, where they have been, or where they are going (v. 14). Judgments are often based on fears and misunderstandings that need to be interrogated by truth and justice. Sometimes we fear things we do not understand, even if the fear is merely based on difference instead of evidence. When we shine the light of truth on our fears and misunderstandings, we create an opportunity to learn from a perspective of truth and not fear, and increase our chances of doing justice to the matter.

This example of seeing and hearing the other may seem a bit countercultural. It is easier to treat people as strangers—as "others"—than it is to get to know them. It is often more acceptable to typecast people than to take time to listen to them and consider their points of view. In some instances, it is more financially profitable to use a microphone to bully, insult, and condemn those who are of a different race, class, religion, gender, or sexual orientation than it is to speak out on behalf of the marginalized or disenfranchised in our world. Sometimes we are compelled to give voice to the truth of the experiences of the disenfranchised, realizing that we may risk being becoming judged and isolated. We may find ourselves feeling like a lone witness surrounded by people that do not value our witness on behalf of ourselves or others. In the end, we are called to do justice, love mercy, and walk humbly with our God (Mic. 6:8). May God be our witness.

LEAH GUNNING FRANCIS

1. Paul Ricoeur, *The Rule of Metaphor* (Toronto: University of Toronto Press, 1977), 303.

Exegetical Perspective

Therefore, what begins as a statement about Jesus meeting the spiritual and physical needs of those who follow him now moves to a legal issue. Jesus, as the "light of the world," begins by couching his announcement in political terms, presuming the present power arrangements are "darkness." However, his statement quickly becomes "testimony" that must withstand the challenge of the law. Furthermore, the argument between Jesus and the Pharisees progresses to an exchange that ultimately questions the divinity of Jesus. The Pharisees want to know, who is Jesus and who is his Father? They want to know if the witnesses Jesus presents to justify his actions are credible (v. 19).

It is clear that Jesus and the Pharisees are approaching the matter of testimony to the truth from two different angles. Jesus is engaging language of divinity in order to speak to what the Pharisees maintain is an earthly, legal concern. The Pharisees want to ensure that what Jesus says is credible under their understanding of the Law. Yet Jesus leans on the "if you knew my Father" christological defense. John, as the author and in an almost amusing manner, shows how the two conversation partners are miscommunicating.

At this stage in John's narrative, there is a stalemate between Jesus and his opponents. As the passage points to a theological and christological misunderstanding shrouded in legalistic jargon, John concludes the pericope with "his hour had not yet come" (v. 20). In other words, there is more. The story is to be continued. What is "enlightening" in this passage is the initial remark of Jesus that he came to bring light into the world. He offers the light of life. However, it appears that the exchange does not help to elucidate much. The Pharisees stick to their legalistic modus operandi. Jesus continues to connect the dots between him and God. While in the temple during a prominent religious celebration, the Gospel of John shows Jesus teaching, but it appears that his students are still in the dark.

STEPHANIE BUCKHANON CROWDER

Homiletical Perspective

Perhaps the darkness comes from being in the midst of divorce or alienated from children—or parents; perhaps darkness occurs because of losing a job or facing a medical crisis. Perhaps congregations and individuals are wrestling with issues related to sexual orientation and the meaning of marriage. These contemporary realities need the light of the gospel.

Naming darkness opens us to light, as the living Christ leads us to hear and see life and faith in new ways that create hope. Dark times can cause people to stop, to turn, and to follow Christ's way of forgiveness and love, a way of compassion and obedience that leads from darkness toward light.

A second gospel word in this passage occurs as Jesus points beyond himself to the God who sent him. Jesus is clear: his life and the life of the One who sent him are united. To know Jesus as our friend and redeemer is to know God as our friend and redeemer.

Gospel created anger and fear among the established religious thinkers in Jesus' day. Jesus encountered the religious authorities on their home territory in the temple. He used images of the temple such as lamps and light to interpret his identity and to explain his mission.

The temple authorities were blind to the light of Christ and deaf to his voice. Such blindness and deafness are not causes for the reader to judge them. Rather, their blind eyes and their deaf ears may judge the reader. They sound a loud warning not to become like them.

When Jesus becomes the light of the world, when he is seen as one with God the Creator, he does not separate his followers from other people, especially not from Jewish people or from Christians who see matters of faith differently from us. Rather, Jesus' desire for friendship with all people can empower divided, hostile people to become united through God's friendship with all people. Such is the nature of friendship love and friendship light as proclaimed in John's Gospel.

ART ROSS

John 8:21–30

²¹Again he said to them, "I am going away, and you will search for me, but you will die in your sin. Where I am going, you cannot come." ²²Then the Jews* said, "Is he going to kill himself? Is that what he means by saying, 'Where I am going, you cannot come'?" ²³He said to them, "You are from below, I am from above; you are of this world, I am not of this world. ²⁴I told you that you would die in your sins, for you will die in your sins unless you believe that I am he." ²⁵They said to him, "Who are you?" Jesus said to them, "Why do I speak to you at all? ²⁶I have much to say about you and much to condemn; but the one who sent me is true, and I declare to the world what I have heard from him." ²⁷They did not understand that he was speaking to them about the Father. ²⁸So Jesus said, "When you have lifted up the Son of Man, then you will realize that I am he, and that I do nothing on my own, but I speak these things as the Father instructed me. ²⁹And the one who sent me is with me; he has not left me alone, for I always do what is pleasing to him." ³⁰As he was saying these things, many believed in him.

Theological Perspective

The early centuries of the church's life were marked by rapid growth in the number of Christians and by refined understanding of the shape of the gospel. Central to both was bishops' instruction to new believers about the character of Christian faith and life. Persons wishing to become full participants in the community of faith spent one to three years as *catechumens*, undergoing training and instruction in the faith prior to their baptism and admission to the Lord's Table. This extended period of instruction immersed catechumens in the Scriptures, in a new way of living, and in the church's *rule of faith*.

Catechetical teaching in places throughout the Roman world was harmonious but not identical. Instruction summarized the same scriptural story and shared a common three-part structure, with clauses about God the Father, the Son of God, and the Holy Spirit. Examples of the *rule of faith* in the writings of Irenaeus and Tertullian, among others, demonstrate congruous teaching about Father, Son, and Holy Spirit. Yet some variations, ambiguities, and unanswered questions remained. They centered on the identity of Jesus Christ and the Holy Spirit: Is the Son fully God or an emissary sent from God? Is

* See "'The Jews' in the Fourth Gospel" on pp. xi–xiv.

Pastoral Perspective

In this passage, Jesus is not the bearer of good news. He alerts the religious leaders of his impending departure to an undisclosed and inaccessible location (v. 21), and when they try to figure out where he is going (v. 22), Jesus reiterates that they cannot come with him because their social location is not congruent with his destination (v. 23). For John, Jesus came from God and will return to God. Jesus goes on to issue a final warning that "you will die in your sins unless you believe that I am he" (v. 24). The religious leaders respond to this by asking, "Who are you?" (v. 25). Their frustration leads them to ask this question, to try to get clarity about what Jesus is saying to them, and to understand exactly why he says it.

However, the religious leaders are not the only ones who seem to exhibit frustration. Jesus also seems a bit exasperated at this point when he asks, "Why do I speak to you at all?" (v. 25). The New International Version translates this, "Just what I have been claiming all along." In other words, Jesus is implying that he is telling them the same things over and over, and they still do not seem to get it. Perhaps Jesus is secretly wondering, "Why bother?" or "What's the use?"

Preaching the gospel can be a dispiriting enterprise. Pastors often find themselves returning to the same text and not gleaning any new insights worth

Feasting on the Gospels

Exegetical Perspective

In the Gospel of John, Jesus frequently speaks in the first-person singular subject pronoun, I, pointing to himself rather than to the kingdom of God or the kingdom of heaven, as he does in the Synoptic Gospels. In these verses, Jesus refers to himself six times: "I am going away. . . . Where I am going, you cannot come" (v. 21), "I am from above. . . . I am not of this world" (v. 23), "I am he" (vv. 24, 28).

Unlike the immediately preceding "I am" declaration regarding his being the light of the world (8:12), in verses 24 and 28 "I am" is not referring to how his presence provides for humankind or how he helps to meet some physical need. Rather, the use of "I am" is more in line with revealing his origin and his destiny. His character is unique. He is not like others who have come before him. What he has to offer and what he has come to do are "from above" (v. 23) and so beyond the human realm. As a matter of fact, to comprehend Jesus, one must realize that he is "not of this world" (v. 23).

John wants to reiterate the connection between Jesus and God. In particular, the language of "I am" the author employs in verses 24 and 28 is to guide the readers to correlate Jesus with the same God who orchestrated the exodus and provided for the Israelites in the wilderness (Exod. 3:14). It is this supernatural being and power, this God, who is present

Homiletical Perspective

A revered theology professor once told me that to understand grace, one needs to have long-term friendships. Deep, trusting, friendships are a form of covenant. They endure "in spite of and because of." Respected pastors earn such friendships from congregants, and wise church members offer such friendships to pastors. Such friendships become a means of grace and truth in flesh.

John understands Jesus as a sacred, trusted friend, who is also mentor, confidant, and companion. Such friendship creates trust; indeed, "trust" is another way to translate the Greek word for faith. Trust allows followers of Jesus to experience God as grace and truth. Trust, friendship, grace, and truth are central to "gospel" faith.

This gospel relationship brings forth a new life, a life of redemption shaped by the values and attributes that Jesus embodies. For John, this life creates friendship with God and friendship with the children of God.

"I am the light of the world" is the key phrase in 8:12–20; the question in verse 25, "Who are you?" is key to hearing gospel in this section. By their question, the Pharisees demonstrate that they have not heard gospel; they have not yet received light. They are not yet friends with Jesus.

John 8:21–30

Theological Perspective

the Holy Spirit the Spirit of the one God or a spiritual presence derived from God?

The great ecumenical councils of Nicaea (325 CE), Constantinople (381 CE), Ephesus (431 CE), and Chalcedon (451 CE) were called to resolve ambiguities and disagreements about the rule of faith, to determine Scripture's witness to Father, Son, and Holy Spirit, and to give consistent shape to the teaching of the church. Nicaea and Constantinople fashioned the *rule of faith* into what we know now as the Nicene Creed, affirming that the Son is "God from God, Light from Light, true God from true God, begotten not made, of one Being [*homoousion*] with the Father" and that the Holy Spirit is "the Lord, the giver of life who proceeds from the Father, who with the Father and the Son is worshiped and glorified."

Establishing the divinity of the Son left unanswered the relationship of divinity and humanity in Jesus the Christ. Was Jesus' humanity merely a "costume" worn by God on earth? Were divinity and humanity two separate halves of Jesus? Were divinity and humanity blended together in a god-man mixture? The Council of Chalcedon articulated Scripture's witness by affirming in the Confession of Chalcedon that Jesus Christ is

> perfect in divinity and perfect in humanity, the same truly God and truly human . . . consubstantial [*homoousion*] with the Father as regards his divinity, and consubstantial [*homoousion*] with us as regards his humanity. . . . One and the same Christ, Son, Lord, only-begotten, acknowledged in two natures which undergo no confusion, no change, no division, no separation.

The language of the councils may seem far removed from the idiom of Scripture, replacing narrative and witness with abstract doctrine. It is sometimes said, for instance, that there is no doctrine of the Trinity or the two natures of Christ in the Bible. That is true enough in the sense that there is no *doctrine* of anything in the Bible; no doctrine of creation or salvation or sin or consummation. Doctrine is a summary exposition of Scripture's wide and deep witness. While the councils did not wish to say more than Scripture says, they certainly did not want to say less than Scripture says. The councils gave summary shape to the biblical witness to Jesus Christ, especially at points where diverse interpretations gave rise to views that threatened the integrity of Christian faith and weakened confidence in God's acts of salvation.

Pastoral Perspective

preaching. How many different ways can you say, "Love your neighbor" or "Pray for your enemies"? Congregants may tire of hearing different versions of the same message, or feel that its aims are unachievable. These types of experiences can lead the preacher and hearer to ask, "Why bother?" Perhaps the challenge to follow in the way of Jesus is not always to find new insight in the text or achieve unachievable goals, but to find ways his words can give insight and meaning to the new situations we face.

For many, there are daily opportunities to find ways to implement the teachings of Christ. What are the implications for a follower of Jesus to ask, "What does it mean to be loving in this situation?" Love's expression does not take the same form in every situation, but returning to this imperative again and again allows us to consider the new and perhaps achievable ways this goal can be reached. However, when the goal is not achieved, we may be tempted to ask, "Why bother?" What keeps pastors standing in pulpits in the face of these "what's the use?" type questions? What keeps congregants committed to discipleship in the midst of difficult circumstances? Jesus offers us insight into this dilemma as he shifts the focus from himself to affirming the power and authority of God (v. 26). In doing so, he offers hope.

In the movie *Flight of the Phoenix* (2004), the survivors of an airplane crash are faced with one means of survival: they have to build a new airplane out of the old one. They are in the middle of the Mongolian desert, have few resources, and have to figure out a way to build a new airplane and fly it back to civilization. Amid the hand-wringing and doubting, a voice of inspiration emerges from the group and says, "I think a man only needs one thing in life . . . someone to love. If you can't give him that, then give him something to hope for. And if you can't give him that, just give him something to *do*."[1] They begin to build a new plane, and as they do, they become more and more hopeful.

After all of the declarations that Jesus has made about himself, where he is going, and what will happen to them if they do not listen, he changes his tactic in verse 28. Perhaps he realizes that his strategy is not too effective, as they are still confused after his final declaration (v. 27). He gives them something to do, something to look forward to, and, in essence, something to hope for. He tells them, "When you have lifted up the Son of Man, then you will realize that I am he" (v. 28). The religious leaders now have

1. *Flight of the Phoenix,* directed by John Moore, written by Lukas Heller, Scott Frank, and Edward Burns (Los Angeles: 20th Century Fox, 2004).

Exegetical Perspective

now in Jesus. Whereas Paul writes of the God who delivered God's people from physical slavery through Moses and from spiritual slavery through Christ, John's Jesus speaks here in verse 28 as he did in chapter 3 of being "lifted up" (3:14–15), invoking the serpent lifted up on a pole by Moses that saved people from death in the wilderness (Num. 21) and the Son being lifted up on the cross by those who now do not understand. Unless they believe him who is "I am," they will die in their sin (v. 21).

The writer of the Gospel of John is highlighting the historical ties with the author's present community and their ancestors, who were the seed of Abraham and remnants of those who followed Moses. Members of the audience first hearing John's Gospel are the descendants of a people who have a long-standing history with I AM. If I AM has sent Jesus, persons in John's hearing must accept the message of Jesus.

Not only does the author attempt to underscore the relationship between what was and what is via historical references; there are also literary devices that aid in this thematic presentation. The author once again expounds on motifs initially introduced in the prologue (1:1–18). In verse 23, Jesus avers that he is from above and not of this world. In contrast, persons who hear him—in this case some Pharisees who are challenging him—are from below and of this world. This is similar to the language John employs in 1:9–10: the Word "was coming into the world . . . yet the world did not know him."

The world does not comprehend Jesus because he is not of this world.[1] What was a move of linguistic foreshadowing in chapter 1 now becomes more defined in chapter 8. Throughout his Gospel, John is trying to address intra-Jewish concerns about the christological nature of Jesus, and from the onset there is confusion over Jesus as Messiah and savior. To answer these concerns and confusions, the Gospel of John not only connects the cultural and historical dots within this community of Jews, but the writer uses linguistic turns of phrase to do so.

Note also the questions the Pharisees ask Jesus. After Jesus declares that he is going away, the Pharisees ask, "Is he is going to kill himself?" (v. 22). Suicide in this time and place was an act of familial embarrassment and societal cowardice. In the first century, where codes of honor and shame guided and regulated communal behavior, to take one's life was a poor reflection not only on the individual,

1. The concept of Jesus as truth in verses 31 and 32 resonates with John's initial presentation of "grace and truth" coming through Jesus Christ in 1:17.

Homiletical Perspective

In every age, religious, law-abiding, doctrinally correct people who have not heard or cannot hear gospel become like the Pharisees. As polarizing disputes that fracture the church remind us, debates that create enmity rather than friendship are contrary to gospel.

Somewhere along the way, most, if not all, of us fall into the trap of being confrontational rather than reconciling. Advocacy for a cause that seems righteous to us may lead to ways of darkness rather than light. When our lives no longer reflect grace and truth, we become like the enemies of Jesus whom John describes in his Gospel.

These religious leaders can help us hear gospel in new ways; they can become a means by which we are "born again" or "born from above" (3:3). In this passage, the religious leaders clearly have not received the gift of new birth, for they are asking all the wrong questions about Jesus. His words confuse them rather than redeem them.

The text opens with a warning from Jesus: "I am going away, and you will search for me, but you will die in your sin. Where I am going, you cannot come" (v. 21). Why can the Pharisees not come? Because they will not follow Jesus; they will not be open to knowing him as friend. They travel one road with their hearts, minds, and actions; Jesus travels a different road.

The lack of understanding shown by the religious people becomes a warning to people in every age who are confused by Jesus and an invitation for readers of the gospel to follow Jesus in ways that enable the world to see they are discovering who Jesus is.

The irony in this passage is that the Pharisees will travel the same piece of ground as Jesus: the road to the cross. Indeed, the Pharisees help determine the path Jesus will travel. However, as Jesus travels that road, he does so trusting the ultimate power of God and sharing forgiving friendship, both of which are the essence of grace. As Jesus travels toward the cross, he shares friendship with those who follow him with their hearts and their feet, even though those followers will deny and forsake him with words and actions.

The Pharisees cannot follow Jesus, because their eyes are blind to his friendship toward them, and their ears are deaf to the good news of grace and truth he brings. By rejecting Jesus, they will be lost, not because Jesus condemns them, but because their own actions condemn them to lives of rejection and hate instead of lives of acceptance and love.

John 8:21–30

Theological Perspective

"Who are you?" the scribes and Pharisees asked Jesus. Their incredulous question followed immediately Jesus' declaration, "You will die in your sins unless you believe that I am [*egō eimi*]" (v. 24b). This is the first of four instances in John of Jesus' self-identification using the absolute *egō eimi,* "I am." It has long been recognized that this statement, with no predicate, goes far beyond normal speech. (Note: the NRSV translates *egō eimi* prosaically as "I am he," relegating "I am" to a footnote. The Common English Bible renders *egō eimi* as "I Am.") Jesus' self-reference is both a type of the divine name YHWH (I am who is/who causes to be) and an expression of the way YHWH speaks, "I, I am comforts you" (Isa. 51:12, my trans.). The significance of Jesus' use of *egō eimi* is clear: he identifies what he says with God's word and he identifies who he is with God's being.

"Who are you?" The question is also followed by a second instance of *egō eimi* as Jesus says, "When you have lifted up the Son of Man, then you will realize that I am" (v. 28, my trans.). When the Son of Man is lifted up on the cross, lifted up from the tomb, lifted up to the Father, then many will realize that the answer to "Who are you?" is "I am." This remarkable identification of Jesus with YHWH is coupled with another self-identification of Jesus as the Son of Man (*huios tou anthrōpou*). The Common English Bible has been criticized by many for translating the Greek as "the Human One." But CEB's capitalization signals that it intends something more than simply "a human being."

The backdrop to *huios tou anthrōpou* is found in Daniel's vision of the beasts (Dan. 7). Daniel sees four grotesque beasts, one like a lion with eagle wings, a second like a bear with tusks, another like a four-headed winged leopard, and the fourth a beast with iron teeth and ten horns. These malevolent beasts represent the kingdoms of this world. Then the Ancient of Days takes his throne and, in stark contrast to the evil beasts, "one like a *bar enosh*" (Aramaic; Heb. *ben adam*) is given dominion and glory and kingship. The one who will reign comes as a human, not a malformed beast. In this brief text, the one Jesus is identified with both God and humans. He is both I AM and the Human One. It is all of this and more that is gathered into the creedal "truly God and truly human." The one person, Jesus Christ, makes God known (v. 28), and reveals truly human life (v. 29).

JOSEPH D. SMALL

Pastoral Perspective

a role to play in this endeavor; they have some skin in the game. They are charged with following in the way of Jesus, and it is in that process that they will come to understand who Jesus is and his relationship to God. It is in their participation with Jesus, not merely questioning him, that they come to know who he is and what he has been sent here to do.

This participation shifts the focus from the "what's the use?" and "why bother?" questions to the power and presence of God in our midst. Frustration abounds on all sides. The religious leaders seem frustrated by Jesus' vague illustrations and harsh words, and Jesus seems frustrated by feelings of rejection and disbelief. However, the tide turns when they emerge from this gridlock and the religious leaders are given a role to play in this saga. They are given the responsibility to "lift up" Jesus or follow him; in doing so, they will come to know the truth.

As Jesus gives the religious leaders something to do, he also encourages himself by saying, "And the one who sent me is with me; he has not left me alone" (v. 29). Perhaps this is also a remedy for the "what's the use?" and "why bother?" questions. When pastors remind themselves the work they do is not theirs alone, but God is with them, they can be refueled for the journey and keep on keeping on. After Jesus gives the people something constructive to do and reminds them of God's presence with him, people become a little more convinced about him (v. 30).

LEAH GUNNING FRANCIS

but also on his or her family. To honor one's family meant to preserve life, regardless of gender or economic or social status.

No matter how low one's social location or class, a person did not kill herself or himself. To commit suicide was an indication of intellectual and mental weakness. Suicide was shameful. Therefore, the question of whether Jesus was going to kill himself was an inquiry regarding what is or is not honorable. It further speaks of the continued miscommunication between the Pharisees and Jesus. What they perceive is of this world. His view is not of this world.

The question, "Who are you?" in verse 25 is the core of the misunderstanding between Jesus and the Jewish leaders. Jesus has tried to explain that his identity is not a new identity. On the contrary, he is that which has already been. He is the I AM that has been present throughout history. John's Jesus wants those hearing him in the temple during Sukkot to understand that he is the continuation, the new revelation of the I AM of the exodus and the Lord of the Sukkot. The Word that was in the beginning, the bread that the Lord provided in the wilderness, the light that the prophets predicted would bring the oppressed out of political bondage, the I AM that was and is and is to come—this is who Jesus is.

Although the writer of the Gospel of John wields much literary finesse in its presentation, the linguistic wordplay becomes more pronounced as the characters in the Gospel communicate and engage in verbal exchanges. The more Jesus and those listening to him talk, the greater their words crisscross. As Jesus continues to divulge his nature, the inquiries surrounding him multiply. While Jesus' use of I AM should immediately correlate his existence to the God of Israel, it is his presence and purpose in John's community in the first century that remain questionable.

STEPHANIE BUCKHANON CROWDER

Jesus' words confuse the Pharisees. The confusion parallels the conflict Jesus has with the authorities in 7:36–52. Both passages are words of warning, especially to those of us who have expressed faith in God much of our lives, those of us who have studied the Scriptures and are sure we know what they mean for our time and for the conflicts we face. When we are sure that our way of knowing and following God is *the* way, we may have become more like enemies of Jesus than like disciples.

However, Jesus also confuses his disciples. John's Gospel is filled with reminders that disciples can become scared, forsaking Jesus and fleeing in the moment of trial. The disciples are faithful friends only because they return, humbled and open, one more time to Jesus' friendship, as God's Spirit transforms their very being. In the Gospels, faithful disciples are not people who follow Jesus perfectly; they are people who come to know the power of Jesus' grace-filled friendship to make them new creations, and then seek to share that friendship with others.

The latter part of the text shares John's powerful Christology. As Jesus responds to the question, "Who are you?" John comments, "They did not understand that he was speaking to them about the Father" (v. 27). Then John shares Jesus' words about the relationship between the Father and the Son. Many readers of this passage hear the words "when you have lifted up the Son of Man" (v. 28) as a veiled prophecy about Jesus' death.

Another important affirmation is that Jesus does not come to proclaim a God other than the God of Abraham, Isaac, and Jacob, the God of the Jews. Jesus comes to bring a new understanding of God, an understanding that rises out of grace and truth. Jesus is a reformer of faith, not the initiator of a new faith. As Jesus will make boldly clear in the next passage, Jesus and the God who called Abram and Sarai are one. To know Jesus is to know God, the creator and redeemer of the world.

John concludes this passage with words that reflect the preacher's great prayer for any sermon on this text: "As he was saying these things, many believed in him" (v. 30).

ART ROSS

John 8:31–38

³¹Then Jesus said to the Jews* who had believed in him, "If you continue in my word, you are truly my disciples; ³²and you will know the truth, and the truth will make you free." ³³They answered him, "We are descendants of Abraham and have never been slaves to anyone. What do you mean by saying, 'You will be made free'?"

³⁴Jesus answered them, "Very truly, I tell you, everyone who commits sin is a slave to sin. ³⁵The slave does not have a permanent place in the household; the son has a place there forever. ³⁶So if the Son makes you free, you will be free indeed. ³⁷I know that you are descendants of Abraham; yet you look for an opportunity to kill me, because there is no place in you for my word. ³⁸I declare what I have seen in the Father's presence; as for you, you should do what you have heard from the Father."

Theological Perspective

Jesus' series of encounters at the Feast of Booths continues here. Compactly, Jesus lays out key elements of who he is and what he does. He describes the momentous change he brings to life in vital terms that take a lifetime to explore and live out.

Continuing in Christ's Word (v. 31). The words Jesus spoke brought some of his hearers to believe in him. Jesus' word was that truly to be his disciples, his hearers must "continue in my word" (v. 31). Whatever sign or indication the "Jews who had believed in him" had given would be tested by the long run, the journey. Would they simply hear and say, "That sounds good," or would they embrace Jesus by faith and persevere, "continue in my word"?

This is always the question, is it not? After we make professions of faith in Jesus Christ—at an evangelistic rally, in response to preaching, or even by confessing our faith and joining the church—will these initial affirmations endure and set meaningful directions for our lives over time? Believing in Jesus and receiving the momentous changes Christ brings are expressed not momentarily, but in a lasting, progressive pattern. Some may profess, but not progress. The early excitement of the Christian

---

* See "'The Jews' in the Fourth Gospel" on pp. xi–xiv.

Pastoral Perspective

The Feast of Tabernacles is the setting for this encounter, a feast of light in the Jewish tradition. The eighth chapter of John appears to be an odd collection of interactions between Jesus and "the Jews," the people of Judea, religious kin who are curious and confused about Jesus' teachings.[1] Beginning with verse 31, readers encounter the final scene of a perplexing interaction with those Jews who believed in Jesus and yet were at odds with him, some even set on killing him. Verses 31–38 frame the familiar claim: "You will know the truth, and the truth will make you free." In anticipation of Pilate's question, readers may ask, "What is truth?" In concert with John's confused hearers, shared questions might be: What does it mean to be "free" indeed? Free from what and for what? What does it mean to tell the truth?

While those first hearers of this Gospel lived under the oppression of Rome and were hungry for political freedom, Jesus talked about a different kind of freedom—freedom from sin. He spoke of a different kind of truth—the kind of truth-telling that sheds light on sin and brings it out into the open so that people can be released from sin and have a new

---

1. Raymond Brown, *The Gospel according to John* (Garden City, NY: Doubleday, 1966), finds analysis of this chapter difficult (p. 342). Brown notes that John often speaks of the inhabitants of Jerusalem or Judea as "the Jews" (pp. 354–55).

Exegetical Perspective

One of the issues in the translation of these verses is whether the two words translated "the Jews" (*hoi Ioudaioi*) should be translated "the Judeans." The Gospel of John presents a three-year period in which Jesus travels back and forth between Judea in the south, where Jerusalem is located, and Galilee in the north, where Nazareth, Cana, Capernaum, and the Sea of Galilee are located. When Jesus travels to Galilee in John 4, the narrator says that "the Galileans welcomed him, since they had seen all that he had done in Jerusalem at the festival" (4:45). When Jesus returns to Jerusalem in chapter 5 and heals a lame man on the Sabbath, "the Judeans started persecuting Jesus, because he was doing such things on the sabbath" (5:16). For some scholars, the best translation of the words in John 8 is "the Judeans," rather than "the Jews." John is concerned with three major regions and their occupants: Judea, Galilee, and Samaria (where Samaritans live). A major issue in John 4 is whether Samaritans (4:39–42) and Galileans (4:43–45, 53–54) "believe" in Jesus; of significance in John 8 is "Judean" belief in Jesus. The focus of this passage concerns some Judeans who believe in Jesus and some who do not (8:30–32).

John 7:40–52 establishes the Judean location for the dialogue that begins in John 8:31–38. On the

Homiletical Perspective

Verse 31 presents a conundrum for interpreters: how do you explain the way this text begins (almost sweetly) and the way it ends? Jesus' "believing" listeners (v. 31a) react with indignation to Jesus' words (vv. 31b, 33). How did this happen? Modern scholars offer mostly literary or grammatical explanations for this incongruous introduction. However, John Calvin provides a distinctly pastoral perspective, suggesting that Jesus was speaking to a "promiscuous crowd," a community from which you might expect a "confused" or mixed reaction to Jesus' message.[1] Jesus implies that his believing listeners were neither as free nor as faithful as they imagined. Their indignant reaction to Jesus suggests their capacity for denial: "We are descendants of Abraham and have never been slaves to anyone. What do you mean, 'You will be made free'?" (v. 33).

One wonders what happened to their memory of the sojourn in Egypt; or the Babylonian deportation; or the reality of Roman colonization. Never slaves to anyone? Ever? Really?

While our own sociopolitical context may be different from the one presupposed by John, this text probes our own capacity for denial. Take, for example, slavery, which for many might be more likely

1. John Calvin, *Commentary on the Gospel according to John*, trans. William Pringle (Albany, NY: Books for the Ages, 1998), 305.

John 8:31–38

Theological Perspective

gospel may evaporate if attention is not given to continuing in Christ's word. In the worst case, this is hypocrisy—roundly condemned in the Gospels. Some falsely claim a commitment to Christ, but do not intend to make Jesus a lifetime companion who orients every aspect of life. Christ's true disciples continue to listen to his word, learn from Christ, and obey the will of Christ. Jesus provides our life trajectories; when we abide in Christ (15:4–7), Christian discipleship becomes real. "Everyone who does not abide in the teaching of Christ . . . does not have God" (2 John 9).

Knowing the Truth (v. 32). Then Jesus continued with the famous words: "You will know the truth, and the truth will make you free" (v. 32). This verse has been quoted and used—and misused—through the centuries.

As we continue in Christ's word, we come to "know the truth." Pilate asked Jesus, "What is truth?" (18:38). Pilate did not know truth, even when he was (literally) staring him in the face! Jesus Christ himself is the truth, just as he is also the way and the life (14:6). John's Gospel establishes what the church has historically believed. Jesus Christ is "the Word became flesh" who "lived among us"; who revealed the glory of God, "full of grace and truth" (1:14). Jesus Christ is truth in person; for he has made known the eternal God, even as he is the eternal God (1:18).

Jesus said, "If the Son makes you free, you will be free indeed" (v. 36). When we know Jesus Christ, we know the truth; and that truth sets us free. We know Jesus Christ by faith, faith being the means by which we are united with Christ and the way our fellowship with Christ is nourished and nurtured. Christian discipleship involves knowing Christ, who is the truth for our lives and for the life of the world. Our knowledge of the truth is our knowledge of a person. As the New Testament scholar C. H. Dodd put it, the disciples' relationship to Christ is

> more intimate than that of disciples to a teacher. To "know the truth" they must not only hear His words: they must in some sort be united with Him who is the truth. Thus even when the concept of knowledge of God is most fully intellectualized, it remains true that it involves a personal union with Christ, which goes beyond mere intellectual apprehension.[1]

1. C. H. Dodd, *The Interpretation of the Fourth Gospel* (repr., Cambridge: University Press, 1998), 178.

Pastoral Perspective

beginning. In particular, Jesus offered them freedom from the enslaving habits that hold people back from their full humanity, and freedom from the fear that keeps some from living the abundant life that is possible when each day is lived in the light of unconditional love and grace. His hearers then and now were unsure about the value of this kind of freedom, this kind of truth.

At times, humans find it hard to face the truth about their lives, just as those who encountered Jesus in person or through John's Gospel sometimes had a difficult time hearing what he had to say to them. Like them, many today live as captives, refusing to turn from the bondage created by the denial of their own brokenness and sin. Like the persons in this story, people become so busy paying attention to the faults and foibles of others that they cannot see their own limitations. For many, pointing the finger at others was and is a convenient way of drawing attention away from one's own brokenness. Denial can become a way of life, so much so that bondage may appear preferable to freedom.

Jesus offered those first hearers release, liberation, spiritual freedom. Even now Jesus offers such release to captives living in denial. Luther said humans are redeemed sinners, *simul justus et peccator*, at once sinful and justified. By that he meant that believers are hardly free of sin; rather, they are recovering sinners, pilgrims in exodus, exiles on their way home. The journey begins with truth-telling, with an honest assessment of the way things are, with that difficult escape from denial, with the grace that allows individuals to see themselves as lovable, forgiven, and beloved of God.

If, as some have said, all are either addicted to something or codependent with someone who is addicted, then one possible way of viewing the human condition is to liken sin to addiction and grace to recovery.[2] Sin, like addiction, involves both rebelling and hiding; it entails believing one has control over life and refusing divine grace. Sin, like addiction, lulls one into the false belief that the comfort of the status quo is preferable to growth and change. Grace and recovery begin with confession and repentance. While recovery involves ruthless self-examination as well as making amends, grace makes room in the self for loving one's self and others, as one has been loved. Recovery, like grace, also

2. Linda Mercadante, "Sin, Addiction, and Freedom," in *Reconstructing Christian Theology*, ed. Rebecca S. Chopp and Mark Lewis Taylor (Minneapolis: Fortress Press, 1994), 220–44; Gerald May, *Addiction and Grace* (San Francisco: Harper & Row, 1988); James B. Nelson, *Thirst: God and the Alcoholic Experience* (Louisville, KY: Westminster John Knox Press, 2004).

Exegetical Perspective

last day of the Jerusalem Festival of Booths,[1] some Judeans believe that Jesus is "the prophet," and other Judeans believe he is "the Messiah" (7:40–41). In John 8:31, Jesus tells those Judeans who believe in him that if they remain in his "word" they will truly be his disciples, they will know the truth, and the truth will make them free. The phrasing is especially strong, since the term Jesus uses for "word" is *logos*.[2] The narrator uses the same term in John 1:1 to describe Jesus' presence as an inner attribute of the invisible God before creation occurred, the inner agency of God through whom all living things "became" (*egeneto*, "came into being," 1:3), and the inner "light" that became the visible being in the world through whom all people could "see" God.

In antiquity, people's identity was especially based on the region in which they lived, their ancestors, their particular history, and the "known" attributes of the people in that region. According to 8:33 the identity of the Judeans is located in Abraham. The Judeans see Jesus' language about truth and freedom in verse 32 to be an assault on their identity, since it implies that they live in slavery. Usually the topic of slavery would take a person to the story of Moses and his freeing of "Israelites" from slavery in Egypt. The Johannine "believing" community that tells this story about Jesus' encounter with "the Judeans" prefers to focus on Abraham rather than Moses, probably because neither the topic of "freedom" nor the topic of "truth" is conventionally associated with Abraham. If the topic were Moses, the Judeans could present quite a strong argument that Moses gave them "freedom" from slavery in Egypt and "truth" about God in God's Torah and covenant with them at Mount Sinai.

In verse 34 Jesus introduces the topic of "sin" to negotiate the topic of slavery with the Judeans. Asserting that the Judeans are "slaves to sin," Jesus focuses on "the son" versus "the slave" in a household. According to Jesus, "the Son" (Jesus) can make the Judeans free, and the Son has a permanent place in the household of God. Theoretically, this should introduce a debate about Jesus' relation to Isaac, because in Jewish tradition "the beloved son" whose life "was laid down by his father" was Isaac. However, the Gospel of John does not allow the Judeans to present "their side" of the issue. Jesus speaks with "complete authority" as "the Son of the Father."

Homiletical Perspective

to be found in a museum than next door. Today the U.S. State Department cites statistics estimating there are 20.9 million victims of forced labor throughout the world at any one time.[2] Servitude registers at other, more subtle levels as well. By denying 11 million undocumented people some sort of legal status (and therefore legal protections), the democratically elected U.S. government maintains an easily exploited pool of cheap labor. Under constant threat of deportation, many become prisoners in their own homes, exploited by "citizen" consumers, haunted by the always imminent risk of deportation.

Meanwhile, the Social Security Administration quietly looks the other way as billions of dollars flow into its coffers from tens of millions of workers. See, for example, Eduardo Porter, "Illegal Immigrants Are Bolstering Social Security with Billions" in *The New York Times* of April 5, 2005. While most North Americans would adamantly deny that they "hold" slaves, North Americans do "hold" on to a financial system that effectively enslaves the most vulnerable to enrich the most powerful.

This might seem like an odd interpretive trajectory, given the way we customarily interpret texts from John. Among some interpreters, John is seen to promote the "personal" or "mystical" Jesus. However, what is less pronounced in our interpretive practice is the historicity of John's Gospel, something that Raymond Brown asserts could be overlooked by commentators who view it primarily as a "theological" text.[3]

If we were to allow this text to offer a cultural critique of our own promiscuity, what might that look like? One possibility comes from cinema. The 1996 British drama *Trainspotting* (based on Irvine Welsh's novel by the same title) seems at first to be a simple morality tale focused on the black hole of addiction, as it chronicles the lives of a small group of heroin addicts in one of the slums of Edinburgh. One of the friends, the central character, seems to "choose life" over death, eventually moving to London. He lands work as a real estate agent; at one point, he likens his new life to his old life as a drug user and dealer. While this comparison hints at the critical edge of this film, the final scene delivers the blow directly. As he walks through London, a wide, almost drug-induced smile spreads across his face. The picture fades until his eye sockets and mouth

---

1. Also called Festival of Tabernacles; see 7:2, 14, 37.
2. An alternative term for "word," *rhēma*, occurs twelve times in John with reference to words either of God or of Jesus (e.g., 8:20, 47).

2. U.S. Department of State, *Trafficking in Persons Report* (June 2012), 45.
3. Raymond E. Brown, *The Gospel according to John I–XII*, Anchor Bible 29 (Garden City, NY: Doubleday & Co., 1966), xli–xliii.

John 8:31–38

Theological Perspective

We know and continue to know the truth as we live lives of discipleship, following Jesus and in union with him.

Free in the Son (vv. 32–38). We know the truth, Jesus Christ; and "the truth will make you free." Our freedom comes from the Son (v. 36). For John, "freedom is salvation, deliverance from sin."[2] This is the great work of Jesus, "the Lamb of God who takes away the sin of the world!" (1:29).

Jesus' hearers did not understand: "What do you mean by saying, 'You will be made free'?" (v. 33). They thought they had always been free, "never slaves to anyone" because they were descendants of Abraham (v. 33). Jesus meant other than and more than political freedom. Freedom goes deeper.

For Jesus, "everyone who commits sin is a slave to sin" (v. 34). Then he contrasted the "slave" who "does not have a permanent place in the household" with the "son" who "has a place there forever" (v. 35). The implication is that no pride of race or pedigree can assure a place in the household of God to those who are slaves to sin. By sinning, Jesus' hearers could find themselves excluded from the household. So can we today. Plotting to kill Jesus showed "there is no place in you for my word" (v. 37). There is no true freedom if there is no freedom from sin.

Jesus Christ has come to bring freedom. Jesus means freedom. As John Calvin put it: "For what He has of His own nature He communicates to us by adoption, when we are engrafted by faith into His body and made His members. . . . Our freedom is a benefit of Christ, but we obtain it by faith, through which Christ also regenerates us by His Spirit."[3] In Christ our sin is forgiven; we are reconciled with God and have been "freed from sin" (Rom. 6:22).

Our true and only freedom is the freedom Jesus Christ brings. Our freedom from sin comes from the gospel. As Christ's disciples, we know he is the truth. Jesus Christ sets us free!

DONALD K. MCKIM

Pastoral Perspective

includes forgiveness. The word that Jesus speaks to sinners/addicts, then and now, is a word of challenge and hope, of judgment and release, of recovery and grace, that can finally be heard as a word of acceptance, encouragement, and healing.

Addiction and sin are personal, but they are also corporate and social. Both individuals and institutions are prone to denial and in need of the radical truth-telling and freedom that the light of Christ can bring. Organizations, including the church, may practice addictive behavior. Indirect communication, exclusion, racism, sexism, greed, and gossip are all too familiar in the church and in other social institutions. Christian disciples have become adept at tuning out the pain of the world, at cushioning themselves from the suffering of those who are poor, weak, hungry, or abused. This habit of denial occurs even within our communities when those who are hurting are our kin, neighbors, and members of our flocks.

In Christian communities graciousness and friendliness tend to be idealized; yet denial of another's humanity is apparent in the ways Christians exclude and judge those inside and outside the church. The truth of which Christ speaks offers liberation from personal and corporate denial. Organizations, including the church, can practice truth-telling in a way that leads to recovery and freedom.

In the end, Christian liberty and political freedom do go together, because individuals too often are in denial about social sins and their participation in the grand schemes of injustice and oppression that defy the liberating grace that Jesus has to offer. The Judeans who approached Jesus were in the grip of an empire whose sinful machinations they experienced on a daily basis and at the local level. They longed for both spiritual and political liberty. Those who enjoy political freedom today can conveniently forget that many in the world still long to be set free socially, economically, and politically. The prophetic truth-telling of Jesus unmasks spiritual and corporate denial. The light of Christ still shines in human hearts and in human institutions. The gospel of grace is at once personal and social.

REBECCA BUTTON PRICHARD

---

2. John Marsh, *Saint John*, The Pelican New Testament Commentaries (repr., Middlesex, England: Penguin Books, 1974), 363.
3. John Calvin, *The Gospel according to St. John: Part One 1–10*, trans. T. H. L. Parker, Calvin's New Testament Commentaries (repr., Grand Rapids: Eerdmans, 1979), 223.

Exegetical Perspective

When Jesus asserts his special identity as "the Son" by claiming that he declares what he has "seen in the Father's presence" (v. 38), his argument moves beyond Jewish prophetic and apocalyptic beliefs to the "precreation belief" described above. Instead of focusing on Jesus at the "end" of time (eschatology), through whom God's prophetic promises about God's kingdom and God's apocalyptic establishment of a new eternal age will occur, "Johannine" Christians focus on the "beginning" of time (protology), with an emphasis that Jesus existed even before time began with the creation of the world. For them, since Jesus was (invisibly) present in the inner being of God before creation and was the personal "agent" of creation through his function as *Logos*/Word, Jesus is the "authoritative" speaker about God, the world, and all that is in the world.

In 8:38 Jesus uses this "Johannine" belief reasoning with the Judeans, arguing that when he was with God "before" creation occurred, Jesus "saw" what was "really true." In John, therefore, while Jesus is on earth, one of his major tasks is to tell people "the truth" about God. Truth, in the Gospel of John, means truth about the inner nature of God's love for the world, how the creation really came into being, and what the tasks of "the Son" really are while he is on earth.

A special aspect of the argumentation here is the occurrence of "my word" (*ho logos mou*) in the opening and closing of the unit.[3] When John's Jesus says the Judeans must "abide in" his own "inner" being as "*logos*/Word" (v. 31) in order "truly" to be his disciples, this statement expands Paul's way of thinking about Christ being "in" a person (cf. Gal. 2:20). Moving beyond Paul's focus on dying and rising with Christ, the Gospel of John asserts that it is necessary to have eternal life "in one's body" by "abiding in" the eternal *logos*/Word.

VERNON K. ROBBINS

Homiletical Perspective

look empty, while the voice-over offers a hyperfast litany of things that he "chooses" that amount to an addiction to a consumerist culture. The film suggests by indirection that we are not so clean or sober as we imagine, just slaves to a different and perhaps even more deadly form of addiction.

Transiency supplies the central motif of the film: shedding images of life in the same way a consumer passes through a laundry list of things to get, buy, hold, and then toss, sacred and profane alike. John's Jesus would have us open our eyes, not only to our captivity to the flesh, but also to the way he, in himself, has reconciled the flesh to his body, making a home of dignity and wholeness through his love. Jesus proposes the freedom of the child of God, and so a lasting place to grow and to be formed and to be in relationship: "The slave does not have a permanent place in the household; the son has a place there forever. So if the Son makes you free, you will be free indeed" (vv. 35–36). If we connect these words with the opening of this pericope, "Continue in my word" (v. 31), we get the sense of a lasting and broadly significant relationship.

The redwood forests supply an evocative metaphor for this kind of community, the kind of community John's Gospel envisions, with an intimate relationality between believing community and incarnate Word. Postcards often show the towering trees of the redwood forests, but perhaps the more radical "forest" is the one beneath the surface of the earth: the very real root system of each tree interlocked into a complex matrix of interdependency, sustaining these mighty trees individually and collectively. Only through that kind of prolonged formation and interformation do we become true disciples: "Dwell in me and I will dwell in you. Instead of being a slave to the anxious winds of addiction and ideology, your life will be rooted in the depths of a lasting community."

ROBERT HOCH

---

3. The term *ho logos* ("the word") occurs six times on Jesus' lips in chapter 8, in vv. 31, 37, 43, 51, 52, 55.

³⁹They answered him, "Abraham is our father." Jesus said to them, "If you were Abraham's children, you would be doing what Abraham did, ⁴⁰but now you are trying to kill me, a man who has told you the truth that I heard from God. This is not what Abraham did. ⁴¹You are indeed doing what your father does." They said to him, "We are not illegitimate children; we have one father, God himself." ⁴²Jesus said to them, "If God were your Father, you would love me, for I came from God and now I am here. I did not come on my own, but he sent me. ⁴³Why do you not understand what I say? It is because you cannot accept my word. ⁴⁴You are from your father the devil, and you choose to do your father's desires. He was a murderer from the beginning and does not stand in the truth, because there is no truth in him. When he lies, he speaks according to his own nature, for he is a liar and the father of lies. ⁴⁵But because I tell the truth, you do not believe me. ⁴⁶Which of you convicts me of sin? If I tell the truth, why do you not believe me? ⁴⁷Whoever is from God hears the words of God. The reason you do not hear them is that you are not from God."

Theological Perspective

The debate between Jesus and his opponents continues here. The point of contention is the claim of his opponent to be the offspring of Abraham. Jesus attributes murderous intentions against him as proof that appeals to being children of Abraham are illegitimate and claims that these motives stem from the devil, "the father of lies" (v. 44). In this debate, Jesus, who comes from God, speaks the truth. Jesus' opponents do not come from God, because they will not hear the words of God that Jesus speaks to them.

Children of Abraham (vv. 39–42). Claims by Jesus' opponents that they are the natural descendants of Abraham do not hold weight with Jesus. To be "Abraham's children," as they maintain, implies a personal relationship with Abraham and assumes the children will act in accord with the character of their parent or ancestor. The reason the claim of these opponents is illegitimate is that they are acting in ways genuinely contrary to Abraham, as evidenced by their efforts to "kill me, a man who has told you the truth that I heard from God." Indeed, "this is not what Abraham did" (v. 40b).

Remember, God said that "Abraham obeyed my voice and kept my charge, my commandments, my statutes, and my laws" (Gen. 26:5). So the actions of those who claim to be children of Abraham do not

Pastoral Perspective

There are times in the Christian tradition of interpretation when particular texts leave a trail of destruction. Sadly, this passage from the Gospel of John has a legacy deeply entwined with the perpetuation of anti-Judaism across centuries of preaching and teaching that fueled the popular Christian imagination. In this text raw emotion boils over, revealing the deep-seated tensions between Jewish communities that survived the Roman destruction of the temple in Jerusalem. The growing rift between Jewish followers of Jesus and their contemporaries is palpable in the antagonistic words placed in the mouth of Jesus. The ferocity of the words intimates frustrations beneath an unsettling context hidden between the lines. There is no escaping the harshness of the vitriol, no satisfactory way to sanitize verse 44: "You are from your father the devil, and you choose to do your father's desires."

While the frustration of the Johannine community is evident in the preceding question, "Why do you not understand what I say?" (8:43), it was the ongoing debate over the significance of Jesus that led to the split with the Jewish community. In this text, framed as a verbal confrontation, fierce words are spoken on both sides. This particular section focuses on what comes from the mouth of Jesus. At least two series of "fighting words" are contained here. First, something

Exegetical Perspective

This unit contains one of the severest assaults by Jesus in the NT. In John 8:39–47, Jesus accuses the Judeans of having the devil as their father, asserts that the devil was "a murderer from the beginning," and says the Judeans do whatever their father the devil desires of them (v. 44). It is hard to reconcile these assertions with statements attributed to Jesus elsewhere that people should love even their "enemies" (Matt. 5:44; Luke 6:35).

There is scholarly agreement that this caustic exchange is part of a Johannine approach in which Jesus is viewed as a divine messenger from another sphere, namely, the divine realm of God, who speaks mysterious "insider" language that only "believers" can understand. The more people "outside" of the group are puzzled by the talk of people "inside" the group, the stronger the sense of community is among the "true believers" on the inside. This way of speaking became an identity marker for Johannine members of emerging Christianity in and around Ephesus in western Asia Minor.

Why is the exchange so antagonistic? Overall, it appears that Jews who did not believe in Jesus were using Greek philosophical insights to interpret the Torah, as Philo of Alexandria had done in Egypt during the early part of the first century CE. In response, Johannine members of the Jesus movement

Homiletical Perspective

Once, as a guest preacher, I walked up the steps leading to the church doors and was greeted with the question, "Friend or foe?" It was spoken in jest, but it seems to capture the spirit of the age pretty well. Today's theological climate seems to be suggested by this exchange: how often do parties battle in order to lay claim to the prized mantle of being "biblical" or truly Reformed or in some way consistent with the tradition? Every "visitor" is questioned accordingly and in an almost mean-spirited way. Hospitality may be present in the church, but it is mostly as subtext to the more important assertion of the legacy that one is guarding and, even more important, who is outside of that legacy.

This lection continues the previous dialogue, but it shifts to what kind of people they, the ruling elite of the temple, would be if Abraham were their father, as they claim (v. 39a): "Jesus said to them, 'If you were Abraham's children, you would be doing what Abraham did, but now you are trying to kill me, a man who has told you the truth that I heard from God. This is not what Abraham did'" (vv. 39b–40). Raymond Brown offers three possibilities for rendering the first half of this verse, which he describes as a "confused situation in the Greek." Brown's renditions may offer interpreters a way of conceptualizing the claim of the sermon:

John 8:39–47

Theological Perspective

conform to the actions of Abraham himself. Deadly designs against the one who speaks the truth disqualify them from genuine kinship with Abraham. In other words, "Jesus insists explicitly now that moral kinship is the only kinship that matters: to cherish murderous intentions against someone who has imparted the truth of God to them is not the mark of children of Abraham."[1]

"If God were your Father," said Jesus, and if they were genuinely Abraham's children, then "you would love me, for I came from God" (v. 42). Jesus' claim that God "has sent me" (v. 42) rests on his person and his mission. Some have seen in this verse an explicit statement of Jesus' divinity, indicating Jesus' divine origin as "from [Gk. *ek*, "out of"] God." Certainly, from the church's historic perspectives of Christology, this is true. However, on the face of it, Jesus' assertion here is that Jesus in himself (his person) is conveying the message from God, who has sent him, which is a divine message, not of earthly origin. Opponents seeking to kill Jesus are denying the truth of God. They do not truly love God as Abraham's genuine children. For "everyone who loves the parent loves the child" (1 John 5:1). There is no love for God when God's child (Son) is rejected.

Lies and Truth (vv. 43–45). Jesus says that his opponents "cannot accept my word" (v. 43). They are "from your father the devil," who was a "murderer from the beginning," not standing in the truth and is "the father of lies" (v. 44). Because Jesus tells the truth, "you do not believe me" (v. 45).

The starkness and vehemence of the language here shows what is at stake. To reject Jesus and the word he proclaims from God indicates an allegiance with "the devil." This is in opposition to the truth of God—which entails believing Jesus' word and believing in him. The Dutch theologian G. C. Berkouwer wrote about the "*contra*-character" of sin. Sin is that which is *contra* to God; *contra* to God in Jesus Christ. With the coming of Jesus as "the Word made flesh" (1:14; the incarnation), "*from this time forth* all sins and aberrations from God will be focused or centralized in this one decisive act of *un*belief or *dis*obedience to Jesus."[2]

For persons confronted by the truth of God in the person and words of Jesus Christ, this becomes life's most important reality. Either living *contra* to God in Christ, or believing and obeying God's truth

Pastoral Perspective

is said that evokes a retort from Jesus' interlocutors: "We are not illegitimate children" (v. 41). Shortly thereafter comes the slanderous charge that Jesus' opponents have the devil as their father (v. 44). This insult is later answered with their allegations of Jesus' own possible demonic connections: "Are we not right in saying that you are a Samaritan and have a demon?" (v. 48). What was at stake here involved contested identities and their theological implications.

To be clear, harsh words exchanged in the heat of argument reflect past conflicts and not present reality. Across the centuries, amid increasing Christian hostility toward Jews, this first-century rhetoric was redeployed in ways that twenty-first-century Christians cannot willfully ignore. The responsibility to redress this destructive legacy is especially urgent for those entrusted with ministries of teaching and preaching.

Fast-forward two millennia to an extraordinary pastoral dialogue between the then-archbishop of Buenos Aires, Jorge Mario Bergoglio, and his dear friend, rabbinic seminary rector Rabbi Abraham Skorka. Together they published a small book reflecting their free-flowing conversation on faith and interreligious relations. They shared on matters great and small, theological and practical, in a book published only in Spanish—that is, until one of them was elected the bishop of Rome in 2013.

Tucked among the various topics covered in *On Heaven and Earth*—from God to prayer to death—is a chapter "On the Devil." The views of these two friends diverge to some degree. Bergoglio articulates a belief in the existence of the devil, "a being that opted not to accept the plan of God," whose fruits always bear destruction: "division, hate, and slander."[1] He takes care to distinguish between the devil and demonizing people, something he suggests is best avoided. Rabbi Skorka proposes that "evil occurs when good is removed from a situation" and "cannot exist by itself." He goes on to summarize their conversation succinctly, addressing their differing perspectives yet acknowledging common cause: "What remains clear is that something exists, whether it is instinct or the Devil, which presents itself as a challenge for us to overcome so that we can uproot evil."[2]

What a difference two millennia make! At the heart of the dialogue between Skorka and Bergoglio is a relationship of trust born of intentional moves that led to genuine friendship. Their dialogue does not mean that they must agree on everything; rather,

1. F. F. Bruce, *The Gospel of John* (repr., Grand Rapids: Eerdmans, 1984), 199.
2. G. C. Berkouwer, *Sin*, trans. Philip C. Holtrop (Grand Rapids: Eerdmans, 1971), 223; cf. 239.

1. Jorge Mario Bergoglio and Abraham Skorka, *On Heaven and Earth* (New York: Image, 2013), 8.
2. Bergoglio and Skorka, *On Heaven and Earth*, 10, 11.

Exegetical Perspective

developed even more special insider religious-philosophical views to distinguish themselves. When the believers in Jesus added the concept that Judeans had killed Jesus, they intensified their language into what Bruce Malina calls "anti-language."[1] Jesus speaks to the Judeans with anti-traditional understanding, and whatever the Judeans say is considered to be anti–true understanding. Jesus says things beyond anything the Judeans can understand, because he brings a truth from heaven that convicts the Judeans of having only earthly understanding.

One way to begin to understand Jesus' accusation in John is to compare it with Jesus' statement to Peter in Mark 8:33 (par. Matt. 16:23): "Get behind me, Satan! For you are setting your mind not on divine things but on human things." The Gospel of John expands this exchange into an entire belief system "from heaven" that Jesus presents to "the Judeans" in a context where he accuses them of wanting to kill him.

The unit opens with an "Our Daddy is . . ." argument that should be appropriate within a first-century-CE Christian community. The Judeans are proud to tell Jesus, "Abraham is our father" (v. 39). This claim sounds very close to Paul's assertion in Galatians 3:29: "And if you belong to Christ, then you are Abraham's offspring, heirs according to the promise." The problem is that Jesus' statements earlier in the conversation make the claim of the Judeans an implicit denial that God is their father. The Judeans do not want to deny this. In fact, later they assert that they have "one father, God himself" (v. 41b). The Judeans are trying to tell Jesus he is overreaching when he says he was "in the presence of the Father." Indeed, Jesus' function as the personal agent of creation (1:3–4) could suggest that believers in Jesus actually have two divine fathers: God the Father of all (like Greek Zeus) and Jesus "the Father" of creation (like the philosophical Greek demiurge who created the world).

Instead of arguing with the Judeans in the mode of Greek philosophy, Jesus accuses the Judeans of trying to kill him. Then he asserts that their intention follows the desires of their father the devil, who was a murderer from the beginning. This accusation is probably based on the early tradition that Cain was born of Eve and the evil angel Samael, who became Satan when he persuaded other angels to rebel against God and bring murder, fornication, and even cannibalism into the world. Cain then was

Homiletical Perspective

- Real Condition: If you are . . . do;
- Contrary-to-Fact Condition: If you were . . . you would be doing;
- Mixed Condition: If you are . . . you would be doing.[1]

Effectively, Jesus implies that they are Abraham's children, but their actions suggest either incompleteness of will, division, or ambivalence about that identity. By contrast, the theological center of gravity within this text rests with Jesus, in whom there is neither contradiction nor inconsistency: "I did not come on my own, but [God] sent me" (v. 42b).

Initially, however, the conflict emerges as a battle for a legacy, for the right to claim the name of a beloved but now absent ancestor. The ancestor, Abraham, cannot speak for himself; so it falls to the descendants to sort out who speaks most adequately in his name. Jesus asserts it is more than a blood relationship that counts. What counts, he says, is what you do, the life you exhibit to and for the other. Jesus may be recalling the example of Abraham's response to the visit of the three strangers in Genesis 18:1–8. When confronted by the unknown and the strange, Abraham did not arm himself or prepare an interrogation of suspicious persons; instead, he opened the doors of his tent with "little" gestures of hospitality, signifying openness to and for the stranger.

So is Jesus a stranger or a member of the family? The text plays on the paradox of known and unknown, familiar and unfamiliar. Note Jesus' self-description in verse 40a: "You are trying to kill me, *a man* who has told you the truth." Jesus appears as someone familiar, like them and known to them, if imperfectly (v. 41b). Yet John concludes this chapter with that most divine expression of self-identification: "Before Abraham was, I am" (v. 58b).

If Jesus speaks from the truth of his humanity, he also speaks to us in order that we might hear from the mysterious depths of his participation in the divine life. In the Word become flesh, the divine I AM has opened the tent of Christ's own freedom and life to estranged humanity, not a "little," but by emptying out the divine life in the word made flesh.

While initially the text seems like a battle for the Abrahamic legacy, by verse 42 it is clear that there is one greater than Abraham. Jesus identifies himself as one with God, come from God and sent by God,

1. Bruce J. Malina and Richard L. Rohrbaugh, *Social Science Commentary on the Gospel of John* (Minneapolis: Fortress Press, 1998).

1. Raymond E. Brown, *The Gospel according to John I–XII*, Anchor Bible 29 (Garden City, NY: Doubleday & Co., 1966), 356–57.

John 8:39–47

Theological Perspective

in the person and words of Jesus: this is our decisive choice. When God's truth is rejected in favor of lies of all kinds, through actions that are *contra* God, Jesus' word is rejected, and Jesus himself is put to death. The responses of Jesus' opponents are a continuing paradigm of the question Jesus posed to Peter: "Who do you say that I am?" (Matt. 16:15).

Hearing the Words of God (vv. 46–47). Despite the hostility toward Jesus, he could not be convicted of sin—Sabbath breaking and blasphemy (v. 46; 5:18). Although he is faultless—which should have led the opponents to recognize the truth of Jesus' words— the opponents do not believe him. They obstinately reject the truth; they are "not from God" (v. 47).

The word of God comes from Jesus who is sent by God (v. 42): "He whom God has sent speaks the words of God" (3:34). Those who are true children of Abraham, true children of the covenant, and true disciples of Jesus Christ will "hear the words of God" (v. 47). Later, Jesus says to Pilate, "Everyone who belongs to the truth listens to my voice" (18:37). Hearing the voice of God through Jesus Christ is our source of knowing God. For the church, it is the sustaining, life-giving word that guides and comforts us. In another context of rejection, Jesus says, "My sheep hear my voice. I know them, and they follow me" (10:27). The temptation to hear another voice, listen to and follow another "shepherd" is to be rejected. Only Jesus Christ, who "came from God" and is sent by God (v. 42), is and speaks the truth.

John Calvin said of the teaching of Christ that "if we embrace it cheerfully, we have, as it were, a visible seal of our election. For [whoever] has the Word enjoys God Himself; but [whoever] rejects it deprives himself of righteousness and life."[3]

DONALD K. MCKIM

Pastoral Perspective

it carries the expectation that in each other's company they are safe respectfully to disagree. This was not an option that could have been foreseen by their first-century ancestors in the faith, who struggled with issues of communal identity and survival under the heel of oppressive imperial power. Opportunities for dialogue often withered into mutual recrimination and violent name-calling.

Dialogue of mere words is insufficient. Consider seriously the wisdom of the Catholic Federation of Asian Bishops Conferences and their call for dialogue in their religiously pluralistic contexts. They identify what can be called a "popular dialogue," an engagement of and among ordinary people in their quotidian relationships. For them, this interreligious endeavor is not some intellectual exchange exclusive to theologians and religious leaders but a fourfold presence embedded in grassroots, local, daily, and lived experience as

- a dialogue of life, where people strive to live as neighbors, sharing in the comings and goings, highs, lows, and anxieties that characterize the mundane;
- a dialogue of action, a collaboration across differences for the purpose of liberating people from all that oppresses;
- a dialogue of theological exchange, where specialists seek to understand their own religious traditions, and grow to respect the spiritual values and ways of others;
- a dialogue of religious experience, where persons, rooted in their own faith inheritances disclose the richness of their particular ways of praying, being, and seeking the holy.[3]

In some ways this approach to dialogue is captured in the striking image of three Latin American friends—a Jew, a Christian, a Muslim—traveling together as pilgrims to the Holy Land in May 2014. A moment at the Western Wall in Jerusalem, caught by photographers, illustrated what interreligious peace nurtured in years of "popular dialogue" looks like: Abraham Skorka, Francis, and Omar Abboud shared an intimate embrace—among friends. Abraham's children celebrated their kinship and recommitted themselves to peace.

CARMEN NANKO-FERNÁNDEZ

---

3. John Calvin, *The Gospel according to St. John: Part One 1–10*, trans. T. H. L. Parker, Calvin's New Testament Commentaries (repr., Grand Rapids: Eerdmans, 1979), 230.

3. Peter C. Phan, "'Reception' or 'Subversion' of Vatican II by the Asian Churches?: A New Way of Being Church in Asia," *Australian eJournal of Theology* 6 (February 2006): 11, http://aejt.com.au/__data/assets/pdf_file/0004/395185/AEJT_6.3_Phan_Reception_or_Subversion.pdf.

Exegetical Perspective

not "like Adam"; he killed Abel "in the likeness" of his murderous father Samael/Satan (Gen. 4:8; 1 John 3:12–15).[2] This view is supported by God's giving to Eve, after Cain killed Abel, another son, Seth, who was "in the likeness" of Adam and was created in the image of God (Gen. 5:1–3).

When Jesus tells the Judeans they are not doing what Abraham did but what their father did, they tell Jesus they are not illegitimate children (v. 41). With their response, they may be implying that Jesus was an illegitimate child, since there was an early tradition that Jesus was born of fornication rather than a legitimate marriage.[3] Jesus responds on the basis of special precreation beliefs about himself and God discussed in the exegetical perspective on John 8:31–38 in this volume. Jesus tells them that if God were their father, they would love Jesus, because he is from God. He explains that he did not come on his own, but God sent him. Then he tells them they are not able to understand him, because they cannot accept his "word [*logos*]," upon which precreation belief is grounded.

Jesus' response also accuses the devil of being a liar. This probably is a reference to Genesis 3:4–5, where the serpent tells Eve she will not die if she eats of the tree of the knowledge of good and evil. When she and Adam eat from the tree, God's punishment is that they will "return to the ground," from which they came (Gen. 3:19). Jesus counters the lie Satan told to Eve with "the truth" he brings from heaven. This brings Jesus to a most startling statement: only people who are "from God" are able to hear the words of God and understand them (v. 47). Jesus appears to be restating that only those "born from above" (3:3, 7) can understand. Distinguishing between "believers," whose origin lies in God, and "outsiders," who belong to the realm of the devil, points toward strong experiences of division in emerging Christianity; other Johannine passages on love and Jesus' laying down of his life for others emphasize a servant life of Jesus "for the world."

VERNON K. ROBBINS

Homiletical Perspective

and now the fully present I AM. This, according to John's account, is what gave the greatest offense to the temple elites. According to Brown, one may have expected the narrator to write, "though Jesus told the truth, they did not believe him; but John actually says that they did not believe *because* he told the truth."[2] It is the truth of the word made flesh that offends.

While visiting with the Cherith Brook Catholic Worker Community in Kansas City, I was invited to experience what they called the "reverse hospitality of the streets." They would walk the streets anticipating how the people they encountered would show the peaceable reign of God in a neighborhood most people would avoid. Their trust in God's faithfulness opened them to see Christ where others saw only ruin or despair. Sometimes God's peace would show itself through ordinary celebrations of new birth, finding affordable housing, or the journey through addiction recovery. While each member of the community subscribed to a community discipline, they deliberately opened themselves to the other, lest their discipline become so tightly secured that they would be resistant to the way the Spirit acts through the stranger.

Likewise this text challenges congregations that are perhaps suspicious or fearful to be ready to hear God speaking through the stranger. Maybe our own setting would view Jesus as a potential member of our particular denominational tribe, but one who needed to be assimilated into our particular tradition, our particular tent. Against this tendency, Calvin reminds us that our knowledge of Jesus remains limited: "Believers . . . are in some measure ignorant of what they know."[3] Jesus may join us in this human tent, and indeed he comes to incarnate the New Human Being, but he is never reducible to "our" particular tribe. There is always a sense that Jesus simultaneously inhabits and surpasses our human tents, always leading us to open the flap of our little houses to the world God so loves.

ROBERT HOCH

2. Raymond E. Brown, *The Gospel according to John I–XII*, Anchor Bible 29 (Garden City, NY: Doubleday & Co., 1966), 358.
3. Origen, *Against Celsus* 1:28; *Acts of Pilate* 2.3; Brown, *Gospel*, 357.

2. Brown, *Gospel*, 365.
3. John Calvin, *Commentary on the Gospel according to John*, trans. William Pringle (Albany, NY: Books for the Ages, 1998), 304.

John 8:48–59

John 8:48–59

⁴⁸The Jews* answered him, "Are we not right in saying that you are a Samaritan and have a demon?" ⁴⁹Jesus answered, "I do not have a demon; but I honor my Father, and you dishonor me. ⁵⁰Yet I do not seek my own glory; there is one who seeks it and he is the judge. ⁵¹Very truly, I tell you, whoever keeps my word will never see death." ⁵²The Jews said to him, "Now we know that you have a demon. Abraham died, and so did the prophets; yet you say, 'Whoever keeps my word will never taste death.' ⁵³Are you greater than our father Abraham, who died? The prophets also died. Who do you claim to be?" ⁵⁴Jesus answered, "If I glorify myself, my glory is nothing. It is my Father who glorifies me, he of whom you say, 'He is our God,' ⁵⁵though you do not know him. But I know him; if I would say that I do not know him, I would be a liar like you. But I do know him and I keep his word. ⁵⁶Your ancestor Abraham rejoiced that he would see my day; he saw it and was glad." ⁵⁷Then the Jews said to him, "You are not yet fifty years old, and have you seen Abraham?" ⁵⁸Jesus said to them, "Very truly, I tell you, before Abraham was, I am." ⁵⁹So they picked up stones to throw at him, but Jesus hid himself and went out of the temple.

Theological Perspective

The controversial debates between Jesus and his opponents continue here. Jesus is accused of being a "Samaritan" and of having a demon (v. 48). He responds by saying, "I honor my Father, and you dishonor me" (v. 49). It is not his own glory he seeks, but God's (v. 50). His promise is that "whoever keeps my word will never see death" (v. 51). Then follows controversy over Abraham and Jesus' affirmation that "Abraham rejoiced that he would see my day; he saw it and was glad" (v. 56). Climactically, Jesus asserts: "Very truly, I tell you, before Abraham was, I am" (v. 58). This leads to potential violence. Jesus' opponents "picked up stones to throw at him, but Jesus hid himself and went out of the temple" (v. 59).

The contentiousness of Jesus' opponents against him has served to highlight and focus Jesus' claims about who he is and what he does. His theological comments transcend the specifics of these particular antagonisms. What Jesus says about himself helps define what the Christian church came to believe and articulate through the centuries. In the context of the controversies at the Festival of Booths (7:14), Jesus reveals the realities that his life, death, and resurrection portend.

* See "'The Jews' in the Fourth Gospel" on pp. xi–xiv.

Pastoral Perspective

Throughout the Fourth Gospel, Jesus is at odds with "the Jews." This puzzling encounter in chapter 8 seems to demonize even those "Jews" who believed in Jesus. The evangelist's use of this label has helped to sow the seeds of anti-Judaism among Christians from early times until now. The first followers of Jesus were Jews, yet "the Jews" have been blamed for Jesus' crucifixion in Christian tradition. An anti-Jewish reading of John's Gospel sees Jesus as leaving Judaism behind in favor of a better way. Biblical scholars interpret this term "the Jews" as applying to those who lived in Judea, to the leaders who resisted Jesus' teachings, or to the temple conservatives who ejected the Johannine community.[1]

The Fourth Gospel is prone, at times, to binary thinking, to pitting light against darkness, seeing against blindness, abiding against denial. Jesus' opponents demonized him; they called him a "Samaritan" and assumed he was demon possessed. Samaritans were the "alien other" to those who saw themselves as insiders, as guardians of their version of the Abrahamic tradition. Anyone who deviated or questioned the guardians' dominant way of seeing

1. Raymond Brown, *The Gospel according to John* (Garden City, NY: Doubleday, 1966), 354–55. Brown notes that John often speaks of the inhabitants of Jerusalem or Judea as "the Jews." R. Alan Culpepper, in *The Gospel and Letters of John* (Nashville: Abingdon Press, 1998), 42–45, speaks of the conflicts between the Johannine community and the synagogue.

Feasting on the Gospels

Exegetical Perspective

The unit begins with the Judeans asserting that Jesus is a Samaritan. From their perspective Jesus "identifies" himself with Samaritans (4:4–42). Judeans contrast themselves to these people, who have an incorrect version of the Torah and worship on a wrong mountain, Mount Gerizim. The Judeans dissociate themselves from traditional arguments whether Jesus is from Galilee (Nazareth) or Judea (Bethlehem) by saying he is from a thoroughly unacceptable place, Samaria! One of the ironies in John is that Jesus really is "from above" (8:23).

Jesus does not respond to the assertion by Judeans that he is a Samaritan. Rather, he addresses their claim that he has a demon. In John, Jesus performs no exorcisms, and eternal life and eternal light are present in him. All the references to a demon or being demonized focus on Jesus himself.[1] Jesus responds by simply saying, "I do not have a demon," and this statement starts a progression of argumentation featuring topics central to the Johannine precreation identity of Jesus. The topics are: honor, glory, keeping *logos*/word, death, Abraham, knowing, and understanding Jesus through his "I am" statements.

Jesus begins with a statement about honor: Jesus honors his Father; in contrast, the Judeans dishonor

1. John 7:20; 8:48–49, 52; 10:20–21.

Homiletical Perspective

This pericope does not begin with anything that Jesus says of himself. Instead it begins with suspicions, with the accusations of those who pose as his interrogators: "Are we not right in saying that you are a Samaritan and have a demon?" (v. 48). These questions resemble the way an interrogator might question a suspect, almost coercing a confession through innuendo and outright lies: "We have you at the scene of the crime, we *know* it was you, and you know it too, and, well, we do not really buy what you have been telling us." John portrays the temple as an interrogation room, where confession is exacted by way of coercion.

Most preachers understand that the sermon actually begins with the oral-aural performance of the text. John's language begs to be "sounded out" as interpreters give oral-aural expression to the sarcasm and biting nature of this dialogue. Interpreters may glean the meaning from the text read in silence, but the text as sound proves at least as instructive: "Are we not right?" spoken with contempt, and "Who do you claim to be?" and "You are not yet fifty years old and have you seen Abraham?" spoken with sneering disbelief. Experiment with this text through a form of readers theater as a way of mining the possible sound of John's acerbic exchange. Where one places the emphasis will shape the way the congregation experiences this text.

John 8:48–59

Theological Perspective

Defeat of Death (v. 51). To those who accuse Jesus of having a demon, Jesus declares he does not seek his own glory and that "whoever keeps my word will never see death." This promise is given explicit and dramatic form when Jesus raises his friend Lazarus from the dead and issues the promise: "I am the resurrection and the life. Those who believe in me, even though they die, will live, and everyone who lives and believes in me will never die" (11:25–26).

The promise of eternal life in Jesus Christ, comprising a new quality of life here and now (3:16) and life forever in fellowship with God, is given so that "whoever keeps my word" will not fear death and will have confidence that the power of death is defeated. This is made certain, specifically, in the resurrection of Jesus Christ himself. In his resurrection, death's power is vanquished. Christ is the "first fruits of those who have died" (1 Cor. 15:20). The promise is that God has given us "eternal life, and this life is in his Son" (1 John 5:11). For "whoever believes has eternal life" (6:47). Faith in Jesus Christ is the means by which eternal life is received (5:24) as a gift (10:28). "When faith quickens a [person's] soul," said John Calvin, "the sting of death is already blunted and its poison wiped off, and so it cannot inflict a deadly wound."[1] Death is defeated, promises Jesus.

Glory from God (v. 54). When wondering how Jesus can make this promise that his disciples will never "see death," Jesus' opponents ask if he considers himself "greater than our father Abraham, who died" (v. 53). Then they ask him: "Who do you claim to be?" Jesus answers, "It is my Father who glorifies me" (v. 54). Jesus is not trying to elevate himself or strive for glory. He is not testifying to himself (5:31). Jesus' glory is bestowed from the Father. For "the only glory that matters in Jesus' eyes is the 'glory that comes from the only God.'"[2] Jesus knows this God as his Father and keeps God's word (v. 55).

With these words, Jesus points to what counts most in life: receiving approval and glory from God. All "glory" received from human sources is trivial and ultimately of no account. Human ambitions—or whatever it is that drives individuals toward goals they calculate will bring them glory (successful careers, amassing money and power)—in the end mean nothing, if true glory does not come to us from God. As Paul wrote, "For it is not those who

Pastoral Perspective

must be possessed by a demon. Jesus did not neatly conform to the religious status quo. As the conversation went on, his detractors became increasingly sure of his deviance.

In John, Jesus also demonized those opponents by calling them liars. There is a drawing of lines, a setting apart, an "us-and-them" situation, on both sides. When Jesus makes yet another bold "I am" statement, it is simply too much for them. The detractors pick up stones and are ready to hurl them.

Raymond Brown prefers the term "demented" to demonic. A contemporary, post-Enlightenment, scientific way of seeing would prefer that label as well. Some twenty-first-century Christians tend to look upon first-century folk as naively invoking demons to explain away aberrant beliefs and behavior. For example, mental illness may resemble descriptions of what the Scripture calls demon possession, but now, with the benefit of the health sciences, there are clinical names for many of these conditions. Today expressions like "wrestling with our demons" tend to use the word in a symbolic, psychological sense. The ancient world believed in extrahuman forces of good and evil and called them *daimones*. Some believers will blame evil on devils, while others doubt their existence. C. S. Lewis describes this dichotomy well:

> There are two equal and opposite errors into which our race can fall about the devils. One is to disbelieve in their existence. The other is to believe, and to feel an excessive and unhealthy interest in them. . . . They themselves are equally pleased by both errors.[2]

There is certainly a spectrum of Christian views on the subject; yet Lewis is reminding people of the all-too-human tendency to demonize the alien other. Such designations occur in relatively harmless, playful rivalries in sports, among schools, across geographic regions, or between denominations. Demonizing is also accomplished in harmful, hurtful ways through bullying, in sexist and racist put-downs, and in the perpetuation of stereotypes. It is done in hateful ways with devastating effects in communities, in churches, and in politics on a global scale. Christian communities and church politics are not exempt.

From the very beginning, Christians have demonized other Christians. The Gentiles and the Judaizers; the gnostics and the true believers; Antioch, Alexandria, Rome, Corinth—church fights are evident in the letters of Paul. They are nothing new. Christians

---

1. John Calvin, *The Gospel according to St. John: Part One 1–10*, trans. T. H. L. Parker, Calvin's New Testament Commentaries (repr., Grand Rapids: Eerdmans, 1979), 231.
2. F. F. Bruce, *The Gospel of John* (repr., Grand Rapids: Eerdmans, 1984), 204.

2. C. S. Lewis, *The Screwtape Letters* (New York: Macmillan, 1961), 3.

him. Jesus does not seek his own glory (v. 50) by glorifying himself (v. 54). Instead, Jesus presents a distinctive way of speaking about glory. As D. Moody Smith has explained, in John the Father reveals his own glory through Jesus, and specifically through the death of Jesus (12:23–25).[2] Jesus emphasizes that God is the judge of "appropriate" glory (v. 50), and God has chosen to reveal his glory by glorifying Jesus (v. 54).

For Jesus, the concept of glory leads to the topic of keeping Jesus' "*logos*/word," which in turn leads to the topic of eternal life. In Luke 11:28 Jesus says, "Blessed are those who hear the word of God and obey it." In a distinctly Johannine manner, Jesus extends the meaning by saying, "Whoever keeps my word [*logos*] will never see death" (v. 51). In other words, Jesus' *logos*/word is eternal life, and those who find a place in themselves for this word and keep it will never die (v. 52).

However, Jesus goes even one step further, since the accusation is against him. He asserts that he himself "knows" God and keeps God's *logos*/word (v. 55). It is not simply that humans "keep God's word." Rather, Jesus keeps God's eternal *logos*/word (cf. 14:31) and brings this word to people on earth. People in turn must believe this *logos*/word, find a place for it inside themselves, keep it there, and "know" that this word is eternal life that caused all things to come into being. This argument is one more way to think about the result of precreation belief that guides understanding in the Gospel of John. Jesus "honors" God, who is his Father. This honoring reveals that God's glory is revealed by God's glorifying of Jesus. Since Jesus knows God and keeps God's word, Jesus brings God's eternal life into the presence of humans. This is simply the setup for the finale in Jesus' argument!

At this point the Judeans return to the topic of "their father Abraham." They assert that they "know" that Jesus has a demon, and they "know" that Abraham and all the prophets died. In this context, they ask Jesus just exactly who he is claiming to be (v. 53). The real issue here is the identity of Jesus, and the hearer has an opportunity to come to know even more clearly who Jesus is through comparison with Abraham. Jesus tells the Judeans that if they "truly knew" God and understood how God worked, they would know "their father" Abraham rejoiced that he would see the day of Jesus; and indeed he saw it and was glad! (v. 56). Again this is special reasoning

At the level of logical development, the text follows the trajectory of suspicions that the temple elite hold with regard to Jesus. Those suspicions seem to be groping for a target, and failing to find their target, they turn into sarcastic disbelief and finally violence: "So they picked up stones to throw at [Jesus]" (v. 59). Despite not "finding" their mark, they nevertheless act out of their fears and prejudices: "They have no ears to know the cause," writes John Calvin, "but they have hands ready to commit murder."[1]

Ironically, Jesus does not speak in the language of suspicion, fear, or prejudice. His words do not grope for a target, for the telltale "Gotcha!" moment. Instead, he speaks plainly: "I do not have a demon; but I honor my Father, and you dishonor me" (v. 49). He speaks boldly: "Whoever keeps my word will never see death'" (v. 51). He speaks mysteriously: "Before Abraham was, I am" (v. 58b). He does not "hide" himself from their suspicions because his profession (of faith?) is incomparable; it is almost as if their suspicions are glancing blows that never enjoy a direct hit. Jesus, who speaks the truth and knows to whom he speaks, does not lash out in violence.

Although Jesus is in a position to execute judgment, he continues the narrative with the temple elite and beyond. According to John, Jesus sees clearly. He knows his whence and whither. He knows the word he keeps. If there is a light in the temple, it is not the understanding of Jesus' interrogators but the light that has come into the world. Perhaps what stands out most with this text is the degree to which Jesus' interrogators trust in their capacity for correct seeing. The narrator of John makes it abundantly clear that they cannot "see" Jesus clearly enough even to strike him with a stone: "Jesus hid himself and went out of the temple" (v. 59b).

It may be difficult to read this particular text in isolation from the surrounding narrative. In the same way that this text needs oral/aural expression, it also begs for embodiment through narration or metaphor. Narratively, interpreters might find chapter 9 helpful, as it continues to develop the theme of blindness. Paradoxically, in order to give a "blind" person sight, Jesus applies mud to his eyes—the opposite of what we might prescribe. However, this clay, according to John Calvin, serves as an anointing of mud.[2] Perhaps one way of receiving the wisdom of this text is to "confess" our blindness, particularly

---

2. D. Moody Smith Jr., *John*, Abingdon New Testament Commentaries (Nashville: Abingdon Press, 1999), 188.

1. John Calvin, *Commentary on the Gospel according to John*, trans. William Pringle (Albany, NY: Books for the Ages, 1998), 324.
2. Calvin, *Commentary,* 332.

John 8:48–59

Theological Perspective

commend themselves that are approved, but those whom the Lord commends" (2 Cor. 10:18). Our "glory" is only in Jesus Christ. By grace we have the "hope of sharing the glory of God" (Rom. 5:2). Now we "set our hope on Christ," so we "might live for the praise of his glory" (Eph. 1:12; 14).

"I am" (v. 58). Jesus' opponents try to say Jesus is claiming to have seen Abraham when he says, "Your ancestor Abraham rejoiced that he would see my day; he saw it and was glad" (v. 56). They say that because Jesus is "not yet fifty years old," he cannot possibly have "seen" Abraham (v. 57). Jesus refutes their claim.

Jesus' emphatic word is: "Very truly, I tell you, before Abraham was, I am" (v. 58). By saying "I am" (Gk. *egō eimi*), Jesus invokes the quintessential divine name, revealed to Moses (Exod. 3:14). By echoing the language used of the God of Israel (cf. Isa. 41:4), Jesus is offending his opponents to the highest degree.

Theologically, Christians may recognize that in the statement "before Abraham was, I am" Jesus is expressing his timelessness, his eternity, his divine preexistence. John's Gospel begins with the assertion: "In the beginning was the Word, and the Word was with God, and the Word was God" (1:1). With Jesus' statement here, "no clearer implication of divinity is found in the Gospel tradition."[3]

Jesus' divinity was confessed in the church's early creeds and remains foundational for christological understanding. The doctrine of the Trinity affirms Jesus as the eternal Son of God, who is fully entitled to say, "I am." All that Jesus has said to his opponents is grounded in this assertion. His opponents get the message: "They picked up stones to throw at him" (v. 59).

DONALD K. MCKIM

Pastoral Perspective

have engaged in battles and crusades in order to stamp out heretics and infidels. Even now the unity of the church seems to be embattled by a kind of either/or, us/them demonization. Old School or New School? Contemporary worship or traditional? Evangelical or Liberal? What is it that makes people want to retreat into camps of like-minded individuals and hurl imaginary stones and real insults at one another?

The demonizing that went on in Jesus' encounter had to do with belief, but it also had to do with culture and heritage, with "difference." Jewish leaders saw the Samaritans as separatists. The religious leaders had particular interpretations of the law. Jesus' teaching and practice were at odds with these religious leaders, in part, because he ministered to those who were "different," to Samaritans, women, tax collectors, prostitutes, lepers. These people were demonized by the privileged in their day as surely as people are demonized on the basis of race, wealth, poverty, gender, sexuality, health, age, and many other ways today.

What is it that makes people seek that alien other, in order to put themselves in the best possible light? Those who consider themselves to be inclusive and tolerant fall into this trap as well. Judgment and prejudice can cut both ways. History is full of those liberated, only to become oppressors themselves. How can Jesus' encounter with those who were at odds with him help people today to overcome alienating and polarizing tendencies?

Jesus was humble. He sought not to glorify himself. Although this confrontation is sharp and direct, Jesus' words and actions remind readers that even one's opponents in a debate are of value to God. Though Jesus is the Christ and makes some stunning claims in this conversation, though he is physically threatened, he does not fight back or resist, but simply slips away and disengages. How can a pastor/preacher help her parishioners disengage and respond with humility to those who tend to make tempers flare?

Jesus also knew that God alone is judge. Judgmentalism and demonization go together. If we can see those who are different, those who make us uncomfortable, those who challenge our deepest values, as "different" or as a threat, then we can look down on them. God is the judge, Jesus said. If we can see the "others" as beloved children of God, we can begin to leave the judging up to God.

REBECCA BUTTON PRICHARD

---

3. Raymond E. Brown, *The Gospel according to John I–XII*, Anchor Bible 29 (Garden City, NY: Doubleday & Co., 1966), 367. Cf. Brown's Appendix IV on the "I AM" sayings.

in the Johannine community. Jesus not only claims that Moses wrote about him (5:45–46); John also claims that Isaiah saw his glory and spoke about him (12:41). Here Jesus claims he personally knows Abraham and Abraham has special joy over what Jesus is doing! If this is based on a special incident in Abraham's life, it may be the birth of Isaac, which started a chain of promises that led to Jesus, or it may be the announcement of Isaac's birth, when Abraham laughs (Gen. 17:17, which the later rabbis interpret as joy).[3]

The final step in the argument occurs when the Judeans challenge Jesus' ability to see Abraham, because he is not yet fifty years old! Jesus responds by saying, "Before Abraham was, I am" (v. 58). To comprehend this, one must understand the Johannine "program" of "I am" sayings. Up to this point, Jesus has asserted through these sayings that he is the bread of life from heaven (chap. 6), the light of the world (8:12), from above (8:23), and "I am he" (8:24, 28). Moses came to know God's identity when God told him, "'I AM WHO I AM.' . . . say to the Israelites, 'I AM has sent me to you'" (Exod. 3:14). Here Jesus says, "'I am' before Abraham." Again, this is an internal part of precreation belief: Jesus is both from God and an internal aspect of the being of God before creation, before Abraham, Moses, Isaiah, and so forth (1:1).

The story ends with a remarkable relation to Luke 4:29–30, where people in Jesus' hometown of Nazareth drive him out of town to the brow of a hill, with the intent of throwing him off the cliff, but he passes through the midst of them and goes on his way. In John 8:59 the Judeans pick up stones to throw at Jesus, but he hides himself and goes out of the temple. Various stories in the Gospels, then, have a memory of occasions when people try to kill Jesus but he escapes from them. In John, the event is depicted in the temple in Jerusalem, rather than in Jesus' hometown of Nazareth.

VERNON K. ROBBINS

in contexts where our questions and actions are prompted more by fear than faith.

This leads to a second, related thread of interpretation, namely, the danger of ordering our faith and action according to our understanding, rather than our understanding and action according to the rule of faith. Suspicion and prejudice are powerfully seductive forces, often substituting faulty understanding for genuine hearing and receiving. This text would caution against that kind of creaturely knowledge. The narrative of the cross and tomb certainly apply "mud" to our comprehension. The empty tomb functions that way for Mary Magdalene, who "sees" the empty tomb but does not really understand it until she receives the testimony of the risen Lord (20:2, 11–18).

Another way this text may probe the congregational imagination is through the metaphor of the interrogation chamber, which seems fitting, given the way the temple appears throughout chapter 8. An interrogation is freighted with urgency, with a determination to ferret out a deceitful truth (oxymoron intended) and, absent that truth, to coerce it through violence. In the very act of coercion, truth is already compromised. By contrast, Jesus, according to John, "knew what was in everyone" (2:25b). Jesus goes beyond the rule "innocent until proven guilty." He knows human guilt already, but loves the world still. Christ enters the "locked house" of the human heart, captive to its illusions, not by force but by mysterious love.

In the same way that Jesus will "leave the temple" in this text, interrupting the cycle of violence and coercion, the resurrected Jesus will enter the human house locked with fear. In that "lock-down" world, he speaks a liberating word: "Jesus came and stood among [his disciples] and said, 'Peace be with you'" (20:19).

ROBERT HOCH

---

3. Raymond E. Brown, *The Gospel according to John I–XII*, Anchor Bible 29 (Garden City, NY: Doubleday & Co., 1966), 360.

John 9:1–12

¹As he walked along, he saw a man blind from birth. ²His disciples asked him, "Rabbi, who sinned, this man or his parents, that he was born blind?" ³Jesus answered, "Neither this man nor his parents sinned; he was born blind so that God's works might be revealed in him. ⁴We must work the works of him who sent me while it is day; night is coming when no one can work. ⁵As long as I am in the world, I am the light of the world." ⁶When he had said this, he spat on the ground and made mud with the saliva and spread the mud on the man's eyes, ⁷saying to him, "Go, wash in the pool of Siloam" (which means Sent). Then he

Theological Perspective

At the center of a Gospel riddled with light and darkness, blindness and sight, truth and lie, John tells the story of a man born blind from birth. From birth he knew nothing but darkness. That Jesus sees the man who cannot see him is a literal fact. It is also a theological truth. From Nicodemus in the middle of the night and the Samaritan woman at the well to Judas in the garden and Pilate at the headquarters, those who dwell in darkness cannot of their own volition see the God who has come to them in Jesus Christ. Rather, God in Christ sees them in the darkness of the human condition without God and pitches his tent.

The disciples see the same man, but they see in a wholly different way. "Who sinned," the disciples ask at the sight of the blind man, "this man or his parents, that he was born blind?" (v. 2). Of course they ask this question, because this is how their eyes have been formed, how the world has taught them to see. They see by the lesser lights of the institutions into which they were born; they see the man born blind and begging at the gate according to the dictates of religion or tribe or nation. They see him through the first-century lens of shame, as some people today see those reduced to begging in society through the lens of culpability and guilt and blame. To Jesus' first disciples his tragic circumstances were a sign of

Pastoral Perspective

In typical Johannine style, the writer writes with palpable paradox and dramatic irony. Ultimately, it is only the man blind since birth who can truly see. The physically sighted people throughout the text—disciples, the blind man's parents, the Pharisees, and nameless others—are the sightless ones. The presence of the miracle-performing Jesus in their midst exposes this irony and paradox. This Gospel turns the miraculous event of one man's receiving sight into an ethical imperative for the disciples themselves and for the church in relation to the world.

As this particular scenario begins, Jesus is in motion: "as he walked along" (v. 1). The meticulous setting of the scene is as important as the dialogue between its characters. This mobile Christ is keenly aware of his surroundings. The readers and the communities in which this story is retold and/or read must move as Christ does, paying full attention to every detail.

Born blind, the man has never seen. He cannot distinguish between the cool blue of a sea and the fiery red of a flame. In his current circumstance, the best he can do is imagine. He cannot recall from memory the colors of things or the expression on a face. His blindness from birth is a significant detail in the story's movement. The detail about his lifelong physical condition ensures that the miracle

went and washed and came back able to see. [8]The neighbors and those who had seen him before as a beggar began to ask, "Is this not the man who used to sit and beg?" [9]Some were saying, "It is he." Others were saying, "No, but it is someone like him." He kept saying, "I am the man." [10]But they kept asking him, "Then how were your eyes opened?" [11]He answered, "The man called Jesus made mud, spread it on my eyes, and said to me, 'Go to Siloam and wash.' Then I went and washed and received my sight." [12]They said to him, "Where is he?" He said, "I do not know."

Exegetical Perspective

The "Light of the World" (8:12) now gives sight to a man born blind. John 9 is one of the finest short stories in the Bible. Following the convention that only two characters interact in a scene (Jesus and the blind man in vv. 1–7, the neighbors and the blind man in vv. 8–12), the chapter is easily divided into seven scenes. As elsewhere in John, light is a metaphor for sight, revelation, spiritual illumination, and Jesus himself (e.g., 1:4, 9; 3:19–21). Given John's episodic structure, in which Jesus meets and interacts with one character after another in successive episodes, the question is how the blind man (and those around him) will respond to Jesus: will they recognize him as the Christ? In this instance the question is "How does one come to the light?"

The disciples' question, "Rabbi, who sinned, this man or his parents, that he was born blind?" (v. 2), sounds odd to modern ears. How could they stand before one who had never seen the light of day and debate theology? The assumptions behind their question were that God causes everything that happens and that God is just. We still hear echoes of this theology among well-meaning Christians who attribute even terrible tragedies to "God's will," as though this presumed stability in the world is more comforting than the implications of random, senseless violence and tragedy. The disciples' logic,

Homiletical Perspective

In most congregations at worship each week, some of those present yearn for a faith that they can touch—a faith that arises out of the ordinariness of life. Things like mud, spit, direct instructions, and specific acts draw them closer to the gospel and evoke faithful living. Sitting adjacent to the person who yearns for such specificity, there likely will be one who hopes to encounter the holy by a revelation of divine action and intention. Reading this text, the first of these listeners may delight that Jesus spat and used his saliva to make mud as a means of bringing sight to the one born blind. The second listener is lifted up by the reassertion, "As long as I am in the world, I am the light of the world" (v. 5).

Bringing these two hearers of the word together in response to this text is a challenge and opportunity for the preacher. It is certainly one of the challenges and opportunities that John presents in this account of Jesus' healing of the man who was born blind by emphasizing both the means of divine action and the unlikely focus of God's intention. What does it mean that Jesus uses the very specific, common stuff of life to restore wholeness? How is it that these specific elements and acts are done by Jesus who proclaims "I am the light of the world"? Those who encounter this text—either as a preacher or as a listener—will have to deal with the tension

Theological Perspective

sin passed from generation to generation. Likewise, faithful Christians today ask the minister: What did I do wrong that my daughter is dying, my grandson is paralyzed, my great-granddaughter was born blind? Faithful ministers ask in return: Is the God who visits infirmity and suffering on the least of these the God made known in Jesus Christ?

In response to the disciples' question, Jesus says that the man's dwelling in undeniable darkness has become the condition for his unequivocal testimony to the light. It is not that his blindness was caused by God; rather, his blindness becomes the occasion for the revelation of God's nearness in Jesus. "Neither this man nor his parents sinned; he was born blind," Jesus says, "so that God's works might be revealed in him" (v. 3). Here is a man who cannot mistake the darkness for light and whose condition does not allow him the illusion of sightedness. Therefore, if the light should happen to shine in his life, the light can only be from God.

"I am the light of the world," Jesus has just said to religious leaders a chapter before and now says to his disciples. "As long as I am in the world, I am the light of the world" (v. 5). The words are surely akin to the Word in the beginning with God (1:2), spoken against the chaos and the darkness: "Let there be light" (Gen. 1:3). So, like the great God almighty at creation, Jesus bends down and takes the dust of the earth, mixes it with living water, and spreads mud on the blind man's eyes. The act is an act of creation.

John's theological anthropology would be that human beings are born into the world prematurely as regards their humanity, born with God's image not yet fully formed, born as creatures who may exist but do not live in the fullness of life for which they have been made. They look but do not see, said the prophet Isaiah, hear but do not listen, think but do not understand (Isa. 6:9–10). They beg to receive life from the things and powers that may promise life but cannot give life. Creation is incomplete and their humanity unfinished until the light of the world should see them and say, "Here's mud in your blind eye! Let there be light."

Jesus next tells the man to wash in the pool of Siloam, which is interpreted "the-one-who-was-sent" (v. 7, *ho hermēneuetai apestalmenos*). With the man's eyes remade, now his way of seeing, of understanding, of interpreting the truth, is about to be born anew by water and the Spirit. While the story's setting is not specified, it follows a cycle of stories that take place around the Feast of Tabernacles, when the living water, the flowing water from the pool of

Pastoral Perspective

cannot be explained in another way that would allow detractors to question the veracity of the miraculous transformation from blindness to sightedness. This would be the claim of those who were determined to discredit Jesus and this miracle. What is about to happen to him has to be viewed as a totally transformative event.

Jesus is not the only one who sees the blind man. The disciples see him also, but they see him differently. Although Jesus does not say anything about the man initially, the disciples feel compelled to beg an explosive theological question: "Who sinned?" How they get from "blind" to "sin" is a peculiar leap for some! Nevertheless, because of this question, the readers of this story enter the heart of a theological discussion that is ages old. What is the nature of sin? What does a sinner look like? Are we born with sin or into sin, or do we acclimate to sin as we sin? At first, it appears that they are asking a seminal theological question. These types of questions are perhaps good for us to ask, but as simplistic as the question asked appears, it is weighted down with many presuppositions.

Jesus responds with exacting deftness: This is not a question about consequential or hereditary sin, as the disciples seem to imply in their query. This particular blindness is an opportunity to participate in the works of God as a community together. The task for the faithful is not to give the correct answers (orthodoxy) but to give ample framing for the questions of the human condition. This framing is "correct" only when it leads the community of the faithful to raise questions about their role and responsibility in getting from malady to wholeness.

Think here of a prism and the ways in which the light is first received and then bent within it. In essence, Jesus turns the prism on the disciples' question, changing the way in which they see the scenario. The question is reframed thusly, "Are there some conditions, circumstances, and maladies in our world that are troubles and troubling from their inception?" Can we see these troubles in our world beyond the consequence of someone's sin, see them, rather, as an opportunity to help set things right? Jesus transforms this theological question into a communal ethical imperative, with such precision that it implicates all who would be called Christian. He was born blind not because of sin but that the works of God might be revealed *in* him. In other words, do not talk about what is wrong with the world; rather, engage it until it is transformed into a locus for the works of God.

following the common theology of the day, is that it must have been God's will that this man was born blind, and if it was God's will, it was justified. Blindness was viewed as punishment for sin (e.g., Nahum of Gimzo, in *b. Taanit* 21a), so the instance of a baby born blind raised the intriguing question of whether he was being punished for his parents' sin (Exod. 20:5) or for sin that he had committed before birth: "who sinned, this man or his parents?" By the end of the story Jesus will completely reorient the assumed understanding of sin. The blind man is an "everyone character"; we are all born blind and need to come to sight. Sin consists not in being born blind but in choosing not to see (9:39–41).

Little words, like minor characters, are often important, and that is the case with the disciples' question: "who sinned, this man or his parents, *that* he was born blind?" (v. 2). The word "that" translates the Greek conjunction *hina*, which commonly introduces a *purpose* clause; but obviously no one sinned with the purpose of having the child born blind. In other occurrences *hina* introduces a *result* clause, which makes better sense here: "who sinned *with the result that* he was born blind?"[1]

The problem returns in the next verse. First, Jesus categorically denies that the man's blindness was the result of sin, either his or his parents'. Instead, it was "so that [*hina*] God's works might be revealed in him" (v. 3b). Again, interpreting the conjunction as conveying result rather than purpose works best; the man was born blind, not with the purpose that Jesus could heal him, but with the result that "God's works might be revealed in him." Taking *hina* as expressing result rather than purpose resolves nonsense in one instance and bad theology in the other. One might also choose to put the period after "his parents sinned" and then begin a new sentence with "But he was born blind . . ."

The means of the healing is described in great detail: first anointing the man's eyes with clay made from Jesus' saliva, and then washing in the pool of Siloam. Spittle was thought to have healing power (Mark 7:33; 8:23), and clay was often used in healings, so Jesus' actions would be recognized as those of a folk healer. It is tempting to find symbolic significance in both steps in the man's healing.

In John 20:22 the risen Lord breathes the Holy Spirit into the disciples, echoing the account of the

that comes from the smallest and largest elements of life being brought into relationship with each other in service of healing and wholeness.

After Jesus' act of healing the one born blind, this text proceeds to the reaction of the (formerly) blind man's neighbors. They are all speculating on what really happened and on whether or not the one before them right now is, in fact, the one born blind. All the while, the text records: "He kept saying, 'I am the man'" (v. 9). It almost plays as a comedy sketch, complete with mistaken identity and willful confusion on all parts.

In his 1933 movie *City Lights*, Charlie Chaplin plays his signature role of the Little Tramp. The story unfolds as the Little Tramp meets a blind girl selling flowers on the sidewalk who mistakes him for a wealthy duke. When he learns that an operation may restore her sight, he sets off to earn the money she needs to have the surgery. In a series of comedic adventures typical of a Chaplin movie, he eventually succeeds, even though his efforts land him in jail.[1] While he is there, the girl has the operation and afterwards yearns to meet the one (whom she believes to be the wealthy benefactor, not the Tramp) who gave her the opportunity to have her sight restored.

With her sight restored, the girl opens a flower shop. One day, when a rich man comes into the shop, the girl wonders if he is her mysterious benefactor. At the same time, the Tramp is outside the shop, looking in. Seeing a flower that the Tramp has retrieved from the gutter falling apart in his hand, the girl kindly offers him a fresh flower from her shop, and a coin. The Tramp begins to leave, then reaches for the flower. The girl takes hold of his hand to place the coin in it; recognizing the touch of his hand, she realizes who he is. "You?" she asks, "You?" She then holds his hand to her heart as the film ends.

In a touch between a Tramp and the once blind flower girl, assumptions are shattered and truth is revealed. At the heart of the matter is the identity of the "benefactor." Likewise, John's account of the healing of the man who was born blind moves the reader to focus on identity. Who is this one who claims to be the light of the world? Who is the one who sees this man born blind and, without waiting for a request for healing, goes ahead and initiates healing with his touch? Who is this Jesus?

The scrambling disorientation of verses 8–12 shows how easy it is to misunderstand the works

1. Frederick William Danker, *A Greek-English Lexicon of the New Testament and Other Early Christian Literature*, 3rd ed. (Chicago: University of Chicago Press, 2000), 477; Daniel B. Wallace, *The Basics of New Testament Syntax: An Intermediate Greek Gramma*r (Grand Rapids: Zondervan, 2000), 301.

1. Roger Ebert, "Roger Ebert's Great Movies-City Lights," www.rogerebert.com/reviews/great-movie-city-lights-1931; accessed April 10, 2013.

John 9:1–12

Theological Perspective

Siloam, the "waters of purification," washed God's people clean in the temple. No doubt those waters have become, in John's understanding, the waters of baptism, the waters of birth by the Spirit. Stumbling into the pool a blind man, he emerges from the water as one who sees everything through the lens of his encounter with Jesus. One can imagine him dating his life from the day when he first saw the light.

Without a word, Jesus disappears from the story, and life in the village resumes. How often is this the case with faith? Light shines in the darkness, a moment of understanding is given, and then we are on our own to make sense of the gospel in a hostile world. Certainly this was the experience of the early church and is the present experience of Christians still waiting, late in time, for Christ to come again. The church bears witness to the light that the rest of the world cannot see. It is a community given stories like this one and sent into the darkness with the great privilege and enormous responsibility of representing the light that is light to a world that prefers the darkness.

There is no joy in his hometown over the former beggar's good fortune, only questions and doubts. No one can agree about the sighted man's identity, because to see him as he is in the light of Jesus would be to acknowledge their own blindness. They cannot. The man's repeated testimony to the momentary encounter that changed his life is not credible to the neighbors' way of knowing. Ironically, they ask to see Jesus again for themselves, to hear his word on the matter firsthand. The exchange is painfully familiar to any whose testimony to the light is met with the epistemology of those who prefer the darkness. The man could only reply, "I do not know" (v. 12).

CYNTHIA A. JARVIS

Pastoral Perspective

Some translations of verse 4 can lead to a very dangerous privatization of religious identity. Instead of "We must work," some manuscripts read "I must work." How quick we are to let Jesus do all the redemptive and transformative work in the world, while abdicating our responsibility to be the difference in times of brokenness and tragedy. The better rendering is that the pronoun be read as first-person plural, "We must work." Reading the pronoun as "we" draws every reader or reteller of this story into the expectations the pronoun implies. We (Jesus and his disciples) cannot raise theological questions as distanced, objective observers. The life of faith draws us into the "we" and the imperative of doing redemptive and restorative work in the name of Christ.

No one who sees the blind man in his condition and identifies with the faith of this Christ and hears this story can be exempted from the personal and communal responsibility to address the maladies and misfortunes of his or her own time. These faults, maladies, and conditions are too easily in our time personalized and privatized. "I must work," but not alone, because the work cannot be accomplished by single or solitary efforts. I must be connected with others who share my communal identity and a commitment to the transformation of creation. Here we see the inescapable imperative for anyone who professes to be motivated by Christ to believe.

No one in the story is exempted from responsibility, not even the formerly blind man. Jesus takes dirt and spit to create a salve for the blind man's eyes and instructs him to go and wash in the pool of Sent (Siloam). By this simple directive, the blind man too is called forth and commissioned. He comes back seeing.

GARY V. SIMPSON

creation of human life in Genesis 2:7. Is Jesus fashioning new eyes for the man born blind by putting clay made of his spittle and dust in his eyes, and does John suggest an allusion to Genesis 2:7 here also? The significance of the washing is more explicit. The pool of Siloam of Jesus' day, which was the largest public *miqveh* or washing pool in the first century, was discovered in excavations in 2004–6 CE.[2] As a blind man he would have been in need of ritual purification, and John points to the further significance of the name Siloam by translating it: "which means Sent" (v. 7). The connection with Jesus becomes all the more suggestive because in the Gospel of John Jesus is the one "sent" (e.g., 9:4). As in the provision of wine in the vessels for ritual purification at the wedding at Cana (2:1–11), so here Jesus uses the Jewish instruments in his revelatory and healing work.

In the second scene (vv. 8–12), the process of verifying and interpreting the sign starts with the neighbors questioning the man. The neighbors ask the wrong question when they ask "how?" rather than "who?" but the man recounts his healing briefly. He sees but has not yet truly gained his sight. When they ask him where Jesus is, he replies simply, "I do not know" (v. 12). At this point, like the blind man in Bethsaida in Mark 8:22–26, and like many of us, the blind man sees but not clearly.

R. ALAN CULPEPPER

of light in a world of darkness. Even so, John keeps a steady focus on Jesus. In this case, it is the touch of Jesus, using common elements of daily life for a holy purpose, that restores sight for the man born blind. Metaphorically speaking, what remarkable event is necessary to penetrate the self-imposed darkness of those who may choose not to see beyond themselves?

Finally, the man who had his sight restored has things done to him and tasks assigned to him by Jesus. Then, in the wake of the healing, he has people discussing and debating about him. Only in the last four verses does the man speak for himself. First, he says, "I am the man" (v. 9) in response to the crowd's inquiries. Second, he once again describes verbatim what Jesus' instructions were and how he followed them to the letter (v. 11). Finally, to the crowd's inquiry about the location of Jesus, he says, "I don't know" (v. 12). First a confession of identity, second a testimony to obedience, and finally an expression of humility. He is not Jesus' keeper. He has been touched by the light of the world, but he does not claim any special purview or power. Grace intruded on his life, and he obeyed its call—even as Jesus shattered assumptions and opened the way to a new life. Any congregation dealing with this text and any preacher who proclaims it may receive a similar gift, and a similar call to obedience.

MARK RAMSEY

---

2. Urban C. von Wahlde, "The Pool of Siloam: The Importance of the New Discoveries for Our Understanding of Ritual Immersion in Late Second Temple Judaism and the Gospel of John," in *John, Jesus, and History,* vol. 2: *Aspects of Historicity in the Fourth Gospel*, ed. Paul N. Anderson, Felix Just, and Tom Thatcher (Atlanta: Society of Biblical Literature, 2009), 155–73.

John 9:13–17

¹³They brought to the Pharisees the man who had formerly been blind. ¹⁴Now it was a sabbath day when Jesus made the mud and opened his eyes. ¹⁵Then the Pharisees also began to ask him how he had received his sight. He said to them, "He put mud on my eyes. Then I washed, and now I see." ¹⁶Some of the Pharisees said, "This man is not from God, for he does not observe the sabbath." But others said, "How can a man who is a sinner perform such signs?" And they were divided. ¹⁷So they said again to the blind man, "What do you say about him? It was your eyes he opened." He said, "He is a prophet."

Theological Perspective

Just as the newly sighted man was met with only questions and doubts from his neighbors, likewise only accusation and judgment attend his encounter with the religious authorities. The neighbors' last question had to do with Jesus' whereabouts. "I do not know," the man replies. They next bring him to the religious authorities. Do they think the authorities will know where Jesus is, or are the neighbors hoping the Pharisees can shed some light on what has just happened? In relation to Jesus and the light they are blind; they can do neither.

The Pharisees' first question of the man is a question of technique. How did he receive his sight? Theology often gives way to technique when the survival of religious institutions is at stake. Once the man tells them what Jesus did, their attention shifts from "how" his eyes were healed to the moral status and religious authority of the man who gave him sight. The work was done on the Sabbath, when healing is permitted in life–and-death situations. "What *was* the hurry?" the Pharisees must have wondered. "The man has been blind from birth!" Yet it is the man's blindness that becomes, on the Sabbath, an occasion not for human work to be done but for the *work of God* to be revealed (9:3). In order to see this at any time in human history, religion (humanly devised ways to God) would have to acknowledge its

Pastoral Perspective

Often pastors find themselves woefully inadequate or cautiously hesitant in addressing the pressing challenges and issues of their day. How often do seminary students comment: "That is a wonderful insight/challenge, but I could never preach that in my church"? In this section of the story of the man born blind, opportunities exist to speak about some contemporary issues, namely, the relationship between worship and action, the need to be careful not to perpetuate anti-Judaism, the role of the institutional church in restorative and prophetic action.

The story of the healed man continues, and the reader is given another significant detail about the context of this miracle. The man formerly blind is brought to the religious authorities, and readers discover that Jesus healed him on the Sabbath day (v. 14). Verses 13–18 are instructive for the contemporary church and believers because they invite consideration of the relationship between worship and service. Some believers really do think that all they need to do on Sunday is to spend an hour or two at a local church singing the songs, professing the beliefs, and participating in the rituals and practices that define what it means to be a "Christian" in their particular community, congregation, or denomination.

In their minds, this participation guarantees that they are in good standing as part of the faithful. It is

Exegetical Perspective

What do you do after a miracle occurs? Most modern Christians have probably never considered this question, because miracles are not part of the experience of many. If someone were to report a miracle, a first response would probably be to dismiss it. In that respect the ancients were no different from many contemporary people.

First, the blind man's neighbors wondered if he was really the man who used to sit and beg (vv. 8–12). Then they took him to the Pharisees (vv. 13–17), who persisted in asking how the healing occurred—the wrong question! The important issue was "who," not "how." Each time the story is repeated—and this is the third time (vv. 6–7, 11, and 15)—it is reported more briefly. The abridged account of the story can highlight particular elements of it (cf. the repetition of Paul's experience on the road to Damascus or the reporting of the confession of Cornelius's household in Acts 10–11). After questioning the man, the Pharisees went to his parents (vv. 18–23). In all three scenes the suspicion and the intent are the same: they suspected a hoax, and they sought to prove that the man who could see was not the man who had been born blind. All three times their efforts were thwarted: the man verified that he was indeed the (formerly) blind beggar; he testified that he was blind but now could see (vv. 15,

Homiletical Perspective

This text in John's Gospel is a continuation of the ensuing discussions and consequences swirling around Jesus' actions that resulted in giving sight to a man who was blind from birth. It encompasses an exchange between the Pharisees and the healed man. This portion of the text reflects a failure of imagination on the part of those who witness the fruits of Jesus' healing action. The restoration of sight becomes an occasion where fear and defensiveness overwhelm the ability of all but the man once blind to perceive the hand of God at work in the world. It is notable that the religious authorities are questioning the healed and now sighted, man; however, they are not questioning the healing itself, but Jesus. Their exchange displays no imagination for the possibilities of how and when and through whom and on whom God may work. A sermon on this text may want to explore the openness of the imagination to God's unexpected ways in people's lives.

Fear is a cause for a stifled imagination. American writer John Cheever once described fear as "the taste of a rusty knife."[1] Fear paralyzes. It suffocates faith. In this text, the fear is that there is on the loose in the person of Jesus a power that the temporal powers that be know nothing about. As the Pharisees try

---

1. John Cheever, *The Wapshot Chronicle* (New York: Vintage Books, 1992), 307.

John 9:13–17

Theological Perspective

blindness to revelation. Religion cannot. Therefore the one born blind, who now sees things differently, is seen by the defenders of truth to be a threat to the future of the institution that guards the truth.

The theological dilemma of the Pharisees parodies a popular question: How can good things be done by bad people (sinners)? Given the fact of the man's restored sight and the fact that his sight was restored on the Sabbath, the Pharisees now must ask themselves if God can work outside the bounds of God's own established limits (only life-and-death matters can be addressed on the Sabbath) and through one whose actions oppose those limits (a sinner). Even a cursory reading of salvation history leads one to conclude that either God is a notoriously bad judge of moral character as humanly conceived, continually choosing to work through people whose behavior falls outside the established moral norms; or else the self-assured defenders of what God has done throughout that history are incorrigibly blinded to what God is doing.

Viewing the situation through what God *has done*, Jesus is a sinner, because he does not observe the Sabbath; viewing the situation through what Jesus *is doing and will do*, he could only be from God. "God's action and God's freedom are never more plainly misunderstood," Paul Lehmann wrote, "than by those who suppose that God has acted and does act in a certain way and cannot, therefore, always also act in other ways. Of course God is bound *to* what God does and has done. But [God] is not bound *by* what God has done."[1]

John reports that the authorities were divided, foreshadowing the divisions of the church on matters of Scripture, theology, and ethics for the next two thousand years. Remarkably, they ask the man who has no authority on matters pertaining to God other than the authority of his own experience with Jesus, "What do you say about him?" John invites us to watch as the light slowly begins to dawn in the mind of the man whose understanding must catch up with his experience.

A physiological analogy is apt. In a chapter on "Seeing" Annie Dillard reports that when doctors first began removing cataracts from the eyes of those who had been born blind, the patients had no understanding of what their eyes were seeing. Unable to assign meaning to what appeared to be blobs of color, they only slowly, often painfully, were able

Pastoral Perspective

worth asking whether the habitual performance of religious observances and practices in and of itself brings about the radical transformation of society. There are so many opportunities on the way to and from these sacred gatherings that call Christians to embody the claims of their faith. In church cultures where religious power is equated with professionally choreographed and precise worship events that are evaluated in terms of celebrity and performance, there is a danger that the rolled-up sleeves and dirty hands of the faith are lost. Sometimes such well-intentioned worship experiences can be too polished or too clean for everyday people to find their own lives included in what can appear to be a service for lofty and high piety alone. Care should be taken to ensure that the work done by those dirty hands of faith is not sanitized or overly spiritualized or even disconnected from worship.

Much has been written and said about the anti-Judaizing elements found in John's Gospel. This story, if not carefully scrutinized, could be interpreted in ways that naively contribute to the violence done by interpretations that perpetuate anti-Judaism, even in contemporary Christian contexts. Throughout the Gospel, the writer refers to "the Jews" and in this particular story to "the Pharisees," meaning those religious leaders in opposition to Jesus and to the Johannine community of Jesus followers. Preachers especially need to be careful with their use of language here and remain mindful that the content of this Gospel reflects the context and intra-Jewish relations of its times.

This passage invites consideration of how sometimes churches use their institutional life as an excuse for not participating in the restorative work of God or in the prophetic dimensions of living the gospel. In other words, concerns about the "order of worship," or church constitutions and by-laws, or pastoral programming can sometimes obstruct the field of vision of pastoral leaders and their Christian communities. While these institutional matters are important to the operations of a congregation, they may also distract attention from those in immediate need—in their midst or in the moment. What happens if a person who is homeless wanders into the sanctuary and "interferes" with the "order of worship," or "disrupts" a scheduled event, or knocks on the door at an inopportune moment? What constitutes a scheduling conflict? Is there a moratorium on grace and mercy in the observance of the implicit or explicit codes of our own Christian communities?

---

1. Paul Lehmann, *Ethics in a Christian Context* (New York: Harper and Row, 1963), 72–73.

25); and his parents supported his testimony: he was indeed their son, and he had been born blind (v. 20).

Along the way, the situation is complicated by the delayed report (v. 14; cf. 5:9) that the healing occurred on the Sabbath. Sabbath law allowed intervention in a critical, life-threatening situation, but blindness from birth obviously did not meet this test. The manner of the healing violated the command to keep the Sabbath holy. Making clay (which is specifically mentioned again in v. 14), anointing, and washing were all proscribed activities (*m. Sabbat.* 7.2; 14.3; *m. Moed* 8.6).

The man's claim that his sight had been restored by actions that violated the Sabbath presented the Pharisees with a perplexing dilemma. Only one who was from God could exercise healing power, but one who was from God surely would not violate the Sabbath. The division among them illustrates another of John's themes: the more clearly the revelation was perceived, the more it brought division. When Jesus challenged the crowd in John 6, saying that the bread he offers is his flesh, they argued among themselves (6:52). At the Festival of Booths in Jerusalem there was a division in the crowd over him (7:43), and again in John 10 the people were divided (10:19–21). After the raising of Lazarus, some plotted to kill Jesus, while others cheered his entry into Jerusalem. When the voice spoke from heaven, some said it thundered, while others said an angel had spoken (12:29). When light dawned, some greeted it while others turned back to the darkness (3:19–21).

Before berating the Pharisees for failing to accept the healing of the blind man, it is important to remember that adapting to new truths is always difficult. Jesus told his disciples that he still had much to tell them that they were not able to bear (16:12). George Bernard Shaw keenly observed, "You have learnt something. That always feels at first as if you had lost something."[1] New truths are particularly difficult for those who live within traditions that reach back centuries. What do we do when God works outside our theology, our tradition, and our structures? Often those who have less invested in the status quo see new realities more quickly than those who maintain it. The question for the blind man and those around him, as it is for all who hear this story, is whether there is truth here or not, and how to respond to it. How does one discern what is of God and what is not?

to parse what is an acceptable and an unacceptable "holy work," they do what fear provokes: they begin to be divided among themselves. Lack of Sabbath observance on Jesus' part leads some Pharisees to judge that he is not from God. Others wonder how Jesus can perform "such signs" if he is such a sinner (v. 16). Mostly, they are afraid of what they do not understand.

The experience of feeling threatened is closely related to fear, and it also shuts down imagination. When one feels threatened, one can rarely be imaginative. What is most often threatened in daily life is power and control—and Jesus is a threat to both. Many people who engage this text may come with an inventory of values, goals, and beliefs to protect. Each one may be trying, at some level, to keep control of life. Religious tradition and practice can at times be co-opted in attempts to maintain control or demonstrate power. However, Jesus demonstrates that the power of God to heal and make whole is beyond human attempts at control.

Every person in the scene reacts to this unexpected event. For the man born blind, there is astonishment and a dawning realization of the power of Jesus. For many of the others—bystanders, observers, authorities—there are subtle and not so subtle attempts to fit this extraordinary event back into familiar categories. There are appeals to law, justice, righteousness, as well as recognition of their own confusion on these matters. John seems to be using these reactions to inspire the imaginations of listeners/readers to see a new life, a new power, a new hope that Jesus embodies.

Finally, imagination thrives in an atmosphere where strange new things can happen and be embraced. The man born blind stands in the middle of this scene and with gratitude receives his new life without question or caution. In his memoir *The Sacred Journey,* Frederick Buechner remembers the words of *Rinkitink in Oz* as they apply to Buechner's own life and faith: "Never question the truth of what you fail to understand, for the world is filled with wonders."[1] This is the truth that the man who was formerly blind has embraced. He is the only person in this entire scene, from the point of his encounter with Jesus through its aftermath, who was not asking any questions. Why is he blind? Who sinned? the disciples wonder (9:2). Who is he? the neighbors query: "Is this not the man who used to sit and beg?"(9:8). What happened? both the neighbors

1. From *Major Barbara*, in *The Collected Screenplays of Bernard Shaw*, ed. Bernard F. Dukore (Athens, GA: University of Georgia Press, 1980), 329.

1. Frederick Buechner, *The Sacred Journey* (San Francisco: Harper, 1982), 55.

John 9:13–17

Theological Perspective

to let go, literally, of the world they had known by touch, in order to inhabit a world they were growing into knowing by sight. One twenty-two-year-old girl did not open her eyes again for two weeks because of the dazzling brightness of the world. When at the end of that time she opened her eyes again, she did not recognize any objects, but, "the more she now directed her gaze upon everything about her, the more it could be seen how an expression of gratification and astonishment overspread her features; she repeatedly exclaimed: 'Oh God! How beautiful!'"[2]

John offers similar accounts of the slow process of coming to belief (Nicodemus, the Samaritan woman, Martha, Mary Magdalene, to name a few) as those who encounter Jesus begin to let go of their previous ways of knowing God and gradually direct their gaze more and more on Jesus until astonishment at God's nearness overtakes them. Previously the man has said to the neighbors that he did not know where Jesus was. Now he says to the religious authorities, "He is a prophet." Soon he will say more as he continues to assign meaning to who he sees in Jesus.

This is not the case with the religious authorities. The cognitive dissonance involved in believing that Jesus is doing the work of God on the Sabbath has to be resolved one way or another. This is the case with everyone who has or will encounter Jesus: either it is true that he is in the Father and the Father in him (14:10), or it is not true. Rather than see God in him, the religious authorities close their eyes and set out to fit God into what they already know. Likewise, as Richard Lischer observes, the church in the time between Jesus' resurrection and promised return "has always been pretty good at investigating irregularities but not so good at acknowledging the power of God that can be contained by no religious premises."[3] Religion's investigation of irregularities continues as the man's parents' are asked to testify next.

CYNTHIA A. JARVIS

Pastoral Perspective

In the immediate past, "It is not the right time" or "Can we opt for a less threatening way of proceeding?" was often used to dissuade faith-based social change. For example, in the struggle for racial equality in the United States of America, religious leaders in Alabama wrote a document appealing to the high moral "Christian" sensibilities of the time to try to persuade Dr. Martin Luther King to refrain from carrying out the public protests in Birmingham. While in jail, King wrote an exacting indictment of religious appropriateness, now known as the classic "Letter from the Birmingham Jail."

Consider that the formerly blind man's first sighted experience of the religious leaders was this encounter. How did he now see this ancient institution that opposed him in his blindness and now was ready to oppose the one who healed him? How can people who have been part of the institutional church all of their lives see it with new eyes? What are the voices that challenge the status quo in favor of the always surprising work of the Spirit? For example, traditionally patriarchal communities of faith are sometimes challenged to be open to varying ways of seeing these texts from the perspectives of women. Feminist singer and songwriter Carol Etzler captures this best in her anthem about seeing anew in a world held hostage by the pain and suffering inflicted on women by patriarchy, :"Sometimes I wish my eyes hadn't been opened, But now that they have, I'm determined to see."[1]

Finally, there is a lot of contemporary conversation about the word "prophetic"—a word too easily used. What was prophetic about Jesus? Note well that he used few words. Prophetic actions do not need an abundance of utterances or proclamations. Prophetic action can confound religious authorities. Perhaps by calling Jesus a prophet, the man once blind himself gives prophetic witness (v. 17). Doing prophetic work may lead to rejection, even by religious people. That too often is the prophet's lot.

GARY V. SIMPSON

2. Annie Dillard, *Pilgrim at Tinker Creek* (New York: Harper Perennial, 1998), 31.

3. Richard Lischer, "Acknowledgment," *The Christian Century*, vol. 116, no. 7 (March 2, 1999).

1. Carol A. Etzler, "Sometimes I Wish," *Sometimes I Wish: Feminist Songs by Carol Etzler* (Samray Music-Sisters Unlimited BMI, 1976), http://queermusic heritage.com/sep2013etzler.html.

Exegetical Perspective

So the question comes back to the man who had been healed: "What do you say about him? It was your eyes he opened" (v. 17). Like others who encounter Jesus in one episode after another in this Gospel, the once-blind man offered a study in the process of responding to the light and coming to faith. His first response was simply, "I do not know" (v. 12). This time he responded, "He is a prophet" (v. 17). As in the experience of the woman at the well, recognition that Jesus was a prophet (4:19) was a step on the way to a fuller recognition of Jesus' identity (1:21; 6:14; 7:40). It affirmed that he was sent from God and that God was working through him. Moreover, it was widely thought that there were no longer any prophets in Israel, that the spirit of prophecy had been taken from Israel. When the Maccabees cleansed the temple after it had been defiled by pagan worship, "they tore down the altar, and stored the stones in a convenient place on the temple hill until a prophet should come to tell what to do with them" (1 Macc. 4:45–46). Many looked forward to the appearance of a prophet at the end of time (Deut. 18:15, 18; Mal. 4:5); so the appearance of a prophet was in itself a dramatic development.

For those who know Jesus by loftier titles (Christ, Messiah, Son of God, Lord), the confession "prophet" is inadequate, but here, as with the Samaritan woman, it is the confession of one who was on his way to a higher level of faith (9:35–38). Confessions represent work in progress, understanding distilled from experience. Rather than quibble over the orthodoxy of a confession, should we not celebrate the dawning light in every confession?

R. ALAN CULPEPPER

Homiletical Perspective

(9:10) and later the Pharisees ask (9:15). How have you received sight? Where is he, the one who healed you? (9:12) "How can a man who is a sinner perform such signs?"(9:16) Who do you say he is since he opened your eyes? (9:17) Even the man's parents are not spared interrogation (9:19).

The man born blind endures the questioning of the skeptical; however, he has given himself over to the God of wonders, and a world of grace. Others in this text respond out of fear, perhaps for what they cannot control. The strangeness of the situation—so outside of their common expectations or assumptions—does not allow them to imagine even for a moment that God can act in this wondrous way. They do not know what to make of Jesus. They recognize the work he does, but it confounds them, and they are unable to appreciate it or give thanks for the miracle in their midst.

One final word about imagination: when the world God has created and redeemed can be imagined, behavior has a way of falling in line behind that imagination and may be manifest as discipleship. Those who can perceive God's new heaven and a new earth are likely to find, over time, that their lives are conforming to that vision. Kindness, patience, goodness, hope, love, and faith are quickened in the lives of those who can imagine how God is alive and at work through Jesus and through the lives of those who follow Jesus. Such openness to the uncontrollable God allows for healing, restoration, and transformation to occur. This is an openness that the man formerly blind demonstrates. While everyone else is distracted by fear and responding defensively, this faithful, healed disciple makes his affirmation of faith in Jesus: "He is a prophet" (9:17).

MARK RAMSEY

¹⁸The Jews* did not believe that he had been blind and had received his sight until they called the parents of the man who had received his sight ¹⁹and asked them, "Is this your son, who you say was born blind? How then does he now see?" ²⁰His parents answered, "We know that this is our son, and that he was born blind; ²¹but we do not know how it is that now he sees, nor do we know who opened his eyes. Ask him; he is of age. He will speak for himself." ²²His parents said this because they were afraid of the Jews; for the Jews had already agreed that anyone who confessed Jesus to be the Messiah would be put out of the synagogue. ²³Therefore his parents said, "He is of age; ask him."

Theological Perspective

With the newly sighted man standing by his story, the religious authorities now turn to question his parents in their attempt to discredit the man's claim that he had once been blind. Their answers foil the authorities' investigation of irregularities for a second time. As is often the case in John's Gospel (e.g., the exchange of Jesus and Martha at Lazarus's death [11:21–27] and the standoff between Jesus and Pilate in the praetorium [18:37–38]), the facts are the facts; but the truth requires a new way of seeing. Yes, his parents testify, he was indeed born blind; no, they were not witnesses to the light.

Although the man's parents say they did not see what or who caused their blind son to see, John is not so sure that this is the case and takes the occasion to remind the reader of the situation his community presently faces. If the man's parents had been contemporaries of John and had confessed to "seeing" Jesus as the giver of light, they would have had reason to fear the power of the authorities to put them out of the community, to exclude them from the people who were their own by reason of birth and blood.

Alongside the obvious tension between the parents and the authorities, John's prologue suggests

Pastoral Perspective

In the spirit of Johannine dualism, there is another subtle dialectic revealed in this story located in the relationship between the parents and their once-sightless child. Exploring these roles within the passage may lead the church to a significant and necessary conversation on parenting.

In 9:18 John's story turns to the role and responsibility of the parents, the characters included in the initial theological query of the disciples ("Who sinned, this man or his parents?" 9:2). Although the authorities still do not believe this is the same man who was born blind, the parents are called as first witnesses in this public hearing. Their confirmation of the authorities' suspicions would make this "an open and shut case" and this whole Jesus-and-his- miracle business would simply go away. If the parents say the man was not born blind, the miracle is easily discredited. This scene invites the reader to consider parental authority and power in relation to the future faith and life of a child.

Often parents have a false notion of what it means to be parents, a notion formed in them by their own parents, who said things like, "Do not do as I do, do as I say." Domineering parents always believe their authority to be final. This miracle sign in John's Gospel puts the newly sighted adult child way beyond the reaches of his parents' authority. Because they

* See "'The Jews' in the Fourth Gospel" on pp. xi–xiv.

Exegetical Perspective

Following the literary convention that only two participants appear in a given scene, verses 18–23 form the fourth scene in this tightly plotted short story from Jesus' ministry. The Pharisees question the blind man's parents. Neither Jesus nor the blind man appears in these verses. As in the previous two scenes, the Pharisees seek to expose as a hoax the report that Jesus has healed a man who has been born blind. Surely his parents can give credible testimony to the contrary!

These verses proceed with a report of the reason for this meeting and its significance (v. 18). The Pharisees ask questions: Is this your son, who was born blind? How is it he can see now? (v. 19). His parents respond: He is our son. He was born blind, but we do not know how he can see now or who opened his eyes. Ask him (vv. 20–21). The evangelist's comments on their response have become a major point of discussion in current scholarship (vv. 22–23).

In verse 18 the Pharisees of verse 13 become "the Jews," who here are not all Jews, but the "religious authorities" or previously mentioned Pharisees who are concerned that the law of Sabbath observance not be broken. The story assumes that the society in which Jesus lived was Torah observant. Sabbath violation, moreover, was not just an individual matter. The community was responsible, so violations implicated the whole community.

Homiletical Perspective

As the narrative in John 9 continues to unfold, it is becoming increasingly clear that this Gospel text is asserting that there is more than one kind of blindness. On the surface, this is an account of a man born blind whom Jesus heals one day as he is "going along." This healing happens without any request from the blind man—it is just what the Light of the World does. Now the Gospel homes in on a crucial point: there is more than one kind of blindness. There is physical blindness, as can be seen in this man, and now his sight has been restored. From the reaction of the crowd, the Pharisees, and the man's parents, this text seems to indicate blindness is also a spiritual condition that manifests itself as an inability to recognize the work of God in one's midst.

It is important, however, to appreciate that sometimes the inability to see may also be a response to violence, resulting in what some specialists have called functional blindness. For example, the Khmer Rouge ruled Cambodia from 1975 to 1979; that time was marked by the "killing fields" of mass execution and terror. After that oppressive political regime had been defeated, doctors discovered a significant number of blind women among those who had suffered during those times. A survey determined that almost all of these women between fifty-one and seventy years of age were constantly depressed. Many had

John 9:18–23

Theological Perspective

that something even more significant was happening to the relationship between the man and his parents: "But to all who received him, who believed in his name, he gave power to become children of God, who were born not of blood or of the will of the flesh or of the will of man, but of God" (1:12–13). Not only had the man been born blind; he also had been born of blood, and by blood he could trace his status as God's child to God's call of Abram (Gen. 12:1–3; 15:4–6). Because he was born of their blood, the parents reply that they "know" he is their son who was born blind (v. 20).

However, because the one through whom all things were created has taken the dust of the ground to make new eyes (eyes that are the beginning of a whole new life); and because in the waters of the pool of Siloam the man born blind has been reborn sighted (or at least he is on the way to "seeing from above"), his parents' knowledge of him has come to an end. They do not "know" how it is that now he sees or "know" who opened his eyes (vv. 20–21) for two reasons. First, they themselves remain in darkness; and second, the man is becoming a child of God who was born not of blood or of the will of the flesh or of human will, but of God. His origin is in the Word who was "in the beginning" (1:1) and through whom "all things came into being" (1:3).

The whence of *Christian* existence has to do, not with human lineage, but with divine will. One's identity as a Christian has to do, not with a person's father and father's father, a person's mother and mother's mother, whose bloodline can be traced back to the point in salvation history when God chose one people out of all the peoples on the earth to be God's people. Rather, the Christian's origin is in One whose origin is in God. According to John's prologue, even though the radical new beginning and relationship created by God's gracious and free claim upon a human life in the person of Jesus Christ is made manifest in time and space, God determined that relationship from the beginning in love.

The difference between these two elections lurks beneath the surface of this text. The relationship between Christian parents and the faith of their children has been obscured, according to Karl Barth, by a church that, in league with the culture, presumes the children of Christian parents to be Christian by birth/adoption. In John's time, it was clear that what constituted the community gathered around Jesus was belief, not blood. As fewer and fewer parents raise children in the life of the church, offspring who believe later in life often do so in spite

Pastoral Perspective

had nothing to do with their son's miraculous "seeing," they could not dismiss what had happened to their son with the proverbial parental trump card: "No, you cannot see . . . *because* we said so!"

Given their inclusion in the disciples' initial question, the parents are more than idle bystanders. Depending on the answer they give, they face the possibility of being ostracized and dismissed from the synagogue. In John's time as in our own, religious leaders and institutions threaten to "drive out" (9:34b) those who "see" in new ways. How many church members "in good standing" have faced expulsion when forced to choose between the policies and doctrines of the institutional church and the binding love they rightly possess for their own LGBTQ children? The wrath of the institution seems to know no boundaries, as even clerics have been defrocked for living the truth of this kind of love. In John's story, the parents of the man born blind face this possibility.

At first the man's parents appear to represent their own fallibility honestly and humbly. Good parenting starts with the realization that parents too have limitations. While these parents have limited options, to use the Johannine metaphor, they cannot say any more than they can "see" themselves. They know two facts, which they verify: this is their son, and he was indeed born blind. However, beyond these facts, they can say only what they themselves do *not* know or understand. "We do not know how it is that now he sees, nor do we know who opened his eyes" (v. 21a).

To confess that we do not know how our children "see" is brutally honest. Parents can prescribe a means and a method for seeing, based on their own experiences and knowledge; however, such prescriptions often fail when a child is faced with the mysteries of life. Further, we do not know by what light they see, because we have not looked beyond our traditions to see by the light of Christ ourselves. Then there are fully capable children who are still dependent on parents that interfere far into adulthood with their children's life choices of companionship and family. On the other hand, there are times when a little dependence on parents can make up for the indiscretions of youth that betray children's absence of wisdom.

It is curious that the son, who surely had been completely dependent on his parents since birth, has left them in the dark concerning how he came to see and who gave him sight. Likewise, the current paucity of intentional intergenerational conversation is unfortunate. Many of those "conversations" begin

Exegetical Perspective

Professions of knowledge and ignorance are important in this story and will become more prominent in the following scenes. In verse 12, the blind man responds, "I do not know." In this scene the parents say first, "We know that this is our son, and that he was born blind" (v. 20). There is no arrogance or presumption to this claim of knowledge, as there is in the later claims of the religious authorities. Then, in response to the question of how their son now sees, the parents say, "We do not know" (v. 21). Pay attention to the claims of knowledge and ignorance in the rest of the story, where in typical ironic form, the ironist claims less knowledge than he has and his counterparts claim more knowledge than they have.

The parents' challenge to the authorities, "Ask him; he is of age" (v. 21), is shocking. Underlining what is going on, the evangelist explains that the parents said this because they were afraid of the authorities (see 7:13; 12:42; 19:38: 20:19). Quite apart from the reason offered in the next verse, the intimidation and threat become dramatically clear. Rather than protecting their son, the parents protect themselves by deflecting the attention of the authorities from themselves to their son.

The reason for this fear, the evangelist explains, is that "the Jews" (here, again, the Pharisees or religious authorities) had "already agreed" that anyone who confessed that Jesus was the Messiah would be "put out of the synagogue" (a phrase that translates a single Greek word, *aposynagōgos*, that appears elsewhere only in John 12:42 and 16:2). To be separated from the synagogue would have meant being cut off from their community and bringing shame on the whole family.

The story assumes that the threat of exclusion is real. The problem is that the rest of the New Testament provides evidence to the contrary, portraying the boundaries between Jews who followed Jesus and those who did not as much more porous in the first century. There is no evidence that Jesus' disciples were excluded from the synagogues because they followed him. In Antioch of Pisidia, when the Jews turned against Paul because of the excitement of the Gentiles about his message, they stirred up persecution and drove him from their region (Acts 13:50). The pattern continues in Acts (e.g., 14:5–6, 19–20; 18:12–13, 28), but there is no reference to any decision that those who confessed Jesus would be separated from the synagogue.

In a very influential monograph, J. Louis Martyn contended that in this chapter John wrote on two levels, overlaying what happened during the ministry

Homiletical Perspective

been starved and spent significant time in refugee or forced-labor camps. A number reported that their vision began failing shortly after they had witnessed and/or survived atrocities: "'I was just crying, crying, crying, and when I stopped crying, my eyes were swollen and I couldn't see.'"[1] Doctors sought explanations and concluded that these women just chose not to see anymore, especially those who had witnessed the slaying of loved ones before their eyes. In the medical examinations they made while treating the women, they found no physical reasons for the women to have impaired sight; the cause appeared to be psychological. For these survivors, blindness was not the result of a physical condition but in response to trauma that impacted them at a profound level. In order to cope, they literally shut out the ugliness of the world around them.

As with the Gospel of John, this example too demonstrates yet another way of interpreting and understanding blindness. One kind of blindness is physical, like the man born blind in John 9. Blind from birth, he lives in a world deprived of the use of one of his senses. Another manifestation is a psychological condition that arises in response to trauma and functions to protect a person from what has disturbed them. Another way blindness is used is metaphorically to describe an absence in spiritual terms—as is evident in the people, the religious leaders, and the crowd in this text. They are physically able to see, but spiritually they are unable to perceive the work of God among them. In this sense they are blind to the ways and purposes of God.

Similar challenges in perception and various reactions to this text can be expected from those who engage and interpret this text today in the context of their own lives. For some, this amazing, assumption-shattering, healing act of Jesus represents a gospel too good to be true. The good news may be too difficult to see in its fullness and with hope when those who are exposed to it are living in fear and/or possess a need to control tightly their own lives in ways that obstruct their vision.

On the other hand, for the man born blind, this is good news—too good not to be true. While the Pharisees interrogate the man's parents, to find out more about the source of his healing, the parents direct the interrogators back to their son; after all "he is of age" (9:21, 23). They tell the Pharisees to return to the one

---

1. Alexandra Smith, "Long Beach Journal; Eyes That Saw Horrors Now See Only Shadows," *The New York Times*, September 8, 1989; http://www.nytimes.com/1989/09/08/us/long-beach-journal-eyes-that-saw-horrors-now-see-only-shadows.html.

John 9:18–23

Theological Perspective

of their parents' nominal involvement during their formative years.

This difference in election has to do not only with the individual Christian but also with the Christian community. "Although [the church] is a people, . . . it is not . . . a natural society linked by race and blood and the sequence of generations, but a people gathered solely by the preaching of the Word and the free election and calling of the Spirit."[1] Barth goes on to acknowledge that

> of course the individual Christian has a father and mother. He [*sic*] too is a member of a family, tribe and nation. And it may well be by this natural mediation that he is led to Church and pointed to his origin and beginning in the grace of God. But this is obviously not necessary. And the fact that he may live in faith and have assurance of faith in the light of that origin and beginning, that he may become a '[child] of God,' is not created for him by his parents, family or nationality. He does not have this privilege either by birth or descent. Indeed he does not have it through the Church, but from God. . . .[2]

Put simply, being born or adopted into a Christian family does not a Christian make! On one hand, this is a great relief, because parents may trust the faith of their children or lack thereof into God's hand. It is also an incredible privilege if a child, who has been told by the great congregation of the God who gave her birth, comes one day by God's grace to "see" and to "know" the God revealed in Jesus Christ with all of her heart, mind, soul, and strength.

The parents send the authorities back to their son saying, "Ask him; he is of age. He will speak for himself" (v. 21). What he says will prompt the authorities to drive him out of the community of his birth and into a life born of God's will.

CYNTHIA A. JARVIS

Pastoral Perspective

with vitriolic questions: "Why in God's name would you do that?" "Are you crazy?" "How long have you been using drugs?" "Are you having sex?" Children cultivate self-expression through conversations that are not interrogations. Simple, open-ended questions over time give children the space and opportunity to develop their voices to speak for themselves: How was your day? Where does it hurt? What do you think about . . . ? Such questions give rise to those moments and occasions when children begin to speak for themselves.

Acknowledging parental limitations is only half the struggle. Too often the voices of the rising generation are silenced within communities of faith. When does a child's self-expression become an essential part of community? Here is an opportunity for religious communities to create spaces and meaningful ritual practices that do not force families to decide between their own generation and the next, but instead value the miracles that are alive and well in new life-giving ways in our children. Instead, the experiences of the older generation are all too frequently used as a way to cancel out the authentic and unique experiences of the younger generation. The reasons often involve the unfulfilled dreams and profound disappointments of parents that are visited on the child.

Involved parents who have come to terms with their own past are better able to bless their children's own decision making. What is the age at which a child can speak for himself or herself? Certainly that varies, but one of the goals of parenting has to be to give children the tools to articulate and communicate for themselves. In the early part of the child's life, the decisions are made for him by the parents, in the hopes that his best interest will be protected by their answers. When the child comes of age and is able to discern and accept responsibility for her own words and actions, can parents say, "She is of age; ask her"?

In one sense, this is a very awkward place to leave this story. In reality it is the actual place known to parents who must release their children into a world of uncertainty, not knowing, but trusting that they are ready to both speak and live for themselves.

GARY V. SIMPSON

---

1. Karl Barth, *Church Dogmatics*, III/2 (Edinburgh: T. & T. Clark, 1957), 584.
2. Barth, *Church Dogmatics*, 585.

of Jesus with what was happening at the time the evangelist was writing, thereby inviting the audience to understand what they were experiencing in light of what had happened to Jesus.[1] By the time the Gospel was written, Martyn argued, the Pharisees meeting at Jamnia had adopted the twelfth benediction (the *Birkath ha-Minim,* or blessing against the heretics), the twelfth of the Eighteen Benedictions (*Shemoneh Ezreh*) recited daily by observant Pharisees. If a believer refused to recite the *Birkath ha-Minim*, the authorities would "put him out of the synagogue."

Martyn's proposal has enormous explanatory power in making sense of the conflict with "the Jews" (religious authorities) in John, but important elements of his proposal have been qualified or abandoned by most Johannine scholars. Little is known about Jamnia, its date, or how the *Birkath ha-Minim* was used. The Pharisees at Jamnia probably adopted practices that were already current in various communities. Other scholars have advocated that the theory that John was responding to the expulsion of believers from the synagogue should be abandoned.[2] The early believers may have withdrawn to form their own communities and framed the story in this way for polemical reasons. Regardless, conflict with the synagogue authorities is a distinctive theme in the Gospel of John, but one that requires great care and caution in the way it is interpreted today.

Apart from its historical basis, the dramatic confrontation between emerging faith and looming persecution in these verses should provoke serious reflection from all believers. How faithful would we be if our Christian discipleship exposed us to suspicion and the threat of social dislocation?

R. ALAN CULPEPPER

person who has experienced this overwhelming act of grace; he can speak for himself (9:21).

Flannery O'Connor once said: "All human nature vigorously resists grace because grace changes us and the change is painful."[2] That statement may provide the best orientation as to why John spends such a long time on this healing, but focuses so little of it on the man who was healed. The one who now can see says very little throughout the entire narrative, except for slightly different versions of "All I know is, I was blind, and now I see" (9:11, 15, 25). However, everyone else in this greater story presented in the whole of the ninth chapter of John's Gospel is questioning and being questioned, commenting on, speculating about and judging the miraculous event. John portrays an array of people in different situations trying to resist grace, perhaps because recognition of grace requires a change of perception.

What God knows, what Jesus knew that day, what the blind man experienced and came to know, and what those who engage this gospel word, by grace, may come to know is that there is no resisting the grace of God. One may choose not to "see," but it is relentless, searching, bold, and intrusive. The presence of God changes people, ready or not. Once one has experienced the healing touch of Jesus, the truth about Jesus is known. Those who encounter this gospel text in its entirety are invited, like the man born blind, to experience this grace that is too good not to be true. Those who engage this text are challenged to remove the obstacles that distort their vision and see the work of Jesus as the embodiment of the good news of God.

MARK RAMSEY

1. J. Louis Martyn, *History and Theology in the Fourth Gospel* (Nashville: Abingdon Press, 1968; rev. ed., 1979, 2003).
2. See Adele Reinhartz, *Befriending the Beloved Disciple: A Jewish Reading of the Gospel of John* (New York: Continuum, 2001).

2. Flannery O'Connor, *The Habit of Being: Letters of Flannery O'Connor* (New York: Farrar, Straus & Giroux, 1988), 213.

John 9:24–34

²⁴So for the second time they called the man who had been blind, and they said to him, "Give glory to God! We know that this man is a sinner." ²⁵He answered, "I do not know whether he is a sinner. One thing I do know, that though I was blind, now I see." ²⁶They said to him, "What did he do to you? How did he open your eyes?" ²⁷He answered them, "I have told you already, and you would not listen. Why do you want to hear it again? Do you also want to become his disciples?" ²⁸Then they reviled him, saying, "You are his disciple, but we are disciples of Moses. ²⁹We know that God has spoken to Moses, but as for this man, we do not know where he comes from." ³⁰The man answered, "Here is an astonishing thing! You do not know where he comes from, and yet he opened my eyes. ³¹We know that God does not listen to sinners, but he does listen to one who worships him and obeys his will. ³²Never since the world began has it been heard that anyone opened the eyes of a person born blind. ³³If this man were not from God, he could do nothing." ³⁴They answered him, "You were born entirely in sins, and are you trying to teach us?" And they drove him out.

Theological Perspective

These verses continue the narrative of the man born blind, a story that is told in three stages. In this portion of the narrative, the man Jesus cured of his blindness on the Sabbath is being interrogated by the Jewish authorities for the second time (v. 24). The Pharisees implore him to be faithful to God and to turn aside from Jesus, because Jesus is a sinner. The man seems unconcerned with the topic of sin. He is not interested in whether Jesus is a sinner or not. This reaction may derive from his own experience of being cast as a sinner from the time of his birth, since in the ancient world blindness could be viewed as a condition that occurred because of one's own or one's parents' sin (9:2).

Jesus makes no connection between the man's physical condition and his moral state. Rather, he tells the disciples that the man's blindness provides an opportunity for God to be revealed through Jesus' healing action (9:3). The cured man's response to the Pharisees redirects the focus of the conversation from sin to the outcome of his interaction with Jesus. His focus is on the practical result of Jesus' action. He knows "that though I was blind, now I see" (v. 25). This proves to be an unsatisfactory response for the Jewish authorities. Even though the cured man has already explained the process by which

Pastoral Perspective

Some stories bear repeating. The happenings in John 9 have all the elements of an oft-told story: a rabbi whose Sabbath activities ignite debate, a man whose vision is restored when a mud-and-spit poultice is spread over his eyes, parents who are both amazed and frightened by what happens to their son, neighbors who do not recognize the man now that he can see them. It is not hard to see why the Gospel storyteller decided to record this story and why contemporary Christians continue to hear it proclaimed in worship. The plot is exciting. Tensions escalate throughout the tale. Risky actions lead to unexpected outcomes.

This is a good story to tell and tell again. Indeed, Christian communities have been retelling this story since the first century, and many contemporary Christians regularly encounter it in the lectionary on the Fourth Sunday in Lent in Year A.

As good as the story is, however, and as life-changing as it might have been for those present when it happened, John 9:27 hints at the healed man's frustration when the religious leaders begin not to relish the story but to probe its details.

In verse 26, they ask the man to repeat his story yet again: "What did he do to you? How did he open your eyes?"

Exegetical Perspective

How obstinate can a person be? To what lengths will a stubborn person go to avoid seeing what she or he does not want to see? This intricate conversation in chapter 9 explores the mental gymnastics that Jesus' opponents undertook in order to avoid seeing the most obvious explanation for a healing.

This passage starts with the second conversation the religious leaders have with the healed man, but the third overall conversation, counting the one with the man's parents. In each case they try to complicate the simple truth that Jesus healed the man's blindness.

The whole incident with the conversation following the healing represents a historical anachronism. The conflict between synagogue and church, with Christians expelled, took place well after Jesus' death. John presents an example of such a conflict, but sets it during Jesus' earthly ministry. As did all the Gospel writers, John offers instruction to a community struggling with certain issues in its own life. Perhaps by presenting a narrative of a conflict during Jesus' ministry, John tells his community of Jesus' solidarity with them. John presents the religious leaders in an unflattering light, but it is possible that the connection with Jesus' ministry and the humor of the passage brought comfort to a community who felt

Homiletical Perspective

Monty Python's *The Life of Brian* is perhaps one of the best religious satires ever written. Set in the time of Jesus, the main character, Brian, is constantly being mistaken for the Messiah. In one scene, Brian is walking through a crowded street when he is solicited by a fit, tan young man who bounces along beside him crying, "Alms for an ex-leper?" He answers Brian's surprise with this story: "I was hopping along, minding my own business, all of a sudden, up [Jesus] comes—cures me! One minute, I'm a leper with a trade, next minute my livelihood's gone!"[1]

The ex-leper's story, like all good satire, simultaneously is ridiculous and makes a strong point. It is rare to get any follow-up stories from those Jesus heals. Little to nothing is said about how they fare after being raised from the dead, cured of leprosy, or rescued from resident demons. Occasionally there is an immediate word of gratitude or a promise of belief, but rare is the description of the new convert's life after the healing and conversion.

Monty Python's silly ex-leper points out this lack of development: what does a leper do with his life after he has been cured of the incurable disease? He is no longer eligible to beg and has never been

1. *The Life of Brian*, dir. Terry Jones (Orion, 1979).

John 9:24–34   303

John 9:24–34

Theological Perspective

he regained his sight, he is asked a second time to explain how he came to be cured.

It is interesting to note that just as the man's blindness was cured through a process (some sort of mud mixture followed by washing), everything in this story also involves a process. The cured man explains his newfound sight and comes to understand who Jesus is through a process. Likewise, the Jewish authorities' lack of understanding increases through a process that begins with their questioning of a healing on the Sabbath and ultimately ends in their incapacity to see or hear the truth that Jesus offers.

There is a skillful use of metaphor in this narrative. The healing emphasizes and foreshadows the triumph of Jesus' resurrection. Just as Jesus will conquer death, the healing of the blind man may also be viewed as a conquering. This is one of the seven signs in the Gospel of John that Jesus performs to affirm his identity. The physical state of blindness is tied to the metaphorical sense of being unfaithful or spiritually ignorant.[1] Throughout this narrative, the Gospel author works with literal blindness or the inability to see, and not being able to perceive who Jesus is or being spiritually blind. Jesus is the one who brings light (9:5) and who enables the blind man to become physically and spiritually healed.

In his interactions with the Pharisees, the cured man accuses them of failing to listen. While his own physical condition involved only the inability to see, it appears that the Pharisees are not only spiritually blind; they also cannot hear the truth, even though they are capable of hearing literally. Their predicament seems more perilous than the cured man's condition ever was. The man who was born blind mocks them, asking why they "want to hear it again" and whether they "want to become" disciples of Jesus (v. 27).

At this point in the narrative, competing knowledge claims are made. Just as the cured man focuses at the beginning of this section on his knowledge that he can see and has been healed, now the Pharisees claim what they know. They know that "God has spoken to Moses," and that this knowledge is authentic and reliable. Jesus is an unknown and cannot be trusted. Thus the Pharisees must be correct, and the cured man must still be sinful.

After this intense interaction, the response of the cured man once again takes on a practical tone. There has never been a time since the very beginning

---

1. Jennifer Koosed and Darla Schumm, *Out of the Darkness: Examining the Rhetoric of Blindness in the Gospel of John* (New York: Palgrave Macmillan, 2011), 79–80.

Pastoral Perspective

The man answers, "I have told you already, and you would not listen. Why do you want to hear it again? Do you also want to become his disciples?" (v. 27).

What, indeed, compels people to watch some movies more than once or to read certain novels multiple times? The man in this story seems to be asking a similar question: "What motivates you to want to hear my story again?"

John 9 provides listeners an opportunity to explore the link between human stories and God's story of healing and redemption. Mud, spit, and blindness healed become the focal point for this link. What is striking about the characters in the story is that some of those present appear to be less concerned about the grace and gift of what happens to the blind man than about whether or not Jesus acted inappropriately on the Sabbath. For them, the story of God's presence in a human life gets lost in the debate about sin.

Why does this matter? Much truth resides in the stories of people's lives. When Jesus mixes dirt with spit and places the earthy concoction on the man's eyes, Jesus creates between that man's story and God's story a life-giving, light-creating link. Much as God in Genesis lights up the night with a moon and stars, Jesus restores light to what for that man had been a lifetime experience of starless nights. Much as God in Genesis takes dirt and fashions human life, Jesus takes spit-watered mud and restores a part of that man's life that had been lost. Truth resides in this story and in how this story is retold.

Lectionary patterns sometimes shape how listeners hear biblical stories retold. John 9:24–34 is part of a larger unit (9:1–41) appointed for the Fourth Sunday in Lent. This particular Sunday is sometimes called Laetare Sunday. "Laetare" in Latin means "rejoice." To some, this title for the Sunday may seem peculiar. Why is there a Rejoicing Sunday in the midst of Lent's somber emphases on introspection and austerity? The midpoint of the Lenten season is the Thursday of the third week of Lent. Connecting this midpoint to ancient mid-March Roman festivals called the *hilaria* (related to "hilarious"), some Christians in earlier eras viewed the Fourth Sunday in Lent as a brief reprieve from Lent's solemn disciplines. Laetare Sunday is also referred to as Refreshment Sunday, Holy Humor Day, or Laughter Sunday, and liturgies for this day include moments for unexpected rejoicing in the midst of Lenten penitential practices.

Resonant with the Laetare Sunday theme, in 9:24–34 the man who is healed, his neighbors and

betrayed by those who expelled them. The "Jewishness" of the leaders does not cause their obstinacy, because the healed man is himself a Judean.

The dispute arises because Jesus healed on a Sabbath. When the man's neighbors and others bring him to the Jewish leaders, they dispute among themselves about the healing (v. 16). The three conversations seem to serve as a way to settle the dispute among the leaders themselves, but perhaps also to convince the neighbors that Jesus has sinned by healing on a Sabbath. Nevertheless, the conversations do not center on the acceptability of healing on a Sabbath. At issue is whether Jesus really did heal the man. After the second conversation, the leaders no longer try to disprove the miracle itself.

In this third conversation, the leaders open with an ad hominem argument, that Jesus is a sinner (because he healed on a Sabbath). Even if they cannot disprove the miracle, they believe that they can discredit Jesus. The leaders speak with one voice in this conversation; the internal dispute seems to have faded. They speak with an air of confidence; they *know* that Jesus is a sinner.

The healed man models a process of coming to faith. At first he admits that he cannot even attest to Jesus' status as a sinner, responding to the confidence of the leaders with self-effacement. He insists on his own experience (v. 25). The Johannine literature frequently uses firsthand experience as an encouragement for faith (20:26–28; 1 John 1:1). The man displays a humorous naiveté when he asks the leaders if they want to become Jesus' disciples. Their indignant reply likely generated a laugh among John's first audience. The healed man seems not to grasp that they want to discredit Jesus, not follow him.

Despite his simplicity, he utters the most cogent line in the entire conversation when he puts the leaders in their intellectual place in verses 30–33. This comment displays spiritual insight (that God would listen to one who worships) and seems well-informed (about the unprecedented nature of healing a man born blind). The leaders cling to tradition, citing their discipleship to Moses. John and this passage do not repudiate Moses, but the leaders do not recognize the new ways God has begun to work in Jesus (3:8). He does not profess his faith in this conversation, but he makes a well-reasoned theological affirmation. Despite his lack of sophistication to this point, he recognizes that the healing indicates that Jesus comes from God.

The leaders cannot disprove the miracle. They cannot outargue the man. They cannot discredit

trained to do anything else. Life without leprosy, in that satirical world, was not as fruitful and exciting as it should have been.

By contrast, through the story of the man born blind, John's Gospel approaches the subject of the life of those Jesus has healed with depth and sensitivity. In the readings that precede this one (9:1–23) Jesus heals the man using spit and dirt (9:6), dispelling his physical blindness but not the social speculation about the healed man. There is the gossipy disbelief that this is the actual man born blind (9:9); an investigation into the method and motives of Jesus (9:14–16); and a question about the truth of the formerly blind man's identity and honesty (9:19).

The investigation into the sinfulness of the healed man and the sinfulness of Jesus continues in this pericope. It is an ugly, unfair investigation, made so by the insistence of the investigating body that they get to the root of the brokenness and ascertain the timing of the event of healing. The new life surely present in the promise of new sight is completely ignored. The man with newly restored sight calls them out on their misguided obsession: "We know that God does not listen to sinners, but he does listen to one who worships him and obeys his will. Never since the world began has it been heard that anyone opened the eyes of a person born blind. If this man were not from God, he could do nothing" (vv. 31–33). The boldness of his response has dire consequences.

Even the hardiest Christians—those who know that discipleship is costly and sometimes feels Sisyphean—may have a difficult time with the final words of this passage from John: "And they drove him out" (v. 34). This seems like a painful punishment for the crime of what? Being cured? Being sighted? Being bold?

This man is driven out from a community that has known him for years, by community leaders and people whom the Gospel writer calls his "neighbors." The reason for his dismissal appears to be his standing up to the religious authorities, but one wonders if he is no longer acceptable in the community because now his identity of "broken, needy, and sinful" no longer applies. In either case, he is driven out and unmoored for turning his attention toward that which matters: a life of faith, forgiveness, and freedom.

So many in congregations, lay and ordained alike, want to believe that belief is the magic solution, and that once lives have been changed by acceptance of the life and teachings of Jesus and acceptance into the community of faith, suffering and pain will be

John 9:24–34

Theological Perspective

of the world when "anyone opened the eyes of a person born blind" (v. 32). Only an individual who comes from God could perform such an action. This is the only conclusion that the cured man can make, a conclusion that assists his developing understanding that Jesus must be from God.

However, the Pharisees reject his claim. While the conclusions drawn by the man who was born blind may seem to make sense, the Pharisees are unable or unwilling to draw any similar conclusions. It cannot be, in their view, that someone "born entirely in sins" could have any valuable knowledge to share with those who are authorities on Moses and the Law (v. 34). This is the great irony of this portion of the narrative. The cured man, once blind, now not only has literal, physical sight; he also is in the process of developing spiritual clarity and sight. The Pharisees, schooled in wisdom, are proving to be incapable of hearing or seeing what should be obvious, even though they possess these physical capabilities. Their reaction is to drive the man away, refusing to listen or to see.

The tensions that exist in this passage invite the reader to wrestle with ambiguities. Does the blind man have to be physically healed to come to a fuller understanding regarding the identity of Jesus? The Pharisees have their physical sight, yet lack understanding. This passage calls the reader to consider what it means to be physically and spiritually whole. It also raises questions about God. Apparently, this man's blindness became the occasion for God to be revealed. What does the author want the reader to conclude about God by framing the narrative in this way?

Finally, when the Pharisees throw the man out, the reader is asked not only to consider the tensions that existed in the first century CE as the community of Jews that believed Jesus was Messiah began to differentiate from the Jews that did not. The reader is also required to consider what it means to see or not see, to be included or excluded, in the world today.

SALLY SMITH HOLT

Pastoral Perspective

parents, and the religious leaders are all responding to the unexpected story of refreshment that unfolds when Jesus, on a day intended for religious practices other than healing, does something that, at least for the man healed, is a cause for rejoicing. Again, this is a story that begs to be retold, but when the healed man retells his story, instead of experiencing the shared joy of others, he is driven out of the synagogue.

Contemporary Christians may at times find themselves in situations similar to that of this ancient story's characters. Biblical scholar Gail O'Day points out that Jesus appears early in this story, in verses 2–7, but then disappears from the action until verse 35. During Jesus' absence (vv. 8–34) we witness the other characters' responses to what has happened. Some rejoice; others resist and criticize.

O'Day emphasizes that "even though Jesus is absent, he remains the catalyst for all that takes place" in verses 8–34. Jesus is present throughout the retelling of the healing story, even though he is physically absent.[1] This means that the healed man's question is as timely now when his story is retold, including on the Fourth Sunday in Lent, as it was when the Gospel writer first placed the question on his lips centuries ago: "Why do you want to hear [the story] again? Do you want to become his disciples?"

Indeed, how do we ensure that telling Jesus' story again and again today, even though Jesus is physically absent, means that Jesus is nevertheless a catalyzing presence as we debate and discuss? Retelling the story invites contemporary listeners to decide how to respond not only to spiritual realities, but also to complex issues such as health care or physical disabilities. How do we, as disciples of Jesus, reflect what we know and have encountered in our own stories about Jesus' prophetic compassion in our decision making about concrete social problems? Through our work to respond to these questions in light of the themes of John 9, we shape our contemporary response to the question of the man who is healed: "Why do you want to hear [the story] again?"

JILL CRAINSHAW

---

1. Gail R. O'Day, *The Word Disclosed: Preaching the Gospel of John* (St. Louis: Chalice Press, 2002), 62–63.

Jesus. They close the conversation the way they began it, with an ad hominem attack against the healed man, accusing him of having been born in sin (presumably because of his blindness), an interpretation Jesus has already refuted (9:3). When they cannot win, they react with force, driving the man out. As noted above, the experience of having the synagogue leaders drive Christians out of the community reflects the situation of John's first audience.

In the passage, the leaders refuse to see the obvious, that Jesus has healed the blind man. When they cannot disprove the miracle or discredit Jesus, they simply become more obstinate. Christians today cannot point to irrefutable proof of Jesus' significance or identity. No one can reduce skeptics to a caricature of willful obtuseness, as the man does to the leaders. All "evidence" for the validity of Christianity comes with ambiguity. Even in the text, one could have made the argument that the water of Siloam healed the man, not Jesus; so some ambiguity exists.

The church nurtures its faith despite the ambiguity, drawing strength from the firsthand experience of grace and healing (of whatever kind). Just as the man could not win over the leaders, so the church may not win over atheists and skeptics. The church continues its ministry nonetheless, without frenetic worry about how to silence disbelievers, who deserve respect. The church uses the critique of skeptics to push it to deeper levels of understanding and sounder theology, but recognizes that no end to the arguments appears on the horizon. The church may also gain some comfort in the passage for the arguments that take place within its walls. It may seem self-serving to place one's opponents in an argument in the role of the religious leaders who refuse to understand. Yet the arguments over biblical interpretation and social issues seem to go on unabated. Perhaps the church can recognize that arguments in which one side does not change have a long history. The church continues its ministry in spite of these disagreements.

CHARLES L. AARON

left behind. The faithful will no longer be blind to the ills of the world or to their own shortcomings. Spoken plainly, that assertion may sound absurd to some, but in the eyes of a new convert or of anyone who was once spiritually blind but now "sees," the new life of faith can seem an island of refuge equaled only by Eden before the fall—which at first it very well may be.

However, as is the case with the man born blind in John's story and with Monty Python's ex-leper, eventually there will be new sets of challenges. Perhaps, like the man born blind, one experiences disbelief in the community being left behind, either disbelief in Christ and Christianity or disbelief in the new practitioner's motives or method. Perhaps, like the ex-leper, one finds oneself as a square peg in a round hole, no longer fitting the expectations that have grounded one for so long.

Those who find themselves straddling two worlds—like Monty Python's amusing ex-leper or John's man born blind, like new converts or those trying to bridge sacred-secular gaps in the world— can find themselves temporarily connected to neither. They may live in a cast-out state that was never part of their plan.

A sensitive preacher interpreting this passage in John may need to remind a congregation that Jesus is present to those who are cast out and/or in between. On the other hand, a congregation—perhaps having rested too long on its laurels—may need a reminder that Jesus never promised the life of faith would be a life of comfort. Rather, Jesus invites his followers into the discomfort, edginess, and dislocation experienced by the newly emboldened man who was given both sight and the insight that led him to question the status quo. Either response gives weight to John's willingness to tell more about the life of this man after he was healed by Jesus and called into a new life of faith, filled with challenges but also filled with grace.

NOELLE M. YORK-SIMMONS

John 9:35–41

³⁵Jesus heard that they had driven him out, and when he found him, he said, "Do you believe in the Son of Man?" ³⁶He answered, "And who is he, sir? Tell me, so that I may believe in him." ³⁷Jesus said to him, "You have seen him, and the one speaking with you is he." ³⁸He said, "Lord, I believe." And he worshiped him. ³⁹Jesus said, "I came into this world for judgment so that those who do not see may see, and those who do see may become blind." ⁴⁰Some of the Pharisees near him heard this and said to him, "Surely we are not blind, are we?" ⁴¹Jesus said to them, "If you were blind, you would not have sin. But now that you say, 'We see,' your sin remains."

Theological Perspective

In this final segment of the narrative of the man born blind, the Pharisees have driven out the now-healed man (v. 35). Previously the parents of the man born blind had been questioned about their son's healing and responded in a noncommittal manner, afraid that if their answer in any way displeased the Pharisees, they would "be put out of the synagogue" (9:22). While the fears of the parents are not realized, the healed son, responding in sarcasm to the questioning of the Pharisees, does suffer this fate.

The historical context out of which this text emerged appears to have been marked by tense and even hostile relationships within the synagogue of the Johannine community.[1] There is disagreement about who belongs. Should Jews who believe that Jesus is Messiah be a part of synagogue? John's Gospel provides a creative answer to this question by illustrating throughout the text that Jesus is the truth. He is the true vine (15:1–8), the light sent from God (8:12). Jesus, in John's Gospel, poses a threat to Jewish institutions and rituals, even to the point of redefining Israel itself. Inclusion is no longer centered on the idea of a place like the synagogue. To belong to God, to be included, for John, means that one belongs to Christ. This first-century-CE conflict

Pastoral Perspective

In John 9:35–41, the man born blind meets Jesus for a second time. In the initial encounter (9:1–7), Jesus heals his physical blindness. Having been healed, the man almost immediately looks not only into the faces of other human beings but also into the face of all kinds of trouble.[1] He begins to see and hear the complexities and challenges of faith, justice, and healing in his world.

Then, in verse 34, the man is driven out of the community. When Jesus hears about this, he seeks the man out. In 9:35–41, the man looks again into the face and eyes of the one who has healed him. He looks into the face and eyes of Jesus, and he recognizes something about him. He sees someone worth believing in.

In the verses just before this chapter's conclusion, as the religious leaders debate who Jesus is and the theological meaning of Jesus' healing actions, the man marvels at what has happened to him: "Never since the world began has it been heard that anyone opened the eyes of person born blind" (9:32). Now, as the chapter ends, the man with new sight seeks new insight as well: "Tell me [who the Son of Man is], so that I may believe in him" (v. 36).

---

1. J. Bradley Chance and Milton P. Horne, *Rereading the Bible: An Introduction to the Biblical Story* (Upper Saddle River, NJ: Prentice Hall, 2000), 404–7.

1. Thomas G. Long, "Once I Was Blind, But Now . . . ?" in David Fleed and Dave Bland, eds., *Preaching John's Gospel: The World It Imagines* (St. Louis: Chalice Press, 2008), 53–61.

Exegetical Perspective

These verses exude spiritual and emotional joy. This last section draws to a conclusion an intricate, well-written story, packed with meaning and theology. It also sets up the next section of material. The healed man has talked to neighbors and to the religious leaders, but now he talks to Jesus. This short passage contains two significant conversations of Jesus, and an important theological statement from Jesus' mouth.

After the religious leaders drive the man out, Jesus finds him. In their conversation we see how this entire episode demonstrates John's pastoral theology. "Believe" serves as a key theological term for John, as 20:31 famously declares. In that verse John teaches that belief leads to life, another important term for John, connoting abundance of life. The whole episode of the healing of the blind man shows the process by which he comes to believe. The description of this process gives the reader a valuable insight, because here John shows in full detail what he only summarizes on other occasions. In chapter 2, for example, the disciples believe after they see the miracle of the water turned to wine at the wedding, but the story reports only the end result and does not show the process.

Throughout the narrative the man has come to successive insights about Jesus. At first he can only recite the details about the healing, but he does not

Homiletical Perspective

This is not the Jesus of platitudes, of simple truths, or of gentle answers. Much like Matthew, who has Jesus turning over the tables in the temple (Matt. 21:12–17), John has Jesus confronting the religious authorities with vinegar and ire. In the passages previous to this one, Jesus has healed a man physically blind since birth (9:6). As a result, the man has been cast out from the society he knows (9:34). It also causes the man to take on a new belief in the power of God and in the power of Jesus to heal and make whole.

For the religious authorities of the time, however, this is not a new awakening but an unacceptable nuisance. This Jesus person is undermining their authority and leaching their power. Jesus is breaking the rules and, in doing so, is subverting hundreds of years of established and respected authority. Predictably, the authorities are not happy.

Jesus has not only healed a man blind since birth, an action unheard of and outside the order of the universe. He has done it on the Sabbath, thereby disregarding what the religious establishment believes to be God's command. He has simultaneously been divine and profane, and they cannot make sense of it (9:30–33).He has done so unmindful of who the man and his parents are or of what possible sinful condition has made him this way by birth.

John 9:35–41

Theological Perspective

may even have involved a component of an inter-Christian dispute between a marginalized group and the emerging mainstream of the early Christian church.[2] Whatever reasons lay behind this conflict, John's Gospel suggests that people who are included in the true community of God are those who belong to Christ.

The man once blind and now cured had always been marginalized because of his blindness, and now that he has been driven out, he appears to remain marginalized. However, this is not really the case, as the reader is about to learn. At this juncture in the narrative, the action takes a dramatic turn. Jesus learns that the healed man has been driven out. Taking the initiative, Jesus searches out the man (v. 35). He inquires whether or not the healed man believes in the "Son of Man"; the healed man responds by asking, "Who is he, sir? Tell me, so that I may believe in him" (v. 36). Jesus then identifies himself, reminding the healed man that he has "seen him"; the healed man then recognizes, believes in, and worships Jesus (vv. 37–38).

It is interesting for the reader to consider how and why this recognition of Jesus is realized. Why does the healed man fail to recognize Jesus from their previous encounter? Does the healed man simply fail to understand Jesus' true identity, even though he recognizes him as the healer? Did the healed man not only physically see Jesus at the moment that his sight was restored, but also see Jesus with a spiritual insight that has yet to be fully integrated into his understanding? Whatever the case, when Jesus identifies himself as the one who has been seen and who is the "Son of Man," the man born blind experiences a harmony of physical and spiritual sightedness.

Now this man has experienced complete healing. While his physical sight has already been restored, it is in this instant that his spiritual sight becomes whole. At this moment, he understands fully and sees completely. In contrast to Matthew, Mark, and Luke, where the miracles of Jesus often require faith on the part of the one being healed and where miracles may not occur because of unbelief, this wondrous sign of Jesus healing the blind man is at Jesus' own initiative and requires no faith on the part of the man.[3] In fact, the faith of the healed man is not realized, even at the moment of his healing. It is an understanding that progresses and becomes

2. J. Scott Martin, *Eerdmans Commentary on the Bible* (Grand Rapids: Eerdmans, 2003), 1185–86.
3. Jennifer Koosed and Darla Schumm, *Out of the Darkness: Examining the Rhetoric of Blindness in the Gospel of John* (New York: Palgrave Macmillan, 2011), 79–80.

Pastoral Perspective

Several questions emerge for contemporary hearers of this ancient story. What does it mean to believe? How is believing related to seeing—physical seeing or metaphorical seeing? How does this story challenge our preconceptions about sin, believing, and community? What does this Gospel writer want us to recognize about ourselves, others, and faith?

A danger in interpreting this story, especially in interpreting these final verses of John 9, is that we may inadvertently conclude or imply that physical blindness is somehow connected to lack of spiritual insight. Now, as in the Gospel writer's time, some people either believe or at least worry that physical illness has something to do with human sin or wrongdoing. Not a few pastors have had congregants with physical illness seek their guidance, saying words similar to these: "Pastor, I have confessed every sin I can recall, but I am still dying with this cancer. What have I done wrong that God is punishing me in this way?" Such questions arise when people equate sin and physical illness.

Jesus turns this notion on its head by insisting that the ones who think they can see spiritually are really the ones without sight. Jesus' actions and words are clear. Sin does not cause physical illness or disability, but sin can cause people to lack clear and compassionate insight about life, faith, and the people and world around them.

The Gospel writer in this story casts the religious leaders as onlookers and eavesdroppers on Jesus' conversation with the man whose sight he has restored. Jesus' last words in John 9 are intended for these as well as for contemporary eavesdroppers on this story. They are judging words: "I came into this world for judgment so that those who do not see may see, and those who do see may become blind" (v. 39). Again Jesus' Sabbath healing actions in John 9 are clear. People, not religious rules or rituals, come first. God first and foremost has compassion on those who suffer. Compassion leads to worship. At least this is suggested by the narrator's brief commentary on Jesus' conversation with the man he has healed: "And he worshiped him" (v. 38).

Contemporary communities face challenges similar to those faced by the first hearers and readers of the story in John 9. People struggle to understand who Jesus is and what it means to be Jesus' disciples. They also struggle to understand how sin manifests itself in people's lives. These struggles are reflected in denominational creeds and polities over many centuries, as well as in the efforts of individual communities to describe or name their theological and ethical

interpret them (9:11). He cannot even keep up with Jesus. At the end of his first conversation with the Pharisees, he concludes that Jesus is a prophet (9:17). In his second conversation with the leaders, he gains the insight that Jesus comes from God and is not a "sinner" (9:31–33).

In this scene between the man and Jesus, the man initially does not fully understand Jesus' identity. When Jesus tells him explicitly that he is the Son of Man, the healed man believes. In showing the man's progression, John plays on the word *kyrios*, translated "sir" in verse 36, but "Lord" in verse 38. Jesus tells the man who has regained his physical sight that he has "seen" the Son of Man. When the healed man fully understands Jesus' identity, he believes, which leads to worship. Contemporary church leaders might appreciate that John shows such a pastoral understanding of the gradual process of coming to believe. Despite John's goal to enable the audience of his Gospel to believe, he shows remarkable understanding and patience for those who need time to achieve belief, and who may need to regain that belief more than once.

Even though the disciples believed after the wedding in chapter 2, they must reinforce that belief in chapter 6 after a lack of understanding and struggle (6:7, 60, 69). The much-maligned Thomas receives understanding from the risen Christ when he asks for evidence of the resurrection (20:27–28). In this narrative of the blind man, John shows that some people need time and careful instruction to find belief and that they may arrive at partial answers along the way. John's pastoral theology encourages church leaders (then and now) to give careful guidance to those moving toward belief.

The reader may have trouble picturing the scene for the last three verses. Does Jesus utter verse 39 to the man, with the Pharisees listening in? If not to the man, to whom does he say it? John intends the verse for the reader, of course, but within the narrative world of the scene, John does not make the audience clear. Do the same Pharisees who interviewed the man speak to Jesus in verses 40–41? This group seems less truculent than those who conversed with the man, so perhaps they come from a different group. The reader does not know the tone with which they ask their question in verse 40, but they do not explicitly condemn Jesus as a "sinner." Jesus' response indicates that at the very least they do not yet fully understand. By 10:19 the Pharisees again reveal division about Jesus' identity.

Jesus then, in this passage, takes it one step further. He upends the moral teachings concerning the cause of the man's blindness, and he goes so far as to call those who tried to uphold this moral teaching "blind." His response to them is both a riddle and perfectly clear and completely infuriating. They are no longer the sole guardians of truth, right, and wrong. For John, Jesus knows the Father; so what he says and does exposes the religious authorities' misrepresentation of God's will.

Jesus is not mincing words when he addresses the temple authorities. He is confronting them with the fact that using the law to oppress the people they are called to serve is not only outside of God's law; it is actually the opposite of God's will. The authorities in this pericope are obsessed with getting to the bottom of the exact cause of the blindness: who sinned to cause such a thing? They are also obsessed with ascertaining the exact cause of the healing: there is no way in their understanding that this breaker of the Sabbath could be of God.

In sum, they have completely failed to address the miracle of the event at hand. They have lost sight of the *person* in front of them, because their lens for seeing is their interpretation of the law. They are blind to the circumstance of the man who was blind, blinded by their own need for control. They have lost sight of God's presence in all of it.

John's Gospel is full of tension and hostility between Jesus and the Jewish authorities, possibly reflecting the late-first-century situation in which the Gospel was written.[1] In order to avoid preaching a dangerous anti-Judaic message, the preacher needs to remember that in John's story of the man born blind, Jesus' difficulties with the religious authorities were not as much about their religious beliefs, that is, their rejection of Jesus' claim of knowing the Father. Neither was he challenging the law itself. Instead, Jesus was challenging their *use* of the law, that is, their using the law as a tool of divisiveness, as a tool to create dramatic power differentials, or as a tool to oppress, control, and punish. Used in this way, the law becomes a stumbling block to community, a stumbling block to connectivity between people. According to Jesus, the law as used by the authorities is blinding and no longer of God.

Again, this is not the Jesus of platitudes and simple truths. Jesus is going to stand counter to that which oppresses and divides. Jesus is going to upend

---

1. David K. Rensberger, "John: Introduction," in *The HarperCollins Study Bible* (New York: HarperCollins, 1993), 2012.

John 9:35–41

Theological Perspective

complete after Jesus has sought him out and questioned him.

As this narrative concludes, the reader has become increasingly aware of the tremendous irony that the situation entails. Jesus, as the "Son of Man," claims to bring judgment to the world "so that those who do not see may see, and those who do see may become blind" (v. 39). The man born blind has physical sight and spiritual insight. Jesus has brought him to this reality where he sees fully and clearly. The Pharisees, on the other hand, while in full possession of their physical sight, only move further into spiritual darkness. When they observe Jesus and the healed man, when they hear their conversation, they still do not understand, and Jesus condemns them. The condemnation seems to occur because the Pharisees remain so obtuse. In the final verse, Jesus tells the Pharisees that if they were blind, they would not have sin. Since they claim to see, their "sin remains" (v. 41).

According to Jesus, blindness is not a condition that results from sin, as the Pharisees claim. In this instance, Jesus provides the blind man with physical and spiritual healing, and even though this is a healing that happens in stages, Jesus remains steadfast until the man born blind is fully restored. The Pharisees, in contrast, have every opportunity to witness this miraculous sign, to question the healed man, and to believe his testimony. They fail at every stage. In a final moment of irony, they wonder about their own sight or lack of sight. This is what brings Jesus' condemnation. They have failed to respond to Jesus' initiative, and claiming to see clearly, they really remain in darkness and sin.

Returning to the issue of inclusion, readers realize that the healed man is no longer marginalized at all. Through his acceptance of and worship of the "Son of Man," he is now included in the people who belong to God.

SALLY SMITH HOLT

Pastoral Perspective

perspectives. Mighty theological and even physical battles have ensued as differing groups claimed to have the right beliefs. Some people have been forced out of communities because of their stances on particular theological doctrines or social issues. Some, like the man in John 9, are judged either to have been born into or inherited sin due to their physical or other circumstances. They are looked upon and treated as outsiders almost as soon as their lives begin.

John 9:24–35 reminds believers of every era: the only true gospel "insider" position is the position of compassion—compassion for all people. The Gospel storyteller puts this wisdom on the lips of the formerly blind man when the man resists entering into the theological debate about sin and instead states: "I do not know whether he [Jesus] is a sinner. One thing I do know, that though I was blind, now I see" (9:25).

Jesus' actions toward the blind man set the example for believers then and now. In John 9, Jesus reveals his identity to the one who has been excluded: "You have seen him [the Son of Man], and the one speaking with you is he" (v. 37). What is the result? The man now sees fully—physically and spiritually—and he proclaims his newfound recognition and belief. To take up Jesus' actions of courageous compassion is to embody spiritual sight and insight. What this meant in John 9 is still true today: to be prophetically compassionate is to seek out those who have been excluded and with them to work toward a future when all of God's children recognize each other and worship together in a spirit of justice, love, and grace.

JILL CRAINSHAW

Exegetical Perspective

However the scene unfolds, Jesus makes a profound theological statement in verse 39. The one who did not come to condemn the world (3:17) nevertheless comes in judgment. The judgment does not take the form of punishment. Simply choosing darkness or choosing not to see serves as its own judgment (see 3:19–20). The "punishment" for remaining in darkness or not opening one's spiritual eyes is to miss out on the light, to fail to see. John carefully articulates that physical blindness does not result from sin (9:3), but one chooses spiritual blindness.

This part of the passage provides a transition to chapter 10, the discourse on the good shepherd. The religious leaders cast the man out of one community, but Jesus provides an alternative community, of which he serves as good shepherd. Jesus even models the role of shepherd by finding the man in verse 35. He then leads the man to belief and worship.

For the preacher and teacher, this passage models the familiar, but needed advice to people in their current spiritual state. The healed man comes to faith in stages, with guesses about Jesus' identity that reflect an incomplete understanding. John does not indicate that the man rejoiced or experienced emotion immediately after the healing. If the miracle affected his spirit as well as his eyes, John does not say. Jesus' question to the man discerns his current status, without pressure (v. 35). Jesus shows no impatience or frustration when the man does not yet understand at that point.

The passage gives the church much material for reflection on its ministry to seekers and to those who consider themselves "spiritual, but not religious." The passage demonstrates the value of patience, honest dialogue, and living witness in leading people to faith. The church has a ministry to those already on the membership rolls, who profess a creed every week. For John, to believe entails more than intellectual assent. Belief results in abundant life and worship.

CHARLES L. AARON

Homiletical Perspective

the social order, and it will not be gentle. As early as the second chapter of John, Jesus is overturning the money changers' tables in the temple (2:13–22). Later, in chapter 3, he answers Nicodemus's challenges with powerful though enigmatic answers, "Are you a teacher of Israel, and yet you do not understand these things?" (3:10b). This picture being painted of Jesus is a challenge to the image of the quiet, gentle teacher.

However, Jesus' response to the man with new sight is very different. The first line of this passage speaks volumes: "Jesus heard that they had driven him out, and . . . he found him" (v. 35). Jesus *finds* the man who has been driven out. In this way, Jesus performs a second act of healing on this man. He is welcomed into the new community of faith, as one once blind but now sighted, as one once cast out and now home. Jesus sees the person as far more important than the misused principles of law.

Jesus' finding of the man with new sight is, on one hand, yet another example of Jesus' relationship with the least, the lost, and the lonely. Yet there is a particular piece of this relationship that makes it unique: Jesus *found* him. When Jesus heard the news that the man had been cast out because of his new sight and new faith, Jesus went *looking for him*. A preacher might emphasize the full cast of outcasts that Jesus sat with, walked with, touched, and healed—and note that most of them came to Jesus. In this case (and a few others), however, Jesus came to him. Jesus not only *came* to him, but *looked* for him, *sought* him out, and *found* him.

Where the authorities had used the law to separate and destroy life, Jesus had used love to seek out and mend. For those in the congregation feeling separated or cast aside, a message from the pulpit that even they are within the realm of Jesus' healing grace can be a balm for the body of Christ.

NOELLE M. YORK-SIMMONS

Contributors

Charles L. Aaron, Pastor, First United Methodist Church, Terrell, Texas

Richard Manly Adams Jr., Reference and Systems Librarian at Pitts Theology Library, Emory University, Atlanta, Georgia

James A. Brashler, Professor Emeritus of Bible, Union Presbyterian Seminary, Richmond, Virginia

Alexandra R. Brown, Jessie Ball Dupont Professor of Religion, Washington and Lee University, Lexington, Virginia

Gary W. Charles, Pastor, Central Presbyterian Church, Atlanta, Georgia

Jaime Clark-Soles, Associate Professor of New Testament and Altshuler Distinguished Teaching Professor, Perkins School of Theology, Southern Methodist University, Dallas, Texas

Joseph J. Clifford, Pastor, First Presbyterian Church, Dallas, Texas

Jill Crainshaw, Blackburn Professor of Worship and Liturgical Theology, Wake Forest School of Divinity, Winston-Salem, North Carolina

Stephanie Buckhanon Crowder, Adjunct Faculty, New Testament Studies, McCormick Theological Seminary, Chicago, Illinois

R. Alan Culpepper, Dean and Professor of New Testament, McAfee School of Theology, Mercer University, Atlanta, Georgia

Mary R. D'Angelo, Associate Professor of Biblical Studies, University of Notre Dame, Department of Theology, Notre Dame, Indiana

Magrey R. deVega, Pastor, Saint Paul's United Methodist Church, Cherokee, Iowa

Mark Douglas, Professor of Christian Ethics and Director of Master of Arts in Theological Studies Program, Columbia Theological Seminary, Decatur, Georgia

Peter Eaton, Rector and Dean, Saint John's Cathedral, Denver, Colorado

Mary F. Foskett, Kahle Professor of Religion and Director of WFU Humanities Institute, Wake Forest University, Winston-Salem, North Carolina

Leah Gunning Francis, Assistant Professor of Christian Education, Eden Theological Seminary, Saint Louis, Missouri

Jean E. Greenwood, Pastor, Presbyterian Church (U.S.A.), Minneapolis, Minnesota

Howard K. A. Gregory, Bishop, The Anglican Diocese of Jamaica and the Cayman Islands, Kingston, Jamaica

Deirdre King Hainsworth, Assistant Professor of Ethics and Director of the Center for Business, Religion and Public Life, Pittsburgh Theological Seminary, Pittsburgh, Pennsylvania

Charles Hambrick-Stowe, Senior Minister, First Congregational Church, Ridgefield, Connecticut

Davis Hankins, Lecturer, Appalachian State University, Boone, North Carolina

Gary Neal Hansen, Associate Professor of Church History, University of Dubuque Theological Seminary, Dubuque, Iowa

Karen M. Hatcher, Minister, Loft Mountain, Shenandoah National Park, A Christian Ministry in the National Parks, Midlothian, Virginia

Robert Hoch, Associate Professor of Homiletics and Worship, University of Dubuque Theological Seminary, Dubuque, Iowa

Sally Smith Holt, Professor, School of Religion, Belmont University, Nashville, Tennessee

Michael J. Hoyt, Pastor, Fourth Presbyterian Church, Greenville, South Carolina

David W. Hull, Senior Pastor, First Baptist Church, Huntsville, Alabama

Philip D. Jamieson, President, United Methodist Foundation for the Memphis and Tennessee Annual Conferences, Nashville, Tennessee

Cynthia A. Jarvis, Minister, The Presbyterian Church of Chestnut Hill, Philadelphia, Pennsylvania

Raquel St. Clair Lettsome, Itinerant Elder, African Methodist Episcopal Church, Campbell Hall, New York

Daniel F. Lewis, Pastor, First Presbyterian Church, Statesboro, Georgia

Donald K. McKim, Editor, *These Days; Joining the Feast; Being Reformed*, Germantown, Tennessee

Alicia D. Myers, Assistant Professor of New Testament and Greek, Campbell University Divinity School, Buies Creek, North Carolina

Carmen Nanko-Fernández, Associate Professor of Hispanic Theology and Ministry, Catholic Theological Union, Chicago, Illinois

Gail R. O'Day, Dean and Professor of New Testament and Preaching, Wake Forest School of Divinity, Winston-Salem, North Carolina

Amy Plantinga Pauw, Henry P. Mobley Jr. Professor of Doctrinal Theology, Louisville Presbyterian Theological Seminary, Louisville, Kentucky

Buran Phillips, Pastor, Westminster Presbyterian Church, Knoxville, Tennessee

Cornelius Plantinga Jr., Senior Research Fellow, Calvin Institute of Christian Worship, Grand Rapids, Michigan

Joseph L. Price, Genevieve Shaul Connick Professor, Department of Religious Studies, Whittier College, Whittier, California

Rebecca Button Prichard, Interim Pastor, Shadow Hills Presbyterian Church, Los Angeles, California

John Proctor, General Secretary, The United Reformed Church, London, United Kingdom

Rollin A. Ramsaran, Dean and Professor of New Testament, Emmanuel Christian Seminary, Johnson City, Tennessee

Nancy J. Ramsay, Professor of Pastoral Theology and Pastoral Care, Brite Divinity School, Fort Worth, Texas

Mark Ramsey, Pastor, Grace Covenant Presbyterian Church, Asheville, North Carolina

David Rensberger, Independent Scholar and Writer, Atlanta, Georgia

Vernon K. Robbins, Professor of New Testament and Comparative Sacred Texts, Department and Graduate Division of Religion, Emory University, Atlanta, Georgia

Art Ross, Pastor, Retired, Presbyterian Church (U.S.A.), Raleigh, North Carolina

Gilberto A. Ruiz, Assistant Professor of Scripture, Loyola Institute for Ministry, Loyola University New Orleans, New Orleans, Louisiana

Clayton J. Schmit, Provost, Lutheran Theological Southern Seminary of Lenoir-Rhyne University, Columbia, South Carolina

Carol L. Schnabl Schweitzer, Associate Professor of Pastoral Care, Union Presbyterian Seminary, Richmond, Virginia

Edwin Searcy, Minister, University Hill Congregation, United Church of Canada, Vancouver, British Columbia, Canada

Katherine A. Shaner, Assistant Professor of New Testament, Wake Forest University School of Divinity, Winston-Salem, North Carolina

Marguerite Shuster, Harold John Ockenga Professor Emerita of Preaching and Theology, and Senior Professor of Preaching and Theology, Fuller Theological Seminary, Pasadena, California

Gary V. Simpson, Senior Pastor, Concord Baptist Church of Christ, Brooklyn, New York, and Associate Professor of Homiletics, Drew Theological Seminary

Joseph D. Small, Presbyterian Foundation, Jeffersonville, Indiana

O. Benjamin Sparks, Pastor, Honorably Retired, Presbyterian Church (U.S.A.), Richmond, Virginia

Nibs Stroupe, Pastor, Oakhurst Presbyterian Church, Decatur, Georgia

Monya A. Stubbs, Associate Professor of New Testament, Austin Presbyterian Theological Seminary, Austin, Texas

Jessica Tate, Director of NEXT Church and Specialized Minister, National Capital Presbytery, Washington, D.C.

Barbara Brown Taylor, Butman Professor of Religion, Piedmont College, Demorest, Georgia

Nancy S. Taylor, Senior Minister, Old South Church in Boston, Boston, Massachusetts

Marianne Meye Thompson, George Eldon Ladd Professor of New Testament, Fuller Theological Seminary, Pasadena, California

Craig S. Troutman, Pastor, Raleigh Moravian Church, Raleigh, North Carolina

Gilson A. C. Waldkoenig, Professor of Church in Society, Lutheran Theological Seminary at Gettysburg, Gettysburg, Pennsylvania

Thomas W. Walker, Pastor, The Palms Presbyterian Church, Jacksonville Beach, Florida

Sharon Watkins, General Minister and President, Christian Church (Disciples of Christ), Indianapolis, Indiana

Audrey West, Adjunct Professor of New Testament, Lutheran School of Theology at Chicago, Chicago, Illinois

Mark D. White, Pastor, Chamberlayne Baptist Church, Richmond, Virginia

Daniel L. Wong, Director of Modular Programs and Assistant Professor of Christian Ministries, Tyndale University College and Seminary, Toronto, Ontario, Canada

Oliver Larry Yarbrough, Pardon Tillinghast Professor of Religion, Middlebury College, Middlebury, Vermont

Noelle M. York-Simmons, Associate Rector, All Saints' Episcopal Church, Atlanta, Georgia

Brett Younger, Associate Professor of Preaching, McAfee School of Theology, Mercer University, Atlanta, Georgia

Randall C. Zachman, Professor of Reformation Studies, University of Notre Dame, Notre Dame, Indiana

Author Index

Robert Hoch	John 8:31–38 HP; 8:39–47 HP; 8:48–59 HP	Joseph L. Price	John 7:1–13 TP; 7:14–24 TP; 7:25–31 TP
Sally Smith Holt	John 9:24–34 TP; 9:35–41 TP	Rebecca Button Prichard	John 8:31–38 PP; 8:48–59 PP
Michael J. Hoyt	John 6:52–59 PP; 6:60–65 PP; 6:66–71 PP	John Proctor	John 6:52–59 EP; 6:60–65 EP; 6:66–71 EP
David W. Hull	John 6:22–29 HP; 6:30–40 HP; 6:41–51 HP	Rollin A. Ramsaran	John 3:22–30 EP; 3:31–36 EP; 4:1–6 EP
Philip D. Jamieson	John 1:1–9 PP; 1:10–13 PP; 1:14–18 PP	Nancy J. Ramsay	John 4:31–38 PP; 4:39–42 PP; 4:43–54 PP
Cynthia A. Jarvis	John 9:1–12 TP; 9:13–17 TP; 9:18–23 TP	Mark Ramsey	John 9:1–12 HP; 9:13–17 HP; 9:18–23 HP
Raquel St. Clair Lettsome	John 1:43–51 PP; 2:1–12 PP; 2:13–25 PP	David Rensberger	John 7:1–13 EP; 7:14–24 EP; 7:25–31 EP
Daniel F. Lewis	John 5:19–24 HP; 5:25–29 HP; 5:30–38 HP	Vernon K. Robbins	John 8:31–38 EP; 8:39–47 EP; 8:48–59 EP
Donald K. McKim	John 8:31–38 TP; 8:39–47 TP; 8:48–59 TP	Art Ross	John 8:12–20 HP; 8:21–30 HP
Alicia D. Myers	John 7:32–36 TP; 7:37–52 TP; 7:53–8:11 TP	Gilberto A. Ruiz	John 7:32–36 EP; 7:37–52 EP; 7:53–8:11 EP
Carmen Nanko-Fernández	John 5:39–47 TP; 6:1–15 TP; 6:16–21 TP; 8:39–47 PP	Clayton J. Schmit	John 7:1–13 HP; 7:14–24 HP; 7:25–31 HP
Gail R. O'Day	John 1:1–9 EP; 1:10–13 EP; 1:14–18 EP	Carol L. Schnabl Schweitzer	John 5:1–9a PP; 5:9b–15 PP; 5:16–18 PP
Amy Plantinga Pauw	John 3:1–8 TP; 3:9–15 TP; 3:16–21 TP	Edwin Searcy	John 3:1–8 PP; 3:9–15 PP; 3:16–21 PP
Buran Phillips	John 1:19–28 TP; 1:29–34 TP; 1:35–42 TP	Katherine A. Shaner	John 4:31–38 EP; 4:39–42 EP; 4:43–54 EP
Cornelius Plantinga Jr.	John 1:1–9 TP; 1:10–13 TP; 1:14–18 TP	Marguerite Shuster	John 5:1–9a HP; 5:9b–15 HP; 5:16–18 HP
		Gary V. Simpson	John 9:1–12 PP; 9:13–17 PP; 9:18–23 PP

Joseph D. Small	John 8:12–20 TP; 8:21–30 TP	Thomas W. Walker	John 4:7–15 PP; 4:16–21 PP; 4:22–30 PP
O. Benjamin Sparks	John 7:1–13 PP; 7:14–24 PP; 7:25–31 PP	Sharon Watkins	John 4:31–38 HP; 4:39–42 HP; 4:43–54 HP
Nibs Stroupe	John 1:43–51 HP; 2:1–12 HP; 2:13–25 HP	Audrey West	John 4:7–15 EP; 4:16–21 EP; 4:22–30 EP
Monya A. Stubbs	John 5:1–9a EP; 5:9b–15 EP; 5:16–18 EP	Mark D. White	John 5:19–24 TP; 5:25–29 TP; 5:30–38 TP
Jessica Tate	John 5:19–24 PP; 5:25–29 PP; 5:30–38 PP	Daniel L. Wong	John 3:22–30 HP; 3:31–36 HP; 4:1–6 HP
Barbara Brown Taylor	John 6:52–59 HP; 6:60–65 HP; 6:66–71 HP	Oliver Larry Yarbrough	John 7:32–36 HP; 7:37–52 HP; 7:53–8:11 HP
Nancy S. Taylor	John 7:32–36 PP; 7:37–52 PP; 7:53–8:11 PP	Noelle M. York-Simmons	John 9:24–34 HP; 9:35–41 HP
Marianne Meye Thompson	John 5:19–24 EP; 5:25–29 EP; 5:30–38 EP	Brett Younger	John 3:1–8 HP; 3:9–15 HP; 3:16–21 HP
Craig S. Troutman	John 3:22–30 PP; 3:31–36 PP; 4:1–6 PP	Randall C. Zachman	John 3:22–30 TP; 3:31–36 TP; 4:1–6 TP
Gilson A. C. Waldkoenig	John 5:1–9a TP; 5:9b–15 TP; 5:16–18 TP		

Printed in the USA
CPSIA information can be obtained
at www.ICGtesting.com
LVHW081217211123
764192LV00006B/17